PUBLIC SPIRIT: DISSENT IN WITHAM AND ESSEX, 1500-1700

JANET GYFORD

ILLUSTRATED BY RAY BROWN

'The best townsman of a publique spirit'
Witham burial register, 16 August 1666, describing Robert Jackson

The illustration on the front cover is from a painting by Ray Brown showing the road to
Terling, seen from Chipping Hill. Witham parishioners went this way to hear the
preaching of Thomas Weld between 1626 and 1631. Dame Katherine Barnardiston lived
behind the long brick wall.

Published by
JANET GYFORD
Blanfred, Chalks Road,
Witham. Essex. CM8 2BT

© Janet Gyford 1999

British Library Cataloguing in Publication Data
A catalogue record for this book is available from the British Library

ISBN 0 946434 03 4

Designed by the author
Printed by the Owl Printing Company
East Street, Tollesbury, Maldon, Essex CM9 8QD
Tel: 01621 869201 Fax: 01621 869811

CONTENTS

LIST OF FIGURES (TABLES, GRAPHS, MAPS AND FACSIMILES)

LIST OF DRAWINGS BY RAY BROWN

Members of the Essex Militia kindly posed for the photos on which the drawings of soldiers were based. The drawings of the outside of the barn at Witham Place, and of the Southcott monument, are based on a photos which are Crown Copyright and used by permission of the National Monuments Record. The drawing of Howbridge Hall is from a photo by the late Harry Loring, and the one of Moat farm and Chipping Hill is from a photo in Lester Shelley's collection, with permission.

PREFACE

It is now two and a half years since I produced the companion volume to this one, *Witham 1500-1700: Making a Living*. That time has been very pleasurable, meeting and hearing from so many kind and friendly readers. I apologise to them that they have waited so long for *Public Spirit*. Even after all this time, it can only be an interim report. There is more to be discovered. Nevertheless, it is a pleasure, though rather a frightening one, to pause and set something down in print.

My new objective has been to try and discover what Witham people did in some of their spare time - praying, meeting, and quarrelling, for instance. I have tried to write for local readers, who may, like me, feel unsure about their history. Some of them have been kind enough to say that they thought they would find this theme interesting, whilst others have confessed that they are not too sure about it. I feel myself that this book actually has a more exciting plot than the previous one, and it gathers momentum as time goes on. So I hope some of you doubters will give it a try. If you find it complicated, that is a good sign. As they say, if history seems simple, you must be missing something.

Many fascinating books, articles and theses have been written about different aspects of Essex life as it was during the sixteenth and seventeenth centuries. So in places I have been able to suggest that the reader consults these other works for more information about the county background. At times, however, when I have wanted to know something that has not already been available, I have myself investigated what was happening in Essex as a whole. This means that the space devoted to county affairs in the book is uneven, but it seemed the best solution. No doubt in future the mysteries of both Witham and Essex will be unravelled further by others. Perhaps this is a good point to reassure those people who think that the study of the sixteenth and seventeenth centuries must be difficult because of the handwriting. In fact, there are more than enough documents in print or in typescript in Essex to inspire a beginner. Then before long, you will be eager to find out more and keen to learn the handwriting as well.

Much of the book is purely descriptive, which is deliberate. However, anyone writing about this period must wonder what it all means. Historians constantly debate the interpretation of behaviour and belief during the sixteenth and seventeenth centuries. The resulting controversies are of great interest, but they are somewhat intimidating to someone like myself who is not an academic. I have kept my references to them as brief as possible, and generally consigned them to an 'overview' at the end of each chapter. Hopefully this will prevent them being too intrusive for those readers who can understandably manage perfectly well without them. Other people, who really are interested in the wider issues, will often know more about them than I do, and will be able to provide their own explanations for the events described.

Inevitably, much of the book is about Christianity. I am not a Christian myself, but I feel that most Christians come out of the story well. Many of them were incredibly brave, and furthermore they were still flourishing in 1700 in spite of two centuries of immense trial and tribulation. I have become just as attached to them as I am to my modern Christian friends. Some of the latter have been amongst the people who kindly read my drafts. On a few points they did not all agree with each other. This shows that even a primarily factual account can be contentious, and I must apologise for not having been able entirely to please everyone in the end.

This experience of sharing and discussing the drafts was extremely rewarding and interesting. The following are the people who generously read some or all of the text at varying stages of preparation: David Appleby, Bill Cliftlands, John Craig, Chris Edwards, Amanda Flather, John Gyford, Michael Jones, Betty Loring, Canon Laurence Reading, Lesli Wheeler, and John Walter. I have often seen lists like this in other books, but never fully realised what an onerous task such readers had, until I came to solicit them for myself, and to ask them to give up their precious time and energy for my benefit.

Many historians have provided other help, information and advice; they are mentioned in specific chapters and notes. Meeting and talking with such people is one of the chief pleasures of preparing a book such as this one. I shall limit myself here to mentioning two people by name. Arthur Brown has a been a tremendous inspiration ever since I started local history over thirty years ago. Engendering enthusiasm in other people is perhaps the greatest of his many prodigious achievements. John Walter has the same flair also. He introduced me to the seventeenth century during a 'Week of Study' run by the Essex W.E.A. in 1980, and without his selfless encouragement ever since, I would never have reached this point.

The staff of many libraries and Record Offices have provided much help and assistance, in particular at the British Library, Essex Record Office, Guildhall Library, House of Lords Record Office, London Metropolitan Archives, Public Record Office, and Suffolk Record Office.

It was a great delight when Ray Brown first suggested that he might be able to draw me some pictures. But I then had no idea how many hours of devoted work he would dedicate to the task, and how special the results would be. Furthermore he has remained completely cheerful, however complicated, difficult or boring the tasks which I have set him. It has been a great honour and privilege to work with him. We agreed together that I would try and explain something here about the drawings, which is that they have not tried to show Witham four hundred years ago, because we do not know exactly what it looked like then. They are usually based on photographs taken some time during the twentieth century, but the more obviously modern features such as street lights and cars have been omitted. They have been chosen to illustrate particular points made in the book, and these are explained in more detail in the captions.

Phil Gyford generously took much time and trouble to draw the maps for me, and to prepare the writing on the front cover.

My friends and family have been endlessly supportive through years of alternating progress and crisis.

I am very grateful indeed to all these people for their contribution, and for making what could have been a lonely project into a sociable one.

Finally, a few 'technical' points:

People with exactly the same name are distinguished from each other in the text by numbers in brackets. These correspond with the numbers used in my previous book, in which more information about them will also be found.

The spelling of surnames was flexible during the sixteenth and seventeenth centuries, but I have used a standard form for each one. Some of the variants are shown in the index.

In naming Witham's church, I have used the spelling which was in use during the sixteenth and seventeenth centuries, 'St.Nicholas'. It was altered to 'Nicolas' during the 1930s.

Until 1752, the year ran from March 25th to March 24th. We now refer to this system as 'Old Style'. It is common in modern writing to convert the period between January 1st and March 24th into 'New

Style' dating, by adding a year. For instance, March 17th 1627 in an original document, near the end of the Old Style year 1627, is written as March 17th 1628 in New Style. After some agonising I have adopted this convention. In my previous book, I chose one of the alternatives, which is to use the form March 17th 1627/8. Some readers found this helpful, but others did not like it. A few of my tables use 'Old Style' years, but this does not alter their overall message so I have left them as they are.

Money is given as it was before 1971:
    12 old pennies (d.) = one old shilling (s.)
    20 old shillings (s.) = one old pound (£)
    1 old penny (d.) = 0.417 new pence (p.)
    1 old shilling (s.) = 5 new pence (p.)
    1 old pound (£) = 1 new pound (£)

Distances are given in miles. One mile = 1.609 kilometres.

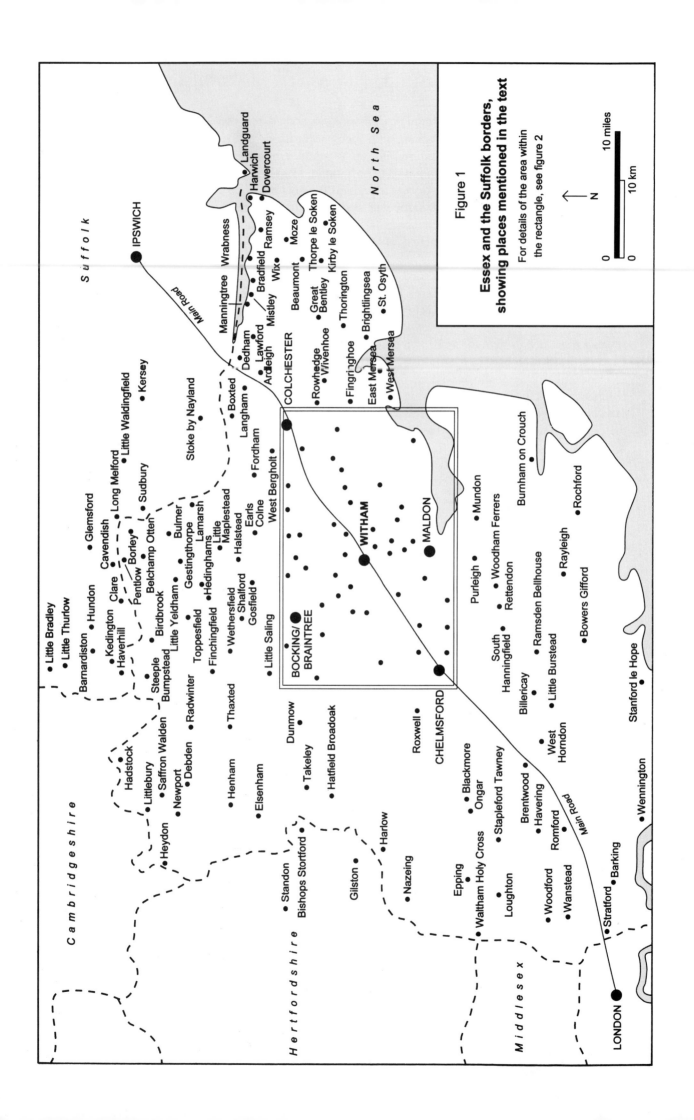

Figure 1

Essex and the Suffolk borders, showing places mentioned in the text

For details of the area within the rectangle, see figure 2

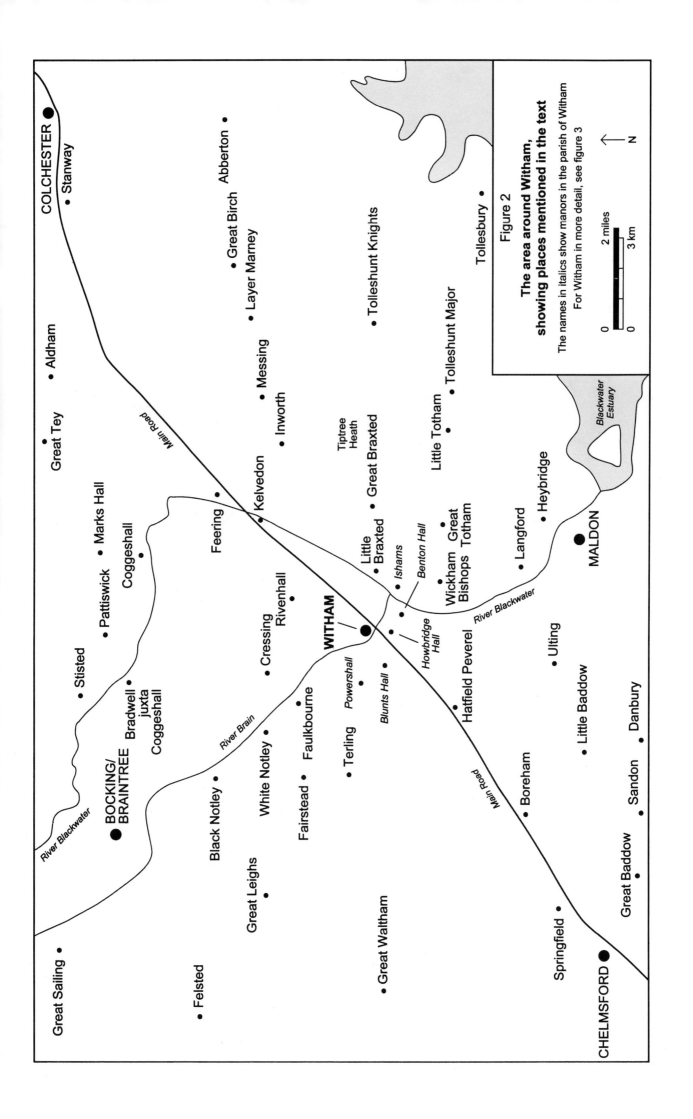

Figure 2

**The area around Witham,
showing places mentioned in the text**

The names in italics show manors in the parish of Witham
For Witham in more detail, see figure 3

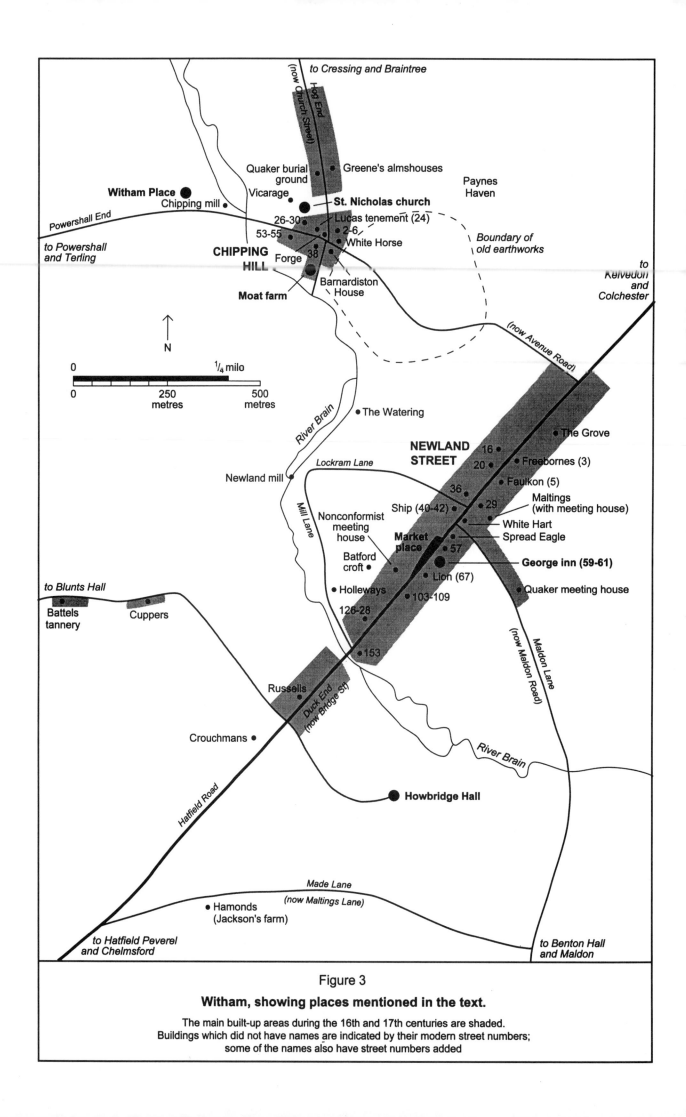

Figure 3

Witham, showing places mentioned in the text.

The main built-up areas during the 16th and 17th centuries are shaded.
Buildings which did not have names are indicated by their modern street numbers;
some of the names also have street numbers added

1. WITHAM

Witham is in the middle of the county of Essex, by the road which runs from London north-eastwards towards the coast and East Anglia. Its heyday was perhaps between the fifth and the thirteenth centuries. During that time it came to possess a royal estate, a minster church, a hundredal meeting place, a market, and a fortified site. It may have been the only place in the county with all these five important features. Its centre was at Chipping Hill until a second settlement was established a mile further south in about 1200. This was the town of Newland, built by the Knights Templars along the main road. [1]

By the year 1500, several other settlements in the county had become relatively more important, but Witham did retain most of its earlier features. The former royal estate, the manors of Chipping and Newland, belonged to the Knights Hospitallers, the successors of the Templars. They were based at Cressing Temple, three and a half miles further north. Within their territory, Newland Street had become the chief settlement and trading place. Chipping Hill, the original centre, still survived, and it was there that the church stood. Dedicated to St.Nicholas, its parish was large, containing the centres of six additional manors to its west and south. Howbridge Hall and Benton Hall are pictured on the following two pages. The others were Powershall, Blunts Hall, Ishams, and the Vicarage. These manors were mostly rural, but they did include some small hamlets, as well as a continuation from Newland Street in a south-westerly direction, then known as Duck End. It is now called Bridge Street and is illustrated on page 6. Witham was still the centre of a half-hundred containing sixteen parishes, whose officers had a significant role in law enforcement. The weekly market, now held in the wide part of Newland Street, attracted people from other places to buy and sell there, and was supplemented by a fair once or twice a year. The defensive earthworks near Chipping Hill, which may have been the former Saxon burh, had lost their function. But they were still very visible and probably somewhat mysterious; even today we have not fully explained them.

During the sixteenth and seventeenth centuries the layout of the parish remained the same as in earlier years. There may have been four or five hundred people living here in 1500, making Witham about the twentieth ranking place in Essex. There were four other urban settlements within ten miles, Braintree/Bocking, the county town of Chelmsford, the port of Maldon, and lastly Colchester, by far the largest, to the east. The population of the county and indeed of the country as a whole increased after 1520, rapidly at first and then more slowly. By the 1670s Witham may have housed 1,100 or 1,200 people. Today it is hard for us to imagine such a town, with only two or three hundred households. Some people stayed here for decades, but there was also a great deal of coming and going. Much of the movement took place within Essex, but we also know of residents who were born more than a hundred miles away. Not all the town's inhabitants knew each other.

Life was hazardous. For instance there were drastic harvest failures during the 1580s and 1590s, and many crises in the cloth industry, of which the best known was in 1629, at which time agriculture was also in difficulties. Plague appeared in localised outbreaks such as the one in Witham between 1638 and 1641, and culminated in the well-known epidemic of 1665, which caused many deaths in large towns and cities. There were fewer losses in Witham, but one of the people who died was the 'best townsman of a publique spirit', clothier Robert Jackson(1). Even normal times could be difficult. When concluding my previous book, I found I had mentioned nineteen separate families whose fathers had died leaving young children. These are only the families who were quite well-known. For most of the time no parish register survives to tell us of the others.

There were not many new sites built on, so the increasing population caused more crowded conditions, and fewer people had the space to produce some food for themselves. Today, it is around the green at Chipping Hill that we can most readily picture what the buildings of Witham looked like before 1700. Newland Street has been altered considerably since then, particularly by the addition of elegant brick frontages during the eighteenth century. Where we do have traces of building work that took place between 1500 and 1700, its quality varies. Owner-occupiers who might have indulged in lavish construction were in the minority, and several owners lived outside the town or in London. Tenants were able to leave readily if they wished, though some did stay in place for many years. Many people lived in the same buildings in which they worked; this contributed to making their houses dirty, messy, dusty, smelly and unhealthy. It could also be unpleasant outdoors in the street, where domestic sewage, overflowing from ditches, mixed with the offal from brewing, tanning, fulling, and the slaughter of animals. However, the various local courts did try to supervise these matters, and in addition there were some improvements to life after 1500. Thus assets such as window glass, wall hangings, decoration, and brick chimneys became more common amongst people of middling wealth. Brick did not often appear in the walls of the buildings until after 1700, but it may have been used for the mansion house at Witham Place, built by its new lay owners in about 1550 on a site previously owned by St.John's Abbey in Colchester. This was very much the largest house in the parish during our period. The brick boundary wall in front of it, of a similar age, still survives in Powershall End.

Roads, tracks and paths suffered intermittently from people digging in them for clay, or allowing their ditches to overflow into them and their hedges to overhang them. Furthermore, in most directions, entering and leaving the town entailed crossing either the river Brain or the wider Blackwater, and there was continual debate about the condition of the wooden bridges and the responsibility for their upkeep. Some private coaches came into use during the seventeenth century, but only the extremely rich owned them. In Witham they were restricted to the successive residents of Witham Place, the Southcotts and the Barnardistons. Other fairly prosperous people might own a riding horse, which could be a valuable beast. Horses could also be hired at the few larger inns in Newland Street, of which the George was the grandest (now the Town Hall, no.61 Newland Street, and the site of no.59). Their position on the main road between London and the coast gave these establishments an important role, particularly in the developing postal service of the seventeenth century, which caused local innkeepers many problems. But most people made their way about

Howbridge Hall

This attractive manor house is situated in Howbridge Road, next to the river.
It was built in about 1580, when it was surrounded by its own fields.

Benton Hall

Another manor house and farm, on the road towards Maldon. Abraham Lake, the yeoman
who lived there during the 1660s, was in trouble for listening to nonconformist ministers,
and allowed two of them, Robert Billio and George Lisle, to preach in Benton Hall itself.

by walking, helped by an occasional ride on a
commercial waggon.

A large part of the parish was agricultural, and the
yeomen who farmed it were often well-off, though like
their urban colleagues they frequently rented their land
from a variety of landlords. Most of the largest farming
units were demesnes of the manors, with several
hundred acres each. The largest demesne of all was the
central one belonging to the combined manors of
Chipping and Newland, but for most of our period it
was rented out in small pieces to local yeomen and
tradesmen. After the dissolution of the Hospitallers in
1540, these two manors were taken over by the
Smith/Nevill family, together with Cressing Temple,
where they lived. They sold the Witham manors in
1659. After this, the owners were London families; after
1670 they took a renewed interest, reviving and
probably inventing various customs.

Outside their demesnes, most of the manors had some
land occupied by free and copyhold tenants. One new
development between 1500 and 1700 was the
emergence of three sizeable new farming units from
areas that were previously let in smaller sections. This
reflected a general trend in the county. Thus the
Witham Place estate was put together during the
sixteenth century, probably farmed in two units. The
owners, the Southcotts, later owned Powershall manor
too, as a result of which they held around 800 acres
altogether, about a quarter of the parish. The estate of

the Moat house, below Chipping Hill, was assembled
during several years before 1600, eventually reaching
about 120 acres. Unusually, it was held by owner-
occupiers, the Garrard family, who also owned other
property in the parish, and figured very prominently in
the town's affairs. Jerome Garrard(1) may have been a
clothier during the 1570s when he first arrived, but soon
he was a yeomen, and his descendants sometimes called
themselves gentlemen. In the mid-seventeenth century,
there were still only one third of the agricultural units
with more than fifty acres, but they covered most of the
parish. The third new large farm, Freebornes, was
created after about 1675, from part of the demesne of
Chipping and Newland that had previously been leased
out in parts. It was named after the previous occupant
of its farmhouse in Newland Street, Quaker clothier
John Freeborne.

Farming was mixed in nature, providing both crops and
animals, and probably increasing in intensity as the two
centuries progressed. Some of its products, especially
wheat, are known to have been exported from Essex,
particularly to London. Although power for farming
was limited to the strength of men and horses, its
organisation was complex and entailed links with distant
parts of the county. Within Witham, the extensive
meadows along the rivers, and the woodlands further
out, were usually owned by the lords of the manors.
Their tenants had rights in them, but these were closely
regulated. Many successful townspeople owned or
rented land and benefited from its produce whilst still

4

Chipping Hill

This was where the centre of Witham was, until Newland Street was built in about the year 1200. Several medieval buildings survive here, one of which is the blacksmith's forge on the right of the picture. It is still in use. In the mid-17th century John Adcock was the blacksmith. He was also a 'horse-leech' or vet, and had some books to help him. Behind on the right is the tower of St.Nicholas church. The houses on the green were demolished during the 1930s.

carrying on a business, or moved from trade into farming altogether. Farm animals were a particularly valuable part of many people's possessions, and were often mentioned individually in wills, along with their characteristics such as their white faces. Before the Reformation, milking cows were often bequeathed in ones and twos to fund prayers for people's souls.

Nevertheless, people who specialised in agriculture were always in a minority in Witham, probably comprising between one seventh and one fifth of the total. Most of the population lived and worked in the built-up areas of Newland Street, Bridge Street and Chipping Hill. In contrast, in neighbouring villages like Terling most people worked on the land, even though there were also some tradesmen and craftsmen. We know that such villages looked to towns like Witham to help provide them with commercial services. Like most places of a similar size, Witham had large-scale processing industries such as milling, brewing, tanning and malting. In general the town did not have specialist areas for particular activities, but brewing was concentrated on the river at the bottom of Newland Street. People who conducted these activities needed expensive fixed equipment. Usually less prosperous were the craftsmen, such as the several tailors, shoemakers and joiners who were always found in the town. Their premises were often adaptable and they could move from place to place. However, the blacksmith's shop at Chipping Hill, shown above, has stayed in its same crucial position at the crossroads since the late sixteenth century or earlier.

Tradesmen seem to have increased in number during the seventeenth century, when there were usually four or five butchers and two or three grocers, together with smaller numbers of other specialists. Grocers had a much more general trade than their counterparts today. One of them, Samuel Wall, who died in 1673, mainly kept fabric, in many varieties, together with a few ready-made clothes. There were also innumerable victuallers and alehousekeepers providing ale and food, as well as the inns already mentioned in connection with the hire of horses. Tradesmen were usually more prosperous than craftsmen, and many had other interests such as farming. However, after about 1680 they seemed more likely to stay in their trade, perhaps under the influence of what some historians have called a 'Commercial Revolution', which continued into the eighteenth century. The market continued to be important too, and in addition to the open stalls there was a market house or 'cross' with an upper floor. This was a landmark. For instance, when someone shot at the Irish captain Ross Carew in 1628, the event was said to have occurred 'neere the markett Cross'.

Most of what I have described so far could have happened in any Essex town. The making of cloth for local use could also have been found anywhere. However, in addition Witham made woollen cloth for export through London. This was a specialised activity limited to certain areas. Suffolk and north Essex had been the scene of a prosperous medieval cloth industry which was still flourishing during the first half of the sixteenth century. Witham seems to have played a part in this, and housed wealthy fullers like Richard Radley during the early 1500s. However, there was a general decline around the 1550s. In some places this was permanent, but in others new techniques from the continent were already being introduced. These 'New Draperies' were so successful in north-east Essex that it became one of the foremost industrial areas of Britain during the seventeenth century, the most important centre being Colchester. The products were light-weight fabrics which were exported to warm countries like Spain. Between 1550 and 1600 a few leading clothmakers came into Witham and there were also some weavers here. Then in around 1600 the town seems to have experienced a fairly sudden expansion of the industry, when many new people arrived. Clothiers also became more numerous. These were the men who organised the system, providing the necessary long-term finance, and selling the finished product. Some of the cloth belonging to Witham's Richard True was at Leadenhall market in London waiting to be sold when he died during the plague epidemic of 1665. The building where he lived and worked is shown in the picture below. Clothiers arranged for other contributors to the process to carry out the various stages of the work in their homes. Amongst these were master weavers, who owned their own looms and were sometimes able to employ other people also. Women and children in villages as well as towns carried out the spinning.

Newland Street

There was already a main road here in about 1200 when the Knights Templars laid out the plots which are the basis of the street. This is a view of its lower, south-western end, looking up. During the seventeenth century Richard True, a clothier, lived and worked in the gabled building in the right foreground. He died during the plague epidemic of 1665.

Bridge Street, formerly known as Duck End

Here we are looking north-eastwards, towards Newland Street, which is on the other side of the river Brain.
The right-hand side of Bridge Street used to be in the manor of Howbridge Hall and the left-hand
side in the manor of Blunts Hall. The three timber-framed buildings on the right
probably date from the 16th century. Decorative wood-carving can still be seen on them.

The first thirty years of the seventeenth century were the most successful for the cloth industry everywhere, and by the 1620s it is possible that about one third of Witham's population were engaged in clothmaking, with clothiers being some of the wealthiest people in the town, particularly the successive John Graveners. Then the war with Spain which began in 1624 cut off the main markets, causing a crisis which reached a peak in 1629. Petitioners to Parliament from Essex claimed that fifty or sixty thousand families in the county depended on clothmaking. Their impoverishment affected other trades and crafts in turn. Full prosperity never fully returned, and the Civil War caused further difficulties. However, considerable numbers of people continued to be employed in the industry well into the eighteenth

century, with some temporary revivals from time to time. The prosperous Jackson family were the most eminent clothiers in Witham towards the end of the seventeenth century. But at that time, the town's lesser participants, such as woolcombers and weavers, probably suffered a downgrading of their relative status. Many of them lived near the river in the Mill Lane area, outside the main centre.

From certain specific times, there survives information from taxation records about the relative wealth and status of the parishioners as a whole. One such source is the Lay Subsidy return of 1523 and 1524. It seems that at that time the inhabitants of Witham were rather less prosperous than many of their counterparts elsewhere in the country, but that they shared this position with some other towns in Essex such as Colchester. Amongst the better-off people assessed in Witham were two wealthy fullers, whilst the middling ranks included tailor Christopher Raven, about whom we shall read more in chapter 3 (pages 32-35). The next views of the parish can be taken from the Ship Money assessment in 1636 and the Hearth Tax returns of the 1660s and 1670s. By this time we have more information about occupations, and we can see that these overlapped considerably in status. However, in very general terms, the gentry had the town's highest assessments, followed by people in agriculture, led by the yeomen, then those working in clothmaking with clothiers at their head, and then those with the collective description of 'processing, crafts and trade'. The poor were another group again, not taxed and often not mentioned.

During the seventeenth century, the most wealthy people had influence outside the parishes where they lived, and could perhaps be called 'county' gentry. Several such families lived in the rural parishes surrounding Witham, and had influence in the town. But within Witham itself it was only the successive occupants of the mansion at Witham Place that came into this category. They were usually members of the Southcott family, the first of whom was judge John Southcott, who arrived in 1567. His Catholic descendants headed the listings of both 1636 and 1673. In 1636 they had just reclaimed their house at Witham Place after the death of their equally prosperous tenant, the Puritan Dame Katherine Barnardiston. She had lived there since 1600 with her second and third husbands, Sir Thomas Barnardiston and William Towse. The 'parish gentry' were the next in rank. Their influence, although considerable, was concentrated within the town itself. Thus near the top of both the 1636 and 1673 assessments were the Garrards, who were gentleman/yeomen, and the Graveners, who were gentlemen/clothiers. Both of these families had been prominent in the town since before 1600, though they seemed to suffer something of a financial decline between the 1660s and 1680s. The same thing happened to the clothier Jacksons, but one of them, John(A) senior, revived the family fortunes after about 1680. A new arrival at the top in 1673 was the Quaker clothier, Robert Barwell(1), who had probably moved to Witham from Coggeshall in about 1650.

Most of the rest of the people who were taxed in Witham during the seventeenth century could be said to be 'middling' in rank, being neither gentry nor poor. They were extremely varied, ranging from the larger yeomen and clothiers to the small master tailors and weavers. Surviving documents help us to get to know

many of them as individuals. However, the lives of the needier inhabitants are more obscure. We do know that they included not only the sick and elderly, but some of the workers themselves. In 1673 over half the town's households were exempt from paying the Hearth Tax on grounds of poverty. This high level was typical of Essex clothmaking towns. In the early sixteenth century some of the poor had probably been helped by money from Witham's two chantries, and then during Elizabethan times a poor rate began to be levied in order to give a more regular provision. There were seven almshouses provided by individual bequests, and in 1633 Dame Katherine Barnardiston left funds for twelve loaves to be provided weekly in the church porch 'untill all the poore be sarved thorow out the Towne .. for ever'; this arrangement continued into the twentieth century.

This chapter set out to be a general scene-setting exercise, to make readers aware what sort of town the rest of the book relates to. But three particularly relevant points seem to have emerged. The first is the fragility of life and of prosperity. Ill-health and death never seemed far away at any age, and nor was the possibility of economic disaster. To people who believed that this was God's way of showing his displeasure, it is easy to see how very frightening it could be when dissenting members of the community appeared to be causing him offence. Perhaps they might be worshipping him in the wrong way, or not worshipping him at all and misbehaving instead. So campaigns to put the parish to rights were deeply heartfelt. Secondly we may note the need for co-operation in many aspects of the parish's life, ranging from managing the meadows and the market to looking after the poor. Thus it could often be helpful for everyone to work together even if their beliefs differed. Thirdly, there were present in Witham several features which historians have suggested might make dissent particularly likely. For instance, because there were such a large number of different manors, there had never been one dominant single figure of authority in the parish as a whole. New trends during the sixteenth and seventeenth centuries accentuated this situation, as more landed estates came into the hands of distant owners, some of them from the City of London, which was itself notoriously independent of the Crown. The cloth industry may also have fostered dissent, in that it provided economic independence in good times, a source of grievance in bad, and contacts with other places and other countries. However, it will be seen in later chapters that accidental occurrences, and in particular the arrival of certain people in the parish, could also affect attitudes to authority amongst the inhabitants of Witham.

2. USEFUL INFORMATION

Most of this book is arranged chronologically, with each chapter moving on in time. So I thought that it would be helpful here to discuss some subjects in a more general way. The first is the role of Christianity. Related to this there are also two sources of information which have no modern parallel. These are the religious preambles to wills, and the records of the Church courts, or ecclesiastical courts. Lastly I shall say something about education and literacy.

CHRISTIANITY

There has been much discussion amongst historians about what Christianity, particularly Protestantism, really meant to individuals during the sixteenth and seventeenth centuries.[1] In many people's minds there may have been a mixture of magical or superstitious beliefs on the one hand, and Christianity on the other. This is symbolised by the evidence of Witham's Elizabeth Rawlin, a maid servant, to the court of quarter sessions in 1593. She reported that a man who had demanded sexual favours had threatened to 'fetche love pouder which woud mak her whether she would or not'. But when she wanted to describe the time of a visit from this man and his friend to another servant in the same house, she said that it had taken place 'about Evening Prayer time'. The house faced Witham's parish church, St.Nicholas, across Chipping Hill green (it is now nos.53/55 Chipping Hill). So she would be well aware of the bells and the assembling congregation.[2] Elizabeth Rawlin and her fellow-parishioners were all compulsory life members of the official state Church, until separate sects and denominations began to be tolerated at the end of the seventeenth century. So nearly all religious debates and changes took place within this Church, and they affected ordinary people much more directly than they do today, when both religion and politics are optional interests.

The supremacy of Christianity is also illustrated by its role in secular affairs. Even foreign and military policymaking were affected by the religious dispositions of the different countries concerned. As a result, archbishops and bishops could be as powerful in government as their secular counterparts such as the Chancellor. Essex was in the diocese of London, whose bishop was frequently particularly influential. The monarchs and their advisers often issued instructions about what the character of the Church was to be. At times it could be dangerous for parishioners not to conform to these orders. Indeed the better-off were obliged to make themselves available for election as churchwarden, and help to enforce them. On the face

of it, religious doctrine was dictated from the centre. In fact, however, there were many local variations of belief and practice, whose nature and meaning constantly exercise historians. One variant of Protestantism, known broadly as Puritanism, became particularly significant from the reign of Elizabeth onwards, and is discussed in chapters 5 to 10 (particularly on page 50).

Even parishioners who did not exercise their minds much about Christianity would frequently be involved with the parish church as a building. Some surviving illustrations may serve as examples of the many others which we do not know about. For instance, in 1516 Robert Herris of Cuppers farm was told to hand over his half-yearly rent payments to his landlord in the 'parish church of Witham' (Cuppers farmhouse is now no.19 Blunts Hall Road). In 1544 the early Protestant Christopher Royden asked for the inventory of his goods to 'remayne within the Upper Revestry of Witham in the Custodye of the churche Wardens' (the 'revestry' was the vestry, which formerly had an upper floor, as can be seen in the drawing on page 39). In 1575 'a public proclamation was made in the Church at Witham' asking a new tenant to pay his entry fine to the manor of Blunts Hall; it was not successful. And in 1583 we learn that the tenants of the main manors of Chipping and Newland customarily paid their manorial rents twice a year in the church's south porch, 'other orders and customs to the contrary notwithstanding'. The porch is shown on the opposite page. These tenants were numerous, so rent-day must have been a busy occasion in the churchyard. In addition, willmakers sometimes decreed that legacies should be paid in the church porch. Examples were the regular payments to be made to the widows of clothier John Gravener(2) in 1611 and yeoman Edward Johnson in 1669.[3]

There were in addition many ways in which parishioners' lives were involved with the Church as an institution. They were obliged to pay tithes annually, which entailed giving up a tenth of their produce and their garden crops, or the monetary equivalent. They also paid an Easter offering towards the cost of the communion. In addition they were liable to censure in the Church courts, not only for offences against the Church itself, but for their general behaviour. The Church's parish organisation was used by much of the new administrative machinery introduced during the period, notably that relating to the care of the poor. Furthermore, after the 1580s the allocation of seats within the church became a significant proclamation of the parishioners' social status.[4] Thus the Church was very dominant in day to day life. In addition, as will be shown in this book, there were always some local

The porch and tower of St.Nicholas church

Arrangements for rents and legacies often specified that the people concerned should meet
in the church porch to make the payments.

people who were even more involved in religious affairs than their neighbours. Their activities in Witham were frequently so visible and dramatic that the whole town must have been aware of them.

Clergymen

When parishes were first established in about the eleventh century, all their income was granted to one person or institution, known as the rector, who also provided the clergyman. Where rectories were owned by religious houses, some of their rights and obligations, including that of ministering in the parish, were often granted on a permanent basis to a deputy or vicar, whose parish thus became a vicarage. This happened in Witham in 1223. Vicars received some of the tithes, called the small tithes. Sometimes they leased the income out to other people for a time.

Even where there was a vicarage, the rectory continued in existence as a separate institution. The rector retained the right to receive the great tithes, levied on corn and hay, and to occupy one of the chief seats in the church, and was also obliged to maintain the chancel. After the Dissolution the rights of the rectory of Witham eventually came into the hands of the bishops of London, who usually leased them to lay people. In places where a vicarage had never been set up, the local clergyman continued to be known as the rector and retained all the tithes. The use of the title of 'rector' since 1994 to describe one of the clergy serving Witham's parish church, does not have any relationship to this system.[5]

In many parishes, the advowson, which is the right to appoint the clergyman, belonged to a lay person or an institution, but the bishop of London always chose Witham's vicars. Witham's vicar in turn owned the advowson of the neighbouring parish of Cressing.[6] Before the dissolution of the chantries in 1548, Witham also had two chantry priests, who will be discussed in the next chapter (page 38). In addition, a parish frequently had a curate to assist. It is usually unclear who nominated him. It could have been the bishop, the patron or the clergyman. Curates required licences from the bishop, but they rarely stayed very long in one place, and sometimes moved on before being licensed. On occasion this may have been a deliberate ploy to avoid subscribing to the Church's Articles. At times, prosperous lay people with no official standing would also introduce a man into a parish to preach or 'lecture', with no licence. Sometimes curates seem to have been called lecturers and vice versa. Thus although assistant clergy are important and interesting, it is often difficult to discover what was really happening to them. Most parishes also had parish clerks, who held the post for life, to assist with a variety of duties.

Witham vicarage was unusual in that it owned a manorial estate, the Vicarage manor, in addition to the usual glebe land and vicarage house (now the 'Old Vicarage' in Chipping Hill, probably a seventeenth-century building enclosed in nineteenth-century brick). However, by the early seventeenth century, and probably earlier, many of its manorial rents were 'decayed' and no longer paid. The total annual value of the vicarage in 1535, at £22, worked out at about four shillings for every person appearing in the Lay Subsidy of 1523, and this was also the average sum for the other eleven vicarages in the area around Witham called the deanery. In comparison, the value for the eleven rectories, who received all the tithes of their parishes, was about ten shillings per person. This difference may have affected the quality of the incumbents of the vicarages, and made them more likely to seek additional appointments elsewhere to supplement their incomes. As we shall see, this was sometimes the case in Witham. However, in general the attainments of the clergy increased over time, so that by 1600 the majority of those newly recruited in the diocese of London were graduates. Jay Anglin investigated the newly appointed incumbents in the archdeaconry of Essex, and found that the proportion with university degrees increased from thirty-five per cent during the 1570s to seventy-two per cent during the 1590s. The change was often slower in other parts of the country.[7]

Churchwardens

Churchwardens will be mentioned frequently in later chapters. They had existed since medieval times and were part of a system of parish organisation that continued to be very varied and ill-defined up to 1700 and beyond. Like the parish constables, they were given new obligations by various enactments during the sixteenth century. At the same time, the other unpaid parish posts of surveyor and overseer of the poor were established. Within the parish the roles of the different officers were closely connected. But it was only the churchwardens that were directly chosen by the parishioners. They also had the distinction of being responsible to the Church and its courts. They were assisted by sidesmen.

The duties of wardens were many. In particular they were usually obliged to enforce church attendance, to ensure obedience to the Church's moral demands upon parishioners, and to maintain the fabric of the church. Studies of various parishes in England have shown that the type of people chosen as churchwardens varied considerably from place to place. Women occasionally held the post in some counties, but this was unusual. It may have resulted from local customs requiring householders of particular farms and holdings to take a turn. It will be seen later in this chapter (pages 27-28) that the Witham wardens tended to have a high level of literacy, helping to suggest that they were chosen from the better-off parishioners, though officially there was no particular qualification required. But although the post was a source of prestige and power for its holders, it could also bring stress and conflict, particularly at certain times. So it did not appeal to everyone. In 1636, Witham's Thomas Freshwater persisted in refusing to act as churchwarden in spite of four excommunications

The interior of St.Nicholas church today

Most of the church was built during the 14th century. The base of the ornate
wooden rood screen dates from the 15th century, but the upper part is a more recent addition.

'being published in church against him'. It was probably he who had just finished a term as county coroner, so perhaps he felt he had done his duty already.[8]

Most parishes, but not all, had two churchwardens, elected at an annual meeting of parishioners, which was usually attended only by the better-off. The details of the system differed according to local custom. In a study of Cambridgeshire, Eric Carlson found considerable variations in this respect. The law allowed a continuation in office for more than one year if the people concerned were satisfactorily re-elected, but there may have been a general move in the late sixteenth century towards regular changes. In Terling, which adjoins Witham, it was said of the retiring wardens in 1598, Thomas Hewes and Henry Rayner, that 'thes two were Churchwardens 40 yeares'; they had begun in the first year of Elizabeth's reign. Such long service was probably rather exceptional. After their departure Terling had a change every three years for a while, and then after 1611 different names appeared there annually. In nearby Coggeshall, a pattern of annual changes was established sometime between 1586 and 1609, the previous practice having been for fairly long periods of service there too.[9] In Witham, there were annual changes for nearly all the periods that we know about, which are from 1570 to 1640 and from the mid-1660s to 1700. The main exception was a brief spell from 1600 to 1605 where the same wardens stayed in office continuously; this is discussed later, on page 80.[10]

Samuel Cardel, one of the churchwardens in 1700, had his name inscribed above the church door. where it can still be seen today. It is shown in the drawing above.

New wardens had to be sworn in by the archdeacon, but neither he nor any other higher Church authority had any powers over their selection. The role of the parish's own minister in the choice varied and was often disputed. New canons issued by the Church in 1604 attempted to formalise it by instructing that if he and the parishioners could not agree, he could select one of the wardens himself. In some places he probably began to exercise this right even if there was no such disagreement. The rector of Chelmsford tried to do so in 1611, occasioning a feud which lasted for several years. In other places older customs probably continued. Eventually the vicar does seem to have played a part in Witham, because in 1636 it was said of Thomas Freshwater that he had been 'lawfully elected and chosen by the minister'.[11] This is rather ambiguous, leaving us unsure whether the parishioners had also played a part. It is unfortunate that we do not know the local procedure more precisely, because the choice of the churchwardens for Witham was sometimes very important in parish affairs.

WILLS AND WILL PREAMBLES

Wills are used in local history to an extent which may surprise the modern reader. They can give information not only about a willmaker's occupation, relatives, friends, and possessions, but also their ability to sign their name, and their religious beliefs. However, only a minority of people made wills, and even when they did, the document may not always survive, especially if it was not taken to probate. There are 338 surviving wills from Witham during the two centuries. This probably means that we only have wills for about ten to twelve per cent of the town's adults between 1520 and 1700 (there were only a very few before 1520). Only twenty per cent of the wills were made by women, representing perhaps four or five per cent of adult women. Most of them were better-off widows. About seventeen per cent of Witham's adult men left wills.[12] Comparable estimates by historians for other places have produced varied results. For instance, Motoyasu Takahashi found almost twice as many men as this making wills in parts of East Anglia and the Midlands. He also found that one third of the men there were husbandmen or labourers. In contrast, only about six per cent of the men making wills in Witham described themselves as husbandmen, and none were labourers. Witham's late seventeenth-century weavers were the most recognisable body of the employed poor, and no wills survive for any of them. The last Witham weaver to leave a will was Hugh Parson in 1655, when weavers still had some status; he left £7 to each of his three grandchildren, to be paid 'at or in the Market Crosse' in Newland Street when they reached the age of 18, and another £6 to his daughter.[13] So wills only tell us about a minority of the people, and this minority excludes the less well-off.

Preambles

During the sixteenth and seventeenth centuries, when a person decided to write a will, they nearly always began their text with the bequest of their soul. This was not only the first item, but the most important. So to Margaret Freeborne in 1607 it was 'above all thinges'. This part of the will is known as the preamble. The wording varied considerably, and may, if considered with care, give an added dimension to our speculations about the beliefs of parishioners. The most basic distinction has been described by Margaret Spufford as follows:

> Any will which mentions the Virgin, the saints, or the angels may be suspected of Catholic tendencies. Any which stresses salvation through Christ's death and passion alone, or the company of the elect, may be thought of as Protestant.

I have adopted this interpretation myself, but historians do not all agree about the details of these definitions and some have added refinements. A particular difficulty is that modern attitudes, particularly of those of Catholics, differ considerably from sixteenth and seventeenth-century ones. The debate is often grounded in wider contention about the relative strengths of Catholic and Protestantism in England at different times. Amongst the many other complicating features is the fact that some preambles combined both types of wording together, as will be discussed in chapter 4 (pages 45-48). Others were entirely non-committal or had no preamble at all, which could itself be significant. Witham's Solomon Turner, whose will of 1646 had no preamble, was described elsewhere as a 'schismatic'. This meant that he sought separation from the Church, as did the later Quakers, whose wills did not usually have preambles either.[14]

Another matter for discussion has been whether it is right to assume that a preamble represents the willmaker's own beliefs. If at a particular time a certain religious viewpoint was virtually illegal, this put a constraint on a person's inclination to express it openly in their will. However, this does mean that those willmakers who were bold enough not to conform were probably doing so deliberately. It is also possible that a willmaker might be influenced by the other people around him, including the scribe. The influence of friends and relations is usually unknown. We can obtain a glimpse of it in one case dated 1638, from the evidence of Edmund Halys of Witham and another witness. They were cross-examined about the will that Halys had written for Gilbert Pickett of Rivenhall. Their evidence claimed that Pickett's wife Susan had 'importuned' her husband, and that if she had not done so, he would probably not have left her 'so much as he did by one halfe'. However, Pickett may have been unusually vulnerable, because at the time of the willmaking, he 'did talke very idly, speaking of Simnells and other things impertinent [i.e. not pertinent] to the business' (at this time, simnells were probably small cakes made by boiling). In spite of this, Halys had included in the will the usual declaration that Pickett was 'in body sick but of good and perfect memoreye'.

So perhaps we should not always take this assertion at face value. However, one historian who has studied several parts of the country has concluded that the testators were in fact usually 'firmly in control of proceedings', even if they were unwell.[15]

Only a very few people wrote their own wills. Witham's nonconformist ministers George Lisle and Edmund Taylor both did so at the end of the seventeenth century, but they were the exception. It was usual for a willmaker to engage someone else to write the will down for them. There was often a choice of scribes available in the parish, particularly after about 1550, when the task began to be done by people who were not connected with the Church. Sometimes these lay scribes were specialists like Edmund Halys, discussed in chapter 7 (pages 77-78), or Francis Lichfield in the 1650s, who was known as a 'scrivener', though he also ran an unlicensed alehouse. Very often the scribe also witnessed the will, and by this and other means, it has been possible to make an educated guess about who actually wrote just over two hundred Witham wills during the two centuries, sixty per cent of the total. A further twenty-nine (nine per cent) were nuncupative, meaning that they were stated verbally and written down by witnesses after the person's death. This is what Hugh Sol of Witham did in 1571, when he was:

> sicke of bodye and in extreme paynes having not a Clarke ready to put his last will and testament in Wrightinge and fearinge Deathe which to all fleshe ys Dewe and the tyme and houre thereof uncerteyne.[16]

Nuncupative wills did not normally have religious preambles.

Whoever the scribe was, the usual procedure for writing a will was designed in theory to ensure that the willmaker's own wishes were obeyed. The system is described several times in depositions relating to contested Witham wills. Edmund Halys figures again in one example, when in 1634 he wrote a will for John Burchard, a member of a large Witham family of gentlemen and yeomen. John may have been a young man when he died; he was the son of Richard, but was lodging with his cousin Robert(3) in Newland Street (in a house on the site now occupied by nos.103/109, on the northern corner of Kings Chase). John Burchard sent for Halys:

> to come to him ... where he then lay sick ... told him that he had sent for him to make his will and forthwith gave him instructions.

Halys came down the street from his own house at the top of the town (now the site of High House, part of no.5 Newland Street, in 1998 the Lian restaurant). He heard what John had to say, returned home to write the will, then took it back again, and read it out 'with an audible voyce', in the presence of the witnesses. Later on, one of them was confident that John:

> did well understand all the guiftes and bequests and did verie well like of the same and said it was according to his mynde and ... did sett his marke.

He lived for another two or three months afterwards. The main variation on this procedure seems to have been that sometimes the will was actually written at the willmaker's bedside rather than in the scribe's own home. This happened particularly where speed was called for, as in the case of the Witham woolcomber Cutlake Matthew in 1632, when his wife Ann called in a passer-by to be a witness.[17]

This procedure would allow a willmaker to express an opinion about the preamble if he wished. We might also note what happened when victualler Thomas Gilder was thinking about amending his will in 1588. His Newland Street premises were called 'the Ship' (on the site where nos.40/42 now stand; in 1998 Lisa Marie and part of Boots). He asked James Hurrell to visit him there to discuss the matter. Hurrell was a schoolmaster and perhaps Witham's curate, and when he arrived, he began by giving Gilder 'good instructions ... in his religion'.[18] These instructions had no obvious effect on the will, as the preamble written two years previously by the vicar remained unaltered. But the episode does remind us that some people would put themselves in the hands of others in religious matters. This is also suggested by the fact that certain scribes tended to have favourite preambles which they used several times for different people; on occasion they were quite elaborate ones. Some were probably taken from text books or other printed examples.

However, there were scribes who used different texts for different people, some of them so distinctive that it seems most unlikely that the willmaker did not endorse them. In any case the possible influence of the scribe in choosing the preambles does not necessarily invalidate their significance. First, the scribes were usually residents of the town, and their religious beliefs are of interest in themselves. And because they were often well-known people, these beliefs would often be common know-ledge, and a determined willmaker could 'send for' a scribe to his liking. Furthermore, information is sometimes available about a willmaker's religious views from other sources, and this can be used to support impressions obtained from their will preamble. One recent writer has examined all the various objections to the study of preambles, and put forward many warnings. Nevertheless he concludes that 'an exceptionally expressive and pious preamble does reflect profound and personal faith'. Thus historians continue to study preambles, particularly in local research. I have attempted to present the changing character of Witham will preambles in diagrammatic form in figure 4, with a view to illustrating some of the changes which are discussed in later chapters.[19]

THE CHURCH COURTS

Secular courts such as the quarter sessions and assizes do have parallels in the twentieth century, so the modern reader can go some way towards understanding them. However, there is no modern equivalent of the sixteenth and seventeenth-century ecclesiastical courts, or church courts. Today they deal merely with the management of the Church of England itself and its

employees, whereas in earlier years they also judged the morals of the population at large. Their main authority for doing this was canon law; the canons were the rules of the Church. Some of the business overlapped with that of the secular courts, but much of it did not. The church courts dealt with many matters which would not otherwise have been recorded. So they are of great interest to the historian, in spite of the fact that their affairs and their documents are very complicated. One estimate suggests that altogether about ten per cent of the adult population were involved in cases in the church courts between 1300 and 1800, with a particularly high proportion between 1450 and 1640.[20]

Organisation

Church courts have a long history, but they became more active from the second half of the sixteenth century, after the Reformation. When people criticised the Church establishment, these courts were often amongst their targets. As a result, they were suspended in 1641, and when they were re-established after the Restoration of 1660, it was in a modified form. There was a hierarchy of courts, under the control of different levels of senior churchmen, who usually did not attend themselves, but appointed someone else to supervise or to find other deputies. The most widely surviving documents are usually the Act books, which summarised the court proceedings. As one historian has written, these 'do not yield up their secrets upon the first assault'.[21] Sometimes other types of document survive also.[22] The archbishops of Canterbury and York controlled the two courts of High Commission. Below these were the bishops' courts. In the diocese of London, the Bishop's Consistory court periodically toured the outer areas such as Essex, hearing selected unresolved matters from the lower courts, and sometimes new cases also. These were followed up at later hearings, usually either in St.Paul's cathedral or in the rooms of the judge.[23] There were also several Bishop's Commissary courts which met more frequently, outside London, each under the control of a deputy known as a commissary. A small part of south-west Essex was under the control of the commissary of London, Middlesex and Barking, but most of the county was served by the commissary of Essex and Hertfordshire. The lowest and busiest courts were those of the three archdeaconries of Essex, Middlesex and Colchester.[24] There were also some 'peculiars', which were parishes or groups of parishes coming under the jurisdiction of specific bodies such as cathedrals and university colleges. All the courts charged fees to the people appearing, and the sums raised were distributed between the various officers. There were also regular 'Visitations' which mainly surveyed the clergy and the parish officers. In various ways, the hierarchy was not as neat as it may sound. For instance the bishop had direct jurisdiction over some parishes, and also cases from any parish could sometimes go straight to a higher court for various reasons. And Archdeacon's courts were not generally entitled to deal with the gentry, except for accusations of absence from church.[25]

FIGURE 4

TYPES OF WILL PREAMBLE IN WITHAM:
PERCENTAGES BASED ON 5-YEAR ROLLING AVERAGES

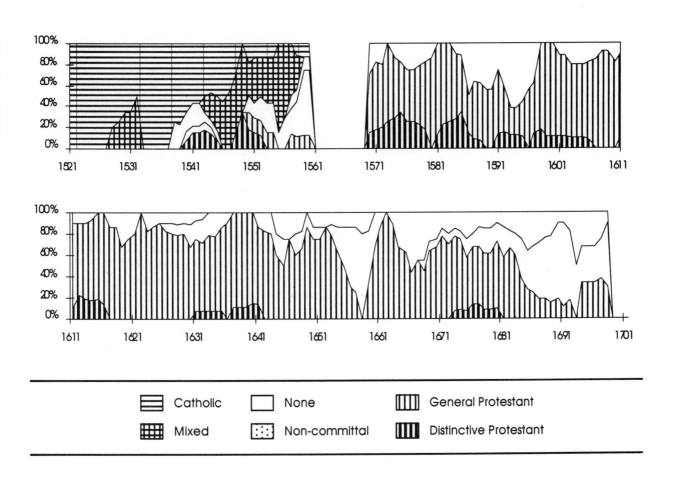

	Catholic		None		General Protestant
	Mixed		Non-committal		Distinctive Protestant

Meeting places, Colchester archdeaconry area

The Bishop's Commissary court for Essex and Hertfordshire had five usual meeting places after 1619; they were probably different in earlier years, for which hardly any records survive. It was accustomed to hearing business from particular archdeaconries at specific centres, but these arrangements were quite flexible. Although some parishes were the direct responsibility of the bishop rather than an archdeacon, more than half the business in the Commissary court came from other parishes whose business on that occasion took them to the bishop's court rather than the archdeacon's, either for some particular reason or for convenience.[26]

The deanery of Witham, containing twenty-three parishes including Witham itself, was in the archdeaconry of Colchester, for whose own courts continuous records survive from 1569. This archdeaconry was in two widely separated sections. The larger part, containing the deaneries of Witham, Colchester, Tendring and Lexden was in north-east Essex. The smaller, consisting of Sampford and Newport deaneries, was in the far north-west of the county, where the archdeacon's jurisdiction was considerably broken up by groups of parishes which came directly under the bishop's court. The Archdeacon's court was always 'on circuit', not having any permanent headquarters. Each part of the archdeaconry was dealt with every three or four weeks.

The sittings were held in parish churches, often at their west end. For the Witham deanery they were usually conducted in Kelvedon church, which meant that most suspects had to walk or ride some distance. Witham itself is three miles from Kelvedon, and other parishes were further away. Tendring, Lexden and Colchester deaneries had combined courts, which made them even less accessible; they were held in Colchester or nearby. Courts for the Sampford and Newport deaneries were usually at Henham or Saffron Walden. Urgent matters from one deanery sometimes went to the court for one of the others. In addition, suspects could be interrogated and sentenced on an individual basis in different places, between court days. Occasionally this is recorded in the Act books themselves, but at other times separate sheets were used, of which many may have since been lost.[27]

Court officers

In many respects the conduct of the ecclesiastical courts was similar to that of the secular courts. 'Proctors' or lawyers approved by the court could act for the parties in a dispute. The hearings were before a 'judge'. This latter position could be taken by various people. The bishop and the archdeacon were entitled to act as judge in their respective courts if they wished. However, they both usually appointed permanent deputies who took charge of the courts. The bishop's Vicar General supervised the Consistory court and the bishop's commissaries the Commissary courts, whilst the archdeacons used chancellors or 'officials'. Temporary substitutes or surrogates could also be called upon to officiate at individual sittings, and some of them appeared quite frequently, particularly in those places which were distant from the home of the relevant permanent officer. Sometimes these surrogates were lawyers, and sometimes local clergy. Witham's vicars did not act as judges often, but Edward Halys did so at the Archdeacon's court in 1570, probably because the official failed to arrive, and Robert Tinley supervised the Consistory court when it unusually came to Witham church in 1611.[28]

There were three successive archdeacons of Colchester during the period 1570-1641. George Wither or Withers, the new archdeacon in October 1570, began in a determined fashion by presiding personally in courts at Colchester, Kelvedon and distant Saffron Walden in the space of four days, and continued until his new official was appointed. After that he only appeared at his Visitations, which took place twice a year in these same three places. When he died in 1595 his son Thomas, rector of Fordham, took his place until his own death in 1617; his tenure seems to have been ignored by recent reference books. He presided at many of the courts for his first nine months, and at other times when there was no official. However, his successor, Henry King, archdeacon for twenty-five years, until 1642, seems to have come to court very rarely, if at all. He was appointed at the age of 25 by his father, John, the bishop of London, and at about the same time he became one of the chaplains of James I. He continued to serve Charles I, held other posts in Kent and London, and went on to have a distinguished career in the Church, finally becoming bishop of Chichester. So for him the archdeaconry of Colchester was probably little more than a source of additional income.[29]

The archdeacons chose their own chancellors or officials, though they had to be approved by the bishop. Until 1617 they had fixed contracts and held office for only about four or five years. I have listed those whom I could discover in the Colchester archdeaconry in appendix 1 (page 162). From 1569 to 1575 and from 1590 to 1617 there were two of them at a time, one for each of the geographically separate areas. One of the earliest officials was William Harrison, rector of Radwinter, who held many other posts, and was also a writer whose vivid descriptions of his times are still much valued today. He supervised the north-western area during the early 1570s, occasionally coming south also; on one occasion he officiated at a court held in Witham's St.Nicholas church. His successor, Fabian Wither, took charge of the whole archdeaconry for a time; he was brother of George the archdeacon, and vicar of All Saints in Maldon, where he promoted Puritan preaching. By 1617 the national policy for appointing officials had changed. Short fixed contracts were replaced by appointments for life, and lawyer Robert Aylett of Feering, appointed by the new archdeacon Henry King, took charge for the next twenty-four years, until the courts were disbanded in 1641. In 1619 he also became the bishop's deputy or commissary for Essex and Hertfordshire, having previously been acting temporarily for some time, and stayed in that post until 1641 also. He was an important figure, and is discussed further in chapter 9 (page 98 in particular).[30]

Even Robert Aylett left the courts in the more distant parts of his territory to be presided over by surrogates. The furthest he travelled to act as judge was to Chelmsford, about fifteen miles from his home. However, the judges' main assistants, the deputy registrars, had a more arduous life. They were obliged to attend all the sittings of the courts in their jurisdiction, and those who worked in the Colchester archdeaconry must have become wearily familiar with the thirty miles of winding roads between Saffron Walden and Colchester. Nevertheless they stayed for a long time; there were only three of them between 1569 and 1641.[31] The one about whom most information survives is the last of the three, gentleman and lawyer Edmund Tillingham of Great Dunmow, who had a remarkable career. He was deputy registrar of the Colchester Archdeaconry court from 1604 until 1641, and for the last twenty-two years of that time he also served the Bishop's Commissary court for Essex and Hertfordshire. The second appointment probably arose out of the first. When Robert Aylett became the archdeacon's official in 1617, Tillingham was no doubt able to give him the benefit of his years of experience. So it is not surprising that a month after Aylett also became the bishop's commissary in 1619, Tillingham

Act books of the church courts

These books were both taken around Essex by Edmund Tillingham, deputy registrar. The one on the right was used in the court of the archdeacon of Colchester from 1625 to 1627. We can see the remains of the leather lace which was used for holding it shut. The one on the left was used in the Bishop's Commissary court between 1625 and 1628. Its lace wore a hole in the cover which has been patched on the inside, but then another hole was worn in the patch also. Both volumes are now in the Essex Record Office.

was appointed in that court too. This duplication may have helped to avoid the 'poor communications' between the two systems that were noted by Jay Anglin in his study of the archdeaconry of Essex. Edmund Tillingham died in 1645, but when the courts reappeared after the Restoration, his successor in the Commissary court was Christopher Tillingham, perhaps his son, who also helped on occasion in the Archdeacon's court. [32]

A deputy registrar like Edward Tillingham had many duties of a general nature, such as receiving and distributing notices and instructions from people like the bishop, but his most demanding role was organising and attending all the court hearings. In court he would often be asked to examine witnesses himself, and his record of the proceedings, mostly in Latin, was an important document. Court business often moved very quickly. We know for instance that an earlier Archdeacon's court sitting in Colchester was completed between the hours of 9 a.m. and 11 a.m., and this was probably usual. Less than a dozen of the accused people seem to have attended on that occasion, but nevertheless over 120 cases appeared in the book, and a future course of action had to be decided for all of them. In a sample year of 1626, Edmund Tillingham went to virtually all 114 sittings of both types of court. In addition he would have gone to the six meetings of the archdeacon's two Visitations, and probably to at least one series of Visitations by the commissary. He must have had a good horse and good health. He

arranged to have active periods of about ten days at a time, when the two types of court were mixed, but carefully arranged geographically. Each cycle was slightly different, but to quote the middle of March 1626 as an example, he held four courts for the bishop and three for the archdeacon over a period of eleven days, beginning at Billericay on a Monday, and then proceeding to Chelmsford, Kelvedon and Colchester on successive days, covering thirty miles. Sometimes both types of court were held at Colchester on the same day, but this time there was only one. After a long weekend free, perhaps spent at his home in Dunmow, he appeared on the next Monday thirty miles away from Colchester, at Bishops Stortford, and then travelled the five miles to Henham in time for a Tuesday court. He probably managed to spend Wednesday at home again before going on to his last hearing in Braintree, fifteen miles from Henham, on the Thursday. Then he had ten days' break, some of which would have to be spent planning the next round of courts, and making sure that the relevant people were informed and summoned, not an easy task in view of all the deferments which took place. He would also write out the details into the Act books in advance, with spaces in between each case, ready to be filled in during the hearing. We can see today that his books suffered a good deal of wear and tear, doubtless making these journeys in saddle bags through wind and rain. Two of them are shown above. Soon after he had become responsible for both courts, Tillingham had wisely introduced a system whereby he only used one book for the Bishop's court and one for the Archdeacon's. Previously there had been two for one court and three for the other. He also dealt with all the money, collecting fees and fines in court, and distributing them to the right people afterwards. As a result he was accused at quarter sessions in 1615 of taking an unjustified payment for the probate of a will; the result is not known.[33]

Assisting the judge and the deputy registrar were several men known as apparitors or mandatorys. They each dealt with particular deaneries, and were local men. They also served the Bishop's courts. It was they who delivered the summonses for people to appear, and they also served as ushers in the court room. Another of their responsibilities was to report on matters such as the upkeep of the churches, and whether penances had been carried out. Jay Anglin suggests that although apparitors were often, not surprisingly, unpopular, some of them could be reasonably reputable and efficient. On the other hand, an earlier Essex writer, W.J.Pressey, wrote about the failings of Essex apparitors, giving examples from the Archdeacon's courts of their neglect of their duties, their succumbing to bribery, and the abuse which they received from suspects. As he pointed out, their fictional counterpart, Chaucer's 'Summoner', a specialist in 'bribery and blackmail', had as bad a name as his real-life colleagues. From time to time irreg- ularities were also presented in the Bishop's Consistory court. Several Essex apparitors were criticised there in 1606. For instance Robert Fishpool of Coggeshall was said to have neglected the correct procedure when he went to Boxted to summon some parishioners.[34]

It was also at the Consistory court that in 1622 there was a more serious complaint from Black Notley about William Salter, a victualler from Witham who was apparitor for the Witham deanery. It was said that he had been 'taking money for suppressing and cancelling of presentments'. However, nothing more seems to have been heard about this, and Salter continued in the post until he died ten years later, after more than thirty years in office. In 1600, at the beginning of his career, he had summoned a fellow parishioner, gentleman Thomas Bayles, for not paying his rates, and Bayles 'dyd strike Salter the mandatarye saying that he cared fore never a straw of the Courte'. One of Salter's most onerous tasks occurred in December 1631, when he attended a lively meeting of the Bishop's Consistory court at Kelvedon and certified that he had served summons on nearly one hundred people in the deanery. Half of them were from Witham itself, including his own churchwardens. He did the job well, as most of them came to court. He seems rather an unlikely choice for the post, having appeared several times himself in court for offences such as unauthorised beer sales, and having a disorderly alehouse. He was adequately off but not wealthy, leaving goods worth £19 when he died.[35]

Nature of court business and punishments

Certain disputes between individuals, known as 'instance' cases, could be taken up in the Church courts,

and the probate and administration of the estates of the deceased were also dealt with. But what I shall mostly discuss will be the 'office' business, whereby the court's officers or the parish's own churchwardens took action against alleged wrongdoers. The offences included working or playing or drinking on Sundays, non-attendance at church or communion, teaching without a licence, and sexual misdemeanours such as fornication, adultery, and bearing illegitimate children. The churchwardens themselves could be presented for not undertaking their duties satisfactorily, and so could the local clergymen. For 'office' accusations the suspects normally spoke for themselves; I only noticed one Witham case where a lawyer was sent instead.[36]

The approachability of the court was increased by its ability and willingness to receive cases merely on the basis of a rumour, known as a 'fame'. So for instance, at a witchcraft hearing in 1588, the deposition of John Barker, a Witham tailor, was made on the basis that he had 'herde yt reported in the parishe of Witham'. However, more specific evidence was also used sometimes. For instance in 1590 Witham's William Salter, the one who was later a court messenger, had been 'taken suspiciously with one Dorothy Priste by the watchemen at an unlawful time in the night'.[37]

The procedure for testing the allegations often went through many court days, spread over several months. Thus I found that only about one third of the Witham entries in the Act books of the Colchester archdeaconry related to new business, whilst the rest were continuations of cases heard at previous courts. As was common in the other types of Church court too, this was frequently a result of the non-attendance of the persons accused. The reasons for their absence were not usually given; probably they were often just avoiding judgement. But there does survive a letter from William Robinson, a Witham grocer, excusing himself on grounds of bereavement in 1625; his alleged offence was 'selling wares on the Sabath'. He wrote:

> Mr.Tillingham I Comend me unto you. I am presented by our Witham Churchwardens and I pray spare me to day I will appeare the next Court if it please god For it hath pleased god that my Father is departed yesterdaye morninge therefore I Cannot Come todaye in some haste.

Having been a churchwarden in the previous year, he would be familiar with Edmund Tillingham, the deputy registrar, to whom he was writing.[38]

When people did appear in court, they could either confess, make excuses, or deny the rumour. The court could dismiss the case without punishment, sometimes with a warning. Alternatively the suspects could be asked to come back to a future sitting. In matters of neglect such as church attendance, they would be expected to certify their reform at this next appearance. If they were accused of positive wrongdoing such as adultery, they had to bring back evidence for their defence, often by producing a certain number of friends in court as witnesses, known as compurgators. This was no easy task, as the friends had to be persuaded to leave their work and travel to the court, and would expect the suspect to pay their expenses. Thus in 1617 it was said that a woman from Bradfield was 'wholie unable' 'to undergoe the charges of a purgacion'. If, as usually happened, no compurgators came, or if some came but the court did not accept their version of events, the accused was normally ordered to perform a penance, the severity of which could vary considerably. Serious accusations occasioned a public confession in church, or a notice displayed in a public place. A blanket or sheet would be worn during the proceedings, and one of these might be kept in the church chest in readiness. Examples of Witham people undergoing penances were Benedicta Wilson in 1600, and Amy Burton alias Shepard, and Barbara Creek, both in 1604; all had given birth to illegitimate children. Benedicta was to wear a white sheet in Witham market place, and the other two in the church.[39] There survives a description of another Witham penance. It was undergone in 1583 by William Newman, for adultery with his servant girl, Jane Pullin, and was recalled five years later thus:

> In the parishe church of Witham upon a Christmas daye ... the said William Newman did publiq and open pennance ... acknowledging at the same tyme to the hole congregation then present that he had committed adultery or fornication ... and desyred the Congregation to praye for him that he might be a newe mann.

Another witness added that Newman had 'promised amendment to his liff houlding up his handes, then being present ... all or most of the inhabitants of the sayd parishe'. Newman was a yeoman, victualler, innkeeper and draper, probably at the White Hart in Newland Street. He had been parish constable in 1583, the year of his offence. In 1589 he and his wife Mary went to the Archdeacon's court again, this time concerning adultery by their son Francis. On that occasion William reported that Francis was in Flanders, and 'while he was in England that he had no rule and government of him'; the case was dismissed.[40]

Many suspects never appeared in court even after being given several chances to do so, and it was for this rather than for the offence itself that excommunications were issued, excluding them from the Church. Excommunication could be revoked later if the person attended court to seek absolution, but more often than not, this did not happen, and many people may have gone to Church in due course without absolution. This form of 'lesser' excommunication seems to have been regarded as a fairly routine punishment and could sometimes cause a 'catch 22' situation. Thus when woolcomber Edward Spradborough and his wife Ann were taken to the Bishop's Consistory court in 1622 for not coming to Witham church, Edward said that 'the cause of his absence' was that he was excommunicate. However, there were some penalties. In 1600 a Lawford woman was buried 'out of the common place of burial because she died excommunicate'. Theoretically there was disqualification from some secular roles, and furthermore, after a person had been excommunicate for forty days, proceedings could be taken by the bishop to the court of Chancery for a writ of full excommun-ication, which was more serious. This does not often seem to have happened.[41] Finally, some cases still continued to be reported in court long after the points at issue appear to have been resolved. This was because payment of a fee was required at many stages in the proceedings, and non-payment was in itself an offence, which could remain on the books for a long time.

There has been some discussion amongst historians about how people viewed the church courts and their punishments. This must have varied greatly with the circumstances. We have seen how the messenger could be abused, and there were other similar occurrences. It may be that the frequent and familiar Archdeacon's court had less impact than the others. Thus in 1602 Witham's John Tabor, alias Heard, ignored its pleas for six months when he was in arrears with his rate payment towards 'the castinge of the bells and repayeringe the steeple', but after appearing in Chelmsford before Sir Edward Stanhope, the bishop's Vicar General, he went home and paid the churchwardens the next day. However, two other Witham men, Robert Bunny and William Nicholls, seem to have welcomed the relative anonymity of less well-attended higher courts. Professor Collinson has suggested that although 'lawlessness was not the prerogative of the poor, and not necessarily a shameful thing', 'someone with a stake in the community ... could not afford to remain excommunicate from one Easter to the next'.[42] The cases of Bunny and Nicholls show that men with such a position to uphold were even more alarmed at the prospect of a public penance. Widower Robert Bunny was keeper of the town's most important inn, the George, in the market place in Newland Street (part of it is now the Town Hall, no.61 Newland Street). In November 1619 he was called to the rooms of the bishop's Vicar General, Sir Henry Martin, in London, and admitted having a sexual relationship with his 'resident servant', Bridget Sammon (though the suggestion that he was the father of her child was deleted). When he was told to perform public penance in Witham church on Sunday, wearing a sheet, he pleaded to be allowed to pay money 'to good and charitable uses' instead, saying:

> that he is a howsholder and lyveth in good reputacion amonge his neighbours who knowe not of this offence committed, neyther is he presented nor hath byn complayned of for this matter to any ecclesiasticall or temporall magistrate. And he further alledgeth that he kepeth a publique Inne in Witham for travaylers to resorte unto, and should be ashamed to go amonge his guestes to give them interteynement if he should be so muche disgraced as to performe the publique penaunce injoyned him, and if his guestes should thereuppon forsake his howse it might be his undoing. And moreover he sayeth that he is a widower and should loose his preferment in marriage and may also be contemned of his owne children.

Martin agreed to think about it. Bunny stayed away from two hearings of the Consistory court in St.Paul's cathedral but made three more pleas in private, and was eventually absolved in June 1620. He had been a churchwarden three years previously and was a probable Royalist in later years.[43]

Meanwhile, William Nicholls, a yeoman and gentleman who lived at Benton Hall, was presented by the officers of the Bishop's Commissary at Braintree in April 1620, following a 'rumour'. He appeared and admitted that:

> about our Lady day was twelve moneth, he had the Carnall knowledge of the body of ... Mary Parrant within the parish of Witham ... for which he is very heartely sorry, and therefore prayeth forgiveness of god for the same and sayth that there is noe speech thereof within the parish where he dwelleth, neither that there is any presentment made by the Minister or Churchwardens there for the same business and submitteth himselfe to the order and answere of the Judge of this Courte for his said offence, humbly praying fauvour in this behalfe.

Like Robert Bunny, he was at first ordered to do penance in Witham church, but he pleaded that he was:

> now a married man, and well thought of amongst his neighbours, and married to an antient widdow with many Children and to doe the pennance injoyned in such publique maner, would be unto him and her a great scandall where he dwelleth, and a greefe and discontent unto his wife and feareth an occasion of some breach between them by reason thereof, and therefore humbly prayeth some Commiseration to be had of him and the said pennance to be Commuted into some pecuniarie somme of money to be imployed to good uses.

His plea was successful and he escaped with a fine of £6 13s.4d. This was not permitted very often, and usually only the bishop's officials could authorise it. When Nicholls was presented in his absence by the Witham churchwardens three weeks later at the Archdeacon's court, it was merely for allowing his pregnant servant to leave the parish. His other role in the affair was not mentioned, and he was not punished. That court was supervised by exactly the same people who had fined him at the Commissary court, Robert Aylett the judge and Edmund Tillingham the deputy registrar, so they were well aware that the matter had already been dealt with discreetly.[44]

Volume of court business

The graph in figure 5 shows the increasing volume of new cases concerning Witham parish. There were over seven hundred of these altogether between 1569, when surviving entries first become reasonably continuous, and 1640, the last complete year before the closure of the court. A similar increase over time was found by the historians of the adjoining parish of Terling, although in Witham there was a temporary reduction in the 1610s, which was not found in Terling, where there was instead a falling off of activity in the 1630s. Overall, Witham had about twice as many cases as Terling, as befitted their relative population sizes. The table in figure 6 gives a breakdown of Witham's new cases. It can be seen that about a quarter of the total was made

FIGURE 5

NEW BUSINESS FROM WITHAM IN COURTS OF COLCHESTER ARCHDEACONRY SHOWN AS PERCENTAGE OF ANNUAL AVERAGE

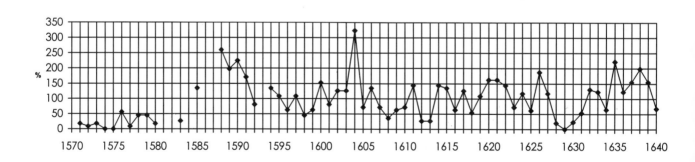

Years are 'Old Style', i.e. 25 March to 24 March.

In the following years, there were in addition more than ten new cases from Witham heard in the surviving records of the Bishop's Consistory Court: 1612 (24), 1618 (24), 1627 (17), 1631 (47), 1634 (16). Not all these records survive.

Some adjustments have been made where all the information does not survive. Gaps have been left where not enough survives for this to be possible.

FIGURE 6

NEW CASES APPEARING IN ARCHDEACON'S COURT FROM WITHAM

DATES	TOTAL 1570 TO 1639	1570s	1580s	1590s	1600s	1610s	1620s	1630s*
TOTAL NUMBER IN THE PERIOD GIVEN	751	21	105	116	131	101*	136*	141*
Of which percentage in each type:-								
The court against the churchwardens	8	14	12	14	15	3	1	2*
Sexual offences	25	14	24	31	27	26	25*	19
Not paying rates	12	0	7	13	17	16	8	11
Non-attendance at church or not taking communion	28	10	20	19	26	25	38*	37*
Games or work on Sunday (all work after 1601)	6	0	8	4	4	12*	10	3
Drunkenness & disorderly houses	6	0	5	2	2	8*	15	4
Irreverence in church, esp. wearing hat or not kneeling	3	0	0	0	1	1	1	15*
Offending court officers	2	0	5	3	1	1	1	1
Presentment of vicar or curate	1	0	3	2	1	0	0	4
Others: including unknown, blasphemy, libel, teaching without a licence, witchcraft	10	62	17	13	7	9*	2	5
Percentage said to be presented by churchwardens	61	9	25	40	66	70	93	73

Years are 'Old Style', i.e. 25 March to 24 March.

* For these figures in particular, there were in addition a considerable number of new cases heard at the Bishop's Consistory courts of 1612 (24 in all), 1618 (24), 1627 (17), 1631 (47) and 1634 (16).

Approximately four years' records are missing altogether, of which about half a year is in the 1570s, a little over three years in the 1580s, a third of a year in the 1590s, and one tenth of a year in the 1600s. If both parties are named for sexual offences, the offence is counted as one; similarly if someone was presented for allowing sexual offenders to go away unpunished, it is counted as part of the original offence.

FIGURE 7
ESTIMATED OLD AND NEW BUSINESS FROM ALL AREAS IN COURTS OF COLCHESTER ARCHDEACONRY
SHOWN AS PERCENTAGE OF ANNUAL AVERAGE

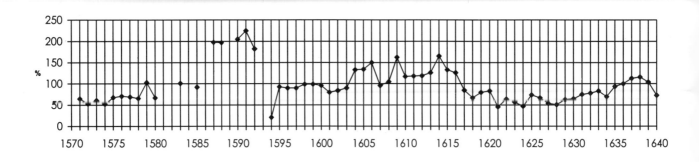

FIGURE 8

OLD AND NEW BUSINESS FROM WITHAM IN COURTS OF COLCHESTER ARCHDEACONRY
SHOWN AS PERCENTAGE OF ANNUAL AVERAGE

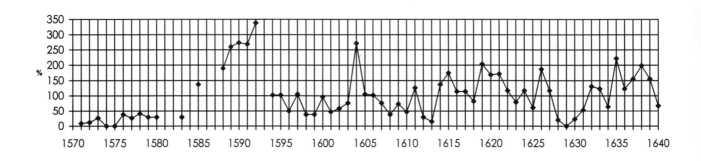

Figures 7 and 8

Years are 'Old Style', i.e. 25 March to 24 March.

In the following years, there were in addition more than ten new cases from Witham heard in the surviving records of the Bishop's Consistory Court: 1612 (24), 1618 (24), 1627 (17), 1631 (47), 1634 (16). Not all these records survive.

Some adjustments have been made where all the information does not survive. Gaps have been left where not enough survives for this to be possible.

up of sexual misdemeanours, and that this rate stayed fairly steady throughout, whilst other types of offence were more common at specific times, as will become more apparent in later chapters. In Terling nearly one third were sexual offences, and the rate reached one half in the early 1600s.[45]

As already noted, these new cases only comprised perhaps one third of the overall volume of business. It is the total volume, including old and new cases, which is shown in figures 7 and 8. Figure 7 is an attempt to assess what was happening in the archdeaconry as a whole. I did this by the somewhat crude device of counting pages in the Act books; the page layout remained remarkably consistent throughout the period, so that the count may at least be taken to show any major peaks in activity. Comparable figures for Witham in figure 8 were derived from a count of entries. As one might expect in a single parish, the level is very volatile. However, there is one unmistakable feature that the archdeaconry in general and Witham in particular have in common. This is the peak of activity between about 1586 and 1591, which will be discussed in chapter 6 (pages 64-66). Other fluctuations will be mentioned in the appropriate chapters.

EDUCATION, READING, AND WRITING

Some writers have suggested that the years from 1560 to 1640 saw an 'educational revolution' in Britain, though the rate of change varied, and only a minority of people were affected. Historians have often pointed out the contribution of the written word, particularly the Bible, to the development of new forms of Christianity, from early Protestantism, through Puritanism, to later nonconformity. Furthermore, the literate were at an advantage when participating in the administration of the Church, the manor, the parish, the county, and the country, as well as in organising their own businesses. However, other writers have also emphasised the contribution of illiterate people, both to radical movements and to the economy, noting that it was common practice for people to ask others to read and write for them, to make good use of the spoken word, and to use practical methods such as accounting with notches on sticks.[46]

The purpose of education

Some Witham people saw teaching as having a moral and religious intent, however imprecise, as we can see from their financial bequests to help their children. Thus in 1584 Joan Jolly wished hers to be brought up 'in the feare of God'. In 1616 the wealthy clothier William Weale combined morality and practicality in asking his wife Ann to 'educate my daughters in the feare of god and good nurtriture of huswivery'. Others concentrated on secular requests alone. Thus in 1555, Emma Reerye was asked by her husband Richard to:

see that my Chyldern be honestly educatyd and brought up And to lerne On mysterye Scyens of

occupacion Wherby they maye be able to gett their lyvynges honestly Another daye.

In 1634 yeoman George Skingley of Powershall arranged for his grandson John to 'be placed in service to some good trade with some honest sufficient man', whilst two years later the young John Markes was left £40 by his father John, the Bridge Street maltster:

for his bringeinge upp and educacion in some good order and waie of life whereby in tyme to come he shall or maye be able to gett his liveinge.

More vague was singlewoman Sarah Jackson, who in 1676 left a fund for the 'tuistion or scoolinge' of her young niece Elizabeth. Sarah was one of a prosperous family of clothiers, and Elizabeth was the daughter of Dalton Clarke, a former innkeeper and postmaster at the George inn.[47]

Very few willmakers tried to provide for university education. It was expensive, and from the late sixteenth century onwards it was probably coming to be dominated rather more by the better-off than it had been in medieval times. The only universities were Oxford and Cambridge, and Essex had stronger links with Cambridge, partly because it was nearer, and sometimes also because of a common interest in Puritanism. The majority of graduates became clergymen, though some took up other opportunities such as the law. Thus in 1616 Witham's vicar, Robert Tinley, left money for his eldest son, Martin, to be 'put forth to schole either in the Cuntrie or at any of the Universities or ... the Innes of Courte or Chancery'. His three younger sons were merely to be brought up 'either to schoole or to some honest occupation'. The later vicar, Thomas Cox, who died in 1676, also had varying expectations of his sons. He left his 'library' to his son Thomas. If Thomas died without male heirs, it was to go to Edmund, but only if 'he shall be brought up in a capacity to use it'. If not, it was to be sold.[48]

Only two lay people in Witham mentioned universities in their wills. One was William Nicholls of Benton Hall, whose concern for his good name we noted earlier. He provided in 1638 for 'the maintenance and bringing up' of his son Cyprian at Cambridge. Cyprian probably became a clergyman, but died soon afterwards. Ten years later, William's widow Dorothy made a less ambitious donation to her grandson William Davies, namely 'five shillings towards his schooling'. In 1633 the wealthy Puritan Dame Katherine Barnardiston of Witham Place left £400 for the education of three poor men at Cambridge. If possible, her relatives were to be chosen, but failing that the money could be used for 'any of the parish of Wittham' who 'shall bring up theire sonn to be a schollar and are not able to maynteyne him at the University'. It is not known whether anyone from Witham ever benefited from this gift.[49]

Teachers

Some families may have taught their own children, but there were also a number of specialised teachers, who will be mentioned in the appropriate chapters. In the

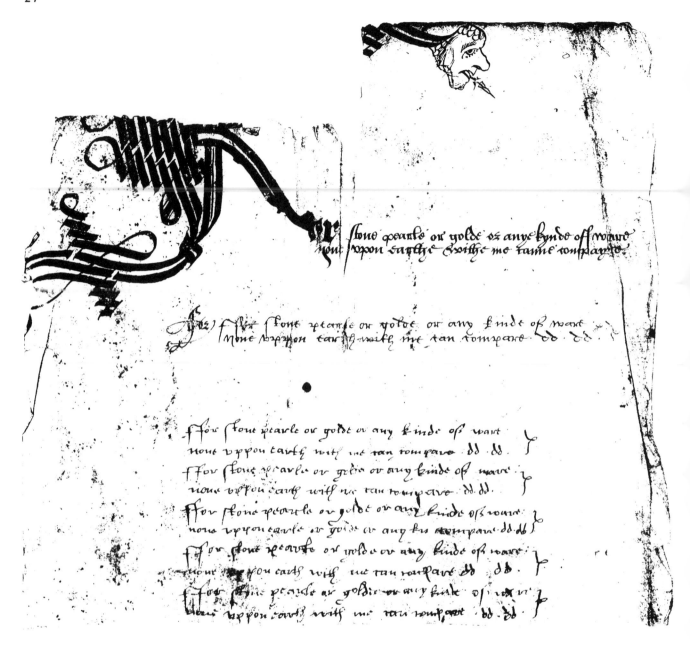

Figure 9. Part of a piece of writing practice, dating from about 1586

Filed by mistake with the will of Witham victualler Thomas Gilder of the Ship in Newland Street.
The teacher who wrote the example at the top and drew the face was probably vicar Edward Halys, who wrote the will.
(Reduced: reproduced by courtesy of the Essex Record Office; reference E.R.O. D/ACW 2/28)

early and mid-sixteenth centuries it was the clergy who fulfilled this role exclusively. The remains of a piece of writing practice have been preserved, accidentally folded into a will which was written in 1586 by the vicar, Edward Halys. It is probably his example at the top of the sheet that the pupil struggled to copy (see figure 9). Several curates were specifically said to be schoolmasters. In 1630 curate Thomas Young was authorised to 'teach grammar school in [the] church of Witham', which suggests that teaching carried out by churchmen was actually done in the church building, perhaps in the vestry.[50]

After 1559, teachers required a licence from the Church, and laymen as well as clergymen began to receive licences from the bishop in the diocese of London. Even the laymen were obliged to sign a declaration accepting the Articles of the Church. Some of them were given a monopoly in the parish. The majority of them ran 'petty schools', which taught children under the age of about ten, probably all boys. The first known layman licensed in Witham was Richard Brodway, authorised to 'educate scholars' in 1577.[51] Smaller parishes also had lay teachers, including many of those adjoining Witham, such as Fairstead and Rivenhall. Some of the men probably taught in their own homes, but others, such as Witham's Richard Redman in 1612, was referred to as teaching 'in the parish church' even though he was not a clergyman. He already had a university degree and was probably waiting to be ordained and obtain a post. One historian has pointed out that 'schoolmastering' was 'commonly regarded as a stopgap' amongst the clergy, and there were other examples in Witham. The qualified teachers were usually given a fairly general remit, but those who did not have a degree were restricted to a specific purpose, such as 'the rudiments of grammar', 'the rudiments of reading English books and the art of writing' or 'schole in the English tongue'. In 1619 Witham had the unusual honour of a teacher in French and another unspecified language, in addition to 'writing and calculation'. Licences for teaching foreign languages were common in London, but less so in Essex.[52]

Teachers doubtless carried out other tasks for which fluent reading or writing was required, for instance preparing documents such as wills. Conversely, other literate people may have been called upon to do some teaching even if they did not have a licence. The existence of unauthorised teachers who had not subscribed to the Articles of the church was understandably a matter of concern for the ecclesiastical authorities, and several such people incurred the disapproval of the Archdeacon's court, particularly between about 1590 and 1615. Some were ordinary tradesmen, and one, in 1590, was a woman. She was Margerie Rainbye, the 'servant' of Richard Rippingale, who was a shearman in the newly developing cloth industry.[53]

None of the Witham establishments developed into formal 'grammar schools', as happened in some other towns. The licensing system was suspended during the Civil War, but re-introduced in 1660. In 1664, in addition to the licensed teacher, Witham had, according to the churchwardens 'some private schooles taught by women soe farr as horne booke and plaster and learning Children to knit and Sowe'. Horn books were boards displaying the alphabet and numbers. Perhaps 'dame' schools like these had always existed without need of official consent, though they may have benefited from the reduced regulation since 1642.[54]

Literacy: reading

Literacy incorporates several skills. The easiest to acquire was the ability to read print; 'Gothic' or 'black letter' type was regarded as the simplest. In 1633 when Francis Barrett, a mariner from Dover, was arrested in Witham for talking about Jesuits, it was reported that 'he denieth that he can either writte, or reade anie other hande than printed hande'. This statement was made in his defence, meaning that he should not be suspected of treason, because he could not read manuscript, so it is also an illustration of the fact that literacy was sometimes thought of as a dubious skill if acquired by the wrong people. Reading handwriting was much harder than reading print, but would be particularly helpful for local office-holders, because most of the documents they would need to deal with would be in manuscript. Some were in Latin, giving those few who understood it an added advantage. Writing was a more

complicated skill again, so by no means everyone who could read could write as well. Students of literacy have suggested further refinements, namely 'functional literacy', which is the ability to understand and write enough for everyday needs, and the more demanding 'cultural literacy' necessary for other purposes.[55]

Reading may have been the easiest skill to acquire, but it is one of the hardest to find evidence of. We do not know whether all owners of books could read them; some, particularly Bibles, may have merely been revered objects. Wills are one of the main sources of information about the ownership of books, but they do not detail every possession, and during the sixteenth and seventeenth centuries only about a dozen Witham willmakers out of over three hundred mentioned books specifically. We may note that all of them were after 1600, the great majority being after 1640. The second half of the seventeenth century is known to have seen a great increase in book production, though some historians suggest that this was not necessarily associated with improved rates of literacy. Many of the Witham people with books were clergymen, nonconformist ministers, or their relatives. But there were a few exceptions, such as weaver John Perry, who left his son 'my biggest brass Pott and a Bible' in 1636, and the Quaker clothier John Freeborne, who left each of his grandchildren 'a bible containing the old and new testament' in 1675. Both men could also sign their names. All the books named in Witham wills were religious ones except for blacksmith John Adcock's veterinary or 'horse leech' books in 1654, and a copy of 'Haylins Geography' left by John Ponder to his uncle Thomas, a clergyman and teacher, in 1678; it was accompanied by 'Andrewes Sermons'. Although the geography book sounds secular, its author, Peter Haylin, was a Laudian theologian, as was Lancelot Andrewes.[56]

Literacy: writing and signatures

Writing was taught after reading, and separately. For want of other sources of information, historians often investigate the ability to write by looking at how many people could sign their name on documents. Those who could not sign made a mark, usually a cross. Some people may have been able to sign but not to write anything else. We have one source of such information which includes nearly all the householders in Witham. This is Essex's petition to the House of Commons in January 1642, which is discussed in chapter 10 (pages 121 and 129-30). It contained 223 names in all, probably all of them were heads of households. Over ninety per cent were men. One writer has suggested that such petitions are 'so confused as to be almost useless' in examining literacy. There is certainly a problem in that many of the Witham names were all written in by the same person, as was customary. These amounted to forty-six per cent of the total, and we do not know whether those people could have signed if asked. However the information we have about some of them suggests that they could not. So the fact that twenty-seven per cent of the names were signed is worth

FIGURE 10

ABILITY OF WITHAM'S WILLMAKERS TO SIGN THEIR NAMES

Percentage is out of those whose ability is known, 1581-1700
(excluding those proved outside Essex)

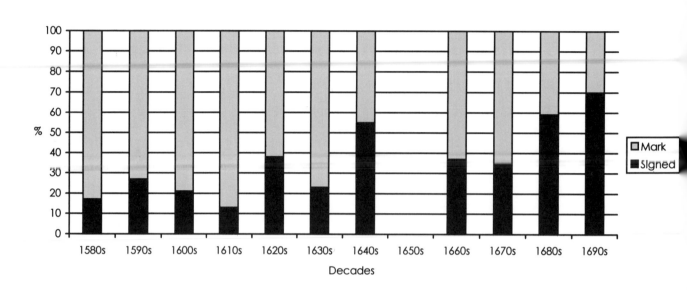

Decade	Total	No. where ability known	Made mark		Signed	
			No.	Per cent	No.	Per cent
1580s	22	12	10	83	2	17
1590s	19	11	8	73	3	27
1600s	24	19	15	79	4	21
1610s	21	15	13	87	2	13
1620s	20	13	8	62	5	38
1630s	26	22	17	77	5	23
1640s	16	11	5	45	6	55
1650s	(mostly proved outside Essex)					
1660s	22	19	12	63	7	37
1670s	27	23	15	65	8	35
1680s	23	22	9	41	13	59
1690s	12	10	3	30	7	70

The difference between the first two columns in the table is accounted for by nuncupative wills and a
few where it is not clear whether the name is signed or not.

FIGURE 11

ABILITY OF KNOWN WITHAM CHURCHWARDENS TO SIGN THEIR NAMES

Percentage is out of those whose ability is known, 1570-1700.
Not all the churchwardens have been identified

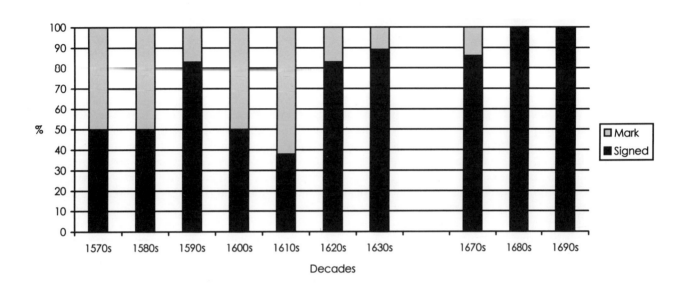

Decade	No. of church-wardens known	No. whose ability is known	Made mark		Signed	
			No.	Per cent	No.	Per cent
1570s	9	4	2	50	2	50
1580s	14	10	5	50	5	50
1590s	15	6	1	17	5	83
1600s	11	8	4	50	4	50
1610s	10	8	5	62	3	38
1620s	8	6	1	17	5	83
1630s	11	9	1	11	8	89
-----	--	--	--	--	--	--
1670s	19	14	2	14	12	86
1680s	20	11	0	0	11	100
1690s	16	13	0	0	13	100

noting. About the same number made marks. One writer has suggested that one third of the population of England and Essex could sign at this time, though there were many local variations. The historians of Terling suggest a much higher figure there.[57]

Signatures on wills have often been studied in connection with literacy, and can give an idea of change over time. They present various problems. People who could write may not always have signed their wills. For instance, Witham yeoman Jeffrey Whale signed a return in 1642 as parish surveyor, but eleven years later, when he was 'aged and weak in body', he only made a mark on his will. In 1672 John Sams of Tolleshunt Major had an even more specific problem; he was obliged to make a mark on his will 'by reason he had the palsie in his hand'. Furthermore, only an untypical minority of people made wills, as discussed earlier in this chapter (page 12). In addition, their writing ability would usually have been acquired many years earlier. Nevertheless, the study of their signatures has been said by one writer to be 'remarkably sensitive' to changes in literacy.[58] In Essex as in many other places, wills before about 1580 usually only survive as copies, and so do not tell us anything about signatures. But there are over two hundred wills surviving for Witham between the 1580s and 1700, and figure 10 shows how many of them were signed in each decade. The proportion increased gradually, though unevenly, from about one fifth in 1580 to more than half by about 1680.[59]

It is also interesting to try and assess literacy levels amongst different sorts of people. Firstly we may note that not one of the nineteen female householders from Witham whose names appeared on the petition of 1642 signed their own name, although it has been suggested by one historian that one tenth of women could write their names by this time. Those few Witham women who made wills rarely signed them. Until near the end of the seventeenth century, those who did sign were from gentry families, though even there, not all women signed. Later we do find signatures from two of 'middling' rank, though they were by no means poor. One was Ann Lisle, the widow of George, the nonconformist minister, in 1689, and the other was Dorcas Robinson in 1694, the widow of George, probably a grocer.[60]

We often have more information about the literacy of influential officials than about the population in general. For instance, we know whether or not about two-thirds of Witham's known churchwardens could sign or not. As shown in figure 11, the proportion who could do so increased, with perhaps the main change having been in around 1620. The level was usually considerably higher than for willmakers, themselves an elite group. Between 1670 and 1700, out of thirty-eight wardens of known ability, only one could not sign, or at least he did not in 1673 and 1678. He was a glover at the site known as the Watering (next to the river, in what is now Guithavon Valley).[61] By 1700 it was probably taken for granted that a churchwarden would be literate. There was a similar pattern amongst the officials of the Witham half-hundred, whose roles are discussed in chapter 5 (page 53). Those high constables and bailiffs who came from Witham itself could usually sign after the 1620s, but not all could do so before that date.[62]

We can also try and assess whether the ability to sign bore any relation to people's wealth or occupations. I have tried to do this by using the petition of 1642. It does not itself give occupations, but many of them can be discovered from other sources. Three-quarters of the people on the petition who were known to be clothiers signed their own names, but only one out of the fourteen weavers. All but one of the yeomen and gentlemen petitioners signed, whilst all but one of the husbandmen and labourers did not. More than half the known shopkeepers signed, but only about one in five of the craftsmen. Of the latter, half of those who signed were blacksmiths, an occupation which appeared to have no non-signers. We may recall that it was blacksmith John Adcock in 1654 who had books to help him in curing horses' ailments. The comparison between shopkeepers and craftsmen is similar to that found in other surveys by historians of Kent and of the diocese of London as a whole, though the particular ability of blacksmiths was not found there. And many studies have found that people of higher wealth and status were in general more likely to be able to sign their names, as is suggested by the comparisons of different occupations given here for Witham.[63]

The relationship to wealth can also be illustrated directly by investigating what rank the signers of the petition held in the Ship Money assessment of 1636. For various reasons only half of the people in the latter also appeared on the petition, but the exercise is still possible. To be assessed for Ship Money at all was a sign of status, because some of the population were regarded as being too poor (the criteria for inclusion are not known). Forty-four per cent of Witham's petition signers appeared in the assessment, but only fifteen per cent of the non-signers. And of those who did appear, the signers had an average assessment of 6s.4d. and a median of four shillings, whilst the non-signers had an average of 2s.7d. and a median of two shillings. However, there was considerable overlap. For instance, five of the signers did have the lowest assessment of one shilling. Conversely, yeoman/innkeeper Thomas Nicholls was assessed at the high sum of fourteen shillings, but, as is confirmed by other sources, he could not sign his name. No doubt he managed his business affairs successfully on the basis of verbal agreements, and simple accounting methods, with occasional assistance from his friends and family.[64] This is a useful reminder of the variety of ability that may be concealed by generalisations.

3. HENRY VIII, 1509-1547

BACKGROUND

In 1496 Christopher Tenant came briefly to be the vicar of Witham. Before that he had been one of the chaplains of 'the King's son Henry, duke of York'.[1] In 1509 this Henry became King Henry VIII, and he reigned until his death in early 1547. Changes that took place during this time and afterwards have since become known as the Reformation. Previously the Church in Europe was Roman Catholic, with the Pope at its head. The Reformation eventually resulted in the emergence of Protestant Churches in much of the northern part of the continent, including England. Many of the points discussed by Christians at that time will be familiar to their counterparts today, but during the sixteenth century they were given added significance by the much greater dominance of the Church in society.

The changes were complicated, particularly during Henry's reign. Detailed official policy in England moved back and forth as a result of such matters as diplomatic expediency, negotiations about the King's marriages and divorce, and the varying relative power of the King, his advisers, and other groups of influential people. The Act of Supremacy of 1534 made Henry VIII the head of the Church in England, and separated it from Rome and the Pope after eight hundred years. After this, allegiance to the Pope became a dangerous thing. In the early years in particular, some suspected papists were executed. Much of the doctrine of the English Church was still Catholic.

However, individual reforms were sometimes included in official pronouncements issued by Henry and his advisers, and most of the new ideas on which they were based, were ones which in due course became associated with Protestantism. Here I should say that some recent writing is cautious with the use of the words 'Catholic' and 'Protestant' during Henry's reign, preferring to use terms such as 'traditional' on the one hand, and 'evangelical' or 'reforming' on the other. Nevertheless, many writers still do talk about Catholic and Protestant belief in discussing this period, and I have done so myself sometimes as a convenient way of indicating a body of ideas and practices with which readers will be familiar.[2]

During the early reforming years after 1534, an influential publication was the cautiously radical book called *Institution of a Christian Man*, or 'Bishop's Book', which appeared in 1537. One of the contributors was John Edmondes, Doctor of Divinity, son of the John Edmondes of Cressing Temple who had earlier held the lease of the Witham manors of Chipping and Newland.[3] After 1538 official policy moved back somewhat towards the Catholic tradition. This was symbolised by the execution of some Protestants in 1540, including Thomas Cromwell, the King's Chancellor, and Robert Barnes, who had associates in Witham.

Nevertheless, it was also during this period that the dissolution of Catholic institutions such as the monasteries was at its height. This had begun in 1536. In 1539 the Abbey of St.John in Colchester, owner of the Witham Place estate, was closed, and in the following year the Knights Hospitallers, lords of the manors of Chipping and Newland, were disbanded. Some writers suggest that the chief motives for the dissolution were financial rather than ideological. In due course much of the property formerly belonging to the religious houses was granted to laymen.

To interpret national policy is complex enough, but to find out what was actually happening in the thousands of English parishes is even more difficult and controversial. There has been much debate amongst historians about whether or not the Reformation was welcome in England. Some of the writers who have suggested that it was, have been inspired by the fact that there were a number of ordinary people who criticised Catholicism even before Henry VIII's break with Rome in 1534. Particularly well-known were the Lollards. They began as followers of John Wycliffe during the fourteenth and fifteenth centuries, but the term is often used to describe their successors at the beginning of the sixteenth century too.

By the 1520s some people in England were also beginning to be influenced by the more formal anti-Catholic movement on the continent of Europe, particularly the Protestantism of Luther. They could be liable to punishment as heretics, meaning that they disagreed with the Church's official doctrine. A return to the scriptures was an important basis of their belief, and often they used versions of the Bible which were illegal, notably William Tyndale's English translation of the New Testament with its strongly Protestant marginal notes, which first appeared in England in 1526. Many of them scorned ritual, pilgrimages, and the worship of saints, and sometimes they rejected transubstantiation, which is the belief that the body and blood of Christ are present in the bread and wine of the communion. Their emphasis on the important role of the individual was also seen as a potential threat to authority. Although there were some changes in the English Church during Henry's reign, they were never sufficient to make people with such beliefs feel secure.[4]

EARLY PROTESTANTS IN ESSEX

In this chapter and the next, I have investigated some aspects of the county as a whole, to give a background to the local information. Lollardy was known in parts of Essex, and in addition, the county was well-placed geographically to receive new Protestant influences. Firstly it had good access from London along the main roads, whose importance for the dissemination of ideas has been stressed by historians. Secondly it had ports on the east coast facing the continent. One of these was Colchester, then the county's largest town. Writers of all opinions have stressed that Essex in general and Colchester in particular were amongst the areas where new ideas made the most headway. Essex has been called 'the most strongly Protestant county in England', and reference has been made to 'the intensity of its popular convictions'. However, even here it is impossible to assess how many people were actively involved. Jennifer Ward has warned that they were only a small minority even in Colchester, and that although the new ideas took more hold there from the 1540s onwards, Colchester could not really be called a 'Protestant town' until the reign of Elizabeth. On the other hand, writers like A.G.Dickens have suggested that many Protestant believers everywhere went unrecorded.[5] So in considering dissenting views in Essex, it should be remembered that either of these interpretations is possible. There are two main sources of information available about early Protestantism in Essex, and indeed in most parts of the country. I shall consider them in turn. Firstly there are records of people who were actually criticised and persecuted for their faith, and secondly there are the preambles to wills.

Accusations of heresy in Essex

Most people who were formally accused of heresy were said to have been actively passing their opinions on to others. Occasionally they were executed, usually by burning. However, during Henry's reign they were often released after being examined by the Church authorities and allowed to 'abjure', which entailed declaring under oath that they had abandoned their heretical views. Frequently their continued activity showed that the abjuration was not genuine. For a few of the examinations there are original records surviving, and many more were later described by the Elizabethan Protestant writer John Foxe, in what became known as his 'Book of Martyrs', which was first published in 1563. It was relentlessly devoted to the promotion of Protestantism, and probably inaccurate at times, but for many incidents it is our only surviving source of information. [6]

Foxe mentions several large groups of people in Essex and Suffolk who were examined, abjured and sent home again during Henry's reign. For many we do not know which parish they lived in, though in 1532 or 1533 they included forty from Steeple Bumpstead and nine from Colchester. Christopher Raven was mentioned twice; we know from other information that he came from

Witham and he will be discussed later. These lists all included family groups of parents and sons and daughters. Of the twelve Essex parishes named specifically, many were associated with people who were punished. One of these was William Sweeting. In about 1509 he had been accused of 'turning' the prior of St.Osyth towards heretical opinions, but he and the prior both abjured and they were released. By 1511 he had moved out of Essex and was employed to look after the cattle which belonged to the town of Chelsea. He was just setting out into the fields with them when he was arrested and taken before the bishop of London, Richard Fitzjames, and accused of speaking against pilgrimages, against worshipping of images of the saints, and against the doctrine of transubstantiation. He was burnt at the stake in Smithfield in 1511 with one of his friends, James Brewster, an illiterate Colchester carpenter. Thomas Mann suffered a similar fate in 1518. His original residence is not clear, but he was said to have 'instructed very many' over a period of several years, and to have spoken in 'divers places and countries in England', including Billericay, Chelmsford and Stratford in Essex. The other Essex people whom Foxe names as having been executed during Henry's reign were three men from Dedham and West Bergholt, in the north-east of the county. They were in fact hanged for theft rather than burnt for heresy. However, they were of interest to Foxe because their offence was to have allegedly walked ten miles to Dovercourt in 1532, removed the crucifix from the church there, carried it away for a quarter of a mile, and set fire to it. A fourth man escaped. Foxe wrote that their motive was to disprove a widespread superstition that the 'idol' in question was so powerful that it prevented the church door being 'shut' (probably meaning 'locked').[7]

Protestant will preambles in Essex

The interpretation of will preambles was discussed in chapter 2 (pages 12-14). Altogether, nearly 1,400 wills survive which were proved in Essex between 1537 and the end of Henry VIII's reign. Their preambles were dominated by traditional Catholic forms, as they were in the country as a whole, but other influences began to appear also, particularly after 1540, and it is these which have interested historians studying the progress of the Reformation. For instance, a number of wills had very brief and non-committal preambles, merely bequeathing the soul to God, with no further embellishment.[8] Thomas Tilling of Witham provides us with an example in 1530; he merely bequeathed his soul 'to Almyghtie god'. His religious affiliation is certainly unclear; in the previous year he had been executor for the traditional Catholic will of his mother-in-law, Joan Bedfield, but he was also close to the early Protestant Christopher Royden who is discussed below.[9] Other preambles mixed both Protestant and Catholic elements; these I shall discuss in the next chapter (pages 45-47).

In looking for 'Protestant' will preambles in Essex, I only picked out the ones which appear to include a definite and committed statement about salvation by

Christ, and nothing about the virgin or the saints; there are more details in the endnotes. Some researchers would be more restrictive in their definition, and others more generous. I found forty-nine of them in Henry's reign, making up about 3.5 per cent of the total. There was a gradual increase; before 1543 they constituted only two per cent, whereas from 1543 onwards the figure was about seven per cent. Peter Clark's study of the Canterbury diocese in Kent showed a similar change, though at a lower level.[10] So Protestant preambles were still unusual and daring. Occupations are known for only eighteen of the forty-nine Essex people who used them. Two called themselves gentlemen, and five were yeomen; both descriptions indicate wealth and status. The others were two husbandmen, five widows, and four craftsmen or tradesmen, namely two tailors, a shoemaker and a mercer.

The earliest of the Essex examples was written in May 1537, when Robert Martin of Rochford omitted the customary reference to the virgin and the saints, and instead left his soul 'to god Almyghty that yt thorowe the meryttes of Cryste Jesus may inherytt the eternall glory'. Two other men followed later in the same year, with rather more expansive versions, and they both obtained the assistance of clergymen, who witnessed the wills and may have written them. Thus Clement Causton of the adjoining parish of Rayleigh had John Gilded, 'clerke' as a witness, and Augustus Yeman of Dedham, had curate John Worthe. Amongst the later examples there was tailor John Coole of Littlebury, near Saffron Walden; his will was dated 1545. Again it was probably written for him by his curate, who was John Halywell. It read:

> First and before all other thinges I comytt me unto godd and unto his mercye trusting without any doubte that by his grace and the merytes of Jesus Christe and by the vertue of his passion and of his resurrection I have and shall have remyssion of my synnes and resurrection of my bodie and soule and eternall lyf accordyng to my faith as my savior christe hath promysed me.[11]

These words are noteworthy because they are taken from the well-known preamble of William Tracy, though they omit many of Tracy's more emphatic adjectives, and part of his text. Tracy, a gentleman from Toddington in Gloucestershire, had died in 1531, and as a direct result of the fervent wording of the preamble, his corpse was removed from consecrated ground and burnt for heresy, after the Church officials at Canterbury had refused to prove the will. This shows that the adoption of a format which opposed the Church's teaching was not to be done lightly. The exhumation was supported by higher authorities, though it was eventually decided that the burning itself had been excessive, and the chancellor responsible was fined the enormous sum of £300. The adoption of the preamble elsewhere in the country has been investigated by John Craig and Caroline Litzenberger. In view of Tracy's fate it was particularly symbolic, and illustrates how new ideas spread around England. The text began

to be circulated in 1531, the year that it was written, when two London men were separately in trouble for possessing copies. Then it was printed in Antwerp in 1535 with a commentary by William Tyndale, who, like Tracy, was a Gloucestershire man. He had been on the continent for some years, having begun in 1525 the printing of his pioneering English translation of the New Testament. He was put to death for heresy in 1536. Tracy's preamble appeared as far north as Halifax in Yorkshire in 1548.[12] As will be discussed more fully in later chapters (page 45, and pages 56-57), I have also found it in Essex later on, once during Mary's reign, and six times during the years 1573 to 1589. I have not fully searched the intervening periods.

The Essex places from which I have quoted examples so far were part of a distinct geographical pattern. In both Kent and Essex, Protestant preambles are concentrated in certain parts of the county. This is shown for Essex on the map in figure 12 overleaf, which also shows the places mentioned by Foxe. Similar conclusions arose from an attempt to assess the frequency of preambles in relation to the level of population.[13] Thus the importance of the coast was illustrated by the Rochford hundred, in which Robert Martin and Clement Causton lived. The Colchester area, including Augustus Yeman's home in Dedham, was near both coast and main road. Colchester itself was rather later in taking up Protestant will preambles. Jennifer Ward has noted that with one exception, none of that borough's wills had them until 1545. However, after this the borough had far more examples than would be expected from the size of its population, several of them witnessed by local clergy. So also did the neighbouring hundred of Tendring.

Other significant places situated on the roads from London were the Saffron Walden area including John Coole's home of Littlebury, and the Liberty of Havering, including Romford. In Romford itself, very near to London, there were eight Protestant wills, more than in any other single parish. Marjorie McIntosh has noted an early readiness to accept Protestantism there, and in the other urban parts of Havering, particularly amongst the leaders of the community. Three of the Romford wills, written between 1540 and 1544, were witnessed by the vicar Robert Samuel, and one by another clergyman. During the same years, six of them used a common wording. The indications are that they were written by several different people, so very possibly the text was circulating in the parish. It read along the lines:

> I commende my soull unto Christe Jesu my maker and redemer in whome and by the merites of whose blessed passion ys my whole truste of clene remyssyon and forgevenes of my synnes.

Another Protestant will from Romford was witnessed by a 'citizen and draper of London' called John Stockar, emphasising the importance of links with the capital. This was the will of John Carowe the elder, whose preamble was a vey elaborate one referring to the Trinity.[14]

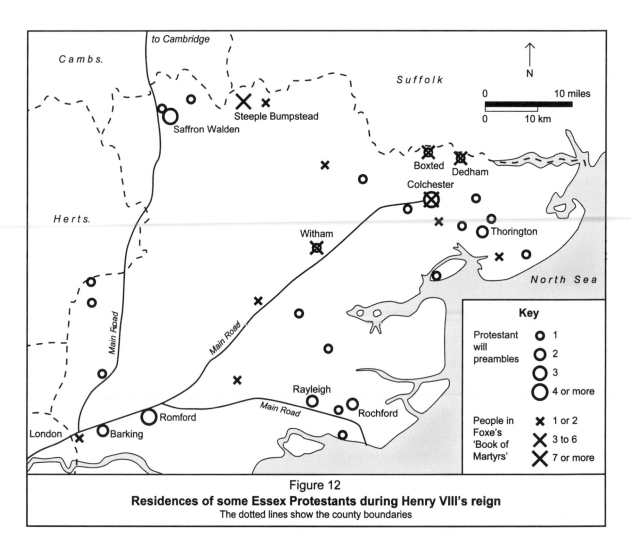

Figure 12
Residences of some Essex Protestants during Henry VIII's reign
The dotted lines show the county boundaries

Key

Protestant will preambles	○	1
	○	2
	○	3
	○	4 or more
People in Foxe's 'Book of Martyrs'	✕	1 or 2
	✕	3 to 6
	✕	7 or more

The Witham half-hundred, also on the main London road, had two Protestant wills, about in proportion to its share of the county's population. They were both from the parish of Witham itself and will be discussed in more detail later (pages 34 and 35). Several areas of the county are noticeably blank on the map, with no mention in Foxe and no known Protestant will preambles. In some of these places there are additional sources of information which can confirm this impression, and show that they had a conformist tradition. For instance, a recent study has shown that this was the case in Maldon.[15] It may be more difficult to illuminate the situation in other such areas, like the countryside to the west and north of the county town of Chelmsford.

Because of the very restricted nature of the evidence, only a few Essex names appear both in John Foxe's work and in wills with Protestant preambles. However, amongst the writers and witnesses of the forty-nine Protestant willmakers of the reign, I did identify five or six people who were probably also mentioned by Foxe. They included John Turke of Romford, John Mell of Boxted, and weaver John Cavell of Thorington; the last two places are near Colchester. All three witnessed wills, and Turke also made one of his own. The first two abjured when accused of heresy, but Cavell was burnt at the stake in 1556, during Mary's reign.[16] Two other people whose names appeared in both sources were the Witham men, Christopher Raven and John Chapman; their friend Thomas Hills was possibly another. I shall discuss them in more detail in the next section.

CHRISTOPHER, DYONISE, AND JOAN RAVEN, THOMAS HILLS, AND JOHN AND RICHARD CHAPMAN, OF WITHAM

Christopher Raven was a tailor. Dyonise his sister, and Joan was his wife. Thomas Hills and the two brothers John and Richard Chapman were his 'servants', which probably meant that they were assistants in the business, possibly skilled men, living with the family as was customary. They have been quoted by one writer to show the importance of the household in the circulation of new ideas. In fact several historians have discussed the Raven 'group', assisted by the survival of some of the original documents relating to their cross-examination in 1527.[17] Here it is also hoped to add a little information from local records to enlarge the picture.

There were two separate inquiries in which Christopher Raven was involved, in 1511 and in 1527. This was when the English Church was still headed by the Pope. Unusually, some original records of the statements made on the second occasion still survive. We know it was the same man on both occasions, because the clerk of 1527 obligingly made a note that Raven had abjured before Fitzjames, who had been the bishop in 1511. Thus Raven's activities can be said to link the Lollardy of the beginning of the century with the new Protestant influences which began to arrive from the continent during the 1520s. As there are so few records surviving, it is rare for us to have two such references to the same person, and when we do, it is very helpful to writers who investigate continuities between different periods of dissent. For the 1511 inquiry we have to rely on Foxe's report, which gives Christopher and his sister Dyonise amongst twelve people who were arrested and taken to London for examination. He says that the Ravens and eight of the others were 'of one fellowship and profession of faith', and that they all agreed with Richard Woolman, who:

> termed the church of [St.] Paul a house of thieves, affirming that the priests and other ecclesiastical persons there were not liberal givers unto the poor (as they ought to be) but rather takers away from them of what they could get.

Such criticism of the clergy was not confined to Protestants. But Foxe also wrote of the Ravens and their colleagues that:

> many of them were charged to have spoken against pilgrimages, and to have read and used certain English books repugning the faith of the Romish church.

Like many others, the Ravens abjured and escaped punishment. However, it was in that same year of 1511 that the Essex men William Sweeting and James Brewster were burnt for heresy at Smithfield.[18]

The later investigation, in 1527, was carried out by representatives of the bishop, Cuthbert Tunstall, as a result of anxieties about heresy. I will concentrate on the hearings relating to Witham here; descriptions of the others may be read in the works of several writers.[19] It was from John Hacker, one of the most active Lollard preachers in Essex and London, that the bishop obtained the names of Christopher Raven of Witham and his friends. Hacker is described by one historian as an 'experienced heretic ... one of the senior generation', and by another as a 'veteran'.[20] His statement includes the main features that were regarded as Protestant heresy. According to the bishop's clerk, Hacker said that:

> One Christofer Ravynes, Taylor, of Wyttham, had convercation with hym about A quarter of A yere last past, at his owne house in the parish of Witham. And also that ons or twise a yere by the space of 4 yeres he hath resorted to his house, and tawght hym other comaundementes. And that in the sacrament of the aulter was not the very body of god but a remembraunce of god that was in hevyn, and that worshypping images and offeryng and goyng on pilgremages, was nowght; and that the one tawght the other in such lernynges. Also he said that one Thomas Hills, servaunt to the said Ravyn is one of the same secte and can Rede well and hathe a boke of the new testament in English prynted, which he bowght at London. Farthermore he saith that the said Christofer had 2 servantes which wer borne in Colcestre called John Chapman and Richard Chapman brethren whych folowed the Redyng and Doctryne of them and hered many of these opinions. And he said that the said Thomas Hilles is a great Reder amongst them.[21]

The importance attached to the scriptures and to reading is notable, as is the fact that the Chapmans were said to have come from Colchester, the place which recurs so often in discussions of early Protestantism.

Many of the people named by Hacker were taken to London to be examined. Foxe implies that this happened to Christopher Raven himself and his wife, whom we know to have been Joan, and to the Chapmans and Thomas Hills. In a story which well illustrates his exaggerated style, Foxe purports to describe what happened to Richard Chapman when he was going through the process of repentance after the hearings. He says that:

> As he was in his coat and shirt enjoined, bare-head, bare-foot and bare-leg, to go before the procession, and to kneel upon the cold steps in the church all the sermon time, a little lad ... came to him, and ... brought him his cap to kneel upon; for which the boy was immediately taken into the vestry, and there unmercifully beaten, for his mercy showed to the poor penitent.[22]

We do not have confessions from the Ravens or the Chapmans, but we do have a long statement from the other servant, Thomas Hills, made in October 1527. It is not signed, but can be identified as his by relating it to information given by other people. He said that his 'errors' had begun about four years previously. He was instructed by Quintin Bocher of Coggeshall, six miles north of Witham. Bocher was 'a young man unmaryed, now ... beying ded'. From him Hills had learnt the second chapter of James, and had also been taught that:

> The articles and errors folowing first that in the blessed sacrament of the aulter is not the body of crist but only bred and don for a remembraunce of cristes passion, also that men shuld not go in pilgremage for they did not perfect a man ner set up any lightes before Images in the Churche, but shuld have a burnyng love to god. Also that men wer not bownd to kepe no manner of holy day except sonday and that no holy day except sonday was made by god but men of the Churche for ther vantage.

In addition Hills often travelled the rather tortuous twenty-five miles from Witham to Steeple Bumpstead, which is in north Essex, near the main road from Cambridge to Colchester. One of the parishes on this journey was Finchingfield, where he had been taught the first chapter of James by Joan Dyer. He had intended to marry her but she had since died. At Bumpstead itself the curate, Richard Fox, was another of the 'brothers in Christ', or 'known men', as he called his colleagues. Five years later, forty of his parishioners were taken together to London to abjure before the bishop.[23] Fox was said to have taught John Chapman there as well as Thomas Hills, who admitted that he went 'dyverse tymes' to several different houses in Bumpstead, and read to groups of people from 'the new testament and the epistoles paule and other, and ther had convercations together many tymes of diverse heresies and errors'.

One of the Bumpstead men was John Tyball. When he was later taken to London with his neighbours for

examination, he was accompanied by his mother, his
wife, his two sons and his two daughters. He had
previously been one of a similar group in Colchester. It
was with him that Witham's Thomas Hills went to
London in 1526 on what has been called a 'famous
visit', to buy a new testament, and there spoke to Robert
Barnes in his chamber. Barnes was an Augustinian friar,
originally based in Cambridge, who had been examined
earlier in the same year by Cardinal Wolsey, then Henry
VIII's Chancellor, for an allegedly heretical sermon.
After examination, he had abjured at a lavish ceremony
in St.Paul's, but remained in prison for some months
and was then put under 'house arrest' with the friars in
London. This had probably helped to make him well-
known to people like Hills looking for new information
and publications. On his visit to Barnes' room in the
friary, Hills:

> fownde a young gentelman whom he did not know
> havyng a chayne about his neck to whom the said
> frear did rede in the new testament ... [they] herd
> hym rede a chapiter of powle.

The friar gave Tyball a long letter for his priest, and,
according to Hills, the pair:

> eche ... bowght a new testament in English of hem
> and paid 3 shillings for a pece ... in which new
> testament he [Hills] red in Roger a tanner's house of
> Bowres Gifford, Bowerhall, mother bocher's and
> mother chaut's, and at last sold the said new
> testament to ... Richard Fox.

The testament must have been Tyndale's new and
forbidden translation. John Tyball's confession added
that Barnes had likened the Latin testament used by the
Catholics to 'a cymbal tinkling and brass sounding'. Hills
was required to do several acts of penance, including
offering a candle to the image of the Virgin, fasting, and
making a pilgrimage to Ipswich Abbey. He was lucky
that the emphasis of the authorities before 1529 was on
burning books rather than people. Friar Barnes was to
be less fortunate. He escaped to spend some time with
Luther on the continent, and came into favour with
Henry VIII during the 1530s, being recruited to help in
negotiations with European princes. However, in 1540
he was burnt at the stake at Smithfield for heresy with
several others, two days after the execution of the
Chancellor, Thomas Cromwell, during a period of
reaction against reform.[24]

The Witham people and their friends seem to have
continued with their beliefs and activities, in spite of
their promises to repent. For instance, it was probably
the same John Chapman who is reported by Foxe to
have been imprisoned for five weeks, three of which
were spent in the stocks, in 1533. This was for
sheltering an alleged heretic at Smithfield in London.
John Tyball, his Steeple Bumpstead friend, was with
him there, and as a punishment was forbidden to go
near his own house in Essex, which he was therefore
obliged to sell. The London man whom they sheltered,
Andrew Hewit, was burnt with another for heresy. Over
ten years later, it was very probably the same Thomas
Hills and John Chapman who respectively witnessed the
Protestant wills of William Trayford of Rayleigh in

1546, and of John Pytte (whose residence is not known)
in about 1550. Rayleigh was very near Bowers Gifford,
which Hills had visited in 1526. Even more clearly, a
persistence of belief is shown by Christopher Raven's
own will, written a few days before his death in
February 1542.[25] Protestant preambles had only
appeared in Essex in 1537, and since then, they had only
been used in four or five surviving wills per year in the
whole county. It is particularly unusual and rewarding to
be able to correlate a preamble with other sources of
information, as we can with Christopher Raven. He
bequeathed his soul to:

> almyghtie god the father, throughe the merytes of
> our onely savyor Jhesus Criste to be emongyst his
> sayntes and electe.

The concept of the 'elect' was particularly associated
with the views of John Calvin, the French theologian
who lived in Switzerland and whose ideas became the
basis of many future Protestant Churches. The elect
were the few who were thought to be predestined for
salvation. It was this belief in particular that
distinguished Calvinism from the German Protestantism
of Luther. Raven's was only the second of the surviving
wills proved in Essex to refer to the elect, the earlier
one having been written in 1539. It was only found in
eight others in the county between 1535 and the end of
Henry's reign in 1547. Except for Christopher Royden
of Witham, discussed below, all the other willmakers
who used it were from the area around Colchester.[26]

Christopher Raven's will also reveals a certain amount
about his material status, to which can be added a few
facts from other sources. With at least three assistants,
he must have been a master tailor. In the Lay Subsidy of
1523 he was assessed on his goods at forty shillings, a
'middling' amount. In the same year he witnessed the
will of Richard Radley, a prosperous fuller. And in 1526
he bought a freehold tenement in the Chipping Hill
area; it is probable that this was his home, and stayed
with his descendants until the eighteenth century (now
the site of nos.2-6 Church Street; the present buildings
probably date from the later sixteenth and seventeenth
centuries, after Christopher's time). He also held some
land in Blunts Hall manor, and a lease and stock worth
£7 a year in land which belonged to St.Mary's chantry.
In his will he left six and a half seams of barley amongst
six friends, including his servant John Chapman (a seam
was a pack-horse load or eight bushels). Chapman was
also a witness of the will. A priest, George Parkes, was
another witness; nothing more has been discovered
about him. William Danon of Witham was to be
overseer; he himself made a Catholic will five years later.
Another of Raven's bequests was a gift of twenty pence
to the parish church of Witham for repairs.[27] So it
seems that he was able to live comfortably in the local
community, and was not estranged from it or from the
parish church, in spite of his beliefs, which must have
been well-known since his two excursions to London
for cross-examination.

Most editions of John Foxe's 'Acts and Monuments'
state wrongly that Christopher Raven was still alive in
the 1560s. They give Foxe's first complete edition as

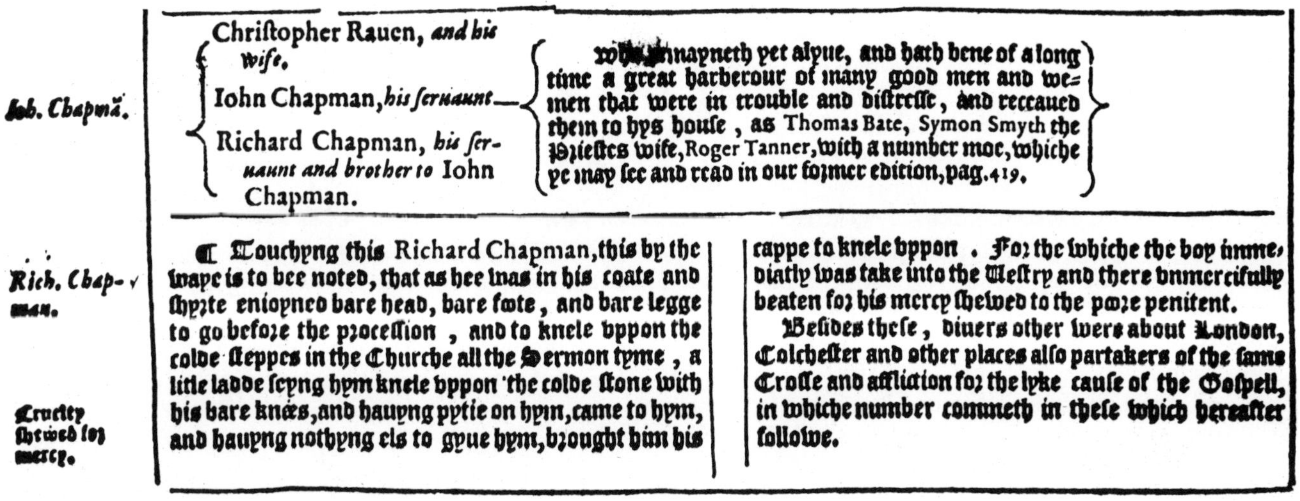

Iob. Chapmā.

Christopher Rauen, *and his wife.*

Iohn Chapman, *his seruaunt*

Richard Chapman, *his seruaunt and brother to* Iohn Chapman.

roͧ remayneth yet alyue, and hath bene of a long time a great harberour of many good men and wemen that were in trouble and distresse, and receaued them to hys house , as Thomas Bate, Symon Smyth the Priestes wife, Roger Tanner, with a number moe, whiche ye may see and read in our former edition, pag. 419.

Rich. Chap-man.

Crueltye shewed for mercy.

❡ Touchyng this Richard Chapman, this by the waye is to bee noted, that as hee was in his coate and shyrte eniopned bare head, bare fote , and bare legge to go before the procession , and to knele vppon the colde steppes in the Churche all the Sermon tyme , a litle ladde seyng hym knele vppon 'the colde stone with his bare knees, and hauyng pytie on hym, came to hym, and hauyng nothyng els to gyue hym, brought hym his cappe to knele vppon . For the whiche the boy imme, diatly was take into the Westry and there vnmercifully beaten for his mercy shewed to the poore penitent.

Besides these , diuers other wers about London, Colchester and other places also partakers of the same Crosse and affliction for the lyke cause of the Gospell, in whiche number commeth in these which hereafter followe.

Figure 13.   Extract from Foxe's *Book of Martyrs*, 1570 edition

Tailor Christopher Raven lived in Witham with his wife Joan, and his servants John and Richard Chapman. This is part of an account of their appearance in London in 1527 to be examined for heresy. It gives Foxe's view of what happened to Richard Chapman when he was going through the process of repentance. It also suggests that John Chapman was still alive in 1570. Foxe's later editions say that Christopher Raven himself survived until that date, but in fact he died in 1542. (reproduced by permission of The British Library; shelf mark BL 4705.h.4)

their authority; it was published in 1563. The misconception has been used by at least one historian to illustrate continuity forward in time from the Protestants of Henry's reign to those of Elizabeth's. In fact, the information does not appear in the 1563 edition of Foxe, but in the enlarged edition of 1570 edition. Furthermore, as shown in figure 13 above, it actually reads as if it was intended to refer not to Christopher Raven but to John Chapman, his former servant, which makes much more sense; we have already seen indications that Chapman continued his activity after Raven's death. Foxe states that he:

> remayneth yet alyve, and hath bene of a long time a great harberour of many good men and women that were in trouble and distresse, and received them to hys house.[28]

Amongst the other survivors of the Raven 'group' were Christopher Raven's widow Joan, who lived until 1572, probably in the same house in Church Street that they had shared together. She and their son John seem to have retained strongly Protestant beliefs for the rest of their lives, to judge from their later will preambles. And I am fairly confident that their descendants included the late seventeenth-century dissenters, the Quaker Ravens. In particular there was Edmund Raven of Cressing, whose sons, also Quakers, married Witham women. In the absence of parish registers from either place, the connection has to be made through the rather incomplete records of descent of the family house. However, in contrast, one of the great grandsons of

Christopher and Joan was John Gravener(3), an important but primarily law-abiding figure in seventeenth-century Witham.[29]

CHRISTOPHER ROYDEN OF WITHAM

The Royden and Raven families were close friends, and probably near neighbours. Christopher Royden made a will with a Protestant preamble, referring to 'the elect', about two years after Christopher Raven did. Royden does not seem to have been noted hitherto by any of the commentators on early Protestantism. His will was written in November 1543, and he died some time during the following year. He bequeathed his soul:

> to almyghtie god my Creator and maker and to Jesus Christe his onely sone my Savior throughe whome and in the merites of his moost blessed passion I truste to be one of the Electe and chosen and partaker of the Rewarde of everlastynge life.

Royden's will reveals the many links between his family and the Ravens. Joan Raven, Christopher's widow, was described as Christopher Royden's 'gossip', which had several meanings connected with godparenthood; probably in this instance it meant that Joan was the godmother of the Roydens' children. Although godparents were part of the Catholic tradition, they are also known to have been used by Lollards to cement closeness with fellow believers. In turn, Royden requested in his will that his own wife Katherine should be 'a contynuall goode frende' to the widowed Joan Raven and her children. In addition, he himself was godfather to two of the Ravens' children, Joan Blowes and Edward Raven. They were already adults, so the bond between the two families must have been a long-standing one, extending back over twenty years, from well before the time when Christopher and Joan Raven were taken before the bishop for heresy in 1527. Edward Raven (known in some other documents as Edmund), was also one of the witnesses of Christopher Royden's will, and Royden left him the lease of the twelve-acre field 'Paynes Haven' or 'Paynes Herne' (whose site was mostly occupied by Safeway, in Braintree Road, in 1998).[30] The two Joans and Edward also received bequests of money and barley in Royden's will.

Christopher Royden, who was always known as a gentleman, seems to have been even more wealthy, and more integrated into the community, than Christopher Raven. This situation seems to have dated from very early in Henry's reign. In 1519, he and the curate, Richard Knight, had together witnessed the will of the priest Miles Leper. And Witham's Thomas Tilling asked in his will of 1530 that Royden should be 'good to my wyff'. In return he was to be allowed to pay only sixteen shillings instead of the twenty-five shillings that he owned Tilling for a 'furre of Blake bridge' (a 'furre' could be a garment trimmed or lined with fur; 'bridge' was probably a black woollen cloth of a type formerly made in Bridgwater, Somerset). Royden was chosen as a trustee of Greene's almshouses, and was also associated with St.John's chantry. He was said to have been one of the chantry's 'elect persons', presumably those who managed its affairs, but he was also accused, with others, of replacing its officially appointed chaplain with someone else, and of himself accepting a lease of its land from this unauthorised chaplain. In this dispute, which was taken to the court of Chancery, he was associated with several Witham notables and with Thomas Pannatt, the curate. When Royden died, he entrusted the inventory of his goods to the church-wardens, asking that it should be kept in the vestry (on the upper floor, which no longer exists, though its windows can be seen in the drawing on page 39). Furthermore, Royden's baby daughter Mary was one of the nineteen godchildren of Witham's vicar, William Love, discussed in the next chapter (pages 48-49), who in due course was to make the last wholly Catholic will in Witham. And a favoured beneficiary and witness of Royden's will was Edmund Stanbanke, the priest of St. Mary's chantry, who lived nearby in Chipping Hill. He was to receive Royden's own saddle and a horse, his 'bay ambelynge geldynge'. It was this chantry from which Christopher Raven had leased some property.[31]

We also know that Royden was a considerable landowner. The debts of £80 which he owed at his death were to be met out of his land. He was lord of the manor of Parkers, otherwise known as Reydon or Royden Hall, in the parish of Ramsey in north-east Essex near the port of Harwich. It had been owned by his family since at least the fourteenth century. One source says that Christopher had lived there before coming to Witham.[32] He held other property in Wrabness and Mistley, near Ramsey, with more in the neighbouring county of Suffolk, and also in Cressing and Rivenhall, adjoining Witham. In Witham itself he owned a tenement 'in Witham High Street by the bridge', some land called 'le Roose', probably nearby, and a house called 'Rekedon's Ermitage'. The latter was by the 'old market' on Chipping Hill green; its garden adjoined the churchyard (the house, dating from the fifteenth century, is now no.24 Chipping Hill and Mole End; during the late seventeenth century it was the home of nonconformist minister George Lisle).[33]

Although Royden owned it, it is not known for certain whether his family actually lived at the Chipping Hill house. However, it does seem significant that its Church Street entrance is only a few steps across the road from the place where their close friends the Ravens are thought to have lived. This close proximity can be seen in the drawing on the opposite page. Later on, the Roydens' house became known as 'Lucas tenement', after John Lucas, who married Mary Royden, Christopher's daughter, and thus took all the Royden family property; he seems to have retained the Witham house until the 1580s. He had first been Mary's guardian, as she was only two years old when her father died. There is a story that the wardship and the hand of Mary were the prize in a game of dice between the Earl of Oxford and Lucas's father, John the elder, who was Town Clerk of Colchester and owner of St.John's Abbey there.

After the marriage, John Lucas the son rented out the Witham property and went to live at the Royden family home in Ramsey. He probably rebuilt the latter, as the present house there is thought to date from the mid to late sixteenth century.[34] He was later involved in a property dispute with the new husband of Christopher Royden's widow Katherine. There are no indications that Mary Royden's new relatives shared her father's beliefs; as far as we know they were conformists. In fact her direct descendants included Sir John and Sir Charles Lucas, who were royalists during the Civil War; Sir Charles was executed in 1648 after the siege of Colchester.[35] In making a match like Mary's, social position may have been rather more important than belief.

It could well be that Royden's wealth and status enabled him to become a patron of early Protestantism, whilst escaping the persecution to which his lesser associates, like the Ravens, were vulnerable. It is of course possible that he was in fact in trouble with the Church, either alone or with the Ravens, but that the record has been lost. However, Andrew Hope, discussing the Lollards, has suggested the existence of prosperous 'shadowy households', which may have sheltered secret meetings but escaped prosecution themselves. Some of the families which he discusses were based in the area around Colchester.[36]

Normally the funeral of such a wealthy man as

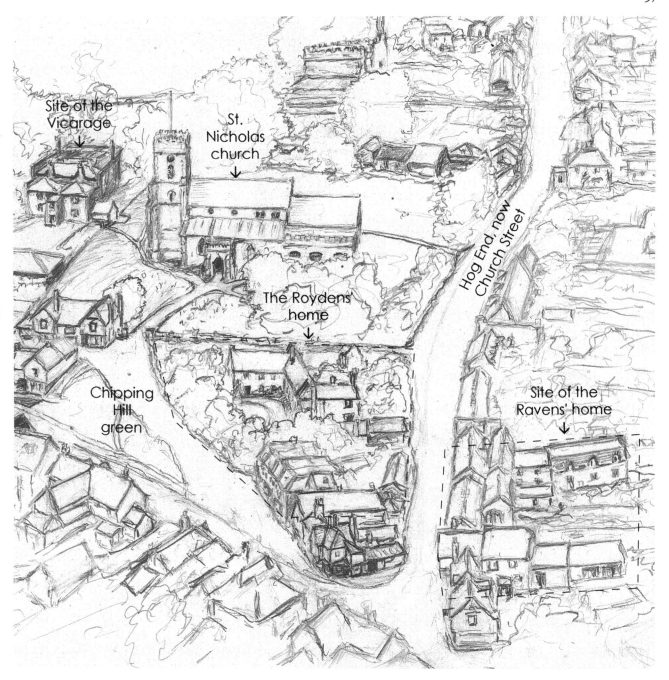

Part of Chipping Hill, showing where the Ravens and the Roydens lived during the 1520s and 1530s

These two families were early Protestants, and close friends.
The dotted lines show the approximate boundaries of their homes

Christopher Royden would have been an extravagant affair. However, William Tracy of Gloucestershire had written in his will that burial ceremonies were 'rather the solace of them that live than the wealth or comfort of them that are departed.' And Royden seemed to feel the same way. He asked to be:

> buried in Christian buryall with no pompiouse funerall but Accordynge to the laudable custome of this realme honestly to be brought on earth with moderate charges.

This wording was later to be echoed by his friend Joan Raven, who wished her burial in 1572 to be only 'accordyng to the laudable institution' of the Church and the law.[37]

TRADITION AND ITS EROSION IN WITHAM

Clergymen

The Ravens and the Roydens were particularly distinctive in their beliefs and behaviour. As Henry's reign progressed, other Witham parishioners began to modify some of their traditional religious behaviour, though in a very much less emphatic way. Before looking at how this happened we may note that we do not know a great deal about the Witham clergymen of the period, so it is hard to assess their influence in the matter. The best-recorded vicar was William Love, who was here for a long time, from 1536 to 1560, and was probably basically traditional in outlook. He did not become very visible until after 1550, and so will be discussed in the next chapter (pages 48-49). There were other supporting clergy, though the Knight's Hospitallers' probably no longer had a chaplain serving a manorial chapel here as they had done in medieval times.[38] The minor clergy often seem to have been more active than the vicar himself. A particularly visible curate was Thomas Pannatt, who witnessed eleven out of the thirty-eight surviving Witham wills between 1540 and 1550. As described in more detail in the next chapter (pages 47-48), their preambles adapted to the changing times as required. Some time around 1540 he was also accused of 'pretending' to be the priest of St.John's chantry; one of his allies was said to be the gentleman Protestant Christopher Royden.[39] A chantry was a medieval bequest to enable prayers and masses to be said for the soul of its founder and his or her friends and relatives. Their funds often came from a gift of land. Witham had two of them, St.John's and St.Mary's. Each had a chapel added to St.Nicholas church; St.John's is now the North chapel and St.Mary's the Lady chapel. Money was also provided for a priest to say daily prayers, and to maintain priest's houses in Newland Street and in Chipping Hill respectively. Such priests often performed many general duties in the parishes. In 1502 Thomas Wotton, chaplain of St.Mary's chantry, witnessed two Witham wills.[40]

It was one of Wotton's successors at St.Mary's chantry, Edmund Stanbanke, who is the best-known of the supporting Witham clergy of this period. His earliest known appearance in the town was in 1535. In 1548 he was said to be 'of the age of 54 yeres', and to hold no other position. He acted as a teacher, which was by no means a usual activity for chantry priests. Thus in 1545 Robert Burche left him twenty shillings and his 'worsted doublet garded with velvett', 'for teching of Robert Burche my sonne'. Stanbanke was also involved in the administration of Greene's almshouses, and appeared at the Archdeacon's court to certify a payment made to the parish. In addition, he witnessed and probably wrote two of the rather scarce surviving wills during his tenure. One of them was for his near-neighbour in Chipping Hill, the Protestant Christopher Royden. The association of Pannatt and Stanbanke with Royden may of course be an indication of Royden's influence rather than a clue to the pair's beliefs. However, if Stanbanke did act as the scribe for the will, he would have needed to be willing to write the striking Protestant preamble about 'the elect'.[41]

Tradition in Witham wills

The changes in Witham's will preambles were generally comparable to those of Essex as a whole. They are summarised in the graph on page 15. Catholic forms were dominant until about 1540. For instance, in 1502 John Hut left his soul to 'almyghti god and lady the moder of Crist and to the hole company of hevyne', and in 1529 Joan Bedfield left hers to 'almighti god and to our lady saynt mary and to all the holy company of hevyn'.[42] There were a few completely non-committal preambles, the two Protestant ones already discussed, and then after 1545, Catholic forms were equalled by a 'mixed' form of preamble which was peculiar to certain areas. The latter continued after Henry's reign and will be discussed in the next chapter (pages 45-48).

Other bequests also had religious significance, and from these we can see how some of the ideas of the early Protestants began to be more widely adopted. People who wrote their wills under the influence of the Catholic tradition frequently made particular sorts of donation connected with the Church. After the 1530s these became fewer, and some kinds disappeared altogether. Many such gifts were associated with the concern of willmakers for the fate of their souls after death, and in particular with their wish to ensure a safe passage through Purgatory. One way of doing this was to give a donation for a candle to be lit in the parish church. Records only survive for a few of these gifts in Witham, mostly early, but they do help us to picture the interior of St.Nicholas church at that time, crowded with statues and paintings, each surrounded by flickering candles. The representations of the saints were collectively known as 'images'. In 1486, Hugh Smith had left three cows, each intended to fund the light before a different saint; these were 'Our Lady of Pity', St.James, and St.Anthony. In 1519, the priest Miles Leper asked for four candles in all, to be provided for five years. He wished for 'a taper of 7 pounds weight at Easter tyme afor the sepulcare in Witham', another weighing one pound, to burn before the 'ymage of oure lady of grace', another of the same weight before 'the pety of our lady', and one of half a pound before the image of St.Katherine. In 1526, weaver Henry Baker left two pounds 'of wax to kype a light afore saynt george' in Witham, and in 1535 Thomas Smart left one shilling for the 'mayntenance of the lyggt kept before the ymag of St.Margret'. This was the last such donation in Witham. The notion of Purgatory, and the offering of money and candles to images, lost favour amongst Church leaders during the reformist period of the mid-1530s, and were disparaged in the Ten Articles of 1536, and in Thomas Cromwell's Injunctions shortly afterwards, which referred to images as being 'devised by men's phantasies'. In some other parishes, the church accounts survive, and students of these have deduced that the commands to extinguish the lights were universally obeyed. Many of the images were also removed, and in Bristol it was said that some were given to children to play with.[43]

To arrange for suitable prayers to be said after one's death was another way of aiding the passage of the soul. Such prayers were known as obits. Willmakers often made bequests to fund their own obits, and sometimes included their deceased friends and relatives and others also. It was quite common for people to leave a cow to the church in order to provide an income for the purpose; otherwise land or money might be given. The chantries were a particularly lavish form of this practice, where the willmakers paid for their own priest and chapel. The more usual arrangement was for the money

The chapel of St.Mary's chantry, on the south side, now the Lady chapel.

This chantry was founded in 1444 and its chapel was built soon afterwards.

The chapel of St.John's chantry, now the North chapel. It is behind the large window in Perpendicular style.

This chantry was founded in 1397 but may not have had this chapel of its own until nearly a hundred years later. It now houses the organ. To its left is the vestry, which can be seen to have previously consisted of two stories. When he died in 1544, gentleman Christopher Royden asked that the churchwardens should keep the inventory of his goods in the 'Upper Revestry'.

to be given to one of the existing priests, for him to say the prayers required; this enhanced his regular stipend. For instance, in 1525, the smith William Bridgeman asked that after his death, his wife Mary should buy two 'good and lawfull mylche kyne [milking cows]' and deliver them to the vicar of Witham, so that twopence a year could be taken from the profits by the churchwardens to pay for a yearly obit to be said perpetually. The prayers were to said 'for the soulles of my father and mother, my soule and all my fryndes soulles and all cristen soulles'. The cows were to 'always remayne and be goying on the groundes of the said Vicarage so that the said kyne be not taken away nor commited to other use by any Vicar or curat'. Occasionally full services or masses were asked for too; in 1529 Joan Bedfield left her house and garden to her niece, provided that she and her heirs paid two shillings a year for masses to be said on the anniversary of Joan's death, for ever. In some places there were guilds, or associations, whose members contributed to this practice. None of these are known in Witham, though there were some in neighbouring parishes. For instance, in 1519 the Witham priest Miles Leper left a shilling to the guilds in Ulting and Great Braxted. The Ulting guild was also mentioned in the will of Reynolde Hammond, discussed later. Occasionally the willmakers asked for , the members of one of the religious houses to say prayers for them also. For example, in 1513 the fuller John Algore gave 3s.4d. each 'to the Fryers of Chelmesford Colchester Maldon and Sudbury to be prayd for'. [44] With one exception, such requests were confined to the period between 1504 and 1519. They inevitably ceased at the time of the dissolution of the religious houses which began in 1536.

Until 1533, requests for prayers and obits of all sorts appeared in about three quarters of the Witham wills. It has been suggested by one writer that in the country as a whole, the proportion was around two-thirds during the mid-1530s, though it varied considerably from one area to another. However the Articles and Injunctions of 1536 appear to have been heeded by most people, because in Witham as elsewhere, the practice virtually ceased thereafter. Many Witham willmakers had requested their obits to be said for ever. Edmund Quyke did so too, but he also showed some foresight. When he left a house in 1527 to provide 6s.8d. for a yearly obit, he added that it was only to continue 'if the lawe will suffre it'; if not, the house was to be sold. A historian of other areas has found such doubts beginning in 1529, so Quyke was rather advanced. There were only two further bequests for prayers after 1533. In 1541 yeoman John Payne left a cow to Witham's church:

> to kepe a yerly obit ... to pray for my soule, the
> soules of my wives Jone, Alis, and Elizabethe, my
> frendes soules and all chriscen soules.

He probably lived at 'Crouchmans' (in 1998 the site of the Bridge Hospital and Poplar Hall in Hatfield Road). Lastly, as will be discussed in the next chapter (pages 48-49), George Armond(1) asked in 1564 for prayers at two of the 'Spitle' or Hospital Houses; these had survived the friaries to which they had been attached. [45]

The enhancement of the state of the soul may originally have been the basis of another common type of bequest. This was the making of a donation to 'the high altar', meaning the parish church's funds, as a safeguard in case the willmakers had incurred any debts to the church during their lifetime, particularly in connection with the obligation to pay tithes. However, by the sixteenth century, fears about the soul were not usually expressed specifically in connection with such donations, so it may be that they had become merely customary, without any such implications. This made them less susceptible to doctrinal changes than other types of bequest. Usually the gift left by Witham's parishioners to the high altar of St.Nicholas church was in the form of money, but in 1504 Joan Pye of Duck End (now Bridge Street) asked her executors to buy a vestment worth five marks for the purpose. The proportion of Witham willmakers making donations to the high altar was already falling by the 1530s, but altogether about three quarters of Witham wills before 1540 included such gifts, and this was one of the most long-lasting practices. There were still nearly half adopting it between 1540 and 1547, long after the official instructions of 1536, and after most other traditional types of bequest had ceased. However, they did ultimately disappear. After the will of William Danon in 1546 there was only one much later reference to the high altar and to a donation made in case of forgotten tithes. This was by yeoman Thomas Harding in 1557, during the return of Catholicism under Mary. [46]

Many people left simple donations to churches without reference to either their soul or to their debts. Until about 1530, about half the makers of surviving Witham wills gave a donation to St.Paul's cathedral in London. Witham was in the diocese of London, so this was their 'mother church'. For instance, in 1502 John Hut left fourpence to go to the 'olde warkes of Pawlys'. 'Paul's Walk' was the nickname of the nave of the old Gothic St.Paul's cathedral, which was used as a public passageway; this was facilitated by the presence of two outside doors facing each other across the nave, and its attraction to troublemakers was a continual cause of concern. Other churches outside Witham sometimes received gifts also. And before 1530 about a third of willmakers gave money to the parish church of Witham itself, over and above donations for prayers and for the forgiveness of debts. The gifts were usually for repairs; thus John Hut left twenty pence for 'the reparacion of Witham church', as did Thomas Richard in 1528. Occasionally other purposes were specified. For instance in 1513 Reynolde Hammond left the generous sum of £6 to pay for an 'antyfoner' for St.Nicholas church; an antiphoner was a book containing antiphons, which are musical compositions consisting of passages sung alternately by two choirs. Hammond lived twelve miles away in Ramsden Bellhouse but he owned land in Witham, known appropriately as 'Hamonds' (in Maltings Lane, now known as Jackson's farm, after Witham's well-known Jackson family who were its owners in later years). He left the land to the wardens of the 'Gylde or fraternite of our blyssyd Lady' at Ulting, south of Witham; they were to pay for the antiphoner out of the profits. After 1545, there were no more donations from Witham people for the fabric and equipment of the church for nearly twenty years. This may appear to suggest that in some ways such gifts had been particularly associated with traditional Catholicism, though Protestant Christopher Raven had made a donation for church repairs in 1542.[47]

OVERVIEW

Although we do not know of large numbers of early Protestants in Essex, they were probably more numerous than in other counties, and their visibility increased during Henry's reign. Known investigations and punishments connected with Protestantism tended to be found in similar areas to Protestant will preambles, particularly near to the coast and to the main roads from London. Many of the wills with Protestant preambles appeared to have been made with the assistance of clergymen.

A closer study of the Protestants of Witham produced examples of the continuities which have interested historians, with links both before and after Henry's reign. It also suggested that they were literate, in wealthy households, integrated into the community, and participating in parish affairs. Some of the recent writers about other parts of the country have come to the same conclusion, though it is a matter for debate. In Witham the Protestant gentleman Christopher Royden may have helped and sheltered others, particularly his close friends the Ravens and their household.[48]

Thus although some parishioners in Essex were willing to hand over early Protestants to the authorities, many were prepared to accept them. Some willmakers who did not commit themselves entirely to Protestant forms may have been showing a tentative sympathy when they used non-committal or mixed will preambles. We saw that in other aspects of will-making in Witham, such as gifts for prayers and for the church, most people appear to have waited for the instructions issued by the Church before they departed from traditional practice, though there was already some decline beforehand, for instance in the giving of donations for images and to the high altar. Some forms of donation, such as those to church repairs, persisted until the mid-1540s. A very similar pattern has been found by two students of Colchester.[49] To balance the early dissent of people like the Ravens

and Roydens, we found John Payne asking for prayers for the souls of his three wives and his friends in 1540, seven years after his fellow-parishioners had given up this practice.

In spite of all the interesting material that is available, no firm assessment can be reached about how many people really subscribed to all the different religious viewpoints in either Witham in particular or Essex as a whole. This illustrates the continuing and fervent debate amongst historians about the beliefs of 'ordinary' sixteenth-century people, to which there have been many new contributions even while I have been writing this book. How much did people care, and if they did, were they pleased or distressed by the innovations of the Reformation? When did the change begin, how long did it take and how deep-rooted was it?

The idea that the Reformation was welcomed, and that Catholicism had already been in decay, was supported from the late 1950s to the 1970s by several writers using detailed information from various localities. However, others, particularly since the late 1980s, have suggested either that most parishioners were indifferent and merely carried out official instructions, or that very many of them held deeply felt Catholic sympathies, which continued in spite of national policy. The original champions of early Protestant enthusiasm have in turn defended their view with new research, though one of the best-known of them, Professor A.G.Dickens, has also stressed 'territorial diversity' between different places.[50]

The impact of the debate may be illustrated by the varied conclusions which three different writers have come to about the destruction of the crucifix at Dovercourt in Essex in 1532. Diarmaid MacCulloch and Patrick Collinson suggest that the men who did it intended to 'avenge' the death of Thomas Bilney, an East Anglian preacher executed the year before, and Collinson says that they were 'probably part of a well established dissenting current'. Christopher Haigh does refer to a possible connection with Bilney, but considers that such events were 'most unusual and are not evidence of any wider rejection of images'. And Eamon Duffy describes the incident at Dovercourt as part of a 'minor epidemic' of iconoclasm in Eastern England; he does not mention Bilney at all.[51] It would probably be possible to make a case for all these varied points of view by using evidence from Essex and Witham.

4. EDWARD VI, 1547-1553, and MARY I, 1553-1558

EDWARD VI, 1547-1553

Henry VIII died in January 1547, and was followed on the throne by his three children in turn, Edward, Mary and Elizabeth. Edward and Elizabeth were Protestants, but Mary was a Catholic. Edward VI reigned until July 1553. He was only nine years old at the time of his accession. This gave a clear field to the men who took the position of regent in his stead, and to Protestant reformers who had previously been restrained by the caution of Henry VIII, notably Thomas Cranmer, Archbishop of Canterbury. Many of them were influenced by their colleagues on the continent, and in particular the Swiss, led by John Calvin. It was during Edward's reign that the English Church was established in the form we know today, whose essentials have survived the centuries in spite of several interruptions. The Prayer Book was introduced in two stages, setting out the required forms of service, the English Bible was to be provided in churches, and forty-two Articles and a Catechism set out Church doctrine. Thus by 1551 it was forbidden to subscribe to the Catholic belief in transubstantiation. However, the bishops and the cathedrals were retained, and this has always distinguished the Church of England from nearly all the Protestant Churches on the continent, and from those in Scotland.[1]

Witham church in Edward's reign

Chantries were dissolved in 1548, their association with prayers for the dead putting them out of favour. The Witham ones were found to have been quite wealthy compared to many others in Essex. St.Mary's had a silver chalice weighing 9½ ounces, and St.John's had one weighing twelve ounces. One of the charitable activities of St.John's, the relief of five 'pore folkes', was allowed to continue; such concessions were unusual. The fate of the chantry priests is unknown. In due course their two chapels in St.Nicholas church were put to general use, as they are today. The loss of their adornments would have made an impression even on parishioners who were indifferent to changes in the form of service, and there were many other similar alterations within the building. The orders were to remove any remaining images and statues, demolish stone altars and replace them with communion tables, and hand over equipment not required by the new procedures. As seen on the facing page, at Witham a niche remains today in the Lady chapel which may once

have contained a statue. It was possibly during Edward's reign that the ornately carved fifteenth-century wooden rood screen was reduced in height. Only the lower part remains today, up to a level of about four feet, topped by a late nineteenth-century addition, shown in the drawing on page 11. It is also likely that a pulpit and seating would have been introduced at around this time. In addition, the walls were probably whitewashed to hide the pre-Reformation wall paintings, and texts were inscribed in their place. We certainly know that the Creed, the Lord's prayer and the ten Commandments were written up on the walls at Witham by the 1630s, when the churchwardens were in trouble for whitewashing over them in their turn.[2]

In 1548 a royal survey of church goods was conducted. Andrew Weston and William Hayward were then the Witham churchwardens. In advance of official instructions, they had already sold 'two Candlestycks of sylver and a pyxe of Sylver' weighing fifty-nine ounces, worth £14 7s., and 'a paxe of sylver' weighing ten ounces worth fifty shillings. A pyx is a container for the bread of the sacrament, and a pax is a small plate or tablet used during the Mass. Weston and Hayward claimed that the sale had been carried out 'with the assent of the whole parryshe'. The proceeds had gone towards the repair of the church and the payment of the 'church debtes'. Edward Dickin has studied the 1548 survey in Essex, and feels that the most goods had been sold in places where Protestantism had been strongest, particularly in the deaneries of north-east Essex, including that of Witham. Thus the parishioners' motives may have been ideological, in that they wished themselves to hasten the change from Catholic to Protestant ways. On the other hand, some writers have thought that they merely wished to keep the proceeds for the parish, rather than having to hand them over to the Crown. Another survey was carried out in 1552, but for most of Essex, including Witham, its records do not survive.[3]

Dissent during Edward's reign

Some Protestants, such as Anabaptists, were still regarded as too extreme by the authorities, even in Edward's reign. It has been said that they saw themselves as 'a sort of permanent opposition' to a corrupt establishment. Some meetings in Essex caused concern but cannot be fully explained. For instance, several Essex and Kent people were reprimanded for gathering together to discuss various matters of doctrine

An empty niche in
the Lady chapel
of St.Nicholas church

This niche may have housed
a statue of the Virgin Mary
before the Reformation.

at Bocking in 1551; they confessed to having refused communion for two years. Some suspicious men meeting at Witham in March 1550 may not have had any religious motives. All we know of them is a rather mysterious order issued by the Privy Council about 'certeyn light fellowes that came out of Suffolk to Wyttam, in Essex, where they drynke all day and looke uppon bookes in the night'. They were to be examined, have their books taken away, and to be put 'in sure holde'. This was the only recorded decision taken by the Privy Council on that day, at a meeting of twelve notables including the Archbishop of Canterbury (Cranmer), the High Chancellor, the Lord Treasurer, the Lord Chamberlain, and the bishop of Ely.[4]

Will preambles in Essex and Witham during Edward's reign

There was an increase in the number of preambles with Protestant expressions in Essex, but they did not become as widespread as we might perhaps have expected. A sample suggests that they were found in nearly twenty per cent of the wills during Edward's reign, compared to about seven per cent during the last four years under Henry. Meanwhile, Catholic forms of will preamble continued to be used in about seventeen per cent of wills, although they gradually diminished. Thus about three-quarters of the solely Catholic preambles were found before 1551, whilst three-quarters of the Protestant ones were found after 1549, when they started to exceed Catholic ones.

However, most preambles used in the county under Edward were non-committal, and avoided referring to the symbols of either Protestantism or Catholicism. This was also true of Kent. An Essex example was Witham's Robert Payne in 1552, who merely bequeathed his soul 'to almyghty god, my maker and redemer'. His will was probably written by the gentleman Alexander Warner, which made it the first surviving will from Witham to be written by a person who was not connected with the Church. Warner probably wrote another similar preamble during Mary's reign, in 1554. His role helps to support the suggestion that non-committal wills were often associated with Protestantism, because his own will, written 'at a great age' in 1586, used the famous preamble of the Protestant William Tracy, who was discussed in the previous chapter (page 31). The use of lay scribes in the parish became more common after the 1550s and often had Protestant associations.[5]

Those few people in Essex who used Protestant will preambles were rather unevenly distributed around the county. Most of the areas where they were found under Henry, also had a number of examples under Edward, but willmakers in some of the other areas began to use them also. For instance, they started to appear in some of the villages around Witham. There were two Protestant preambles in Witham itself, one from gentleman John Moone of Blunts Hall in 1550, and one from John Wynwell in 1552. Wynwell was known as a husbandman, a relatively humble description, but he did own a house and also some land in Wickham Bishops.[6]

There continued to be some places in the county whose will preambles avoided Protestant terminology entirely even at this time, For instance a historian of Maldon found that in that town, no wills gave 'even a broad hint of Reformist beliefs before the 1560s'.[7]

MARY I, 1553-1558

This caution stood Maldon in good stead when the Catholic Mary arrived on the throne in 1553. The enactments of Edward's reign were repealed, and new Injunctions issued to restore Catholic ceremony in the parishes, which re-equipped themselves accordingly. However, images of saints and the provision of obits and prayers for the dead were not generally restored, and nor was the former authority of the Pope ever fully re-established. Only a few lands were given back to revived religious houses. They included the Witham manors of Chipping and Newland, which were re-granted to the Knights Hospitallers. The lordship of the two manors was already leased out to Sir John Smith of Cressing Temple, so the restoration of the Hospitallers may not have made much difference to local affairs.[8]

Accusations of Protestant heresy in Essex during Mary's reign

The re-imposition of Catholicism was welcomed by some people, but this welcome was a quiet one about which we know comparatively little. The fate of those Protestants who suffered is better recorded. About eight hundred of the more prosperous English Protestants exiled themselves temporarily to more congenial parts of Europe. The Government attempted to trace and confiscate their land; for instance, the property of three men from Great Braxted, two miles east of Witham, was taken. At home, nearly three hundred people were burnt to death in England for their Protestant beliefs during Mary's reign, including Thomas Cranmer, the Archbishop of Canterbury. Between fifty and sixty of them were inhabitants of Essex, and Colchester people are said to have suffered more executions during Mary's reign than those of any other town in England except London and Canterbury. The burnings themselves were used as a warning to the spectators, as well as a punishment, and were staged in various Essex parishes not always connected with the case itself. John Foxe is one of our main sources of information, as he was for Henry's reign; in reading him we again need to remember his aim of glorifying Protestantism. He wrote that of all the parts of England, 'there is none ... that hath bene more frutefull of godly martyrs, then hath Essex'.[9] I will concentrate here on some examples which illustrate specific points.

Most Protestants who were detected and arrested seem to have attracted certain punishment. We do not hear of many who were allowed to abjure and continue life as before, in the way that Witham's Christopher Raven and many others had done during Henry's reign. So it was probably a surprise when a group of twenty-two men and women from the Colchester area were questioned in London and released after 'repentance' in 1557; they made a confession claiming that they accepted transubstantiation. The bishop, Edmund Bonner, had hoped that they would be brought to him early in the day and 'quietly', but instead they travelled through Cheapside in mid-morning, and Foxe claimed that they collected about a thousand sympathisers on the way. He attributed the outcome to the authorities' fear that 'by the death of so many together, some disturbance might rise peradventure among the people'. Three of the people who were released were William and Alice Mount, and Alice's daughter, Rose Allen, all of Great Bentley. Due to a complaint by their priest, they were arrested again later in 1557 for examination at Colchester, and were burnt to death on the bishop's instructions in the Castle Yard, with a man from Thorpe le Soken. Earlier in the day, six others had suffered the same fate just outside the town walls. Foxe asserted that most of the 'thousands' of spectators called out support for them.[10]

As the State and the Church were so close, it was only a short step for a religious dissenter to be regarded as a traitor too. Thus George Eagles, known as 'Trudge-over', was hanged, drawn and quartered at Chelmsford in 1557, after being accused of praying 'that God should turn Queen Mary's heart or else take her away'; he admitted the first part of the prayer though he denied the second. He had travelled far and wide in his preaching, particularly in the Colchester area. The number of burnings of people from around Colchester recalls the strength of Protestantism in that area during Henry's reign, and a similar continuity can be found in Saffron Walden. A pewterer from Maidstone in Kent was burnt in that town, and Foxe notes that a well-known travelling preacher called John Bradford wrote a letter to 'the faithful dwelling at Walden' in the 1550s. A few years later he was burnt at the stake for his beliefs.[11] But some who suffered were from parts of the county about which little had been heard before. For instance a draper from Billericay in the south was burnt at Chelmsford, and four clothworkers from Bocking were burnt at Smithfield. Their offence was refusing to attend the Latin church services in their parish churches.

By this time these clothworkers of Bocking, together with those of Colchester, were involved in the revival of clothmaking, using new techniques. This increased the economic independence of communities and individuals, and because it depended largely on exports, it enhanced opportunities for contact with new ideas on the continent. It was probably not until nearly 1600 that Witham's parishioners began to participate fully in the new industry. However, Coggeshall, not far away, was one of the pioneering clothmaking towns of the mid-sixteenth century, as well as having been involved in the industry previously. It is therefore interesting to note that it was often mentioned by Foxe, and that some of the references were to clothmaking occupations. We may recall that one of Coggeshall's residents had instructed Witham's Thomas Hills, servant of Christopher Raven, during the 1520s. There was also a report of a crucifix 'in the highway by Coggeshall' having been destroyed in about 1532. It was probably during the 1550s that William Flower, a travelling preacher from Cambridgeshire, taught children there, and also visited Braintree nearby; he was later burnt at the stake for his activities in London. In 1554 six men from Coggeshall were reported by the town's constables for not receiving communion and for 'holding of divers other opinions, contrary to the faith of the church'. Four of them were weavers, and two were fullers. After examination by bishop Bonner in London, three escaped with instructions to do penance, but the others were put to death at different places in the north-east of the county. In the following year Thomas Hawkes was taken to Coggeshall to be burnt 'with no small multitude of people on every side compassing him about'. He was described by Foxe as a gentleman, 'brought up daintily' somewhere in Essex. As a pre-arranged signal he raised his hands over his head whilst in the fire; this was to show his friends that the pain was 'tolerable' and that his mind was still 'quiet and patient'; Foxe alleged that 'there followed such applause and outcry of the people ... that you would have thought heaven and earth to have come together'.[12]

I will lastly mention the well-known group of thirteen men and women who were examined in London and then burnt there, at Bow, known as 'Stratford le Bow', in 1556. The event earned an illustration in Foxe's book. Of the thirteen victims, ten were from Essex, all from different parishes apart from two residents of Colchester St.James. They came from places as far apart as Waltham Holy Cross in the west and Wix in the east, Great Dunmow in the north and Stanford le Hope in the south. Amongst them was a 20-year old tailor called George Searles from White Notley, three miles north-west of Witham, who had first been taken to Colchester castle. Growing up at this time in the adjoining parish of Black Notley was the young boy Jerome Garrard(1). He and his descendants were to be notable and fervent Puritan Protestant activists in Witham in later reigns.[13]

Protestant will preambles in Essex and Witham during Mary's reign

People like the Garrards must have heard of the fate of their neighbours, and of those in other nearby towns such as Coggeshall and Bocking. But nevertheless, some Essex willmakers were still bold enough to express their Protestantism in their will preambles, even under Mary. About 2,200 wills survive which were proved in Essex during her reign, out of which I found sixty-nine, or about three per cent, which had Protestant preambles. This was, not surprisingly, a great reduction compared to the twenty per cent of Edward's reign. One of them, made by John Graygoose of Epping in the west of Essex in 1554, uses several phrases which are recognisably taken from the notorious will of William Tracy, discussed in the last chapter (page 31).[14] Occupations are known for twenty-seven of the sixty-nine. Six were husbandmen, six were widows and six were tradesmen and craftsmen. There was one parson, John Hornsey from Birdbrook. Four were involved in

clothmaking, of which one was from Saffron Walden, and three from the area around Colchester, namely a clothier from Dedham, a shearman from Manningtree, and a weaver from St.Osyth. There were no gentlemen and only four yeomen. Thus the Protestant willmakers were perhaps rather less prosperous than their fellows from Henry's reign, of whom over a third with known occupations had been yeomen and gentlemen.

The map of Essex in figure 14 overleaf relating to Mary's reign, is drawn on the same basis as figure 12 on page 32 which relates to the later part of Henry's. In the Witham half-hundred, there were three Protestant will preambles. They came not from Witham itself but from three adjoining parishes, Kelvedon, Cressing and Faulkbourne, the last two being witnessed by clergymen.[15] One Essex clergyman was found who witnessed and probably wrote Protestant wills in both Henry's and Mary's reigns. He was John Thorpe or Thrape, vicar of St.Peter's parish in Colchester. It was probably he who had been in trouble with the bailiffs there in 1543, for not conforming to the King's instructions in his church. More parishes are represented under Mary than under Henry, but the pattern is similar; continuity like this was also found in Kent. In Essex it was in the area around Colchester that there was still most evidence of Protestantism, and the vicinities of Saffron Walden and Romford, on the London roads, continued to be well represented also. The three wills from Romford were witnessed by the priest John Saunder in 1556 and 1557. He probably wrote them too, as the same preamble was used for all of them, with the soul being bequeathed to:

> Chryst Jesus my maker and redemer in whom and by the meryttes of whoss most blessyd passyon ys my trust and clene remyssyon off all my synnes.

Similarly, the same hundreds were under-represented in Mary's reign as in Henry's, particularly in the centre and west of the county. For instance, there continued to be a relative lack of evidence of expressed Protestantism in the county town of Chelmsford. One Chelmsford resident, saddler John Living, did make a will with a Protestant preamble in 1555, but as witnesses he chose men from the nearby village of Sandon and from London, so he may not have expected much support in his own town.[16]

'MIXED' WILL PREAMBLES IN WITHAM AND ESSEX, 1543-60

Some wills had 'mixed' preambles, containing both a Protestant reference to Christ's passion and a traditional Catholic reference to the Virgin and the 'holy company' of heaven (there were also some modified versions which I have omitted from my figures). They were used over four reigns in Essex. Some writers classify them as Catholic, but others do not accept this suggestion. They have an exalted pedigree, having been used in the wills of both Henry VIII and the conservative bishop of Winchester, Stephen Gardiner. However, they were surprisingly uncommon. I found them in less than one per cent of Essex wills, thirty-two in all, between 1543,

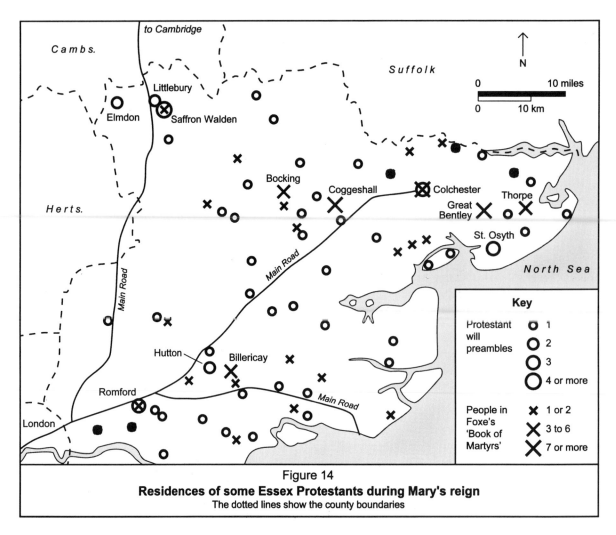

Figure 14
Residences of some Essex Protestants during Mary's reign
The dotted lines show the county boundaries

Key

Protestant will preambles	⊙	1
	○	2
	○	3
	○	4 or more
People in Foxe's 'Book of Martyrs'	✕	1 or 2
	✕	3 to 6
	✕	7 or more

FIGURE 15

NUMBERS OF WITHAM WILLS WITH DIFFERENT SORTS OF PREAMBLE DURING DIFFERENT REIGNS, 1545-58

	Pt. Hy: 1545 ----- 1547	Edw: 1547 ----- 1553	Mary: 1553 ----- 1558
Total	6	6	8
Fully mixed	4	1	4
'Modified' mixed	0	1	2
Non-committal	0	1	2
Catholic	2*	1	0
Protestant	0	2	0

*Counting William Danon as one, though there were two versions of his will

when the earliest one was found, and 1560. Margaret Spufford found only one example in her study of three Cambridgeshire parishes, dated 1552. There were some in the diocese of York in the time of Mary, but they only represented about two per cent of all the wills studied there.[17]

So it is particularly striking that for a time, between 1545 and 1558, mixed preambles were the single most important type used in wills in the parish of Witham, particularly at the end of Henry's reign and during Mary's. This is shown in figure 15. With nine examples, Witham had more than any other Essex parish. There were six more in White Notley, four miles to the north of Witham, the home of George Searles, one of the Protestants who were burnt at the stake in 1556. So these two parishes together had nearly half of the mixed preambles found in Essex as a whole. Most of the other examples were in an area further north, as shown on the map opposite (figure 16). Here, the only parishes with more than one were Gosfield and Pentlow, with two each, all witnessed by clergymen who may have been the scribe. Occasionally the spread of influence across parish boundaries was suggested by the use of similar wording, or the same people as witnesses, in adjoining parishes. Particularly noticeable in this respect were Sible Hedingham and Gosfield.[18] However, rather surprisingly, I could not trace any such personal link between Witham and White Notley.

Geoffrey Jones, vicar of White Notley from 1537 until

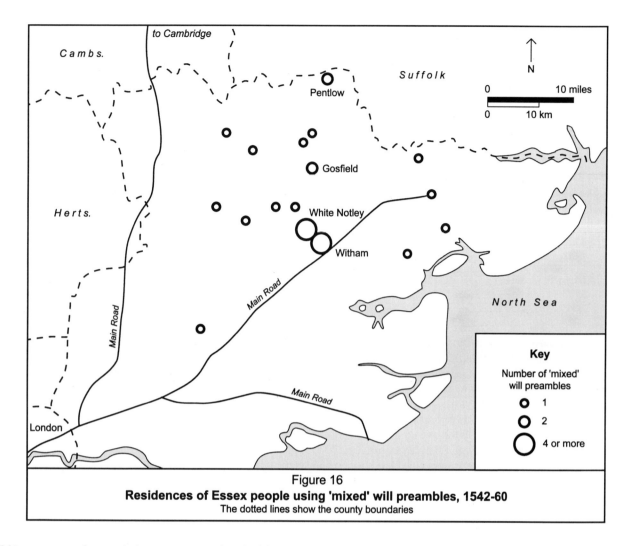

Figure 16
Residences of Essex people using 'mixed' will preambles, 1542-60
The dotted lines show the county boundaries

1562, was one of several clergymen associated with mixed preambles. He also held two rectories in London. In about 1550 he left Essex for Wales, a stronghold of traditional religion. He was deprived of his living at Notley in 1562, in Elizabeth's reign. I found fourteen wills probably written by him, spanning the whole of his incumbency. In general he followed what might be seen as a relatively 'safe' course, with a mixture of Catholic and mixed preambles in Henry and Mary's reigns, a Protestant one in the reign of Edward, and two mixed ones at the beginning of Elizabeth's reign. His 'mixed' preambles all had practically identical wording. However, in 1555, during Mary's reign, he also wrote the Protestant preamble of Richard Mabbe of Faulkbourne, between White Notley and Witham. Another clergyman connected with mixed preambles was William Jolly, rector of Pentlow. Like Geoffrey Jones he had traditional associations, having been a canon of St.Osyth's priory before its dissolution, and being in trouble for saying Catholic masses for the household of Sir Thomas Wharton at New Hall in Boreham in 1561, after he had left Pentlow. I have not found wills written by him before Mary's reign, when he wrote two mixed preambles and two whose preambles are unknown but which included a traditional donation to the church for tithes forgotten (both by clothmakers). Then in Elizabeth's reign he wrote a rather restrained Protestant preamble. One clergyman whose own will had a mixed preamble was Edward Popley, whose temporary deprivation during Mary's reign for marriage is mentioned later.[19]

Minor Witham churchmen writing mixed preambles

In Witham as in White Notley and Pentlow, most of the mixed preambles seem to have been prepared by men who wrote other forms at different times. One was Thomas Coleman, who was sexton; this office originally implied care of the fabric of the church and its contents, as well as gravedigging and bell-ringing. He witnessed five of the seven Witham wills with mixed preambles between 1545 and 1553. The first three were all for widows, Edie Christmas, Jane Haven and Joan Holder, and they used exactly the same words:

> I bequethe my soule unto Almyghtye god thorough the Intercession of our Lady saint mary virgin and all the hoolye blessed companye in hevyn to be partaker of the merites of Christes bloode and passion.

These three were written over a period of four years, suggesting that Coleman possessed a version already written down to which he could refer. He also witnessed a wholly Catholic will during Edward's reign for the wealthy William Halle of Witham Place, who left him 3s.4d. Curate Thomas Pannatt was even more adaptable. He witnessed wills during four reigns, beginning in 1540. The first six, in Henry's reign, were all Catholic, and then during Edward's reign he witnessed the Protestant will of husbandman John Wynwell. Under Mary he became associated with mixed preambles, whilst his last appearance was just into Elizabeth's reign, with the will of Walter Jolly, another husbandman, which had no preamble at all. Two of his mixed preambles, both in 1557, used the same quite distinctive wording, this time with the Protestant section first; these were for shoemaker Thomas Bentley and husbandman John Sweeting, whose souls were entrusted:

> unto Allmyghtie god trusting that through the merytts of Chrysts death and passyon and be the intercessyon of oure blessed lady and all the holye company of heaven to be partaker of the heavenly kyngdome purchased by our savyoure Jesus Chryst.[20]

WILLIAM LOVE, VICAR OF WITHAM, 1536-1560

Like his curate Thomas Pannatt, and like Geoffrey Jones of White Notley, Witham's own vicar, William Love, saw his parish through four reigns. He came in 1536 and stayed until his death in 1560. In common with many of his colleagues at this time, he probably did not have a university degree. He also became rector of Rivenhall in 1539 and may have rebuilt the rectory house there. The income of the Witham vicarage was not particularly high, and in 1548 Love sought to make the best of it by leasing out all its financial rights for sixty-one years, for £22 a year, thus giving him and his successors a fixed income whilst someone else had the trouble of collecting the rents and the vicar's share of the tithes, called the small tithes. This was quite a common practice. He himself was to retain the use of a chamber for himself, another for his servants, and another for his deputy if any, together with the garden next to the hall window and a buttery; this wording was repeated in a later lease so it may have been a customary arrangement. I shall digress briefly to say a little about the man who took the lease from Love in 1548. He was Jerome Songar of Witham, a gentleman and lawyer. Six years later he also leased the rectory of Tolleshunt Knights. On that occasion it was suggested that he was seeking to help the rector Edward Popley to try and retain his living on the accession of Mary. Popley feared removal because he had married, which had become temporarily legal under Edward. In the end he was in fact deprived, as were a number of his Essex colleagues, but he was reinstated elsewhere later.[21] During a dispute about this, Songar was referred to as a 'verey craftie and busy person'. He was also accused of extortion and breach of promise when serving as deputy sheriff of Essex. Not long after taking the lease of Witham's vicarage, he also bought the Witham Place estate. He probably held a lease in the Witham rectory too, entitling him to the great tithes.[22]

It is just possible that when William Love leased out Witham's vicarage, it was because he feared for his position under the new Protestant Church of Edward's reign. His limited role in willmaking reveals little about his views. His first contribution was to witness a predictably Catholic one in 1544. In Edward's reign, he was appointed to the respected role of supervisor by gentleman John Moone of Blunts Hall in 1550, whose will had a distinctive Protestant preamble. Then in 1552

Love joined sexton Thomas Coleman in witnessing the will of gentleman William Halle, who was a tenant of Witham Place before Jerome Songar bought it. This had a brief but solely Catholic preamble, the only one in Witham during Edward's reign. Then he witnessed one with a mixed preamble in Mary's reign, and a noncommittal one at the beginning of Elizabeth's.[23]

There is one particular aspect of his life which is puzzling. It would seem that Love did not marry. He was not removed from his post with his married colleagues when Mary came to the throne, and he does not mention a wife or any children in his will. The only person he refers to with his surname is an Oliver Love. Yet in 1564, four years after William's death, his friend George Armond(1), discussed below, left £5 to 'young William Love', who was still under 21. Who was he ? Could he have been the vicar's son ? Some clergymen survived the changes in official attitudes to their marriages by putting their wives away, or by illicit liaisons. Perhaps William Love was one of them, but we shall probably never know for certain.[24]

Love's own will was written in 1560, during the early years of Elizabeth's reign. He had provided a stone for his burial in the choir of St.Nicholas church, but was happy to be buried elsewhere if he should die away from the parish. He displayed great generosity, leaving money to a wide variety of people, including the poor of seven parishes and some of their priests, sixpence each to 'forty poore howshoulders', £10 to 'thirty poore maryages', and money to nineteen godchildren. One of these was Mary Royden, who had been born just after he became Witham's vicar, and was the daughter of the early Protestant Christopher Royden (for whom see pages 35-37). But nevertheless, William Love's will had the last exclusively Catholic preamble from Witham.[25] It perhaps represented his fundamental feelings as a man who had been ordained in the early years of the century, and this idea is supported by his close association with George Armond(1), discussed below.

Traditional associates of William Love

William Love may have had a small group of relatively 'traditional' people who were particularly close to him, led by George Armond(1), whose grandson George(2) was one of Love's godchildren. George(1) was a prosperous clothmaker who had come to Witham from Coggeshall during the 1550s. We earlier noted the presence of several enthusiastic Protestants in Coggeshall, but George Armond(1) was clearly not one of them. He was made the executor of Love's will, and was his main beneficiary, receiving money, silver, linen and houses. When George(1) himself eventually died in 1564, his will in turn was very generous, and also very revealing in that it showed how traditional were his beliefs and associations. In particular, he made various requests for prayers to be said for himself and other people after their deaths, a Catholic practice which had virtually ceased in the 1530s. Thus he left five shillings each to the 'poore Spitle howses' in Chelmsford and

Colchester, in order that their inmates could pray for him and for William Love. These 'hospital' houses were previously attached to the Friaries, to which pre-Reformation Catholics had sometimes made requests for prayers. Armond also left £5 to his sister to pray for both himself and for William Love, and he asked both 'Father Crane' and John Harte to pray for him. Harte had been witnessing wills in Witham since 1524, long before Henry VIII had rejected the supremacy of the Pope, most of them Catholic ones. His last two appearances in this role were for Love and Armond themselves. Armond's executors were to answer at the 'Dredful Daie of Judgment' for the successful performance of their tasks; this is a concept common to Christians of many varieties, but it does not appear very often in wills. The original preamble does not survive.[26] Although George Armond(1)'s son John made a quite strongly Protestant will in 1600, his grandson-in-law, Richard Brodway, is thought to have had Catholic sympathies. The family's descendants in the late seventeenth century, the clothier Jacksons, were not Catholics but were probably conforming members of the Church, and were certainly not enthusiastic Protestant dissenters like many of their fellow-parishioners.

OVERVIEW

There are many very different historical interpretations of this period. To some observers it was the Catholic Mary's reign which was out of place and unwelcome.[27] This view has the benefit of hindsight, there having since been over four hundred years of almost uninterrupted established Protestantism. But to other writers, Edward's reign merely postponed a grateful return to Catholicism under Mary. There is however some agreement that Essex continued to welcome Protestantism more than most other counties, particularly in certain places; some of these were associated with the reviving cloth industry. Even writers who consider that Protestantism made little advance in the parishes under Mary cite Colchester as an exception, as they did for Henry's reign. We know that in many parishes, including Witham, the Catholic equipment of the church was sold by the parish officials before the official investigations began under Edward.

A number of Essex Protestants lost their lives for the faith during Mary's reign, and in several instances, they appeared to have the support of the watching crowds, if we are to believe John Foxe. One historian, Christopher Haigh, considers that such sympathetic crowds were limited to 'London and other centres of Protestant success: Coggeshall and Colchester for example', and that elsewhere the observers were merely curious. Inadequate evidence makes it impossible to arrive at a conclusive view about this. However there must certainly have been some Protestant believers in Essex in addition to those who were actually executed, though it is impossible to say how many. For instance, we continue to have some Protestant will preambles, some of them written by clergymen. There were also families living in the county whose Protestant beliefs we know of from other reigns, such as the widow, descendants and friends of Christopher Raven. One writer suggests that 'the sympathetic silence of the majority of their neighbours ensured the survival of the nonconformist communities'.[28] The severity of the times may have encouraged, rather than discouraged, mutual acceptance in a place like Witham, in which we know that people held many different beliefs, and whose residents were aware from the example of nearby parishes that lack of tolerance could actually lead to executions. Someone who would consider informing on their neighbours in order to secure them a reprimand might hesitate if it could mean them losing their lives.

The population at large were not all swayed by official changes. For instance, only a minority of Essex will preambles in Edward's reign were Protestant in nature, and only a minority in Mary's reign were Catholic. However, the use of Protestant preambles did appear to extend further down the social scale than in Henry's reign. Some began to be associated with lay scribes, but many probably continued to be written by clergymen, as were wills of all kinds. Over a long period of time, many people avoided a clear-cut choice by adopting non-committal preambles, and some, particularly in the Witham area, used a mixed form. It was perhaps surprising that the latter were not more common. It is difficult to interpret them, though some of their writers appear to have been clergymen with traditional associations.

Some long-serving clergy, like William Love of Witham and Geoffrey Jones of White Notley, managed to survive many reforms, but appear to have retained a traditional Catholic belief themselves. There has been some discussion amongst historians about the interpretation of careers such as theirs. For instance, did their beliefs really remain constant or did they develop with changing circumstances? Even in the case of a well-known and well-documented figure like William Shepard, vicar of Heydon in north Essex from 1541 to 1586, historians do not entirely agree.[29] Whatever its basis, the adaptability of William Love at Witham did enable him to have links with people of a variety of different beliefs, but his closest friend, George Armond(1), boldly asked for outdated traditional prayers in his will. It was in Elizabeth's reign rather in Henry's or Edward's that traditionalists like William Love and Geoffrey Jones eventually began to seem out of place.

5. ELIZABETH I (part 1), 1558-c.1583

BACKGROUND

Elizabeth I was a Protestant, and when she became Queen she appointed Protestant advisers to replace those of the Catholic Mary. The Act of Uniformity of 1559 declared the established English Church to be Protestant also, with the monarch at its head. In a short time, what had been the essentials of the Church under Edward were re-introduced, with ceremony and doctrine set out in a revised Prayer Book, new Injunctions, and the Thirty-nine Articles, which were derived from the original forty-two Articles of Cranmer. It became compulsory to worship in the forms prescribed, and the Mass and Catholic practices were abolished. So the people in the parishes witnessed another series of changes in their own churches. There is a debate amongst historians about their readiness to accept this, just as there is for the pre-Elizabethan period. But most agree that by the 1580s, personal belief had become predominantly Protestant in character, the new generations having known nothing else.[1]

PURITANISM

However, the situation was by no means simple. Elizabeth's was a very long and varied reign, influenced by different events and pressures from one year to the next. These all coloured the attitude of the Queen herself, of officials at every level, and of ordinary parishioners. In practice there was frequently a considerable toleration of diversity in the Church. In particular, the term 'Puritan' began to be used to describe certain people, though they themselves preferred to use the term 'godly'. They played an important part in English life until the mid-seventeenth century, though their exact role and significance changed as time went on. The details are a matter of considerable discussion. Some historians try to avoid the term 'Puritan' altogether because it is hard to define. I have continued to use it, though I appreciate that it is sometimes an oversimplification. Even writers who disagree about terminology acknowledge that Essex was one of those areas where enthusiastic Protestantism, or 'Puritanism', was strongest.[2]

There were certain Puritan attitudes that were fairly constant. These included anti-Catholicism, from which arose a hostility to specific symbolic features such as the wearing of the white surplice by the clergy. Puritans favoured individual access to God, and laid stress on the scriptures, with a liking for sermons, the reading of the Bible and the singing of psalms. Some of these interests recalled those of the early Protestants of Henry's reign. Most of them were already a part of the Elizabethan Church. Nevertheless they did result in variations of emphasis, and disputes sometimes arose. In places lay people began to use their influence to achieve the style of worship they preferred. Thus at Colchester the borough appointed an independent preacher from 1562, and in Maldon, the aldermen were patrons of sermons from 1566. Such religious enthusiasm was not new to Colchester, but in the more traditional town of Maldon it was an innovation.

Puritans stressed the Calvinist belief that only the elect would be saved, which we have seen was also important to some of the early Protestants of Henry's reign. Nevertheless, they feared that God's displeasure would be attracted even to the elect, if they failed to reform the behaviour of society as a whole. So Puritanism was frequently associated with moral crusades against other people. The nature of these, the way they developed over time, and their association with social structure, has been of particular interest to many historians.[3]

SECULAR OFFICIALS

A particularly important aspect of Elizabeth's reign was the apparent increase in local administration and discipline, though some historians urge us not to under-estimate what went before. It is easy to be misled by the fact that so many more documents survive from this period.[4] Whether they represent a real change or not, they allow us to examine the local officials and their activities, both secular and ecclesiastical, in more detail than for previous times. With very few exceptions these officials were all men, as they continued to be until relatively recently.

Magistrates

The people who were appointed by the crown as magistrates, or justices of the peace, were all high-ranking gentlemen. In this period there were only fifty or sixty of them in Essex. The numbers increased fitfully in later years, but did not regularly reach a hundred until the late seventeenth century. They played an important part in administrative matters such as poor relief and the regulation of commerce. They also adjudicated on criminal cases in the courts of quarter sessions, and formed the grand jury at the assize courts, which were supervised by the two visiting circuit judges. In addition, one of the duties of a magistrate was to examine local suspects and witnesses; for many types of offence he could do this alone. If he thought that there was a case to answer, he would then prepare and sign documents called recognisances, which he later took to quarter sessions or assizes; many of these still survive in the quarter sessions rolls. These recognisances in effect extracted a promise from the people concerned; if they failed to keep it they were liable to pay a considerable sum. Sometimes they were to 'keep the peace', and sometimes to attend at the next quarter sessions or assizes. They were also needed by people authorised to keep alehouses. They are particularly useful to the historian because they indicate which magistrates dealt with which cases.[5]

Judge John Southcott, who came to Witham Place in

1567, was entitled to act as a magistrate. However, he only rarely seems to done so in Witham itself; he probably spent much of his time serving as a judge on the assize circuit. He is discussed in the next chapter (pages 67-69) in the context of his Catholic relatives.[6] There were no other magistrates living in Witham itself during this period, so men from nearby parishes dealt with the town's business, as indeed they did for most of the sixteenth and seventeenth centuries. One of the men who helped most in Witham was Henry Fortescue who had served since at least the beginning of Elizabeth's reign, and remained on the bench until his death in 1576. His home was at Faulkbourne Hall, shown below, only about a mile and a half from Witham's Chipping Hill by road. He could probably see

Faulkbourne Hall

This 15th-century brick mansion in the parish of Faulkbourne is a mile and a half away from Chipping Hill in Witham, and can be seen from the fields in the north-west of the parish. It was the home of Henry Fortescue, who acted as a magistrate in the town for many years in the first part of Queen Elizabeth's reign.

The monument to Francis and Mary Harvey in St.Nicholas church

Francis and Mary lived at Cressing Temple, three and a half miles north of the centre of Witham.
Although it is in the parish of Cressing, it is not far outside the Witham parish boundary.
Francis was an active magistrate in the town at the end of the 16th century, and held a lease
of the Witham manors of Chipping and Newland. Mary was the grandmother of Henry Nevill,
who also lived at Cressing Temple and who fought for the Royalists during the Civil War.

Witham church from his windows, and he owned property in the parish, notably the manors of Powershall and Blunts Hall. But his successors were short-lived, and this convenient spot did not seem to provide members of the bench again for a long time. Instead, Cressing Temple was often one of the nearest places to Witham with a magistrate. It was rather further away than Faulkbourne, being about two and a half miles from Chipping Hill, and nearly another mile from Newland Street. However, its residents were lords of the manors of Chipping and Newland until the mid-seventeenth centuries, and so had a particular interest in the town. Francis Harvey of Cressing Temple was appointed a magistrate in about 1570, and after the death of Henry Fortescue he frequently acted alone in Witham cases. He continued for thirty years until his death in 1602.[7] The monument in St.Nicholas church to him and his wife Mary is shown opposite.

Officers of the half-hundred

Because there were so rarely any magistrates living within Witham's own boundaries, particular responsibility fell on the shoulders of the officers of the half-hundred, who frequently lived in the town itself. The half-hundred bailiffs were chosen by the Queen's representative in the county, the sheriff. Their particular task was to issue writs, and to summon the half-hundred jury to quarter sessions to hear presentments of nuisances and cases of neglect of duty in their area. In some places the bailiffs were renowned for accepting excessive fees or bribes to excuse jurors. The bailiffs of Witham half-hundred often held office for a considerable period. Thus John Dawson, a Witham yeoman, was in the post from at least 1559 until 1576, when he was succeeded by Witham clothworker Richard Dyer. John Dawson was probably unable to sign his name, drawing an axe instead when he made his will. Thus although being a yeoman meant that he may have owned a horse to help him about his business, he would have needed to seek help to read any written instructions or to prepare any documents. This was not an uncommon situation even in early seventeenth-century England.[8]

The responsibilities of the sheriff and the bailiffs were gradually eroded during the following century by the quarter sessions and its own officers, particularly the high constables of the hundreds or half-hundreds. These men had originally been chosen by hundred juries, but by the sixteenth century they were appointed by quarter sessions. As that court itself acquired a greater role, so did these high constables, who became the chief administrative officers of the county, providing contact between quarter sessions and the parishes in a variety of ways. They had considerable responsibility. For example they presented public nuisances, tried to ensure that the parish constables did their work, and had some law-enforcement powers of their own; for instance they could order vagrants to be whipped.[9]

Although originally the high constables probably only

served for a year, they seem by this time to have held long-term appointments. For instance John Choppin of Witham itself served during the 1550s and 1560s. In 1572 John Garrard(1) of Black Notley took the post, but he did not survive to serve for long, as he died in 1574. He was a considerable property owner and left the Moat farm in Witham to his son Jerome(1), who lived in it, and was followed there by prominent Puritan descendants.[10]

From time to time the half-hundred officials seem to have met together at a 'petty sessions' in Witham, sometimes with local magistrates also attending. To begin with, these were probably arranged informally for convenience, particularly for licensing alehouses; they became more systematic in later years. Peter Clark's study of Kent found a similar pattern of development there. From the eighteenth century onwards the petty sessions came to be presided over by magistrates only.[11]

Parish constables

The parish constables' main responsibility was to the high constables and the magistrates, whom they assisted. Nevertheless they were elected annually by the manor courts. The busiest men must have been the constables for the central and most populated manors of Chipping and Newland, but Blunts Hall and Howbridge Hall manors did include one side each of Duck End, an urban area (now Bridge Street), and Blunts Hall also had its own hamlet. It is not known whether the other more rural manors in Witham had constables. The only ones for whom we know names during this period are a few of the Blunts Hall ones. In some parts of the country, poor men were often chosen as parish constables because of the unpopularity of the job, which was unpaid. But elsewhere they were reasonably prosperous. Other information about them is limited. One, Richard Wheeler, was a husbandman; his enthusiastic will preamble is discussed below. Another, Thomas Smee, was a yeoman, but he could not sign his name.[12] It would usually be these men who were obliged to ride or walk out to the magistrates' country houses with suspects and witnesses to have them examined.

CLERGYMEN

Edward Halys, vicar of Witham 1560-1587

The traditional but accommodating William Love, discussed in the last chapter (pages 48-49), did not survive long into Elizabeth's reign; he died in 1560. There is no record of his reaction to the new instructions to destroy images in the church and to amend his services yet again. He was replaced as Witham's vicar by Edward Halys, who stayed until his death in 1587. As far as we can tell, like many of his contemporaries, Edward Halys was not a graduate. We know of two of his sons, Eton and Edmund. Edmund, who was born in about 1564, is discussed in chapter 7 (pages 77-78) and mentioned in several other chapters, particularly as a writer of wills in Witham. The grand-daughter of this Edmund, and thus great-granddaughter of the vicar, was Deborah Davies, who married Edward Eatney. They were late seventeenth-century Witham Quakers, unusual descendants for an Elizabethan vicar.[13]

There was a shortage of clergymen at this time, one result of which was a temporary increase in pluralism, whereby clergy held several posts at once. Halys appears to have been vicar of nearby White Notley as well as of Witham, and he also held some land next to the church at Tollesbury, ten miles to the east, where he was involved in a dispute with the churchwardens about fencing. It may have been because of these other interests that his participation in Witham's will-writing did not begin until 1567. However, during the twenty years after that he was involved in about one third of Witham's wills, as overseer or witness, and in the 1580s he took part in some land transactions in Witham. He was in the parish frequently enough to acquire an enemy; Edward Dawny took him to quarter sessions in 1570 for enticing his servant away, and Halys was fined 3s.4d. as a result. In 1583 he leased the vicarage's income to a London haberdasher for twenty-one years, retaining the same accommodation for himself as William Love had done before him. Halys's son Edmund was at that time apprenticed to another haberdasher in London, so perhaps that contact helped with the arrangement of the lease, or perhaps the family had earlier associations with the haberdashers which occasioned both arrangements.[14]

A group of reform-minded or Puritan churchmen carried out a review of Essex clergy, probably in 1584, and considered many of them to be unimpressive. They allocated Edward Halys to the one third of the ministers whom they felt were the least suitable and capable, calling them 'unpreaching'. He was mentioned as having more than one post. It was claimed that he 'gave a summe of money to two men to conceile his pretensed whoredoome at Islington', and, in accordance with a promise made then, had never since spoken out against adultery. He was said to have 'made a confirmed lease of his benefice to his sonne for a small thing yeerly, and that for manie yeers'. If the latter accusation had any basis, it must have occurred before the lease of 1583, which was made at the recognised value of the vicarage, £22 per year. He was accused in the same review of '[moral] incontinence' and 'evil manners', and it was also said that he was 'no preacher'. Not all clergy were licensed to preach, and if they were not, they were obliged to employ a preacher to fulfil the requirement that a sermon be given in every parish four times a year. This was the subject of one of the first Injunctions issued on Elizabeth's accession. The preaching of sermons was an important part of Protestantism, and in particular of godly Puritanism. Reading was not sufficient. There was understandably a shortage of preachers when the English Church first became Protestant.[15] But by the time of the survey Halys had been in Witham over twenty years, so there had been time to adapt himself if he had the inclination. He may have been indifferent or incompetent, but on the other hand he may have preferred to retain the conservative ways of his youth, and reject Protestant fervour.

Certainly none of the wills which Halys wrote could be described as enthusiastic in their preambles. A typical example left the willmaker's soul 'to allmightye god beseching him of his mercy by and thorough Jesus Christe my onely advocate and Redemer'.[16] All the Witham willmakers in this period who did require particularly fervent preambles employed other scribes. For instance yeoman John Harding brought in Francis Sea, the vicar of the neighbouring parish of Ulting, to help him.[17] Others employed laymen such as John Glascock, discussed later in this chapter (pages 56-57).

Curates

At the time of the bishop's Visitation of 1574, Nicholas Day was recorded as Witham's curate, but below his name it was noted that he was not admitted into the ministry, and was forbidden to exercise ecclesiastical functions; the reason was not given. He seems to have stayed in the town nonetheless, to judge from his role in willmaking thereafter. He nearly always used a standard wording which was only marginally more enthusiastic than the forms used by Halys; in it the soul was left to 'Almighty God my only saviour and redemer by whose mercy and meryttes I hope to be partaker of his kingdom'. The Visitation of 1583 was dismissive of his being recorded as the town's schoolmaster; it was written that he was 'inhibited', namely forbidden. Nevertheless Edward Halys later appointed him to the vicarage of Cressing, where the Puritan survey of 1584 found him to be 'unpreaching'; this perhaps suggests that the pair were theological allies at this time.[18] Day returned to Witham again later on.

TEACHING

It would appear that if Nicholas Day did teach at this time, he was not authorised to do so. But there are records of licences being issued for Witham and the surrounding parishes from the 1570s onwards, beginning in Witham itself in 1577 with Richard Brodway, licensed to 'educate scholars' in the parish and elsewhere. His wife Margaret was the granddaughter of the clothmaker George Armond(1) of Witham, who had died in 1564 leaving a will which suggested Catholic sympathies. So it is interesting that Richard Brodway seems to have had similar associations in later life. In 1588, by which time he was in Maldon, four men with Catholic connections recommended him for a teaching post in Colchester, saying that he was:

> well knowne unto us to be one of honest living and good conversacion, and of long time a teacher ... a mann mete for that office as wee are fully perswaded.

It is not known whether he was accepted there, but by 1594 he was master of the Chelmsford free grammar school. Whilst he was there he was alleged to be a Catholic himself, or, as Sir Thomas Mildmay called him, a 'temporysinge papist'. He died in 1608, after some vehement disagreements with some of the people involved in running the school. He must have kept in touch with his Witham relatives after he left the town, because he was made executor of the will of his father-in-law John Armond in 1600, and his son Thomas Brodway was still living in Witham as late as 1632, when he briefly inherited the Armond family property.[19]

WILL PREAMBLES

From this time onwards, personal declarations of belief become more difficult to find than previously. When the Elizabethan authorities moved against offences of a religious nature, they were usually acting against behaviour, such as not attending church, rather than against actual belief.[20] So we do not have any statements from Witham parishioners to compare with those of the 'heretical' friends of Christopher Raven during the reign of Henry VIII. We have to make the best of other sources, such as will preambles.

From 1560 to 1567 we do not even have this information for Witham or for other places whose wills were proved in the Colchester archdeaconry, because the wills only survive in a register whose compiler has abbreviated all the preambles to a few words, with the addition of 'etc.'[21] However, in the Elizabethan preambles which do survive for Witham, there were no Catholic sentiments apart from those of the two wills mentioned in the last chapter (pages 48-49), of vicar William Love in 1560 and of the teacher Richard Brodway's grandfather-in-law George Armond(1) in 1564. Nor were there any of the 'mixed' style of preamble which had so often been used in Witham since 1545. By 1568 when full preambles become regularly available again, a brief but definitely Protestant form had become the norm in the town, with more enthusiastic versions from time to time. There were also some willmakers who retained an extremely brief and non-committal form, referring only to god, and it is difficult to judge the significance of this.

The Puritan sympathies of some of the residents of Witham are indicated by a small number of wills, first appearing in the early 1570s, which express very elaborate Protestant sentiments, with a fervent and lengthy expression of faith. For comparison it may be noted that in the adjoining village of Terling, the earliest Elizabethan will showing any similar degree of commitment did not appear until 1583.[22] The local churchmen were not invited to participate in these enthusiastic wills. This may have been because the willmakers concerned considered themselves to be superior to the Witham clergy, either socially or in the strength of their faith.

Joan Raven

The first example of these extreme wills is that of Joan Raven, made in 1572, who by this time must have been fairly elderly. We saw in chapter 3 (pages 32-35) how she was accused of Protestant heresy in 1527 with her husband Christopher Raven. She had survived him by thirty years, retaining rights in his property, probably continuing to live in his house at the bottom of what is now Church Street. Like him she left money towards the repair of Witham church, asking the vicar and churchwardens to bestow 3s.4d. 'where and when most nede is'. Bequests for the fabric of the church had ceased in Witham for a time after the 1540s, together with other donations then associated with Catholicism, but gifts for repairs to the newly Protestant church had begun to be made during the 1560s. Joan also seems to have continued the family's relationship with the gentry. In earlier years this had involved close ties with the prosperous Protestant Roydens, Katherine Royden having been asked by her husband to continue her friendship with Joan after she too was widowed. But now in 1572 the main gentry connection was with the Harveys and Smiths of Cressing Temple, who were often said to be interested in Catholicism. Thus one of the supervisors of her will was Francis Harvey, lord of the manors of Chipping, in which Joan was a tenant, and Newland; the other was gentleman Clement Roberts from the neighbouring parish of Little Braxted, who owned some land in Witham. And Francis Harvey and William Smith, the brother of Francis's wife Mary's first husband, were witnesses.[23]

However, Joan's will suggests that she may not have been thought of as the social equal to the gentry herself. A similar impression was obtained from Christopher's will thirty years earlier. Thus the goods which were named in her will were fairly ordinary. She left her son John her:

> best Fether bedd bolster to it, the best coverlet and a payre of blankettes and the curteynes to the same, a presse and a square boorde or table, three platters, three disshes, three sawcers, three pottengers, a bason and a pewter Pott and a great brasse panne.

She said that he was also to have 'my great powderyng troffe and my great Spytte', 'my leade, my mouldyng borde and a great Cowpe'. A press was a cupboard, pottengers were bowls, a powdering trough was for salting meat, a lead was a large open vessel, and a moulding board was a board on which dough was shaped. She also left 3s.4d. each to four of John's servants, and two 'mylche kyne [milking cows]' to her daughter and son-in-law, Agnes and John Martin, who had four children. They were also to have a 'little Tenement' called Caters in Witham which she had bought. Christopher's former property went to their eldest son Edward under the terms of Christopher's will.

Joan's will of 1572 was written for her by Thomas Hunt, a Witham gentleman. At the time he had just acquired some property in Blunts Hall manor by means of a marriage to Elizabeth Songar, widow of Henry, and was in dispute with Elizabeth's sons about their father's goods. He was the supervisor and probably the writer of another will twelve years later, whose preamble had some marked similarities to that of Joan's; this was for Clement Clarke, a gentleman from Stisted. The main expression of faith in Joan Raven's will took the form of a 'pre-preamble'. Thus before bequeathing her soul she noted that in making her will she was:-

> Calling to my remembraunce the certentie of death to all persons assured and the uncerteintie of tyme when it shall please Almyghty God of his infynyte goodnes and mercye to call me out of this frayle transitory life the vale of mysery and wretchednes in comparison of the life to come, whereof I most assuredly trust thorough the merites of Cristes passion and his most precyous bloud shedd for me and all mankynd onely to have fruycion with joyes incomparable in his celestyall kyngdom which is prepared for all them that die in him, Mynding and entendyng by goddes grace and sufferaunce to despose soche worldly goodes and substance as he hath lent me in this world (of his infynyte goodnes and dyvyne provydence more then any thing by my desert) to soche my posterite as it pleases him I shall leave behynde me in the wretched world.

She wished her body to be:

> bestowed in godly and decent ordre accordyng to the laudable institucion of the Churche and the Quenes highnes lawes and proceedings in the Church yard of Witham.

Her friend Christopher Royden had used similar wording in 1543 when he asked that his burial should not be embellished by additional ceremony. Joan's beliefs seem to have been supported by her son John, who, as seen below, witnessed another will with an enthusiastic Protestant preamble in 1586; he also left one himself in 1599.[24]

Preambles taken from William Tracy

The other three particularly lengthy and fervent preambles of this time from Witham were identical with each other. They were those of Robert Richolde, written in 1576, Richard Wheeler in 1577, and Alexander Warner in 1586. They read:

> I comend me wholly unto gode and most humbly submytt my selfe to his mercy, belevinge stedfastly withowte any Dowbte or mystruste that by his grace and the merytes of Jesus Christ his only sonne oure Lorde And by the vertue of his blessed passion his gloryous resurrection I have and shall have free remyssion of my synnes and resurrection of body and soule accordynge as it is written. I beleve that my Redemer lyveth And that in the last daye I shal Aryse owte of the earthe and in my fleshe see my Savyour this my hope is layde upp in my bosome. And the grounds of my faythe and beleffe is that their is but one mediator betwene gode and man which is Jesus Christ. All other be but peticioners in receyvinge of grace but none able to gyve influence of grace and therfore my truste is in the assured promyisses of gode.

This wording was taken directly from the will of William Tracy of Gloucestershire, which had been composed in 1531 and has already been mentioned (pages 31 and 45). When it was first written it had occasioned the burning of Tracy's corpse because of his Protestant heresy; the words were used in two Essex wills of 1545 and 1554 but only in a much abbreviated form. The 1570s and 1580s were more confident times for Protestants, and Tracy's preamble had been drawn to the attention of new generations by being reproduced in John Foxe's 'Book of Martyrs', beginning with the first and second editions in 1563 and 1570. It was expected that each church would display a copy of Foxe's book. However, the particular associations of Tracy's words meant that even now they were not likely to have been used lightly. In a search of around five thousand Essex wills between 1573 and 1589, I found only six altogether whose preambles quoted at length from Tracy, including the three from Witham. Of the others, one belonged to an esquire from Terling, adjoining Witham, one to a yeoman from Black Notley, four miles away, and the other, which only uses part of the wording, to a yeoman from Tollesbury, about ten miles away. When John Craig and Caroline Litzenberger studied the effects of Tracy's preamble they found only fifteen instances of its use in the whole of England at any time, though of course others remain to be discovered.[25] The only Essex one included in the fifteen was the one from Terling mentioned above, which was written by John Rochester for himself in 1583. It is interesting to note that not only did Rochester possess a Geneva Bible, which was an extreme Protestant edition, but his son-in-law John Shaa owned a copy of Foxe.[26]

The Witham and Black Notley versions contain particularly full and faithfull renditions of Tracy's preamble. The originator of all four must have been John Glascock, who witnessed all four and definitely wrote three of them. He also wrote another Black Notley will in 1585 with a more conventional preamble. He lived at the manor house of Blunts Hall in Witham, and in 1572 was called 'a gentleman of wealth and friends' during a dispute about rent. The fact that the Black Notley yeoman Nicholas Collin who used Tracy's preamble travelled the six miles to Witham to seek out John Glascock, helps to emphasise the deliberate nature of his willmaking. Richard Garrard was one of his witnesses. Richard was the brother of Jerome(1), both being sons of the late John Garrard(1), former high constable and fellow parishioner of Collin's in Black Notley. By this time Jerome(1) was settled at Witham's Moat farm. His son Jerome(2) and his grandson Robert(2) were to become aggressive leading Puritans in Witham during the seventeenth century.[27]

The three clients from Witham for whom John Glascock used Tracy's preamble were all primarily involved in agriculture, not in the more urban activities which are sometimes thought likely to have harboured extremism. It is probable that the cloth industry, a 'notorious hotbed of Puritanism', was not yet very prominent in the town. Two of the three, Robert Richold and Alexander Warner, were fairly prosperous yeomen. In addition to having Glascock write the will,

Richold made him his overseer, described him as 'my very assured friend', and said that he had 'special trust' in him. Richold and Glascock either shared or sublet from each other the lease of Blunts Hall. Richold asked that after his death his wife Thomasine should have a regular supply of wheat and malt from this land to keep herself and her two youngest daughters. He probably lived at his 'mansion house' in Newland Street; and also owned a tenement in the same street, together with Batford croft behind it. His son Henry, who inherited the property, later had some lively encounters with the courts. In 1591 it was for speaking ill of the 'honest women' of Witham, and fighting with the man who took him to court, and in 1594 it was for joining a group of men who were said to have attacked the estate of Cecily Sandys, widow of the bishop of London, at Woodham Ferrers.[28]

When yeoman Alexander Warner had his will prepared by Glascock using Tracy's preamble, one of his other witnesses was John Raven, the son of early Protestants Christopher and Joan. Warner's daughters were married to local tradesmen, and he himself was an established figure in the community, being a 'great age' when he wrote his will. He had probably been the first person not connected with the Church to act as a scribe for wills in Witham, the first having been written in 1552, during the reign of Edward VI. He had been a churchwarden in that same year, and was also an almshouse trustee, and a juror at quarter sessions and assizes on occasion.[29] In his will he left 6s.8d. to the repair of the church and 6s.8d. to the poor, and wished to be buried 'agaynste the Chancell dore where my Father and Grandfather were buryed'.

Glascock's third Witham client whose will used Tracy's words, Richard Wheeler, merely referred to himself as a husbandman, and appears to have owned no land or property. He did leave seven separate sums of 6s.8d. to members of his family. In relation to four of these, he wrote that if they all died, 'which god forbidd', their money was to go to his wife Elizabeth. In 1545 either he or his namesake had been accused of taking a cow from the rector of Rivenhall. However, around 1570 he was a parish constable for Blunts Hall manor. In 1590 his widow Elizabeth appeared in the Archdeacon's court for publicly quarrelling or 'scoulding' with Sarah Turner, a dispute which was settled by the vicar.[30] Thus Wheeler does not seem to have been as well-off or well-established as the other two users of the same preamble, nor as well-connected as Joan Raven.

On balance, however, the noticeable aspect of the enthusiastic Protestant preambles which have been mentioned is that the scribes and most of the willmakers were associated with the gentry. This makes it likely that the believers knew each other. In particular, willmaker John Rochester and the scribes Thomas Hunt and John Glascock were probably all near-neighbours, associated with an area in the west of Witham. Finally we should note that Glascock's son-in-law Edmund Allen, who also lived in this vicinity, at Hatfield Priory, was involved in a dispute during this same period which revealed him to be an assertive Puritan. It concerned the minister whom Allen had placed in the parish, who was suspended by the anti-Puritan bishop of London, John Aylmer, for not wearing a surplice, and accused of many other strikingly radical beliefs and practices such as persuading the parishioners that there was no need for water at baptism because 'they have the worde'. They also sat with their heads covered in church, which was to become an important issue in similar later disputes. The bishop called Allen and his associates 'puritans, fooles, knaves', and committed him and the minister to the Fleet prison for a time.[31]

OFFENCES TAKEN TO COURT

Secular courts

The assizes and quarter sessions were normally held in the county town of Chelmsford, ten miles from Witham. There was a relentless and accelerating increase in the number of serious criminal cases which they received during Elizabeth's reign. Theft was a particular feature of this phenomenon, which was at its most dramatic in the period after 1585. However, recorded offences were unevenly distributed, so many places could go for years without being affected at all. There are only six surviving indictments concerning Witham from the assizes between 1558 and 1580. Five involved theft; judge John Southcott of Witham presided over these. The other was an isolated instance of suspected witchcraft, heard by Gilbert Gerrard, the Attorney General. This was when Joan Haddon, a spinster, was accused by several people of obtaining money from them by witchcraft in 1560. The jury however found her only guilty of fraud, for which she was sentenced to stand in the pillory. It is thought by some historians that accusations of witchcraft increased at this time, encouraged by the return after Mary's reign of Protestant exiles whose awareness of the concept had been heightened on the continent.[32]

The courts dealt with administrative matters too, and a high proportion of the surviving Witham cases concerned bridge maintenance, but there was also one instance of suspected extortion, two of poaching, a theft of bushes and thorns, and a burglary. In 1576 it was reported that the town lacked a 'cucking' stool; this was a chair to which offenders were fastened as a punishment, in order to suffer either jeers or ducking or both. And five unlicensed 'tippling' [drinking] houses were presented before 1580, a foretaste of the more extensive attempts to control such matters in later years.[33]

Church courts

As shown by the graphs in chapter 2 (pages 20 and 22), activity in the Archdeacon's court was less at this time than during the later years of the reign. Most of the initiative was still being taken by the court officials. During the 1570s only nine per cent of Witham cases were brought by the churchwardens, and in fact much of our surviving knowledge about the wardens is fairly negative. In 1569 and 1573 the court criticised them because Witham's church and churchyard were 'in decaye'. One of the most striking cases was in 1571, when it was reported by the court's officers that there were 'none of the parishe at service the sondeay before Michaelmas'. In punishment John Ligett, one of the churchwardens, was to pay his large fine of thirteen shillings to the hospital at Colchester. This seems to imply that nobody was at church at all, though it is possible that it merely meant that none of the parish officers was in attendance. The 1559 Act of Uniformity required that parishioners should all attend morning and evening service, but it is thought that this was not generally enforced. Nevertheless, to have 'none of the parishe' there at all was rather surprising. These cases may all go to support the suggestion made earlier that Edward Halys was not a particularly conscientious vicar. Other references to Witham in the Archdeacon's court show hints of matters that were later to become of great concern, such as rate collection and the taking of communion. Two Witham men were accused in 1569 of detaining funds which had been intended for the use of the poor. There were also several appearances for sexual misdemeanour, especially after about 1570.[34]

OVERVIEW

It can be seen that surviving indications of the religious life in Witham at this time are rather intermittent, and do not allow a study of its dynamics such as can be undertaken for places with additional information like borough records. For instance, in his research on Colchester, Mark Byford was able to examine the changing situation there, which was symbolised by the existence of separate Protestant and Catholic alehouses in 1560.[35] As in earlier decades, we are only aware of the religious interests of a very small number of Witham people. There may have been between 150 and 200 families in the parish, and the views of most of them are unknown to us. However, we saw that Catholic sentiments did continue to be held into the 1560s, as demonstrated by the examples of the vicar William Love and his friend George Armond(1), and very probably into the 1570s with Armond's grandson-in-law, teacher Richard Brodway. Some of the relatively few reported absences of other people from Witham church may have been for this reason, but if so it was not considered important enough in this period for the documents to say so.

There is also evidence that some particularly fervent Protestants lived in the town, notably Joan Raven, who was able to maintain into a less hostile reign the beliefs which she and her husband Christopher had shown during the time of Henry VIII. Witham and some of its neighbouring parishes were notable in Essex for another echo of Henry's time, the use of the will preamble of heretic William Tracy, particularly by prosperous gentry and yeomen. These particular wills provided links with both Witham's past and its future, in that one was witnessed by John Raven and another by Richard Garrard.

Some historians have argued that 'middling' or even quite humble people were absorbed in enthusiastic Protestantism at this time. However, others, such as Marjorie McIntosh in her study of Havering in Essex, have found that it was mostly the preserve of the better-off members of the community. This is what most of the limited evidence available for Witham seems to suggest, except for the involvement of husbandman Richard Wheeler.[36] Although the writer of the wills using Tracy's preamble, John Glascock, was father-in-law of an assertive Puritan in neighbouring Hatfield Peverel, we do not yet have evidence in Witham itself of the type of moral Puritanism which sought to impose itself on the behaviour of other people. Clergy and parish officers here were often more noted for their neglect than their enthusiasm. But the apparatus of administration and justice was in place and ready for whatever obligations might befall it in later times.

6. ELIZABETH I (part 2), c.1583-1603

ECONOMIC AND SOCIAL DIFFICULTIES

This second half of Elizabeth's reign was more dramatic than the first in many ways. In particular, the 1580s and 1590s were times of serious economic crisis. The whole century had been one of rapid population increase and high inflation, but matters were brought to a head by some drastic harvest failures. 1586 was a bad year, but 1594 to 1597 in particular were years of unremitting disaster. War with Spain also imposed severe financial pressures during the 1590s. In the ensuing atmosphere of panic, the number of criminal prosecutions in Essex soared even higher than during the previous decades, during which they had already been increasing. People at all levels of society suffered. Thus in spite of owning his own house near the bottom of Newland Street, and several acres of land nearby, the butcher Peter Snow was not able to pay his rates in 1595 because he had 'gone away for debt'. Some of the land he had only received in 1594 on the death of his elderly yeoman father, another Peter, but he sold most of it in 1596, no doubt because of his financial problems. He managed to return, because he was practising as a butcher again in 1608 when quarter sessions ordered him not to sell meat during Lent.[1] The recovery of his business and others like it may have been helped by the fairly sudden transformation of Witham in about 1600 from a market town to an industrial centre making cloth for export.

Religion continued to be a major issue, as different factions sought power at court. A new law was passed in 1593 which sought to restrain separate Puritan activity. It not only enforced attendance at the parish church, but forbade other forms of religious assemblies or 'conventicles'. Together with other legislation, it also penalised Catholics, against whom feeling continued to run high. This period saw dramatic feuds in several Essex places which historians have studied recently. In these, a common theme was the power struggle between different Protestant factions for control of the parishes and the churches, often involving an element of personal as well as theological competition. Examples are Maldon and Heydon. In Colchester there had been similar disputes during in the 1570s.[2]

SECULAR OFFICIALS

Magistrates

The county's magistrates became involved with these problems, and their work continued to expand during this period, in both the administrative and the judicial fields. Essex is said to have been particularly 'closely governed'. A number of new magistrates seem to have been recruited in the county around 1590, their number increasing from fifty or sixty to nearly seventy during the early 1590s, and to eighty in 1593. There was about one magistrate for every five parishes by 1600. Similar increases were to be found in other counties; by the same date Kent had one for every four parishes. Magistrates began to receive regular instructions or 'charges' about dealing with social and economic problems from the government; these were delivered to them by the assize judges on their bi-annual visits. The assizes and quarter sessions became important meeting places for the powerful men of Essex, giving a magistrate power and influence outside his own immediate locality, though there has been some discussion amongst historians about the exact nature of such county 'society' and its relationship to national affairs.[3]

Judge Southcott of Witham Place, who was qualified to act as a magistrate, died in 1585. His wife Elizabeth and many of his descendants were Catholics, and the family is discussed later in the chapter in that context (pages 67-69). Although they owned about a quarter of the area of the parish of Witham, the Southcotts did not again become figures of authority here until the very end of the seventeenth century. They were usually disqualified on religious grounds, and in addition they sometimes lived elsewhere.

Francis Harvey of Cressing continued as a magistrate. His somewhat intermittent activity on Witham cases was supplemented at times by men from other villages adjoining Witham, particularly William Ayloffe and John Sams of Great Braxted and Kelvedon. In about 1600 Ralph Wiseman of Rivenhall was also appointed to the bench. He had arrived in that parish ten years earlier, and his family were to deal with very many of the Witham cases during the seventeenth century. But often it seems to have been necessary to call on men from five or more miles away; examples were Sir Edward Huddleston of Pattiswick, Christopher Chiborne of Messing, and Peter Tuke of Layer Marney.[4]

In addition, for a time there was a decidedly unusual figure on the scene. This was magistrate John Sterne, who was Witham's vicar and also suffragan bishop of Colchester. This post was additional to, but lower in rank than, the main establishment of bishops. Sterne appears to have become a magistrate in about 1598 and served until his death in 1608. At times he dealt with nearly all the town's cases. His appointment must have been by virtue of the post of suffragan. The lists of magistrates were carefully arranged in order of rank, and the men probably sat in a similar format at the sessions. Sterne always came high on the list in the position reserved for bishops, just after the peers. The only previous representatives of the Church on the Essex bench had been the successive bishops of London themselves, whose role was probably only nominal. In the country as a whole, churchmen other than bishops who became magistrates at this time were usually administrators, and there were only a very few of them, although their numbers increased somewhat from the 1620s onwards.[5] So Sterne was not only unusual in that he was an active magistrate who was resident in Witham parish itself, but in that he was a vicar and a magistrate at the same time.

Half-hundred and parish officers

Mark Goodwin, a Witham yeoman and innkeeper, became bailiff of Witham half-hundred in 1582, and stayed until his death in 1598. During this long tenure he was involved in various disputes. One of the high constables was Leonard Aylett, a Witham yeoman who probably could not write his name; he and his colleague helped to preside over a petty sessions held at Witham in 1590. His son Robert, a lawyer, became a man of influence in the Church in Essex during the 1630s.[6]

Most of the constables for the manors of Chipping and Newland are known from this period. These being the central manors, the holders were in effect the parish constables, and the post seemed to be taken seriously and filled with men from the better-off ranks of the middling occupations. All owned land in the manors. A quarter of the known men were innkeepers or victuallers, often with an additional occupation as well. The rest were evenly distributed between shopkeepers, yeomen and clothmakers, the latter starting to appear during the 1590s. Except for one tailor and one tailor/innholder, there were no craftsmen, who were generally less prestigious than people in the occupations mentioned. This reasonable status was reflected in the fact that of those parish constables whose writing ability is known, twice as many could sign their names as could not. For comparison, amongst willmakers in general, themselves a select group, only about a quarter signed their name during the 1590s. On average the parish constables whose date of death is known, lived for another sixteen years after their period of office, so they were 'middle-aged' when constables. A number of them also became churchwardens in due course, usually about three or four years after they were constables.[7]

CLERGYMEN

John Sterne, vicar 1587-1608

John Sterne became Witham's vicar after the death of Edward Halys in 1587; he had a Cambridge degree, and was thus the first graduate vicar here since before the Reformation, a fact which reflected a trend towards increasing educational standards amongst the clergy. He was previously in Hertfordshire, and whilst there, in 1584, he had been elected to the Lower House of Convocation of the ecclesiastical province of Canterbury; this body consists of two clergymen elected from each diocese. The papers concerning the election survive, which is most unusual. In commenting on them, Professor Collinson refers to Sterne as a 'carpet-bagger', and suggest that he 'may have had official backing' in the election.[8] A 'carpet-bagger' is someone 'interfering with the politics of a locality with which he is thought to have no permanent or genuine connexion'. The term originates from the period after the American Civil War of the 1860s, so its application to John Sterne is somewhat anachronistic, but the meaning is clear !

After Sterne was appointed to Witham he also continued as rector of Bygrave in Hertfordshire, which produced a bigger income, but he seems to have spent at least some of his time in Essex, because in 1589 he witnessed two wills of Witham people, and probably wrote them. One of their preambles was totally non-committal, reading 'in the name of god', whilst the other was a very brief Protestant one. He also gave evidence about Witham on various matters in the Archdeacon's court. His life as a career clergyman progressed further in 1592 when he became suffragan bishop of Colchester. The post had been set up in 1534, but had remained unfilled since the death of its first holder in 1540. Mark Byford has suggested that in reviving the appointment, the bishop of London, John Aylmer, was seeking revenge for the borough of Colchester's earlier refusal to accept Sterne as its preacher. The bishop had earlier suspended a 'full-blooded Protestant' there. The implication therefore is that Sterne himself was not comparably full blooded. In an early seventeenth-century survey of Essex clergymen, Sterne was not included in a list of ninety-four 'dilligente and sufficiente preachers'. However, a separate list of 'double beneficed' and other ministers it was conceded that he was at least 'a sufficiente preacher'.[9]

After his appointment as suffragan, Sterne appears to have stopped carrying out mundane tasks such as will-writing in Witham, but this may partly have been because Edmund Halys had begun to do much of this work from 1593 onwards. Sterne's active work in Witham after his appointment to the bench of magistrates in 1598 suggests that he did spend time in the town. Another indication of this was that in 1594 his servant Henry Beckwith was alleged to be the father of an illegitimate child in Witham.[10]

Curates

The curates during John Sterne's incumbency changed frequently and played varying roles. The first known is John Cooke, recorded in 1588 and 1589; he made various appearances at the Archdeacon's court, once supporting an alleged sabbath breaker, once for not appearing in church, and another time for conducting a marriage ceremony for a couple who had already been excommunicated for living together. He was replaced briefly by a Mr.Smith who was referred to in the Archdeacon's records of 1590 as Witham's 'new curate and schoolmaster'. But Smith never showed his licence in court, and a year later it was recorded that 'he is gone'. Three other curates are recorded; there was Lewis Bromley in 1593, a John Hawsted or Hastye from 1596 to 1600, and John Luther from 1602 to 1605. The first two were schoolmasters but the last was specifically stated not to be one.[11] Lewis Bromley may have come from a similar position in the small neighbouring parish of Fairstead, where he was licensed to teach grammar in 1592. Whilst in Witham he baptised the servant Margaret Dawson's baby daughter Elizabeth, who was discussed at length by the court of quarter sessions at Chelmsford. The justices could not decide whether her father was the young Witham man Robert Westwood, or Abdias Maye, a Rivenhall tailor. They made calculations about the number of weeks which had passed between the encounters of the two men with Margaret at her master's house, and the date of the birth of the baby (the house is now nos.53-55 Chipping Hill). When he had prepared the baptism certificate Bromley had opted for Westwood, whose father's will of 1593 decreed that he should not receive a legacy of £20 until he was discharged from the accusation.[12]

TEACHING

In addition to recording some of Witham's curates as schoolmasters during this period, the churchwardens told the bishop's officers in 1602 that their schoolmaster's name was 'Mr.Brethwayt'. However, I did not find any record of licences issued to laymen to teach in the town in this period. Instead we begin to come across people who were in trouble for teaching without a licence. Thus in 1590 the Witham churchwardens presented Margerie Rainbye to the Archdeacon's court for being 'a mayd livinge suspiciously at the house of Richard Rippingale which teacheth children without a licence'. She was forbidden to continue. Rippingale was a shearman in the cloth industry, who was later to have a fairly enthusiastic Protestant will preamble. She was the only woman teacher found in Witham, though Peter Clark's research in Kent suggests that there were many female teachers there. Far fewer women than men were literate everywhere, though one writer has recorded a female scrivener (writer of documents) in Suffolk in this same period.[13]

In the following year, 1591, it was reported that Nicholas Day 'teacheth and kepeth a scole without lycence in Witham parish', and a few months later that he 'doeth not come to Churche'. Having earlier failed to be accepted as Witham's curate and schoolmaster, he had returned from a few years as vicar of Cressing during which he had been in a good deal of trouble for various mistakes. It is not clear whether he ever did obtain a licence, though his name was put down as a teacher in the record of the bishop's Visitations in 1592 and 1598. He died in Witham in 1601 without leaving a will; his son Thomas is not known in later Witham records.[14] In spite of the fact that his name appears so often in the records, he remains something of a mystery; there is no obvious ideological reason for his having been in so much trouble. Perhaps he was just inefficient or indifferent to authority. There may yet be more to be discovered about him.

WILL PREAMBLES

There were quite a number of Witham wills with very non-committal preambles, in addition to the two written by vicar John Sterne. Some were written by laymen. However, others provide some assurance of the devout strength of Protestant feeling amongst some Witham residents, as they did in the earlier part of the reign. Edmund Halys, the newly returned son of the former vicar, began to make a considerable contribution to will-writing, and at this time his preambles were fairly varied. A very individualistic and elaborate one was for the prosperous John Westwood, who left specific sums of money totalling £140 to his relatives, and property in several parishes. Another was in 1599 for yeoman John Raven, whose enthusiastic Protestant family background has been traced in earlier chapters (pages 32-35 and 55-56). He had been a churchwarden in 1588 and was an almshouse trustee. His long preamble was appropriately ardent, concluding that he willed his body to the earth:

> untill the generall daye of Judgment at which time I doe undoutedly beleve I shall with theise my eyes behoulde my alone lord and saviour Jesus Christe to my endles joye and comfort.

Halys' other preambles were less ornate but varied, suggesting that some of the willmakers contributed to the choice. One of the more distinctive ones was written in 1600 for another well-off property-owner, John Armond, who wished to have a 'godlie preacher that shall make a sermon' at the funeral, and left five shillings for him.[15] This is quite surprising, because he was the son of George Armond(1) who had retained Catholic sympathies into the 1560s, and the overseer of the will was his son-in-law, teacher Richard Brodway, a suspected Catholic during the 1590s.

THE SECULAR COURTS

Crime

The heightened anxiety of the times made the authorities anxious about talk of a sort that may more usually have been regarded as habitual gossip. Thus in 1590, Denise Derrick of Chipping Hill was alleged at the assizes to have said that Queen Elizabeth 'hath had alredye as manye childerne as I, and that too of them were yet alive'. She claimed that the Earl of Leicester was the father, and that he had disposed of the children who were no longer alive in the chimney piece when they were born. She was sentenced to be put in the pillory during Witham market time with a paper on her head (probably describing her offence). The secular courts had already seen a continuous increase in business throughout Elizabeth's reign, but appear to have responded in a particularly dramatic way to the second of the major harvest failures, in 1597, after several years of dearth. Joel Samaha has calculated that in that year the number of prosecutions in the county for serious crime at assizes and quarter sessions was twice as many as in any previous year. The level subsided after that, and Peter King has pointed out that the rate of prosecution achieved in Essex during the late 1590s was not reached again in the county until the nineteenth century. Samaha's study excluded assaults, but the main prosecution from Witham during 1597 concerned two labourers and ten labourers' wives who were taken to the assizes for riotous assembly and assault, to which they confessed. Their motives are not known, but it is tempting to surmise that the affair may have been connected with food shortage.[16]

For a single parish such as Witham the number of serious offences per year varied between one and four, too few to discern any trends. But recognisances for people to appear at quarter sessions were more numerous; some did not proceed and some were for lesser offences. During the 1580s and 1590s as a whole there were an average of less than three recognisances per year originating in Witham, so the fact that there were six in 1598 and ten in 1600 is particularly noticeable. However, it was in about 1598 that John Sterne, Witham's vicar and the suffragan bishop began to serve as a magistrate, and he was involved in the great majority of the relevant recognisances. So it was almost certainly his appointment rather than a local crime wave that caused the upsurge. Witham had not previously had an active magistrate resident in the town, and suddenly the parish constables found it much easier to be conscientious and follow up their suspicions. They could obtain the necessary paper-work and signature from the vicarage, rather than having to walk or ride out to one of the country houses. From what we have seen of John Sterne, it seems probable that if his own initiative played any part in the increased activity, this would have arisen from a general concern for law and order, rather than from any Puritan zeal. The quarter sessions cases he was dealing with were not of any distinct moral character - they included stealing a plough chain and a bushel of peas, cutting a purse, and stealing a doublet.[17]

Accusations made against Witham people at assizes for theft included taking a bay horse worth five marks (£3 6s.8d.), a smock wrought with silk worth ten shillings, and a gold chain worth £80, together with £40 in cash. They were all acquitted. For people found guilty of serious offences or felonies such as theft, the fate decreed by law was hanging, but some people were able to escape execution by 'benefit of clergy'. This meant that they demonstrated the fact or pretence of being able to read. This was only permitted for a first offence. The punishment substituted was probably whipping. One Witham man who was able to survive by this means was Thomas Marshall, found guilty in 1596 of taking a silver bowl worth thirty shillings, a pair of

sheets worth ten shillings, and a bolster worth five shillings, from Nicholas Lowe. Lowe was a yeoman, who also dabbled in victualling and teaching. He had just been left £40 by his father, John, a yeoman, so possibly the thief hoped for a bigger haul. Less fortunate was Clement Bawley, a Witham currier. By benefit of clergy he escaped hanging in 1587 when accused of stealing a sheep in Wickham Bishops, and was found not guilty of some thefts in early 1589. But as far as we know he was hanged later in the same year for stealing two cows worth £4 and a steer worth twenty-six shillings at Langham. He could not be allowed clergy a second time, though his accomplice was saved by that means, being a first offender.[18]

Vagrants and lodgers and employment

Clement Bawley and several other Witham offenders came under suspicion when they were away from their home parish. This fear of strangers is characteristic of many periods including our own; James Sharpe has described the phenomenon in the adjoining parish of Kelvedon during the early 1600s. There was an interesting precedent in Witham in the will of Richard Reerye, made in 1555. He asked that his tenement should be sold for the best price, but that if any of his brothers and sisters wanted it, they could have it for less. As he remarked, 'better cheap than a straunger'. In late sixteenth-century Essex many parishes saw larger numbers of strangers than they were accustomed to. The cloth industry contributed to this, but economic distress also caused people to travel about looking for work, so that places like Maldon, not a cloth town, were affected too.[19]

So 'vagrants', with no means of support, attracted suspicion. Magistrates probably penalised many of them out of court, but some were taken to court also. For instance, in 1583 and 1584, two groups of Witham vagrants appeared before the assizes; in total there were two men and five women; three of the women were said to be single. A study of Salisbury found that the majority of vagrants in that town were single women during a crisis caused by dearth and high prices, whereas in more normal times most of them were usually single men. None of the surnames in the Witham cases are known from other records of the town, so the people concerned were probably strangers here. Anxieties about lodgers, vagrants and poverty were neatly combined in the terms of a presentment against John Greene, an alehousekeeper of Chipping Hill, in 1590; he was said to be:

> maintaining ill rule in lodging and receiving rogues and vagrant persons with other simple and poore people in his house.[20]

In the following year Ralph Wiseman, newly arrived in the adjoining parish of Rivenhall, was High Sheriff of Essex, and issued some comprehensive instructions on the subject of vagrants to the county's high constables. He said that his earlier warrants had been ineffective because the proposed times of the searches had not been kept secret, so that the 'wicked Lyvers' had escaped. So on this occasion, the high constables were to 'Respect the Secrecie hereof', and instruct the parish constables to:

> apprehend all vagarant persons, as well Iryshe and of the Ile of Man, as all pedlers pettie chapmen Tynkers or Egyptians and all other vagarant persons of what sortt or kynde soever not being Lawfullie licensed and Allowed to travell and all other suspycyous persons ... which cannot Render a good Accompte of their lyvyng.

The message concluded ominously, 'Fayle ye nott att your perills'.[21]

Even if a stranger found a place to live, the could still be regarded with suspicion. Once settled, if ever they needed financial support they became the responsibility of the parish officers. So there were some attempts to use the manorial courts to deter lodgers, though manorial activity was primarily concerned with land transfer by this time. At Blunts Hall in Witham, a general declaration had already been issued in 1572 against lodgers who had lived in the parish for less than three years, and in 1585 two people were presented in the manorial court for allowing men to lodge with them. In the urban manors of Chipping and Newland, the homage, or jury, showed their renewed concern about order in a general way by ordering the repair of the stocks at Chipping Hill in 1583 and 1588, and by restating their bye-laws in 1587. But during the difficult period 1585 to 1587 they became particularly concerned about lodgers, and issued a series of orders that five men and four women should be removed and expelled out of the houses of residents of the manors. The penalty for not complying was set at forty shillings. The offenders were all living in different houses except for 'both those women living in the house of Webb'. All the inhabitants were ordered to ban the culprits from their houses in future.[22]

It may be that these cases which were brought to court involved some extra problem which made them worthy of attention. One of them concerned a man called Osborne, lodging in Chipping Hill, who had come from White Notley, and was a pauper living on the town's charity, which emphasises one particular cause for concern. Two of the other lodgers were widows, possibly also needing support. And unruliness may have attracted attention to two more, James Biatt and Clement Complin. Complin was a shearman working in the cloth industry. Both of them appeared at the Archdeacon's court a few years later for unruly and irreverent behaviour. They were still living in Witham, having presumably found other accommodation meanwhile. It is thought that overcrowding was symptomatic of many towns, particularly those involved in clothmaking.[23] Witham had become industrialised by 1600, and controlling lodgers probably became futile thereafter; certainly it was not tried again in the manorial courts.

On the face of it, some positive attempts were made to solve the problems of these tumultuous years. The magistrates conducted a particularly extensive inquiry into employment in early 1590. As a result, several people in the county were ordered to find masters within a month; they included Witham residents Mary Martin, husbandman William Freeborne and weaver Henry Brooke. These three were involved later in alleged sexual offences, so it may be that one motive was to control 'undesirables'. The magistrates also invited prospective employers to take on a number of 'free' employees, who included eight from Witham; three of these were also in trouble at other times. These measures were not repeated.[24] It may well have become evident that comprehensive action was not feasible.

THE CHURCH COURTS

Churchwardens

Witham had new churchwardens every year up to 1600, and during this period most of them only served once; this seems to have been the pattern since 1550. The majority of the wardens were yeomen. Only about a quarter were non-agriculturalists, including a miller, a brewer, an innkeeper and a grocer. In general we do not know much about their religious views. On the one hand they included Thomas Campion, whose family were allegedly Catholics, and on the other, two of the wardens were John Westwood and John Raven who later had enthusiastic Protestant will preambles. We are fortunate to know of John Westwood's views on one matter of discipline. He announced during the bishop's Visitation to Essex of 1589 that 'he hopeth the drunkerdes will amend if there be anie in the parishe'.[25]

Because John Sterne, the vicar, had so many other duties, and the curates only stayed for short periods, Witham's churchwardens potentially played an important part in keeping order in Church affairs. They were indeed gradually increasing their role in making presentments to the Archdeacon's courts, though they still appear to have been responsible for less than half the Witham cases, the rest being brought by the court officers. Later, in the decades after 1600, the wardens' contribution was at least two thirds of the total. There were only a few instances where they were reprimanded for neglecting to present specific offenders. Quite frequently they were complained of for more general matters such as not attending Visitations, but usually many of their colleagues from other parishes were equally neglectful.[26] Their other main failing was neglect of the church fabric. Patrick Collinson has suggested that by the 1580s many churches were in what contemporary traveller Philip Stubbes called a 'lamentable' condition. We need to be aware of the difficulties of interpretation. Words like 'decay' and 'ruin' may indicate poor maintenance rather than a state of collapse. Nevertheless, modern churchwardens would sympathise with their predecessors in Witham. In 1585, the sexton's house, the churchyard wall and gate, the bells, and the windows were all in need of repair, whilst in 1595 the churchyard was 'in ruin and decay'. In 1600 it was said that 'the steeple is in ruin', and a bell, seats and the wall were all damaged. In 1602 the pavements and windows were broken, the 'stooles' were 'full of holes', the 'whiting' was not done, and the church fence was ruinous. At different times there were lacking a bible, a hearse, and a font cover.[27] However, the fact that the nature of the complaints changed from time to time does suggest that some progress was made.

We also know that some of the bells were improved, because the two oldest bells still hanging in the church today were made in 1601 by Richard Bowler, a noted Colchester bellfounder. Payment was a problem. The churchwardens tried for six months to get the money from John Tabor, alias Heard, towards the rate levied 'for the castinge of the bells and repayeringe the steeple'. Eventually he came before the bishop's Vicar General himself, Sir Edward Stanhope, in March 1602 in the church at Chelmsford. Taber must have been impressed by the occasion, because he paid his twenty shillings to the wardens the next day. A different bell was cracked by 1608, and another new one, still surviving, was made by the prolific founder Miles Gray of Colchester in 1627. Very possibly the metal from existing bells was re-used. We only have occasional earlier references to Witham's bells. In 1525 blacksmith William Bridgeman had left 6s.8d. to be spent by the parishioners 'in and aboute the mendyng or exchangeyng of the firste and lest of the v [five] belles hayngying in the steple of Witham'. And in 1515 and 1524 Margaret Nicholas and Felice Kele left twelve pence and fourpence respectively to 'the great bell'.[28]

Amount of business

The number of cases from Witham in the Church courts seemed to fluctuate in accordance with the business from the Colchester archdeaconry as a whole during this period, rather than indicating any individual initiatives. Much the most striking feature shown by the graphs in chapter 2 (pages 20 and 22) was the very marked temporary upsurge in the total amount of activity in the court in about 1586, which was sustained until 1592. In particular, the number of new cases from Witham itself averaged twenty-four per year between 1588 and 1591, whereas there had only been an average of 2½ per year between 1569 and 1583. Mark Byford found a similar increase in the borough of Colchester in the years 1586 and 1587, but it was not sustained to quite the same extent as in Witham, except for another burst of activity in 1593-94. The situation in Colchester was however complicated by the fact that the borough courts took many of the cases instead.[29] This increase in the activity of the Archdeacon's court at the end of the 1580s followed the first of the major harvest crises, and coincided with other pressures such as a wave of anti-Catholicism. However there does not seem to have been such a striking reaction to the economic problems of the mid-1590s, whose effect on the secular courts were so marked.

Figure 6 on page 20 shows the make-up of new cases in Witham during the 1580s and 1590s. Apart from a high rate of abuse of court officers, the level of different types of offence was roughly similar to that for the whole of the period 1570-1640, with sexual offences and non-attendance at church each accounting for roughly a quarter of the total, and non-payment of rates around a tenth. Concern about sexual offences was often aggravated in such times of crisis because of the fear of having yet more dependants added to the parish's responsibilities. Studies of other areas have found considerable increases in illegitimate births at the turn of the sixteenth century, to the extent that it has been called a 'national phenomenon', but this cannot be investigated for Witham because the parish registers do not survive.[30]

Non-payment of rates

Problems arising out of the collection of Witham's church rate were, perhaps understandably, almost all raised by the churchwardens, rather than the court officers. The wardens needed the money to carry out their duties, particularly the never-ending repairs and maintenance. Some historians have suggested that the collection problem was symbolic of a new impersonal system, which replaced traditional means of fund-raising such as church ales, when ale was sold in the church. Many of Witham's non-payers seem to have been merely negligent. In 1590 Richard Skinner, a weaver, claimed that he had never been asked for the money, and in 1595 butcher Peter Snow had 'gone away for debt'. The more vociferous of them, such as gentleman Rooke Fitche, in 1588, and yeoman Andrew Sayer, in 1602, objected that the rate was made before they came to the town. Fitche also claimed that 'there was no reparacions done towards the churche or the bells sythence his comynge to Witham'. He accused one of the churchwardens of presenting him without cause. This was Thomas Slater, the miller at Chipping mill (at what is now no.1 Powershall End). Fitche was presented on two subsequent occasions for non-attendance at church. Andrew Sayer went away to sea soon after his problem with the rates, and died on board ship in 1606, making a codicil to his will in which he distributed his ship-board possessions, including four pieces of eight and two Paradise birds. His will had a distinctively Protestant preamble, in which he said that he hoped to 'enjoye ... the kingdome of heaven amongeste the elect'.[31]

Discipline

General discipline in Witham was almost entirely the preserve of the court officers rather than the churchwardens during the 1580s. In that decade the wardens only presented one of the parish's twenty-five sexual offences which went to court, one of the eight cases concerning games and working on Sundays, and one of the five cases of drunkenness and disorder. After about 1590 this changed considerably. During the 1590s they were responsible for half of the thirty-six presentments for sexual offences, and four out of the five sabbatarian ones concerning games and working on Sunday, though both the drunk and disorderly cases were brought by the court.

One type of offence which did concern the court in particular was disrespect to its own officers. This was particularly common in this period, during which such cases took up a much higher proportion of the Witham total than at any other time. Either the court room was particularly unruly, or the court was especially sensitive during these crisis-ridden decades. For instance, when Mark Goodwin was presented at the court in 1588 for being drunk on a Sunday, he told the judge, Thomas Taylor, to 'never geere [jeer] at me'. Three years previously he had been presented in the same court by the churchwardens of neighbouring Fairstead, because he did 'contemptuously call our parson Henry Robinson Peltinge Prest'; 'pelting' meant paltry, petty, and contemptible. On that occasion he was ordered to apologise during a church service but did not do so. He was a yeoman and innkeeper, and was also bailiff of the Witham half-hundred. He owned several properties in Witham, including the Lion inn, and at his death in 1598 he had goods worth the considerable sum of £146 (the Lion was on the site which is now no.67 Newland Street, in 1998, Bakers Snacks and Woolwich Property Services).[32]

Other Witham people also mocked the officials. Most of them were less wealthy than Mark Goodwin but many had recognisable occupations; they included a shoemaker, a joiner, a yeoman, a barber and a mason. One asserted 'that he might accuse the Judge as well as the Judge in this cause cold accuse hym and he dyd contemptuously behave hym self'. The 'process' or charge sheet was a symbolic and vulnerable document. Another man, whose sister was being presented, said 'shite on her process, your cowrte is a bawdie cowrte. I care not for yt nor your courte neyther', and two others took their process 'out of the mandatoryes hande and rent yt in peces'. The mandatory was the apparitor, the messenger who delivered the processes and tried to keep order in court, a difficult task, as seen in chapter 2 (page 18). One apparitor was told by a Witham suspect 'that he would be even with him and bad hym look to hymself', and Thomas Bayles 'offered to strik and dyd strike Salter the mandatarye saying that he cared for never a straw of the Courte'. Bayles' familiarity may have been encouraged by the fact that the unfortunate court official, William Salter, a victualler, was a Witham man himself, with a not entirely unblemished reputation.

Some of Witham's own church officials were also said to have been attacked. Thus a yeoman appeared in court for 'scoulding and fighting with one of the sidemen for that he presented him the last Cort daye' (the sidesmen assisted the churchwardens). His original offence had been 'diffaming of the honest women of the towne saying that ther ys not one amongst them of honest conversation'. Of two other suspects it was said that 'they did strike our sexton in the steple'.[33] Not one of these unruly offenders came back to the court to answer the charges of making offensive remarks, and all were

excommunicated as a result; one or two were later absolved as part of occasional general dispensations.

Disorder of a more general nature also caused the court unusual concern. Some of it was seen to be particularly offensive because of its connection with the Church. Thus one Witham man was said to be 'a common and great swearer and blasphemer of the name of god', one had been 'abusing Mrs.Frogmorton in the Chauncell in service tyme' and another, who was also said to have been drunk, 'did quarrell in the Church Yeard'. There was also a sensitivity to other forms of abuse. One suspect was alleged to have defamed the wife of a Mr.Hull, 'calling her whore'. An innholder was said to have called one of his fellow-townsmen 'thowe Knave, scowdrell and shitten fellow'. And in 1592 Joan Greene of Chipping Hill was accused of being 'a scoulde and sutche a one as setteth and maketh debate and discorde between neighbours'. Five years later she was found not to have attended church because she had been 'going to Typtre faier'. She was the wife of the John Greene who kept ill-rule in his alehouse.[34]

Sundays, and church attendance

In some later periods, accusations in the Church courts about drunkenness in Witham related almost entirely to drinking on Sundays, but during the 1580s and 1590s less than half did so. Not many were accused of playing games on Sundays either. When they were, it was always because the offence took place during the time of the church service. Thus two brothers played at scales (nine-pins), and another played at scales with 'a great many more whom he can name', whilst a victualler allowed 'bowling in Divine Service time in his groundes upon the Sabaoth'.

More common at this time was the accusation of working on Sunday. Examples of this during the increased court activity of the late 1580s were a couple who were presented for making hay, a man who was doing his work as a glover, and another who was making armour. In addition, Roger Brewster's servant was said to have been setting Newland mill to work and grinding corn (this mill was on the site of the present Old Mill House in what is now Guithavon Valley).[35] The case against the armourer was dismissed on the grounds of the urgency of the task, and Brewster established that he had not been responsible for his servant's actions. There was a later flurry of sabbatarian presentments, in which the churchwardens played more of a part, between 1597 and 1603. Thus the brewer Thomas Campion had two accusations of Sunday working dismissed, firstly because the work was urgent, in that he had to send his cart for barrels after evening prayer 'to save his brewing', and secondly because his servant had been hooping tubs and barrels without his leave. He had been a churchwarden two years previously, but his family were later said to be Catholics. It was also found that the miller George Bright 'went to Chelmseford with meale and came home and went to Maldon and fetchd corne upon the Sabaoth'. He had occupied Newland mill after Roger Brewster. Yet another miller, Goodram Upcher, set his mill to work, whilst others were ploughing and carting. They all admitted their offences, which must have been difficult to conceal.[36]

General concern about absence from Witham church figured more prominently than at the beginning of Elizabeth's reign, but less so than during the seventeenth century. There is no obvious theme dominating either the motives for the accusation or the reasons for absence. In 1591 Clement Complin had been:

> demanded by the churchwardens wher he was, he sayd no where but sayd he was at home drinking with his frends and ... sayd further that he was absent and wolde be absent the next sondaye alsoe.

Complin, whom we have already noted as an unauthorised lodger, was a shearman, working in the cloth industry. A relatively poor man, he left goods worth only £4 when he died in 1616.[37] However, in most instances, no particular reason for absence was given, except for a few plausible excuses such as sickness. In about one third of the cases, the alleged offence was specifically stated to be not taking communion, rather than absence from church.

The anti-Puritan legislation of 1593 gave the secular authorities power to act against absentees from church in addition to the Church courts, but in Witham this power hardly seems to have been used at all against Protestants. However, Catholic absentees were presented in both the Church courts and in quarter sessions.

ANTI-CATHOLICISM

As mentioned previously, most historians agree that Protestantism had become the predominant form of personal belief in England by the 1580s. And everyone was nominally a member of the Church of England. However, there were always some people who retained varying degrees of commitment to Catholic belief. Many of them took part in the services in their parish churches without any difficulty, though they may have found some ministers less congenial than others. Some of those who attended services were conscious enough of their differences to try and avoid actually taking the Protestant form of communion. But in addition to these 'church papists' there were people who felt so strongly that they did not attend the parish church at all. These were the 'recusants', or refusers; usually the term 'recusant' was used specifically to refer to Catholics at this time. The available information about Catholic believers probably indicates when official concern about them was particularly strong, rather than any changes in their activities and beliefs. Michael O'Boy has suggested that prosecution in Essex was often very sporadic at this time, due to inefficiency or lack of inclination on the part of the authorities. He found that visible signs of sympathy with Catholicism were not very great in the archdeaconry of Colchester, in which Witham lies. They were rather more evident in the south and west of the county.[38]

In the last chapter we left the Witham Catholics with a sole known representative during the 1570s, teacher Richard Brodway (pages 54-55). There were no Witham men or women included in a diocesan return of suspected recusants made in 1577. But since the mid 1570s a more confrontational situation had begun to develop in the country as a whole. It was then that Catholic priests who had trained on the continent had begun to come to work secretly in England, often protected by sympathetic members of the aristocracy. Historians differ about the strength of their influence. But for various reasons there were a number of official moves against Catholicism by the Queen's advisers after this time, and several anti-Catholic statutes were passed. The fines for recusancy were increased, and the secular courts were given responsibility for prosecuting recusants, in addition to the ecclesiastical courts who were already concerned in the matter. Several priests were executed under the new legislation. In fact the 1580s have been called 'an extraordinary decade' of hysteria against Catholicism. This cannot be attributed to fervent Protestantism alone; nationalism was extremely significant, and was particularly stirred in East Anglia and Essex by Queen Elizabeth's journeyings in 1578.[39]

Further incitement was provided by the execution of Mary Queen of Scots in 1587, the destruction of the Spanish Armada in 1588, and war with Catholic Spain from then until 1603. The Armada was sighted off the Scilly Isles on June 19th but was recalled temporarily to Corunna. At about the same time, Witham's armourer and cutler Robert Armond, who lived in Lockram Lane, was working hard on 'diverst armers and harnesses which weis comitted to hym to mak clean readye to the training'. This training would be for the local militia, and the harness probably described the whole equipment of a soldier and his horse. Armond was so busy that he continued on Sunday, but by the time the officers of the Archdeacon's court presented an objection to this, the court had probably heard about the Armada's first visit, and Armond's excuses about pressure of work were sufficient for them to dismiss the complaint.

The Spanish set sail again for England a week after the court hearing. Witham men were amongst those who were called upon to help defend the coast in 1588; and they were also sent to fight in the Low Countries in the 1590s. The soldiers who went to the latter engagement were armed with:

> newe armes ... and newe apparrelled with coates of broade cloth, russet gullos lined with cotton, dublettes of fustian, cloth hose ... knitt stockinges, shoes, shirt and shirte Bandes', 'for the better service of their countrye.[40]

So we can see that the threat of Spain was near at home to many people. This made them even more vulnerable than usual to any propaganda which suggested that Catholicism was also to be feared.

The Southcotts and Southwells

The new level of opposition brought to light several Witham Catholics, all of fairly high social status. The first was Elizabeth Southwell, who was first prosecuted during 1589. She had formerly been the wife of the judge, John Southcott, who had died in 1585. He had been made a judge in 1563. They had owned Witham Place from 1567 onwards, and probably lived there for most of the time. Its front wall still remains in Powershall End and is shown below. With the estate they held a lease of the rectory, and the great tithes.

I do not know of any suggestions having been made during the judge's lifetime that he himself was a Catholic, and in fact he was involved in several anti-Catholic committees and hearings. However, his Catholic descendants later claimed him as one of their flock. Thus nearly 150 years later his great-great grandson Sir Edward suggested in a letter that the judge had neglected the faith for most of his life in pursuit of fame and fortune, but that he had returned to the fold in the end when faced with sentencing a priest at Norfolk assizes. The story was that:

> rather than give the sentence of death against him, he stood up in the open court and pulled off his robes of Judge, declaring that he there resigned his office rather than he would bring upon himself and family the guilt of innocent blood.

Original records of this case do not survive. So the main contemporary evidence about the judge's beliefs at the end of his life comes from the preamble to his will, which has a firmly Protestant tone. It was originally written in 1580, which would perhaps have been before the alleged change of heart, but he added a codicil about a year before his death, and did not alter the preamble. The Lord Chancellor and Lord Chief Justice were to be overseers of the will, a good indication of the judge's status in the country.[41]

However, he must have had fairly close contacts with the Catholic community, as a result of the marriage of his son John Southcott esquire to Magdalen Waldegrave, probably during the 1570s. Magdalen's sister Mary was Lady Petre of West Horndon, who was known during the 1580s as a recusant, although her husband, Sir John Petre, a successful public figure, favoured church attendance. The father of Magdalen and Mary was Sir Edward Waldegrave, who had been a member of the Catholic Queen Mary's Privy Council, and had died in the Tower of London in 1561 after accusations of attending Catholic mass; he had also been imprisoned earlier, under King Edward VI. John and Magdalen Southcott did not live in Witham during Elizabeth's reign. To begin with they were probably based in the family's Surrey house at Merstham, but had accommodation in London too. John was reported by an informer to have been seen at a Catholic mass in London in 1584, before his father's death. Several surviving reports from the ten subsequent years suggest that he was widely known to have been a Catholic, but probably avoided trouble because of his friends in high

The front wall of Witham Place

The mansion of Witham Place was the home of the Southcott family, except for the years 1599 to 1633 when it was rented from them by the Barnardistons.. The house no longer survives, but this long brick wall which stood in front of it still stands in Powershall End. It dates from the late 16th century.

John Southcott and his wife Elizabeth, later Elizabeth Southwell

This is part of their monument in St.Nicholas church. It still survives, although it has been moved from its original position. John, who died in 1585, is shown wearing judge's robes, which would have been bright red. Some traces of the colouring remain on the monument. After he died, Elizabeth married Richard Southwell, and was said to be absenting herself from Witham church; she and her descendants were Catholics.

places. Although most of the information about his activities comes from London, family tradition recorded that he was also 'often' at the Petres' home. In particular he and Magdalen were said to have attended a mass there in 1590. By 1594 the couple had moved to Bulmer on the Essex and Suffolk border, adjoining the Waldegraves' parish of Borley, and after being presented to quarter sessions as recusants they were able to avoid further prosecution by paying regular large fines.[42]

Meanwhile, John's mother Elizabeth, the judge's widow, continued to live at Witham Place. Although we know that young John was already participating in Catholic activities before his father died, we only know about Elizabeth's involvement after she was widowed in 1585,

and her beliefs during the lifetime of the judge must remain a matter for speculation. Both Queen Elizabeth and the judge himself seem to have regarded her with some caution, and it is possible that her religious beliefs played a part in this. Thus there was a family tradition that Judge Southcott might well have:

been Lord Chief Justice but for a conceit of the Queen's who said she should govern too like a woman if she suffered a woman to be Chief Justice of England. The occasion of this reflection was that he being a good-natured man had a reputation in the world of being governed by his wife.

Furthermore, the judge altered some of the intentions of his will between 1580 and 1585, stating that he no longer wished his wife to be one of his executors. He blamed her 'wante of skyll and understandinge', adding that 'she ys not fitt', and that 'evil disposed persons' might influence her. In addition, she was only to receive her bequests if she handed over the will to their son, John.[43] As we have seen, this John was himself already a Catholic, so if the judge did exercise any religious discrimination in his choice of executor, he was either prepared to waive them in the case of his son, or was not aware of his clandestine attendance at mass. It may be that his doubts about Elizabeth were not religious at all, but that they genuinely arose from her lack of business skills and the danger of suspected fortune hunters.

The gentleman Richard Southwell may have been one of these. Within three years after the judge's death he had become Elizabeth's second husband. If he was a Catholic he managed to keep it from the Essex authorities, not being subject to any of the accusations about church attendance levelled against his wife. There was a prominent Catholic family of Southwells in Norfolk, but I have not found any close connection with Richard.

Richard and Elizabeth continued to live in Witham, and between early 1589 and early 1590 Elizabeth was presented three times at quarter sessions for not attending Witham parish church. On the first occasion it was reported that she 'laye at hir howes wthein the parrishe of Witham for the space of ii monthe and never came at our churche all the tyme she laye there'. The second presentment recorded the same offence and complained that in spite of it, 'she goeth aboute everywheare'. Although no details are given, I think that we can take it that the offences were associated with Catholic belief, in view of what we know about the rest of her family. I have wondered whether her example, and even support, might have encouraged other Witham people to become more demonstrative in their Catholic belief. She probably knew Nicholas Ridgley's wife, one of the recusants mentioned later, because Nicholas himself had once been a servant of the judge, who had him witness his will, and left him £10. She also appeared at the Archdeacon's court in 1595 and 1598 for non-attendance, causing some confusion by moving between Witham and another family home in Little Totham. In addition, some of her family servants were presented in connection with illegitimate children in 1587 and 1588, perhaps part of a campaign against the family. However, on one of these occasions, the Witham churchwardens had to be persuaded by the archdeacon's officers to take action, having not chosen to do so themselves.[44]

After Elizabeth died in about 1600, Richard Southwell seems to have left Witham. A monument to her and her first husband, the judge, is still one of the most striking features of St.Nicholas church; it is illustrated on the facing page. The mansion house at Witham Place was subsequently let to the Puritan Barnardiston family, and John Southcott, the son of the judge and Elizabeth, did not return from Bulmer to live there until the 1630s.

Other Witham Catholics of the late sixteenth century; the Bayles, Ridgleys and Campions

Elizabeth Southwell had not actually been called a 'recusant' by the courts. The first Witham person to be specifically given this description was Mrs.Bayles, in the Archdeacon's court in 1598. It seems safe to assume that the several other accusations of non-attendance made against her and her servants between 1597 and 1604 also had Catholic implications. The pregnancies of two of the unmarried servants were also reported. The court of quarter sessions joined in with five presentations against Mrs.Bayles for absence from church between 1599 and 1602. It is possible that her husband Thomas himself had joined her by early 1601, though the record is not very clear. He certainly expressed some antagonism to the establishment. In July 1600 when he was accused in the Archdeacon's court of not paying his rates towards the upkeep of St.Nicholas church, he struck the apparitor and expressed his contempt for the court. He was again in trouble for not paying the rates in 1604.[45]

We know of two men and two other women from Witham who were probably colleagues of Mrs.Bayles during Elizabeth's reign. This is because when they were all referred to as 'popish recusants' in the archdeacon's records of May 1605, it was said that they had offended 'before the kinges Majesty's Reign'. Three of them had also been accused of absence or not taking communion in various courts during 1603 and 1604. In March 1605 the bishop's representative had raised the question of whether one of them might actually be a recusant, and all the archdeacons had just received new instructions on the subject of recusancy.[46] The two men were gentlemen Thomas Ridgley and William Campion. The women were Anastasia or Agnes Campion, who was William's sister-in-law, and Mrs.Ridgley, who was probably a relative of Thomas, and was the wife of the Nicholas who had been the servant of Judge Southcott. They were all excommunicated in 1605, so that they were barred from the church, but this made little difference as they were not attending anyway. Afterwards all except Thomas Ridgley were regularly accused of recusancy until 1608, particularly at quarter sessions. In 1606 Anastasia Campion was also said to have 'laboured to induce her mother and others from the true religion'.[47]

The earlier beliefs and behaviour of these people is obscure. We do not know at what point during Elizabeth's reign they had begun to absent themselves from church. The male Campions and the Ridgeleys had probably been living in Witham since at least the mid 1580s; we do not know about the wives. The Bayles may possibly have been more recent arrivals. Michael O'Boy suggests that court appearances for recusancy may only have been occasioned by a refusal or inability to pay the one shilling fine.[48] So there are various possible explanations for the eventual appearance of the Witham people in court during the late 1590s. They could have been new converts to Catholicism, or they could have been long-term believers who decided to adopt a new policy about church attendance or fine-paying. Another alternative is that the authorities could have become increasingly intolerant of previously acceptable behaviour.

Thomas Campion

When Anastasia Campion was said to have refused communion in 1604, her husband Thomas was included in the accusation. He was a brewer, who lived in Newland Street (where no.57 now stands, the Midland Bank in 1998). He came to the Archdeacon's court and blamed 'a little falling out between him and her' for their refusal. Sadly we do not know whether they had been arguing about church affairs or not. They were given several chances to certify that they had made amends, but never did and were excommunicated. By May 1605 the couple seemed to have agreed to differ; she and her friends absented themselves from church altogether whilst he attended but did not take communion.[49] It seems likely that Thomas's motives also derived from Catholic sympathies, but that his wife interpreted her duty more rigidly than he did.

Thomas Campion was no stranger to the court, having made various appearances during the previous twenty years in connection with such matters as failing to present two pregnant maid servants, and for working on Sundays. In 1602 he was asked to appear at quarter sessions for 'misbehaviour against my lord suffragan'; this was John Sterne, Witham's vicar and suffragan bishop of Colchester. We do not know any other details. Perhaps the most notable information about Thomas Campion is that he had actually been one of the parish's churchwardens just prior to 1596, in which year he was held responsible for the 'ruin and decay' of the churchyard. Did he manage to obtain and sustain this role in a sympathetic or indifferent parish in spite of being a 'church papist'? Or did he only begin to find the Protestant communion distasteful eight years later? Before leaving the Campions I should point out that it has been suggested that they were connected with the Catholic martyr, Edmund Campion, who died in 1581, and that one of them was suspected of harbouring him. A link has also been suggested with the physician, poet, and musician, Thomas Campion. However, as far as I know, neither of these claims is proven.[50]

Other possible Catholics

For people who did not have 'popish' relatives as Thomas Campion did, it is more difficult to interpret accusations of their not taking communion. There were seventeen of these from Witham between 1570 and 1603, half of them during the 1580s. None were accused more than once. The majority were excommunicated for failing to certify that they had made amends. One, in 1589, was Eton Halys, son of the former vicar, Edward, and brother of Edmund; he appeared with his wife. Rarely were any further details given, but in the case of Ralph Holden in 1585, we are told that 'he doth refuse to receve the holy communion and ys suspected to incite others to do the lyke'. He confessed but was eventually excommunicated for not paying his fees. Sometimes there were other accusations made against the same people; for instance John Hutt in 1572 was also said to have refused to pay the church rates.[51] But not enough is known about these cases for us to be able to tell whether we can add any additional determined Catholics to the list of six or seven gentry whom we already know about.

WITCHCRAFT

Like Catholicism, witchcraft involved both the ecclesiastical and the secular courts. Recorded anxiety about it in Witham is concentrated in the 1580s and 1590s. The only other incident we know about had taken place in 1560, when Joan Haddon had been accused of defrauding people by bewitching them. The assize court had found her not guilty of being a witch, but nevertheless decided that she had been 'cozening money', for which offence she had to spend some time in the pillory. In 1563, some types of alleged witchcraft had been made punishable by death, and so became much more visible in the records than previously. The number of known cases in England remained high from about 1570 until 1600, with Essex represented far more than other counties. Historians have associated this series of prosecutions with such matters as a breakdown in traditional social links, and the increasing numbers of the poor.[52]

The best-recorded affair in Witham took place in 1587, and was rather complicated and bewildering. It was mentioned during a dispute in the Archdeacon's court about the will of victualler Thomas Gilder. He was a relative of Thomas Wayland, a brewer, and was also the landlord and neighbour of armourer Robert Armond, 'a pore man'. It was reported that 'Robert Armond and his wiff having a childe sicke in ther house and they saying and alledging that the sayd childe was bewitched by one Elizabeth Miller alias Harris wife of George Harris of Witham, did seeke out and make enquiry to other witches for helpe for the recovery of the helthe of the sayde childe'. One of these other witches was said to be 'a woman about Shalford'. Robert Armond and Thomas Wayland, were heard 'speaking helpe and helthe to witches or cunning men as they call them'. However, Thomas Wayland's own son Gildern died a month later, and Thomas then alleged that this was 'murder by witchcraft' by the aforementioned Elizabeth Harris. She was taken to the assizes accused both of this offence and of similarly murdering a woman called Ursula Netherstreet, but she was found not guilty. It was also 'notoriously reported within the parish of Witham' that Robert Armond and his wife 'theraboutes did fall out and quarrell with the sayd Elizabeth Harris'. Elizabeth, alias Bess, was later excommunicated twice by the Archdeacon's court, once for not going to church and once for adultery, suggesting the possibility of alleged witches being perpetual victims of suspicion. Soon after the witchcraft affair Robert Armond also made two more appearances in court. One, mentioned earlier, was for working on a Sunday, and the other was for 'offering adultery' to Elizabeth Beckwith, probably a relative of his landlord. Before this could be resolved he moved, no doubt with relief, to Bocking.[53]

There were two more allegations of witchcraft in Witham. In 1588 Thomas Harding and his wife were presented to the Archdeacon's court on the basis of 'a fame [rumour] in the parishe of Witham', for witchcraft and speaking scandal, but the case was dismissed. Lastly, in 1592 Margaret Hogden, a single woman, was acquitted by the assize court of bewitching Ann Gowers, wife of Robert, who had languished eight months before dying.[54]

OVERVIEW

These later years of Elizabeth's reign in Witham did have some similarities to the earlier ones which were described in the previous chapter. It seems that the local clergy still tended to be anti-Puritan. There were again a few lay parishioners, mostly prosperous ones, who left evidence of particularly fervent Protestant beliefs in the preambles to their wills. The contribution of John Raven provides a link between the enthusiasts of the earlier part of the reign and their successors in the later part. A newly revealed element of these later years was unofficial teaching, some of which may have been inspired by religious zeal.

There were again small numbers of fairly prosperous Catholic believers in the town, but it is not possible to establish any personal links with earlier years. We do not know the antecedents of Witham's few recusants of the end of the reign. They were revealed by new official policies and by anti-Catholic 'hysteria', rather than local initiatives, and the indications are that local tolerance may well have prevailed previously. Several of the Witham recusants were women, and it is Judge Southcott's widow Elizabeth who is most likely to have earlier Catholic connections. Historians differ on the question of whether we should be looking for new manifestations of Catholicism to be a revelation of long standing behaviour, or to be the result of a sudden change. [55]

These years were distinguished by other turbulent features in addition to the wave of anti-Catholicism. The church courts recorded an unusual number of cases of irreverent behaviour, and increases in the general level of presentments and prosecutions at both the secular courts and the church courts appeared to coincide with particular harvest crises of the 1580s and 1590s. However, we also noted the probable effect of the appointment in 1598 of a resident magistrate in Witham, John Sterne, in increasing the number of prosecutions in the town. Apart from his cases, the activity had generally subsided by the very end of the reign, as had specific campaigns in the secular courts concerning employment, lodging and vagrancy. The abandonment of these efforts may partly have arisen from adaptation to new economic circumstances. The harvest crises passed, and the cloth industry was established in Witham by 1600. The appearance of strangers in the town must have become the norm, and new types of work were available.

We might justifiably refer to the increased activity in the courts as a 'moral panic', meaning that it reflected heightened official anxiety as much as a real increase in offending. However, this does not necessarily mean that it was moral in the sense of being Puritan. There is some controversy amongst historians about what Puritan morality really entailed, and some say that features such as action against sexual misbehaviour may not have been specific to Puritanism. It is however generally conceded that concern for church attendance and for the sanctity of the Sabbath were important aspects. There was some evidence to suggest that the Church courts were taking notice of such matters, and that towards the end of the period they began to have more support from Witham's churchwardens, some of whom we know to have been enthusiastic in their beliefs. It is of interest to note that many of the people whom they presented, even for unruliness, were reasonably well-off. At this time, much the same could be said about the adjoining parish of Terling. One of the best-known themes of the renowned study of that parish by Keith Wrightson and David Levine was the development of a concerted campaign to control the poor by such means as presentment in the Church courts, but this they found to have developed primarily after 1600.[56]

7. JAMES I, 1603-1625

BACKGROUND

After the death of Queen Elizabeth, the natural and the man-made crises of the later period of her reign subsided. James I made peace with Spain in 1604, heralding a very successful period for the exporting cloth industry of Essex. The Thirty Years War began on the Continent in 1618, but England did not become involved in it until after the end of James' reign. In religion James was generally regarded as moderate. He seemed able to assure Protestants that he was opposed to Catholicism, and the Gunpowder plot of 1605 assisted him in this. On the other hand some Puritan leaders felt that he was not sufficiently sympathetic to their own views, particularly after the Hampton Court conference in January 1604. This discussed reform of the Church, but not many innovations resulted. The most notable was the Authorised Version of the Bible, which eventually appeared in 1611. Even this had been opposed by the anti-Puritan Richard Bancroft, bishop of London, and Puritan anxiety increased when he was appointed as Archbishop of Canterbury shortly after the conference. He was largely responsible for the 141 far-reaching new canons or rules issued by the Convocation of the Church of England in June 1604. These were the first since the Reformation. In due course Parliament reacted with a declaration limiting the authority of Convocation, whose powers have been restricted ever since. Bancroft was followed in 1610 by an archbishop more sympathetic to Puritanism, George Abbott. Most of the bishops of London were also of his mind. Writers about both Essex and Kent have felt that Puritanism met little official opposition during James' reign. In Essex it began to be associated in particular with the Earls of Warwick, whose political and military activities gave religious zeal an added dimension.[1]

In Witham, some very wealthy clothmakers became established during the prosperous years of the industry after the peace with Spain, and there were no agricultural crises to match those of the 1580s and 1590s. Bequests to the poor by Witham people reached a peak during the first decade of the century, when forty-two per cent of the wills included them, perhaps inspired by the earlier economic crisis, but they declined thereafter. During the next decade the proportion was only twenty-four per cent, and in every decade in the seventeenth century after that it was less than twenty per cent. Some aspects of the 'moral panic' of earlier years subsided. Thus there was a lower rate of criminal prosecutions in Witham than during the last twenty years of Elizabeth's reign, though it remained fairly high, and was marked by suspicion against clothworkers. Prosecutions of Witham's Catholics in the courts ended for the time being in 1608, and did not recommence until the 1630s.[2] So when some riotous and aggressive visitors caused a disturbance outside the large Newland Street house of Elizabeth Archer in July 1611, it was said to be surprising because of Witham being 'so peaceable a town'.[3]

THE BARNARDISTONS

Katherine Soame and Thomas Barnardiston were married in 1599, having both been recently widowed. Thomas's first wife, Mary, had been the daughter of a notable Northamptonshire Puritan, Richard Knightly, who was related to many eminent people including the Duke of Somerset, uncle and Protector of Edward VI. Katherine and Thomas came to live in Witham with Thomas's teenage children, including Nathaniel and Arthur; Katherine had no children of her own. Thomas's father was Sir Thomas of Kedington in Suffolk, who made a settlement of two hundred marks a year on Katherine (£133.6s.8d.). Her signature on the document is dwarfed by the large and confident hands of her father-in-law and her brother, John Banks. The couple lived in the largest house in the parish, the mansion at Witham Place. Its imposing front wall still survives, and is illustrated on page 67. With the house they also held a lease of Witham rectory, and thus the right to receive the great tithes and to sit in a prominent pew in the church. Our first sign of Katherine and Thomas's arrival in the parish is that Thomas 'Barston' esquire appeared in a list of eight prosperous Witham residents who agreed to set the church rate in early 1603; the name was probably pronounced 'Barnston'. Houses of the size of Witham Place probably did not become available very often; it was leased from the Catholic John Southcott. There were Southcott residences near the previous homes of Katherine in London and of Thomas in Suffolk, so acquaintance amongst the families probably led to the letting, in spite of the fact that the Southcotts were Catholics and the Barnardistons definitely were not.[4]

It was Katherine in particular who was to have a very strong Puritan influence in Witham and elsewhere during the following three decades. Her powerful figure is shown in her monument in Kedington church, illustrated on page 101. Professor Collinson has discussed the important role of prosperous women in sustaining preachers and introducing a matriarchal element into local Puritanism.[5] Katherine had many well-connected relatives to assist her, as shown in the charts in appendix 2 (pages 163-66), which also indicate which of them she seems to have kept in touch with, as far as can be judged from the later donations in her will.[6] In her own generation and the next, she eventually had twelve close relatives who were knights, and six who were Members of Parliament. The parents of Katherine and of both her first two husbands had at one time lived within a few miles of each other on the Essex/Suffolk border, in Hadstock, Little Bradley and Kedington (these parishes and those of other family members in Suffolk mentioned later, are shown on the map on page x at the beginning of the book). So all three families may have known each other a long time, and several generations of them moved between there and the City of London during the rest of the seventeenth century, often keeping in touch with both places and with each other, as well as with Dame Katherine. The busy parishes around Cheapside and St.Paul's Cathedral were particularly well-known to them.

Katherine had herself been born and brought up in the parish of St.Michael le Querne, in the shadow of the old St.Paul's cathedral. Its church stood approximately on the site of what is now no.5 Cheapside, but was subsequently destroyed in the Great Fire of 1666, so the only remaining sign of it today is a nineteenth-century boundary marker on the wall of the cathedral's choir school. Katherine's father, Thomas Banks, had made his life there since he moved to London from Hadstock on obtaining an apprenticeship during the 1550s. He was master of the Barber Surgeons three times, and when he died in 1598 he left the Company a cup made of an ostrich egg set in silver. His daughters and their families continued to keep in particularly close touch with each other throughout their lives. One of them, Katherine's sister Mary, married Sir Richard Deane, who was born in Great Dunmow in Essex, and was a son of George, bailiff of the Dunmow hundred. He became a London skinner and was Lord Mayor in 1628. The elder of Katherine's brothers, Richard, had quarrelled with the family and may have left the country. It is just possible that this was connected with the fact that some of the Banks family who had remained in Hadstock appear to have been Catholics.[7] However, she was close to her other brother John Banks, a very wealthy London mercer who shared her religious beliefs. His company, the Mercers', had a considerable Puritan tradition, and was the only company in the City which regularly chose Puritan ministers for its livings before 1640. It was also the only one with its own chapel, and in 1619 John endowed sermons to be given there seven times a year. Five of them are still given today. He was Warden of the Company twice and was eventually elected Master in 1630, but he died four days afterwards, leaving bequests worth thousands of pounds in total, including £1,600 for his tomb and funeral. The sums going to charity included £5 each to twenty poor Puritan ministers. Some of his gifts still survive, including silver cups and silver gilt badges bearing his motto 'Thinke and thanke God'. The badges were for the residents of Whittington College, almshouses founded by Dick Whittington. Katherine received silver plate worth £120.[8]

Her first husband, Bartholomew Soame, had moved to London from the country like her father, He was born in Little Bradley in Suffolk and the Soames then went to Beetley in Norfolk, but he subsequently became a London girdler. He had died in early 1596 when they must both have been quite young, and Katherine paid the churchwardens of St.Michael le Querne 3s.4d. for the ringing of his 'knell'. When leaving her the residue of his possessions he wrote 'I do thinke it too little if it weare tenne times so much', and she later referred to him as her 'dearest and first husband'. She continued to keep in contact with the Soame family. Her brother-in-law Sir Stephen Soame was Lord Mayor of London in 1597, and was also a Member of Parliament. He had a country home in a 'greate mansion house' in Little Thurlow in Suffolk, and his wealth dwarfed even that of John Banks. In his will of 1619 he frequently expressed gratitude to God for this good fortune. He had land worth £5,000 a year including about sixteen manors in several counties, goods worth £40,000, many 'greate adventures abroad' and 'greate Sommes of money' owing to him. He had already made many gifts to Little Thurlow, including almshouses and a free school, whose residents and pupils were to attend prayers and church frequently if they wished to keep their places. The scholars were not to absent themselves for 'idle buisynes' such as gleaning in the cornfields. Little Thurlow was only a few miles from the Barnardiston family home of Kedington, and Sir Stephen's daughter Jane, Katherine's niece, married Nathaniel Barnardiston. Nathaniel was Katherine's stepson through her second marriage, so she became twice related to the illustrious Soame family. Jane had already received a large sum of money from her father when she married, and in his will Sir Stephen also lent Nathaniel £1,000 until he inherited his own family property, and gave money to their children.[9]

The wealth and influence of the Barnardiston family itself was also very great, though concentrated in Suffolk rather than in London. In due course the Barnardistons became as important to Katherine as the Banks and Soames. For instance she was godmother to the first born child of each of her Barnardiston stepchildren. However, her marriage to Thomas Barnardiston was brief. He was knighted in 1603, making her Dame Katherine, but he died in 1610 before he could inherit the family estate from his father, Sir Thomas the eldest. Because he was in Witham for such a short time, nothing can be discovered directly about Thomas's own particular beliefs. His connections were varied, though the best-known was a Puritan one, in that his father had been brought up in Geneva under Calvin. He left Katherine the lease of Witham Place and of the tithes, and she continued to live there. By this time she was wealthy. Not only had she received bequests from her father but, as she had no children, she had received nearly all the property of her first two husbands. In 1612 her name was mentioned in the Bishop's Consistory court, which noted that the chancel in Witham church, for which she was responsible as owner of the Rectory, was 'not well repayred'. However, she was said to be 'at London', and the matter was not pursued.[10]

She may have been visiting her many relatives in the capital at the time, but very possibly she was also meeting with a third husband, because it was in around 1612 that she married lawyer William Towse, with whom she spent the next twenty years, until her death. He was in his early sixties when they married; she may have been rather younger.[11] As with her second marriage, the very rapid match can probably be explained by previous family associations. Firstly, although Towse's country house was by this time at Takeley in Essex, he had originated from Hingham in Norfolk, and was there when Katherine's first husband Bartholomew Soame had lived ten miles away at Beetley. Secondly, Towse and Dame Katherine's second father-in-law, Sir Thomas Barnardiston, were both members of the Inner Temple. Towse's chief claim to fame is that he was a friend of diarist and Middle Templar John Manningham. Manningham recorded some of Towse's witticisms and high class contemporary gossip in his diary in 1602, including a story about William Shakespeare. But Towse was also a hard worker. Since being admitted to the Inner Temple in 1571 he had continually joined committees for such matters as investigating the water supply and auditing the accounts. He became a Member of Parliament in 1586, and had sat in the Temple's own 'Parliament' since 1596. He was one of four men appointed in 1602 to make arrangements for a preacher to give two lectures every week in the Temple church, and was Treasurer in 1607. He must therefore have been familiar to Kedington's Sir Thomas Barnardiston, whose own membership dated from about 1590. Barnardiston's interests were mainly in Suffolk, and he was less assiduous at the Temple than Towse, but he was several times elected as one of the six 'officers for the Grand Christmas', and on at least one of these occasions Towse was amongst the men who chose him.[12]

When Katherine married William Towse, he came to join her at Witham Place and she lent him £1,000. His career continued to develop; he became a Serjeant at law in 1614, a post which entitled him to sit as a judge in the court of Common Pleas. He was Town Clerk of Colchester from about 1620 to 1632, and Member of Parliament there from 1620 to 1625. When he signed a recognisance as a magistrate in 1623 he was 'at Colchester'. The couple were closely associated with several of the Puritan Witham clergy of James' reign, and Katherine gave a silver almsdish to St.Nicholas church in 1617. They were well-known elsewhere in Essex too; a sermon was dedicated to them in 1623 by Thomas Barnes, a well-known Puritan preacher at Great Waltham.[13] Katherine's contribution to the parish continued also into the turbulent times of Charles I, as will be seen in chapter 9.

SECULAR OFFICIALS

Magistrates

The role of magistrates continued to be extended during James' reign, particularly with the formal authorisation by the Privy Council of extra meetings of magistrates in the form of petty sessions, held in each local division. These were also given new powers concerning the regulation of alehouses. Although there were occasionally rumours at court that Puritans on the one hand, or suspected Catholics on the other, might be removed or disqualified from the magistracy, in practice people of both sorts served alongside each other in Essex as elsewhere.[14] Witham's vicar and magistrate John Sterne continued to act on Witham cases until he died in 1608. When Dame Katherine Barnardiston's new husband William Towse arrived about four years later, Witham again found itself in the relatively unusual position of having a member of the bench resident in the parish. Towse had already been an Essex magistrate for ten years. To judge from the surviving recognisances, his participation in Witham's own cases was only moderate during James' reign. A busy man elsewhere too, he was much travelled, and was particularly concerned about the state of the Essex roads, about which he had already complained before he came to Witham. He must have been extremely familiar with them. Probably he returned periodically to his own home of Takeley, as he continued to sign recognisances in that area of north-west Essex. And like all magistrates he was expected to go to Chelmsford about six times a year for the quarter sessions and assizes. However, it was confirmed in the papers concerning a case from 1624 that he was one of 'two justices dwelling next to Witham', and he may been influential in the town in ways of which there is no longer any surviving record.[15] In another case in that year he took the evidence when a fellow-magistrate, Edward Allen of the Priory in neighbouring Hatfield Peverel, was said to be the victim of 'scandalous and disgracefull speaches'. Allegedly these had been made by Witham's Alexander Brooke, innkeeper at the White Hart. There was a family connection in that Allen's wife Elizabeth was cousin to William Towse's son-in-law, but it is possible that the case also had some political or religious element which particularly concerned Towse. William Brooke, the son of the suspected scandalmonger, was a Royalist in later years, whilst Edward Allen had Puritan associations, not only on his own account, but through his father Edmund and also his grandfather, Witham willwriter John Glascock, both of whom were discussed in chapter 5 (pages 56-57).[16]

Allen himself signed recognisances in several Witham cases during the early 1620s, but only for a short time. The magistrates who were the most attentive to Witham business were usually not at all likely to be sympathetic to Puritanism. In particular there was Sir Thomas Wiseman, who lived in the adjoining parish of Rivenhall, and seems to have been a man on whom the officials of the half-hundred and of Witham parish relied very heavily. He and his father Ralph had been knighted with many others on the accession of James I in 1603. Sir Ralph died in 1608, and Sir Thomas joined the bench almost immediately. From then until the end of James' reign, he signed half the recognisances concerning Witham people. It was unusual for any one magistrate to take such a high proportion of the town's cases. Sir Thomas also continued to watch over Witham thereafter. In spite of many allegations that he and his family had Catholic sympathies, he did not lose his position as a magistrate until the beginning of Civil War. He died in 1654. Among the other magistrates who played a part in Witham affairs during James' reign were Sir William Ayloffe of Great Braxted and Sir Henry Maxey of Bradwell juxta Coggeshall; like the Wisemans, these families did not regard Puritanism favourably. At this time there were no active magistrates at Cressing Temple, which was occupied by William Smith/Nevill, a younger brother of the Nevill family; he was however a Deputy Lieutenant of the county.[17]

Half-hundred and parish officers

The bailiff of the half-hundred until 1608 was Nicholas Kent, who was a yeoman and innholder, and previously a servant of Henry Smith of Cressing Temple. He was several times in trouble for not taking communion, sometimes at the same time as fellow-parishioners who probably had Catholic sympathies. He died in 1608 and was replaced by Alexander Brooke, whom we have already observed criticising the Puritan magistrate Edward Allen; he was variously known as a yeoman, ploughwright, wheelwright and victualler.[18] I have not discovered the names of any of the high constables of the half-hundred during James' reign, and have only traced one parish constable. This was haberdasher Robert Allen, who attended the 'riot' outside Elizabeth Archer's house in 1611, and went off to an inn with the troublemakers. Elizabeth's prospective son-in-law Richard Gwynne, of Norfolk, subsequently took Allen to court for neglect of duty, alleging that he had 'kyndely with Capp in hand desired [the men] to desist and departe, not once takeing [the King's] name or his authority of constable'. As the men were 'well-horsed and armed', Allen's deferential approach to them may have been wise.[19]

CLERGYMEN

Vicars

The vicarage of Witham was still held by the conformist career clergyman John Sterne, suffragan bishop of Colchester, until he died in 1608. The Bishop's Consistory court came to Chelmsford in March 1605, and the record book conveys a sense that Sterne should perhaps have been making more effort in the parish. Several notes about him appear in the margin, probably written in advance by the bishop's Vicar General Sir Edward Stanhope to advise the surrogate judge, who was Thomas Corbett, rector of Stanway and Abberton, and inferior in rank to Sterne. For instance the notes suggest that Sterne should be 'entreated' to make an order for the setting and collection of the church rate, which was long overdue, and expressed a hope that he would take 'more payns' with persistent refusers to take communion. Another omission was noted by the same court in 1606.[20] Although he was still active as a

magistrate, he left no other evidence of participation in Witham's life during James' reign.

After Sterne's death, successive bishops of London provided the town with two Puritan vicars. The first was Robert Tinley, an Oxford graduate, who was appointed in 1608, and continued until he died in 1616 at the age of about 55, leaving his widow Ann with four daughters under 18 years of age and four sons under 21. He held several other appointments, all acquired before he came to Witham. Thus he was archdeacon of Ely, rector of three Cambridgeshire parishes, and prebend of Kentish Town. The total annual income of these five other posts together was over £200, whilst that from Witham was only £22. We do have a few glimpses of his presence in the town from the records of the Bishop's Consistory court. He acted as judge when that court unusually met in Witham church in 1611, and in December 1612 he was asked by another judge at Chelmsford to follow up some of the Witham suspects, a role which was probably quite a usual one for the vicar. Six months later he wrote a letter for shearman John Haven, successfully 'requiring favour for him' in spite of the fact that Haven had not performed his penance for 'lurking in the alehouse and being drunken on the sabboth'. But Tinley's will particularly showed his interests in Ely and in Cambridgeshire. He left £3 each to the poor of Duxford in that county, and of Witham, but he only added these donations as an afterthought, with the engaging explanation 'I am sorrie I had almost forgotten'. His monument in St.Nicholas church said that 'his great learning and integrity of life was a worthy light in God's church'.

One of the overseers of his will was his brother-in-law, Sir John Borlase, who was a distinguished soldier in the Low Countries, later to become a lord justice and Master of the Ordnance during the 1640s. The other was Dr.Richard Crakenthorpe, vicar of the nearby parish of Black Notley, who was once one of the King's chaplains; he was said to have been 'conspicuous among the puritanical party for his great power as a disputant and preacher', and 'replenished with all kinds of virtue and learning, being a great philosopher'. Tinley's own will preamble was fervently Puritanical, and he asked to be buried 'without all Charge of mourning weedes or superstitious and dissolute sounde of bells'. The question of mourning display may have been one of controversy amongst Puritan adherents. Although they disapproved of ringing bells at unauthorised times, they do seem to have used them to mark special occasions, so some would probably have accepted funeral bells. Social status could take priority in such matters. In particular, we shall see later that Dame Katherine Barnardiston asked for an extremely elaborate funeral. Although do not know of any direct contact that she had with Robert Tinley, she left £8 to his widow and son, so that they could buy black clothes in which to mourn her.[21]

At the same time, she also referred to Tinley's successor, Roger Webb. Thus she provided more black clothes for 'Sir George St.John he that his wife lay in at our late

Vicker Mr.Webb's house in Witham'. One St.John family became noted Parliamentarians in the eastern counties, and were related to Oliver Cromwell, but Sir George so far remains a mystery. Webb, who was vicar from 1616 until about 1624, was an Oxford graduate from St.John's college, and must have been about 58 years old when he was appointed. We know little about his activities in the parish, but he did appear at the Archdeacon's court in 1617 to certify that grocer Arthur White, an alleged sabbath breaker, was behaving himself, and in 1624 Thomas Greene, a Witham gentleman, left him twenty shillings.[22]

Curates and a lecturer

If, as seems probable, the vicars were frequently absent from Witham, the curates potentially had an important role. Information about them is incomplete, and it seems that they changed fairly frequently. This was usual; curates were poorly paid and were often seeking a living of their own. The first two Witham curates known from James' reign were John Luther and John Gaye; the latter was suspended temporarily in 1607 for not appearing at the Archdeacon's Visitation.[23] More is known about two later holders of the office, Dr.Abraham Gibson and Thomas Holmstead. Both had Puritan connections, particularly with Dame Katherine Barnardiston and William Towse.

Abraham Gibson was only 24 when he came briefly to be Witham's curate in 1611, his first appointment. He subsequently became a well-known and well-liked figure in the Church in London and East Anglia. Dame Katherine was godmother to his eldest son, so perhaps the boy was born in Witham. In 1612, Witham yeoman Leonard Aylett asked in his will that 'Mr.Gibson the Curate of our towne shall preache at my buriall', and left him ten shillings 'for his paines'. Soon afterwards Gibson left for Suffolk, to become vicar of Little Waldingfield, north-east of Sudbury. In early 1614 he returned to Witham on a visit, to talk to Dame Katherine's new husband William Towse about an invitation to become occasional preacher at the Temple Church in London; as we saw earlier, Towse was very influential there. A full-time trial period had been suggested, and a surviving letter from Gibson shows his unhappiness about this proposal, which would have meant temporarily deserting his new parishioners, whom he called 'my people'. In a postscript written at Braintree on his way home, he asked that his neighbours should not be asked to carry messages, as they had not been informed of the problem.

The matter must have been resolved as he did become the lawyers' preacher and also stayed at Little Waldingfield. Then in 1618 he sent a curate there instead, on being appointed as rector of the Barnardistons' family parish of Kedington by Sir Thomas Barnardiston, Dame Katherine's former father-in-law. Very possibly she and William Towse recommended Gibson to Sir Thomas, having been close to him at Witham. Whilst in Kedington he was

influential in the successful election of Dame Katherine's stepson Sir Nathaniel to Parliament in 1628. Sir Symonds D'Ewes, a contemporary Puritan writer and a relative of the Barnardistons by marriage, called Gibson a 'kind friend', and referred to his 'witty and pleasant conversation'. Gibson died in London in his early forties in 1630, saying that he 'had little' to leave to his family, and was buried in the Temple Church to the accompaniment of a eulogistic funeral sermon. His widow Marabella, their son Abraham, and Marabella's second husband Mr.Lambard, were later left mourning clothes by Dame Katherine Barnardiston, who also left young Abraham, her godson, £100 in cash, 'two silver tankerds that are wreathed aboute', and the bed, furniture, chest and linen from her 'White Chamber', whilst the other Gibson children received £20 each.[24]

Nothing is known of 'Mr.Stone', who followed Abraham Gibson as Witham's curate, and little more of Edward Salter, who was here in 1615; he may have become vicar of Little Braxted later. But there are several interesting references to Thomas Holmstead, who took the post during the 1620s. Although some references call him the curate, Dame Katherine Barnardiston said that he had been 'Leckturer of Witham'. She may have helped to provide for him; 'lecturers' were usually sponsored by lay people, particularly Puritans. They were preachers who had often not formally committed themselves to the requirements of the Church such as the obligation to observe Prayer Book ritual. In 1623 Holmstead witnessed the will of a Witham husbandman, John Coleman, in 1624 gentleman Thomas Greene left him ten shillings, and in 1625 clothier Thomas Creswell left him the same amount 'to preach at my buriall'. By this time he may have been in charge temporarily after the departure of Roger Webb from the vicarage. The special nature of the preaching requested by Creswell was indicated by a case heard at the Archdeacon's court in 1624. Robert Smith had been absent from his own church in the adjoining parish of Hatfield Peverel, and told the court that he:

> of absolute necessitie repayres to other Churches for his soules health for he cannot learne jesus Christ by whome he onely hopeth to have salvation, from Mr.Stable his owne minister so well as from other ministers, one namely Mr.Holmstead of Witham.

The emphasis on salvation by Christ alone was a characteristic of Puritanism. The court sent for Holmstead himself to appear on the next court day, but he did not do so. The case was left to stand and he was not summoned again. No later references to his presence in the parish have been found. However, he was still known to Dame Katherine when she made her will in 1633, because he was yet another recipient of money for mourning clothes. It seems very probable that he was the Thomas Holmstead who in December 1631 was curate of Great Burstead, south of Chelmsford, and was accused in the Consistory court of 'preaching a lecture' in the chapel at Billericay, having earlier been suspended from the curacy of Dartford in Kent by the bishop of Rochester.[25]

EDMUND HALYS

Edmund Halys has been mentioned several times already. His life in Witham spanned three reigns and also extended into the Civil War period, so it would perhaps be helpful to summarise it here in one place. He was the son of Witham's earlier 'unpreaching' vicar, Edward Halys, and was born in about 1564, four years after his father had arrived in the town. At a young age he was sent to London as an apprentice to William Earnesbie, a haberdasher, and he was admitted to the Haberdasher's Company in 1583, at the age of about 18. By this time, however, the pair had moved to Colchester in Essex, where Earnesbie became one of the two bailiffs, the equivalent of a mayor, in 1586. Colchester's government was going through a period of considerable disruption at that time; Mark Byford has suggested that the borough officers included both extreme and moderate Protestants. Then in 1588 Earnesbie fell ill, and wrote to the bailiffs and aldermen to ask them to make Halys a freeman so that he could run the business. His letter reported that Halys was 'acquainted with my affayers' and 'very necessary aboute them', and was 'so honest and so good behaviour that I doubt not but that your worships will well lyke of him'.

Earnesbie died soon after writing this letter, leaving considerable bequests of money and property, and twenty shillings for a 'recreation or drinckinge' for 'the companye of Capthickers and Capdressers' in London and Southwark. He left Halys twenty nobles, worth in all £6 13s.4d.; his other servants received ten shillings each. His letter had achieved the desired result; four days after the funeral in December 1588, Edmund Halys was made a free burgess of Colchester. For this he paid forty shillings; he was then aged about 24. Free burgesses had trading and voting rights in the town, but it was not necessarily a greatly prestigious position.[26] It might seem, therefore, that Edmund Halys was set up for life as a Colchester haberdasher. But only a few years later he returned to Witham, the town of his birth. Thereafter he was always known as a gentleman, became Witham's best-known and oft-used scribe, and haberdashery was never mentioned again. This move may have been prompted, and perhaps even financed, by the death of his father Edward, the vicar, in 1587, though Edmund was not the eldest son. In 1635 he said that he had been in Witham for about the previous forty years, implying that he had returned in about 1595. In fact he started writing wills in Witham in 1593, when he was about 29 years old.[27]

For the following fifty-five years, he personally wrote about one third of Witham's wills, and witnessed other documents such as deeds. He also carried out work for people in other nearby parishes. As can be seen below in figure 17, his signature became more subdued as he aged, and when he finally wrote his own will in 1648, at the age of 'almost 84', he abandoned the flourishes and used his ordinary writing.[28] I have wondered if he was the parish clerk, but no information on the subject survives. His only known official position was as an

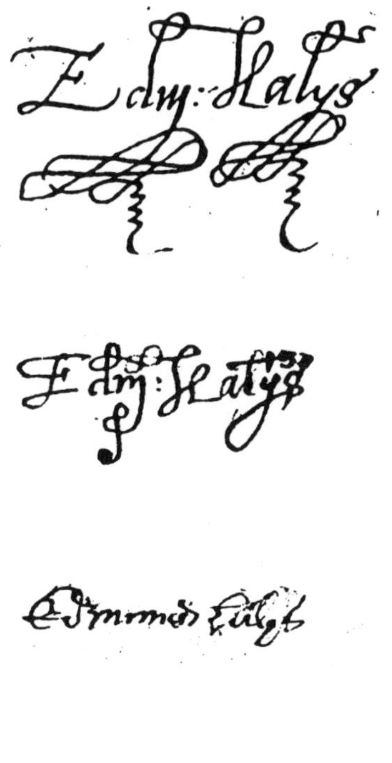

1597, aged about 33

1632, aged about 68

1648, signing his own will
at the age of 'allmost 84'

Figure 17.   Signatures of Edmund Halys

Edmund Halys was born in Witham in about 1564, the son of vicar Edward Halys. He went away to London and Colchester as an apprentice haberdasher, and then returned to Witham in the early 1590s and became one of Witham's most prolific scribes, particularly of wills, until his death in 1648. As can be seen above, his style of signing his name changed during his long life. He lived in Newland Street, in a house on the site now occupied by 'High House' (part of no.5).
(reproduced by courtesy of the Essex Record Office; references E.R.O. D/ACW 3/156, 11/264, 15/85)

almshouse trustee. He seems in many ways to have taken the role which professional men began to fulfil in later years. However, he appears to have been less prosperous than many of his fellow-parishioners who were involved in commerce and the cloth industry. When he first came to Witham he owned half an acre of land which had been his father's, and the lease of another three acres, but he did not keep them long. After this his only property seems to have been his own house and the one adjoining it, at the Colchester end of Newland Street; he had bought these by 1608 (they were on the site now occupied by High House, in 1998 the Lian restaurant, part of no.5). In the Ship Money returns of 1636 he was assessed at the relatively humble sum of two shillings; the median value for all those assessed was three shillings. His will mentioned furniture which was solid and comfortable rather than opulent; it included a 'walnut tree chayer with a leather backe and seate' in the 'studdy parlor', where he had perhaps done his writing.

It is perhaps surprising that he was only very briefly recorded as a teacher, and this not until 1628, when he was licensed to teach 'English schoole' 'and to Wright and sipher' under Christopher Webb. Eighteen months later the new curate was licensed as a teacher and this seemed to disqualify Halys. When this matter went to Consistory court, reference was also made, somewhat incongruously, to a rumour that he was 'a Common drunkard'. Perhaps he was engaged in some feud with the curate. He sent a lawyer to a later hearing to secure his absolution; this was unusual.[29]

His earlier work in will writing was varied, but often associated with enthusiastic Protestant preambles. Possibly the rather flowery language of some of them, referring to the 'socyety and Companie of Jesus Christe and of all the blessed Aungelles and Saintes in the kingedome of heaven', 'the generall resurecion att the laste daie', and 'the generall daye of Judgment', may have derived from what Halys had heard in his youth from his traditionally minded father, and been adapted by him to a Protestant format. Many of these phrases and ideas were also similar to the ones used in the elaborate preamble of his former master William Earnesbie. After about 1600 his preambles were less complex but did vary and included some quite elaborate ones. His own, written in 1648, was extremely cautious; he merely commended his soul 'unto the most holy and blessed Trinity the Father the son and the Holy Ghost'.[30]

We have an unusual chance to hear Halys' own words in the record of the disturbance outside Elizabeth Archer's house in 1611. In Newland Street afterwards he met Richard Gwynne, Elizabeth's prospective son-in-law. He and Halys talked together, and when they saw the rioters again, Halys 'most earnestly entreated [Gwynne] to plaie the parte of a wise man'. This seems to summarise our impression of Halys' cautious contribution to Witham's life. His only appearance in the Archdeacon's court records was when he complained about the height of new pews in 1623. In 1634 he was one of thirty-six men and women who

were said to have attended an 'unlawful meeting', but the people attending held quite varied views, and the purpose of the meeting is unknown. Eight years later the great Parliamentarian petition of 1642 was prepared, but Halys' name did not appear on it. This was such a comprehensive document that any absence must be suspected as being deliberate, though of course it cannot be conclusive. Halys was in his late seventies by then, but he was still witnessing wills.[31]

In spite of his apparent moderation, Halys had two connections with the later Quakers, although he himself died just before they became established. One of the witnesses to his will in 1648 was Paul Gattaway, a cordwainer who later became a Quaker. This might have merely been an act of neighbourliness, as Gattaway and Halys lived only about sixty yards apart in Newland Street. But Halys's own grand-daughter, Deborah Eatney (nee Davies), also became a Quaker in due course.[32]

TEACHING

During James' reign the curates probably did some teaching, and the licensing of other teachers by the bishop continued. In September 1612 Richard Redman or Redmayne, was licensed as a schoolmaster both 'in the parish church of Wittham' and elsewhere in the diocese. He must have been living here already, as he had witnessed the will of a Witham man seven months earlier. Then in 1617 John Hanson, M.A., obtained a licence to teach grammar in the town. Just possibly he was the John Hanson who had received his B.A. from Cambridge in 1604, and wrote what has been called a 'turgid poem' telling of 'Elizabeth's death, of James I's accession, of the plagues of 1603, and of the vices of London'; it is chiefly known today for its rarity. He was followed in Witham by John Burrowes, who presented a much grander portfolio of subjects than had been offered in the parish hitherto; he was to be allowed:

> to teach children and others to understand and pronounce the French language and ----- language, and the art of writing and calculation.

The second language was left blank.[33] He did not appear to have a degree, and I did not discover anything else about him. This was at the height of the prosperity of the cloth industry in the parish, and perhaps knowledge both of languages and calculation helped with the negotiations in London about the export of cloth to other countries.

Anxiety about unlicensed teaching continued until 1614, but lessened thereafter. The unofficial teachers of this time were varied. Little is known about Henry Kitchen, who appeared at the Archdeacon's court in 1603 as 'Mr.Kitchen, schoolteacher', for 'keping a schole', and again in 1609 because 'he teacheth boyes to Wright but whether he be allowed we know not'. But three others seem to have been ordinary tradesmen of the town. Edward Gould, presented in 1603, was a tailor; the case against him was dismissed. In later life he was presented again, but this time as a 'common drunkard'. He lived in a cottage in Newland Street which was subsequently pulled down and incorporated into the site of 'the Grove' by the Barwell family.

Nicholas Lowe, who taught boys without authority in 1607, was a yeoman. He had appeared earlier at quarter sessions for arresting people with false writs, probably as parish constable, and also for victualling without a licence. It was alleged at the Archdeacon's court in 1611 that he had absented himself from church. He had inherited £40 from his father in 1595, but when he himself died in 1617, all his goods were only worth £14, and his son was excused from paying court charges on grounds of poverty. Finally, Henry Pickett, who was said in 1614 to have been 'teaching school being not licensed', was a wheelwright; his case was dismissed. We find him later amongst Witham parishioners going to Terling church to hear the Puritan Thomas Weld in 1631, and he was again presented for having an unlicensed school in 1639. [34] The picture of these unauthorised teachers is that some may have held some religious conviction, but that they were generally men of fairly humble means, for whom the added income could well have been an important motive.

WILL PREAMBLES

Gentleman Edmund Halys, discussed earlier, was the single most important writer of wills in Witham during this period. On average during James' reign he wrote a third of them, and between 1615 and 1625 the proportion was two thirds. One effect of his influence was that for the first fifty years of the century, only one Witham will appears to have been written by a clergyman, whereas during the previous fifty years the clergy had probably written more than half. After his flowery start during Elizabeth's reign, his preambles became muted between 1600 and 1610, though like all the others of this period, they were firmly Protestant. After that, many of them were more extended. Although less elaborate than his very early ones, they were not standardised. There were some common features, but he found a slightly individual wording for each one, perhaps to suit the will-maker. An example was the preamble for yeoman Thomas Pye in 1616, which read:

> I comende my soule unto the handes of Almighty God the father the sonne and the holy ghoste assuredly believynge that all my sinnes ar washed awaie by the precious bloodsheddinge of my onely Saviour and redemer Jesus Christe and that after this sinfull and painfull liffe ended I shall have and enjoy everlastinge liffe and felicitye in the kingdome of heaven. [35]

Usually, where we know the value, people with this fairly extended sort of will preamble had goods worth over £50. After 1610, the few wills of Halys which had only brief preambles were written for people with relatively few goods, like yeoman and victualler William Wood of Chipping Hill, and husbandman Richard Freeborne. [36]

DISCIPLINE AND THE COURTS, 1603-c.1611

The accession of James I in 1603 was accompanied by some increase in activity in the court of the archdeaconry of Colchester as a whole. Although there were fluctuations, the level seemed to stay above average until about 1616, although never approaching the 'panic' rates of around 1590. The pattern in Witham itself was much more volatile, as would be expected in a single parish. Here, surges of activity, usually lasting for only one or two years, were interrupted by quiet periods of similar duration. During the decade from 1600 to 1609, the proportion of Witham cases of different types was very similar to the average for other periods. Thus although there was concern for particular sorts of offence in certain years, there were none that dominated the decade as a whole. Accusations of drunkenness and abusing the Sabbath were in fact somewhat below average, and it could not be said that there was any definite evidence of a concerted Puritan moral crusade during this decade. Figures 5 to 8 on pages 20-22 illustrate these features.

The events of 1604

During James's reign as a whole, over two-thirds of the Witham cases in the Archdeacon's court were brought forward by the churchwardens. However, they were influenced by outside events as well as by their own inclinations, and one of the most marked features of this period in Witham may not have been solely their responsibility. This was the increase in business in the year 1604. In that year there were more new Witham cases than in any other; the total was thirty-six. The fact that this was accompanied by an increase in activity in the Colchester archdeaconry as a whole, suggests some influence from beyond Witham. It seems very probable that the events of 1604 were in fact connected with the 141 new canons or rules issued by the Convocation of the Church of England in June of that year. On 9 July, Witham's churchwardens presented twenty-seven of their parishioners, of whom twenty-three, including six married couples, were accused of absence from church. Three people had been presented for this offence in 1602 but, before that, there had only been one since 1597. Half the people appearing in 1604 were said to have failed to receive holy communion. Amongst them were the Catholic Campions and Mrs.Bayles, but we do not know the allegiance of the other absentees. As often happened, most of the suspects did not appear at the following court hearings and were excommunicated, with later attempts to revive the cases being unsuccessful. When the Bishop's Consistory court visited Chelmsford in March 1605, outstanding cases from the Archdeacon's court accounted for two-thirds of the unusually large number of twenty-four Witham people whose names were presented, but none of them were resolved even there. This was the occasion on which vicar John Sterne was urged to make more effort. The year 1604 saw a similar surge of activity in neighbouring Terling. In discussing that parish, Keith Wrightson and David Levine considered that there were 'no purges initiated from above' until the later seventeenth century. However, the comparable pattern in Witham and in the archdeaconry as a whole suggests that in fact the 1604 canons may have had some influence.[37]

In the same year, the state of the church was complained of by the Archdeacon's court. This was a recurring theme and often it may have implied a concern for maintenance rather than a dire emergency. The churchwardens responded by saying that:

> we cannot get our money which we have layd out, neither cann have a rate made, for that they which are willinge have payd and the other be not Compelled to paye; also we have sett our accompt in the Churche book but they will not tak yt.

Later they reported that they had:

> often presented divers in the parishe for rates towardes theses reparacaions and cannot gett yt at ther handes but refuseth to pay it.

They put forward similar pleas to the Bishop's Consistory court when it visited Chelmsford. We may well be hearing a certain amount of exaggeration and self-justification from the wardens here. However, there were a considerable number of presentments for non-payment of rates at this time.[38]

Churchwardens, 1603-c.1611

My suggestion that the wave of new activity in 1604 was stimulated by the newly issued canons of the Church, is supported by the fact that the same churchwardens had been in office in Witham since 1600, but had previously done very little. So something must have roused them. No other long take-over of the office was found in the parish. There had been annual changes since at least 1583, and this pattern was restored after 1605. But for five and a half years, from 1600 to 1605, John Gravener(1) and John Savill held the posts continuously. John Gravener(1) was the wealthiest clothier in the town, although he probably could not write his name. John Savill was a tenant farmer at the manor house of Blunts Hall; he had become a warden earlier, giving him a total tenure of seven years. He could write, so the pair reflected the situation in this decade that only half of the churchwardens whose abilities were known could sign their names. Another notable feature of Gravener and Savill's period of office is that it marks the beginning of a time when it was usual to have a clothier as one of the churchwardens. Hitherto the majority of wardens had been yeomen, and in fact there was only one previous occasion when one of them is known to have been a clothier. This was in 1588, when John Gravener(1) had a year's earlier experience of the task. The participation of clothiers after 1600 was so new and so regular a feature that we might suppose some sort of formal agreement on the subject, perhaps instituted by Gravener himself. A comparable arrangement was known in Brighton, where one warden was a fisherman and the other a 'landsman'. This was said in 1570, when it was confirmed, to be an ancient custom.[39]

The termination of Gravener and Savill's period of office in 1605 could well have been connected with the canons of 1604, which gave ministers a role in the selection of wardens. It is hard to be sure exactly how that role was exercised in Witham. Although vicar John Sterne's local contribution appeared to be rather deficient by this time, he may have felt it was time for a change, and as suffragan bishop he was in a good position to try and enforce it. The replacement of the pair did not mean that no more was heard of them. In November 1606 they were presented at the Archdeacon's court by the new churchwardens because they 'did and do detayne from us the Register book of the names of the marriadges, christeninges and Burialles belonging to the parish of Witham'. There are no further details, but the episode suggests something of a power struggle. One historian has noted that possession of the registers was sometimes important during arguments about the control of parishes during the 1640s. The conclusion of the Witham dispute is not clear. The register from that period does not survive today, but its loss probably dates from later times. Retiring warden John Savill was also presented by his successors for not paying his church rates. He never appeared to answer and was ultimately excommunicated. This was the last reference to him found in the Witham records, so he probably died or moved away soon afterwards. His partner John Gravener(1) died in 1607, leaving a fairly emphatic Protestant will written by Edmund Halys. He also left goods with a higher value than any Witham person for whom we have this information before 1640. His son John(2), another clothier, died soon afterwards in 1611, having been a warden himself in 1609. The widow of John(2) was Mary, granddaughter of the early Protestants Christopher and Joan Raven; she moved away to Colchester. John(2)'s and Mary's son John Gravener(3) was then a minor, but in later years he became a dominant figure in Witham like his grandfather. Unlike some of his colleagues he was primarily law-abiding.[40]

In early 1607, the first new churchwardens after Gravener and Savill were presented by the Archdeacon's court:

> for not providing of bread and wine upon Christmas daye last past and for not presenting of divers [sexually] incontinent persons within the parish of Witham.

It was also stated that they should provide 'a stope or pott for the Communion table for the wine'. Yeoman William Sone, one of these new wardens, appeared a month later to certify that all had been seen to, and the case was dismissed, so the omission may have been a matter of negligence rather than defiance. Possibly after the long tenure of Sone's predecessors, no-one else knew how to do the job properly. But it is most noticeable that during the first five years of the resumption of annual changes in office, there was less activity in the court by the Witham churchwardens, and the cases that they did bring forward were mostly for sexual offences rather than 'religious' ones, apart from some presentments of Catholics in 1605. During this period also, the churchwardens themselves were sometimes accused of inactivity by the court. On one occasion they were said to have omitted to present 'divers offences' of their parishioners, and on another to be lacking 'the book of constitutions', but more frequently their neglect related to the continuing problem of the physical state of St.Nicholas church. Thus it was alleged that there was a cracked 'great bell', broken windows, and decayed arches, whilst some of the parishioners were said to have been digging up the path between the town and the church.[41]

DISCIPLINE AND THE COURTS, c.1611-1625

Churchwardens, c.1611-1625

In 1615 the bishop's Visitation still found that Witham's church 'wantes pavementing in many places and it wantes leadinge for it Rayneth in in many places'. However, in general the decade of the 1610s saw a very marked reduction in the numbers of presentments against Witham churchwardens by the Archdeacon's court, and they continued at a similarly low rate thereafter. In the previous forty years such cases had comprised fourteen per cent of the total of Witham cases, but for the thirty years from 1610 onwards they represented only two per cent. At the same time the churchwardens of Witham began to show an increased interest in supervising the parishioners. Thus their activity revived in 1611, when they made several accusations about absence from church and non-payment of church rates, and, their successors became increasingly concerned about various other matters. The number of Witham cases in the Archdeacon's court varied considerably from year to year for the rest of the reign, but many years were above average, whilst in the archdeaconry as a whole, the level appeared to be below average after 1616. The Bishop's Consistory court took an unusually large number of new cases from Witham in 1612 and 1619, but I have not discovered whether there was any particular reason for this.[42]

The office of churchwarden continued to change annually amongst Witham's tradesmen, farmers and clothiers, with the latter usually occupying one of the places. Men holding this position of authority often attracted criticism from other parishioners. For instance, in 1613 it was said that shopkeeper Anthony Bentall had abused the Witham churchwardens on the day of the Archdeacon's court. They reported that:

> he has this morning spake in disdayne in executing our office and us in contempt thereof and of the ecclesiastical lawe in coming to the Corte he willed us to bring our great dogg with us to the Corte.

His original offence had been 'selling wares on the Sabbath'. He was warned and dismissed; six months later he had died, leaving goods worth the considerable sum of £126. He could sign his name, and had some experience of office himself, having been manorial aletaster in 1601.

The annual change of office and the readiness of the

Archdeacon's court to hear cases on the basis of rumour, made it easy to take revenge on past churchwardens. The list of known wardens is rather incomplete during this period, but we do know that in 1617 the clothier Thomas Creswell, then a churchwarden, presented grocer William Robinson and others to the Archdeacon's court for selling goods on Sunday, whilst seven years later, Robinson himself became a warden and in turn presented Creswell for not paying his rates. There are other cases of wardens appearing in court not long after their period of office, but usually we do not know who their accusers were. They included innkeeper Robert Bunny, churchwarden in 1616-17. We saw in chapter 2 how he was embarrassed to be presented at the Bishop's Consistory court in 1619 for a sexual relationship with his maidservant (pages 19-20). And a year later he came before the Archdeacon's court for non-attendance at church, the case being dismissed on the grounds that:

> he being a single man and no housekeeper in Witham is often out of the town and at other parishes and there doeth heare divine service upon the Saboth daye.

He was a widower. A pattern of counter-accusation against prosecutors has been noted by Keith Wrightson in a study of another Essex parish at this time, Burnham on Crouch.[43]

Adultery and fornication

The proportion of the new Witham cases at the Archdeacon's court which related to the sexual offences of adultery and fornication remained at its usual level of about one quarter during this period. However, as shown in figure 18 overleaf, during the decade of the 1610s in Witham, it is notable that one third of these accusations concerned sexual relations between people who eventually married, whereas during the previous forty years the proportion had been less than one tenth. Nearly all of the new cases were presented by the churchwardens. If the couple married, there were no financial repercussions for the parish, because the baby would be provided for, and the objection was purely moral. The historians of Terling therefore suggest that cohabitation before marriage only became a matter of official concern during times of increased Puritan activity. In Terling, action against this offence began to become more common during the 1620s.[44]

The majority of the Witham people said to be cohabiting during the 1610s, nine couples in all, were probably mostly of fairly low status. None is known to have owned property or been able to sign their name, and generally their other appearances in the records were for offences such as being drunk, assault, theft, or having an illegitimate child. There were two weavers, a comber and a tailor. The only one of an apparently more noted position in the town was tailor Nathaniel Garrard, who went on to hold several parish offices during the 1630s and 1640s, and appeared in the Ship Money assessment of 1636, though at the relatively low level of 1s.6d.[45]

FIGURE 18

NEW CASES APPEARING IN THE ARCHDEACON'S COURT FROM WITHAM: SOME SPECIFIC TYPES

(for overall figures see figure 6 on page 21)

DATES	TOTAL 1570 TO 1639	1570s	1580s	1590s	1600s	1610s	1620s	1630s
Number of sexual offences	**187**	3	25	36	36	26	34	27
Of which cohabitation before marriage	**28**	0	3	2	3	9	2	9
As % of all sexual offences	*15*	---	*12*	*6*	*8*	*35*	*6*	*33*
Number of offences of drunkenness & disorderly houses	**40**	0	5	2	2	8	20	5
Of which relating to Sundays	**23**	0	2	0	0	8	10	4
As % of all drunkenness & disorderly houses	*58*	---	*40*	---	---	*100*	*50*	*80*

Years are 'old style', i.e. 25 March to 24 March.

Approximately four years' records are missing altogether, of which about half a year is in the 1570s, a little over three years in the 1580s, a third of a year in the 1590s, and one tenth of a year in the 1600s.

If both parties are named for sexual offences, the offence is counted as one; similarly if someone is presented for allowing sexual offenders to go away unpunished, it is counted as part of the original offence.

Alehouses and drinking

Although a licensing system for alehouses had been established by Act of Parliament in 1552, enforcement had been spasmodic at first. However, the Government took a new interest from the beginning of James' reign, for a variety of reasons including the possibilities for collecting fees. Thus several new regulations were introduced from 1604 onwards increasing the powers of magistrates to control alehouses. In 1605 the main responsibility for issuing licences was given to the newly regularised meetings of magistrates in local petty sessions. We do not generally have petty sessions records from this period, but quarter sessions and assizes did continue to consider some of the establishments which were unruly, or unlicensed, or both. Thus we hear in 1620 about Essex magistrates 'in and out of sessions', having suppressed alehouses. In many places the magistrates are known to have used their new powers with enthusiasm, and Keith Wrightson has written that 'at the level of the local community, the struggle over the alehouses was one of the most significant social dramas of the age'. He considers that during the early seventeenth century it was the way in which parish officers themselves took up the campaign that was particularly significant, and has calculated that Witham was one of the most frequent presenters of unlicensed alehouses in the secular courts of Essex between 1616 and 1629.[46]

For the first few years of James' reign, before the petty sessions took over and we lose sight of the records, Essex quarter sessions had regularly licensed about a dozen people in Witham to keep 'inns, common alehouses or tippling houses, and to sell ale, beer bread and other victuals'. It may well be that this number continued to receive approval in subsequent years also. To begin with, we only hear of a few problems with disorderly alehouses in Witham, but after the magistrates had noted in 1616 that there were 'too many alehouses in Witham by six', the secular courts always received several complaints about the town each year, generally in the form of presentments, which were usually drawn up initially by local juries. Most of the suspects were men.[47] One feature of alehouses at this time was their encouragement of newly popular indoor games, in contrast to outdoor activities such as archery. Many of the establishments which were complained about continued unabashed. Thus nearly half of the twenty-eight different Witham people appearing between 1616 and 1625 were named more than once, some of them several times. So we have the impression of there having usually been about a dozen unauthorised alehouses supplementing perhaps a similar number with licences. This was to serve a population of the order of a thousand people, in perhaps only about two hundred households, many of whom would also be brewing for themselves. Travellers and visiting traders provided additional customers. The Church courts also played a part in the campaign against drinking, beginning at much the same time. Accusations by the Witham churchwardens recommenced in 1612 after a break of several years, and became a regular occurrence from 1615 onwards. Some related to people who were running alehouses or entertaining others in their houses, which seems to have amounted to virtually the same thing, but more than half concerned individuals, variously described by such phrases as 'being drunk', 'common drunkard', 'notorious drunkard', and 'often overcome with drink'.[48] The secular courts very occasionally dealt with such individual drinkers also.

It may be that the number of alehouses in the country had already been increasing since late Elizabethan times, and that their greater visibility in the records after 1610 reflected new involvement by the authorities for a variety of reasons. There was often a combination of religious feeling, economic concern, and anxiety about public order, which is illustrated in the new orders issued by the Privy Council to magistrates and town authorities in 1622. These urged greater control, and neatly mixed several requirements. They noted that barley was 'in time of Scarcitie the bread corne of the poore', who were suffering from its high price; a reason for this was the amount which was used for 'excessive quantities of strong Beere and Ales spent in Alehouses'. Therefore, the authorities were to suppress:

> all such Alehouses as shall not bee needfull for the ease and convenience of his majesties Subjects, the same being now growne to so great a number, and for the most part places of disorder and intertainment for Lewd and ill-governed persons.

In those alehouses which were allowed, the strength of the beer was to be:

> so moderated and reformed as that there may bee no vaine consumption of the graine of the Kingdome whereof this yeare there is such scarcitie.[49]

Drinking and disorder on Sundays and feast days

Symbolic of a new concern about Sundays was the alteration of arrangements for holding one of Witham's two annual fairs. Important events in the trading calendar, these provided an opportunity for working, playing and drinking. One of them had previously been held on a Sunday at Chipping Hill since 'time out of mind', but it was moved to a Monday in 1616 by order of the King because it profaned the sabbath. During this period the Archdeacon's court records continue to express the problem of drinking in terms of general public order, as they had done previously. However, as shown in figure 18, it appears on closer examination that the offences with which they were now most concerned took place on Sundays, even if the record does not always mention the fact. All the eight drinking cases in that court between 1615 and 1619 took place on Sundays, there having been no others which did so since the 1580s.

This pattern continued to a lesser extent into the 1620s, when about half were on Sundays and the other half unspecified.[50] In those cases which concerned alehouses and groups, the court often reiterated the fear of crowds and strangers noted in the last chapter (pages 62-63). For instance, in 1619 Richard Canom of Witham was drinking in Hatfield Peverel 'with other aliens'. In 1621, Joan Purcas had been 'entertayning other drunkards upon the Sabbath day'; she was the wife of bricklayer William Purcas, 'a common drunkard' and alehousekeeper. And in 1622 Francis Ellis, a tailor, had been 'suffering Company to be drinking in his house in the sermon tyme ... being strangers'. The mention of sermon time in several of the accusations is significant, as the sermon was a particularly important part of the service to Puritans. Francis Ellis successfully defended himself on the grounds that 'he and his wife being in Church, his maid servant entertayned two strangers in his house who did drinke onely two peniworth of beere and departed presently'.[51] Most of these people were presented in other years for different offences, and Ellis in particular was continually in trouble; in 1614 he was even accused with another man of the 'felonious killing' of John Lane. They had thrown him down some stairs and he had died six weeks later. The jury decided that Lane had died 'by divine visitation' and Ellis and his companion were acquitted.[52]

The magistrates in quarter sessions also occasionally heard cases relating to Sundays, and at the midsummer session of 1624 a group of seventeen Witham men were presented there together for 'keeping disorder on the Sabbath day', meaning that they received other allegedly disorderly people. It is interesting to examine who they were. Half described themselves on other occasions as alehouse keepers or victuallers, though in every case they had another occupation as well, such as husbandman, yeoman, tailor, weaver, or barber. Three quarters suffered other prosecutions for similar offences, often several times. Only three seem to have ever actually held a licence for victualling or having an alehouse, but the record is probably incomplete in this respect. Various measures of status, amplified in the notes, suggest that the alleged offenders included a wide range of people, but that most of them were of at least lower 'middling' status or above, and that they were unusually literate.[53]

It is more difficult to compile a picture of the individual drinkers, and this in itself probably indicates that they were of lower rank. Fifteen of them from Witham, all men, appeared in the Archdeacon's court between 1615 and 1625, which is not really very many; their hosts were what really seemed to concern the courts at this time. As amplified in the notes, most of the fifteen were probably fairly poor, much more so than the alehousekeepers.[54] There were certainly none who matched Mark Goodwin, the prosperous yeoman and innholder who had been accused of 'being drunk' in 1588.[55]

Sunday games

The Archdeacon's court heard hardly any accusations from Witham in this period for playing games on Sundays, but this activity was now coming under the authority of the court of quarter sessions. Thus in 1618 it was reported there that John Brewer, a Witham weaver, on 13 September, 'being the Lord's day, and on diverse days before and since, entertained and received in his house divers persons of ill fame and conversation together with divers servants of his neighbours and allowed and maintained in the night time unlawful games ... cards, dice and gaming tables'. Brewer was eventually committed to gaol in Colchester castle for three days, fined ten shillings, and forbidden to keep any unlicensed alehouse in future However, he was running a victualling house again by 1634, when he managed to have one of his customers sent to the same gaol. In 1620 it was the turn of prosperous innkeeper and former churchwarden Robert Bunny of the George to be in trouble, He was accused of 'admitting unlawful assemblies into his house upon the Sabbath day ... spending their time in drinking, playing and the like in the time of Divine Service'.[56]

Sunday working

Although Sunday working had been one of the concerns of the Witham churchwardens around the crisis times of the late 1580s and the 1590s, they had been less conscientious about the matter since then. In 1611 the Archdeacon's court actually took one of the current Witham churchwardens to task for working on religious feast day himself. Some feast days were subject to the same prohibitions as Sundays. He was yeoman

William Tanner, who was alleged to have carried straw on May day. He claimed that he actually did it on Ascension day, and the case was dismissed. In that year Ascension day was on the second of May, the day after May day, so it was a narrow escape. In 1612 there were nine Witham cases of working on Sundays heard at the Bishop's Consistory court; they concerned seven shopkeepers and two millers. Again in 1615 the bishop's Visitation found that on Sundays and holy days 'their be two watermylles which goe very much', and 'a fulling myll which goeth commonly'. This perhaps implied that the churchwardens were not controlling such matters adequately, but from 1617 and for the following ten years, they regularly took their parishioners to the Archdeacon's court for working on Sundays. The offences were varied, and included opening shop windows, setting mills going, selling shoes, selling meat, hedging, driving hogs and brewing.[57] Often a group of people was presented together. The campaign particularly caught up several of the 'middling' people of the town. It must have been extremely difficult to avoid suspicion for this offence at a time when home and work were so inextricably intertwined, and the problem is illustrated by the defences which were put forward. They leave an impression that many of the activities were commonplace and even essential, and that at other times, when the wardens were not being so particular, they would not have attracted attention.

An example of such a frequent suspect is Arthur White or Wright. He lived at the Eagle, now the Spread Eagle, in Newland Street, owned by George Armond(2), and also had a close of land behind. He seems to have run it as a general trading place rather than as an inn, as he was variously described as a grocer, haberdasher, or mercer. He was accused three times of working on Sundays, in 1617, 1618 and 1625, and each time the case was dismissed, suggesting that the court did not take his offence as seriously as did whoever complained about him in the first place. In 1617 his offence was 'setting open his shopp windowes and keeping markett contrary to the lawe upon the lords day'. In 1618 it was 'hedging upon the Lords day 13 September last and for absence from Church the two Sundays following', to which he responded that 'upon necessetie upon one Saboth day in the morning prayer he did set up one pale in his orchyeard and that he was at Church the same day'. The fact that this slight offence was not brought to court until over three months after the event adds to the impression that it was part of a deliberate crusade of some sort, either against Sunday working or against Arthur White. Finally, in 1625 he was again in trouble 'for selling wares upon the Saboth dayes'. This time he said that 'one Saboth day he did sell wares to some pore people for which he is very sorry'. Several other people seem to have been frequently pursued by the courts, such as shoemaker John Hussey for selling shoes, miller Francis Hunwick for grinding corn, and butcher William Allen for 'driving of hoggs ordinarily upon the Sabath Day', and 'selling mete upon the Saboth day'. In the same year, Allen was also presented at the manorial court of Newland for the nuisance caused by his not killing his pigs in the proper place.[58]

Wall painting at no.53 Chipping Hill, dated 1606
This painting, which still survives, shows three fishes representing the Trinity.

Absence from church

Some of the censure directed at drinking, playing or working on Sundays arose from the fact that these activities kept the offender away from church. In addition, people who were merely absent or had not taken communion continued to be mentioned in court at much the usual rate. The largest number of absentees referred to at any one time was at the Bishop's Consistory court in March 1619, when there were thirteen. Few of them were particularly well-off apart from yeoman James Cosen and his wife of Colemans farm, and there are no indications that they were being anything other than negligent.[59]

Church pews

Since the 1580s, churchwardens had been empowered to seat their parishioners according to rank. This was a sensitive task which caused disputes in many places. Frequently, individuals came to be regarded as owning specific seats, whose structure they then elaborated to emphasise their personal status. Thus in 1623 Edmund Halys complained in the Archdeacon's court that some newly built seats in Witham's St.Nicholas church were 'a great hindrance unto the parishioners for hearing the minister in tyme of sermon'. The churchwardens, one of whom was John Gravener(3), were ordered to investigate. If they found the 'tops of the seats' were 'any inconvenience to the parishioners', they were to 'admonish those that sitt in them to pull them downe or els to present them' in court. This would have been a difficult task. They failed to certify that they had fulfilled it, but the matter was eventually left to stand. The offending structures or their successors may have remained for some time, as the former presence of what he called 'Puritan pews' in the church was recollected by a writer in 1862, although by then they had disappeared. Whether such pews were really more favoured by Puritans than their fellow parishioners is in fact debatable.[60]

OVERVIEW

At the end of Elizabeth's reign it had seemed that Witham's local affairs could move in any direction, and for the first ten years or so of James' reign there was still no evident trend. Certainly Christianity continued to permeate many people's lives. We are reminded of this by a wall painting dating from 1606, showing the three linked fishes representing the Trinity. This still survives in a house in Chipping Hill (no.53), and is illustrated on the previous page. But the records do not at first suggest any noticeable local campaigns or conflicts. The main recorded innovation in the town was the apparent custom whereby one churchwarden was always chosen from the cloth industry. This was marked by five years with the same wardens from 1600 to 1605, one of which was the town's wealthiest clothier, John Gravener(1). They did not appear to be guided by any reforming zeal; their only additional activity against their fellow-parishioners was probably inspired by the new canons of the Church in 1604, and was temporary.

However, after about 1611 there are several indications of a quickening of Puritan feeling amongst some of the Witham parishioners, particularly those in authority. These may have been facilitated by the relative absence of national opposition to Puritanism, the support of some of the people who were involved in county administration in quarter sessions, and the availability of new regulations, particularly those concerning alehouses. In particular we may note that the town's vicars and some of the curates had Puritan sympathies, and were closely associated with the prosperous and very well-connected Dame Katherine Barnardiston and her new husband William Towse. After 1610 the Protestant will preambles written by Edmund Halys became generally more elaborate, particularly those for the better-off willmakers. The churchwardens' activity in the Archdeacon's court revived in 1611, and although it fluctuated thereafter, they showed a new interest in controlling several matters that might normally have been overlooked, especially sexual relations before marriage, drinking on Sundays and working on Sundays. Suspects were varied in character. For instance those accused of Sunday working, or accommodating drinkers in unofficial alehouses, were often of middling rank, but individual drinkers and people who cohabited before marriage were probably mostly poor.

But it was a complicated town, and other feelings were also present which were relevant to later conflicts. For instance, the hand of Sir Thomas Wiseman's anti-Puritan sympathies extended from beyond the parish boundary to administer much of the civil control of Witham. And the wise Edmund Halys probably represented another strand, in which Protestant feelings were tempered by restraint and by little obvious inclination either to supervise the behaviour of others or to criticise authority. Halys' power was perhaps restricted by his limited wealth, but another cautious parishioner, the prosperous John Gravener(3), made a first appearance in James' reign. So although by 1625 public Puritan zeal had returned to Witham after a quiet time, we could not be sure it would continue. I will continue the chronological story in chapter 9, but first I will describe a particular event which serves to illustrate some of the wider pressures on Essex in general and Witham in particular.

8. CHARLES I - interlude -
THE FORCED LOAN OF 1626,
and ST.PATRICK'S DAY 1628

BACKGROUND

The reign of Charles I was an eventful time in Witham.
But before proceeding to describe it in general, I shall
deal separately in this chapter with one particularly
dramatic episode and its background. It is the dispute
which took place on 17 March 1628, St.Patrick's Day,
between some billeted soldiers and the townspeople. It
was unusually well-recorded and several historians have
written about it.[1] The story really starts in 1625, when
Charles I succeeded James as King. Almost
immediately, he and the Duke of Buckingham, who was
general of the army, put into effect England's entry into
the Thirty Years War on the continent. A historian has
pointed out that 'the war effort combined the maximum
of disruption at home with the minimum of success
abroad'. The county of Essex was particularly affected
by the atmosphere of crisis because of fears of invasion
of its coast in 1625, the death of many of its soldiers at
Cadiz in the same year, and the use of the port of
Harwich for the movement of troops. Furthermore,
many of the Puritan gentry of Essex, led by the second
Earl of Warwick, Robert Rich, were beginning to
oppose the King in debates on national affairs.[2] In
north-east Essex this all took place against a
background of increasing crisis in the cloth industry
caused by the loss of markets during the war with Spain.

THE FORCED LOAN OF 1626

Charles I dissolved Parliament in June 1626 to curtail its
members' criticisms of himself and Buckingham. In its
absence, he needed other means of raising money for
the war. Various schemes were tried and failed, and then
in September 1626 he ordered the collection of a
'Forced Loan', of which Essex's share probably
amounted to about £10,000. Reaction to this varied
from one place to another, and was later to affect the
discussion about which parishes should receive billeted
soldiers, which is why it is relevant to this chapter.[3]
Loan commissioners chosen from the county gentry
supervised the arrangements, whilst collectors were
responsible for actually getting in the money from the
individual parishioners and paying it to the Exchequer.
There were between one and three collectors in each
hundred according to size, Witham half-hundred having
two. The collector for the part which included Witham
itself was the town's John Gravener(3). As can be seen

from figure 19 overleaf, he worked extremely quickly.
The Exchequer received over a thousand sums of
money from the country as a whole over a period of
fifteen months, and out of these, the third payment that
arrived came from Gravener, on 28 November 1626.
On that day he paid in two-thirds of the total amount
due from his area. His colleague for the rest of the half-
hundred, William Sams, handed in a similar proportion
of his dues on the next day. He was probably the
gentleman from Rivenhall who was later to be accused
of collecting arms for the King's supporters at the
beginning of the Civil War. There were a few individuals
in some villages who resisted paying the Loan, which
accounts for Gravener's failure to achieve his complete
total immediately. Two apparent non-payers from
Witham itself had probably left the parish. So by August
1627 the only real defaulter from the town was said to
be 'William Warde ... a poore man and not able to paie'.
Other information about Warde sheds some doubt on
this description.[4]

It has been suggested by Richard Cust that there were
two main influences on the reaction to the loan in
Essex, though it was a complex issue. He considered
that where there were loan commissioners loyal to the
King, such as Earl Rivers of St.Osyth who supervised
the Tendring, Thurstable and Winstree hundreds,
collection tended to be speedy. In contrast, Puritan
commissioners delayed payment in areas like the
Hinckford hundred. In the Witham half-hundred he felt
that there was a general readiness to pay because of the
loyalty of commissioners Sir Thomas Wiseman of
Rivenhall and William Smith/Nevill of Cressing
Temple, but that there were pockets of resistance from
Puritan landowners in specific places like Terling and
Hatfield Peverel. In other parts of the county he
suggests that links with the cloth industry were a feature
of resistance.[5]

Witham was a clothmaking town, but as we have seen, it
was not slow to pay. It is interesting that its successful
collector was the clothier and yeoman John
Gravener(3), who was one of the most wealthy people
in the town, and remained an important figure for many
decades afterwards. The collection returns in fact call
him a gentleman, and later, during the 1660s, he began
to use that title himself. We do not find him recorded as
participating on either side during the confrontations
involving Witham's Puritans during the 1620s and
1630s; probably his concern was above all to maintain

FIGURE 19

PROGRESS OF PAYMENT INTO THE EXCHEQUER FROM SIX ESSEX HUNDREDS, OF MONEYS FROM THE FORCED LOAN

Payments began on 24 November 1626

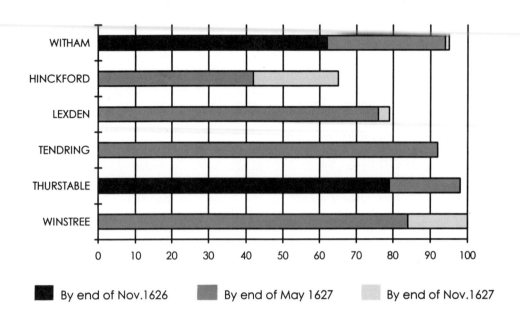

By end of Nov.1626   By end of May 1627   By end of Nov.1627

HUNDRED	TOTAL DUE (£)	PERCENTAGE PAID BY:		
		END OF NOV. 1626	END OF MAY 1627	END OF NOV.1627
WITHAM:	**405**	**62**	**94**	**95**
Of which John Gravener's part (including Witham parish)	205	66	92	92
Of which William Sams' part	200	58	96	98
HINCKFORD	**1292**	**0**	**42**	**65**
LEXDEN	**648**	**0**	**76**	**79**
TENDRING	**424**	**0**	**92**	**92**
THURSTABLE	**122**	**79**	**98**	**98**
WINSTREE	**107**	**0**	**84**	**100**

law and order. His apparent enthusiasm for collecting the Loan, and his willingness to co-operate with commissioners Wiseman and Smith, helps to support this interpretation. The fact that he succeeded in spite of the considerable potential for resistance in the town is perhaps a sign of his influence. Another interesting point is that the presence of the Puritan couple Dame Katherine Barnardiston and William Towse of Witham does not seem to have exerted any serious influence to delay Witham's payments, even though Dame Katherine's stepson Sir Nathaniel was a fierce opponent of the Loan in Suffolk, as a result of which he was imprisoned. His case, along with those of John Hampden and others, resulted in an argument between Parliament and the King about the legality of their confinement. Gravener and Sir Nathaniel probably knew each other, as they both spent their youth in Witham.[6]

BILLETING SOLDIERS IN ESSEX

Whenever they were on home territory for any reason, soldiers were usually billeted in private homes. Their 'diet' could be provided by the local organisers, by the householders, or by the soldiers from their meagre and often unpaid allowance of sixpence per day. An interesting bill survives from Colchester, in which Thomas Nevill was claiming £3 12s. from the bailiffs because he had taken in some soldiers. He had two of them on an 'all charges' basis for three shillings a week, but for others he was merely claiming extras such as salt and vinegar on their food, washing and starching 'table Clothes and napkines', providing 'fyer and candell', and 'a supper' on 'the first nighte they come'. Such costs were supposed to be reimbursed by the county's Deputy Lieutenants. They in turn raised funds for the purpose from a combination of private loans and levies on the county at large. Ultimately the money should have been refunded by the Privy Council, who were administering the country whilst Parliament was suspended. The Deputy Lieutenants were knights and peers, the Essex ones usually being about six in number at this time, and responsible to the Lord Lieutenant, the Earl of Sussex, for military matters. They had no supporting administrators and their proceedings were necessarily informal. During 1625 and 1626 some of them had been dismissed and others appointed, the overall result being a reduction in the number who supported the Puritan Earl of Warwick.[7]

Places on the main road to the coast were particularly likely to be visited by soldiers. Thus in one of their petitions, Witham's inhabitants pointed out that it 'a great roade towne', so that in spite of its great poverty due to the problems of the cloth industry, it had been 'extraordinarily sercharged with billitinge of great companies of soldiers passing to other places and continual postinge betweene London & Langarde'. Landguard was a fort on the Suffolk coast which protected Harwich. Furthermore, the town had also suffered from the 'great Charge and burthen of ... the Companyes of Soldiers which went to Colchester [and]

were billited as they passed thither'. On that occasion, Colchester was destined to provide more permanent accommodation, and it was the arrangements for such long-term billeting which caused particular problems. New demands were heralded by a letter from the Privy Council to the Essex Deputy Lieutenants on 17 December 1627. This asked for billeting to be arranged for soldiers returning from the failed expedition to the Isle of Ré, led by Buckingham, during which about half the original force had been killed. Some were sent to other counties such as Kent, where they caused tension. In mid-January 1628 the nine companies of Sir Piers Crosby's regiment of Irish soldiers, totalling over six hundred men, were settled in the homes of various Essex parishes and boroughs. Captain Ross Carew's company was sent to Maldon, the port six miles south of Witham.[8]

This imposition on the county of Essex was not accepted quietly, and correspondence flowed to and from the Deputies about their two prime concerns in the matter, money and public order. They raised £100 in loans and sought to levy £1,000 on the county's inhabitants; Witham half-hundred's contribution was to be £30. This was to be collected by the local high constables and sent to the Deputies' Treasurer, who at first was William Smith/Nevill of Cressing Temple. His was a difficult task. As well as receiving and paying out the county's funds, he seemed to be personally responsible for keeping track of weapons and ammunition. During a mutiny at Harwich in April 1627, he had sent off cash, letters, instructions and encouragement every few days by messenger to local officials, and sometimes visited there himself. He 'voluntarily' resigned his position as Deputy a few weeks after the new loan for billeting had been sought. It is worth noting in view of later events that he may have been the only Deputy with any knowledge of or interest in Witham, where he had a life interest in the main manors. He was replaced by the two Sir Henry Mildmays, one of Graces in Little Baddow, and the other of Wanstead, who will figure later in this story. His departure may have been because of illness; he was already over 70 and died two years later in 1630. But it may also have been precipitated by his lack of success in raising money for the soldiers, in spite of the Privy Council's provision of two 'messengers' to assist. It was reported that whole hundreds and towns were refusing to pay, so it was not possible for the messengers to identify and apprehend any disobedient individuals. The Deputies were not surprised, writing of the other recent demands made on the county, including 'these Warlike preparacions', 'his Majesty's house', and the 'losse of nere fortie thousand pounds in the Sea Walls'. A further source of anxiety was whether or not the expected reimbursement would be forthcoming from the Chancellor of the Exchequer. Although promised in March 1628, it is not known whether it was ever received.[9]

The Deputies had reported at the outset that 'the poorer houses' would not be able to keep the soldiers even if they did receive the official allowance, because it was inadequate, and that the better-off were 'absolutlie refusinge' to take them. Soon they found that there was insufficient money even to pay what should be paid, and towns and individuals who were not able to reclaim their costs were refusing to give any more credit. As a result, the soldiers were said to be helping themselves to food. This illustrates the other main fear of the householders and of the Deputies, the disruption of public order. Naturally the magistrates and the constables of the hundreds and the parishes were also concerned, so there was yet more correspondence with them. The Deputies warned of 'stragglers, fellons and other disorderly souldiours'. The Privy Council issued special regulations under martial law, and asked the civil authorities to co-operate in enforcing it. Nevertheless, before long there were reports of daily 'offences and daingers', and accusations of rape, robbery and disrespect, even to 'ministers of the peace.' Two specific points were to become particularly relevant to Witham. One was the petition of Captain Ross Carew, saying that his men had been badly used by the inhabitants of Maldon. The other was a complaint from the Deputies to the Privy Council about the soldiers being Irish, and 'of a Contrary Religion', namely Roman Catholics, which allegedly made them 'offensive above others'. As a result, householders who would otherwise have been co-operative refused to pay or receive them, and this opposition was 'not by a few private men, but by a generall consent'.[10]

With some foresight, the Deputies were anxious about the future. They expressed 'feare of much mischiefe which will speedily fall upon us', and said that 'the dainger wee ... would prevent is much greater and not yet Come'. One of the Privy Councillors' responses was to urge the proper enforcement of the existing martial law, and as a result the Deputies issued new directions. Among other constraints, the soldiers were not to draw their swords, not to abuse their hosts or anyone else 'either in base speech or action', and not to 'offer anie violence' to females. They were also to be in their lodgings by eight or nine o'clock at night when the bell was rung. But without enforcement, these regulations were nothing new, and the Privy Councillors began to blame the Deputies for the problem, claiming that the billets were in remote places where supervision was difficult, and telling them that 'Wee require you to see better order taken'.[11]

THE MOVE TO WITHAM

One solution that was soon mooted was to move some of the soldiers to different places, but the idea caused some confused debate, about which our information is probably only partial. Whilst considering the idea, the Deputies and the Privy Councillors both tried to take into account the willingness with which different places had paid the Forced Loan of 1626, and whether they were paying the current billeting levy. The Deputies threatened that they should be 'forced to billett the souldiours in those places which shall refuse to paie towards theire billetinge'. By about the end of January,

Witham, Kelvedon and Coggeshall had heard that they were being considered as places to take some soldiers. The inhabitants dispatched two petitions in their defence; from Witham alone one went to the Privy Council, and all three together wrote to the Duke of Buckingham. Drafts of these documents can still be found in the Leicestershire archives of the Nevill family, who had a home in that county as well as at Cressing Temple. This suggests that one of the Nevills may have contributed to their preparation. The petitioners stressed that they had already accommodated passing soldiers, that they had paid the Forced Loan and all other contributions demanded, and that their livelihood came mostly from the cloth industry:

> wherein trading is soe badd, & their number of poore soe great & unruely that they are not able to releve or governe them.

Lists of other more suitable towns were added.[12] It may have been one or both of these petitions that caused a change of heart amongst the Privy Councillors. On 3 February they had suggested to the Deputies that Witham should receive the soldiers from Maldon and that its two neighbours should take the ones from Horndon and Billericay, but a week later, on the 10th, its clerk wrote a rather confusing memorandum apparently recording a decision of the Council, which is shown in the illustration on the facing page. It stated:

> that the souldiers may be continued in Maldon for the reasons herein expressed. And that Witham may have none of them.

Chelmsford and Braintree were to take the others; they were amongst the places suggested by the petitioners. The conclusion of the memorandum makes clear the intention to punish four towns which had been 'very obstinate in their Loanes'. Chelmsford in particular had seen some prosperous resisters to the Loan. Because of the alterations to the document, it is not clear which the other two difficult towns were besides Chelmsford and Braintree; they may have been the two which were deleted and are illegible.[13] One historian implies that the document gives Witham as one of the recalcitrant towns which needed to be punished. However, as we can see, it really instructs that Witham should be excused, and of course the town had actually paid the Loan extremely promptly. On the same day, 10 February, the Privy Councillors wrote again to the Deputies informing them of this new decision. However, it seems that this amending letter was ignored or not received at the time by the Deputies.[14]

In any case, the Councillors had changed their minds yet again by 6 March, a month later, when they reported that 'some things' had 'fallen out' between the inhabitants of Maldon and the soldiers. They had received a petition from Maldon complaining that the Irish soldiers behaved 'as if they were our Lords and wee there slaves', drank three times their allowance, insisted on having 'two candles and a great fire' until nine o'clock at night, and took up all the room at the fire, claiming that 'the King dothe allowe it them'. It was asserted by the Maldon petitioners that their borough, hitherto prosperous, was not so any longer. There may also have been an element of rivalry with Witham. We

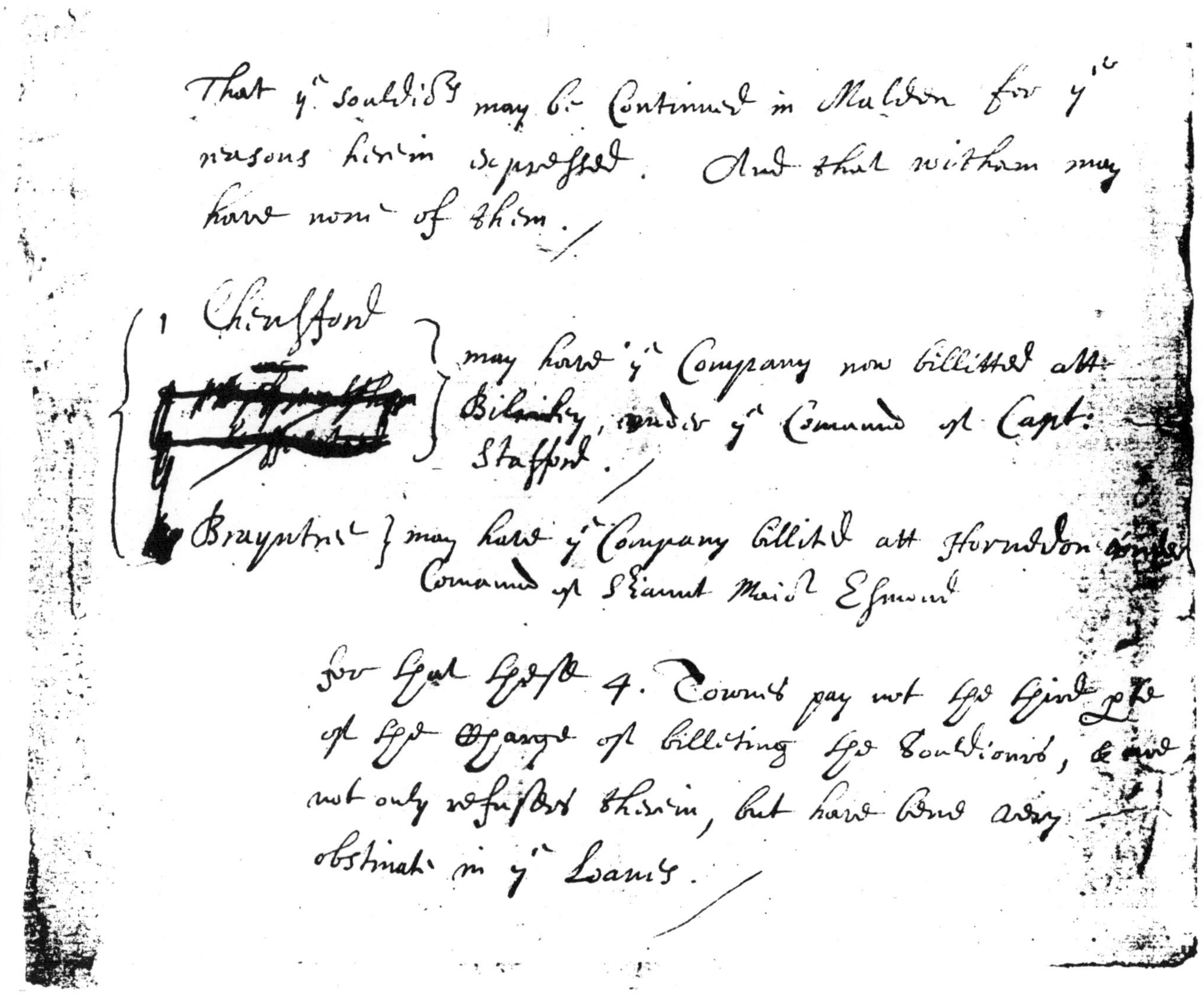

Figure 20.   Memorandum by the clerk of the Privy Council about billeting soldiers in Essex, 10 February 1628.

This memorandum seems to make clear that the Privy Council did not intend to billet soldiers in Witham at this point., though it has sometimes been interpreted otherwise. It also shows that it was planned to send some to Chelmsford and Braintree, because they had not paid enough either for the soldiers or for the Forced Loan.. The names of the other two of the '4' towns appear to have been deleted.
(Crown copyright material in the Public Record Office, reproduced by permission
of the Controller of Her Majesty's Stationery Office'; P.R.O. reference SP 16/92, folio 86)

know from another source that one of the fishermen from Maldon who complained about the soldiers, James Brownesword, later referred to some Witham jurors as 'bloodsuckers', and on the same occasions he also 'spake many other words ... not fitt to be repeated'.[15] The Privy Council's new request on 6 March was that the soldiers be moved from Maldon after all, to either Witham, Dunmow or Thaxted, with a preference for the latter. On the same day the Lord Lieutenant asked the Deputies to 'follow the Councells letter for the billetinge of the souldiers at Thaxted'. However, a memorandum in the Deputies' letter book recorded that in actual fact 'the souldiours were by the three Sir Henry Mildmays sent to Witham upon the Receipt of the said letteres'. It was later recalled that the move had taken place on 8 March, and that Witham had been chosen because of 'the povertie of Dunmoe and Thaxstead'. The Mildmays were all Deputy Lieutenants but it would appear that they acted without the agreement of their colleagues. Two of them were the new appointees of only about one month's standing who had replaced William Smith; they were probably more inclined to the Puritan faction of the Earl of Warwick than their more long-established colleagues.[16]

The moving of the soldiers to Witham provoked some strong reactions, which is not surprising in view of fact that so many people seemed to be opposed to it. A single unnamed Deputy wrote to the Duke of Buckingham that his colleagues were unhappy, and pointed out that if abusing the soldiers became seen by other towns as a way to have them removed, then there would be even more trouble in future. Furthermore, he reported that Witham was genuinely 'a verye poore Clothing Towne, and not able to keepe their poore', particularly as trading was so bad at the time. Maldon on the other hand was 'a farr more wealthier Towne and a fitter place for there billeting', and had been deceitful in its claims to be poor.[17] A historian of seventeenth-century Maldon has suggested that claims to poverty, which were frequently made by that borough's inhabitants, were indeed misleading, and that in spite of some stagnation in its economy, poverty was not a serious problem there. It seems that a further protest was issued by a meeting of some of the Deputies, in which they blamed the Privy Council for the decision, pointing out that Witham's townsmen had been 'most Conformable' in paying the Loan and the billeting money, and that soldiers should instead have been sent to some of the towns and hundreds which had paid nothing.[18] This declaration was said to have been sent out as a letter from the Deputies, but if it was, the document does not survive. We only know how they felt because Sir Thomas Wiseman told Henry Nevill of Cressing about it when the two met on the way to London, and then reported the conversation in a letter which he sent on 12 March to Henry's uncle William. Wiseman did not record his own opinion, but his tone suggested concern about the situation. He reported that his 'neighbor Garret' had been present at the Deputies' discussion, and had been asked by them to draw up a petition 'on behalfe of their town' of Witham. We do not know whether it was customary for the meetings to include interested outsiders in this way. The petition which resulted is almost certainly one of the ones addressed to Buckingham that now only survives in the Nevill archives. It makes the same points and names the same defective towns as the Deputies were said to have done. It stresses in addition that the number of poor were 'soe greate and unruly' that the town was 'not able to releive or governe them'. As 'Garret', the petition's compiler, was obviously a Witham man, he must have been the gentleman and yeoman Jerome Garrard(2), who was to become high constable of the half-hundred in the following year. He and Forced Loan collector John Gravener(3) were at this time the most prosperous and influential people in the town after Dame Katherine Barnardiston and her husband William Towse.[19]

ST.PATRICK'S DAY, MONDAY, 17 MARCH 1628

Matters came to a head in Witham on St.Patrick's day. The company which had marched from Maldon to Witham on 8 March consisted of about eighty Irish soldiers under their captain, Ross Carew. They had been billeted in the local houses, which only numbered two or three hundred in all. As we have seen already, the townspeople were unwilling participants in this arrangement, because of the probable financial burden, the Catholicism of the soldiers, and the fear of disorder. The first week must therefore have been one of considerable upheaval. The only report which we have

of it claims that it was a time of 'good peace and Contentment', but this was written later, when it was being compared to St.Patrick's day itself. That was the day that everyone remembered, and when the 'mischief' foreseen by the Deputy Lieutenants occurred. St.Patrick was of course the patron saint of Ireland, and of the visiting soldiers. The most detailed descriptions of the event occur in the evidence taken down on the following day from sixteen different people, on several closely written sheets, and sent to the Privy Council. The following summary is taken from those; it will be seen that sometimes the depositions appear to contradict each other or to be selective.[20] Some of the variations may be lapses of memory, but it is also hard to escape the impression that witnesses were understandably anxious to show their own behaviour in the best light, and also that some of them favoured the soldiers whilst many did not.

When St.Patrick's day dawned, as Captain Carew himself later reported, the Irishmen were all wearing red crosses in honour of the saint. This was to become significant. Most of the trouble took place in Newland Street. Two local boys, John Wasse and John Kemett, were the first participants. John Wasse was aged nine, and was probably the son of a weaver of the same name, who lived in a house which is now part of the White Hart. John Kemett was older. He died two years later, when his savings amounted to £3. He left the money to his parents 'in regard that they had most need of it'. His father was also called John; he was a barber and victualler who had earlier been in the courts for disorder and other offences.[21] Before eight or nine in the morning, young John Wasse was 'playeinge in the street' when John Kemett called him into the shop of William Parmenter, a tailor, and gave him 'a redd cross'. He told him to put it on the whipping post that stood by the shop. This is what he was doing when Parmenter's journeyman, Richard Cornell, saw ten Witham boys 'gathered about' the post, which was probably in a prominent position in the market area of the street. Word of the deed reached William Johnson and Edward Pond, two of the assistants of John Hussey, a shoemaker. As Johnson had 'redd coten of his owne', he made two more crosses and tied them on John Hussey's dog, 'one to his head and another to his tayle'. Hussey probably lived at the bottom of the street (on the site that is now nos.126/28 Newland Street, in 1998 formerly Coates' shop, partly Four Seasons). He was no stranger to conflict and may have been something of a local scapegoat. Amongst other troubles, in 1625 five of his fellow townsmen had taken him to quarter sessions, where he was fined for extorting money from twenty-seven people in his role as a collector of funds for supporting troops.[22] So he had good reason to be cautious. His later report about St.Patrick's day claims that on receiving a comment from a soldier about the 'contempt' expressed by his dog, he himself made a civil reply and removed both crosses from the creature, because even though they had not been his doing, he wished 'to avoide offence'.

Not long afterwards, at about nine or ten in the

A captain

This soldier is wearing the uniform of a captain such as Ross Carew, the leader of the Irish soldiers who were billeted in Witham.

morning, Ralph and William Wiseman rode into Witham from Rivenhall. They were sons of the Royalist and near-Catholic magistrate Sir Thomas. Three days previously, two days after he had written to William Smith/Nevill about the soldiers, Sir Thomas himself had been arrested for election irregularities, and appeared before the Privy Councillors in London on St.Patrick's day itself. They decided to send him to the Fleet prison 'till farther Order'. He was however able to continue his public life afterwards.[23] The Wiseman brothers came to Witham on that day because they had 'business' with Robert Bunny. Bunny was one of the men whom we encountered in chapter 2 successfully attempting to keep their immorality from the public eye (pages 19-20). Fifteen years later, he was to be amongst the relatively few people from Witham to sign a Royalist petition, so perhaps his relationship with the Wisemans was friendly as well as commercial. He was innkeeper of the George, the greatest of the Witham inns, centrally situated in the market place (part of it is now the Town Hall, no.61 Newland Street). When the Wisemans arrived, the soldiers were 'dancing with Swords in their hands', having been given 'money to Drinck and to be merry' by Captain Carew. In due course the Wiseman brothers sent for the Captain, and soon they were all 'being merry together'; perhaps religious sympathy helped their friendliness.[24]

Carew's evidence recalls that during the merriment he heard about the affair of the dog, and sent for Hussey, its owner, who retorted that Carew should pacify his soldiers. Neither Hussey nor the Wisemans mention this exchange in their own depositions, but the Wisemans do report that William Skinner, one of the parish constables, then came to them all and reported disorder amongst the soldiers. The next event which the Wisemans recollect was a disturbance at the house of John Hussey, the owner of the offending dog. William Wiseman remembers finding a Lieutenant and some soldiers 'breakinge downe the Lettice of a Windowe', whereupon he pacified them with the help of a message from the Captain, so that they did 'little or no hurt'. Ralph Wiseman recalls that he and Captain Carew went there, that a maide 'looked out of a windowe' and told them that Hussey was hurt, and that while they were investigating, the Captain was called down to quieten some soldiers, which he did by speaking to them 'in Irish'. The depositions of Hussey and his fellow-townsmen give a more dramatic account. Hussey claims that ten soldiers came and 'asked him if he would have a crosse, and he answered he had received crosses enoughe allready from them, because one of them had taken from him a payer of shoes'. At this, they 'drewe their weapons', wounded him, and then 'followed him up to his Chamber'. More soldiers and the Lieutenant came up, threatened to kill him, 'ryfeled his house and tooke awaye his foode'. Carew himself does not mention this visit at all in his own account.

It was the afternoon by this time, because 'not long after', parish constable William Haven intervened, and he had not returned home until one o'clock, when he had 'found the soldiers in fowle disorder quarrelling with the Townesmen'. He was a clothier. He either spoke to Captain Carew, or asked Ralph Wiseman to do it for him, with a request that the Captain keep the peace 'for feare of further Danger'. Both Wiseman and Haven recall in their evidence that as a result of Haven's representations, the Captain 'beate' some of the soldiers and brought them to order. Haven remembers being asked by Ralph Wiseman to hold either the Captain's or Wiseman's horse. On hearing a drum the horse broke away, and Haven was attacked by one of the soldiers whilst a Lieutenant was 'crying out kill him kill him'; he managed to escape to his own house 'by a backe way'. Ralph Wiseman also left for home at this point because he believed that 'all had been pacified'. He does not mention the affair of the horse or the attack on Haven in his report.

He was mistaken about the pacification. According to his brother William, who had stayed behind, Captain Carew then 'Drewe his Sword, and all the Soldiers likewise, and brought out their Colors, and beate upp the drum, and came down the streete towarde London'. The deposition of another observer mentions that some of the soldiers also had their 'pikes chardged'. William Wiseman claims that soon after they had passed the market cross he himself asked the Captain to make a proclamation for the men to put away their weapons, but 'the Captaine marched on'. The market cross was in the wide part of Newland Street, shown below.[25] The Captain asked Wiseman to stay, but he began to leave,

and then heard a shot, though he saw nothing. The Captain does not mention the swords and the drums in his account, and claims that at the time of the shot he was still attempting to pacify the soldiers. He remembers being 'Hett upon the forehead with a bullett out of a window'. Although he thought it was only a graze he went 'to his Chamber to be Dressed of the said Wound', and stayed there. Wiseman wanted the local magistrate, William Towse, sent for, but he was told that Towse was not at home, so instead he asked one of the local men to try and restore order. He later called this man a constable, but it was probably Thomas Browne, a clothier who had earlier been asked to help the constables. Browne himself and some of his other assistants were then attacked by some soldiers and 'very much hacked and ... almost slayne'; both Browne and Wiseman confirm this attack. Wiseman claims that he himself then persuaded the lieutenant to call 'all the soldiers togeather into the George Yarde' (the yard of Robert Bunny's inn, the George). After visiting Captain Carew, whom he found 'faynting and very ill', and being shown 'the Muskett and the bullett', he heard that the soldiers had all been 'quieted'. So 'seeing all at peace', he 'toke horse and rod home' to Rivenhall.

This may have been towards evening, as two parishioners recall seeing Captain Carew in the street as late as four o'clock, which must have been before his injury if the latter really confined him to his room. They said he had been at the door of saddler John Hopkinson and had responded 'yes yes yes' when soldiers asked him

Newland Street, the market area

At the height of the disturbance on St.Patrick's day, Captain Carew and the Irish soldiers marched down the street towards us. The 15th-century building with the clock is now the Town Hall and has a 19th-century brick frontage. In 1628 it was the George inn, where the Wisemans came to see the innkeeper, Robert Bunny, and where the soldiers were called together in the yard at the end of the quarrelling.

permission to take revenge in the town.[26] It seems probable that it was after William Wiseman's departure when two of the Sir Henry Mildmays rode into Witham, because they and Wiseman did not mention having seen each other. These were two of the three Sir Henrys who had originally arranged the billeting of the soldiers in Witham; they lived about ten miles away in the Chelmsford area and had been notified of the trouble. With them they brought several magistrates and other gentlemen, so it must have taken some time to gather their party together. If they did reach Witham after William Wiseman left, then Wiseman, like his brother Ralph earlier, had been over-optimistic about the peace. The Mildmays' report says that on their arrival they found 'the Countrye and Town in Armes, tooe Stronge by fare for the Soldiers, and soe inraged by reason of ther wounded Townsmen and neighbours to the number of Thirtye men'. Captain Carew's wound they felt to be 'dangerous, but as wee hope not mortal'. They recall that at first their attempts to 'dissolve the assembly' failed, and two more soldiers were shot, but eventually 'Sergeant Major Esmonds' disarmed the soldiers and the assembled crowd 'quietly departed'.

AFTERMATH

The third parliament of Charles I met for the first time on St.Patrick's day, whilst Witham was in an uproar. Three months later, in June, the King was obliged to sign the 'Petition of Right' in return for Parliament's co-operation. Its best-known and most far-reaching provision was that taxes and loans might only be levied with the consent of Parliament. Amongst its other sections there was one which forbade the billeting of soldiers and sailors, which was no doubt prompted by the recent problems in the counties. This particular relief was to be short-lived; 'free quarter' of soldiers was imposed by both sides during the Civil War.

At Witham, evidence was taken on the day after the affray by the two Sir Henry Mildmays as Deputy Lieutenants, and three magistrates. One of the three was William Towse, who had returned home to Witham, and the other two were Sir William Maxey of Bradwell juxta Coggeshall and Robert Aylett of Feering. They heard the various stories given above, and in addition, Uriah Zebland, a husbandman, and Thomas Shakerley, a butcher, said that during the morning they had seen two men carrying muskets into a house which had 'windows which looke into the ... George yarde'. One of the men they had seen was a prosperous woolcomber from Witham, George Creswell, who allegedly carried his musket in his hand. Later in the year he offended the congregation of St.Nicholas church because he 'did ... a long time rudely and unreverentlie bounce and knock at the churche doore when he might have gone in at other of the church doores being open'. The other man with a musket was blacksmith Alexander King from Hatfield Peverel, who hid his 'under a leather apron', and was said to have been seen 'walkinge about the Chambers of the said house', wearing a 'plunkett [grey] coloured hat'. The information was all sent to the Privy Council,

together with the two Sir Henry Mildmays' own account, to which they added that they would expect similar trouble to occur daily until they received money to pay the soldiers, because people were too 'enraged' to accommodate them. The Mildmays must have drawn some satisfaction from having the earlier predictions of the Deputies proved correct; they did not apologise for their own personal role in selecting Witham to house the soldiers. In letters to the Lord Treasurer and the Chancellor of the Exchequer, they claimed that townsmen and soldiers had been killed in various places, and that the soldiers would soon be 'pinched with hunger' unless more money was found. The Privy Councillors responded quickly, writing back on 20 March, acknowledging that Witham was 'both smale and poore', information which they may have gleaned from the town's earlier petitions. The Deputies were told 'speedily' to send the soldiers somewhere more 'fit and commodious'.[27]

An anonymous letter written on the following day reported a rumour that there were 'on both sides between thirty and forty slain in this incident'. As pointed out by G.E.Aylmer, this claim seems to have been a false one. Probably about that many were hurt, but none were killed. On 26 March the Duke of Buckingham made a statement to the House of Lords. He made no attempt to excuse Witham in the way that the Privy Councillors had done. He announced that:

> a great Outrage was committed by the Inhabitants of Witham, against the Soldiers ... in which Outrage divers were sore wounded on both sides, and had not the Affray been pacified by the good discretion of the Captain, it had proved both very dangerous both to the Town and to the Soldiers.

Two days later the Privy Council issued warrants for two messengers to fetch seven of the people involved at Witham, including Captain Carew and William Wiseman. They were to appear before the Council in London about the 'mutiny'. Nothing more is known about this summons, so perhaps it was not proceeded with, but Captain Carew did appear to be in custody a month later, when his release was ordered.[28]

On 31 March and 8 April the Privy Council announced that the soldiers which were still billeted in Essex, including those at Witham, would be moved into Kent. A week later the Treasurer of the Army was ordered to repay part of the money owing to some of the counties for billeting.[29] However, the Deputies were still pleading for the refund of over £1,000 in August, when the 'private men' who had lent money were 'earnestly' pressing for repayment, and the towns which were still owed money for billeting were 'much impoverished'.[30] The Councillors then wrote to the Lords Lieutenant of several counties involved, including Essex, asking for the sums to be checked in case the King was being defrauded, and requesting information about priorities for repayment, such as 'particular billetters, keepers of victuallinge houses, or others of the meaner sorte'. They said they still intended to refund the money, albeit in instalments, but that 'the defence of the kingdome' and assisting 'his Majesty's friendes and Allies abroad' would have first call on the subsidies voted by Parliament. At the time the King was spending some of these funds on the expedition to relieve the Protestants besieged at La Rochelle, in France. The Duke of Buckingham was assassinated a week later in Portsmouth whilst supervising the preparations.[31]

In October the Deputy Lieutenants responded by sending in 'verie carefull' accounts, but said that they could not single out any priorities because all the people who were owed money were poor, and many in debt, the better off 'refusinge absolutely' to accommodate any soldiers. They also expressed anxiety at the bad feeling between places which had paid the levy and the 'third part' which had not, and suggested that this might prejudice the King's chances of raising such money in future. No written response was recorded to these further pleas. But a fortnight later La Rochelle was relieved and the English expedition sailed for home. Possibly the resultant financial saving allowed the counties to be refunded in due course. By the end of November it was the behaviour of the many soldiers who had been released from the army that was worrying the Privy Councillors, who warned the Essex magistrates about those who 'wander up and downe the Country or behave themselves disorderly'. The Deputies soon turned their attention to the crises in the county's economy, and the billeted soldiers and the Witham affray became history. One author has suggested that Witham gained revenge for its treatment by including an excessive number of 'out-dwellers' in its assessment for the 1636 Ship Money, but in fact this is not the case; there was an error in writing out the assessment.[32]

OVERVIEW

The decision to send the soldiers to Witham was something of a muddle, and we will never entirely understand it. Although the Privy Councillors did appear in the end to be including the town in their list of suggestions, having adamantly excluded it earlier on, Thaxted was their final favourite, and it was the three Sir Henry Mildmays who selected Witham from the list instead. They were acting as Deputy Lieutenants, but it appeared afterwards that they did not have the support of all the other Deputies. The confusion has given scope for historians to put forward differing theories about the reason for the choice of Witham. One suggests that the Royalist Privy Councillors were punishing a Puritan Witham for resisting the Forced Loan.[33] However, as we have seen, Witham actually paid the loan with alacrity. The second theory, put forward by Brian Quintrell, takes the completely opposite view, that the Puritan Mildmays wished to punish Witham for near-Catholic and Royalist tendencies, and for paying

the Loan and other levies so readily. He relates the Mildmays' position of authority to their support for the Puritan Earl of Warwick, who was gaining ascendancy in the election campaign caused by the King's recall of Parliament in1628.[34] In support of his view he says that the area around Witham was less Puritan and Calvinist than other parts of Essex. The Catholic Southcotts, who are quoted by Brian Quintrell as a possible target of the Mildmays' displeasure, were not actually living in Witham at this time. But nevertheless, it may be that in the minds of the gentry elsewhere in the county, the town was equated with people like the Royalist Nevills and Wisemans from the nearby villages. It was men of this rank with whom people like the Mildmays would be familiar, and, as my evidence suggests, both the Nevills and the Wisemans may have helped to promote the interests of Witham in the debate.

However, Witham town itself was to become notable for its Puritan activism within the following three years. If the Mildmays did indeed feel hostile to Witham itself, was it because they were unaware of its Puritan sympathies for various reasons? After all, Dame Katherine Barnardiston was a woman and did not take part in county meetings, William Towse was often absent, and many of the active parishioners were only of middling rank. Or was it because in fact many people in Witham were still behaving in quite a loyal way at this time in spite of the fact that some of them were Puritans in religion? This might be suggested by the apparent co-operation of the prominent parishioners John Gravener(3) and particularly Jerome Garrard(2) with people like the Nevills and Wisemans over the Loan and the petitions. Gravener is not known for any later disobedience, but, as will be seen in the next chapter (page 106), Garrard was already being criticised for leaving the parish to hear Puritan sermons elsewhere.[35]

On St.Patrick's day it must have become evident to the townspeople that their secular masters, the Wisemans, favoured Captain Carew and the soldiers. Even William Wiseman's alarm over the marching did not prevent him and his brother from putting a favourable slant on the Captain during their evidence of the following day. So perhaps the experience of St.Patrick's day 1628 contributed to the development of a suspicious attitude amongst some of the Witham townspeople towards authority, or at least highlighted some latent feelings. Within three years, William Haven, the constable around whom the Catholic soldiers had cried 'kill him', was an assertive Puritan churchwarden, very positively disobeying his vicar and the King's new bishop of London, William Laud. By then he and his colleagues were claiming new provocation, at both a local and a national level. But perhaps they also remembered the Wisemans 'being merry together' with Captain Carew.

9. CHARLES I (part), 1625-1640

BACKGROUND

The affray in Witham on St.Patrick's day 1628 took place during a very turbulent period in England. The economy, always vulnerable to natural disaster, was further disrupted by the war in Europe. The crisis in the Essex cloth industry reached its peak in April 1629 and continued thereafter. Witham's clothiers claimed that they were afraid to go home because they could not pay their workers, or find them more work. Agriculture was also in difficulties, and in May 1629, some unnamed inhabitants of Witham joined the two or three hundred men and women who demonstrated against grain exports at Burrow Hills near Maldon in the second of two riots. The others who came from outside Maldon were from the cloth towns of Braintree and Bocking. Several of the rioters were hanged.[1] The Privy Council was inclined to criticise local magistrates for not restricting prices and not putting the poor to work, but in the circumstances their powers were limited. People in all occupations were affected. When Witham shoemaker Roger Pasfield was accused in the Archdeacon's court of not going to church, he claimed that he dared not appear in public at church because he was so much in debt, and the judge treated him leniently. This happened in both 1633 and 1635. In the latter year, as an extra precaution, he did not go to court either, but sent his wife to explain the situation. Further distress was caused by several epidemics of plague. During an outbreak in Witham from 1638 to 1641, the parish made a number of pleas for assistance. In spite of the troublesome times, a fall in the level of accusations for criminal offences was noticeable in the Witham area during Charles' reign, though there were specific outbreaks of concern illustrated by several indictments for larceny in 1626 and 1629. The decrease in recorded crime in the town continued for the rest of the century, reflecting a phenomenon which has been noted by historians of both Essex in particular and of England in general.[2]

Charles I dissolved his third parliament in March 1629 after a year. It had first met on St.Patrick's day, 1628. Thereafter he ruled with no parliament from 1629 to 1640, relying on his Privy Council for contact with local officials. Financial pressures continued, typified by his decision in 1636 to collect Ship Money from the whole country, instead of merely the coastal areas. Meanwhile, he took a very active interest in the character of the English Church, helped by William Laud, whom he appointed as Archbishop of Canterbury in 1633. Laud had been bishop of London since 1628, so had already acquired influence in Essex. Laud and the King thought that the modification and diversity of Elizabeth's and James's reigns was wrong, and wished to restore what they felt to be the true Church of England. Laud's policies worked against Puritanism. He was opposed to many aspects of the Puritans' faith, such as their Calvinist belief that only a predetermined 'elect' would be saved. In this respect he was often said to be 'Arminian', following the Dutch theologian Arminius, and he and the King were also felt by some people to be sympathetic to Catholicism. He sought practical changes to support his aims. Thus his instructions emphasised the communion, at the expense of the sermon which was so valued by Puritans. He asked that communion tables which had been moved out into the church should go back into the chancel and be railed in. The ritual of the Prayer Book was to be followed exactly, with its required marks of respect such as standing and sitting for certain parts of the service. Laud disapproved of the way in which the influence of lay people in the Church had increased since Elizabethan times, and the additional preachers and acts of worship which they often promoted were to be suppressed. His adoption of the 'Book of Sports' was seen as an encouragement to disregard the Puritan observation of the sabbath, and as a threat to public order in general. As has been written by James Sharpe, Puritans found unexpectedly that they faced a threat 'not from the rude multitude, but from the agents of the Church of England'.[3]

As a result, the earlier compromises broke down at many levels, and many writers have described a newly 'political' dimension to Puritanism dating from this time. In Essex, opponents of both Charles and Laud amongst the gentry continued to be led by the second Earl of Warwick of Great Leighs. In him and many others like him, the causes of Puritanism and Parliament often merged, though the two were not always synonymous. A resurgence of Puritan religious activity was typified by the activities of Thomas Hooker, appointed lecturer at Chelmsford in 1626; men and women came 'from all parts' to hear his lectures.

The power of Laud and the King was maintained until 1640. Then in that year the King's methods of raising funds to quell the Scots began his downfall. Opposition to his independent action was already gathering when in April he recalled the 'Short' Parliament. These elections were perhaps the first to be dominated by religious and political issues. Royalist Henry Nevill of Cressing Temple stood for one of the two Essex county seats and was defeated.[4] The King dissolved Parliament again three weeks later when it refused to grant him money. By September he had been humiliated in the Scottish campaign and was unwillingly forced to call Parliament again. By the time of the new elections for the 'Long Parliament' in October 1640, the balance of power had moved away from him, and the degree of mutual suspicion between him and Parliament had greatly increased.

LOCAL OFFICIALS

Robert Aylett

William,Laud's most important representative in Essex was Dr.Robert Aylett, an ecclesiastical lawyer who also wrote sacred verse. When he was only in his thirties he had been chosen for two posts which obliged him to sit in judgement in the ecclesiastical courts, and also to try and enforce the Church's policies in many other ways. To begin with, in 1617, he had become the official of the archdeaconry of Colchester. His predecessors there had only held short-term contracts of four or five years, and often the area had been divided between two of them. Aylett was responsible for the whole archdeaconry, and a change in national policy meant that his post was permanent. This, together with the preoccupations of the archdeacon, Henry King, elsewhere, gave Aylett a newly powerful position. Two years later, in 1619, he had acquired the even more significant role of bishop's commissary for Essex and Hertfordshire, serving most of the county. He retained both of these positions until the courts were disbanded in 1641. He also became a magistrate during the mid-1620s, and took evidence at Witham after the St.Patrick's day disturbance in 1628, but he ceased to be active locally in this role after about 1630.[5]

His presence was particularly noticeable in central and north-east Essex. His official residence was at Feeringbury, four miles north-east of Witham. In 1630 a Feering man suffered from this proximity when Aylett acted as prosecutor, witness and judge against him, for absence from church and for exhorting others to absent themselves also. Aylett presided over almost all the Archdeaconry and Commissary courts held in Colchester, Kelvedon, Braintree and Chelmsford. More distant ones, comprising about half the sittings in all, he usually delegated to surrogates, often local clergymen. He also held hearings at his home or in London. Probably many records of this latter practice have not survived, but a few examples are to be found in a small collection of papers that has recently come to light. These mix his work for the archdeacon and the bishop, suggesting that the two posts became closely linked whilst he was in office. Three of the cases relate to the turbulent life of Witham during the 1630s and will be discussed later.[6]

Robert Aylett's connection with mid-Essex and with the Witham area was not just a recent one. He was probably born in Witham itself, or possibly in the adjoining parish of Rivenhall, so many of the people he dealt with in court would have been known to him since his childhood. His father was Leonard, a yeoman and former high constable, who lived in Witham when he died in 1612, asking that the town's Puritan curate, Abraham Gibson, should preach at his funeral. Leonard's goods were only worth £19, but he had properties in ten parishes, some inherited from his father. He left these to Robert, together with a musket and armour. In 1624 Robert married as his second wife Penelope, who was the cousin of Sir Thomas Wiseman, the Rivenhall magistrate.[7] During the 1630s Aylett spoke enthusiastically of people like Wiseman and other nearby Royalists and supporters of Laud, like Henry Nevill. He used their assistance in implementing Laud's new policies, which he himself appeared to endorse enthusiastically. We know that he was also very friendly with his cousin's husband, Sir John Lambe, a prominent Laudian ecclesiastical lawyer. In the mid 1630s Laud's Vicar General, Sir Nathaniel Brent, was sent on a long tour of southern England to investigate the state of the Church. After he had visited Kelvedon in 1637, he felt that he 'could not finde any great fault' in the surrounding area. He reported to Laud that its virtue:

> may be ascribed to the care of Dr.Aylett, who
> dwelleth there. I humbly desire your Grace to take
> notice of it, and to encourage him.

However, it has been suggested that Aylett was really a moderate, attracting the respect of people of diverse beliefs, and several documents do show another side to him. For instance in 1637, writing about how to deal with Puritan troublemakers in the Church, Aylett said that:

> it is dangerous to purge out alltogeither lest we
> weaken too much the Body, but such tupping
> overworking ones must be abated.

And although he lost his official positions when Parliament acted against the King's supporters in the early 1640s, he appears to have come back into favour later. Thus in 1642 he signed the great Essex petition criticising the King, in 1646 he was chosen to carry out the induction of new ministers, and in 1651 he was one of the few Essex men whom Parliament re-appointed as magistrates after having dismissed them in 1642. His cousin, Jeremy Aylett of Rivenhall, was one of the Parliamentarian county committeemen for Essex. Robert died in 1654 at the age of 72, so did not live to face the test of the Restoration of the monarchy in 1660. There is a monument to him in Great Braxted church.[8]

Magistrates

As the reign proceeded, Laud and the King called on the magistrates as well as the ecclesiastical officials to enforce their policies. To begin with, the chief magistrates who worked on Witham cases were Robert Aylett himself, who ceased to do so in about 1630, and the Puritan William Towse, Dame Katherine Barnardiston's husband. For a few years Towse became rather more active in this field than previously, but then he moved away to his own home at Takeley after Dame Katherine's death in 1633. The quarter sessions clerk recorded in February 1634 that he was 'old', and he died in October 1634 at the age of 83. Thereafter there were no more magistrates resident in Witham itself for fifty years. So during the 1630s, the town was supervised by representatives of the usual three neighbouring households, namely Henry Nevill of Cressing Temple, Sir Thomas Wiseman of Rivenhall, and to a lesser extent Sir Benjamin Ayloffe of Great Braxted. They were all Royalists, and also often said to be Catholics. Henry Nevill became established at Cressing Temple after the death of his brother William Smith/Nevill in 1630. In 1637 Robert Aylett wrote of Henry as being a more 'forward and active a man' than any other in the service of the King; this was in connection with proposed action against unauthorised Puritan preachers in and around Coggeshall.[9]

Other local secular officials

One of the two high constables of Witham half-hundred usually came from Witham town, and they were successively the two men who were its most senior and prosperous townsmen. Thus Jerome Garrard(2) held the post from about 1628 to 1636. We have already seen how he worked with magistrates Wiseman and Nevill in preparing petitions about billeting in 1628. However, he was also a Puritan activist. He quickly made use of his new post, raising an objection at quarter sessions in 1628 about Witham's vicar Francis Wright, which will be discussed later, and complaining at the assizes in 1630 about disorderly alehouses in Witham that had been 'licensed without the consent of the officers and chief inhabitants'. It is not known whether he resigned or was removed in 1636, though he probably died soon afterwards and so may have been ill. He was succeeded by John Gravener(3), the enthusiastic collector of the Forced Loan, who served from 1638 to 1650, though he tried unsuccessfully to resign in 1644. He was much more cautious than Garrard though he eventually became a supporter of Parliament. From 1626 to 1647 the lesser role of the sheriff's bailiff was held by Witham yeoman/innholder William Brooke, later said to be a Royalist.[10] The names of Witham's secular parish officers do not generally survive for this period, but we can perhaps obtain an overview of the influential men in the town from the list of trustees chosen in 1627 by George Armond(2) when he set up a new almshouse charity. He himself had a Catholic grandfather and a brother-in-law said to have 'papist' beliefs. Nevertheless, the nineteen men he selected held a variety of religious views and included some committed Puritans.[11]

Churchwardens

It will be seen later that the churchwardens were also diverse in their opinions. The two holders usually served for one year only now, the elections taking place at around Easter time. Although the minister played some part in this process, his exact role in Witham is unknown.[12] It was usual by this time for most of the town's wardens to be literate. Out of the nine whose names and abilities are known during the 1630s, only

one, the tanner Richard Barnard, could not write his name. They were thus even more capable in this respect than the select people who made wills.[13] The wardens of the 1630s were also wealthy, with a median value in the Ship Money assessment of twelve to thirteen shillings, compared to three shillings for all those assessed. As had been the case since about 1600, one of them was nearly always a clothier. In some parts of the country, fears began to be expressed at this time that churchwardens could become a threat to ecclesiastical authority, and we shall be able to observe this happening in the Witham of 1631.[14]

DAME KATHERINE BARNARDISTON AND HER FRIENDS

We saw in chapter 7 (pages 72-74) how Dame Katherine Barnardiston had acquired contacts in Essex, Suffolk and London through her own family and her marriages, and had also become wealthy. She and her third husband William Towse had maintained close relationships with the Puritan clergy of Witham before 1625. Here I shall consider her role during Charles' reign, in the last seven years of her life. The main source of information for this is her amazing will of 1633. Most of it was written by her husband William Towse and a scribe, though the many personal phrases suggest that she was probably dictating it. And she wrote the religious preamble down herself.[15]

Her place in society

The will sheds light both on her wealth and on her wide circle of influence. In addition to valuable furniture and plate, and an interest in a manor in Suffolk, specific bequests of money alone totalled £7,700. Some of her fellow Puritans were uneasy about elaborate funerals, but for her the expectations appropriate to her social status carried more weight. She gave about £1,400 for her executors to arrange her funeral with 'blackes and Harolds' in the parish of her birth in London, St.Michael le Querne, where her parents, her first husband, and her brother were also buried. The church was destroyed in the Great Fire of 1666 and leaves no trace (it was approximately where no.5 Cheapside is now). Another £700 was left to individuals to buy 'blackes' or mourning clothes, £20 for her body to be embalmed by the man who had performed the same service for her brother John Banks two years previously, and £100 for the imposing monument at Kedington which provides our only surviving image of her today (shown on page 101).

The largest personal bequests were for her many relatives, as shown in the charts in appendix 2 (pages 163-66). Having no children of her own, she was able to indulge her cousins, sisters, and nieces and their husbands with lavish gifts of money, silverware and furniture. She also remembered some of the well-known family of her first husband, Bartholomew Soame, and in addition left money for mourning to the ageing Puritan parson of St.Mary Colchurch in London, who had been her minister when she and Bartholomew had lived there together forty years previously. But her own and her second husband's families, the Banks and Barnardistons, figured most.[16] For the enormous task of executing her will she appointed two executors from each of those two families, and singled out the Barnardistons in the gift towards education at Cambridge which was one of her many charitable donations. London charities also benefited, some being the same as those helped by her brother John Banks two years earlier. We can see that she had also liaised earlier with her relatives as trustees in property transactions, had lent them money, was godmother to their children, and housed some of them as 'servants' in her household. In addition she had 'undertaken to bring up' her young namesake, Katherine Banks of Hadstock, the daughter of one of her cousins.[17]

Her beliefs

Dame Katherine does not appear to have attracted censure in the courts for religious dissent. Either she avoided specific nonconforming behaviour, or her wealth and status exempted her. However, her will helps us to appreciate her beliefs, particularly as she wrote the religious preamble herself, only three weeks before her death. Her distinctively spiky writing was larger and perhaps more confident than it had been when she had put her name to her marriage settlement over thirty years previously. We can almost hear her voice and feel the depth of her fervour, with its mixture of confidence and anxiety. She began:

> First I bequeath my soule into thy handes of god father sonne and holy ghost whom hast first made me and then hast given thy sonne to become man and died for my sinns o father for thy sones sake have mercye on me O Lord Jesu Christ thou son of god thou hast bought me with thy precious blood by one oblation sufficiently for all that beleeves on thee O Christ god and man which are in heaven have mercye upon me and be thou my merciful mediator for me unto thy father that I may be saved. O holy ghoste coequall with the father and the sonne have mercie upon me worke thy divine power on me thorough thy gratious inspiration drawe me unto Jesu Christ that I may find favour and be saved Amen.

> My Confession: I acknowledge and confesse with all my harte that I am a sinner yea and such a sinner as hath neede of the grace mercye and favour of god. My faith grounded and with hope, I beleeve that the lord will have mercye upon me for he hath made me and he hath promised to save me this I beleeve that whether I lyve or dye I am the Lordes.

> My hope: I hope that I shall find both grace and mercye for my sinns of god the father even for Jesu Christes sake in him I beleeve he is my Redeemer he liveth for ever and ever he maketh intercession for

sinns so I know that I now am a corruptible bodie but I hope through Christ to rise an incorruptible bodye now a mortall body but but [sic] thorow Christ and his merittes I hope to have an immortall body for as many as shall be saved shall shine in the kingdome of god as bright as the sonne this my faithe and hope I laye up in mind the mind of my soule trusting onely to be saved thorow the merittes of Jesu Christe god and man which is in heaven from whiche I looke againe the which shall change my vile body and make it like his owne most glorious body whereby he is able to subdue all thinges to himself O Christe have mercie upon me thou hast redeemed me O Christe save me.

Following this, she wrote a long series of quotations from both the Old and New Testaments.[18]

Her ministers

Dame Katherine asked for the sermon at her lavish funeral to be preached by Stephen Marshall, the vicar of Finchingfield, who had earlier connections with the Barnardiston family. She left him £10 and black mourning clothes for his trouble. He was one of the most famous and active of Essex Puritan ministers, renowned for captivating an audience. A Visitation reported to William Laud in 1637 that Marshall 'governeth the consciences of all the rich Puritans in those partes', and that he was:

> held to be a dangerous person, but exceeding cuning; noe man doubteth but that he hath an inconformable hart, but externally hee observeth all.

This shrewdness enabled him to keep his position during the 1630s, but nevertheless to be invited to address the new and rebellious House of Commons in 1640. Dame Katherine also left £200 for:

> such religious good and charitable worke as my Executors shall, by and with the advice of the forenamed Mr.Marshall the Minister, thinck best to be bestowe upon as may be most for the glory of God.

Local magistrate Henry Nevill later reported this bequest, which was clearly regarded as suspicious, and Marshall was questioned about it during the 1637 Visitation. He had given £150 of it to John Dury, a Scot who had recently begun a long campaign to unite all European Protestants, which brought him into favour with English Puritans. The donation was said to have been made as a result of a complex series of recommendations across the country. The other £50 he gave to an Anthony Thomas who lectured in Wales and 'preacheth in the Welch toung, of which he saith there is greate necessity'. To those who were concerned about such matters, Wales had long been considered a benighted area devoid of Protestant enthusiasm and preaching.[19]

Other famous Puritan ministers favoured by Dame Katherine were two successive vicars of the adjoining parish of Terling; which had close associations with Witham. The first was Thomas Weld, sometimes known

Dame Katherine Barnardiston of Witham

Dame Katherine was born in the City of London, probably during the 1560s. There she met and married her first husband, Bartholomew Soame, a girdler. After he died in 1596, she married Thomas Barnardiston, of the well-known Suffolk family. They rented Witham Place in Powershall End from the Southcotts, and came to live there in considerable grandeur, being by far the most prosperous people in the parish.

Thomas died in 1610 and Dame Katherine married lawyer William Towse. They became a strong force for Puritanism in the county, assisted by her many influential relatives (shown in Appendix 2). She had no children of her own, but many step-children, godchildren, nephews and nieces.

It was through her that the Barnardistons were related to Robert Mildmay, her sister's son-in-law. They all liaised in the appointment by Mildmay of Thomas Weld as vicar in neighbouring Terling in 1624. She was godmother to the Welds' first son, John, born in 1625. Thomas Weld became a very well-known Puritan clergyman, attracting enthusiastic visitors to his church from Witham. He was eventually removed by Archbishop Laud and emigrated to New England.

Meanwhile, Dame Katherine conducted a campaign against Witham's own vicar, Francis Wright. She died in 1633, and left £100 for this monument in the church at Kedington in Suffolk, which also commemorates Thomas Barnardiston and his first wife Mary.

as Wells, who was appointed in 1624. He will be
discussed separately later. The next was John Stalham,
who was newly arrived in Terling when she made her
will in 1633; she left him £6 for mourning clothes. She
also contemplated making a bequest to another nearby
minister, Nehemiah Rogers, 'preacher at Messing', but
she deleted his name. He appears to have had Laudian
friends as well as Puritan ones, and writers seem to vary
in their interpretation of his views, so it may be that
uncertainty prompted Dame Katherine's change of
heart.[20]

In addition to remembering the families of the Witham
vicars and clergy of James' reign, Dame Katherine was
close to one of the new curates in the parish, John
Preston. He had obtained his B.A. at Cambridge in
1622. Although he was quite well-known in Essex, it
should be noted that he was not the same person as the
older and more famous Puritan divine of the same
name, who was closely associated with Parliament and
the court, and died in 1628. Witham's John Preston was
only curate here for a short period during 1628 and
1629.[21] However, he stayed in the town with the help of
Dame Katherine, suggesting that his initial appointment
may well have been as a 'lecturer' funded by her or her
friends. In her will of 1633 she left his family some
money for mourning clothes, and he and his son were
given an additional £10 each. Furthermore, she
instructed that he was to 'have his dwelling in my house
where now he keepes until he be better provided for'.
Perhaps he preached there at Witham Place. The
appointment of private chaplains was common amongst
gentry and aristocratic families, and it was frequently the
women of these households who particularly called
upon them for spiritual reassurance. Laud attempted to
restrict such chaplaincies in 1633, but many probably
continued nonetheless. John Preston did stay for a time
after Dame Katherine's death, because a month after
her will was proved, he witnessed and probably wrote
the will of Elizabeth Greene, a Witham widow.
Furthermore in 1634 he attended an 'unlawful meeting'
with some fellow-parishioners, which will be discussed
later. Soon afterwards he became curate in the adjoining
parish of Little Braxted, and then in the new conditions
of 1642 he came into greater favour and was made vicar
of nearby Messing, where he died in 1656.[22]

Her contacts in Witham

Dame Katherine's male relatives were busy about their
counties and elsewhere as businessmen, magistrates,
Members of Parliament, and seekers after influence in
the government. As a woman these opportunities were
not open to her, despite her wealth and status. So she
was able to take a particular interest in humbler matters
closer to home in her adopted parish of·Witham, and
her will shows that she was familiar with its activities
and people. She gave £18 to the parish 'to make them a
Dynner for the whole parrishe', on which occasion the
'Ringers' were to have £2. Generous funds were
provided for the regular provision of bread for the poor,
and in addition there was a more personal bequest of £1

each to 'all the poore Neighbors that dwell betwixt
goodman Gouldeings howse to goodwife Colemans'.
Her servants and their families received money and
sometimes their bedding. Witham brewer Arthur
Barker, and Mrs.Armond and Mrs.Nicholls, probably
Elizabeth and Joan, widows of the prosperous George
Armond(2) and Hugh Nicholls, were given money for
mourning clothes. We are not sure of their religious
allegiance.[23] However, the rest of her local bequests
were to people who are known to have been Puritan
activists. One of her closest relationships seems to have
been with the gentry and yeoman Garrard family of
nearby Moat farm. Although they were prosperous they
were very much less so than she was. They received
several donations in addition to their mourning clothes.
She was godmother to Bartholomew, the young son of
Jerome Garrard(2), and she left him £20. This was a
special honour; the other ten godchildren mentioned in
her will were either her relatives, or the sons of
ministers. It seems possible that Bartholomew was
named after her first husband. Robert Garrard(2),
Jerome's adult son, witnessed her will. She waived the
tithe payment which Jerome owed her, probably a
considerable sum. In addition, Thomas Bromley, a
nephew of Jerome, was to receive £5 towards the keep
of his children. She made no mention of the other most
prominent Witham family, the Graveners; we saw in the
last chapter (pages 87-89) that John Gravener(3) had
been diligently collecting Witham's Forced Loan while
her stepson Nathaniel was imprisoned for resisting it.
But three more favoured Puritan parishioners were
Jerome Greene, and clothiers William Baxter and
Nathaniel Nowell, to whom Dame Katherine had earlier
lent money; perhaps they had been suffering during the
crisis in the cloth industry. Her will excused them from
some of their debt.

Finally Dame Katherine's will shows us her interest in
Witham church itself. She had already established a trust
in 1630 to provide for preaching there on Tuesday
mornings, to be funded by the rent of a house in
Chipping Hill that still bears her name (shown on the
facing page). Weekday preaching was something
favoured and often sponsored by Puritans, including
Katherine's brother John Banks in London. It was soon
to be specifically outlawed by William Laud.[24] Her
endowment in Witham was probably inspired not only
by her general belief but by a feeling that what was
already provided was inadequate. We can see this from
two other bequests in her will, which made it quite clear
that although she supported many clergymen, Witham's
vicar, Francis Wright, was not amongst them. Firstly she
left £10 to cordwainer or shoemaker James Princet.
This was a considerable sum for an ordinary local
tradesman; and it was given for a special reason, namely
'the greate paynes he hath taken in following the suite
against Mr.Write Vicar of Witham'. Secondly, a bequest
of mourning clothes was only to be given to the town's
vicar if 'it be not Mr.Wright that is now vicar'. Francis
Wright was indeed in charge of the parish when she
died, and the nature of the 'suite' against him and some
of the reasons for her distaste will become apparent
during the rest of this chapter.

Chipping Hill and Barnardiston House

Barnardiston House is the building to the left of centre with a brick frontage and seven windows. The back part of it
dates from the 16th and 17th centuries. It was bought by Dame Katherine Barnardiston in 1626, and in 1630 she set up
a trust so that the rent from the house could pay for preaching or for education in Witham. She did not live there herself.
It is now no.35 Chipping Hill. On the left is the house of the blacksmith at Chipping Hill forge.

LOCAL CLERGYMEN

Francis Wright, vicar of Witham 1625-1643 and 1660-1668

Bill Cliftlands first 'discovered' Francis Wright; he has
been outstandingly generous with his material, and in
encouraging me to find out more. Bill had finished his
research before some of my information, such as the
Barnardiston connection, came to light. I hope he will
find it intriguing.[25]

Dame Katherine's mansion at Witham Place was within
sight of the vicarage and the church, across the river. As
lessee of the rectory and its tithes she was entitled to a
prominent pew and was responsible for maintaining the
chancel. So when Wright was appointed the two would
soon have been well aware of each other. The vicars of
Witham were chosen by the bishop of London, who at
this time was George Montaigne, the predecessor and
staunch ally of William Laud. We do not know how
deliberate the selection was. Bishops were often limited
in their choice and could not know their whole diocese
intimately, but on the other hand, Witham was well-
known to Robert Aylett, the bishop's adviser. I have
only very recently discovered anything of Wright's
background. He was born in Newby, just outside Ripon
in Yorkshire, in an area where nearly all the local gentry
were of Catholic and Royalist sympathies. He went to
Queens' College Cambridge and graduated there.[26]
Many Cambridge colleges were Puritan strongholds, but

John Twigg who has studied Queen's in particular,
suggests that it may only have been 'moderately Puritan'
at this time, even though it housed the noted preacher
John Preston.[27] Wright was ordained in November
1621, at the age of about twenty-six, and then spent
about two years in the Middlesex parish of Finchley
before coming to Witham. His sons Francis and
Thomas were born soon after he arrived here. Later
reports say that he had a 'modest wife', but we know
nothing else about her. Their vicarage house may have
been rebuilt by Wright; the record is somewhat
ambiguous. It was said to have had twenty-one rooms
in 1637.[28]

Wright's contribution to the general running of the
parish may have been limited. It was during his time, in
1630, that the income of Greene's almshouses stopped
being collected from the tenant of the charity's land in
Springfield, and although Wright and the
churchwardens were ordered to make amends in 1639,
the matter was not actually put right until sixty years
later in 1699. Wright never wrote or witnessed any
surviving wills in the town. Even the busiest of his
predecessors usually managed to do this occasionally.
Many wills were still being written by the aging Edmund
Halys. The only positive reference to Wright in a will is
by Frances Burchard, wife of yeoman Robert(2). In
1632 she gave him twenty shillings 'if he shall preach at
my buryall'.[29] This seems to be expressing some doubt,
though it is true that the Burchards are not recorded as
opposing Wright.

Curates and teachers

There was something of a revival of teaching during the 1620s, and Laud, appointed bishop in 1628, granted three new licences for Witham in that year. One went to the 25-year old Christopher Webb, M.A., later rector of Great Braxted and a fervent Royalist. The other two were given to local men, namely Edmund Halys, who was to assist Webb, forty years his junior, and John Totteridge. By 1630, however, it was ordered for some reason that Witham's teaching should instead be restricted to a new curate, Thomas Young, who had replaced Dame Katherine Barnardiston's friend John Preston. We know of one other teacher, George Eatney, who was here in early 1637; he was later appointed to his own parish by Parliament. Of two more curates, Thomas Herris in 1631 and Jonas Prost the younger in early 1638, we shall hear again later.[30]

Thomas Weld, vicar of Terling 1624-1631

In November 1624, a year before Francis Wright's appointment to Witham's vicarage, the fervent Puritan Thomas Weld was chosen as vicar three miles away in the adjoining parish of Terling. He was soon to become notorious.[31] Historian Kenneth Shipps has discussed how his arrival may have originated in a promise made by Dame Katherine's stepson Sir Nathaniel Barnardiston. Nathaniel had lived at Witham in his youth, but had been the head of the family in Kedington, just across the Essex border, since the death of his grandfather in 1619. There he began to establish what has been called 'a combination of broad family interests behind the puritan cause ... unparalleled in East Anglia'. In 1623 he offered Samuel Fairclough the living of the parish of Barnardiston, adjoining Kedington. Fairclough, who was then lecturer at Clare, only accepted the place on the understanding that his friend Thomas Weld, another possible candidate, would be provided for elsewhere. Weld had been born in Sudbury, further east along the county boundary, and by this time was a rousing lecturer in nearby Haverhill, with considerable influence at Cambridge University also. It was a year or so later that Weld was appointed to Terling by the patron there, Robert Mildmay. In support of the suggestion that this move was due to the Barnardiston influence, I have discovered that Mildmay was Dame Katherine's 'nephew', as she called him. Her sister Mary Deane was the mother of Mildmay's wife Joan. Furthermore, when Weld baptised his eldest son John in Terling church in June 1625, soon after his arrival, Dame Katherine became the boy's godmother, and presumably attended the ceremony. When she died eight years later she left the boy John £5.[32]

1625-c.1628: WITHAM PARISHIONERS' PROTESTS, AND THE FIRST VISITS TO TERLING

Having described the people involved, I shall now attempt an account of local events during Charles' reign.

As soon as he arrived, Thomas Weld's vicarage at Terling became one of the centres of Puritan activity in Essex. During 1625 a young colleague, Thomas Shepard, soon to be well-known, came there to stay. It was quite common for an established minister to take a new graduate under his wing for a while. Both men visited the lectures of the famous Thomas Hooker at Chelmsford, and met with Hooker and other 'worthies' at regular fast days and other meetings, some of them held in Terling itself.[33] However, we have no such reports of encounters between Weld and Witham's Francis Wright, the two men who were on the one hand Dame Katherine's friend, and on the other her own vicar and enemy. They must have seen each other at events like Visitations, but our knowledge of their rivalry is indirect, the first intimations dating from the second of June, 1626, seven months after Francis Wright's arrival.

On that day twenty-four Witham people were accused in the Archdeacon's court of not attending Wright's church services. For most of them, this was not mere idleness. Sixteen of them were said to have gone to Terling instead to hear Thomas Weld. No-one from any other parish was similarly accused. To get there, many of the Witham residents would have passed Dame Katherine's mansion at Witham Place, as shown in the drawing on the facing page (and also on the front cover). Whether she joined them we do not know. Unlike her, they did not have the use of a coach and horses; most would have walked, though the more fortunate might have travelled on horseback. Another four people were thought to have gone to other unnamed churches, and only four merely to have been absent. Six of the suspects were women. One of the men, Francis Lea, was also accused of disrespect to Wright in Witham, in:

> refusing to kneele at the holy communion being thereunto requested by his minister, and for his unmannerly going forth at that tyme skipping on the pewes and so disturbing and distracting the heart of the congregation.[34]

Kneeling and sitting during certain parts of the service were often at issue in such disputes, some patterns being regarded as scripturally decreed and therefore acceptable to Puritans, whilst others were considered to be Catholic. Twenty-one of the twenty-four suspected absentees went to the court hearing in Kelvedon church and gave their excuses to the judge, Robert Aylett, and his registrar Edmund Tillingham; this was an unusually good attendance. Some were very outspoken and made quite clear that it was the contrast between the two vicars that had influenced them. Thus Daniel Redgwell and joiner Philip Pledger, together with their wives, said that their reason for going away from Witham was because they 'cannott understand their owne minister'. As Wright was a Yorkshireman, the difficulty may have been linguistic as well as ideological. The Redgwells had actually moved to Terling by 1631. And Peter Emmins asserted that he went 'to Terling Church to heare that there which he could not heare at his owne ... namely a good sermon'. The sermon was a particularly important feature of the service for Puritans and Thomas Weld's in Terling were especially notable. Other defaulters said sheepishly that they had only been absent once, or that they had not intended any contempt. John Browne claimed that he had been ill, although his wife confessed to going to Terling. By the end of two more hearings, fourteen of the twenty-four defendants had been excommunicated for not appearing in court at all or for not coming back to certify their attendance at Witham church.[35] A comparison of figures 7 and 8 (page 22) suggests that the particular problems of 1626 were peculiar to Witham and that there was no similar wave of accusations in the archdeaconry as a whole.

The most prosperous of the absentees of 1626 was also the most deliberate. He was joiner Philip Pledger, whose remarks were quoted above. He and his wife Susan were also the most persistent, re-offending several times during the following decade. In due course their son George became a Quaker. Also of reasonable status was the wife of clothier William Skinner; he was a churchwarden a few years later. She had gone to Terling with their son Richard, a weaver, but both pleaded that they were only absent for one afternoon, and were dismissed with a warning; they are not recorded as offending again. In contrast, most of their fellow suspects were of the 'lower middling' or even the poorer sort, although they were unusually literate, with an ability to sign which was comparable to that of willmakers.[36]

The road from Chipping Hill towards Terling

Witham parishioners went this way to hear the preaching of Terling's vicar, the Puritan Thomas Weld,
between 1626 and 1631. Dame Katherine Barnardiston lived at Witham Place, behind the long brick wall,
on the other side of Chipping bridge (there is a coloured version of this picture on the front cover).

The social status of Witham's worshippers at Terling was soon enhanced by the attendance of Jerome Garrard(2), who was shortly to be high constable, and was helping at this time to prepare petitions about the soldiers billeted in Witham. His family had been resident in the parish for over fifty years, and his father Jerome(1) had owned the devout book *The Doctrine of the Gospel*, published in 1606.[37] Jerome(2) was a friend of Dame Katherine Barnardiston and was one of the three most prosperous men in the parish. He and his wife Mary may already have been going to Terling church for some time when the Bishop's Consistory court came to Kelvedon in March 1628, just before the St.Patrick's day disturbance, and heard that they were both 'often absent' from Witham church. Jerome went to court and responded:

> that there being neither sermon nor catechisms in the afternoones on the Sabboth dayes he and his wife have gone to other Churches to heare sermons and namely to Terling Church.

The main accusation against Garrard on that day actually concerned the fact that he had been keeping the key to Witham's church chest, although he was 'neither churchwarden nor officer'. He claimed that this was because he was a charity trustee, and that the contents of the chest all related to the charity, which probably concerned almshouses. At about the same time he appeared in the Archdeacon's court 'for refusing to paye 6s.8d. for the buriall of his daughter in the Church'. Arguments about burials often arose from the form of service used, and in 1626 Witham's Jerome Armond had refused to pay 'for breaking up the Church for the buriall of his late wife' at Kelvedon.[38] Garrard did certify later that he had returned the key and had attended Witham church, but he did not pay for the burial. His family were never far from the various disputes with Francis Wright during the following years.

Sixteen other Witham people were called to the Consistory court at Kelvedon in March 1628 with Garrard. Nearly all of their offences related to Sundays. Some had been drinking or working during the service, whilst seven, including Philip Pledger, who had earlier been the senior absentee in 1626, had deliberately refused to go to their own church, four of them 'wilfully and obstinately', after being 'both in private and in publique admonished by the minister'. These four did not come to court, but clothier William Curtis, another absentee who was also accused of adultery, did attend. It was said that on 'being demanded by Mr.Wright vicar their, why he did not come to Church, he answered "shall I go to hell"'. When he was questioned in court, he admitted to going 'many times' to Terling church. Terling had not been mentioned in the actual accusation against him, which leads us to suspect that some of the other people merely said to be not attending Witham church were in fact visiting Terling.[39]

The significance of absences from Witham church at this time can be shown statistically. From 1570 to 1640 as a whole, absentees accounted for twenty-eight per cent of the accusations against Witham people in the Archdeacon's court, but during 1626 and 1627, they comprised seventy per cent, the other alleged offences being fairly evenly divided between working on Sundays, non-payment of rates, being drunk, and having illicit sexual relationships. But it was not only numerically that the absences from church were distinctive, it was that they entailed visiting Terling to hear Thomas Weld. The 'gadders', as they were known, would have been shamelessly visible on their three-mile journey, riding or walking past Witham's own church, and past Dame Katherine Barnardiston's front gate, perhaps singing psalms as they went. Only rarely were dispensations granted by the bishop for people to go out of their parishes to church. It appears that not only did the other church have to be nearer than their own, but that the parishioner had to be very unwell. Examples were Robert Gravener of Standon in Hertfordshire, who in 1602 was troubled 'both with the gowte and stone', and Thomas and Alice Clarke of Henham in Essex two years later, who were 'ould diseased and decrepit people', separated from their own church by a 'way very fowle and unfitt'. For healthy parishioners to take this decision for themselves was quite a different matter, and implied division of the Church. In fact one historian has suggested that gadding to hear sermons, which had been a tradition in some Puritan communities since Elizabethan times, was the beginning of an unconscious move towards the formation of separate Christian sects.[40]

We do not know the names of many of the Witham churchwardens at this time. Yeoman William Nicholls and clothier Thomas Damatt were wardens in 1628, when they were reprimanded in the Bishop's Consistory court for not reporting the offensive William Curtis in spite of hearing about him from Francis Wright. However, it was mentioned on the same occasion that they had been urging Elizabeth Totteridge to attend Wright's services.[41] And it was they and their predecessors who had made the accusations against all the earlier absentees from church. So it seems that during this period, vicar Francis Wright was able to rely on some support from local office-holders even though he was losing some of his parishioners. However, he was soon to face official opposition too.

1628-1632: OFFICIAL INVOLVEMENT, AND MORE VISITS TO TERLING

The high constable and Francis Wright

In 1628 Francis Wright was presented at the Easter quarter sessions in Chelmsford about his behaviour at St.Nicholas church on Easter day. At Easter more than any other time it was important for parishioners to take communion. It was alleged that he had:

> with much disturbance violently thrust out of the chancel door many of those persons which were prepared to receive the Communion which persons the day before had given their names and paid their offering to him.

This took place 'after divine service and sermon and the people repairing into the Chancel to be partakers of the

Sacrament'. The result is not known. The objection was raised by the new high constable of the half hundred, the prosperous Jerome Garrard(2), friend of Dame Katherine Barnardiston. He had earlier acted in a personal capacity against Wright, as we have seen, but was now in a position to make an official move.[42] In 1628 the Witham churchwardens still showed little sign of joining Garrard. In fact one of them was a personal enemy of his, clothier Henry Wood. Soon afterwards, in 1629, the whole parish was caught up in the major crisis in the cloth industry.

Thomas Weld in trouble

Terling's Puritan vicar Thomas Weld had soon made his mark in his own parish as well as in Witham, and on one occasion in 1627 his zeal even brought him into conflict with his patron Robert Mildmay.[43] In July 1628 William Laud became bishop of London. As was customary, his first Visitation was conducted soon afterwards. It reached Kelvedon church in September, where it was noted by the Vicar General Arthur Duck that Weld was to be asked to certify his 'conformity'. He did not do so, and the case was put onto the agenda of the Bishop's Consistory court in December, also in Kelvedon. When the day came, Weld was not there. The choice before the judge was to ask him to appear at the next court instead, or to immediately inflict the lesser sort of excommunication, the standard punishment for non-attendance. On this occasion he chose to excommunicate. He was John Dodd, vicar of Coggeshall, acting as a substitute to Duck, and he may have taken some pleasure in his task. Two years previously, Weld's friend Thomas Shepard had been afraid to be sent to Coggeshall as lecturer, because he considered Dodd to be 'old, yet sly and malicious'. A recent study of Coggeshall by Chris Johnson concluded that although Dodd may have begun his long career as a religious Puritan, he was strongly opposed to radicalism and to any subversion of authority. His awareness of the situation in Terling and Witham would have been enhanced by his links with Witham's cautious Gravener family. He had been a 'loving friend' of the Coggeshall father-in-law of John Gravener(3). [44]

Weld continued at Terling in spite of Dodd's decision, and his visibility in the records increased thereafter, as did Laud's determination to control his diocese. Just before Whitsun in 1629, 'Mr.Peters, a suspended minister', was said to have preached in Terling church on a Thursday. The churchwardens denied responsibility in the Archdeacon's court before Robert Aylett. He suspended their right to hold lectures, but restored it under strict conditions a week later, after they had made a special plea. The culprit was the famous Hugh Peters, who had lived in both Essex and London, and at about this time was on his way to Holland after a dispute with the previous bishop. He and Weld had a mutual friend in Thomas Hooker, lecturer at Chelmsford, and the three of them must have met many times thereafter during Peters' long career as one of the principal opponents of Laud, and as a

leading Puritan preacher and activist successively in the Holland, New England and Civil War Britain. Later in 1629, Weld and forty-eight other Essex ministers wrote to Laud in defence of the 'peaceable' Hooker, and expressing their esteem for him, but Hooker was removed from his lectureship shortly afterwards and went to New England. Emigration to the American colonies was a solution adopted by several dissatisfied Puritans in Essex around this time. There is no firm evidence of any Witham residents joining them, though emigrant William Freeborne, probably of Maldon, did have relatives and property in the town.[45] By March 1630 a Terling surgeon was planning to follow Hooker, and Weld had sent the settlers £30.

In May 1630 the archdeacon's official Robert Aylett was concerned about weekday lectures given by Weld in Terling; such lectures were not favoured under Laud. The matter was eventually dropped without Weld appearing in court. It was at about that time that Weld had a 'younge scholler' staying with him in Terling, who may have attended a night-time conventicle with some of the parishioners, though when Aylett eventually heard of the accusation a year later, the suspects denied it and escaped with a warning. In November 1630 Laud included Weld in a list of eleven Essex ministers who were 'not conformable in opinion or practice'. On 16 December Weld was called to London for interrogation by Laud himself. So also was his friend Thomas Shepard. By this time Shepard was lecturer at Earls Colne, where he had been criticised by Aylett for being unlicensed. One of his parish officers had been suspended for supporting and praising him. Weld and Shepard attended the London hearings together, and Shepard, not of course an impartial observer, later described Laud's demeanour there, saying that he 'looked as though blood would have gushed out of his face, and did shake as if he had been haunted with an ague fit'. Shepard himself was forbidden to preach in the diocese again until he certified his conformity. Weld, at his own request, was granted more time to consider whether or not he should subscribe to the Articles of the Church. Two days afterwards it was reported in a letter to John Winthrop, governor of Massachusetts, that 'divers godly lecturers and ministers dayly are put by' and that 'Mr.Weld of Essex is now upon the stage and expects his doome'. Correspondence with Winthrop, a relative of Robert Mildmay and hence distantly of Dame Katherine Barnardiston, is one of our most fruitful sources of information about these times. Subsequently, Weld twice failed to appear before Arthur Duck at the Consistory court in St.Paul's, in February and May 1631.[46]

It was also in May 1631 that some of Weld's followers in Witham again visited his church, on Whit Sunday, and they continued to do so on several Sundays during the next four months. It may well be that they had in fact been going there often during the previous five years, ever since we first heard of the gadding in 1626, and that only Weld's own increasing fame had drawn the matter to official attention again. Meanwhile, the final reckoning against Weld himself drew near. On the first of July he went to Fulham Palace for another personal interrogation by Laud, during which he thanked the bishop for allowing him time to consider his position, and told him that 'he was not yet perswaded in his conscence to subscribe, not desired any longer time of Consultacion'. Laud therefore suspended him from his post. Two days later three men and a woman from White Notley went to church in Terling, having often been there previously. They were challenged in the Archdeacon's court by Robert Aylett later in the month. One of the men confessed to not kneeling when taking communion from Weld on earlier occasions, and another admitted telling his own minister 'in derision' that he 'would give sixpence' for his sermon. Also in July, Weld's fourth child, Edmund, was baptised at Terling. On 1 September, Laud and Weld met again at a Visitation in Kelvedon church. When asked to subscribe, Weld answered 'the Lord Knowes I cannot', and Laud issued a full excommunication against him. An attempt by Weld and Shepard to discuss the matter with Laud shortly afterwards in Dunmow church failed and they made a hasty escape on horseback. Weld failed to appear at St.Paul's in October as requested.[47]

The curate of Terling, Nathaniel Bosse 'denounced' the excommunication. He officiated during Weld's absences, and had been in trouble in the courts himself since May for Puritan offences such as not wearing the surplice, omitting parts of the service, and not crossing children in baptism. He and his churchwardens were later accused of neglecting their duties.[48] Witham people continued to go to Terling church during September, and so may have heard Bosse instead of Weld. On 24 November 1631 Weld was finally and permanently deprived of his post by the Archbishop of Canterbury, five bishops, and six other ecclesiastical dignitaries sitting as the court of High Commission in London. Very few other Essex ministers were completely removed in this way, in spite of frequent criticism. Bosse was also suspended shortly afterwards and other ministers preached in his place, allegedly without wearing the surplice. In January 1632 Laud reported to his colleagues that Weld had gone to Amsterdam, and on 9 March Weld set sail from London for New England with his family on the *William and Francis*. He arrived there in June 1632 after an enjoyable voyage, settled in Roxbury, Massachusetts where he acquired several hundred of acres of land, and was much in demand. Many people writing to his fellow-settlers sent him their love thereafter, including Sir Nathaniel Barnardiston. Weld in turn wrote an enthusiastic letter to his former parishioners in Terling in 1633. On his return to England in 1641 with Hugh Peters he mocked Laud and went on to enhance his fame with his work in north-east England.[49]

Soon after Weld's deprivation, both the Bishop's Consistory court and the court of High Commission heard allegations that he had actually been bribed not to subscribe to the Articles of the Church, by having land bound over to him. In the latter court, in January 1632, it was Laud himself who named a figure of £100 a year, a considerable sum, settled on Weld's children. In the former, in December 1631, two of Weld's 'neighbours' were implicated, and it was suggested that Nehemiah Rogers, vicar of Messing, could provide more information, though this does not seem to have been pursued. One of the suspect neighbours was named as 'Gamlee'.[50] So it is interesting that there were two men called Robert Gamlin in Weld's congregation in Roxbury Massachusetts, though they do not seem to have had any great wealth. Robert the elder may have been a Terling man and may have travelled on the same ship as Weld to New England. Robert the younger was from Coggeshall and probably went about a year later. His wife was the widow of Thomas Mayhew, whose father was a Kent man; this caused early researchers into emigration to assume that the Gamlins were from Kent also. I have explained my own interpretation in the notes.[51] There was a Mayhew family in Terling also, whose connection, if any, with the Coggeshall Mayhews is not known. They were prosperous; it will be seen later that Mrs.Elizabeth Mayhew appeared on an unexplained list of Terling and Witham people in the early 1630s.

The Consistory court at Kelvedon, December 1631

Weld's deprivation did not mean that the accusations about the summer's gadding to Terling from Witham were forgotten. They were brought to court in December 1631, together with many other matters. If the Archdeacon had known of the offences he had nevertheless felt it was more suitable for them to await the visit of the Bishop's Consistory court, when it toured various churches in Essex and Hertfordshire over a period of twelve days. Bill Cliftlands discovered the relevant entries in the record and told me about them with his customary generosity. At some of the sittings, the judge was Laud's Vicar General Arthur Duck himself, but at others there were substitutes, Thus the session in Kelvedon church on 14 December dealing with the Witham deanery was presided over by none other than Robert Aylett, who so often supervised the lesser courts held there. The innumerable summons had been issued by the long-suffering apparitor from Witham, William Salter. But regular attenders would nevertheless know that the sitting was something out of the ordinary, by the fact that it was organised and recorded not by the archdeaconry's familiar Edmund Tillingham, but by the bishop's lawyer Robert Cooke. There were nearly a hundred accusations from the deanery heard in all. About half were from the more rural areas, including one against a Kelvedon man 'for entertaining of fidlers to be plaieing in his house in time of divine service', and half concerned Witham itself. No-one from outside Witham was accused of going to Terling church. The Witham 'gadders' were between twelve and twenty in number, including several married couples.[52] Some of them are known to have also gone to Terling in earlier years, notably high constable Jerome Garrard(2). However, their leader this time was Jerome's son, churchwarden Robert Garrard(2), whose wife accompanied him. Many of the Witham people were faced with several accusations, some concerning other matters.

Moat farm and Chipping Hill, from across the river Brain

Moat farm was the home of the prosperous Garrard family, who were Puritan activists.
It is the large house on the left of this drawing, with its outbuildings in front.
It was demolished in the 1950s and the site is now occupied by Chase House in Moat Farm Chase.

Witham churchwardens, 1631

Attention having been drawn to the parishioners of Witham in this way, the Church authorities had also discovered that matters were not at all satisfactory in Witham itself. The town's churchwardens were particularly suspect. They were Robert Garrard(2), William Haven and William Baxter. They served at different times during 1631, but the exact sequence of their appointment is unclear. Robert Garrard(2) generally called himself a gentleman, and may have lived at Moat farm, seen above, with his parents. Not long afterwards, in 1633, he witnessed Dame Katherine Barnardiston's will, and received money to buy black clothes in which to mourn her. William Haven, a clothier, had already had the misfortune to be a parish constable at the time of the St.Patrick's day disturbance in 1628 when he was involved in a rather violent encounter with the soldiers, and with a horse belonging either to their captain or to Royalist Ralph Wiseman. It is possible that he or his son left Witham around 1650 and joined the Quakers in Colchester. Warden William Baxter, another clothier, had come to Witham from Cavendish in Suffolk about twelve years previously and lived in Newland Street (on the site now occupied by no.16, Roslyn House). He borrowed money from Dame Katherine and in her will she forgave him the loan.[53]

Vicar Francis Wright seemed to be losing control of these churchwardens in 1631. They had already

unsuccessfully presented him at the Archdeacon's court in June because in the previous month:

> he hath not gone the perambulation of the circuite of the parish this last yeare according as he is enjoyned by the Canon and for not reading divine service in the Church on Ascension daye.[54]

And the hearings of December 1631 revealed a catalogue of disruption by the wardens, much of it deliberately directed against the practice of the Laudian Church. Some of their disobedience was personal rather than official. Thus Garrard, Baxter and Haven were all complained of for 'seldome coming into Church untill devine prayers be ended'. Furthermore, when Garrard did attend, he did not kneel 'in time of devine prayers but stands bolt upright in his pew', and in contrast remained seated through 'the reading of the Gospell and the Confession of the faith'. We have already noted the significance of gestures such as these.

Just as striking are the accusations levelled against the three men in their official capacity as churchwardens. William Baxter and William Haven had earlier been:

> ordered by Mr.[Robert] Aylet to buy a new bible and a new prayer booke and a larger and longer surplis and hood, according to the King's order, yet have not, and still refuse to buy them being often desired by the curate.

The Prayer Book and the surplice were both associated in many people's minds with Laudian ritual. In addition:

> they were injoyned by Mr.Aylet in his parochial visitacion to white [whitewash] the Church, which

they did and then blotted out the Creed the lords prayer and ten Commandments which were written on the wall of the said Church, and being spoken to by their minister to rewrite and new paint the same, they refuse and say it is an unnecessary charge.

On Whit Sunday, when he was allegedly in Terling, Robert Garrard(2) had not provided wine for communion and 'the people would have gone away had not the minister entreated them to stay'. And in July:

> in the afternoone ... very few were at Church, and being required to take the names of those that were absent and present them, and likewise of those that refused to send thier Children and Apprentices to be catechised, he refused.

Haven, who may have served with Garrard as well as with Baxter, faced a similar accusation, and was also accused of 'dayly absenting himself from his parish Church, and never yet sending any of his owne children to be catechised although he have many'! Two months later, in September, Garrard had not made amends, and:

> Of 150 Children fit to be Catechised, not above two or three at the most came, and the vicar charged the Churchwarden aforesaid to take the name of those that were absent and present them, for that he had heard how strickt the Charge the Bishop of London had given him for the same, but he refused it.

And together Garrard and Haven had been allegedly:

> seldome coming into Church on Sundayes in the forenone untill prayer be ended, but stande at the Church doore and collect money, to the disturbance of the Congregation by reason of the great noise they make there in time of Devine Service, and the same Garrad being reproved for it by the Vicar there, replyed that he had the word of god for it.

Haven denied this in court, whilst Garrard admitted that 'he did gether money at the Church Doore ... but he denieth that he said he hath the word of god for it'. Garrard was also accused of protecting his colleague Haven by not reporting a rumour that he had made his maid servant pregnant, and had then given her '40 shillings and his wives best petticoate' to deny that he was the father. And finally, both Garrard and Haven had omitted to present all the other 'abuses' mentioned in court, including an accusation against John Oliver for having sexual relations with Garrard's maid. The Archdeacon's court at Kelvedon, to which they should have reported, had been noticeably short of presentments from Witham since 1628.

Other parishioners, 1631

It is not surprising that the churchwardens had not presented the 'abuses' to the Archdeacon, because most of the offending parishioners appear to have been committing much the same sort of offences as the churchwardens. A few of them were the subject of the usual sort of accusation, like being drunk, but many of them had been going to Terling church and also making trouble at home. Thus cordwainer James Princet was:

> never present at the reading of devine prayers, he

never kneeles, never stands at the confession of the faith nor the reading of the Gospell, but comes into the Church at the psalmes immediately before sermon.

He was Dame Katherine Barnardiston's favoured beneficiary, of whom we shall hear yet more later.

Two other demonstrators were Elizabeth Totteridge, who had been in trouble previously for not going to Francis Wright's services, and the John Oliver who was said to have had a relationship with Garrard's maid. Elizabeth was said to have been:

> reading aloud the singing psalme in the interim of singing it, and refusing to desest ... though shee were desired by Mr.Wright, who sent first his Clarke and then the Churchwarden to her to that purpose, yet nevertheless did continue her lowdenes to the offence and disturbance of the Congregation.

John Oliver was accused of 'not frequenting prayers and ... for indecently behaving himself, weareing his hat on his head in service time who being reproved by the Curate derided him'. The wearing of hats in church was an issue that was to recur.

Altogether, twenty-three Witham people, including the three churchwardens, were referred to during this Consistory court hearing of December 1631, of whom nineteen were involved in either absence from church or disruption, or both, seven of them women. Eight of the nineteen were members of, or relatives of, the Garrard family. The highest ranking were gentlemen Robert Garrard(2) and his father Jerome(2). Joiner Philip Pledger was typical of most of the rest, the men having their own businesses and known occupations. In contrast, when Pledger had been accused of going to Terling in 1626, he had then been one of the few better-off people amongst a generally lower-ranking group.[55]

In 1631 nineteen of the twenty-three offenders actually went to the court hearing, an unusually high proportion. Two who did not were James Princet and his wife. They were said to be 'at London', where, as we shall see later, they may well have been pursuing their vicar in yet another way. Of those who did attend the court, the great majority admitted their offences. They were called to attend the Consistory court in St.Paul's cathedral on 8 February 1632 before Vicar General Arthur Duck, to certify that they had confessed publicly before their minister and fellow-parishioners. However, only churchwarden Robert Garrard(2) went there, and none of his offences seemed to have been resolved. He denied some of the charges, and was asked again to produce a certificate for others, and to pay his fees. He and some of the others were called there again in November 1632 but to no avail, and we do not know what happened after that because the records do not survive. The only accusation that was pursued rigorously and resolved was the one against William Haven for misbehaving with his maidservant. He went to London to Arthur Duck's offices twice in the summer of 1632 and eventually produced a certificate from fellow-parishioners declaring his innocence, so that the case was finally dismissed on June 6, the day after vicar Thomas Weld of Terling arrived in Boston.[56]

Opposition to curate Thomas Herris

When Robert Garrard(2) waited to face Arthur Duck at St.Paul's in February, 1632, the man just in front of him in the queue was Thomas Herris. Herris was Francis Wright's curate in Witham, and he was in court to certify that another parishioner, who was not present, had made amends for allowing drinking on Sundays. It is unlikely that the two men made a friendly journey to London together. Three weeks previously Garrard had gone to the Archdeacon's court at Kelvedon in his role as churchwarden, and claimed that Herris was 'a Common Alehouse haunter and a comon swearer', who had been 'rayling and usuall talking in Church in tyme of divine service and sermon to the disturbance of the Congregation'. Herris had responded to the effect that these actions were part of his duties, in that he was 'driven sometymes to take his diett at victualling houses and that for his necessary sustenance he doeth go to sutch houses', and that he had only railed in church 'when he hath seen some of the parishioners behave themselves irreverently in the Church in tyme of divine service, as many there ... do'. The case was dismissed.

A year later, in 1633, Garrard repeated the accusations, saying that Herris was 'a Common Alehouse haunter ... and swearer and ... a common rayler and reviler, as the Common fame and reporte goeth in the parish'. Furthermore, when he had been:

> using the accustomed exhortation in the Common prayer booke, and repeating these words in the same, vizt. "I praye as many as be heere present to accompany me with a pure hearte", he added these words or the like in effect of his own invention ... "which you cannot doe or will not doe".

It was said that this caused 'the greate discomforte of the people'. This time Harris failed to appear, and proceedings of excommunication were taken against him, giving the Witham churchwardens their first success in court against one of their clergyman.[57]

1632-1636: POSSIBLE PURITAN CAUTION

Dame Katherine Barnardiston died in 1633. By that time her demonstrative ally Robert Garrard(2) had relinquished the post of churchwarden, but it had not been a peaceful change. Attending the election meeting on Easter Monday, 2 April 1632, was Robert's father Jerome(2). Also present was clothier Henry Wood, who had himself served a term as churchwarden in 1628 just after Jerome and his fellow-gadders to Terling had been in court. A dispute arose between the two men at the 1632 meeting, which continued into several succeeding Sundays. As a result, Wood complained to the Archdeacon's court in May that Jerome Garrard(2) had struck him 'at the communion table', 'rent his cloake by violence', and called him a 'Cosening knave'. Garrard was called to Robert Aylett's house in Feering to explain himself, and said that at the election meeting and at

other times, he had been 'provoked' by Wood's making 'opprobrious and scandalous speeches' He admitted that he himself 'did make replie in a chiding and brawling manner, for which he is sorrie'. Aylett suspended Garrard from entry into the church on the charge of 'chiding and brawling in the Chancell'. But at another special hearing five days later in London, he was absolved.[58] This was unusual treatment, but then Garrard was an important man; he was still high constable and had considerable social status. The dispute may well have had some basis in ideology, with Wood being a supporter of vicar Francis Wright, because the new churchwardens of 1632 who replaced Robert Garrard(2) began gradually to report some of their Puritan parishioners to the Archdeacon's court, in a way that had not been done since 1628. For a time their successors did likewise.

As described later, vicar Francis Wright's behaviour was being discussed intermittently in London by about 1632, but we hear nothing of him in Witham itself during this period except for a strange episode in 1633 when twenty-one year old Ambrose Purcas, a Bachelor of Arts, was called to Aylett's home in Feering to be questioned. Purcas had been in Witham for about six months. He held no appointment, 'not so much as deacon', but admitted that at Wright's request he had often 'read divine service in Witham Church upon Sundayes both in the presence and absence of Mr.Wright', despite having told Wright that he was not in holy orders. He had also conducted a wedding without banns or licence, and 'buried two or three Children in the Churchyard'. Purcas seems to have disappeared soon afterwards, and I have found no record of Wright himself having been censured about him, but other information may have been lost.[59]

The mystery list of names, and the 'unlawful meeting' of 1634

The information about Ambrose Purcas comes from some papers of Robert Aylett, Laud's chief local representative, which have only recently come to light. Amongst them there are two other documents concerning Witham. One is a list of names with no explanation or date; in fact it was probably written between 1630 and 1633. At its head are five prosperous Terling residents. There is the wealthy Puritan Robert Mildmay, lord of the manor there, his wife Joan, who was Dame Katherine Barnardiston's niece, a Mrs.Mayhew (probably Elizabeth, widow of Francis), and a Mr. and Mrs. Bradshaw. A Thomas Bradshaw was to witness Dame Katherine's will in 1633. The other forty-seven people named, mostly married couples, came from Witham and were reasonably prosperous. They included three men who were 'servants' of Dame Katherine Barnardiston, two of whom were her relatives. But the temptation to imagine that we are witnessing a fervent Puritan gathering, perhaps even connected with Dame Katherine and the support of Thomas Weld, is shaken by the character of the remaining Witham people on the list. They were very broadly based in their opinions. They did include Dame Katherine's friends the Garrards, but there was also the cautious John Gravener(3) with his wife Priscilla, and at least two men whom we know later as Royalists, William Brooke and Jeffrey Whale.[60]

The other document is dated April 1634 and lists thirty-six Witham men and women who had allegedly attended an 'unlawfull assemblie in theire parish' and were interviewed by Aylett, probably at his home. The scribe at first referred to the meeting as a 'conventicle' but deleted this word; a conventicle was an unauthorised or secret meeting, and was a term particularly favoured in describing religious gatherings. The suspects were fined, but none of them paid the full sum, and excommunication for non-payment was being considered. I have not yet found any other record of this event, either before or after Aylett's list was compiled, so the outcome is unknown. There were twenty-four households represented, probably not far short of a tenth of the total number in the parish; they consisted of twelve married couples, nine men on their own, two wives on their own, and a widow. Mostly they were notably prosperous, of middling rank and above, and, like the people on the other list, espoused a considerable range of opinion. Thus they included some recognised Witham Puritans, notably the disobedient ex-churchwarden Robert Garrard(2), and his cousin Thomas Bromley, both beneficiaries of Dame Katherine Barnardiston. With them was her clergyman protegé John Preston. But there were also two important men who usually stood somewhat aloof from the parish's disputes at this time, the gentleman and scribe Edmund Halys, and the wealthy clothier John Gravener(3). There were also three men who later put their names to the 'Royalist' peace petition of 1643.[61] The nature of the meeting must remain as difficult to interpret as the earlier list of names, and my initial excitement at discovering the two documents soon turned to puzzlement. Just possibly even these multifarious people all felt the need at this time for some guidance from clergyman John Preston instead of Francis Wright, but we cannot be sure.

Other activity in Witham, 1632-1636

Although we do not know the purpose of the meeting of 1634, it is probable that the suspicion which it aroused came from official fear about the creation of groups separate from the established Church. Such concern was made more explicit in the description of Witham's Solomon Turner, a Witham glover, when in 1635 he was presented with some of his fellow parishioners at the Bishop's Consistory court for non-attendance at church. He was said to be 'a great schismatic', the literal meaning being that he wanted to divide the Church. He was reasonably well-off for a craftsman, and his will was witnessed by two prosperous Puritans, gentleman William Allen and yeoman Jerome Skingley. It had no religious preamble at all, in the style of the later Quakers.[62]

However, since the removal of Robert Garrard(2) in

1632, the Witham churchwardens themselves do not appear to have been interested in joining any schismatic groups, and seem to have been fairly dutiful, particularly in 1635 when they were Anthony Westwood and Arthur Barker. Barker was a brewer who lived in Newland Street (at the site now occupied by no.153 Newland Street, the Swan inn in 1998). An attender at the 'unlawful meeting' mentioned earlier, he had been left money for mourning by Dame Katherine Barnardiston, but if this shows us anything about his beliefs, he nevertheless felt obliged to be obedient when in office. Westwood's name had been on the 'mystery' list of parishioners.[63] The two men presented about a dozen people together in the Archdeacon's court for not attending church or not receiving Communion in 1635. Another group of six appeared for the same offence in 1636. We do not know whether or not they were going to Terling like their predecessors of 1626 and 1631. The new vicar there, John Stalham, who had been given mourning clothes in Dame Katherine's will, had been cautious in public at first. But he was soon in conflict with Laud, and was to become an noted minister of Civil War Essex. The Witham absentees of 1635 and 1636 did include two associates of Dame Katherine. Her ally James Princet appeared on both occasions, whilst Nathaniel Nowell, a clothier to whom she had lent money and then forgiven him some of his debt, was amongst the first group. Nowell retaliated, accusing churchwarden Barker of coursing 'a hare upon the Sunday before Whitsunday last'. This was dismissed after the court heard Barker's defence, that when 'going into his fields upon Sunday after dinner, his bitch going with him started a leverett and killed it, but he had not intent to Course a hare upon that day'.[64]

Catholics

One result of Dame Katherine Barnardiston's death in 1633 was that the Catholic Southcott family reclaimed their mansion at Witham Place, which she had rented from them since about 1600. Her husband, William Towse, moved away after her death. One branch of the Southcott family had since spent some time in the neighbouring parish of Little Totham, and made periodic court appearances from there.[65] John Southcott esquire, the judge's son, owner of Witham Place, was by now in his eighties. He had lived in Bulmer on the Suffolk border, in close proximity to several other Catholic families, from the 1590s to the 1620s, and had then spent some time at another family home, Merstham in Surrey. He must have returned to Witham soon after Dame Katherine's death, as Southcotts appear in the Witham records in December 1633, for the first time for over thirty years. From then onwards John himself, his son Edward with his wife Elizabeth, and his grandson John (later Sir John), were all named along with their servants in regular accusations of refusing to attend Witham church, and not paying rates for its maintenance. Some of these were heard in quarter sessions, doubtless under the auspices of the Puritan Jerome Garrard(2) as high constable, whilst others were presentations in the Archdeacon's court by the churchwardens. At this time it was probably relatively easy to unite people of a variety of different beliefs in hostility to Catholics, particularly as Catholicism was being rumoured to attract the sympathy of the King and of Laud, who had become Archbishop of Canterbury in 1633.⁶⁶ John Southcott the elder died in 1637, leaving a will with a Catholic preamble. His family upheld the religious tradition thereafter, and the assize court began to take an interest in them also. We shall meet them again during the Civil War.⁶⁷

There were now no other visible Catholics resident in Witham of the sort that there had been during the Southcotts' previous residency, at the end of Elizabeth's reign. However, the atmosphere of the 1630s did lead to the arrest of Francis Barrett for remarks that he made when travelling through Witham in 1634. Barrett, described as 'a poor straggling fellow', was an unemployed mariner with an impressively varied history; he was heading for Wivenhoe to seek out a previous employer, having heard that the Earl of Warwick, previously his chief in the navy, was not at his home at Great Leighs. Whilst spending the evening at John Brewer's alehouse at Witham, he had 'called for diverse Juggs of beere, and haveing drunke them with his host and hostess', they asked him if he had heard of a Jesuit lately executed in London for treason. Jesuits were teaching and campaigning Catholics. Barrett allegedly replied that he did know of it, and that 'there is three more of his companye but it skills not wheare they bee, I know not'.⁶⁸ The Brewers had him arrested, and he was sent to Colchester castle for suspected treason, but was probably discharged after a few days. John Brewer, who was a weaver as well as an alehousekeeper, may have been a professional informer. One of his earlier victims was an Ardleigh man accused of criticising the King in 1621, but other cases in which he was a witness were more mundane. He was also in trouble himself several times for allowing disorder in his house, and as a result he, like Barrett, had spent three days in Colchester gaol in 1618.⁶⁹

Francis Wright at the Court of High Commission, 1632-1635

Whilst his parishioners had been involved in these concerns, Witham's vicar Francis Wright had been the subject of an action which had also demonstrated the prevailing suspicion of Catholicism, though at a much higher level. The case took a slow course through the highest ecclesiastical court, the court of High Commission in London, between 1632 or before, and 1635. When Dame Katherine Barnardiston left Witham cordwainer James Princet £10 in 1633 for his 'great paines ... in the suite against Mr.Write', it was this action to which she referred. So she may well have played some part in instituting or sponsoring the proceedings. As we saw earlier, Princet was 'at London' in December 1631; perhaps he was involved in this 'suite' at the time. He was to act as a witness against Wright again later, in 1643.⁷⁰

Records only survive for two meetings during the earlier part of the proceedings, when in May 1632 the bishops and others assembled in court at Canterbury. Vicar General Arthur Duck represented the prosecutors or 'promoters', and Wright's counsel was another well-known lawyer, Dr.Thomas Eden. At the first meeting on 3 May they were told that Wright had been accused of making his maid servant pregnant, the adultery having taken place at an inn in Greenhithe in Kent, just across the water from south Essex. Then at another session on 8 May, William Laud, then still bishop of London, had announced that he had been told of a 'worse matter' also. This was that:

> this Wright, in his Cupps, related to one Sir Thomas Wiseman's sonne and some others, that the Bishop of London was present with Doctor Price when he received the Sacrament of a Preist, and that he dyed a Romane Catholicke. And Sir Thomas Wiseman's sonne saying he thought most of the Bishops were in their judgementes Romane Catholiques. Wright swoare, yea, that they were, and most of the Cleargie too; and for my part, I am of that minde, and wished that if he dyed not soe, that bread which he then tooke up and eate might not doe him good.

Laud said that he had asked Robert Aylett to investigate and that the witnesses had 'stood to' their story. Theodore Price, referred to here, had been sub-dean of Westminster before his death in the previous December, and there had been a well-publicised controversy about his friendship with Laud and about what his religious preferences had been when he died.⁷¹ We have already noted the alleged Catholicism of Sir Thomas Wiseman, a cousin of Aylett's wife Penelope, and we know of his sons as participants in the St.Patrick's day affair of 1628 in Witham.

A month later it was ordered that both sides should put in their evidence before August 1632, but no more information about the progress of the case during the following two years seems to have survived. The next reports which we have, dating from April 1634, show that in the interim Laud's allegations about Wright's religious beliefs seem to have been dropped. By then the charge was 'adultery with Margaret Claydon alias Umpton his late servant, and . . . drunkenness and other miscarriages in his ministerial function'.

Between April 1634 and June 1635 the case was referred to in court on fifteen separate dates, but postponed on each occasion, whilst Wright's representatives quibbled about administration and tried to gather up more witnesses. Except for James Princet, we do not know who supplied information for the prosecution, but the names of eight of Wright's supporters survive. One of them, Laurence Charles, whose residence is not recorded, admitted in 1635 that much of his evidence had been falsified, and he was fined £10. Five of the others can be traced as having lived in Witham. One was John Alexander, a yeoman/innkeeper who later signed two rather contrary petitions during the early 1640s, the Parliamentarian one of 1642 and the more selective Royalist one of 1643. Another was John Parker. Of middling status, he may have been a habitual informer, because in 1634 he gave evidence against a currier accused of not undergoing the proper apprenticeship; that sort of case was often presented by informers in the hope of receiving a share of the fine. Probably the most prosperous lay witness for Wright from Witham was gentleman John Greene, who owned considerable property including a shop on London Bridge. He was enrolled under a 'compulsory process' some time after the others. However, he failed to arrive when called, and there is no record of his coming later. He had also 'informed' on another occasion. His name appeared on the Royalist petition of January 1643, but later in 1643 he changed sides in the matter of Francis Wright, and actually gave evidence against him in the House of Lords. Wright's last two Witham witnesses were newcomers to the town. Gentleman William Thursby had only just arrived from Bocking. He died soon afterwards in 1637, though his wife stayed on. His son and heir Christopher, who lived in Northamptonshire, lent money to Royalist Henry Nevill in the form of a mortgage. Lastly, Matthew Mootham had come to Witham from Great Tey.[72] Thus Wright's Witham supporters do not appear to have been a group of united or established parishioners. Two clergymen from nearby parishes also spoke for him. They were Alexander Bonniman and Edward Strutt. Strutt gave evidence for him again in 1643. They were rectors of Kelvedon and Faulkbourne respectively. Bonniman resigned in 1641, but Strutt was to be deprived of his living by Parliament in 1644, when he was criticised for having supported Wright.[73]

In June 1635, at least three years after the proceedings against Wright had opened, the court of High Commission found that the accusations about drunkenness and 'miscarriages in his ministerial function', were not proved. But concerning the adultery the court felt that 'there was matter sufficient prooved to putt him to his purgacion'. This meant that he had to find six people as compurgators to speak for him; as he was a clergyman they had to be clergy also. Other unspecified charges were deferred until 'the courte shall thinke meet' and were not heard of again; just possibly these related to the Catholic connection.

In October 1635 Wright came back with his compurgators. They were men of noticeably non-Puritan inclinations, four of whom later incurred the displeasure of Parliament, when one of them, Joseph Bird from Belchamp Otten, was alleged to have been 'an excessive drinker', 'often so distempered that he is unfit for his calling', and frequently to be found 'sitting up drinking on the Sabbath till twelve o'clock at night'. Wright swore 'uppon the Evangelists' that he was innocent of the adultery, his compurgators said they believed him, and the court 'pronounced him lawfully and canonically purged and ... restored him again to his good name'.[74]

1637-1640: PURITANS TO THE FORE AGAIN

When Laud's Vicar General Nathaniel Brent visited

Essex in 1637, he was mainly concerned with suspected Puritan clergymen, and did not give Witham any special attention. He remarked on the good control which was exercised in this part of the county by Laud's local commissary, Robert Aylett. At Easter 1637, two prosperous men, Jerome Skingley of Powershall and Henry Bunting were elected as Witham's church-wardens. We know little of Bunting, but Skingley, a yeoman, was probably the first of Witham's Puritan elite to have held the post since his irreverent predecessor Robert Garrard(2) in 1631. He had not been very closely involved in the local debate hitherto, though he was accused of not kneeling at the prayers in 1632, but during the 1640s he showed his Puritan and Parliamentarian sympathies. It was also in 1637 that Jonas Prost the younger arrived to be Witham's curate. Although his activities in the parish are not recorded, we do know that his father, another Jonas, was minister of the Dutch church in Colchester, and had probable Puritan inclinations, having been a pupil of Richard Blackerby, one of the Barnardistons' protegés in Suffolk. Six years later Jonas the younger was to give evidence against vicar Francis Wright. In early 1638 the town began to suffer a three-year epidemic of plague which taxed its finances and organisation, and which was perhaps seen as a judgement by some of the parishioners.[75]

From 1637 onwards there was a revival in the number of presentments by Witham's wardens in the Archdeacon's court relating to the sort of behaviour that was most offensive to Puritans. There had been surprising absences during the previous years. Thus there had been no Witham cases in that court concerning working on Sunday from 1628 to 1634, and none for drinking from 1629 to 1635, though alehouses continued to be presented in quarter sessions as before. It may be noted here that although such prosecutions have not been given much space in this chapter, with other matters coming to the fore, it was found that when they were being made, the suspects continued to include many people of middling rank as they had during James' reign.[76]

Francis Wright at the Bishop's Commissary court

The return of concern for the parish's morals may have helped to prompt another challenge against Francis Wright in July 1638, though the formal presentments were made by the court officials. This time it was in the Commissary court, the regular court held for the bishop by Robert Aylett which did not very often hear Witham cases. Wright claimed there that 'there is no fame or reporte of the premisses within the parish of Witham', though it would be surprising if this were true. The charges were long and comprehensive. It was said that:

within these tymes in severall Innes, tavernes and other tipling houses within the parish of Witham and other parishes thereunto adjoyning at unseasonable hours both in the daye and night he hath behaved himself in a disorderly and unbeseaming maner, being distempered and overtaken with excessive drinking of beere and wyne to the scandall and the disgrace of his calling and profession and contrary to the Canons of the Church.

For the first time Wright admitted his bad behaviour. It was reported that he:

> doeth most humbly submit himselfe to the censure of the judge of the Courte, craving his lawful favour, in this behalfe and promising for the tyme to come a reformation and amendment to his life and Conversation, and ... also he Confesseth that ... he hath omitted to walke the boundes of the parish as by lawe he ought to have done, for which likewise he humbly submittes himselfe to the judges censure.

He was suspended for three weeks, and then Robert Aylett absolved him and restored him to his post.[77]

Irreverence

Soon after their appointment in 1638, the new Puritan wardens were engaged in an unexplained dispute with John Adcock. He was the blacksmith at the Chipping Hill forge, which is shown in the drawing on page 4 (now no.18 Chipping Hill). Two forms or benches had been taken from the nearby church. They were claimed by Adcock's wife to have been a loan from the sexton. In addition, 'a tagg which the Churchwardens had nayled up to hang hatts upon in the Church', had been moved. Adcock said that he had merely put it up again by his new seat. Hats were significant objects; they should have been removed from the head in church to show respect, and one form of Puritan protest was to keep them on instead. In due course this symbolism was to be developed by the Quakers into a refusal to remove hats on meeting their 'superiors'. The Puritan wardens appear to have connived at the wearing of hats in church, and may have supported it, because soon afterwards they were criticised by the officers of the Archdeacon's court for 'not presenting the parishioners for sitting with their hats on in service time'. It was only after this criticism that they took John Wood, clothier Thomas Nethercoate and shoemaker John Hussey to the court for the offence in May 1638, and added a complaint about their 'not standing up at the gloria'. The cases against Nethercoate and Wood were dismissed, but Hussey, a more persistent trouble-maker, was ordered to re-appear later and certify that he had been 'constantly bare' during the service. As he did not do so he was excommunicated. He had been one of the main victims of the arguments on St.Patrick's day 1628. Shortly afterwards, John Coe, Jerome Hussey and Alexander Hussey also appeared at the court for 'sitting with hats on their heads'. Appropriately enough, John Coe was a hatter and feltmaker. Jerome was probably John Hussey's father.[78]

It is not known who were elected churchwardens in 1639, or what their beliefs were; they presented a variety of offences. Included amongst them were accusations of irreverence amongst the parishioners, much of it directed at vicar Francis Wright. Most of the suspects are not known to have been Puritan idealists; our other knowledge of them is for general offences of disorder. In October 1639, six men were presented for sleeping in church. In spite of being reprimanded by Wright, blacksmith John Adcock, who had earlier 'borrowed' the benches, did 'nevertheless sleepe in the Church the Sunday next following'. William Purcas was:

> diverse times admonished by our Minister for his usuall sleeping in the Church in time of divine service and sermon publiquely in the deske and pulpitt and privately by our said minister and the congregacion and to the dishonour of god he wilfully persists in the same.

He was a bricklayer whose more usual offence was drunkenness. Butcher William Allen, similarly accused, claimed that 'his eyes were sore and could not hold them open but he did not sleepe'; at other times he was said to have driven hogs and sold meat on the sabbath. Eventually the charges against the alleged sleepers were dismissed.[79]

At the next court, in November 1639, Thomas Nicholls and Mary Harper were presented because although they were 'often admonished by Mr.Wright our Minister', they continued to 'keep a disordered alehouse neere unto the Church'. The 'men's servants' who were their customers included John Grimes, who had previously been a servant of Wright's, and used to 'stay in their house whole nights together'. There was alleged to be continual 'drinncking and ryotting' all day and night, especially on Sundays, 'to the great dishonour of God and disturbance of the neighbours that dwell thereaboutes' (Thomas Nicholls' alehouse was probably either where the White Horse now is, no.2 Church Street, or adjoining it). At the same court, Jerome Greene appeared:

> for carrying himself very rudely and disrespectfully towards our minister Mr.Wright, and for giveing him very foule language in the Church yard adding in Conclusion ... he cared not a strawe for our said Minister Mr.Wright and bad him do what he could, and these words were all spoken in the Churchyard.

He confessed, and the court later dismissed the case with Wright's consent.[80] In previous decades cases of irreverence in church had never represented more than one per cent of all the Witham offences, but during the 1630s they comprised fifteen per cent of the whole, with twenty-two instances in all, often, as we have seen, directed at 'Mr.Wright'.

Communion rails

The removal of communion rails into the chancel, and their railing in, formed an important part of Laud's new policies. We do not know for certain whether this process caused any dissent in Witham. However, when commissary Robert Aylett reported to the bishop in 1636 that he had 'caused many of the communion tables within my officialry to be railed in, and the people to come up and kneel and receave at the Raile', he did add that there had been 'much opposition especially in great clothing Townes, because they see no such thing they say in London'. Puritans feared that such rails would separate them from God. There was certainly a rail in Witham church by 1639, when James Fisher was taken to the Archdeacon's court on the grounds that 'as soon as he had received the communion, he rose up from the rayle and went out of the Church before the prayers were ended'. His defence was that he was sick. Explaining his absence on another day he said that he 'was driven' to be at home, because his wife was at church.[81]

It was during 1640 that the shift of power against the King and Laud accelerated, and attacks on communion rails were amongst the local symbols of this. There were two Witham men in a party of people who protested against rails in July 1640. They were weaver and clothier Thomas Browne, and labourer Arthur Gooday. It has been debated by historians whether such protesters were Puritan, or anti-Catholic, or just drunk. The backgrounds of Gooday and Browne do perhaps suggest some element of idealism; Browne had been a 'gadder' to Terling church in earlier years, whilst Gooday was later to serve as a soldier with the Parliamentary forces. The attacks in which they were involved took place at the churches of the neighbouring parishes of Kelvedon and Great Braxted, and were part of a wave of popular 'iconoclasm' in Essex, carefully directed at the symbols of Laudianism and suspected Catholicism. Another group was accused of causing damage in the church at Bradwell juxta Coggeshall, and there were three similar incidents in north-east Essex. The men may have been discharged soldiers. Local men had been drafted into the fighting, and Witham's parish constable John Hussey was in trouble later in the year for allegedly demanding money twice over to release labourer Thomas Slater's son, who had been 'prest for his Majesty's service'. It was said of all the suspected iconoclasts that they 'went in a hostile manner armed with staffs, bows and swords', and 'violently and in a war-like manner', 'riotously and unlawfully' broke the rails surrounding the communion tables, fixed in the chancels, and took them out into the churchyards.

In August 1640 Essex magistrates held inquisitions into some of the attacks; the group which included the two Witham men were found guilty. The magistrates included commissary Robert Aylett; most of the rest were Royalists, including Sir Thomas Wiseman. Ten days later the Privy Council rather belatedly issued orders that the Lords Lieutenant themselves should be present at any such trials held in the future concerning 'the late Ryotters and such like offenders'. In August 1640 the King ordered special powers to be given to all the Lords Lieutenant of England 'in this stirring and dangerous tyme'. There were more inquisitions held in Essex in September.[82]

OVERVIEW

Studies of other places

The reign of Charles I has been the subject of innumerable local and national studies. This is partly because of its inherent interest, and partly because of its relevance to the Civil War which followed it. In individual parishes and towns, the development of Puritanism in the face of official opposition has attracted particular attention, as has its varying character. Influences on the parishes have been seen to include the bishop, the patron of the living, and the resident clergy including the unofficial ones. Thus some places, such as Dorchester, came under the authority of bishops sympathetic to Puritanism. In contrast, the extreme Laudian Bishop Wren of Norwich frequently controlled towns like Ipswich, Norwich and Great Yarmouth, in spite of the Puritan beliefs of some of the inhabitants.

In Essex, the influence of Laud and his colleagues was always felt, in various ways, though when he became archbishop in 1633, his successor as bishop, William Juxon, was not as aggressive as Wren. So Puritan ministers in Colchester, for instance, managed to keep their places even after several accusations. A bishop's control over the appointment of ministers was limited, and Kenneth Shipps has shown that between a third and a half of Essex parishes altogether had Puritan ministers. They were even found in ten per cent of the parishes which had ecclesiastical patrons. The local influence of such Puritan ministers has been referred to in many studies. For instance, research by Keith Wrightson suggested that the arrival of a Puritan minister in Burnham on Crouch in Essex was important in bringing that parish into line with the many other places that had already embarked on a campaign of social control.[83]

Investigations have also been made into the influence of local laymen at different levels of society, and this has led to considerable debate amongst historians. Two thirds of Essex ministers were appointed by wealthy laymen, some of whom were committed enough in their beliefs to make deliberate placements. On the one hand there were patrons like the Puritan Robert Mildmay of Terling, and on the other there were those like the Laudian and Royalist John Lucas, who appointed Laud's chaplain to the living at Fordham in 1633. This was therefore an important means of exerting lay influence, particularly as many patrons had other local assets such as the ownership of land and manors; Mildmay and Lucas were both lords of the main manors in their parishes.

The less direct influence of lay people is harder to discover. The study of aristocratic power has sometimes been rather separate from descriptions of what was happening to other parishioners. And ideas about the attitudes and influence of ordinary people vary. Keith Wrightson and David Levine's classic study of Terling, first published in 1979, made that parish a benchmark against which many others have been compared, particularly in relation to the reign of Charles I. It was republished in 1995 with an addendum summarising the intervening debate. The book suggested that in Terling there was a ruling Puritan elite of about twenty men by the 1620s, intent particularly on controlling the ungodly

FIGURE 21: 1625-48 - SOME RELIGIOUS AND POLITICAL INFORMATION ABOUT WITHAM PEOPLE APPEARING IN THE SHIP MONEY ASSESSMENT OF 1636

Names in capitals are known to have been office-holders (magistrate, half-hundred or parish)
Bold text indicates that the information includes some from before 1641

Ship money assess-ment	Evidence that pro-Francis Wright, Catholic or Royalist	Evidence that anti-Wright, Puritan sympathiser, or Parliamentarian		No clear evidence of political or religious sympathies	
£3	John Southcott (1633 onwards)				
£2-£3		JEROME GARRARD(2)			
£1-£2	HENRY NEVILL (of Cressing)	JOHN GRAVENER(3)		Mrs.Ann Jenour	
£1	**John Greene**				
18s.		**WILLIAM ALLEN (gent.)**		HENRY BUNTING WILLIAM NICHOLLS senior	
16s.	**FRANCIS WRIGHT (vicar)**	**JEROME SKINGLEY** ROBERT BURCHARD(3)			
14s.				Thomas Nicholls	
13s.4d.		**ROBERT GARRARD(2)**			
12s.				RICHARD BARNARD (tanner)	
11s.	William Coe	**Christopher Banks** RICHARD PORTER		**ARTHUR BARKER** Thomas Brodway Robert Allen	
	THOMAS PARKER				
10s.				Mrs.Cordilla Parker	
8s.	**William Thursby**				
	John Alexander Mrs.Elizabeth Armond				
6s.		**WILLIAM.SKINNER senior** Jerome Tabor			
5s.6d.				Joseph Tabor	
5s.	ALEXANDER FREEBORNE	Daniel Freshwater		James Wall	
4s.	**John Parker** **HENRY WOOD** WILLIAM BROOKE Jeffrey Whale	**John Adcock** **John Hussey** **James Princet** **John Wood** William Borebanke William Ford	**WILLIAM HAVEN** **PHILIP PLEDGER** **Solomon Turner** Thomas Upcher Mrs.Mary Warde	John Corbett William Nicholls junior	
3s.-4s.		JOHN FREEBORNE William Wyatt			
	John Hopkinson				
3s.	John Hull	**George Goulding Nath'l Nowell**		Jasper Mott Mrs.Margery Symonds	
2s.-3s.	John Robinson	**Thomas Nethercoate**		John Gurton Thomas Massant	
2s.	**Matthew Mootham**	**John Garrard (2)** Richard Dagnet William Linsey William Darby Robert Lord Robert White		Richard Barnard (baker) Miles Dawson Richard Boone Edmund Halys John Brewer Richard Mathew Robert Clarke William Pye George Creswell Henry Robinson Henry Weale John Snow	
1s. - 2s.	William Kendall	**Jerome Greene (1 of 2)** Roger Baker NATH'L GARRARD Jeffrey Cottis John Markes Francis Ellis		Richard Gage Thomas Perkins Jerome Greene (1 of 2) John Peachie	
1s.	John Mitchell William Purcas	Edward Barry Peter Clarke senior John Hasleby		Jerome Bromley Robert Powell Thomas Hasleton Edmund Summers senior John Summers Thomas Hasleton Thomas Totteridge junior Peter Winkfield	
	Francis Mitchell William Norris				

poor. In contrast, David Underdown considered that a similar group in Dorchester targetted people of all social levels, and James Sharpe felt that people of middling rank, rather than the poor, were the main subjects of accusation in the village of Kelvedon, three miles east of Witham.

In Witham too we have seen that the poor were by no means the sole suspects, though it may be noted here that one complication is the definition of the term 'poor'. In other places concerted campaigns were less evident. In Coggeshall, a few miles further north, where the patron of the living was the Puritan leader the Earl of Warwick but the vicar was the relatively conservative and long-established John Dodd, there appear to have been two Puritan factions disagreeing with each other rather than trying to influence others, the less extreme group usually being in the ascendancy. And elsewhere there may have been only individual Puritans, with little influence, and not deserving of being called a group at all. One of the best known analyses of such a place is Keevil in Wiltshire, studied by Martin Ingram. For all these examples we rely on the interpretation of the researcher, which can vary. For instance, Kenneth Shipps and William Petchey reached different conclusions about whether the leading townsmen of the port of Maldon, south of Witham, were primarily loyal or Puritan.[84]

Witham

Witham was complicated. It would be easy just to say that it was a Puritan town, but it was not entirely, by any means. The 1636 Ship Money return showed 106 people of lower-middling status in the town.[85] Figure 21 on the previous page shows some of their religious and political affiliations.[86] This can only give an impression rather than a complete picture, because of lack of knowledge, and the fact that many people came and went before and after 1636. It can be seen that many of the office holders and others were indeed known Puritans, but that there were also a few who were opposed to them, a number whose allegiance we do not know of until after 1640, and of course many about whom we do not know at all. It is not really surprising that there is so much variation and uncertainty. During Charles' reign the town did not come under many of the direct influences which have been shown by other writers to be important in setting a Puritan tone. For instance, there was little sympathy for Puritanism from the bishops and from their local representative Robert Aylett, and those same bishops, as patrons of the vicarage, appointed a non-Puritan vicar, Francis Wright, in 1625.

However, there were several factors which did favour the development of Puritanism in the parish. As we saw in chapter 7 (pages 75-76), Wright's predecessors and their curates, together with their ally Dame Katherine Barnardiston, may well have already encouraged lay Puritanism before 1625. She also developed an alliance with her lay social inferiors in Witham, comparable to others discussed by historian Patrick Collinson. As he wrote, 'there was implicit acknowledgement by both parties that questions of divine law and the will of God transcended the normal respect due to a titular superior'. And from 1625 to 1631 she had the assistance of her protégé Thomas Weld, over the parish boundary in Terling. Lastly, Francis Wright, Witham's own vicar, actually assisted the Puritan cause by his opposition to it, because he became associated with immorality and incompetence. Readers may feel some sympathy for him; he was a long way from his home in Yorkshire and must have found Witham puzzling and indeed overwhelming. However, this did not save his reputation at the time. There were other so-called 'scandalous' ministers in Essex, but Wright was one of the most notorious. We will hear more of him in the next two chapters.[87]

All these factors boosted the morale of Witham Puritans between 1625, when Wright arrived, and 1631. Several of them were freely going to Terling church to hear Weld and avoid Wright. The relatively humble people who were challenged for doing this in 1626 were joined by others of middling and higher rank in 1628. The more senior of them began to take office in Witham itself, and as churchwardens some of them noisily dominated the running of their own church. Their position seems to have been lost for a time after 1631, in which year many of them were challenged in the Consistory court, and Weld was deprived.

Nevertheless, by 1632 a court action assisted by Dame Katherine was under way against Wright for immorality, and even for suspected Catholicism, She died in 1633 but the prosecution continued until 1635. It failed, but another began in 1638; this was more successful though he managed to retain his post. From this time onwards, lay Puritan control in Witham itself became evident again in some years, as did outbreaks of outspoken disrespect for Wright and for Church discipline amongst all ranks of the parishioners. Meanwhile the King and the Church were beginning to lose their authority at a national level.

When Dame Katherine died in 1633, she must have felt that Laud and the King would continue to have the upper hand. But by 1640 her nieces, nephews, and stepchildren in various parts of south-east England were beginning to acquire power. Several were Puritan members of Parliament. And in due course two of them signed the King's death warrant in 1649.[88] The next chapter will show how these developments were reflected in Witham and Essex.

10. THE LONG PARLIAMENT and the CIVIL WAR, 1640-1660

BACKGROUND

In late 1640 the opponents of Charles I were in a very strong position. They probably wielded more authority at that time than they ever did again. As James Sharpe has written, the King was then 'isolated, apart from a clique of courtiers'.[1] The Long Parliament, elected in October, seized the initiative and introduced sudden and drastic measures which completely changed the balance of power. Many of Charles' senior supporters were removed from office, and in March 1641 Archbishop Laud was sent to the Tower after an attempt to extend the Church's independence. However, at this stage there was still almost universal support for the actual institution of the monarchy. The fundamental disagreement was about Charles' attempts to act alone on the 'royal prerogative', without reference to Parliament. In particular there was hostility to his demands for money for war. He had been fighting the Scots since early 1640, and by autumn 1641 there was also rebellion in Ireland to contend with. Antagonism between Parliament and the King increased further after December 1641, when Charles rejected most of the points in Parliament's 'Grand Remonstrance'. On the fourth of January 1642, Charles made an unsuccessful attempt to seize five members of Parliament, accompanied by several hundred armed men. He left Whitehall on the tenth, and Parliament returned there in triumph. Several counties responded to these events with petitions of loyalty to Parliament. During the following months the King gradually retrieved some support. He departed from London for the north in March 1642, and in many respects this was the start of the Civil War. It was a confusing period. There was a certain amount of negotiation, but both sides were preparing to fight. This was not an easy task, particularly as there was no standing national army. 'Trained bands' of militia had existed since medieval times, but were recruited on a local basis.

On 22 August 1642 the King raised his standard at Nottingham, formally heralding the beginning of military action, which was to continue in various parts of Britain for the following four years during the 'First Civil War'. There was no fighting on Essex soil during this time, but Parliament and the King both sought financial and military support from all the counties. To begin with, the armies were recruited on a voluntary basis by men of influence, who also provided funds. However, conscription, together with taxation to support the troops, soon became important. County Committees of gentry 'well-affected' to Parliament were formed, particularly in sympathetic counties like Essex. At first there were separate committees for collecting taxes and for taking over or 'sequestering' the estates of non-payers, but they had similar memberships. Military associations combining several counties were also formed. Much the most successful of these was the Eastern Association, of which Essex was a part. From early 1643 it became the mainstay of the Parliamentary cause, and remained so until the formation in 1645 of the New Model Army, which was directly responsible to Parliament.[2]

The Royalists had some successes in early battles, but the upper hand in the fighting was eventually gained by the Parliamentary armies, culminating in their victory at the battle of Naseby in June 1645. In 1646 the King's headquarters at Oxford surrendered. This marked the end of the First Civil War. Charles escaped and surrendered to Scottish troops, who subsequently handed him over to the English parliament after discussions in which the Parliamentarian general Oliver Cromwell was one of the chief participants. For the following two years there were unresolved and heated debates within both Parliament and the army on many subjects including the roles of the King, the soldiers and the Church. Some of these provoked a series of local Royalist uprisings in 1648, beginning what has become known as the Second Civil War. This time Essex did see some fighting. Royalists from Kent crossed the river in May and joined others at Chelmsford. Together they conducted a peaceful raid on the Earl of Warwick's house at Great Leighs, and then marched to Colchester. They were pursued by a Parliamentary force, who were joined by local men raised by Sir Thomas Honywood of Marks Hall. At the 'siege of Colchester' the Royalists were blockaded until they surrendered in August 1648.[3]

The King was tried and executed for treason in January 1649 after a purge of Parliament instituted by the army, and the failure of further negotiations. Two relatives of Witham's Dame Katherine Barnardiston were leading members of the group of men who sat in judgement on the King and signed the death warrant; they were Richard Deane and Sir Robert Titchborne. The monarchy and the House of Lords were abolished in March. There was a further brief military campaign originating in Scotland and Ireland in favour of the King's son Charles, sometimes known as the Third Civil War. This was finally brought to an end by Cromwell's victory at Worcester in September 1651. Cromwell became Lord Protector in 1653. Parliament continued to be tormented by financial, political, constitutional and military stresses, which caused division on many issues. There were more unsuccessful Royalist risings, particularly in 1655 and 1658. Cromwell died in September 1658, and his son Richard abdicated in 1659. The Long Parliament was finally dissolved in March 1660, and Charles II was brought to the throne in May 1660.[4]

Religion

Historians have long debated the role of religion in the conflict. It was certainly given a high priority. Three days after the Long Parliament first met in November 1640, it set up a committee of the whole House 'for Religion'. Subsequently this committee underwent various subdivisions and modifications. In due course moves were made by Parliament against 'scandalous' clergymen, the most usual complaints being immorality, or allegiance to Archbishop Laud and the King, or both. The majority of these accusations ended in dismissal, with the result that over two thousand ministers in the country as a whole were removed from their livings and replaced by loyal men. In July 1641 the courts of High Commission were abolished, and the other ecclesiastical courts were suspended shortly afterwards, as were some of Laud's allegedly 'popish' innovations.[5]

The organisation of the Church was also a pressing concern. Many members of the English Parliament favoured a Presbyterian system, without bishops. This was how other Protestant churches in Europe, including Scotland, were organised. The Church of England had retained its bishops at the Reformation, and their association with the Catholic Church attracted particular hostility in some quarters, as also did their secular power and wealth. At times Parliament's sympathy towards Presbyterianism attracted the assistance of the Scots in other matters. A 'classis' or presbytery, which was a group of local elders and ministers, was an important part of Presbyterian organisation. In 1646 a group of clergymen from Essex and Suffolk petitioned the Lords in favour of such a scheme, and its establishment in those counties was duly authorised. The Essex names were put forward by the County Committee and approved in January 1647.[6] Similar arrangements were set up in other counties also. But opinion on the subject was divided, and the classis system probably did not become fully established. Another matter of debate at the time was the role of the Prayer Book. Some would have been content to keep it but to reduce its importance. However, in the end it was replaced by the Directory of Public Worship in 1646.

Many Parliamentarians saw a united church as a high priority. Having seemingly dealt with what they saw as the threat from Archbishop Laud and the Catholics, they were soon faced with problems on the opposite front. Separatist radical movements of both a religious and political nature were already evident during the 1640s, and flourished during the 1650s. Amongst them were several which developed into Protestant sects,

A Civil War clergyman

During the Civil War, army chaplains frequently preached to the Parliamentary soldiers, who in turn took part in many of the religious debates of the period.

many of which survive to this day, like the Baptists and Quakers. Their radicalism was social as well as religious. Often they scorned the traditional hierarchy between ranks, and between men and women. Some Quakers were particularly vociferous at this time in petitioning for their rights, and becoming active in the militia. Parliament considered various alternating schemes for both toleration and persecution of separatists, but failed to agree.

ESSEX BEFORE THE WAR, 1640-1642

In the election for the Long Parliament in October 1640, the Puritan Earl of Warwick's supporters were unopposed in the two Essex county seats. Royalist Henry Nevill of Cressing, defeated seven months previously, did not stand. In Suffolk there was a contest, but with the same result; the Puritan Sir Nathaniel Barnardiston, Dame Katherine's stepson, was elected there for a second time. Essex and Suffolk both became important centres of enthusiasm for Parliament in its feud with the King. Essex was the second of all the counties to send the members a petition of support, when on 20 January 1642 'divers Gentlemen' of Essex went to London with an immense roll of names addressed to the House of Commons. This can still be seen today in the House of Lords' Record Office; I estimate it to be about forty-five feet long, with well over ten thousand signatures, marks, and names, amounting to perhaps one tenth of the population of the county, and maybe half the householders. The compilation of these documents has been attributed to the Earl of Warwick. The names seem to have been collected on separate sheets for each parish, which were then stuck onto both sides of the roll. Witham's considerable contribution is discussed later. A smaller petition went to the Lords, with about a thousand names. In their declarations the compilers inextricably mixed what we would today regard as the separate subjects of religion, politics and economics, including the fortunes of agriculture and the cloth industry. And they made it clear that they supported the constitution as a whole, including the monarchy. It was only King Charles personally to whom they objected. In June 1642 the sheriff of Essex received conflicting instructions from the King on the one hand and Parliament on the other about the rights of the population to 'march and muster'.[7]

However, even in Essex there were many people who still hoped in mid-1642 that there would be an agreement with the King and a peaceful solution. Thus about eighty gentlemen of the county made a declaration to the King in July. They included Witham's Thomas Bayles, of whom more will be seen later. Like the other petitioners already mentioned they wrote against 'the practices of Papists' and in favour of the privileges of Parliament. But they also promised:

> that for the safety of your Majesty's royall person, and posterity, defence of your rights and just prerogatives, we will be ready ... to assist your Majestie with our persons, lives and fortunes,

whensoever you shalbe pleased to command us.[8]

LOCAL DISTURBANCES, 1642

There was increased concern about riot and disorder all over the country during the early 1640s, and there was a series of attacks in Essex and Suffolk in 1642 which were particularly aimed at the property of Catholics, who usually supported the King. It was the Royalist propagandists who subsequently gave most publicity to these events in alarming terms. John Walter has made a particular study of the situation, and has argued that it was in fact 'less threatening than has been supposed'. Attacks were on property and reports of personal injury are rare. One of the best-known raids concerned Sir John Lucas of Colchester. He was one of the chief opponents of the Earl of Warwick in the county, though he was a descendant of Christopher Royden, an early radical Witham Protestant of Henry VIII's reign. On 22 August 1642, the same day that the King raised his standard at Nottingham, Lucas was seized by a crowd which had gathered from several parts of north-east Essex. It was said that he had been preparing to go north 'to wait upon the King'. After his capture, his house was plundered, and the properties of several other Royalists in Colchester and East Anglia were attacked. One of the places to suffer such a raid was Melford Hall, the house of the Countess Rivers in Long Melford, just over the county boundary in Suffolk; she had fled there from her Essex estate at St.Osyth. She asked Parliament to institute a search for her missing belongings, claiming they were worth £50,000. The Royalist reporter who described the affair suggested that her total loss was actually £100,000 or more, and that her coach horses were later confiscated to prevent her escaping overseas. Such allegations were something of an embarrassment to the members of Parliament, who issued a declaration urging caution on people who had carried out attacks in Essex. Nonetheless they authorised the imprisonment of Lucas, and received eight of his horses on the grounds that they were intended to serve 'a Malignant party'. They did their best for Countess Rivers, making an order for her security when she came to London, and urging officials to search for her belongings in 'Creekes, Vessels, Waggons and Carts', and to watch the London tradesmen. But she also had arms and ammunition seized by commissioners, and in spring 1643 she complained that her tenants were not paying their rents, 'so her debts are unpaid and her children deprived of maintenance'.[9]

Thomas Bayles of Witham

During 1642, probably on 24 August, there was an attack on the house of Mr.Thomas Bayles in Witham. He later claimed he had suffered damage and loss valued at £1,600. The House of Commons did not receive a report until three months afterwards. This stated that Bayles was 'plundered by divers ill-disposed Persons in that County, and his goods taken from him by Force'. The Commons authorised him and his employees to search for and seize his goods, and constables and officials were urged to help. It was also decided by the House that 'the like Order be made for all other Persons that have been plundered by the King's Forces, or any others', but this may perhaps be taken as an attempt to divert attention from the role of Parliament's supporters, rather than indicating that Royalists took part in the Essex attacks. Bayles, originally from Suffolk, was a lawyer of the Middle Temple who had only recently come to live in Witham. He had briefly become a magistrate with other Royalists in 1641 and, as we have seen, supported a petition in favour of the King with other gentlemen in 1642. However, his religious sympathies are something of an enigma. We do not know of any connection with the Bayles family who had been Witham Catholics forty years earlier. The Thomas Bayles of the 1630s and 1640s did have some connections with the Catholic Southcotts of Witham Place, and it seems just possible that he was living in that house temporarily, in which case the fact that the house belonged to the Southcotts could have attracted a raid there. His other associations with the family were in his official capacity as a lawyer, and on one occasion, in 1650, he may have been appointed as an agent for their estate by Parliament. We hear of him again in 1671, when he wished to practice at the Bar, so that he could 'shutt upp his old age with some signall of his majesties takeing notice of his losses and services'. His petition said that after the Restoration of 1660 he had begun to 'dispatch his majesties service for the publique good', though of course we should remember that at that time it was in his interests to say so. He had 'layd asyde his gowne' as a lawyer in 1662, having 'lost his then only chile'. He then had an income of nearly £1,000 a year, but four years later he had suffered losses of £5,000 or £6,000 in the Great Fire of London.[10]

On the day after the trouble at Bayles' house in 1642, it was reported by two Essex magistrates from Steeple Bumpstead that 'riotous people' were 'assembled in a riotous tumulteous and rebellious manner in this County', and had 'Committed divers riottes and outrages about Colchester, Witham and other places'. They were expected to go next to Audley End and rifle the Earl of Suffolk's house, and 'by the way to plunder and rifle diverse houses of other his Majesty's Liege people'. This suggests that the many of the alleged offenders were a travelling crowd rather than being residents of the places concerned. The parish constables were told to 'warn all the trained bands in their parishes to be ready, completely armed, at an hours warning, to assist'.[11] However, the attacks and riots subsided within a short space of time.

PARLIAMENT'S ORGANISATION AND SUPPORT

The Committees

The arrangements for the Parliamentary committees in the counties varied. In Essex the County Committee had about seventy members, mostly knights, esquires and some better-off gentlemen. So they were the type of people who had habitually acted as magistrates and Deputy Lieutenants, though some of them did not have previous experience of county office. They were at first asked by Parliament to raise £1,125 per week from Essex, and the financial burden increased greatly in subsequent years.

Members also met in six smaller groups or Divisions. Witham half-hundred came into the north-eastern Division with the hundreds of Tendring, Lexden, Winstree, Thurstable and the borough of Colchester. The records of the southern Divisional Committee, which was based at Romford, still survive, but less is known of the activities of the others. The people of magistrate status in the Witham area were by now mostly Royalist, so not eligible. Nor do there appear to have been any Committee members from the town of Witham itself. Although several of its leading figures, such as John Gravener(3) and Robert Garrard(2), referred to themselves as gentlemen, they were only what have been called by some writers 'parish gentry'. Robert's father Jerome(2) had probably died in about 1640. John Walter has suggested that in some counties people like these did in fact gain office. However, in Witham they were presumably not of sufficient repute or standing, in spite of their known support for Parliament. In the end, the nearest committee member to Witham was Jeremy Aylett of Dorewards Hall in Rivenhall, cousin of Robert, the former bishop's commissary. Jeremy and four of his tenants spent a short time in prison in September 1643 for the over-zealous exercise of their duties in sequestering an estate in Norfolk, and, as he complained, he was often taken away 'from the public service' to attend to the subsequent dispute.[12]

Magistrates

In spite of the existence of the committees, magistrates retained some traditional roles, particularly in enforcing the criminal law. Their numbers were added to during 1641, probably in the vain hope of strengthening the King's hand. Amongst the new recruits was Witham's Thomas Bayles, already mentioned. But he and his fellow Royalists were quickly removed from the Essex bench once the war had started. Others who departed in this purge were Henry Nevill, Sir Thomas Wiseman and Sir Benjamin Ayloffe, who between them had been doing much of the work in Witham. Their signatures stopped appearing on the town's recognisances during 1642 and they attended no more at the assizes and quarter sessions at Chelmsford. Between early 1643 and Easter 1644 there were no meetings of quarter sessions, and there were also two years with no assize courts, but they both continued as usual thereafter. The dismissals caused a temporary depletion of numbers on the Essex bench to around sixty, but by 1659 this had been made up to about a hundred by the addition of Parliament's own supporters. This was more than at any time during the previous century, though, as always, the figure included many people who probably did not act, such as members of the government. For instance Oliver Cromwell himself was an Essex magistrate after 1650. Dionyse Wakering of Kelvedon was appointed in about 1647, after which he dealt with most of the Witham cases until 1650. He was involved in the arrest of Quaker James Parnell in 1655, and died in the following year. After 1650, Jeremy Aylett of Rivenhall conducted much of the Witham work, having become a new magistrate as well as a Committee member. He in turn died in 1657; his memorial is still in Rivenhall church tower. John Godbold of Hatfield Peverel was appointed at about this time, and took over in Witham.[13]

Sir Nathaniel and Arthur Barnardiston, Dame Katherine's stepsons, were also Essex magistrates from about 1644 onwards. Sir Nathaniel lived at the family home in Kedington, Suffolk. Arthur, a lawyer, had an estate in Snailwell, Cambridgeshire, from his first wife, Ann. There he accommodated the retired Puritan minister Samuel Fairclough. After Ann died in 1644, Arthur married Joan Mildmay, widow of the Puritan Robert of Terling, about whom we read in the last chapter (pages 104 et al.). Joan was Dame Katherine's niece, so the marriage forged yet another link between Dame Katherine's own family and the Barnardistons. It may be in this connection that Samuel Barnardiston was in Terling at one point during the 1650s, when he was ill. This Samuel was probably the one who was Arthur's nephew, and whom Queen Henrietta is alleged to have described as a 'handsome young roundhead' in 1640, thus giving occasion to the use of the term to describe the Parliamentarians. As an Essex magistrate Arthur dealt with cases in north Essex as well as in the Terling area. He was also one of Cromwell's Masters in Chancery, so his address was usually given at the Inner Temple in London. His other posts included membership of the Essex County Committee, and the Recordership of Colchester. Arthur died at his chambers in London in 1655 and was buried in Essex.[14]

Half-hundred officers

The role of the half-hundred in administering the law was maintained. Witham's John Gravener(3), one of the high constables since 1638, retained the post until 1650. He did ask quarter sessions to let him resign in 1644, because 'his partner haveinge absented himselfe from the service above a yeare now the whole burthen lyeth upon him alone'. He claimed that because of his 'age and inability of bodye, hee is not able further to execute the said Office according to the necessity of the time'. It was resolved to find an 'able man' to replace him, but in fact he seems to have continued for several more years, being finally succeeded by two of Witham's Puritan gentlemen in turn, William Allen in 1650 and Robert Garrard(2) in 1659.[15]

However, the lesser role of sheriff's bailiff seems usually to have been taken by Royalists. Thus Witham's yeoman/innholder William Brooke of the White Hart in Newland Street had held the post since 1626 and

continued until his death in 1647, in spite of being accused of collecting arms for the King in 1642, and having a horse taken from him for not contributing to Parliament in 1643. Two other Witham innholders held the post briefly after him. One was George Starke, who died almost immediately, his will being written by Royalist William Robinson. George's widow married Richard Swinborne, yet another innkeeper. Next there was William Bunny, who was probably related to Royalist Robert Bunny. In 1652 William Mootham took over, an uncle or other relative of the Matthew Mootham who had supported Royalist vicar Francis Wright at court in 1634.[16]

Soldiers and other supporters

In many counties the existing trained bands only played a very limited role during the Wars. However, the well-organised bands from London provided several thousand soldiers for the Parliamentary armies, and in Essex also, some of the bands did play a part, though often the men paid for poorer substitutes to take their places. Essex was also a particularly fruitful area for recruiting new volunteers, though as time went on there was some conscription too. The county town of Chelmsford was one of the main assembly points for the troops raised by the Earl of Warwick as Lord Lieutenant, and saw great disruption as a result. Various messages were forwarded to Parliament purporting to come from the trained bands and the volunteers. One, in June 1642, deplored the fact that 'His Majesty, seduced by wicked Counsel, intends to make War against the Parliament'. In November 1642 Parliament agreed 'to re-pay such Expenses to Freeholders of Essex as will serve in the Army'. So the county was already busy raising men and horses when the Eastern Association was specifically instructed by Parliament in August 1643 to raise 10,000 foot soldiers and dragoons from Essex 'to withstand the enemy'. Amongst the dragoons already enlisted were four men from the Witham hundred including Zacharias Allen from Witham itself. Dragoons rode horses but fought on foot, and were usually from rather higher social ranks than the ordinary foot soldiers, who were mainly poor. Two years later, Arthur Gooday of Witham was said to be away 'in service' of Parliament when he was put on a jury list for quarter sessions. In 1640 he had been an alleged destroyer of communion rails at Great Braxted.[17]

The only other Witham soldier whose name we know is Thomas White, who was a member of a regiment from the Essex trained bands under Sir Thomas Honywood. He was wounded in the last battle of the Third Civil War at Worcester in 1651, and taken with others to the Savoy military hospital in London. There he was put under the care of the 'Treasurers for maymed Souldiers and Widdows, for the recovery of his health, and cure of his maimes', as shown in figure 22 on page 125, together with drawings of foot soldiers like him. Like many of his fellows he could not be entirely cured and was issued with a pre-printed certificate in December 1651, in which the Treasurers pointed out that he had

Foot soldiers

One soldier has a pike and the other a musket.. Witham's Thomas White,
whose certificate is shown on the facing page, was a foot soldier.

been subject 'to the utmost skill of our Physician and Chirurgeons', but that he was nonetheless 'disabled to follow his calling, or to perform any further service in the Army'. They gave him twelve shillings for his journey back from London to his home in Witham, having first written eight shillings and changed their minds. The officials of the places that he passed through on his way were asked to make provision for him. It is probable that he returned to be a weaver, perhaps inheriting the trade of his father-in-law Hugh Parson in 1655. At Easter 1652, quarter sessions awarded him a pension of forty shillings a year, but this would have been withdrawn at the time of the Restoration in 1660. When he died in 1672 he did have his own house, but was referred to as a pauper and left

goods worth only £8, as did his widow Ann when she died in 1680. Neither Thomas nor Ann could sign their names.[18]

Witham men could also be called upon to protect the reputation of Parliament in a less violent manner. Two of them gave evidence to quarter sessions against Parliament's critics. One was John Coe, who in 1644 supported the case against George Bush of Halstead. Both men were feltmakers; Coe, who lived in Mill Lane, had been one of the people who were in trouble in 1638 for wearing hats in Witham church. He alleged that Bush had made 'divers false and opprobrious speeches against the proceedings of the Parliament, tending to the great disheartening of those that take part in them'.

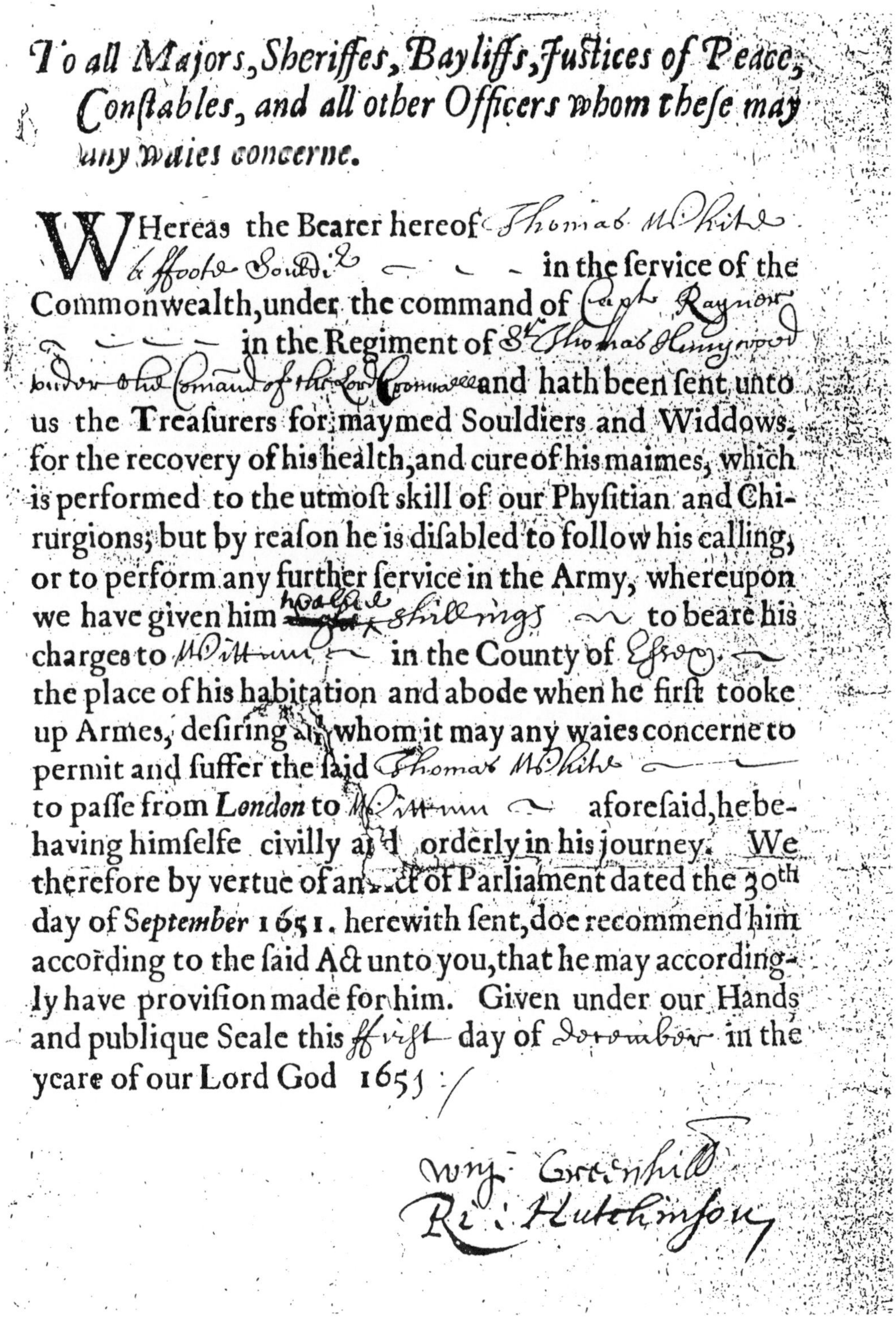

To all Majors, Sheriffes, Bayliffs, Justices of Peace, Constables, and all other Officers whom these may any waies concerne.

WHereas the Bearer hereof *Thomas White* a foote Souldir in the service of the Commonwealth, under the command of *Capt Raynor* in the Regiment of *Sr Thomas Hunnywood under the Comand of the Lord Cromwell* and hath been sent unto us the Treasurers for maymed Souldiers and Widdows, for the recovery of his health, and cure of his maimes, which is performed to the utmost skill of our Physitian and Chirurgions; but by reason he is disabled to follow his calling, or to perform any further service in the Army, whereupon we have given him *hoo gd shillings* to beare his charges to *Witham* in the County of *Essex* the place of his habitation and abode when he first tooke up Armes, desiring all whom it may any waies concerne to permit and suffer the said *Thomas White* to passe from *London* to *Witham* aforesaid, he behaving himselfe civilly and orderly in his journey. We therefore by vertue of an act of Parliament dated the 30th day of *September* 1651. herewith sent, doe recommend him according to the said Act unto you, that he may accordingly have provision made for him. Given under our Hands and publique Seale this *first* day of *November* in the yeare of our Lord God 1651 :/

Wm: Greenhill
Ri: Hutchinson

Figure 22. The certificate of Thomas White of Witham, a foot soldier

This arranges for him to be sent home. He had been wounded in the last battle of the Third Civil War, at Worcester in 1651. After his return, he became a weaver.. The magistrates granted him a pension of 40 shillings a year, but this would have withdrawn at the Restoration in 1660. He died a pauper in 1672. His widow Ann survived until 1680, when she was also referred to as a pauper. (reproduced by courtesy of the Essex Record Office; reference E.R.O. Q/Sba 2/78)

Soon afterwards, in 1645, Thomas Goulston, a Witham gentleman who had only recently arrived in the town, was one of several witnesses against Ralph Wiseman of Rivenhall, whose Royalist family we have already encountered, and who was said to have been referring to the members of Parliament as 'rebels'. It was Wiseman who as a young man had helped to control the affray in Witham on St.Patrick's day in 1628. Goulston's position is rather difficult to discern; as seen below, only two years before he himself had been considered to be a Royalist and had a horse taken from him as a result.[19]

THE KING'S SUPPORTERS

Ralph Wiseman came from one of the many families in Essex who unhesitatingly supported the King. We have already seen that eighty Essex gentlemen expressed their allegiance in writing just before the war. In addition, a desire for compromise turned some people against Parliament, whose members received an extensive 'peace' petition from the county in January 1643 after five months of war. It was headed by loyalist clergymen and asked that an 'accommodation' be sought with the King 'for the Preservation of the true Protestant Religion, His Majesty's Safety and Honour, the Peace and Prosperity of all His Subjects'.[20] There were said to have been 6,619 names on it altogether. The petition in support of Parliament a year previously had contained very roughly twice that number.

People who put such doubts about Parliament into practice became more vulnerable in Essex as the demands of the war increased. For instance, in March 1643, an order was sent to three local officials to seize horses, arms and munitions in the Braintree and Witham areas from 'papists and malignants', and from anyone who refused to appear at musters or to support Parliament's 'propositions'. As well as visiting some of the gentry of the villages, the officials came to Witham itself and took away four horses, one each from four men mentioned elsewhere in this chapter. Two of them were the prosperous gentlemen, John Greene and Thomas Goulston, whose allegiance is somewhat ambiguous, and two were more unequivocally supporters of the King, namely the vicar Francis Wright and the half-hundred bailiff, William Brooke. But it was still possible for a Royalist with sufficient status and funds to exert influence. Thus some of the horses were afterwards handed over to various local civilians; not only did John Greene receive a horse back again, but Lady Ayloffe, wife of the Royalist Sir Benjamin of Great Braxted, was given 'two colts and one mare'. One of the collectors was suspected of taking money for such 'redelivery', though he denied it.[21]

In 1645 it was alleged to a Parliamentary Committee that John Robinson of Witham had sent twenty shillings to someone in the King's quarters at Oxford, and that he had been 'drinking to the confusion of Parliament'. He was lucky to be discharged for lack of evidence.[22] But most of our other surviving knowledge about Royalists concerns the better-off families, and some examples of their experiences in the Witham area are given below. Their family and estate records can often show us their activities in much greater detail than we have for their opponents, and the records of the sequestration of their estates by Parliament can also be informative. This procedure meant that the Royalist families still retained legal title to their property, and could usually retrieve possession of it by paying a fine. The severity of the fine depended on its value and on the circumstances.

Henry Nevill

During the 1630s Henry Nevill had been said by Robert Aylett to be a 'forward and entire supporter' of Archbishop Laud's programme. As well as Cressing Temple, his home, he owned the manors of Chipping and Newland in Witham, but a large part of his estate was in Leicestershire, much nearer to the centre of the fighting. Our information about his role derives from hostile Parliamentary sources. He was among several Essex people accused by Parliament of collecting arms for the Royalists in 1642 during the first weeks of the war. Other suspects near Witham were William Sams of Rivenhall, formerly a collector of the Forced Loan, and probably Christopher Webb, rector of Great Braxted, who had earlier been a teacher in Witham. In investigating Henry Nevill, soldiers had apprehended some men from Witham on suspicion of 'buying and conveying Armes to Cressing Temple'. Only three of these men were named. They were George Betworth, about whom I have found no information, William Brooke, the Witham gentleman/yeoman/innholder who was bailiff of Witham half-hundred, and Hinde Goodale, who was a tenant of Chipping manor and ratepayer in Witham parish. Rather surprisingly, Goodale had signed the Parliamentarian petition to the Commons nine months previously, but William Brooke contributed to the Royalist 'peace' petition in early 1643. The report about Henry Nevill confirmed that he had been a supporter of Archbishop Laud, and 'a man formerly inclined to the late innovations introduced into the Church, & much in favour with the Bishops delinquents'. The arrested men were to be examined, and Nevill was to be sent for. Soon afterwards, in October, Parliament ordered that 'the Horse and Arms of Mr.Nevil' should be seized as part of a move to disarm 'all Papists and Disaffected' people in Essex. However, a few months later the County Committee of Northamptonshire complained of his 'levying War against the Parliament' in that county, and it was resolved to imprison him and to seize his estates, including his Essex ones. It was eventually reported that he had been captured in August 1644 in Leicestershire 'in arms against Parliament', and that he had 'an estate of £6,000 a year in lands'. He was released five months later in exchange for two Parliamentarian captains. Two of his sons were also Royalist officers and one of them took part in the Second Civil War in Essex. Henry retrieved his estate as early as 1646 by paying a fine of £6,000, and Parliament reproved the County Committee 'for threatening to distrain one of his tenants for rent'.[23]

One of his successors as lord of the manor of Chipping and Newland claimed that the manor court rolls had been confiscated by Parliament, but this is unproven. In 1654 Nevill took out a 1,000-year mortgage on the manors in order to pay his debts, and five years later he and his son sold their interest altogether.[24]

John Southcott

John Southcott was another rich Royalist, living at Witham Place with his Catholic father Edward. The monument in St.Nicholas church to his great-grandparents, the judge and his wife, survived the seventeenth century in spite of the family's beliefs. The part which John took in the war provides us with an interesting description of its informality. It was related later by his son, so it emphasises his successes. He was said to have been of 'a sprightly active disposition' and anxious to volunteer. His father was reluctant to allow him to do so, as he was the only male heir. But soon after the beginning of the war in 1642 his family:

> equipped him very handsomely with arms and horses for himself and two or three men, and so he set forward with letters of recommendation to some of their acquaintance in the army, to present this their son to the King ... as one ambitious to serve him as a volunteer, who met with a very gracious reception, and so took his post in the army.

After standing by as reserve in his first battle he found himself near his sister's 'fine house' in Staffordshire, so went to visit her, riding his horse into the hall and up the stairs until he found the family at supper. Then in 1643 he took part in the inconclusive first battle of Newbury, and personally captured Captain Hall, the commander of 'Oliver [Cromwell]'s own Troop'. Southcott took Hall to Reading and treated him well, releasing him when the captain's friends sent a ransom of 'a fine managed horse, a suit of armour, and a valuable diamond ring', together with an offer of instant release if Southcott himself was captured. The account continues by saying that 'the King having heard of this feat, the first time he came into his presence he knighted him'. However, the King also criticised Southcott for letting 'so noted a man' go without obtaining the release of another prisoner in exchange, to which Southcott's friends 'made answer, that being he ventured his life in his Majesty's service, without receiving any pay for so doing, it was reasonable that he should make the best advantage for any lawful prize he could make'.

After surviving more fighting, Sir John returned home to Witham after the King's defeat at Naseby in 1645, and spent some of the subsequent years travelling in France and Italy, and living at the family house of Merstham in Surrey. He struck up two politically unlikely relationships during the later 1640s, conducting a correspondence with Oliver Cromwell's daughter and also having an offer of marriage rejected by the widow of the Earl of Essex, the leading Parliamentarian peer. Instead he married another peer's daughter.[25]

A Civil War officer

An officer like Henry Nevill of Cressing. Soldiers wore their ordinary clothes, which indicated their social position rather than which side they were on, so there was little difference in appearance between Royalist and Parliamentary soldiers.

The Southcott family later alleged that in 1648 their home at Witham Place had been 'severely plundered' by a Captain Foster and some of the Parliamentary forces returning from the siege of Colchester. Sequestration by Parliament also affected the estate, which was still owned by Sir John's father Edward. Two-thirds was taken, on account of the family's Catholicism and non-payment of taxes. If Sir John himself been the owner, the whole would have been sequestered because of his 'delinquency' in fighting for the King. In 1652 Edward died and Sir John inherited while he was 'beyond seas'. In August 1653 the growing corn was in danger of decay whilst the County and Parliamentary Committees discussed which of them should authorise it to be reaped. Another part of the estate was described in 1654 as a 'ruinous farm and barns', when the tenant asked for a contribution to repairs. When Sir John returned to England he asked to have the sequestration lifted. In December 1654 the Committee for Compounding agreed, 'on proof of his being a Protestant'. The claims of Protestantism must have surprised the Committee; perhaps his earlier friendships with Parliamentarian ladies assisted his cause. Much of the farmland was situated within the Witham manors of Henry Nevill, who had been engaged in a dispute with Southcott's grandfather twenty years earlier about the nature of some of the tenures. The political alliance of the two Royalist families did not prevent a renewal of the discord after 1654, when there was another dispute, lasting ten years, about the renewal of manorial leases. As late as 1715, Sir John's son referred to the 'long suit in Chancery betwixt my father and Mr.Nevill'.[26]

The Ayloffes

It is an interesting reflection on the heightened divisions created by the war, that in earlier years the Royalist Sir Benjamin Ayloffe of Great Braxted had been on friendly terms with Jeremy Aylett, discussed above, now his enemy as a County Committee member. Thus Aylett had been amongst those who had 'gone to take dinner att Braxted Magna, one summer day' with Sir Benjamin. Whilst 'seated under the great oak' there, the assembled company had discussed whether the Ayletts and the Ayloffes were related to each other. They compared the family shields inscribed on their signet rings to prove that they were not.[27] As we have seen, Sir Benjamin, formerly a magistrate serving Witham, was removed from the bench with other Royalists in 1642. In addition he was taken before the House of Commons in January 1643, where he confessed that in defiance of an earlier order, he had accepted a commission as sheriff of Essex from the King, and had published a proclamation in Chelmsford 'forbidding the Contributing of any Supplies to the Army raised by Parliament, or the Associating for Defence of the County'. After 'some Debate', the Commons ordered the seizure of his goods, and committed him to the Tower of London. His estate was also sequestered, both in order to pay the costs of the case and to provide 'money, horses, plate and arms'. As we have seen, his wife managed to reclaim three horses from another Parliamentary collection in

March. He was released on bail of £2,000 in 1646 and his property was restored to him in 1649 on payment of a fine, after he had claimed he had 'no livelihood for his six children'. He was said to have grieved for the death of Charles I in 1649 as if he were 'a near kinsman'.

Sir Benjamin's eldest son William left two contradictory pieces of information about his own role in the war. During negotiations about his estate in 1649, he told Parliament that he 'assisted the king in the second war only', whilst in a letter written in 1662 he said that he had not been able to 'goe to His Majesty's aide', being on bail like his father and concerned about friends who would have been obliged to pay if he disobeyed. This letter was written to his youngest brother John, and it also gives us an account of John's own participation. He is said to have raised a troop from the tenants of the Ayloffes and their neighbours when he 'came home from schoole' in 1651, still in his teens. William describes the scene to him as follows:

> That nighte after our Father had kissed and blessed you and you had mounted your good horse, Brighteye, we stood in the front yarde listeninge untill the hoofestrokes of your horses had dyed in the distance, and when we went into the house to the light of the candles, I noticed the tears in the eyes of our dear Father.

John fought in the battle of Worcester in September, where Witham's Parliamentarian soldier Thomas White was wounded. After taking part in one of the Royalist risings of 1655, John escaped to Virginia, where he married and settled. Confusingly, he there adopted the name Aylett, although his English relatives were not happy with the change.

Meanwhile Sir Benjamin and William continued at home in Braxted. A letter sent from William to John in 1658 suggested that Sir Benjamin had still 'never fullie recovered from his Sicknesse brought on by his longe confinement in the Tower', and described the 'stirring tymes' and 'greate unreste' occasioned by the death of Cromwell, when two great storms had led a friend to suggest that 'the olde Devil was in the winde', hunting for Cromwell's soul. William felt then that the return of the monarchy seemed unlikely, though he intended to 'work secretly' for it.[28]

RUNNING WITHAM

Before the war, 1640-1642

In the last chapter we saw some of the disruption in Witham church during the 1620s and 1630s, and how vicar Francis Wright had been challenged in several courts over a period of years, finally being suspended for three weeks in 1638 for immorality. Bill Cliftlands has used Wright's case to illustrate the fact that many of the complaints made by Parliament against ministers during the 1640s had originated in earlier years. And John Walter has pointed out that there was also a new situation after 1640, when the authorities themselves began to encourage people to give evidence against their own ministers. I owe to John Walter the knowledge that Wright's behaviour faced an official challenge soon after the election of the Long Parliament. It was one of the topics for a meeting of the new 'Grand Committee for Religion' as early as January 1641, two months after it had begun its work. We do not know exactly how Wright came to be selected for consideration on that occasion. The committee had called for local information, and many of the hearings at this time arose from parishioners' petitions. The committee's discussion about Wright was witnessed by diarist Symonds D'Ewes, a relative of the Barnardistons, and he reported that the following was 'proved' against Wright:

> that hee was given to dalliance and incontinencie with his own maidservants. That hee was an ordinarie drunkard; yea had made himselfe drunke on the Lordes day with the verie wine that left at the communion, and after hee himselfe had that day received the sacrament. That hee was a common swearer, and speaker of obscenitie. That hee was full of superstitious and idolatrous observations: bowing towards or to the communion table and to the elements in the Lordes supper after consecration; which hee did alsoe elevate: and that he had saied; that hee did conceive that ther was moore then a sacramentall presence of Christs bodie ther.[29]

Some of these assertions recall the suggestion made by Archbishop Laud in 1632 that Wright was sympathetic to Catholicism. However, at this stage the Committee had limited powers, and for the time being Francis Wright retained his post as vicar of Witham.

Other local information becomes scarce with the closure of the Church courts in 1641, but we do have a glimpse of Witham in November 1641. This suggests that Wright had little influence in the parish by then, because we know that two of his leading opponents from 1620s and 1630s were helping to run the parish, very probably as churchwardens. They were joiner Philip Pledger, the senior member of the first known group of gadders to Terling in 1626, who had continued as a Puritan activist ever since, and gentleman Robert Garrard(2), who had been the chief of the gadders and dissidents in the major demonstrations of 1631. In 1641 they and two other men were said to have taken widow Jane Earle from her bed one afternoon and 'by force' put her in into the cage for quarter or half an hour. The cage was a small lockup for casual wrongdoers (it may have been on the corner of Mill Lane and Newland Street).[30] On this occasion her alleged offence was being absent from church. She argued in turn that she had walked fifteen miles on the previous day and was tired. However, her reputation might have attracted particular attention. In 1639 she had been 'commonly reputed and taken to be a woman of very rude behaviour and hath an ill report', according to a note made in the Archdeacon's court book after two allegations of drunkenness. She was also suspected on one occasion of fornication. The cage incident in 1641 only came to light because Jane accused the Puritan parish officers of assaulting her in her own house. The two other men who assisted in locking her up were Nathaniel Garrard, perhaps a relative of Robert's, and John Freeborne, an

active newcomer. At about the same time that John Freeborne had come to Witham, his brother William, of Maldon, had probably crossed the Atlantic to New England. There he had been made a freeman of the Massachusetts colony in 1634, on the same day as Reverend Thomas Hooker of Chelmsford, and the younger Robert Gamlin, probably an associate of Reverend Thomas Weld of Terling. Since then William Freeborne and some of his fellow settlers had left Massachusetts in disgrace after a religious dispute about the nature of salvation, and founded the separate community of Rhode Island.[31]

It is perhaps no coincidence that the two magistrates who took Jane Earle's statement in 1641 were the Royalists Sir Thomas Wiseman of Rivenhall and Sir Benjamin Ayloffe of Great Braxted. Perhaps they even insisted on her making the charge as a small local demonstration of resistance to the new shift of power. As already seen, they were both dismissed after the outbreak of war in the following year.

The Parliamentarian petition of January 1642

Soon after the locking up of Jane Earle, the confidence of Witham's leaders was demonstrated in a grander fashion by their contribution to the great Essex petition to the House of Commons in support of Parliament, submitted on 20 January 1642. It has been suggested that the parish clergy collected the names on behalf of the Earl of Warwick. But although Francis Wright may still have been in the parish at the time, a petition criticising the King was not for him. One part of Witham's sheet is headed by the signature of John Gravener(3), the constable of the half-hundred, the other part by that of Robert Garrard(2). Garrard seems to have been the only Witham person who also signed the shorter petition to the House of Lords; perhaps he put his name to that whilst delivering the Witham names to the Earl of Warwick. Gravener and Garrard were probably the two richest men in the parish apart from the Catholic Southcotts, and it seems a reasonable supposition that they and their friends collected the other names. We have heard much of Garrard's dissent, but this was perhaps Gravener's first public declaration of commitment against the King. As seen in the last two chapters he had conscientiously collected the Forced Loan for the King in 1626, and whilst Charles and Laud had been in power, he does not seem to have publicly joined the parish's Puritan disturbances, even under the provocation of Wright's misbehaviour. His only recorded misdemeanour during the 1630s was when he failed to provide arms for the musters in 1634, after which he had given a 'promise of conformity' to the Privy Council.[32]

The petition to the Commons perhaps included about half the householders' names in Essex as a whole. Witham's contribution was much greater. There were 223 names from the parish, probably ninety per cent or more of the householders, of all ranks. There had been 106 names of people of middling rank and above on the

1636 Ship Money assessment for Witham, whilst the 1673 Hearth Tax return showed 108 householders taxed and another 160 exempt, a total of 268. Many parishes kept a list of inhabitants for the purpose of checking church attendance, so perhaps this was used in compiling the petition. In fact it is very likely that many of the signatures were collected at church, for convenience. Some of the people whose names did not appear were known Royalists or supporters of Francis Wright like gentleman William Thursby, grocer Alexander Freeborne, clothier Henry Wood and yeoman and innholder William Brooke. But two of the men who had earlier been witnesses for Wright did contribute, namely John Parker and John Alexander.[33] Conversely some absentees were hard to explain and may merely have been away from town. One was cordwainer James Princet, Dame Katherine Barnardiston's assistant in the campaign against Francis Wright, and frequently in London for that purpose.

It was common at this time for names on petitions to be all written down by the same person, with no effort to obtain an individual's signature or even a 'mark', which they made with a cross or some other sign if they could not sign their name. Some of the entries from Essex in 1642 were like this. In the Witham section however, only the bottom half, with a hundred or so names, was written in a uniform hand. At the top were signatures and marks, about sixty of each. This format is shown here in figure 23 opposite, perhaps symbolising to some extent the social structure of the town. Not surprisingly those who signed were generally better-off than those who made marks or whose names were written in. The people whose names were written for them included some who were definitely poor, but about one third of them were known to have had specific trades.[34] There is further discussion of the petition in relation to literacy and status in chapter 2 (pages 25 and 28).

The 'Royalist' peace petition of January 1643

In Essex as a whole, the later 'Royalist' petition included very roughly half as many names as the Parliamentarian one a year earlier, but from Witham the proportion was only about fifteen per cent. This time all the names were written in the same hand, even though most of the people would have been able to sign if asked to do so. A number of the lists from the country parishes around Witham were headed by their own vicars and rectors, many of them soon to be removed from their livings by Parliament. They included George Bosvill of Rivenhall, Edward Strutt of Faulkbourne, and William Hull of Ulting. However, Witham's Francis Wright had left the town by this time, and another clergyman, John Heron, headed the Witham list. The other thirty-four contributors were very varied socially, ranging from yeomen and innkeepers to people who were known to have been paupers at one time. A few had other Royalist associations, like William Brooke, Alexander Freeborne and Robert Bunny. But as many as twenty-one out of the thirty-five had also appeared on the petition supporting Parliament a year earlier; seven had actually

signed their names on it, six had made their mark there, and eight had been written in.[35] These who appeared on both petitions included both rich and poor men, as described in the end notes. They included yeoman John Alexander and gentleman John Greene, both of whom had been called to give evidence for vicar Francis Wright in 1634, though Greene failed to appear, and opposed Wright later on, in 1643. There was also Nicholas Greene, a cardmaker, probably John's relative. Both Greenes were professional informers, perhaps a reminder that some names might be 'bought' on such occasions.[36] It seems difficult to generalise about the beliefs of the twenty-one people who appeared on both of the petitions. However when discussing the fourteen individuals who only put their name to the later peace petition, I have sometimes been bold enough to use the term 'Royalist', even though this may be an oversimplification of their position.

The sequestration of vicar Francis Wright, 1643

We know that vicar Francis Wright was still in Witham in January 1642, when parishioner Josiah Lock was called upon to keep the peace towards him. But he had certainly stopped officiating in Witham church by the spring of 1642 and probably sooner. He fled to the house of another parson, Daniel Falconer of Aldham, who kept him 'in his house to secure him from the Parliament officers'. Falconer also persuaded Wright and three other 'scandalous' ministers to preach for him there. Some of his duties in Witham may have been taken over unofficially for a short time by the John Heron whose name appeared in the last-mentioned petition, and who seemed to be the sort of man who was able to secure appointments under both Parliament and the King. By this time Parliament was proceeding to remove ministers of which it disapproved. The complaints against them included 'scandalous' behaviour, their support for the King against Parliament, and their use of rituals said to be Laudian or even Catholic in nature. Eventually about 150 men lost their livings in Essex, there being about 400 parishes in all, and in due course this is what happened to Francis Wright. He and his protector in Aldham, Daniel Falconer, were both discovered there and Wright was taken to gaol in Southwark to await examination. By September 1642 he had been released on bail of £500, provided that he held himself ready 'to make his personall appearance' to defend himself. When he was wanted, word was to be left at the house of a barber surgeon in Carter Lane, near St.Paul's cathedral. This was the street in which Witham's judge John Southcott had his London house sixty years previously.[37]

Meanwhile, as we have seen, in January 1643 Parliamentary collectors took one of Wright's horses. He also claimed later that his house at Witham had been plundered, though if this is true we do not know when it happened. In April 1643 he was finally called before the relevant committee at the House of Commons. In the same way that had happened in the High Commission hearings of the 1630s, the final accusations

FIGURE 23

PETITION TO HOUSE OF COMMONS FROM ESSEX, 20 JANUARY 1641/2: DIAGRAM OF THE 223 NAMES IN THE SECTION SENT FROM WITHAM

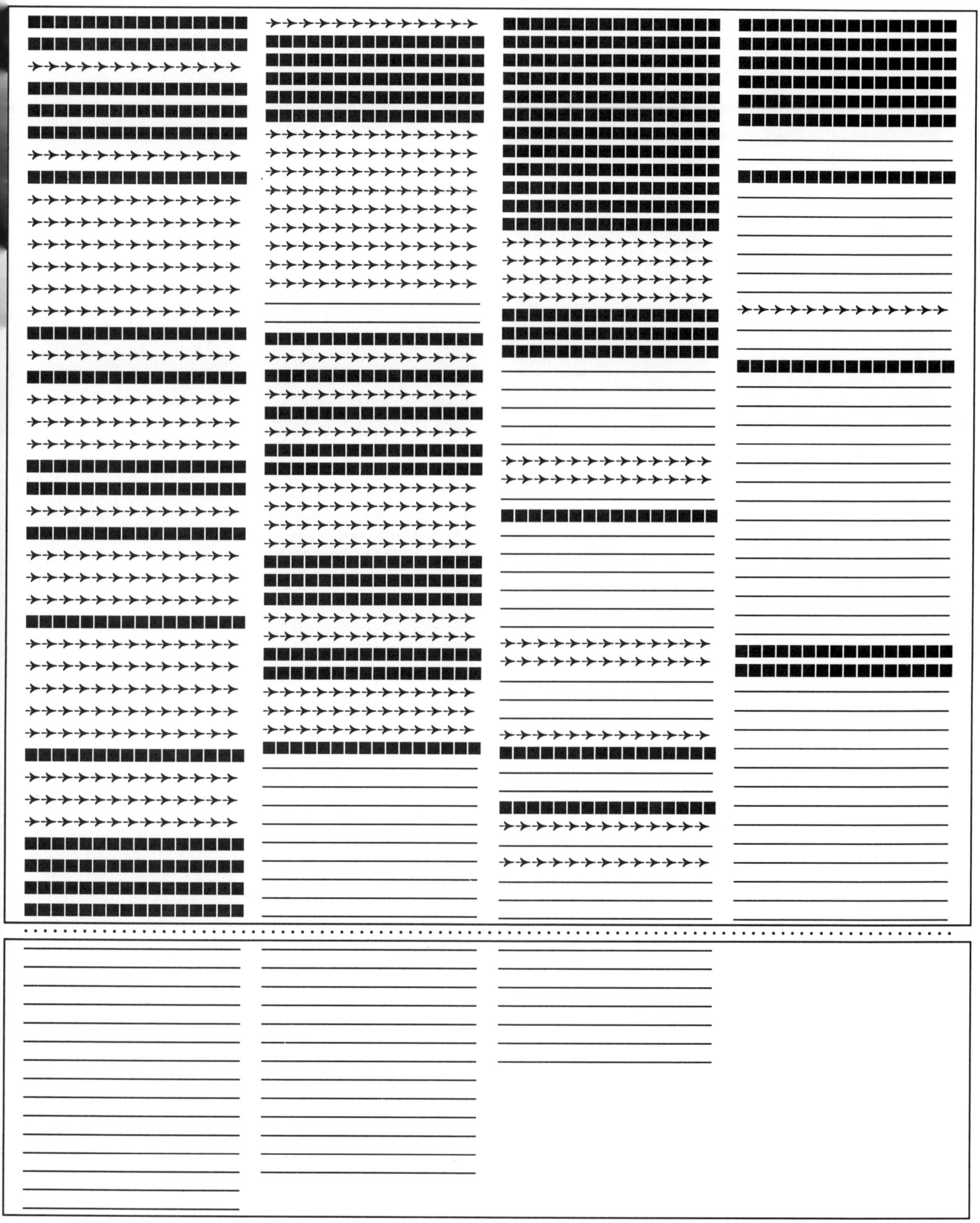

KEY:

■■■■■■■■■■■■■■■■ = signed   →→→→→→→→→→→→→→ = made own mark

――――――――――――――― = name written in by one of the Witham organisers

· · · · · · · · · · · · · · · · · · · = join between main sheet and extra sheet

ignored earlier allegations about his religious preferences, and concentrated on his immorality. Thus they referred to his:

> common temptinge of women his servants and parishioners to Adultery and of being a common haunter of Alehouses and Tavernes and a common Drunckard and Prophaner of the worshipe of God by publique performeinge the same in his Drunckennesse; and a common swearer and a common user of corrupte Communicacion, and other Misdemeanours.

His answer was heard, but the committee found him 'unworthy and unfitte to Execute and hould any Ecclesiasticall benefice or Promocion in the Church', and recommended that the living of Witham should be should be taken away from him, or 'sequestered'. The Commons agreed, and issued an order to that effect, subject to the approval of the House of Lords.[38]

When the Lords heard the case on 1 May 1643, Wright did not appear, although he had been served personally with a notice two days previously. There is a surviving document headed 'Francis Wright, viccar of Witham', purporting to be a list of witnesses against Wright, but, as pointed out by Bill Cliftlands, the heading is mistaken. In fact it relates to the vicar of Stapleford Tawney, who was alleged to have said that he 'hoped to see the Earle of Warwicks head off', and that Parliament was a 'company of factious fellowes and that the Parliament is noe Parliament and that the major parte of the Lords and Commons being with the Kinge, they are the Parliament'. As we have seen, the claims against Wright were more personal. The Lords heard four named witnesses against him, James Princet, John Greene, Jonas Prost, and Elizabeth Croxon; others may have attended also. James Princet was the Witham cordwainer who had been pursuing Wright for over ten years, with the initial encouragement of Dame Katherine Barnardiston. He must have been an accomplished witness by now, with a successful appearance in the House of Lords furnishing a suitable reward for all his efforts. The £10 which Dame Katherine left him had perhaps been supplemented by financial support from other wealthy parishioners. In contrast, John Greene was the prosperous Witham gentleman, known as a professional informer, whose name appeared on the 'Royalist' peace petition of 1643. He seemed keen to ingratiate himself with all sides. Thus although he was now opposing Wright, he had actually been called to court to support him in 1634, though had failed to appear then. And although the Parliamentarian collectors had taken one of his horses in 1643, he had managed to persuade them to let him have one back again. The third witness, Jonas Prost, son of Colchester's Puritan Dutch minister, had been curate of Witham in 1637 and so well placed to observe his vicar at first hand. And the fourth, Elizabeth Croxon, a Witham woman, was perhaps giving evidence of Wright's 'tempting' of women; in 1630 she had been accused of having an illegitimate child by one man, and of 'living incontinently' with another. Like Princet, she would doubtless have needed financial assistance to travel to London. The House of Lords was persuaded

of Wright's wickedness by this rather ill-assorted group, the Commons sequestration order was confirmed, and Francis Wright sent to the Fleet prison, 'there to remain during the Pleasure of this House'. It is not known how long he stayed there. When in the following year his former neighbour, Edward Strutt, rector of Faulkbourne, was going through the same process, part of the evidence quoted against him was that he had said 'Parliament could not by law take away' Wright's living. He response to the various accusations against him was that Parliament was guilty of treason, and was a 'body without a head' in the absence of the King.[39]

Vicars after 1643

Parliament appointed Edmund Brewer to replace Francis Wright in Witham, and reported him to be a 'godly learned Orthodoxe Divine'. A Cambridge graduate, he had been constantly in trouble with the ecclesiastical authorities for his Puritanism during the 1630s. When he was vicar of Castle Hedingham in 1637 the archbishop's Vicar General had reported him to be a 'very inconformable man', frequently omitting the sign of the cross in baptism, not wearing his surplice, and allowing communicants to stand rather than kneel. He had avoided suspension by apologising. He left Witham in 1645 to return to Hedingham. Two other Puritan ministers succeeded him. The first was Richard Rowles, reported by a parliamentary inquiry in 1650 to be an 'able, godly preacher'. When he died in about 1653, he was followed by John Ludgater who stayed until he was ejected in 1660.[40] The evidence suggests that all of these ministers did participate in the affairs of Witham. Edmund Brewer signed a return from the parish about alehouses in 1644, and in 1658, long after he had returned to Hedingham, Mary Lucas of Witham left him twenty shillings to come back and preach at her burial. As she did not die until late 1660, after the Restoration, he may have had difficulty in doing so. She also left ten shillings to the current minister, John Ludgater. In 1657 clothier John True left forty shillings to Ludgater, who probably wrote his will for him, and also wrote two other Witham wills. Richard Rowles wrote one too. Witham clergymen had very rarely contributed to will-writing since the 1590s. The resumption of calls on their services may well have arisen from the death of the prolific lay scribe Edmund Halys in 1648, at the age of 84.[41]

The sequestrators of the vicarage

When a living was sequestered, Parliament appointed local people as 'sequestrators' to take over its administration, and in April 1643 the House of Commons named eight men to carry out the task in Witham. They were the clothier, yeoman and gentleman John Gravener(3), the two gentlemen, Robert Garrard(2) and William Allen, the three yeomen Jerome Skingley, Robert Burchard(3), and Thomas Parker, grocer Alexander Freeborne, and clothier John Freeborne. They or any three of them were to choose collectors 'to gather tithes' and report any difficulties to the Commons or the Lords. John Walter has pointed out the radical nature of arrangements such as these, whereby groups of middling parishioners were responsible directly to Parliament, without the customary mediation of the county's magistrates. The names of the Witham sequestrators are familiar ones from other parts of the political and economic story of the town. It seems likely that wealth was one of the main qualifications. Their median assessment in the 1636 Ship Money return was sixteen shillings, compared to a median of three shillings for all the people in the return. All the sequestrators were assessed at over ten shillings except the Freebornes. It is quite surprising that the Freebornes were included, particularly as they were also relative newcomers to the town.[42]

The duties were primarily administrative, and it has been suggested by Bill Cliftlands that, in general, the people who were appointed need not necessarily be expected to be fervent Parliamentarians or Puritans. This seems to be borne out in Witham. In particular, it seems fairly clear that Alexander Freeborne favoured the King. Not only did he sign the peace petition of 1643, but he was to be given the post of master of Chelmsford House of Correction in 1660, when the restored Royalist magistrates had dismissed the previous holder of the post, and referred to Freeborne's 'honesty, fidelity and fitness' for it. In 1652 he was accused of kicking and whipping Elizabeth Fuller whilst she was gleaning in his harvest fields. The magistrate who took her evidence against him was Jeremy Aylett of Rivenhall, a member of the County Committee appointed by Parliament.[43]

Turning to the other sequestrators, Thomas Parker appeared on the 'peace' petition with Alexander Freeborne, but also signed the petition favouring Parliament in 1642. John Gravener(3) was previously conformist or at least cautious, and probably continued to be so, but he had led the 1642 petition, on which the names of the other five sequestrators were also prominent. Of these, Robert Burchard(3) may have been quite young. His uncle and grandfather of the same name had held office in the parish but none were noticeably involved in any faction, though it was his mother Frances who had rather mysteriously left Francis Wright money in 1632 if he would preach at her burial. Robert(3) himself died in 1647. We know of more clearly defined Puritan affinities for the remaining four men. Robert Garrard(2) is already well known to us for his very active opposition to Francis Wright during the preceding years. Jerome Skingley had been presented for not kneeling at prayers in 1632, had been an active Puritan churchwarden in 1638, and had several other similar credentials. He moved away to Fordham in about 1650. William Allen was newer to the town. With Skingley, he witnessed the will of the 'schismatic' Solomon Turner in 1646, and the Parliamentarian magistrates appointed him to succeed John Gravener(3) as a high constable of Witham half-hundred in 1650. In 1653 he married the widow of vicar Richard Rowles. John Freeborne had joined Garrard in the action against

Jane Earle described above, and later became a Quaker. He was a relative of two of his fellow sequestrators, Robert Burchard(3) and Alexander Freeborne, but probably had little in common with the Royalist Alexander, his nephew.[44]

Local affairs, 1643-1660

This was clearly a dramatic time everywhere. The floor of Witham's St.Nicholas church was still 'much decayed' as late as 1664 'by reason of the souldiers shutting up there in the late unhappy times'. This may possibly refer to the occasion when some of the Parliamentarian army under Colonel Whalley spent a night at Witham on the way to the siege of Colchester in June 1648, and found much of the country thereabouts 'very cordial towards the army'. But in general the records are silent on the sort of alarms and disputes in the town about which the Church court records gave us some insight in earlier years. The local flavour of the drama has only come down to us from a few places. For instance, there survive detailed parish records from Chelmsford, and wonderful diaries from Isaac Archer of Halstead, Colchester and Dedham, from Sir Humphrey Mildmay of Danbury, and from Ralph Josselin, the Puritan vicar of Earls Colne. Josselin was related to the Johnson family of Witham, and during the 1650s he occasionally rode the ten miles here to visit and to preach. Thus in March 1658 he recorded that he 'rid to my Cosin Johnsons', probably Edward Johnson of Blunts Hall. The following day he preached a 'Lecture' at Witham, based on Psalm 78, 'pressing to stedfastnes', and at the same time:

> saw my freinds, who were well, god good to mee in my jorney and in divers of my affaires, lord I see many things in other families, that I blesse thy name are not in mine.

A few months later he found 'very chearfull' audiences at both Witham and Hatfield Peverel. And in November of the same year he was back in Witham, taking as his text 'James 2.23', and again observing 'the troubles attended some persons in their affaires, which allayes mine, and sweetens my mercies and enjoyments'. In spite of these problems, he had 'hopes of good' when he again preached here in June 1659.[45] So we can tell that Witham had its discussions, disagreements and illnesses, as well as its joys, even though we do not have the day-to-day picture of them that Josselin provides us with for Earls Colne. This may be borne in mind when we review the rather static picture of Witham that has come down to us for this period, much of it comprising information about the middling or better-off parishioners who took part in various official activities.

The quarter sessions records are the most helpful in this respect. They suggest that people of Puritan sympathies often obtained positions which allowed them to try and influence the parishioners' morality. In particular, four of the eight men who had been appointed as sequestrators of the vicarage tended to lead the way in other matters too, and they were the four who probably had the closest Puritan connections, Robert Garrard(2),

William Allen, John Freeborne and Jerome Skingley. The first three were 'chiefe inhabitants' who signed a return about alehouses in 1644, when they were joined by vicar Edmund Brewer, Robert Burchard(3), and Richard Porter, a yeoman who died soon afterwards. And together with the new vicar Richard Rowles and magistrate Jeremy Aylett from Rivenhall, the four of them comprised the proposed 'classis' or presbytery for the Witham half-hundred, chosen by the County Committee in 1646. Meanwhile, just across the Suffolk border, four of Dame Katherine Barnardiston's relatives, who had been well-known to her, served on the similar classis of the Risbridge hundred. There were two each from the families of her first and second husbands, the Soames and the Barnardistons, together with some of their renowned Puritan ministers.[46]

We do not really know whether the Witham classis actually functioned as intended, but leading parishioners contributed to a drive against alehouses which was reminiscent of the 1620s. The 1644 return had been a response to a Parliamentary edict which resulted in a county-wide effort. It proposed to permit only eight alehousekeepers in Witham, six in Newland Street and two in Chipping Hill. Earlier in the century there were usually about twelve licences issued for the parish. One of the favoured alehouses of 1644 was the one belonging to the Thomas Nicholls who had allegedly beguiled Francis Wright's servant in 1639. In 1645 the new godly ministers of Essex, feeling 'dejected by the deluge of corruptions', secured yet further restriction in the form of monthly presentments at quarter sessions, not only of disorderly alehouses but of swearers, profaners of the Sabbath, and promoters of schism in the Church. In subsequent years, Witham's officials did challenge some keepers of disorderly alehouses in the courts. They did not appear to be in the same large numbers that had typified the period around the 1620s, though possibly individual magistrates dealt with cases that have not been recorded. One of the offenders from those earlier times, Rooke Allen, was still working, and had managed to be included in the approved list in 1644, but he was in trouble again in 1646 for using short measures and allowing disorder. Another very frequent earlier troublemaker, Francis Ellis, had died, but his widow continued the tradition of keeping an unlicensed alehouse. And a new culprit, brewer Richard Earnesbie, attracted a great deal of attention for unlicensed activity at his two establishments, one at the bottom of Newland Street in Witham, and the other in Heybridge. Witham's two fairs were also suspended at around this time; one of them had already been rescheduled in 1616 in order to avoid Sundays.[47]

There were other administrative roles in the town which had less moral import. One was that of parish surveyor. This could be a somewhat disagreeable post, the holders of which had to persuade the parishioners to contribute labourers and carts for road repairs. In 1642 the surveyors reported well over one hundred Witham people to quarter sessions for not fulfilling their obligations. It seems that one of the two parish surveyors was usually a man who inclined towards the King. Thus yeoman Jeffrey Whale, and grocers William Robinson and Alexander Freeborne, were surveyors in 1642, 1644 and 1651 respectively.[48]

However, when twenty-one new trustees were chosen for the Newland Street almshouses in 1652, none of these three Royalists were invited to join them. Such trustees could exercise moral as well as financial responsibility, in that they selected the residents of the almshouses. The new appointments were necessary because there were only two of the previous trustees surviving. One was clothier Nathaniel Nowell, who had earlier borrowed money from Dame Katherine Barnardiston and had now moved to Bocking, and the other was the prosperous John Gravener(3), whom we have seen as a supporter of Parliament but otherwise perhaps not strongly committed. It is noticeable that he had not participated in either the alehouse return or the classis in spite of his wealth. He had probably been running the charity alone for some time. The new trustees came from thirteen different families altogether. They included seven pairs of fathers and sons; the appointment of young men was customary in the hope of extending the continuous life of the trusteeship, though Gravener's own son John(4), newly appointed, in fact died before his father. Of the thirteen 'adults', five called themselves gentlemen, which seemed to be becoming a more widely used title at this time, and three were yeomen, so it was quite a prosperous group. Two of the others were clothiers. Robert Garrard(2), William Allen, and John Freeborne, three of the four Puritan sequestrators, were included together with their sons. Their colleague Jerome Skingley had moved to Fordham by this time. The rest of the trustee families included three others who had been associated with the 1642 petition supporting Parliament, and also Thomas Goulston, whose position we have seen to be uncertain.[49] There were in addition four families who were newcomers to the scene, all probably later associated with nonconformity.[50] Lastly there was clothier Robert Jackson(1), of whom we shall hear more in the next chapter (pages 140-42). The Jackson family tended towards conformity. He may have been included because it was his great-grandfather, George Armond(1), who had endowed one of the almshouses in 1627. Armond had at that time chosen men of quite varied views as his trustees, but times were different in 1652.[51]

A year later, in 1653, nineteen Witham men signed a petition to quarter sessions, asking for the 'direction' of the court in setting the poor rate, because they had failed to do so themselves even after several meetings. The particular point at issue seemed to be the allocation of responsibility between landlord and tenant. Quarter sessions agreed with the petitioners that the landlords should make some contribution, and made an order to that effect. The nineteen were less prosperous than the almshouse trustees, including only one gentlemen and one yeoman. Again they were a mixture of the cautious and the committed for Parliament. Seven were clothiers, there was one woolcomber, and the rest were tradesmen and craftsmen. The episode serves as a useful indication that there were other people taking an active interest in some aspects of the town's life, outside the fairly select few of most of the groups discussed so far. Newcomers were even more prominent than they had been amongst the trustees. Thus for as many as seven of the nineteen men, their signing of the 1653 petition was their first appearance in the surviving records.[52]

RELIGIOUS SEPARATISM

Although these people were co-operating in the organisation of Witham during and after the War, they must already have held differing views about the unity of the Church. The opinions of many of them can only be discovered with the hindsight of the 1660s, after which some families, like the Jacksons, felt able to stay with the restored Church of Charles II, and others, like the Garrards, did not. But there were already some parishioners who were leaving the Church during the 1650s. Thus out of the thirteen families providing almshouse trustees in 1652, two became Quakers. And as many as one third of the poor-rate rate petitioners of 1653 went on to have Quaker associations, including clothiers John Freeborne, newcomer Robert Barwell(1) from Coggeshall and probably Richard True from the same parish. The Quakers became the dominant separatist group in Witham, where we know nothing specific about the Baptists and Brownists who had already influenced other places like neighbouring Terling and the county town of Chelmsford during the 1640s. It was the national scale of movements like the Quakers and Baptists that made them startling. The idea of schism and separatism was not in itself new. We heard in the last chapter (page 112) how Witham glover Solomon Turner was called as a 'great schismaticke' in 1635. When his will was written in 1646, it did not include any religious preamble at all, and this soon became a characteristic of Quaker wills also. We do not usually know the religious affiliation of the fourteen Witham people for whom we have surviving wills from the 1650s, but it is interesting that half of their wills had either no preamble at all like Turner's, or had an extremely brief one along the lines of 'I commit my soul into the hands of almighty God'. Of the seven wills from the 1650s which did in contrast have longer religious preambles, four were written by Royalist grocer William Robinson, and a fifth was the will of Royalist Jeffrey Whale himself.[53]

Quakerism

Quakers have been influential all over the world during the last three hundred years. Of the many Christian sects which emerged during the 1650s, it was they who made the most impact in much of Essex. The term 'Quaker' was first used in jest by critics of the Society of Friends, but it has since become a generally accepted term to describe its members. Quakers emphasised the direct access of the individual to God, without ministers or ceremony. The implications of this made Quakerism a threatening concept for the civil as well as religious

authorities. Already by the late 1640s some of their founders in the Midlands and the north of England were travelling those areas, and by the early 1650s were linking them into what has been called 'a loose kind of church fellowship'. They sent speakers to undertake successful visits to the south of England in 1654 and 1655, when their 'foreign' speech must have accentuated their striking impact. In the latter year the 18-year old James Parnell visited Essex and attracted attention in Coggeshall, six miles from Witham, by conducting a dispute with a preacher in the parish church and holding a meeting in the street. Kelvedon magistrate Dionyse Wakering arrested him and he was imprisoned in Colchester castle, where the gaoler was instructed not to let any 'giddy-headed people' visit him. He died there after refusing to pay a fine of £40. Wakering is said to have regretted his role afterwards, and when he suffered an unpleasant death from smallpox in the following year, Parnell's fellow-Quakers took it as a judgement. It was also in 1655 that George Fox came to Essex. He lived longer than most of his colleagues, and in due course he became known as the leader of the movement. According to his journal, during this visit of 1655 he:

> came to Coggeshall where there was a meeting of about two thousand people as it was judged, which lasted some several hours, and a glorious meeting it was.

In July 1656, the magistrates at Essex quarter sessions issued an order to all the constables in the county, that they should seek out and arrest Quakers, who were described in a long and hostile tirade. They were said to:

> travaile and passe from County to County and from place to place propagateing and spreading certaine desperate and damnable opinions and Delusions.[54]

John Freeborne, the Witham clothier, was recalled by later members as one of the first Essex Quakers. We have already heard about the part that he had played in the administration of the town, his rebellious brother in New England, his Puritan and Parliamentarian sympathies, and his Royalist nephew Alexander. His house in Newland Street still stands, and is shown overleaf. Very probably John and some of his fellow townsmen went from Witham to hear George Fox in Coggeshall in 1655, because in the next year they began to keep their own register book of Quaker births in Witham (Quakers did not baptise). It begins with five entries for the children of one Witham family, the Howletts, the most recent having been born in 1656 and the older ones having been entered retrospectively. Their father John was a cordwainer who had come to the town from London with his wife Elizabeth and baby son William in about 1648. Continuous entries were made from 1656 onwards, with the birth of Mary Pledger, who was a daughter of George, a joiner, and a granddaughter of both John Freeborne and Philip Pledger, who had together helped to lock up Jane Earle for not attending church in 1641. The first recorded Quaker marriage in Witham was in 1659, when gardener Nicholas Winkfield married Elizabeth Harding. Both came from families which were fairly long-established in the town, but their only known history of earlier

Freebornes

The home and workplace of clothier John Freeborne, one of the first Witham Quakers. After his death in 1675 it continued to bear his name, but became a farmhouse. It is now no.3 Newland Street. The lower picture shows a fireplace in one of the downstairs rooms.

activism consisted of unexplained absences from church by some of the Winkfields. Elizabeth's uncle, John Hull, was another Quaker. John Freeborne headed the list of witnesses at the wedding. Nicholas and Elizabeth occupied land in Witham and Faulkbourne, to which they later moved, and in 1682 they were to donate property in Maldon Road, formerly part of Nicholas's grandfather's land, for the first fixed Quaker meeting house in the town. Their second child, Peter, born in 1662 and entered then in the Quaker register, was eventually baptised into the Church of England in 1718 at the age of 57.[55]

Although we know from this register that the Quakers already had some organisation in Witham by 1656, the records remain silent about their actual behaviour in their earliest years, and about the reaction to them of their fellow-townspeople. Nevertheless they continued to meet, and we know that their fellows elsewhere in the county were active in demonstrations such as speaking in churches after sermons. Furthermore, George Fox passed through Essex again in 1659.[56] Later developments will be described in the next chapter.

OVERVIEW

This was one of the most momentous periods in British history. It continues to be the subject of great debate amongst historians. Could either side have averted war? To what extent did ordinary people in counties like Essex really feel spontaneous support for Parliament or the King, and to what extent were they obeying their leaders? How many people were undecided or changed their minds? How much did political and religious belief coincide?[57] Most of Witham's life at the time has been lost to us. Even more than usual, we feel we are peering helplessly into the darkness. But it is just possible to see that on the one hand the parishioners were fully involved in the stirring affairs of state, and all the conflicts that they created, whilst on the other they worked together to sustain the town and its needs. Thus during the early 1640s, when the King's unpopularity was at its height, the house of Thomas Bayles, Royalist `and possible Catholic, was attacked, and the names of nearly every person in the town were added to the great petition in support of Parliament which was organised by the Earl of Warwick. The rich and law-abiding John Gravener(3), then high constable of the half-hundred, joined the more vociferous Puritan parishioners at the head of the list.

When Parliament removed unsympathetic and immoral clergymen, Witham's vicar Francis Wright was sent away with them. This was in 1643, after he had survived more than fifteen years of criticism from Dame Katherine Barnardiston, many of his parishioners, and from the Church courts themselves. Even before his formal dismissal, Wright's opponents had probably taken charge of the parish. Afterwards they were able to continue in positions of moral influence together with their new more sympathetic vicars. Several of them were appointed as sequestrators to administer the finances of the vicarage.

Nevertheless, Gravener and some less committed colleagues were also chosen as sequestrators, and so also was Royalist Alexander Freeborne. Declared Royalists were in the minority in the town, but Freeborne and several other Witham parishioners had joined in the 'peace' petition supporting the King in 1643, some names appearing on both this and the earlier one in favour of Parliament. Several wealthy families around Witham had always leaned towards the King and what he stood for. They lost their positions as magistrates, but they managed to send their sons to fight in the War, in spite of financial penalties. So did the Catholic Southcotts from Witham itself. And even though much of the local administration had been taken over by Parliament's supporters, the Witham half-hundred bailiffs and one of the Witham parish surveyors were nearly always Royalists. These were doubtless two rather unpopular posts, and it is possible that the men were being given a burden rather than honour. But at least they were allowed to wield some authority over their fellow-parishioners.

By the 1650s, religious separatism, on a far larger scale than before, was adding a new dimension to local affairs. Some of the Witham parishioners who had supported Parliament became Quakers, and were reinforced by wealthy newcomers like Robert Barwell(1). Unlike some other separatist groups, such as the Chelmsford Baptists, many of them were of high status, and they continued playing a part in parish affairs, in spite of the hostility and suspicion with which they were viewed by magistrates.[58] The next chapter will describe how they fared after the Restoration of Charles II, together with those of their fellow-parishioners who had outwardly conformed before 1660.

11. CHARLES II, 1660-1685, JAMES II, 1685-1688, and WILLIAM and MARY, 1689-1702

BACKGROUND

The arrival of the King Charles II in May 1660 was witnessed from a balcony in the Strand by Sir Benjamin Ayloffe and his son William of Great Braxted, adjoining Witham. The King greeted Sir Benjamin personally and recalled the service of his other son, John Ayloffe, in the Civil War. William later reported the 'triumphal entrance' and the:

> brilliante scene, the flashing of steel, the rustleinge of the banners, the dancinge of plumes, the flowers carpetinge the streets, the shouttinge of the hostes, and the brazen blare of the trumpets.

He felt it to be 'the worke of the Lorde' and concluded, 'O it was moste glorious to us Cavaliers'. People like the Ayloffes were generally to be well satisfied by the results of the Restoration. Many of their opponents of earlier years were punished, whilst others came round to supporting them. For instance, Dame Katherine Barnardiston's nephew Sir Robert Titchborne of London, who had sat in judgement on Charles I, was imprisoned after narrowly escaping execution. But her godson and step-grandson, Sir Thomas Barnardiston, an energetic Cromwellian in Suffolk during the 1650s, came to favour the King after 1660, and as a result received a baronetcy in 1663.[1]

Sir Benjamin Ayloffe was himself elected to the new Parliament, though he died soon afterwards. The strictness of the new religious settlement is generally attributed to Parliament rather than the King. The Act of Uniformity of 1662 established a Church in which there was no room for the variety of religious practice and belief that had developed during the previous twenty years. In many ways, its aims were similar to those of Archbishop Laud during the 1630s. Bishops were restored, and adherence to the liturgy of a newly revised Prayer Book was enforced. Clergymen who had been deposed by Parliament during the early 1640s were to be allowed to return to their former parishes if they wished, and about eight hundred did so. One of them was Francis Wright of Witham. The men who had held those posts in the meantime were therefore deprived. A similar number of clergymen in addition were removed because they would not agree to comply with the new requirements. The lower ecclesiastical courts were revived in a modified form and supervised by men loyal to the King.[2]

Religious dissenters now included not only the separate Christian sects which had already begun to form before 1660 like the Quakers and Baptists, but 'nonconformists'. I shall use this term, as is customary, to describe the new dissenters, who had hitherto remained in the Church of England but found that they could not conform to the new requirements after 1660. They were often led by clergymen who had been removed from their parish appointments. Some of these men stayed in their old parishes, like John Stalham in Terling, whilst others moved elsewhere. Nonconformity did not usually entail the same degree of social radicalism as was associated with the older sects.

All sorts of religious dissenters became subject to restrictions. Firstly, in early 1662, there was an enactment announcing that Quaker assemblies were being held 'to the terror of the people' and making it an offence for more than four adult Quakers to meet together. Quakers were to be punished if they refused to take an oath, which they often did because of the implication that they could not be truthful without it. Then in 1664, Queen Elizabeth's legislation of 1593 against dissent in general was revived, with new penalties, including transportation to the colonies for a third offence. Attendance at the parish church was to be enforced, and other religious meetings or 'conventicles' were forbidden. In some places, such as Cambridge, mass imprisonment resulted. Nonetheless, dissent continued. Quaker organisation became more formalised by the end of the 1660s, whilst in early 1672 Charles' Declaration of Indulgence temporarily allowed nonconformist meeting places other than Quaker ones to be licensed. However, the later years of Charles' reign were characterised by fierce religious conflict. His increased hostility to the nonconformists was associated with his friendship with Louis XIV and Catholic France. This inspired a movement against Catholicism which helped to unite the newly emerging Whig party, and was fuelled by the discovery of the so-called 'Popish Plot' in 1678. In Essex, the 1679 election resulted in success for the Whig candidates, who came from families which had been associated with the Parliamentarians during the Civil War.[3]

Charles died in February 1685. His son James II, who succeeded him, was perceived as being even more sympathetic towards Catholicism, and in mid-1685 the Duke of Monmouth, Charles' illegitimate son, landed in

Dorset and attempted a rebellion in support of Protestantism. It was short-lived. The Essex magistrates, meeting in July, recorded their suspicions about 'severall persons ... disafected to the present Government' who had been absent from home during the 'late horrid Rebellion'. In 1686 James suspended the bishop of London, Henry Compton, who was strongly anti-Catholic and favoured co-operation with nonconformists. Ironically, however, nonconformists were ultimately to benefit from James' religious toleration. Thus his moves of 1685 in favour of Catholics were extended in 1687 to abolish all religious penalties, in the hope of securing the support of the nonconformists against the Church of England. His constitutional right to act in these matters without Parliament was questioned, and in 1688 Bishop Compton enlisted the help of James's daughter Mary, to whom he had formerly been a tutor, and her husband, the Dutch Protestant William of Orange. William invaded Britain, James escaped to France, and after considerable debate, William and Mary took the throne. In 1689 the 'Bill of Rights' reasserted restrictions on the power of the monarch, though it was in many ways conservative. The Toleration Act introduced limited acceptance of most nonconformists and Quakers, though not Catholics. It was intended to 'unite their Majesties protestant subjects in interest and affection'. The 1690s were nevertheless times of considerable stress, with disputes about the accession of William and other matters such as his increased taxation. There was also a series of bad harvests, occasioning food riots in several areas.[4] In Essex the economic pressure was increased by the continued decline of the cloth industry, in spite of a temporary revival during the late 1660s.

LOCAL OFFICIALS

Magistrates

Some of the Essex magistrates of the 1650s survived the Restoration. One such was John Godbold of Hatfield Peverel. But many who had been appointed by Parliament were dismissed from the bench. Royalist families who had been deposed during the early 1640s returned in their place. Amongst them were three Ayloffes of Great Braxted in turn, Sir Benjamin, his son Sir William, and then another son Henry. Henry was the most active of the three in Witham, becoming the busiest magistrate working in the town during the last fifteen years of the century. Sir Thomas Wiseman of Rivenhall, who had first begun to watch over Witham's affairs in 1608, had died in 1654 at the age of 84. His grandson William was appointed to the bench in 1660 and knighted in the same year, but rarely seems to have officiated in Witham. The Nevills of Cressing were no longer on the scene, having sold their Essex estates. There were instead some new names, such as Sir Thomas Adby of Kelvedon, Thomas Roberts esquire of Little Braxted, and later Sir Thomas Darcy of Great Braxted.[5] So none of them lived in Witham itself.

Under King James' dispensations of 1685 and 1687, Sir Edward Southcott was briefly appointed to the bench, while still in his twenties. He was an unusual magistrate for Witham. Not only was he young and a Catholic, but he lived in the town itself, at his family's ancestral home, Witham Place. He later recalled being asked to prosecute someone for sheep stealing on Tiptree Heath. The suspect's father, Captain Foster, had allegedly led an attack on Witham Place in 1648, so when Sir Edward rode over to Tiptree in his coach he sought help from a colleague, in case he himself should be thought to be seeking revenge. He was conscientious, helping with the affairs of Witham and the surrounding area, attending assizes, and even becoming one of the honorary County Treasurers and a Deputy Lieutenant. However, under William and Mary, his three appointments were declared in retrospect to have been illegal, each liable to a fine of £500. Sir Edward therefore 'thought it advisable to step just to the other side of the water, to France'. He returned in less than a year, having heard that the Government were not proceeding with prosecutions because they would also have damaged onconformists.[6]

The total number of magistrates in Essex increased from the 1670s onwards, when it continuously exceeded a hundred for probably the first time, and more new recruits were added during the reign of William and Mary. Thus during the 1690s there were usually around 140 on the county bench, and this is reflected in the greater number of different men dealing with Witham's cases. However, it was only with the advent in 1709 of Newman Barwell esquire, grandson of the Quaker Robert(1), that the town again had a magistrate who lived within its own boundaries for a short time.[7]

Half-hundred officers

The two high constables of the Witham half-hundred had hitherto held office for quite long periods. At the Restoration, Robert Garrard(2), Witham's well-known Puritan, had been constable for only about a year, but he was removed in early 1662. No doubt he was not in favour with the new Royalist magistrates, but in any case, terms of about only about three years seem to become habitual thereafter. For many years before 1662, one of the men had usually come from the town of Witham itself, but during the following forty years they were both nearly always chosen from the country parishes. The few known constables from Witham were all yeomen, namely Abraham Lake of Benton Hall and Robert Burchard(4) of Newland Street during the 1670s, and John Lake, Abraham's son, in 1691. Abraham was involved with the nonconformists during the early 1660s.

The less prestigious but hardworking bailiffs also began to change every few years, but some of them held the office more than once. About half were from Witham, and, as previously, several were innkeepers. For instance, Dalton Clarke, bailiff in 1669 and 1681, was at the George in Newland Street. He was also postmaster for a time, and as such was criticised on occasion for inefficiency.[8]

Secular parish officers

We have rather better information about the holders of parish office than in previous years. Various sources show that not all the posts were considered to have the same status, and this has been found to be the case in other places too. The hierarchy may be demonstrated by the progress of Witham butcher Edward Shakerley as he grew older. He was parish constable in 1666 and 1678, overseer of the poor in 1672 and churchwarden in both 1685 and 1692, by which time he was a prosperous property owner. The aletasters and parish constables, chosen by the main manor courts, but working for the magistrates and half-hundred officials, were nearly all tradesmen and craftsmen. Most had two or three hearths, and although the majority could sign their names there were several who could not. It is not clear how often they changed. As with other secular posts, it was possible for some of the holders to be religious nonconformists. One such was Samuel Wall, an innkeeper and grocer, whom we shall encounter later. Another parish constable, tanner Thomas Richmond, who held office in 1671, was a Quaker.[9]

Overseers of the poor were appointed by local magistrates, but in most places the parishioners probably put the names forward. The post had been established in 1597, and its holders had onerous responsibilities. We do not know names of Witham overseers until after 1660, when we have a collection of papers about the putting out of paupers as apprentices. Many overseers were tradesmen and craftsmen, but in addition about a quarter were yeomen. Usually they had four or five hearths, and very nearly all could sign their names. They seem to have changed every year. All religious groups were expected to assist. In a few years one of the overseers had nonconformist associations, but even more noticeable were the Quakers. For six of the eight years for which we know the names between 1664 and 1680, one of the overseers was a Quaker. The next known Quaker overseer after this was in 1699. In 1690 Priscilla Chipperfield of Powershall, widow of the yeoman, Thomas, was appointed. She thus became Witham's first female parish officer, but she did not start a new trend. Only very rarely were women made overseers even in the eighteenth and nineteenth centuries. Their appointment may have arisen from their occupation of certain farms whose tenants were expected to take a turn in the post.[10]

Churchwardens

Nonconformists served as churchwardens in Witham sometimes, but Quakers did not. Usually the holders changed annually as they had done before, but it became usual after 1660 for some of them to take up the office again after six or seven years, though the rotation was not exact. If this was related to any pattern of turn-taking, it may have been newly introduced, not having been in evidence before. Wardens were similar in rank to the overseers. By 1660 there were very few indeed who could not write their names. Some of those who were appointed several times after 1660 were amongst the richest in the parish, where some degree of social polarisation may have been taking place both in farming and in clothmaking, with the rich getting richer and the poor poorer. Prosperous churchwardens were the yeomen Thomas Chipperfield of Powershall and Thomas Hewitt of the newly created Freebornes farm, and various members of the Jackson family of clothiers. But they did have colleagues who were less well-off, such as cordwainer Ralph Bunny who served several times. The pre-1640 custom of always having a clothmaking churchwarden had ceased, and only about a quarter of the wardens were clothmakers now. During the 1660s and 1670s many of the better-off clothiers were in any case disqualified from being churchwardens because they were Quakers.[11]

The churchwardens' burdens had probably increased when the Restoration gave them back powers which had lapsed during the previous two decades. In 1664 a bishop's Visitation was anticipated, and, as was customary, all the churchwardens in the diocese received a long and detailed series of printed questions or 'articles' which they were expected to answer in writing when the hearings reached their area. The Witham wardens were then Robert Jackson(1) and Thomas Chipperfield, and the four-page response which they took to Kelvedon in September 1664 was one of the most long and detailed of them all. I have reproduced a transcript in appendix 3 (page 167). It gives us a magnificent picture of the men's responsibilities and concerns. The church was still under repair after damage by soldiers during the Civil War, which they called 'the late unhappy times', but all its fittings and furnishings were in order, including the 'Stately pulpett'. The churchyard, vicarage, almshouses and schools were also accounted for. But what concerned the wardens most was the distressing behaviour of their vicar and of the parishioners. This will be discussed more fully below (pages 141-42), as will the possibility that the pair were later rewarded by being asked to take over the administration of the vicarage from the vicar.[12]

The two men had different backgrounds. Thomas Chipperfield, a yeoman, had accommodated a nonconformist meeting in his barn in 1663, and he will be discussed later in that context. His colleague Robert Jackson(1) was a clothier, who was to die of the plague two years later, in August 1666. When he was buried, the usually noncommittal compiler of the parish register described him as 'the best townsman of a publique spirit'. The family had been generally noncommittal during the seventeenth century, though in 1631 clothier Adam Jackson, father of our churchwarden, did persuade his servant John Carter to promise to kneel at the appropriate time in church. Adam had died in 1632, when Robert was just a boy, and Robert had only begun to participate in parish affairs during the 1650s, for example as an almshouse trustee and a signatory of the rate petition of 1653. His loyalty to the Church is suggested by the fact that two weeks before he prepared the report in 1664, he and his wife Sarah had taken their daughter Abigail to Witham's St.Nicholas church to be baptised, in spite of the fact that many of their fellow-parishioners, including his colleague Thomas Chipperfield, refrained from doing so because of the vicar's distressingly bad ways. Jackson's allegiance was particularly notable because so many of the other prominent clothiers in the town were Quakers. This distinction recalls the position of his ancestor George Armond(1), who had Catholic sympathies in the mid-sixteenth century, and originated in Coggeshall, where many of his fellow clothiers were early Protestants. The Jacksons continued to be important figures in what remained of Witham's cloth industry at the end of the seventeenth century. One of them was Robert(1)'s brother, John Jackson(A). When John himself became churchwarden in 1680, he found the parish much more agreeable than Robert had done in 1664. Thus at the Visitation of that year he merely reported 'all well' to every single question (appendix 3, page 170).[13]

VICARS

The return of Francis Wright, 1660-68

The vicar about whom the churchwardens of 1664 were so concerned was of course Francis Wright. Under the new legislation of 1660, he had asked the House of Lords for permission to return to Witham vicarage after an absence of seventeen years. For at least some of that time he had been in prison. He told the Lords that he had been 'with the king' in 1643, and that his estate had been 'unjustly kept from him ever since'. The phrase 'with the king' seems to have been personal to Wright; it was not used by petitioners in general. He was re-instated and John Ludgater was removed.[14] Many of Wright's old adversaries in the parish had died or moved away, but some remained, notably Robert Garrard(2), who had led the demonstrations against him in 1631.[15]

Wright soon attracted attention in ways reminiscent of his earlier years in the parish. To begin with we have a stirring series of complaints, most undated but including one from 1661 and one from 1663. We know of depositions made by twelve different parishioners, submitted on some occasion about which other information does not survive. Much of the evidence concerns Wright's drunkenness. We are told that on one occasion he was 'reelinge' along the road near the White Hart in Witham and collided with a horse, and that on another he fell off his own horse in the main road at Springfield, so that he was 'in great danger to be runne over by carts and coaches'. On one occasion strangers 'did laugh and Jeare at him to the great scandall of the ministeriall function'. Furthermore, in 1661 he had drunk 'excessively of the remaineing part of the Communion Wyne that was left'. Most of the people giving evidence were of quite lowly status, but they included the sexton, and two yeomen, brothers Richard and Thomas Chipperfield.[16]

When Thomas became one of the churchwardens in 1664, he and his colleague Robert Jackson(1) soon complained of Wright in the Archdeacon's court because of the state of the vicarage. He failed to attend to answer them, so proceedings of excommunication had already been taken against him when, as we have heard, the bishop's Visitation came to Kelvedon church in September. He appeared there with his colleagues before the bishop, Humphrey Henchman, to certify that he was correctly ordained. At a separate hearing before the Vicar General, Sir Richard Chaworth, on the same day, the wardens handed in their survey of the parish (appendix 3, page 167). They said that Wright had failed to wear the surplice for two years although there was one provided, which may account for the fact that the previous wardens had been accused of not having one at all. People coming to church for christenings and burials had to climb over the gates, which he kept locked in order to keep his cattle in the churchyard. He would not reveal the details of the glebe land. The wardens referred to his 'lewd life' before the Civil War, and to his frequent drunkenness since his return, which had taken him twice before the local magistrates. 'Multitudes of pore miserable Simple Creatures' were following his example in blasphemy and drunkenness. Worst of all was the fact that his behaviour had nearly emptied the church. The parishioners preferred either to join the Quakers, to go to other parishes, or, when the weather was bad, to stay at home, rather than encounter Wright's swearing and his 'threatning Speeches both in and out of his pulpet'. Many would not let him baptise their children. Evidence from the parish register suggests that between a half and two thirds may have abstained from baptism. For some, an additional deterrent to taking communion was that Wright claimed transubstantiation of the bread and wine. The wardens tactfully submitted the acceptability of this idea 'to better Judgments'. Transubstantiation is a Catholic doctrine; we may recall that there were suggestions in 1632 and 1641 that Wright had Catholic sympathies. Finally, Wright had threatened Jackson and Chipperfield over their plans to make the complaints, saying that the registrar and the Vicar General, Sir Richard Chaworth, were both his 'great Frinds', so that Jackson would 'wish his right hand off' if he proceeded. The wardens had chosen nevertheless to do their 'duty'. Some notice was taken, because they were asked to show the report to the Consistory court in March 1665, but we do not know what happened there. A few of their accusations were passed on to the Archdeacon's court, which heard them in the following year, 1665, but Wright never appeared to answer them.[17]

Wright was entitled to receive the 'small' tithes levied on livestock and non-cereal crops, including 'apples, peares, cherries, egges, hoppes, flax, [and] honey'. By this time in Witham these seem to have been commuted into a money payment. At Easter 1664 he took seven Witham men to the court of the Exchequer in London for not paying, and at Easter 1668 he took another thirteen. It was said to have been eight years since some of the latter had paid, but they had not been included in the 1664 list. So it seems quite likely that Wright was suffering from the inadequacy of his own record keeping as well as his unpopularity. The accused men were varied in their beliefs, but more than half, including the ageing John Gravener(3), had no known association with active dissent. We must expect some exaggeration in the claims made on either side in such cases. Wright himself reported that he himself had been 'preaching the Word of God and instructing the People ... and Administering the Sacraments with care, diligence and good conscience'. Some Essex defaulters elsewhere had refused to pay tithes on principle because they disapproved of them. The few men from Witham who did not defend themselves at all may possibly have felt like this, but those who did prepare evidence gave other reasons. Thus in 1664 five of the seven defendants alleged that they had paid for some years, and that Wright would not tell them what they owed for the rest. Innkeeper John Pengelley had asked for an account, and thought that his lack of success in obtaining one was due to the fact that Wright himself owed him an even greater sum. And John Harris asserted that when he went to the Vicarage to enquire what was due, Wright 'forbidd him his house and levelled a gun att him swearing by god he would shoote him'. The joint statement of ten of the thirteen defendants of 1668 was based on another startling allegation, to the effect that Wright had been suspended from office two years previously.[18]

This assertion seems too precise to have been invented, and Thomas Chipperfield, one of those who made it, had first-hand knowledge. He and his fellow-defendants said that he and Robert Jackson(1) had been asked as churchwardens to administer the vicarage after its sequestration by the bishop in June 1666, following the suspension of Wright by the Consistory court in May. This could possibly have been an end result of proceedings begun after the two men had been asked to take their report to that court in 1665, which would explain why their names were given in the decision of 1666 even though their term of office had probably ended by then. Several Essex clergymen did suffer sequestration during the 1670s, but the relevant records for the 1660s do not survive.[19]

Wright died later in 1668, and it is perhaps not surprising that he was then said to be:

> in soe poore and meane a condicion that he left behind him noe visible Estate in so much that noe person or persons tooke any Administration of his Goods.

No burial at Witham is recorded for him. This adds plausibility to the story of his having been suspended, as does the fact that when the appointment of the next vicar was recorded by the diocese, the clerk left a blank in the place where he should have entered Wright's name and what had happened to him. Nearly forty years later, one of Wright's successors, Jonas Warley, was asked to provide information to John Walker, who was preparing a history in defence of clergymen like Wright who had been removed by Parliament during the 1640s. Warley wrote to Walker about Wright that 'I shall advise you to drop him in silence, for I am told he had no very good reputation'. However, Walker did include Wright in his book, but suggested that his being allowed to

return to Witham in 1660 had been 'to the dishonour of the Church'.[20]

John Harper, 1668-1670, Thomas Cox, 1670-1676, and Thomas Brett, 1676-1680

Francis Wright was followed by three Cambridge graduates in succession, who all died in Witham after only a short time in office. The first, John Harper, may have been the man who had been ejected from Nazeing as a Royalist in 1645, and had been a minister in London since 1660. He welcomed an unusual number of growing children to his font, when those who had been withheld from Francis Wright were taken to him for baptism. The vicarage he found to be still 'very much ruined and dilapidated'.[21] The property left by Dame Katherine Barnardiston to pay for preaching, today known as Barnardiston house, was also in a poor condition. Not being able to make any claim on the estate of the destitute Francis Wright, Harper spent £200 of his own on the buildings. Nevertheless, there were still only four hearths recorded in the vicarage in 1670, there having been six in 1662. After Harper died in 1670, 'capable and sufficient workmen' continued the work, but it was said in 1672 that 'the premises still remaine soe ruined and dilapidated' that an additional £150 was needed for 'further necessary' repairs. In that year an agreement was drafted between the bishop and the next vicar, Thomas Cox, whereby Cox would contribute out of his tithes and rents until the buildings were habitable. The number of hearths in the vicarage increased again, between 1670 and 1673, from four to seven. It is probable that Cox also revived the court of the Vicarage manor, which brought in some income. In the following year Sarah Swinborne asked that he should preach her funeral sermon. His will shows that he had relatives in nearby Coggeshall, owned property there and in other Essex parishes, and was able to leave considerable bequests of money.[22]

His successor, Thomas Brett, who came in 1676, also had links with other places, particularly his previous parish of Cottenham in Cambridgeshire. One of his predecessors as rector there had been Henry Compton, who in 1675 had become bishop of London. Brett's will of 1680 does show some ties with Witham also. He was probably young and unmarried. He left £10 to the poor of the parish, and £20 'to be laid out upon the Vicaridge house'. His executor was to be the prosperous Witham clothier, John Jackson(A). Particularly favoured was Benjamin Nussey, a maltster who carried out many clerical tasks in the town, and had been churchwarden when Brett had arrived or just before. Brett left him his 'wearing apparel lynnen and woollen', and also most of the parish's unpaid tithes, provided that 'he deale mildly and kindly with the poorer sort especially'. Elizabeth, Nussey's wife, received a silver spoon and cup and £5, their daughter Ethelburgh was to have £5, their son Gilbert £10 'towards his schooling or apprenticeship', and their maid twenty shillings. Another twenty shillings went to the servants of the Countess of Lavall, who was the widow of Sir William Ayloffe and was soon afterwards alleged to be a Catholic. She lived in part of Witham Place, just across the river from the vicarage.[23]

Jonas Warley, 1680-1722

When Jonas Warley came to Witham in 1680 to follow Thomas Brett, he may have feared that the decrepit vicarage house had been undermining the health of its residents. If so, he need not have worried. He did eventually die in office, but it was not until 1722, when he was 73 and had served as Witham's vicar for forty-two years. In 1704 he was also made archdeacon of Colchester, and immediately undertook a painstaking survey of the state of the churches in his area. He appears to have been an enthusiastic follower of Bishop Compton, the campaigner in defence of English Protestantism who had appointed him. In 1704 Compton headed the list of contributors to the improvement of Witham church with a donation of £13. When Warley wrote his will in 1722 the bishop had died nine years previously, but Warley still recollected him as his 'singular Patron and Benefactor'. He had a portrait of Compton amongst his personal possessions, and also displayed his coat of arms in the east window of St.Nicholas church.[24]

Jonas Warley seems to have taken firm charge of the parish. He may well have shared Compton's sympathetic attitude towards nonconformity, but neither of them approved of Quakers, and Warley was said to have organised a raid on a local Quaker meeting in 1683. He altered the long-suffering vicarage yet again, no doubt benefiting from the experience of improving the parsonage house in his previous parish of Loughton. Major repairs were carried out to the church in 1685, entailing the exchange of the old lead for new by the Witham glazier Charles Clarke and the Chelmsford plumber Robert Justice. By the time Warley made his collection for the 'beautifying' of the church in 1704 he was able to attract a wide range of subscribers in addition to the bishop. Several were from outside the parish but had connections with it, such as family memorials in the church. There were six baronets, a knight, seven esquires, and several titled ladies, as well as the better-off tradesmen of the town. There was also the Catholic Sir Edward Southcott of Witham Place, who had four generations of ancestors buried in the church, including the judge and his wife whose monument still survives there. The Essex writer William Holman found St.Nicholas soon afterwards to be 'so beautiful and adorn'd that it may well vye with any other church in this county'.[25]

The sum collected was enhanced by the use of £67 from the funds of the Greene's almshouse charity, from which the 'balance' was allowed to be used by the church. Its income had been lost during the 1630s but Warley had successfully instituted legal action in Chancery in 1699 to recover it. He probably also re-established the additional sermon provided for by Dame Katherine Barnardiston's will of 1633. It had originally implied criticism of the regular services provided by the vicar and by the Laudian church, but Warley now appropriated it for himself. We have other glimpses of his local influence, for instance in his association with two Witham gentlemen, Augustine Mayhew and Newman Barwell. In 1699 he was asked to preach a funeral sermon by Mayhew, who owned the manors of Great and Little Coggeshall. And he recklessly lent £1,150 to Newman Barwell which was not returned; their descendants wrangled over the debt in the court of Chancery for many years. Further down the social scale, he sometimes intervened in the manor courts of Chipping and Newland to pay the fines for his poorer parishioners. These courts were being revitalised by their London owner, John Bennett, who was busy re-asserting his right to claim rents and fines, and very possibly inventing some new customs in addition.[26]

Warley's will of 1722 shows him to have been quite a wealthy landowner, and his bequests to his wife Deborah, who survived him by twelve years, included:

> a silver cup with a cover, a little silver cup, a silver porringer, a pair of silver sconces, a silver hand candlestick, her gold watch, a diamond ring, a pair of diamond earings, a peice of old gold ... [and] ... the use of ... a silver ladel, a little silver tankard, two silver salts, six new silver spoons cyphered D.W. ... the Silver Tea pott and two small silver salvers.

Several charitable bequests benefited Clare Hall in Cambridge, his birthplace of Elham in Kent, and some national organisations. His gifts to Witham did not fare well after his death. Funds left for bread for poor women were used to rebuild the steeple, whilst one of his successors borrowed the money which he gave for teaching the poor, and disappeared to Ireland with it during the 1780s. He asked that his papers should be burnt after his death, except for a special collection of sermons that had been given on public occasions, whose whereabouts is not now known. So the most enduring survival of his life in Witham is the epitaph on his tomb in the north aisle of the church:

> He was very diligent and constant in the discharge of his Archidiaconal and pastoral office; a great promoter of good works; witness this church, and the recovering 18£ per annum for 4 Almspeople, which had been lost near 80 years. He was ready to oblige every one in his Power, and willingly offended none; was always steady to the Principles and Interest of the Church, yet of so courteous a temper, as all parties respected him. He did, not only in his life do a great many good works, but left considerable Sums to several Charitys of divers kinds when he died, and lamented by most who knew him.[27]

Other clergy and teachers

The teacher Thomas Ponder, probably a Cambridge graduate, and quite elderly, provided a steady presence in the parish during the constant changes before Warley's arrival. His wife Priscilla was one of the Garrard family, whose wealth was starting to decline;

she was the sister of nonconformist Robert Garrard(2). Ponder was authorised by the bishop in 1662 'to teach children and others in the Rudimentes of Grammar and such other English books as are lawfully allowed to be taught in the Realme of England'. In 1664 his was reported to be the town's only licensed school, though there were other 'private schooles taught by women'. He was also curate of the adjoining parish of Cressing. Nine Witham wills were witnessed and probably written by him between 1669 and 1678, many more than were witnessed by the vicars. He lived in a two-hearth house, but was recorded as a pauper in 1662 and again at his death in 1679, when no valuation was made of his goods, even though the parish register called him a 'gentleman'. Two bequests made to him by his Witham relatives may in the circumstances have been acts of charity. His brother-in-law Robert Garrard(2) left him a 'coat that is in John Skinner's hands to be altered', and his nephew John Ponder left him £10, some clothes, and two books by Laudian authors. His widow Priscilla seems to have fared rather better, perhaps with funds from her relatives, as she bought a house in Newland Street in 1687 (where no.20, 'Tiptree Villa', now stands). Her goods were worth £25 when she died in 1696. She left the house to her youngest daughter Elizabeth, together with a Bible. Elizabeth, then aged 30, was 'not in her Right Sences', so her brother was to supervise her property.[28]

Vicar Francis Wright had no curate, but his successor John Harper appointed one, William Howe, in 1669. John Ponder, Thomas's nephew, wanted Howe to preach his funeral sermon in 1678, and left him forty shillings for doing so. Howe also witnessed the will, but did not witness any others in Witham. One other teacher was layman Robert Burchard(5), like Ponder connected with a family of gentlemen and yeomen who had been established in the parish since the late sixteenth century. The Burchards had lived in the same Newland Street house throughout (now the site of nos.103/109, part of the Co-op in 1998). Robert(5) is first recorded as teaching in 1706, but he was already aged about 56 by then, and may have begun earlier. By the 1720s, his establishment seems to have been the only one in the parish that was regarded as a 'school'. Amongst his pupils were five 'Charity Children' paid for by the bequest from vicar Jonas Warley.[29]

DISSENT

The identity of a few of the new nonconformists is known, particularly from the early years, and there survives very full information about who the Witham Quakers were. It is clear that dissent in Witham was very strong after the Restoration. For instance, when Sir Thomas Barnardiston appointed ten new trustees for the Barnardiston charity in 1669, no more than half of them were fully committed to the Church of England. He included at least two nonconformists, two Quakers and the Catholic Sir John Southcott. Figure 24 on the facing page shows what is known of the religious affiliations of the 105 Witham householders who were

liable to pay the 1673 Hearth Tax.[30] It can be seen that known dissenters were well represented, particularly at the highest level. The better-off Quakers were usually clothiers, with other members in different commercial occupations, whilst most nonconformists were yeomen or gentlemen.

Witham had the largest number of dissenters of any of the Essex parishes which responded to the 'Compton census' in 1676 (the twelve Colchester parishes being treated separately). This survey related to the population over sixteen years of age in the southern part of England, and was undertaken by Bishop Compton on the instructions of the archbishop. Only three-quarters of Essex parishes sent in returns. The final figures combined Quakers and nonconformists. Witham had 107 dissenters out of 750 people surveyed in the parish (fourteen per cent). The next largest group, numbering 100, was in Colchester St.James (seventeen per cent). Only fifteen other parishes had a proportion of more than fourteen per cent, two of them being Cressing and Fairstead, adjoining Witham. The percentage in Essex as a whole was four per cent, more than for any other county surveyed. This does not seem high, but Essex was very varied.[31]

QUAKERISM

Success and expansion, 1660-c.1680

In the course of his research, Bill Cliftlands found evidence of Quakers in nearly ten per cent of Essex parishes altogether by 1664. Travelling Quakers continued to visit Essex after the Restoration. George Fox the younger was imprisoned for speaking at Harwich in 1660, and William Caton frequently passed through Essex on journeys to and from Holland, being gaoled in Great Yarmouth in 1663. In that year he wrote that he had 'visited Friends at Coxhall [Coggeshall] and Witham to their and our refreshment in the Lord'. As we found in the last chapter (pages 135-37), Quakers were already well established in Witham in 1656, with their own register book of births and marriages. From the 1660s onwards, Quakers from many of the rural parishes adjoining Witham also began to use the Witham registers.[32]

Thus the strength of Quakers in Witham did not solely arise from the failings of vicar Francis Wright, as implied by the churchwardens in their report of 1664. They alleged that by his 'harsh expresions' he had driven away any separatists who returned to the church 'to be reclaimed', with the result that the parish 'multiplyes with quakers', who 'meete once or twice a weeke as wee are informed, not ever being present with them ourselves'. The wardens directed their displeasure at Wright rather than the Quakers. However, a week after they took their report to the Visitation at Kelvedon, a weekday gathering of Quakers in Witham was visited by an unfriendly shoemaker from Danbury area, ten miles away. He took five of them straight to five local magistrates, who on the same day convicted them of

FIGURE 24

KNOWN RELIGIOUS AFFILIATIONS OF PAYERS OF THE 1673 HEARTH TAX IN WITHAM

HEARTHS	QUAKERS (probably fairly complete)	PROBABLE NONCONFORMIST SYMPATHISERS (very incomplete; includes people supporting preachers etc., and their relatives)	LOYAL TO CHURCH OF ENGLAND ? (very incomplete; mainly people who allowed Francis Wright to baptise their children, and their relatives)	CATHOLICS (probably fairly complete)	AFFILIATION UNKNOWN - NUMBERS AND OCCUPATIONS
11				SIR JN. SOUTH-COTT	
(9 to 14: inns)		(Samuel Wall) (only had many hearths because innkeeper)			(2 innkeepers)
8	ROBT. BARWELL(1), clothier	ROBT. GARRARD(2), gent.			
7		THOS.CHIPPERFIELD, yeoman ABRAHAM LAKE, yeoman/gent. JOHN LAKE, yeoman	JOHN GRAVENER(3), clothier, yeoman, gent. JOHN GRAVENER(4), clothier, gent.		
6	MGT.COCKERILL, widow JN.FREEBORNE, clothier	ROBT. GARRARD(3), gent			2 (1 innkeeper, 1 n/k)
5	THOS.GARDNER, clothier	JN.GOODMAN, clothier JER.BROMLEY LAURENCE ELLIS, yeoman	JN.JACKSON(A), clothier		6 (2 gents., 1 farmer, 2 grocers, 2 n/k)
4	JN.WARDE, clothier THOS.RICHMOND, tanner	THOS.GOODMAN, yeoman THOS.JOHNSON, yeoman	JN.HARPER, vicar MRS.SAR.JACKSON, widow MRS.AB.JACKSON, widow		8 (5 craftsmen etc., 3 n/k)
3	JOHN HULL, maltster GEO.PLEDGER, joiner	RD.CHIPPERFIELD, yeoman RD.GOODMAN, brewer GEO.LISLE, minister SAML.PLUMB	JN.SKINNER MARTIN SKINNER, cardmaker		15 (2 widows, 1 husbandman, 2 clothiers, 5 craftsman etc., 3 tradesman, 2 n/k)
2	DEB.DAVIES, single MRS.MARY MITCHELL, widow JN.OSBORNE, tanner ALEXANDER FRANCIS	JN.GARRARD(3)	THOS.PONDER, teacher/clerk/gent. RALPH BUNNY, cordwainer WM.MEADE, victualler THOS.MITCHELL eldr, barber THOS.MITCHELL ygr., tailor		20 (2 widows, 1 husbandman, 1 gardener, 3 clothworkers, 6 craftsmen etc., 3 tradesmen, 4 n/k)
1	MRS.ELIZ.TRUE, widow of clothier MRS.ELIZ. HOWLETT, widow of cordwainer NICHOLAS WINKFIELD, gardener HUGH NICHOLLS, bricklayer				10 (1 weaver, 2 trades, 2 crafts etc., 5 n/k)

This version of the 1673 returns probably refers to a few years before 1673.

The table relates to the 105 who were liable to pay. In addition there were 160 exempt.

assembling with others 'under colour of the exercise of religion ... contrary to the peace of the King and to the Statute'. It seems almost certain that the arrests had been pre-arranged. Not only did they take place immediately after the Visitation, from which information could have been handed on by the bishop's officers or other observers, but the magistrates had obtained a witness from a considerable distance away, and were themselves already conveniently gathered together, probably meeting in petty sessions. On the same day, eight members of a similar gathering in Coggeshall were sent to the same magistrates by other witnesses from the Danbury area.[33]

The Witham Quakers who were arrested in 1664 were assembled at the house of bricklayer Hugh Nicholls in Newland Street (the site is now part of no.5, the 'old Post Office'). The naming of at least five of them was necessary to achieve a conviction under the Act of 1662. With them were seven other unnamed people in addition to Nicholls' servants. These anonymous seven may have included some of the men's wives, though at Coggeshall a wife was amongst the named people.[34] The Witham offenders were well-known. One was clothier John Freeborne, who had been the earliest active Quaker in the town and had been taking part in Witham's life since the 1640s. By now in his late sixties, Freeborne was known by his colleagues elsewhere to have 'a good testimony for the lord in meetings'. He lived next door to the meeting place (his house is now no.3 Newland Street, Freebornes, illustrated on page 136). Also accused was clothier Robert Barwell(1), very much the most prosperous Witham Quaker, who was also to be most long lived of this generation. He was a relative newcomer, probably from Coggeshall, and lived in a large house on the other side of John Freeborne (later the Grove). He was still working as a clothier during the 1660s, but was rich enough to have attracted the title of 'gentleman', had Quakers not spurned such indications of rank.

Also at the meeting were two of Freeborne's sons-in-law, joiner George Pledger who lived nearby, and clothier Thomas Gardner; Gardner originally came from Glemsford in Suffolk. Lastly there was Thomas Richmond, the tanner at Battels tannery in Blunts Hall green, who had connections with the parish of Langford. The accused men probably spent ten days imprisoned in Colchester castle for not paying their fines. Freeborne and Pledger were also persisting in 'refusing to pay the rates' of the parish in 1665, and as a result continued to 'stand excommunicated' from the Church, a situation which had little power to worry them. It seems to have been the archdeacon's officers rather than the local churchwardens who complained about them.[35]

In 1667, undeterred, the same five Witham men who had been prosecuted in 1664, together with six others, established a Quaker burial ground in the town, practically adjoining St.Nicholas churchyard (next to what is now no.11 Church Street; its present appearance is shown in the drawing on the facing page). Not until more tolerant times, in 1700, when their successors purchased the freehold and discussed having new fencing and 'a good gatte into it', do the deeds admit that the ground in question was in fact the 'burial place for the people commonly called Quakers'. The first trustees of 1667 took a ninety-nine year lease on the sixteen rods of ground from widow Elizabeth True at ten shillings a year. They were to put up a 'fence of palling' round it, and Elizabeth was to be allowed to cut down the trees there if she wished, and to pick the fruit. Her father, her husband and her brother were all clothiers and left her money and property, so that in due course she owned eight or nine houses in the Chipping Hill area. Although she was sometimes referred to as a Quaker herself, she also used her houses to assist the nonconformist ministers.[36]

Among the first trustees of the new burial ground were two men from nearby parishes. One, from Inworth, was a relative of Witham's Nicholls family of bricklayers, and the other was yeoman Edmund Raven of Cressing, who had been imprisoned in 1662 for non-payment of tithes. In 1676 Raven's sons John and Edmund married Susannah and Elizabeth, the daughters of Robert Barwell(1) and Elizabeth True of Witham, in a joint wedding at Witham meeting. Thirty six other people also signed the register; Quaker weddings were customarily witnessed by many of those attending. These Ravens were almost certainly descendants of Witham's early sixteenth-century Protestants, Christopher and Joan Raven. There were however other Ravens in the area who were not Quakers. For instance, William, the other son of Edmund the elder, may not have been a member, and was probably the Cressing constable who acted against a Quaker for non-payment of tithes in 1696. He was assisted by a churchwarden called Richard Raven, who in addition helped to take goods from Edmund the younger in 1704.[37]

The Quakers' new plot began to be used for burials immediately, and the records were entered in the existing register book. The third person to be buried there was John Freeborne's wife Jane, in 1669. John was then about seventy years of age; shortly afterwards he married Hester Hayle. The marriage took place 'in the presence of many friends', as he later wrote in his will. In 1666 Hester, with her sister and other relatives, had been accused of being 'reputed Quakers' and not attending church. This was in her home parish of Billericay, fifteen miles from Witham. It became part of Witham Monthly Meeting, together with Chelmsford and Maldon, when the hierarchy of meetings which is characteristic of Quaker organisation was established. George Fox is said to have 'settled' the Monthly Meetings in Essex in 1667. The minutes of Witham Monthly Meeting survive from 1672.[38]

Quakers often sought to arrange separate education for members' children. Witham Quaker Paul Gattaway was in trouble in 1675 for 'teaching school' without a licence at his house in Newland Street (now no.29); he was a cordwainer or shoemaker. It may also have been at about this time that a permanent meeting place was established in a cottage in Maldon Lane, now Maldon Road. Its owners were the long-standing members Nicholas Winkfield and his wife Elizabeth, whose marriage had been the first to be entered into the Quaker register in 1659. Nicholas was a gardener like his father and grandfather. Some time before 1690 a new building was put up on the site. A replacement built during the early nineteenth century continued in use until about 1875 (it is now the Masonic Hall). Members in Witham were always part of the wider Quaker organisation too, and sent representatives to the county's Quarterly Meeting and the national Yearly Meeting. Grocer Thomas Richmond of Witham, son of Thomas the tanner, left £20 and £10 respectively to the 'Mens Meeting' and the 'Womens Meeting' 'in London'

in 1698, as well as £100 'for the service of Truth and the spreading thereof'.[39]

Quakers' role in the town

Quakers were a noted presence in Witham. Figure 25 overleaf shows that in 1673, at least twenty-six households, or ten per cent of the town's total, were Quakers. This was a remarkable figure. In England as a whole the proportion was about one per cent, in Essex between one and two per cent, and in the well-known Quaker city of Bristol five or six per cent. Looking at the different ranks in Witham, we find that Quakers comprised six per cent of the poorer households who

The Quaker burial ground as it is today

This plot in Church Street was leased by Witham Quakers in 1667 to use as their own burial ground. It is probable that they did not at first have tombstones, regarding them as ostentatious. They did use them during the 19th century, and a few survive from that time. The site is next to no.11 Church Street.; it is no longer used for burials.

were exempt from paying the Hearth Tax. These people made up thirty-eight per cent of the membership. It was a surprise to me that there were so many of them. The more prosperous members, those who paid the tax, took a more active part, which distorts our first impressions. Amongst these payers, Quakers comprised fifteen per cent of the town's total, with a fairly even distribution amongst people with different numbers of hearths. It is particularly noticeable that four out of the leading eight clothiers in the town were Quakers, as shown on figure 24 on page 145. Clothmaking had undergone a temporary revival during the late 1660s.[40]

The role which their numbers and rank gave the Quakers in the town was acknowledged by their inclusion amongst new charity trustees, and in particular by their frequent recruitment as overseers of the poor between 1664 and 1680. The names of the overseers must have been approved by the magistrates, even though one Quaker overseer, maltster John Hull, served in 1664, the same year in which his colleagues were being imprisoned by magistrates for attending an illegal meeting. During the 1670s some of the attenders at that meeting held office themselves; Robert Barwell(1) and George Pledger were overseers, and tanner Thomas Richmond was a parish constable. In accepting these positions, the men would have been expected to swear an oath that they would serve. Quakers disliked taking oaths, but there do seem to have been other occasions too when Witham members must have done so, for instance when Robert Barwell(1) administered his son's

estate in 1697, when they witnessed wills or acted as executors, or when they submitted depositions in the Court of the Exchequer about tithe payments and other matters. John Freeborne seems to have refrained from joining such a deposition, so perhaps he in particular did object to the procedure. The alternative was to 'affirm', which became legally acceptable in the reign of William and Mary. Thus Ann Moore, said to be 'a dissenter commonly called a Quaker', affirmed in 1698 as executor of her husband John. He was the miller at Chipping mill and had been an overseer in 1676 and parish surveyor in 1689.[41]

The Quakers and the poor

In 1675, Quaker clothier John Freeborne acknowledged his connection with the town at large when he asked that eighty sixpenny loaves should be distributed by the overseers amongst the parish poor on the day of his funeral in 1675. In the following year his daughter, Elizabeth Gardner, also died. Her husband Thomas was already dead, so their four children, all under twelve, were orphaned. The eldest, Thomas the younger, was an apprentice. Freeborne had left money for them to have a Bible each, and had also provided £30 for Elizabeth. Elizabeth's chosen executor was woolcomber Joseph Todd. He and her sister's husband, joiner George Pledger, had a disagreement about the direction of this £30 towards the children's welfare, though they were both Quakers. It was not regarded as proper for members to take disputes between themselves such as this one to the secular courts, so the Monthly Meeting took over, paying out regular sums for the children, and supervising the apprenticeship of the other boy, John, to a Great Baddow Quaker, Richard Cass. This continued for some time. Nearly ten years later, in 1684, 'Friends met at Edward Eatney's house about the children's money'. Another attempt by the meeting to solve a dispute was less successful. One of the two parties, from Terling, 'did freely submit himself to the Judgment of Friends', but the other 'utterly refused'.[42]

At this same time we also hear of more regular provision for the Quaker poor. From 1675 onwards a contribution was made for this purpose to Essex Quarterly Meeting from each Monthly Meeting, including Witham. There were individual donations too. When John Freeborne gave bread to the parish poor in 1675, he did not single out the Quakers. But during the 1680s most such gifts from Witham members were directed within the meeting, where, as we have seen, there were several members of limited means. Tanner Thomas Richmond did not leave a donation in his will, but to mark the occasion of the burial in 1688, his son Philip gave ten shillings to Robert Barwell(1) to distribute amongst what the Meeting called 'the pore of Witham'. This must have meant the Quaker poor, as Barwell gave two shillings each to five members. Most of them were probably elderly, as three died within the following four years. Three lived in property owned by the Barwell family. Providing such tenancies was another way to care for poorer colleagues. In the same

---

FIGURE 25

QUAKER HOUSEHOLDERS IN THE 1673 HEARTH TAX RETURNS FOR WITHAM

No.of hearths (people paying)	Total no.	No. of Quakers	% who were Quakers
Over 6	8	1	13%
5 and 6	15	3	20%
3 and 4	38	4	11%
1 and 2	44	8	18%
All payers	**105**	**16**	**15%**
Total exempt	160	10	6%
Total both paying & exempt	**265**	**26**	**10%**

This version of the 1673 returns probably refers to a few years before 1673.
Four innkeepers (none of them Quakers) are excluded, because their large numbers of hearths derive from their inns rather than their personal status.

year, Mary Richmond of Witham, Thomas's daughter-in-law, was left £6 by her mother Jane Woodcock to be given 'to widdowes and fatherless children of the people called Quakeres'. Although she had property in Witham, Jane was living in 'the parish of the Savoy' in London, so this bequest may have gone elsewhere.[43] The next local bequest was forty shillings to 'poor Friends of Witham' by 'our loving friend Hugh Nicholls' in 1689. He was the bricklayer who had provided the house for the unlawful meeting in 1664. Grocer John Baker distributed the sum amongst six people, four of them already having received some of Philip Richmond's gift. A more permanent arrangement was the establishment of a charity in 1693 by Witham's Deborah Eatney, wife of Edward. It was at their house in Newland Street that members had met in 1684 to discuss the Gardner children (on the site now occupied by High House, in 1998 the Lian restaurant, part of no.5). Deborah was a granddaughter of Witham's Edmund Halys, who had lived in the same house, and thus a great-granddaughter of the town's sixteenth-century vicar, Edward Halys. She gave twenty-one acres of land in Hatfield Peverel, Ulting and Langford in trust, so that the rents would be distributed 'from time to time' amongst 'poor Friends usually called Quakers' in the Witham area. The trustees included several non-Quakers like Witham clothier John Jackson(A).[44]

At the end of the century, some of Witham's Quaker willmakers again provided for the poor of the town in general, as John Freeborne had done in 1675. In 1698 grocer Thomas Richmond (son of Thomas the tanner), gave £10 'to the poor in Witham', which could have meant the meeting or the town, but Robert Barwell(1) in 1704 and Elizabeth True in 1705 definitely intended to benefit non-members. Barwell, by then nearly ninety years of age, left £5 to the 'poor people of Witham ... to be laid out in bread', in addition to donations to poor Quakers in Witham, Kelvedon and Coggeshall. And Elizabeth True left £4 for general distribution by the churchwardens and overseers, and only £1 for 'poor people called Quakers'.[45]

Quakers and tithes

Quakers were in principle opposed to the payment of tithes, and in some places they made statements to that effect when taken to court for defaulting. There were only three Quakers amongst the twenty-two Witham men taken to the court of the Exchequer for alleged non-payment between 1664 and 1670. John Freeborne and gardener Nicholas Winkfield were challenged by Francis Wright in 1664, as was Winkfield again in 1668, and George Pledger was accused by John Harper's widow Jane. We do not know whether Pledger made any answer. In both 1664 and 1668 Winkfield's name appeared on the defence depositions, saying that he had already made some payments, so he presumably had no objection in principle. He and a non-Quaker gardener, George Long, were said to owe £5 a year each, as much as the more prosperous yeomen, garden produce being an important part of the vicar's tithe. John Freeborne

refrained from joining the statement, so he may have been one of those who, according to Francis Wright, had claimed tithes to be unjustified in law.[46]

Change in the Quaker meeting, c.1680 onwards

The Quarterly meeting in Essex kept an 'account of Friends' sufferings' in a large book, from which they periodically forwarded information to the Yearly meeting in London. Although doubtless incomplete, it does contain much information not otherwise surviving, particularly relating to warrants issued by individual magistrates. These often ordered the confiscation of goods for such matters as non-payment of tithes. Before 1683 Witham Quakers were rarely mentioned in this book, though some of their relatives in other parishes did appear. However, in 1683 there is a whole page headed 'For meeting together to worship god' and subtitled 'For Meeting at Witham'. Thirteen people are said to have had goods taken from them. Six lived in Hatfield Peverel, four in other nearby parishes, and three in Witham. The three were Elizabeth True, from whom the parish constables took unspecified goods worth £1, Edward Eatney who lost a table worth five shillings, and Paul Gattaway, the unauthorised teacher, whose cordwainer's shop was relieved of two pairs of shoes. A horse was taken from one of the Hatfield Peverel men, who was imprisoned for not finding sureties for his good behaviour. It was also said that:

> there is more warants out against divers Friends for the said meeting ... and in particuler against Robert Barwell the Elder for £20 for the house, though its none of his ... The Constables of Hatfield Peverel affirmed that Justice Tendering bid them take as much for 5s. fine as was worth £5.

This was magistrate John Tendring, probably from Boreham. The names of the people who had informed the officials about the meeting were not known, but:

> the priest of the parish whose name is Jonas Wharley is supposed to be one, for he caused the officers to come to the meeting, and came with them.[47]

There may have been other similar occasions unrecorded, but the compilers of the book do seem to have regarded this one as particularly notable. Jonas Warley had arrived in 1680, and could have been making a new demonstration against the meeting. It is noticeable that Quakers were no longer asked to be overseers of the poor after 1680, the next occasion being in 1699. At the same time, the cloth industry, which had sustained so many leading members, began to decline, and became dominated by the non-Quaker Jacksons.[48] A marked decrease in the numbers of members in Witham meeting began in about 1680.

The main damage to the meeting came from the departure of adult children of founder members. It was particularly the sons who left. This did not seem to cause a complete family rift, because when the Quaker parents died, they still handed on their possessions to those children. None of John Freeborne's three sons seem to have stayed in the meeting. His daughters Elizabeth and Jane did so to begin with, but as we have seen, Elizabeth died in 1676, a year after her father. Jane was married to George Pledger, at first an active member. The couple entered the births of five children in the Quaker register during the 1650s and 1660s, but when Jane and George died (in 1679 and 1689) they do not appear to have had Quaker burials. Possibly they had become estranged from members because of the dispute about Elizabeth's children mentioned earlier. George's will had a Quaker format but he made no donations to the meeting. And none of their children appear to have been Quakers when they grew up. Hugh Nicholls, who died in 1689, had also entered the births of his children in the Quaker register, between 1653 and 1662, but they did not stay. His son Matthew, an innkeeper, had all his own children baptised in St.Nicholas church from 1692 onwards, was a churchwarden there in 1697, and was buried in the churchyard in 1700. His tombstone is the oldest one remaining in the churchyard today, albeit with a hole in it; it is shown below. He took over his father's house, formerly used for an illegal meeting in 1664, and known as 'the Faulkon'. Another of Hugh Nicholls' children, Elizabeth, married Richard Cooper of Hatfield Peverel at a Quaker wedding. Their conversion to the Church of England can be dated to within a couple of years, because they had the birth of their daughter Elizabeth entered in the Quaker register of Witham monthly meeting in July 1682, but then in January 1685 they took her to Hatfield Peverel parish church to be baptised at

the age of two and a half. They had three other children baptised there subsequently. Yet another defector was the son of Paul Gattaway, the Quaker teacher, who had a child baptised in 1677.[49]

Wealthy clothier Robert Barwell(1) and his wife Martha(1) also experienced change. Like the Freebornes they had two daughters who married Quakers. But their son, Robert(2), known as a gentleman, moved emphatically away. In 1676, in his early twenties, he was a witness at the Quaker wedding of his sister Susannah. But in due course he became a prominent member of St.Nicholas church. He was appointed as churchwarden in 1691 when he was about 38, and obtained a faculty from the bishop for a private pew in 1693. This was probably a rare event in Witham. To create the pew he rebuilt at his own expense an 'old and decayed' seat belonging to the bishop on the north side of the chancel. When he had enlarged and enclosed it, he had a space 8 feet by 6¼ feet:

> for himself and his family to sit, kneel and remaine in during the time of divine service and sermons, and the performance of such other religious duties and devotions to Almighty God as are required by the Lawes of the Realme.

Robert(2) died soon afterwards, in 1697, at the age of 44. His burial was at the parish church, but his father, the Quaker Robert(1), administered his goods, as his children were minors. In due course the eldest of them, Newman, provided a white marble monument in the church with an elaborate Latin verse, shown opposite.

The tombstone of Matthew Nicholls in St.Nicholas churchyard

This stone symbolises the decline of the Witham Quakers towards the end of the 17th century. Matthew Nicholls was born into a Quaker family in 1659. But he had his own children baptised in St.Nicholas church, became a churchwarden in 1697, and, as his tombstone informs us, was buried in the churchyard in 1700. It is just outside the south door.

The monument to Robert Barwell(2) in St.Nicholas church

An even more ostentatious defector from the Quakers. Robert was born into one of the leading Quaker families of clothiers in the town, in about 1653. However, as an adult he not only became a churchwarden in St.Nicholas church, but built his own pew there. He called himself a gentleman. After he died in 1697 his son Newman provided this elaborate memorial in the church, which still survives. It is very different from the simple style of the Quakers. Newman himself became a magistrate in due course, and helped to prosecute Quakers for non-payment of tithes.

Newman inherited the pew, and in 1709 he became a magistrate. In this role he signed several warrants ordering goods to be taken from his Quaker cousin John Raven of Feering for non-payment of tithes and similar offences.[50]

Robert(1) and his wife Martha(1) both survived into their eighties and into the eighteenth century, still members of the Quaker meeting. When he died in 1704, Robert left his considerable wealth and property to his non-Quaker relatives, particularly his grandson Robert(3), who was to be executor, with instructions 'not to give to any of my relations or to any other person Black clothes or anything that is called Mourning at or after my funeral'. Such dislike of ritual is characteristic of Quakerism and recalls some of the Puritans earlier in the century. Robert(1) also asked to be 'buried decently after the manner of the people called Quakers in the burying place for Quakers in Witham', and wanted his very prosperous Quaker son-in-law John Raven of Feering to 'have the sole Management and ordering of my funerall and noe other person'. However, no such burial is recorded in the Witham Quaker records, and nor is there any for Martha who died four years later. Assuming this was not just an accidental omission from the register, there seem to be two possible explanations. On the one hand John Raven could have buried them at Feering Hill, where he himself owned a piece of ground used by Quakers for burial. However, there are records there which begin early enough to include Martha (though not Robert). and they do not mention her. So the second alternative is perhaps rather more likely, which is that their non-Quaker grandchildren buried them at St.Nicholas church after all, and ignored Robert's request. The burials are recorded in the parish register, though this does not necessarily indicate a church burial. Somebody certainly managed to have the description 'Quaker' omitted from the entries, even though it was commonly used there for other people. There is a similar query over the burial of Elizabeth True, who wished her Quaker grandson, Edmund Raven of Cressing, John's nephew, to act as her executor in 1705.[51]

Another way to see the decline of Witham meeting is to count the couples from the town having the births of their children recorded in the Quaker register. There were six or more during the 1660s, four in the 1670s, three in the 1680s, two in the 1690s, and none at all between 1700 and 1710 (the number did not exceed two again until the 1790s). John and Mary Baker were having children during the 1680s and 1690s. John, a grocer, became the leading member of the depleted Witham meeting until his death in 1728. He was an overseer of the poor in 1699 and again in 1706, the only Quaker holder of the office since 1680. He was said to have defaulted on tithe payment in Purleigh in 1702, so he must have held property there. As a result the Witham constables were ordered to take linen and woollen cloth from him worth £10. It probably came from his shop, as grocers sold fabrics. After about 1690 there was an increase in births from other places in the Monthly Meeting area which had previously been poorly

represented, particularly around Maldon and Chelmsford. Meanwhile, some of the former Witham members who had left for the Church joined vicar Jonas Warley in voting for the victorious Tory candidate at the Parliamentary by-election of 1693.[52]

Seventeenth-century Quakers have been the subject of close attention from historians. In particular, Adrian Davies has devoted many years of study to Essex Quakers, and I have much valued his kind advice. It seems to be generally agreed that membership declined towards the end of the seventeenth century, as it did in Witham, though the detailed process varied. Other matters are more controversial. It is likely that there were considerable variations from place to place, and that towns were sometimes different from the countryside. One discussion has been about the connection between Quakerism and earlier Puritanism. Certainly both were strong in Witham and there were some personal links, but a number of the town's Quakers came from other parishes and I have not discovered much about their previous lives. Another debate concerns the economic and social status of the members. Many investigations have found that active membership was particularly derived from the middling ranks, with a few of the better-off. But recent research has also shown that there were a considerable number of poorer members in many places, particularly in towns, and this was true in Witham. Lastly, there is continuing discussion about the integration of Quakers into society. Much recent work has stressed the links which were often established between Quakers and their local communities, and also the participation of Quakers in local office holding, in spite of their powerful loyalty to their own members. Adrian Davies felt that such links only developed in certain parts of Essex, and that where they did, they were often not evident until after 1670. However, he found cloth towns like Coggeshall and Witham to be different, in that their Quakers were involved in wider community from the beginning of the movement.[53] This has also been borne out by what I myself have found in Witham.

NONCONFORMISTS

Travelling preachers

Ministers who had been removed from their livings were forbidden to preach even before the Conventicle Act of 1664, and several were presented in the Archdeacons' court for doing so in Witham. The accusations seemed to come from the court itself rather than from the churchwardens. Some of these men lived a rather nomadic existence during the early 1660s after they had suddenly been deprived of their livelihood. One of them was Robert Billio, who had been to school in Castle Hedingham, where he knew one of Witham's Puritan vicars, Edmund Brewer. Billio had earlier been vicar at Hatfield Peverel, adjoining Witham, where he was said to have experienced a miraculous cure from gout whilst praying. He moved to nearby Wickham Bishops in 1658, and was then removed, probably in

The barn at Witham Place

Although this appears to have been originally built as a house in the grounds of Witham Place in the 16th century, it became a barn sometime afterwards. It may therefore have been the barn at Witham Place belonging to yeoman Thomas Chipperfield, where nonconformist minister George Lisle of Chipping Hill preached to fifty people in an 'unlawful conventicle' in 1663. The lower picture shows part of its interior as it is today, part of the Spring Lodge Community Centre in Powershall End.

1661. However, he stayed in the area for a time. Thus in 1661 he witnessed and probably wrote the will of Thomas Goodman, a Witham yeoman, and in October 1663 the Archdeacon's court heard that 'Robert Billio alias Burst of Wickham Bishops' had been 'holding Conventicles' in Witham at the houses of Abraham Lake and Edward Johnson, who lived at Benton Hall and Blunts Hall respectively. Benton Hall is shown in the illustration on page 3. The court was assured that 'Mr.Billio is removed out of this Jurisdiction and hath not since held any conventicles at Witham'. And Edward Johnson explained that 'the said Billio did once come to his house and dine with him, and after dinner he the said Billio sent for several persons who came thither unknown to [Johnson] and he did expound to them, but at no time before or since hath he been there nor shall in the future'. This was probably true, for Billio moved to Felsted, where he was in trouble for holding a conventicle in the following year. One of his sons, Joseph, went on to be preacher in Maldon, where he founded the Independent chapel. Some have suggested that the fervour of Joseph's preaching was the origin of the term 'like billio', though another possible meaning of the phrase is 'like the devil'.[54]

Edward Johnson's interest in nonconformity may have been rather less accidental than his statement in court suggests. Later in 1663 he and Jerome Garrard(3) were said to have been:

> permitting conventicles to be held in their respective houses, and suffering one Clarke late of Stisted to pray and preach there, and for not frequenting the parish Church to heare divine service and sermon.

Preacher Thomas Clarke had been removed from the vicarage of Stisted. Another visitor to Witham was Thomas Lowrey, a Scotsman who had been rector of Great Braxted in the early 1640s, and then of Market Harborough in Leicestershire. Having been removed from there he became a nonconformist preacher in Coggeshall. Elizabeth Read of Witham was presented to the Archdeacon's court in 1663 for 'entertaining' him and 'suffering him with others to keep conventicles in her house'.[55]

George Lisle

George Lisle was Witham's most enduring nonconformist preacher of the seventeenth century. He moved here in 1662 after being dismissed from neighbouring Rivenhall for not conforming, and stayed till his death twenty-five years later. He lived in a substantial house on Chipping Hill green, adjoining the churchyard, shown opposite (now no.24 and Mole End). He bought it in two stages from John Garrard(2), cousin of nonconformist Robert(2). Originating in Hertfordshire, he was an Oxford graduate, and had been at Rivenhall since 1648. Recent research on Rivenhall by the Reverend David Nash has shown that whilst in that parish Lisle was very systematic; he wrote down the exact time of birth of his own children in the register, and seemingly always took Friday as his day off.

In October 1663 he appeared in the Archdeacon's court for holding a conventicle at Benton Hall at around the same time as Robert Billio had done. The magistrates were also taking an interest in deposed ministers, and in the same month Sir William Ayloffe's footman was sent down to Witham from Great Braxted to give a warrant to innkeeper and grocer Samuel Wall, a parish constable, 'to disperse unlawful assemblies'. Clothier John Jackson heard Wall complain that 'they would not send a warrant against swearing, whoring and drunkenness'. So Wall cannot have felt any great enthusiasm when a week later, on the first of November, he was called upon by magistrates to help disperse a meeting being addressed by George Lisle. With him were sent the churchwardens, the other constable, and a soldier. They all went to the barn of yeoman Thomas Chipperfield at Witham Place. This was very possibly the one which still stands (now part of Spring Lodge community centre, shown on the previous page). Chipperfield lived at Powershall but rented land at Witham Place too. There the men discovered what the magistrates later called:

> divers ... persons to the number of fifty ... being disloyal persons, assembled together in an unlawful conventicle ... under pretext of the exercise of religion.

The officials reported that they had 'required them to depart to their houses', but that 'Mr.Lisle and the people would not depart and continued there in contempt of the warrant'. On the following Sunday, 8 November, Lisle preached at his own house next to the church. Lieutenant Henry Leaming heard about the assembly and, on the strength of the same warrant, went there with some troops and one parish constable; we do not know whether it was Wall or his colleague. The Lieutenant 'required the people to depart the house of Mr.Lisle where he was speaking to them, there being ... between about 70 and 80 persons'. When they did not, he arrested Lisle, Abraham Lake of Benton Hall, and Samuel Plumb.[56]

No prosecution seems to have been pursued against Lake, but Lisle and Plumb were taken to quarter sessions in January 1664. Lisle claimed that he had obeyed the orders given him on the first occasion, not having returned to the barn, and that when the troops arrived at his own house in Chipping Hill a week later:

> he did frequently leave speaking, but saith that he must and will preach to his family, and the doors shall be open, if any come to hear him, they may come freely.

The case was removed to the court of King's Bench in London, which decided in the summer to proceed no further. Meanwhile Lisle and Plumb were both sent to gaol in Colchester castle for refusing to give sureties that they would keep the peace, and they were still there in August 1664. The Archdeacon's court continued in vain to call on Lisle to reappear in connection with the earlier conventicle at Benton Hall; eventually, in July 1665, he was excommunicated for not attending. At the same hearing, Samuel Wall, the reluctant constable, was

George Lisle's house at Chipping Hill, next to the churchyard

George Lisle, the nonconformist minister, lived here from 1662 until his death in 1687. A week after preaching in the barn at Witham Place in 1663, he was arrested for preaching here at his home, and sent to Colchester gaol. In 1672 he received a licence for the house to be used for public worship. It is now no.24 Chipping Hill, and the adjoining wing is now Mole End.

said to have been 'frequenting conventicles' and not going to the parish church. He had also been accused a few months previously of having a sexual relationship with his maidservant.[57]

The 'Five Mile Act' of 1665 forbade ejected ministers from living within five miles of their former livings. Whether Lisle obeyed it by moving away from Witham is unknown but perhaps unlikely. He was recorded again as holding conventicles in 1669. Then under Charles's temporary Declaration of Indulgence of 1672 his house was given a licence for Presbyterian worship, and in addition, one of his near neighbours, Elizabeth True, received another licence for him to 'be a Teacher of the Congregation allowed ... in a Roome or Roomes'

in her house. This was across the road from his own (hers now being nos.53/55 Chipping Hill). We have already heard of Elizabeth's assistance to the Quakers. All the licences ordered the authorities 'to protect [the worshippers] in their said Meetings and assemblies'. Officially this indulgence did not last, but Lisle continued in his house until he died in March 1687. In his will, which he wrote himself, he left his 'study of books' to his wife Ann, who outlived him by ten years. Like their fellow nonconformists, they were both buried at St.Nicholas church, next to their house, there being no separate nonconformist burial ground. The tablet commemorating them both, now in the south aisle of the church, describes George's earlier role as the rector of Rivenhall and does not mention any of his dissenting

The monument to George and Ann Lisle in St.Nicholas church

This mentions George's post as Rector of Rivenhall from which he was removed in 1662, but not his activities as a nonconformist minister in Witham afterwards.

activities in Witham. It is shown in the adjoining drawing.[58]

Edmund Taylor

A third licence was issued for Witham in 1672. This was to Edmund Taylor, described in a manorial survey of 1680 as a 'nonconformist parson'. He was a Cambridge graduate, who had been removed from the vicarage of Littleton in Middlesex in 1660 when the former vicar returned. He inherited the 'Hen and Chickens' in London's Paternoster Row from his father, who had worked there as a mercer, but the property was lost in 'the dreadful conflagration of or upon that City in the year 1666'. On coming to Witham he rented a house from Elizabeth True adjoining the churchyard, next to George Lisle, shown below (now nos.26/30 Chipping Hill). Lisle was described as a 'worthy and loving friend' by Ann Sharpe, Taylor's mother-in-law.[59]

Edmund Taylor was imprisoned in Tilbury Fort for preaching in favour of the Duke of Monmouth during the ill-fated attempt to oust James II in 1685. Returning to Witham afterwards, he moved to a different house, and continued there for a few years after Lisle's death in 1687. It was reported in 1690 that he 'jointly with three aged ministers kept up a meeting' in the town, and that for income he had 'somewhat of his own; they give him five shilling per day'. When he died in 1691, he wrote his own will as Lisle had done, saying that his wife Anna

Edmund Taylor's house in Chipping Hill

Like George Lisle's house next to it, Edmund Taylor's house in front of St.Nicholas church was licensed for nonconformist worship in 1672. Edmund Taylor was imprisoned for preaching in support of the uprising against James II in 1685. The house is now nos.26/30 Chipping Hill.

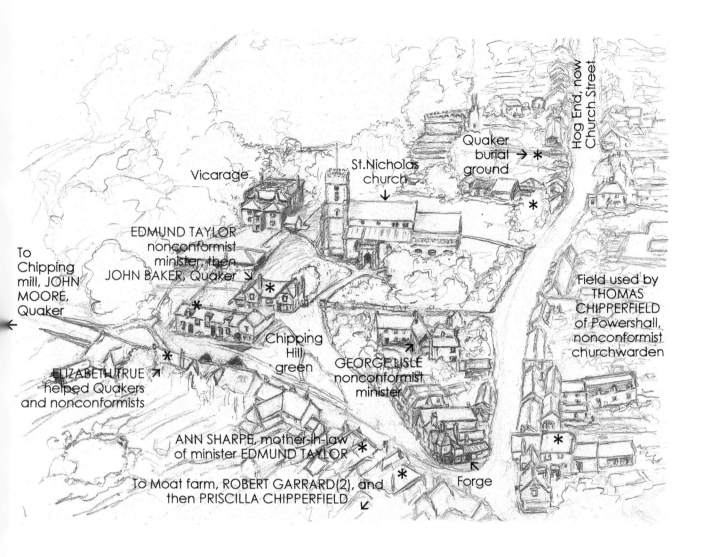

Vicarage

St.Nicholas church ↓

Quaker burial ground → *

*

EDMUND TAYLOR nonconformist minister, then JOHN BAKER, Quaker ↘

To Chipping mill, JOHN MOORE, Quaker

Field used by THOMAS CHIPPERFIELD of Powershall, nonconformist churchwarden

*

Chipping Hill green

GEORGE LISLE nonconformist minister ↗

ELIZABETH TRUE ↗ helped Quakers and nonconformists

*

*

ANN SHARPE, mother-in-law of minister EDMUND TAYLOR *

*

To Moat farm, ROBERT GARRARD(2), and then PRISCILLA CHIPPERFIELD ↙

Forge

Hog End, now Church Street

Chipping Hill and late 17th-century dissent

The names show occupants of the houses at different times after 1660. Only well-known people are included, as the names of most individual nonconformists are unknown to us. Places marked with an asterisk were owned by Elizabeth True, who helped both the nonconformists and the Quakers.

deserveth tenn times more than ever I was worth'. She may have been able to help maintain him, because in 1669 she had been left some furniture, and property in Colchester, by her mother, who was the widow of a Fingringhoe yeoman. All three witnesses of Taylor's will were relatives of his former colleague, George Lisle.[60]

Lay nonconformists

What little information survives about lay nonconformists relates mostly to the early years of the 1660s when some of them were in trouble in the courts. There were said by the officials to have been fifty people at Lisle's first meeting, and seventy or eighty at

the second. These estimates may have been exaggerated, but they do show that it was not just a small furtive group.

However, it is not possible to identify very many nonconformists individually. As can be seen above, there was something of a gouping near their ministers in Chipping Hill. This was of course in the vicinity of St.Nicholas church and the vicarage, and may have added to the discomfiture of the troubled vicar, Francis Wright. Amongst them were Jerome Garrard(3) and his father Robert (2) of Moat farm. Both the Garrards were included when Sir Thomas Barnardiston needed to appoint new trustees for the Barnardiston charity in 1669. We first encountered Robert in 1631.

He was then churchwarden and led the Puritan group who challenged vicar Francis Wright. Neither Wright nor Garrard can have been very pleased to meet each other on Wright's return in 1660, nearly thirty years later. We have confirmation of Robert's own unsurprising affiliation with the new nonconformists from his will of 1677. He left twenty shillings to minister George Lisle, and a dozen wooden plates (trenchers) to Anna, the wife of Edmund Taylor, to whom he may have been related by marriage. However, as already noted, Robert's sister Priscilla Ponder was married to a conformist teacher (pages 142-43).[61]

Most of the other nonconformists who can be identified were prosperous people who housed meetings, and lived elsewhere in the parish in substantial houses. One of them was Elizabeth Read, whose home in Newland Street had eight hearths in 1662 (probably where the Avenue now joins Newland Street). However, the others tended to be yeomen, living in the parish's several rural manor houses. One, Abraham Lake, called himself a gentleman as well as a yeoman, had seven hearths in his house at Benton Hall, where he farmed about two hundred acres, and was high constable of the half-hundred in the 1670s. During the stirring Parliamentary election of 1679 he voted for the successful Essex candidates of the newly emerging Whig party. His will of 1686 mentions a silver tankard and spoons, and he left £90 to one of his daughters.

Abraham Lake's son-in law was Thomas Johnson, son of the Edward who had harboured preachers Billio and Clarke. Edward Johnson's farm at Blunts Hall had about three hundred acres, and at the time he was receiving the ministers he was an overseer of the poor. When he died not long afterwards, in 1669, he left goods worth the large sum of £707. Sums totalling over £500 were to go to his seven children and a grandson. Diarist Ralph Josselin, vicar of Earls Colne, rode the ten miles to Witham to preach at Johnson's funeral; as we saw in the last chapter (page 133), the two were relatives. To his own surprise, Josselin had been allowed to continue as vicar after the Restoration in spite of having offered considerable support to Parliament during the Civil War, and refusing to subscribe to the Act of Uniformity in 1662. He visited Witham at other times also, and met Bishop Compton here in 1678. He was distressed at the removal of so many clergymen from their parishes at the Restoration, so it is not surprising that he was willing to help bury Edward Johnson, who had assisted some of these deposed preachers. The burial was after all at the parish church. The historians of Terling found there that nonconformists used the church for baptism as well as burial.[62] This seems to have happened in Witham too, after 1668 when a new and relatively acceptable vicar arrived.

I have deliberately not referred to any of the nonconformists in Witham as 'members'. Such a term would imply a degree of formality and separation from the Church of England which probably did not exist. This is particularly illustrated by the post of churchwarden. It was different from the other parish offices because so many of its responsibilities related to the church itself. But nonconformists nevertheless became wardens sometimes. This also happened in Terling. In Witham we have the particular example of Thomas Chipperfield of Powershall, who was elected at Easter 1664, less than six months after one of his barns was used for a nonconformist meeting. With his second wife Priscilla, he joined the parishioners who decided not to have their children baptised by Francis Wright. He was very prosperous, renting a large amount of land in the parish. His goods were assessed at over £2,000 when he died in 1680, the highest such value known in Witham between 1663 and 1700. During a later family dispute, one of his sons-in-law claimed they were actually worth £5,000. The family paid for the privilege of burying Thomas in linen rather than the wool which was normally required by law. His funeral sermon was not preached by the new vicar Jonas Warley, but by a Mr.Allen, perhaps the curate. The Chipperfields gave him £1 for his trouble.[63]

We know that Chipperfield's fellow churchwarden in 1664, Robert Jackson(1), was not himself a nonconformist, but nevertheless the report prepared by the two of them for the September Visitation nowhere commented on the nonconformists. Whenever the questions asked about dissenters, it was only the Quakers whom they mentioned specifically in their response. In answer to a query about ministers or lay persons holding 'any Conventicles or Religious Meetings' contrary to law, they did say that many exercised 'Religion in theire private Familyes', but blamed this on Wright's 'raileings in the pulpett'. To another long question about people not accepting the requirements of the Church, they said that they knew of none other than Quakers.[64] Minister George Lisle may possibly have still been in gaol at the time, and his colleague Edmund Taylor had probably not yet arrived, but the dozens who had heard Lisle preach were still here. My impression is that the comparable presentments from other parishes are equally silent on the question of nonconformists.

Thomas Chipperfield was chosen again as a churchwarden during the 1670s, and in that decade and the next, so also were several sons of the nonconformist activists of the 1660s, We do not know anything about the beliefs of those sons in particular.[65] But we do know that unlike the Witham Quakers, the town's nonconformists did still have a considerable number of successors in the early 1700s. This is because they came together to build a meeting house in Newland Street in 1715. Some of the subscribers and trustees were from other nearby parishes, but they also included Robert Chipperfield, Thomas's nephew, and Richard, grandson of Thomas Goodman. Perhaps surprisingly, the conformist Jackson family sold them the site, and William Jackson, nephew of Robert(1), subscribed. At some time prior to that date, meetings had probably been held on the upper floor of a large building in Collins Lane, where six rooms had been made into one for the purpose (later a maltings, then in 1998 the Superdrug shop in the Grove precinct).[66] During the eighteenth century the new 'Independent' church in Newland Street flourished in a more institutionalised form. The site is occupied today by its successor, the United Reformed Church, which largely dates from a rebuilding in 1840.

CATHOLICISM

Bishop Compton's survey of 1676 found three adult Catholics in Witham, probably all members of the Southcott family. They continued to live in the mansion at Witham Place whilst nonconformist Thomas Chipperfield farmed the land there. The attitudes of the Government to Catholics were particularly complex and changeable in this period, and may not always have been mirrored in the parish. For instance, Sir John Southcott, veteran of the Civil War, was presented at quarter sessions in 1667 for absence from church, but in the following year he was appointed to be one of the new trustees of the Barnardiston charity. And his son Sir Edward later reported that Sir John 'always lived very hospitably amongst his neighbours, and for many years ... constantly kept open house at Christmas'.[67] Leases and mortgages helped to sustain the depleted estate, and in addition, a Frenchwoman, Ann, Countess of Lavall, rented part of the house after 1675. She was the widow of Royalist magistrate Sir William Ayloffe of Great Braxted. As we have seen, vicar Thomas Brett left her servants twenty shillings in 1680. In 1682 she was accused at quarter sessions of being a recusant and not attending the parish church. This was at the end of Charles' reign, when Charles' own French wife was attracting particular hostility in some quarters. Ann died in 1683, and her stepson Henry Ayloffe became an assiduous magistrate soon afterwards. In 1687, during the relaxation of penalties against Catholics by James II, a travelling Catholic priest visited Witham and spoke to 'a great confluence of people'. In addition, as already mentioned, Sir Edward Southcott, Sir John's son, enjoyed a few years as a magistrate during James' reign. He returned from his brief voluntary exile in France thereafter to become head of the household, his father having died. The courts of assizes and quarter sessions heard that he had not attended St.Nicholas church in 1690 and 1691, and he complained about the 'iron age of double taxes' when Catholics became liable to pay double land tax in 1692. In 1697 he was given a licence authorising him to remain in Britain, in spite of having been to France without permission. By 1700 he had been made a trustee of two Witham almshouse charities. His house remained a centre for eighteenth-century Catholicism in Witham.[68]

OVERVIEW

This chapter has covered a long and eventful period. Originally I divided it into two, with one chapter being devoted to the reign of Charles II and the next to the years after it. However, I combined them in the interest of providing continuous accounts of the different religious groups. This decision in itself helps to show that the policies of the different monarchs do not always seem to have been the most important influences on local events.

The early years after the Restoration were times of great turmoil in Witham, as the churchwardens' report of 1664 described so eloquently. On more than one occasion, the Archdeacon's court heard complaints all on the same day about vicar Francis Wright, about the town's nonconformist yeomen or preachers, and about its Quaker clothiers. The suspects rarely troubled to attend the court. Prosecutions against dissenters and Catholics were not often initiated by the lay townspeople themselves, though the vicars did take some action against the Quakers. Witham's Quakers comprised a remarkably high proportion of the population, including several clothiers, and also a number of the less well-off. They developed a strong organisation to supervise and support their own members, and also took a part in the secular affairs of the parish until about 1680. After that the founder members began to die out and many of the next generation joined the Church. We know less about the nonconformists, though enough of their names survive for us to see that many of the early activists were yeomen with large farms. It seems likely that within the parish they were not seen as separatists in the way that the Quakers were, and most of them probably attended and used the Church as well as holding their own meetings. Finally, even during Witham's troublesome times during the early 1660s, many parishioners remained true to the established Church. Robert Jackson(1), 'the best townsman of a publique spirit', was amongst several who continued to allow Wright to baptise their children in spite of his failings. Another who did so was gentleman John Gravener(4). The experience did not harm his daughter; she lived to be about ninety years old. We might have anticipated such loyalty from him in view of the law-abiding career of his father John(3), frequently mentioned in earlier chapters. The Church in Witham was finally rescued from its years of embarrassment and change by the arrival in the vicarage of the long-lived Jonas Warley in 1680. No sooner had he arrived than the churchwardens were reporting 'all well' throughout the parish.[69]

12. POST SCRIPT

The research for this book was fun, but I have often found the writing painfully difficult. This chapter is the hardest of all, especially as the sun is shining outside and the birds are singing. I don't really go in for grand and meaningful conclusions. For instance, historians have long discussed the question of when exactly it was that the country first began to possess a serious potential for civil war.[1] Perhaps I should now be able to comment on this. Was it in 1527 when Christopher and Joan Raven were taken from Witham to London to be interviewed about their heretical beliefs, or during the 1570s when Joan and some of her fellow-parishioners were declaring themselves more openly? Or in 1600 when Dame Katherine Barnardiston came to live at Witham Place, or in 1625 when Thomas Weld and Francis Wright came to the vicarages of Terling and Witham? Or in January 1642 when the normally loyal and discreet John Gravener(3) put his name at the head of the Witham's section of the petition supporting Parliament and expressing concern about the King? I feel it would be unwise to try and make such a choice on the basis of what happened in one small area. Instead I shall note a few points of a more local nature that I have found interesting.

ACCEPTANCE

The path of dissent was smoothed by neighbourly acceptance. Since I first started preparing the book, many years ago, this idea has almost become commonplace amongst historians, though there is still much ground for further discussion about how and why it happened. In Witham, local positions of responsibility were given to members of dissenting groups such as early Protestants, Civil War Royalists, and Restoration Quakers. There were also less formal contacts of a secular nature. Dissenters and others witnessed each other's wills, and sometimes acted as executors and overseers for each other. They met together to discuss questions like the billeting of soldiers and the levying of the rates. The Catholic Sir John Southcott is said to have entertained his neighbours at Christmas. Children who did not share their Quaker parents' beliefs were allowed to inherit the family wealth. And when local dissenters did face prosecution, the initiative very often came from outside the parish. Thus it seems that Witham's dissenters were rarely obliged to hide their beliefs from their neighbours for fear of disapproval. And at times they were so well accepted, or even powerful, that in the local context they could hardly be called dissenters at all.

WEALTH AND STATUS

The poor

The poorer inhabitants of Witham were accused of immoral behaviour by the better-off at times. But during the 1620s and 1630s, the time when the control of the poor is thought to have become such an important feature of neighbouring Terling, Witham had other concerns as well. In fact it was then that we first discerned some of the less well-off parishioners joining with others in religious dissent, when in 1626 they went to worship with the Puritan Thomas Weld in Terling. Such participation recurred at intervals after this. Thus towards the end of the 1630s all sorts of people seemed to be joining in the harassment of vicar Francis Wright. Many poor men fought in the Civil War, though not always voluntarily. After 1660, nonconformist preacher George Lisle attracted dozens of people to hear him; the numbers alone imply a cross-section of the population. At the same time, the thorough records of the Quakers allow us to see that they had a number of poor people amongst their members, though the proportion was less than in the population as a whole. However, at all times the most active and vociferous of the dissenters were of at least middling wealth, and many of them were prosperous.

The rich

Although some dissenters suffered for their beliefs, many emerged relatively unscathed even after breaking the law. In Witham, people who survived particularly dangerous situations often appeared to have the support of at least one family of very high status. There is often reason to suspect that these wealthy families served as protectors or even sponsors for dissent. Initially they all moved into Witham from other places. The Catholic Southcotts had the most long-lived presence of this sort. Protestant Christopher Royden was a friend to the Ravens during the 1520s and 1530s. From 1600 and 1633 we saw how Dame Katherine Barnardiston, with her successive husbands and her other influential relatives, helped Puritans in Witham and elsewhere, including Thomas Weld in Terling. For half a century after the 1650s, clothier Robert Barwell(1) and his wife Martha were by far the richest Quakers in the parish. The equally prosperous Thomas Chipperfield, with other local yeomen, joined and assisted the nonconformists, and property owner Elizabeth True helped both groups.

CONTINUITY

On the face of it, the important role of these rich incomers might seem to imply that Witham's dissent was largely due to a series of accidents. Another external factor was the arrival of Francis Wright at two important times, which could be said to have provoked dissent. Nevertheless, there were some continuities too, which perhaps indicate that there was already fertile ground. The descendants of the sixteenth-century Protestant Ravens were very probably Quakers in parishes around Witham at the end of the seventeenth century, though there is a long gap in between those times that remains to be illuminated. More influential for a long time were the Garrards, with a history of Protestant dissent for over a hundred years from the 1570s. This was revealed to us most clearly in the long-lived Robert Garrard(2), Puritan friend of Dame Katherine Barnardiston in the 1620s, whom subsequent national events made temporarily acceptable before he became a post-Restoration nonconformist.

However, continuity was not confined to dissenters. To parallel the career of Garrard we have that of the similarly prosperous John Gravener(3), who maintained an equally long and constant presence. Unlike Garrard, Gravener seems to have been primarily law-abiding. The two must have met frequently about the town and elsewhere, as the leading men in the parish for over forty tumultuous years, and I should love to know what they thought of each other. Their only important collaboration of a religious or political nature that we know of, was when together they headed the great petition supporting Parliament in early 1642. Robert Jackson(1), 'the best townsman of a public spirit' in the 1660s, followed consistently traditional forbears, and was conforming like Gravener. In his case it was a local rather than a national crisis that stirred him to cooperate with a dissenter, the nonconformist Thomas Chipperfield. Together they condemned vicar Francis Wright in 1664.

In view of the influence of a person's upbringing, continuity is perhaps almost predictable, and discontinuity may be what is surprising. For instance, the careful John Gravener(3) was a descendant of the radical Ravens, whilst one of the town's Quakers, Deborah Eatney, had a sixteenth-century Witham vicar as her ancestor. A few families contained contemporary discord; even Robert Garrard(2) had a conformist brother-in-law. In most cases the details of such disharmony are lost to us. However, the sudden defection of second-generation Witham Quakers to the Church of England was very visible. In the process they ceased to be official dissenters, but they were also expressing what Professor Collinson has called 'true dissent', in that they abandoned the convictions of their own upbringing.[2]

In 1700, Witham was still the richly varied place that it had been for the previous two centuries, but its religious life appeared to be relatively calm. Only a few years later, we were presenting ourselves to the world as a genteel spa town. To discover the true nature of the apparent peace would entail moving into the eighteenth century. How much was it an inevitable result of the new post-Stuart Britain? And how much of a part was played by local factors, such as the work of vicar Jonas Warley, changes in the character of the cloth industry, the financial decline of some of the old families, or the ascendancy of new yeomen and shopkeepers? Perhaps someone else would like to think about this. I do have plans to write some more, but probably not about the eighteenth century. And my next projects will hopefully be shorter and less demanding. When the sun shines again I should like to be out there.

APPENDICES

APPENDIX 1: ARCHDEACONRY OF COLCHESTER, PERSONNEL 1569-1641
(compiled from the Act books in E.R.O. D/ACA)

OFFICIALS (JUDGES)	
COLCHESTER, LEXDEN, TENDRING AND WITHAM DEANERIES	**NEWPORT AND SAMPFORD DEANERIES**
William Rust (vicar of Felsted) - from before 1569, to 1570	**William Harrison** (writer and rector of Radwinter) - from before 1569, to 1570
(George Wither, new archdeacon, acted as judge in the interim)	
Thomas Rochester - 1571 to 1575	**Wm.Harrison** (again) - 1571 to 1576
Fabian Wither (vicar of Maldon All Saints, brother of George the archdeacon) 1575 & 1576 to 1579	
Ralph King - 1579 to 1581	
Wm.Bingham (Doctor of Laws, previously official of archdeaconry of Essex and bishop's commissary, afterwards rector of Rettendon) - 1581 to 1587	
Thomas Taylor - 1587 to 1590	
William Rust (again) -1590 to 1594	???
Nicholas Nevill (Doctor of Laws, later rector of Great Tey) - 1594 to 1595	**Richard Hodshon** (rector of Debden) ??? to 1595
(Thomas Wither, new archdeacon, acted as judge in the interim)	
John Cowell - 1600 to 1609	
(Thomas Wither, archdeacon, acted as judge)	
(Thomas Wither continued to act here)	**John Tuer** (vicar of Elsenham) c.1611 to 1617
Robert Aylett (of Feering, Doctor of Laws) - 1617 to 1641 (also bishop's commissary 1619-41)	

DEPUTY REGISTRARS
John Sandford - from before 1569 to 1582
(Edmund Hodilow, acting scribe 1583 to1586)
John Redstone - 1587 to 1603
Edmund Tillingham (gentleman, of Great Dunmow) - 1604 to1641 (also deputy registrar of Bishop's Commissary 1619 to 1641)

APPENDIX 2
THE FAMILIES OF DAME KATHERINE BARNARDISTON OF WITHAM

p.164. Some of her family she was born into, the Banks

Main sources: P.R.O. PROB 11/91/48/372, 11/158/84/156, 11/163/25/205, 11/171/87/358; E.R.O. D/ACW 14/159; Guildhall MSS 2895/1, 4438, 5265; Guildhall MS, Noble Collection C78; *D.N.B.*; *Visitations, London*; Beaven, 1913; Bodleian MS Rawlinson Essex 6, f.125; Bodleian MS Rawlinson Essex 22, f.155.

p.165. Some of her family through her first husband, Bartholomew Soame

Main Sources: P.R.O. PROB 11/87/6/46, 11/108/80/229, 11/133/1/1, 11/133/12/96, 11/135/1/1, 11/163/25/205, 11/182/14/101; Suffolk R.O. FL 535/4/1; Norfolk R.O., N.C.C. will, 200 (Ponder, Thomas Some), 1569; Guildhall MS 4438; *East Anglian Notes and Queries,* N.S., iii; Shipps, 1971, pp.80, 234-35; Pearl, 1961; R.R.Sharpe, 1894; Beaven, 1913.

p.166. Some of her family through her second husband, Sir Thomas Barnardiston

Main sources: P.R.O. PROB 11/163/25/205; E.R.O. T/P 252/4 (though this misses out a whole generation including Dame Katherine's husband Sir Thomas); *D.N.B*; Almack, 'Kedington'; Bodleian MS Rawlinson Essex 6, f.125; Bodleian MS Rawlinson Essex 22, f.155.

APPENDIX 2. THE FAMILIES OF DAME KATHERINE BARNARDISTON

SOME OF THE FAMILY OF DAME KATHERINE BARNARDISTON THROUGH THE FAMILY SHE WAS BORN INTO, THE BANKS

People whose names are in bold received bequests in Dame Katherine's will of 1633

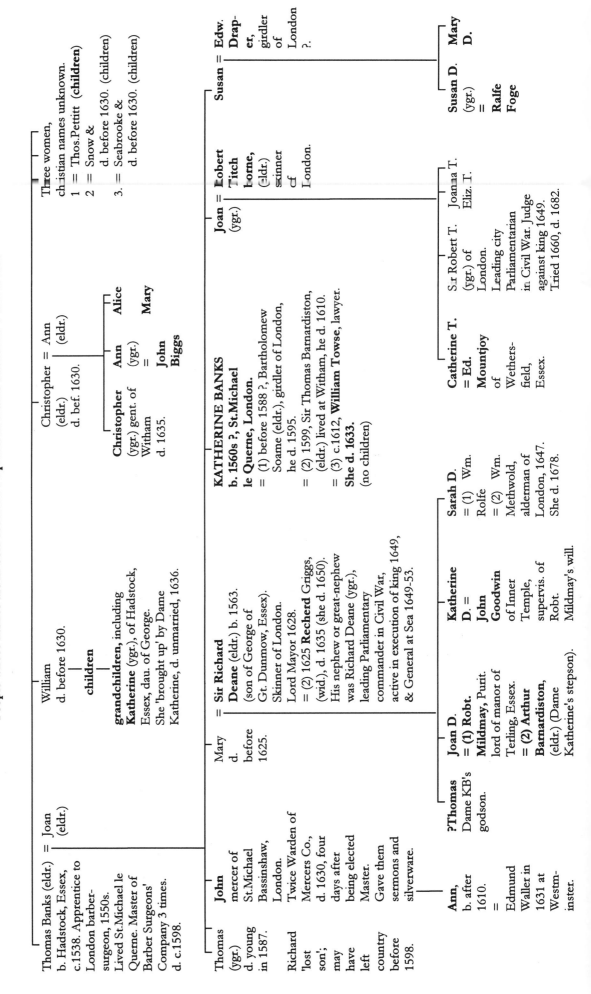

APPENDIX 2. THE FAMILIES OF DAME KATHERINE BARNARDISTON

SOME OF THE FAMILY OF DAME KATHERINE BARNARDISTON THROUGH HER FIRST HUSBAND, BARTHOLOMEW SOAME

People whose names are in italic and bold received bequests in Bartholomew Soame's will of 1595

People whose names are in plain bold received bequests in Dame Katherine's will of 1633

Thomas Soame (eldr.), gent., of Little Bradley, Suffolk, and Beetley, = Ann Knighton, widow of Richard Hunt of Little Bradley, Suffolk. Norfolk, d. 1569 while most of children under 21.

Elizabeth (eldr.) = *Gregory Seaton*, London alderman.

Thomas (ygr.) *gent.* of Little Bradley, Suffolk, d. 1606. = Eliz. Allington d. 1618.

Mary = *Richard Farrington*, London alderman (? who quarrelled with Sir Stephen).

Richard, gent., of Little Bradley, Suffolk, d. 1641.

John (ygr.), gent. of Lt. Bradley, Suffolk. In 'classis' of Risbridge hundred with Barnardistons, 1645. d. 1672.

Sir Stephen (eldr.) Lord Mayor of London 1598, M.P. 1601, d. 1619. Also mansion at Lt. Thurlow, Suffolk. Land etc. worth £5,000 p.a., & goods worth c. £40,000, & overseas investments. = Ann Stone of London.

William (eldr.) of Hundon Suffolk. d. 1631. = Sara Deresley of Suffolk.

John (eldr.) of Wethersfield, Essex.

Bartholomew (eldr.), girdler, of St.Mary Colchurch, London. b. c.1560 ? at Lt. Bradley, Suffolk, then to Beetley, Norfolk, then to London. d. 1596. = *KATHERINE BANKS*, of St.Michael le Querne, London, dau. of John, barber surgeon. **d. 1633.** (no children)

who = (2) in 1599, Thos. Barnardiston (eldr.) of Kedington, knighted 1603. d. 1610.

— by 1st wife —

Jane = **Sir Nathaniel Barnardiston** of Kedington. Puritan M.P. for Suff. 1625 and 1640. (see Barnardiston chart on next page).

Sir Thomas (ygst.) b. 1585, St.Mary Colchurch, London. Grocer & alderman. Briefly imprisoned by the King 1640 for obstructing forced City loan. Master of Grocers 1644. M.P. for City 1640-48. Later anti-Parl. & M.P. again 1660. d. 1672.

Sir Stephen (ygr.) of Heydon, Essex, d. 1640. = --- Platers dau. of Suffolk knight.

Sir William (ygr.) of Little Thurlow Suffolk. In 'classis' of Risbridge hundred with Barnardistons, 1645. = Bridget Barneham dau. of London alderman.

Ann (ygst.) m. c.1601 = Sir John Wentworth of Somerleyton, Suffolk. Puritan M.P. for Yarmouth 1628. d. 1651.

Mercy = Sir Calthrop Parker of Ewarten, Suffolk. Investor in East India Co M.P. for Suff. d. 1618.

Bartholomew (ygr.) of London.

Philip P., Puritan M.P. 1640.

APPENDIX 2. THE FAMILIES OF DAME KATHERINE BARNARDISTON

SOME OF THE FAMILY OF DAME KATHERINE BARNARDISTON THROUGH HER SECOND HUSBAND, SIR THOMAS BARNARDISTON

People whose names are in bold received bequests in Dame Katherine's will of 1633

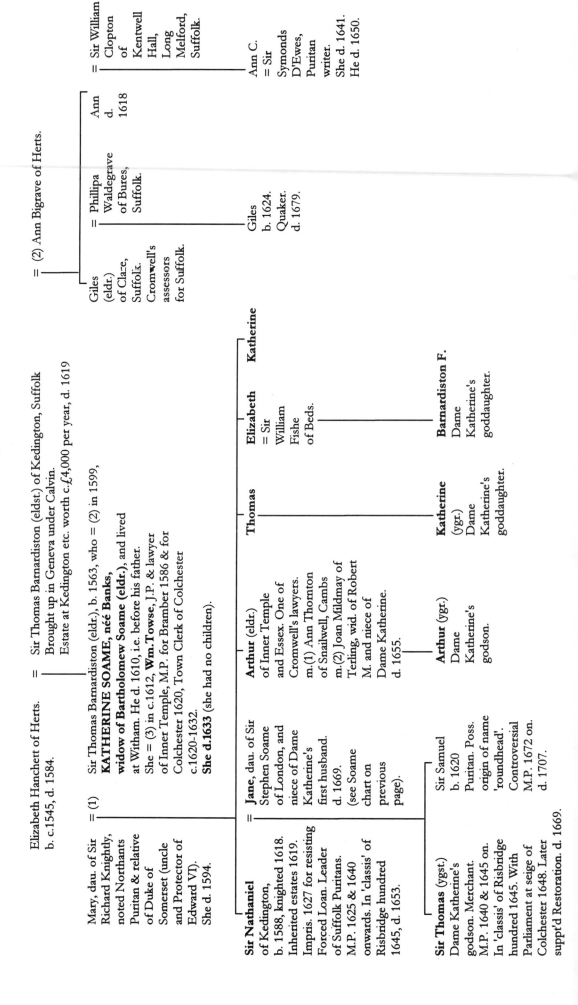

WITHAM CHURCHWARDENS' PRESENTMENTS AT THE BISHOP'S VISITATIONS, 1664 AND 1680

Quoted in full by permission of the Guildhall Library, Corporation of London
(from Guildhall MSS 9583/2, part 3, ff.124-25v, and 9583/5).

PRESENTMENT OF 1664, AT KELVEDON

Note:

The words indicated by asterisks are explained at the end.

The questions or 'articles' to be answered at Visitations were reproduced in printed pamphlets for circulation to the parishes. Different ones were prepared for each Visitation. The numbered articles for 1664, to which the Witham church wardens are responding here, survive in the British Library as *Articles of Enquiry concerning matters ecclesiastical within the diocese of London, in the primary Episcopal Visitation of the Right Reverend Father in God Humfry Lord Bishop of London*, 1664. Humfry was Humphrey Henchman.

[f.124]

The presentment of Thomas Chipperfild and Robert Jackson the present Churchwardens of the parish of Witham given at Kelvedon ... the 12th day of September 1664 before the right Reverend Father in god Humphrey Lord Bishop of London according to Articles sent by his Lordship

Concerning Churches or Chappels

To the first article. The outside of the Church is in present good repayre and last Summer Stood the parish in about 50 li but the pavement is much decayed by reason of the Souldiers Shutting up there in the late unhappy times, but now arepaireing, but the Fabricke is in very good repaire.

To the 2nd. We have a decent Font newly built being formerly Spoyled and A Communion table with a faire Carpet and linnen suitable we have a cup flagon and Chalice belonging to that Sarvice.

To the 3d. Wee have a Complete Deske for the minister and Stately pulpett with decent rich Cloth and Cushow for the Same not any pews erected of late to oure knowledge.

To the 4th. We have a large Bible of the new translation with two bookes of the Common Prayer and a book of Homilies and booke of Cannons.

To the 5th. Wee have a Register booke for Christnings and burialls and to our knowledge those concerned in keeping of them have Done their Duty.

To the 6th. Wee know of noe Stranger hath preach'd in our Church for a yeare last past wee keepe A ledger booke of our churchwardens accounts to register our accounts and for such Strangers as shall preach, if soe happin as to have them, wee shall Sett Downe.

To the 7th. Wee have a faire Surplice provided at the Charge of the parish but for 2 yeares past <u>never worne by our Vicare till the 4th of this September 1664.</u>

To the 8th. Wee have a chest to put in Almes and a chest with three locks to keepe our writings in and another Chest to kepe the ornaments of the church and a good strong Bire for the buriall of the Dead.

To the 9th. Our churchyard is indifferently well fenced but if any annoyance is <u>occasioned by our</u> <u>Vicars Cattell</u> and to keepe his Cattell Safe hee lockes up the gates that at all burialls or christnings or passage to the church the parishioners are forced to horse* over an high gate or Stile.

To the 10th. <u>Our vicars house is in very bad repaire</u> and the greatest part of a great Barne falne Downe and the rest ready to fall.

[f.124v.]

To the 11th. Our Vicar hath a Terriour of his glebe land as hee hath confesed in his possession but keepe it from our knowledge whereby wee cannot give further account of the eleventh article.

To the 12th. Wee knowe of noe change or altration of any of the Glebe land.

Concerning our Minister or Vicar

To the 1st. Wee know nothing to the Contrary but that hee is Episcopally ordeined according to the lawes of the nation.

To the 2nd. Wee doe not know whether our Minister bee licensed by the present Bishop of the Diecesse, hee reads Divine Service and preacheth when at home.

To the 3d. Our Vicar publisheth the bread and wine after Consecration to be transubstantiated and to be the reall body and blood of christ which whether disagreeing to the woord of god and the Articles of christian faith wee Submitt to better Judgments.

To the 4th. Our Vicar hath not used the Surplice these two yeares last past till the fourth of September 1664 either in reading divine Sarvice or at Sacrament, and administers nott the Sacrament above three times a yeare.

To the 5th. Our Vicar for four years last past hath not catechised the youth of the parish and instead of endeavouring to reclaime Sectoryes, by his harsh expresions in pulpett hath driven away those that came to be reclaimed Soe that our parish multiplyes with quakers and most other of the parish, are forced to goe to other Conformable parishes to exercise their Devotion.

To the 6th. Before the late trobles our Vicar was of Such lewd life, though then hee had a modest wife of his owne, that for that Scandall he was Sequestred in the late trobles as we are Informed, and Since his Restoration nere now foure yeares hee hath been twice convicted before the Justices of peace of this County for drunkennes, and was Since being the 16th of November last very drunk againe and that hee is a frequent Swearer, and useth rayling and threatning Speeches both in and out of his pulpet it is his weekly Conversation with most of his parishioners that he discourseth with.

To the 7th. Wee are Informed our minister did refuse to christen the child of Henry Masson brought unto him, but beleeve he gives the Comunion three times in a yeare.

To the 8th. Wee know not of any mariages in private houses by our Vicar but that he obsarves the 8th Article.

To the 9th. Our Minister usualy bids holy dayes and fasting dayes and noe way guiltey of appointing privat fasts or religious exercises, and by reason of his raileings in the pulpett occasions most of his parish to exercise Religion in theire private Familyes when the unseasonablenes

[f.125]

of the weather gives not leave to goe to theire adjoyning parishes but wee have a Sect Called Quakers meete once or twice a weeke as wee ar informed not ever being present with them ourselves.

To the 10th. Our Vicar hath noe Curate & is Sometimes absent as before expressed.

To the 11th. Wee have noe lecture.

To the 12th. Our Vicar about a yeare since excomunicated three or foure persons, but wee know not of any Since.

Concerning parishioners

To the 1st. Wee have in our parish the Sect of Quakers as before expressed but know not of any other of the first Article in our parish.

To the 2nd. Wee know none at present that lyes under the Common fame of adultery fornication or Incest but Drunkards and blasphemers of gods holy name, our Vicars ill Example wee verely beleeve occasions multitudes of pore miserable Simple Creatures that are often Drunke and Dayly Blaspheme gods holy name in theire ordinary Communications.

To the 3d. Many parishioners as before expressed for want of a diligent painefull and loveing Minister neglects the publique holy duty.

To the 4th. Divers parishioners in our parish Both Quakers and others resort not to our Church for the reasons before expressed.

To the 5th. We know none in oure parish that refuse to have their Infants Baptized but Severall refuse to have theire Infants baptised by our Vicar, but baptize them by Orthodoxe ministers to our best knowledge.

To the 6th. Wee have no Catechising as before expressed, and therefore householders doe not send theire children and Sarvants.

To the 7th. Many of our parish refuse to receive the Sacrament of our Vicar hee publishing the Bread and wine after Consecration to be transubstantiated and to be the reall body and Blood of christ [but most of those receive it as we [???] at next adjacent parishes] [part in brackets deleted].

To the 8th. Wee present Hugh Horsnayle and Samuel Davye as were lawfully maryed but lives not with theire wives; but whether lawfully Divorced wee know not.

To the 9th. There ar many as refuse to Come to be churched* oure Vicar of soe Scandalous life.

To the 10th. The widdow Ludgater, George Pledger and Thomas Barker of Dunton are in arreres in paying their rates for the repayreing of the Church, and most parishioners refuse to pay there Ester offerings for that they receive not the Sacrament at our Vicars hands.

To the 11th & 12th. We know Nothing.

[f.125v]

Concerning Officers of the Church

To the 1st & 2nd. Our present Churchwardens are chosen according to law and our former churchwardens have Given up theire accounts according to the 2d Article.

To the 3rd. Wee know not any Misdemeanours of our parish Clerke and Sexton if hee keepes the churche Cleane.

Concerning Almshouses and Schooles

To the 1st. Wee have twoe Almeshouses one Thomas Greene gave and the founders Charity is by a decretall order uppon a Masters reporte in Chancery many yeares Since Misimployed, the other the Charity duly Imployed.

To the 2nd. Wee have on Mr.Ponder keepes a Schoole but licensed by Sr.Richard Chaworth* as wee are Informed and wee have some private Schooles taught by women soe farr as horne booke and plaster* and learning Children to knit and Sowe.

Touching Ecclesiasticall Officers

To the 1st. Wee know none that offend in either article only our Vicar on Thursday last sayd to Robert Jacson Sr Richard Chaworth and the Register weare his great Frinds and if he woold omitt and not make any presentment Hee the sayd Sir Richard and the said Register should keepe us harmless, and that if wee made any wee should repent it and Jacson for doeing it one day woold wish his right hand of, but wee beeleeve hee doth abuse those worthy Gentlemen and woald by his threats have hindered us of our Duty herein.

[signed] Robert Jackson

                         Churchwardens

[signed] Thomas Chipperfield

---

*To horse usually meant to lift but here it probably indicates climbing. Women were expected to go to church to be *churched* after giving birth; this entailed prayers of thanks being given for their safe delivery. *Horn books* were boards displaying the alphabet, and sometimes numbers and other information also, covered with a thin sheet of horn. *Plaster* was perhaps some sort of model-making substance. *Sir Richard Chaworth* was the bishop's Vicar General.

PRESENTMENT OF 1680, AT BRAINTREE

Wytham. A bill of presentment made and exhibited by the Churchwardens ... at the Second Episcopall visitation of the Right Reverend Father in God Henry ... Bishop of London, held in the parish Church of Braintree ... 3d. day of September, Anno domini 1680

Concerning Churches and Chappells	O'ia bene [all well]
Concerning Churchwardens	O'ia bene [all well]
Concerning Ministers	O'ia bene [all well]
Concerning Parishioners	O'ia bene [all well]
Concerning parish Clarkes &	
Sextons Schoolmasters &c.	O'ia bene [all well]

[signed] John Jackson

NOTES

ABBREVIATIONS

Books, articles, and lectures are described in an abbreviated form, as explained at the beginning of the Bibliography on page 193. Full details are listed there in alphabetical order. Volume numbers are given in lower-case Roman numerals.

B.L.	British Library, Department of Manuscripts (formerly British Museum)
E.R.O.	Essex Record Office
et al.	et alia, i.e. and others. I have used this in relation to the Act books of the Church courts, at points where I have quoted one of the main references for a case but there are also other minor references in the same book to the same case
E.U.L.	Essex University Library
f.	folio
ff.	folios
Guildhall MS	Guildhall Manuscripts Library
H.L.R.O.	House of Lords Record Office
L.M.A.	London Metropolitan Archives (formerly Greater London Record Office)
L.P.L.	Lambeth Palace Library
Manor no.	refers to the identification numbers used in the records of the manor of Chipping and Newland after 1686 (mostly E.R.O. D/DBw; see Gyford, 1996, p.231, for a fuller explanation)
p.	page
pp.	pages
P.R.O.	Public Record Office
R.O.	Record Office.
v	verso, i.e. the reverse side of a folio

References to quarter sessions rolls (E.R.O. Q/SR) generally relate to the typescript calendar in E.R.O., though on a few occasions I have also consulted the original rolls. References to assize rolls (P.R.O. ASSI) from 1558-1625 refer to the printed calendars in Cockburn, 1978 and 1982 (for which see the bibliography), whilst from 1625-1714 they refer to the typescript calendar in E.R.O.

Chapter 1. Witham

[1] This chapter is a summary of the main points in my previous book, i.e. J.Gyford, *Witham 1500-1700: making a living*, Janet Gyford, 1996, which is indexed and referenced. So the chapter is only indexed in broad outline, and I have not given references for it.

Chapter 2. Useful information

[1] E.g.: Duffy, 1992, pp.1-2, 277-78, 651; Thomas, 1971, p.53; Wrightson, 1988, pp.199-205; Ingram, 1995, pp.95-123; Haigh, 1984, pp.212-14; M.Spufford, 1995, pp.1-102; Collinson, 'Critical conclusion', 1995, pp.388-96.

[2] E.R.O. Q/SR 124/63; manor no.136 (house of Christopher Greene).

[3] E.R.O. D/DDc T82; E.R.O. D/ACR 4/262; E.R.O. D/P 30/28/14, 13 Nov.1576; E.R.O. D/DBw M26, 6 April 1583; E.R.O. D/ACW 5/234, 18/26 (the registered version of the latter only has half the will, i.e. E.R.O. D/ACR 8/140).

[4] Thanks to Amanda Flather for this point, and for the example of Gough, 1981, based on a list of occupants of pews and their social position in Myddle, Shropshire, in 1702.

[5] *Vicarage (small tithes):* Guildhall MSS 9531/12, f.221, 9531/13, f.102 (leases of 1548 and 1583). *Rectory (great tithes):* with Canons of St.Martin le Grand until 1503, then Westminster Abbey till the Dissolution, then the bishop of London (date of latter not certain: Fowler, 1911, p.5, says 1581, Guildhall MS 9531/13, f.48v, implies already in 1564). Then with the Southcotts and then the Barnardistons of Witham Place, till death of Dame Katherine Barnardiston in 1633; then other leases thereafter (Guildhall MS 12737; PRO PROB 11/69/6/24; 11/116/204). *1994 onwards:* The 'head' clergyman of Witham adopted the title of 'rector' from 1 June 1994; there are still two vicars also ('Parish Magazine', August 1994, pp.1-2).

[6] Fowler, 1911, p.5; Guildhall 9628/4.

[7] Guildhall MS 9628/4; Gyford, 1996, p.84; Collinson, 1982, pp.93-95; J.P.Anglin, 1965, pp.205-206. Values per person calculated from E.R.O. T/A 427/1/4, 427/1/5, and *Valor Eccl.*, i, p. 445. *Vicarage house:* John Bramston, vicar from 1840-73, disliked the 'spirit of sham', represented by the 19th-century outer bricks which had no structural function. Nevertheless his wife Clarissa described the vicarage as 'our most comfortable, most cheerful, most bright-looking Home, which John has done all that taste aided by £.s.d. could do to make perfect'. At some time since then, the size of the building was reduced, and the porch removed. A large new extension was added in 1997 (Bramston, 1855, p.49; E.R.O. D/DLu 15/19; photograph in E.R.O. T/P 339).

[8] Carlson, 1995, pp.193-204; Webb, *Parish and County*, 1924, pp.15-25 (felt, perhaps over-optimistically, that churchwardenship was not very onerous, and therefore attractive); Craig, 'Co-operation' (summarises others' views on the nature of churchwardens, and discusses the use of their accounts as a source, with Mildenhall in Suffolk as an example); E.R.O. D/ACA 51, f.249, ACA 52, f.3 et al.; E.R.O. calendar of assize records; Grieve, 1994, p.31 (re.Freshwater of Chelmsford, possibly the same man); Q/Sba 2/17.

[9] Webb, *Parish and County*, 1924, pp.21-23; Carlson, 1995, pp.168-74, 180-81, 188-204; E.R.O. D/ACA 51, f.249, ACA 52, f.3 et al.; E.R.O. D/P 299/1/3; Johnson, 1989/90, pp.273-74.

[10] *Holders of churchwardenship:* E.R.O. D/ACA 3-4, 6, 8, 13, 18, 20, 22, 30,

32, 40, 43-44, 48-51, 53-55, E.R.O. D/ACV 1-4, 6-8, 10-12, Guildhall MS 9537/1-16, E.R.O. D/P 30/14/1. *Ability to sign:* especially from E.R.O. D/ABW, E.R.O. D/ACW 2-22, H.L.R.O., Main Papers, H.L., 20 Jan.1641/2, petition box.

11 Webb, *Parish and County,* 1924, pp.22-23; Grieve, 1994, pp.28-29; Carlson, 1995, pp.180-91; E.R.O. D/ACA 51, f.249, ACA 52, f.3 et al.

12 Assuming population estimates as in Gyford, 1996, p.3, life expectancy 40 to 45 years, and 2/3 to 3/4 of the deaths being of adults. Similar result from burial register 1664 onwards (E.R.O. D/P 30/1/1). Wills in E.R.O. D/ABW, D/ACR 1-7, D/ACW 2-22, P.R.O. PROB 11.

13 Takahashi, 1990, pp.212-13; see also J.Thirsk quoted in Camp, 1974, pp.xxxvi-xxxviii. P.R.O. PROB 11/248/517; Gyford, 1996, pp.101-07 (weavers).

14 M.Spufford, 1974, p.321; Walker, 'Sects'; Duffy, 1992, pp.505-509; Litzenberger, 1997, pp.171-78 (uses a more restricted definition of Protestant preambles). Further difference is possible over what constitutes a religious preamble in the first place; e.g. Johnson, 1989/90, pp.286-88, says 17th-century Coggeshall wills have none, but several do seem to (e.g. E.R.O. D/ACW 8/284, 10/220, 12/197). *Freeborne:* E.R.O. D/ACW 4/227. *Turner:* E.R.O. D/ACW 14/165; E.R.O. D/ALV 2, f.133v.

15 E.R.O. D/ABD 8, f.53; E.R.O. D/ABW 56/283. The usage of 'simnel' to describe a rich currant cake is a later one (*O.E.D*). Marsh, 1990, p.231.

16 E.R.O. D/ACW 20/214; 21/152; E.R.O. D/ABW 34/125. *Lichfield:* E.R.O. Q/SR 363/16; 376/51; E.R.O. D/ACW 16/7, 16/182; P.R.O. PROB 11/283/577.

17 E.R.O. D/ACW 2/240; 12/98, 12/99; E.R.O. D/ACD 7, ff.58v-59v, 101; manor nos.1, 12, 13; see also E.R.O. D/ABD 7, f.5v.

18 E.R.O. D/ACD 1, f.15v; E.R.O. D/ACW 2/28; manor no.63. *Hurrell:* probably at Cambridge University in 1573, later vicar of Great Saling in Essex (Guildhall MS 9537/6/86v; *Alumni Cantabrigiensis*). Called 'clerk' in 1588 (E.R.O. D/ACD 1, f.15v).

19 Marsh, 1990, p.239 (thanks to Margaret Spufford for advice also, in letter, Oct.1992); Collinson, 1982, p.197; Haigh, 1987, pp.98-99; Craig, 1996, pp.38-39; Litzenberger, 1997, pp.168-85 (an immensely detailed study of Gloucestershire which defines 17 categories of preamble; p.170 has a list of works since 1971 which have used preambles). Figure 4 compiled from: E.R.O. D/ABW 1-41, E.R.O. D/ACW 1-22, P.R.O. PROB 11 various. Definitions as follows: *(a) Catholic:* reference to the Virgin Mary and the saints. *(b) Mixed:* elements of both (a) and (e). *(c) None:* No preamble at all. *(d) Non-committal:* reference to God but none to Christ, usually brief. *(e) General Protestant:* to God and also to Christ, sometimes as saviour and/or redeemer, and/or reference to the merits of Christ, or asking Christ to accept the soul, sometimes also to salvation, forgiveness of sins, eternal life, the resurrection of the self; the wish to be partaker or inheritor of the kingdom of heaven, the wish to be one of the 'elect'. *(f) Distinctive Protestant:* distinctive forms, both long and short.

20 *Amplification:* see e.g. Chapman, 1992 (clear and brief; emphasises the higher courts; figures quoted come from this, p.7); Anglin, 1965 (full, very useful on discussion of operation of courts etc.; interpretation of Puritanism has evolved since then); Emmison, 1973, pp.vi-xiv; Webster, 1997, pp.180-84 (for summary of powers relating to defaulting ministers). *Textual examples:* R.Taylor, 1928; Brinkworth, 1942; Purvis, 1953. Note that Tarver, 1995, does not relate much to office business or to the 16th and 17th-centuries.

21 Brinkworth, 1942, p.xvii.

22 E.g. deposition books (written evidence), books of 'causes' (re.litigation between individuals, which constituted a minority of cases, and to which I have not often referred), visitation books (especially re. the clergy), probate records.

23 *High Commission:* many of the records were destroyed during the Civil War. Some items survive in other sources, e.g. see *Cal.S.P.Dom.*, and Gardiner, 1886. *Consistory court:* Its tours are sometimes known as Visitations, but I have just referred to them as courts, to distinguish them from the main Visitations which reviewed the churches themselves. Records in L.M.A. DL/C, E.R.O. D/AL. Until 1615 Witham deanery's cases were mostly heard at Chelmsford, after 1622 mostly at Kelvedon. The only substantial numbers of new cases from Witham in the surviving records were in 1612, 1619, 1628, 1631 and 1635 (L.M.A. DL/C/319, pp.83-90, DL/C/323, pp.78-82, DL/C/621, pp.147, 154-56; E.R.O. D/ALV 1, ff.25v-26v, ALV 2, ff.25-25v, 133-33v).

24 *Commissary court of Essex and Hertfordshire:* Records in E.R.O. Only survive from 1616 onwards (E.R.O. D/AB) except for a fragment for a single year from July 1561 onwards (part of D/ABR 4). *Archdeaconries of Essex, Middlesex, and Colchester:* Records in E.R.O. (E.R.O. D/AE, D/AM, D/AC). For amplification see: Anglin, 1965; Pressey, 'Affairs'; 'Apparitor'; 'Churchwarden'; 'Records'; 'Seating'; 'Surplice'; and 'Visitations'.

25 *Peculiars etc.:* Chapman, 1992, pp.23-24; Newcourt, 1710, ii, pp.1-2; *Victoria History,* ii, 1907, pp.81-82. *Fees:* Pressey, 'Records', p.5. *Visitations:* e.g. L.P.L. Bishop's Register, Laud 1633-45, f.158v (Archbishop of London); Guildhall MS 9537/1-25 (Bishop of London), E.R.O. D/ABV 1-5 (Bishop's commissary), E.R.O. D/ACV 1-9 (Archdeacon of Colchester), E.R.O. D/AEV 1-7 (Archdeacon of Essex), E.R.O. D/AMV 1-9 (Archdeacon of Middlesex). The records in E.R.O. D/ALV appear to relate to the Bishop's Consistory court itself rather than to the Visitations strictly so described. *Bishop's own parishes etc.:* many in north-west Essex. Jurisdiction for probate could change over time. For inter-personal disputes the Commissary court may have sometimes been chosen as more efficient. Some matters were reserved to the bishop's courts, e.g. the decision to substitute a fine for a penance (Anglin, 1965, pp.115-16, 161-63, 289-90, 305-306). For other complications of the hierarchy see Chapman, 1992, pp.19-20. For detailed jurisdictions see Humphery-Smith, 1995.

26 *Meeting places:* Before 1619, information is fragmentary. In 1561-62, about two-thirds of the Commissary courts for north-west Essex were held in the churches of Stortford or Castle Hedingham, the rest being divided between seven other churches, and two private houses (E.R.O. D/ABR 4). From May 1616 to July 1618, meetings for south and east Essex were at Chelmsford and Colchester (E.R.O. D/ABA 1, ff,1-51v). Then in April 1619 a new county-wide schedule begins (E.R.O. D/ABA 1, f.52). *Usual source of business after 1619:* eastern part of Colchester archdeaconry to Colchester; Essex archdeaconry to Chelmsford and Billericay; Middlesex archdeaconry to Braintree; north-west of Colchester archdeaconry, and part of the archdeaconry of Middlesex in Hertfordshire, to Bishops Stortford (the latter area had more of the bishop's parishes and so more business direct from them).

27 E.g. E.R.O. D/ACA 5, f.140v (in house of George Wither, archdeacon, in Danbury, where he was rector, in 1574); E.R.O. D/ACA 21, f.423 (in house of Nicholas Nevill, official, in parish of St.Nicholas, Colchester in 1595); E.R.O. D/ABR 4 (in house of Thomas Dorell, commissary, in Birdbrook, in 1561, and in house of Richard Rogers, vicar of Great Dunmow, in 1562). Loose sheets referring to individual hearings are found in various of the Act Books, and a few others have recently come to light (E.R.O. Accession A9368).

28 In 1592 the archdeaconry of Essex had the following officers: the archdeacon, the registrar and his deputy, three proctors, four apparitors or mandatories and three servants (Pressey, 'Records', p.4). *Surrogate judges:* E.R.O. D/ACA 3, f.70; L.M.A. DL/C/619, p.279. The bishop's commissaries took most courts near where they lived, with substitutes helping elsewhere, e.g Thomas Dorell of Birdbrook, 1561-62, Robert Aylett of Feering, 1617 onwards (E.R.O. D/ABR 4; E.R.O. D/ABA 3).

29 *John Calfhill:* appointed 1565 so preceded George Wither, but information on his courts does not all survive (Guildhall MS 9531/13, ff.137, 157; E.R.O. D/ACA 3, f.101). *George Wither:* E.R.O. D/ACA 4, ff.2-88, ACA 5, ff.29v, 50v, 125, 140v, ACA 19, f.145, ACA 22, f.168v; E.R.O. D/ACV 1, ff.27v, 32v, 43, 50, 51, 66v, 71. Newcourt, 1708, i, p.92, mistakenly gives him continuing until 1617. *Thomas Wither:* D/ACA 21, f.430 onwards, ACA 22, f.206 onwards, ACA 23, f.86 onwards, ACA 39, f.99v. He is omitted by Newcourt, 1708, i, p.92 and *Alumni Cantabrigiensis*. Thanks to Pat Lewis for information about Fordham, where the parish register gives Thomas Wither as archdeacon in 1598, and has his burial in 1617. *Henry King:* Guildhall MSS 9531/14, f.212, 9531/15, ff..109v-110; Foster, 1891; *D.N.B.* King was followed briefly in 1642 by Josias Shute. *General:* Jay Anglin found that the archdeacons of the Essex archdeaconry similarly presided at the courts for considerable periods when they appeared to have no official (Anglin, 1965, pp.31-32). The Visitations usually took place in autumn and spring, the latter being called the Synod.

30 *Periodic division between two officials:* can be inferred from the Act books but also see e.g. E.R.O. D/ACA 19, f.229v, naming William Rust as official in the deaneries of Witham, Colchester, Lexden and Tendring in 1591, and E.R.O. D/ACA 23, f.1 naming Richard Hodshon as official of the deaneries of Newport and Sampford in 1595. *William Harrison:* Harrison, 1877. For examples of his working in the east see E.R.O.

D/ACA 3, ff.9 (Witham), 21, 27 (Kelvedon). *Fabian Wither:* Petchey, 1991, pp.199-202. *Appointment policy:* Chapman, 1992, p.31. *Robert Aylett:* presided as a temporary substitute, before his appointment (e.g. E.R.O. D/ACA 39, ff.121, 130v, 133v, ACA 40, f.54; E.R.O. D/ABA 1, ff.1, 39). First referred to in the Act books as archdeacon's official in May 1617 (E.R.O. D/ACA 39, ff.140, 62); the bishop himself called him 'official or surrogate' of the archdeaconry in the previous month, April 1617, so his appointment was clearly anticipated (Bodleian MS Top.Essex c.17). First mentioned as bishop's commissary in June 1619 (E.R.O. D/ABA 1, f.60). His biographer and other commentators mention the latter post, but not the former (Round, 'Aylett').

31 *Deputy registrars:* John Sandford 1569-82, John Redstone 1587-1603, Edmund Tillingham 1604-41. They were often 'acting' before their appointment. Also, Edmund Hodilow was 'acting scribe' 1583 to 1586 (E.R.O. D/ACA 3, f.9, ACA 10, ff.102-108v, ACA 14, ff.120v-151v, ACA 27, ff.26-101). The reason for the term 'deputy registrar' is that the registrar himself usually seemed to be a more senior appointment serving the bishop himself and all parts of the diocese e.g. William Sherman in 1636 (L.P.L. Bishop's Register, Laud 1633-45, ff.158v-66).

32 *Ship Money, 1636:* Tillingham's assessment was fourth highest in the parish of Great Dunmow (£1 6s.) (E.R.O. T/A 42, 42A). *Cambridge University:* Two people called Edmund Tillingham there, but probably not our man, i.e. one too late (scholar 1606, L.L.B. 1610) the other said to be our man's son (M.A. 1639) (*Alumni Cantabrigiensis*). *Appointments:* Archdeaconry court began June 1604 (previously a substitute for his predecessor, John Redstone, since March 1603) (E.R.O. D/ACA 27, ff.30-101). Bishop's Commissary began July 1619; his predecessor had prepared the book, but Tillingham entered the proceedings (E.R.O. D/ABA 1, f.64). *Communications:* Anglin, 1965, p.116. *Family etc.:* E.R.O. D/P 11/1/2. Tillingham probably married Ann Marlar in Colchester in 1611 and then Ann Pomfret, widow, in Little Saling in 1617. Two sons Edmund and William baptised Great Dunmow 1614 and 1615. Edmund the younger to school in Halstead and thence to Cambridge University (*Visitations, Essex*, pp.74, 243; E.R.O. D/P 178/1/1; E.R.O. D/P 297/1/1; E.R.O. D/P 11/1/2; *Alumni Cantabrigiensis*). I have wondered whether Aylett and Tillingham may have been related; they both had associations with Kelvedon (*Visitations, Essex*). *Christopher Tillingham:* No baptism Great Dunmow though a marriage there 1641. Deputy registrar in Bishop's Commissary 1662-69 (E.R.O. D/ABA 10-12). Acted as registrar sometimes Colchester archdeaconry 1663-64 but not actually in office (E.R.O. D/ACA 55). Not all relevant records survive.

33 *Duties:* Anglin, 1965, pp.41-44. *Time:* E.R.O. D/ACA 24, f.357. *1626:* E.R.O. D/ACA 45; D/ABA 3. Occasionally no names are given making it unclear who attended. *Visitations:* no archdeacon's records for the 1620s, but in 1611 they were held at Colchester, Kelvedon and Saffron Walden, once at each place in April, and once at each place in October or November (E.R.O. D/ACV 4). *Books:* The few surviving records before 1619 imply separate books (E.R.O. D/ABR 4; E.R.O. D/ABA 1). The latter book has courts only for the southern part at Chelmsford and Colchester, from May 1616 to July 1618; then, after a break, Tillingham appears and enters courts in it for all areas from April 1619 onwards. *Quarter sessions:* E.R.O. Q/SR 214/28.

34 Anglin, 1965, p.47; Pressey, 'Apparitor'; Pressey, 'Records', p.4; Chaucer, p.313; L.M.A. DL/C/304, pp.697-98, 712-13, 721-24, 729-30.

35 L.M.A. DL/C/325, p.82, DL/C/319, p.73; E.R.O. D/ACA 25, f.115, ACA 49, f.15; E.R.O. Q/SR 228/10, 244/9, 245/32, 261/27. For the Bayles family see chapter 6.

36 L.M.A. DL/C/322, f.89 (Edward Campion, a notary public, went to the Consistory Court to represent Edmund Halys, who is discussed in chapter 7).

37 E.R.O. D/ACD 1, f.37v; E.R.O. D/ACA 18, f.180v.

38 Collinson, 1982, p.214, points out that 'a high proportion, sometimes even the majority of those cited to appear in court for all kinds of offences, but especially for sexual crimes, failed to present themselves'. E.R.O. D/ACA 45, ff.93v (including separate sheet), 104v, ACA 44, f.131. A lead farthing token of William Robinson's has recently been found at Tolleshunt Major; a large hoard of tokens of George Robinson, probably his son, is already known (Pryke, 'Token', p.283; Thompson and Gyford, 'Hoard'; thanks to Robert Thompson for this information).

39 Pressey, 'Records', p.13; Ingram, 1996, pp.65-66; E.R.O. Acc.A9368; E.R.O. D/ACA 25, f.110, ACA 27, f.114v, 118.

40 E.R.O. D/ACD 1, ff.36-37; E.R.O. D/ACA 12, ff26v, 28v, ACA 16,

f.114 et al., ACA 18, f.5v.; manor no.30; E.R.O. D/DBw M26, 6 April 1583.

41 L.M.A. DL/C/325, p.86; E.R.O. D/P 347/1/1; examples of the roles from which excommunicate people were theoretically barred were serving on juries, giving evidence in court, suing for debt, or acting as guardians (A.Davies, 1986, p.111).

42 E.R.O. D/ACA 25, ff.177, 192, 194, 197; L.M.A. DL/C/303, p.743; Collinson, 1982, pp.214-30.

43 L.M.A. DL/C/621, pp.288, 292, 308, 335, 392, 401; E.R.O. D/ACA 40, f.10.

44 E.R.O. D/ABA 1, f.131v; E.R.O. D/ACA 40, f.182; Anglin, 1965, pp.305-306; Pressey, 'Records', p.17 (gives an example of the Archdeacon's court accepting payment instead of a penance in 1662).

45 *Figures 5 to 8:* calculated from E.R.O. D/ACA 1-13, 16, 18, 20, 22, 25, 27, 30, 32, 34, 34A, 37, 40, 43-55. The Witham figures come from a count of individual cases, whilst the figures for the archdeaconry as a whole are from a count of pages in the Act books. The figures quoted in figure 5 for the Consistory court come from: L.M.A DL/C/319, 323, 621, and E.R.O. D/ALV 1. *Terling:* Wrightson and Levine, 1979 and 1995, p.119.

46 Haigh, 1993, p.276; Haigh, 1987, p.11; Wrightson and Levine, 1979 and 1995, pp.152-54; Cressy, 1980, p.85; Byford, 1988, p.428; Thomas, 1986, pp.104-114.

47 E.R.O. D/ABW 21/130, 31/95; E.R.O. D/ACW 7/249, 12/25, 13/21, 18/353, 19/20; Gyford, 1996, pp.60, 198.

48 Lawson and Silver, 1973, pp.126-27; P.R.O. PROB 11/129/7; E.R.O. D/ACW 19/20.

49 P.R.O. PROB 11/178/155, 11/25/205; E.R.O. D/ACW 15/108; Gyford, 1996, pp.83, 223-24, 234(#23).

50 E.R.O. D/ACW 2/28; L.M.A. DL/C/343, f.87.

51 DL/C/333, ff.89v, DL/C/341, f.20; Haigh, 1993, pp.276-77; M.Spufford, 1974, pp.192-218; Cressy, 1980, p,85, pp.142-74, and p.19 (quoting Stone, 'Revolution'); Wrightson, 1988, pp.184-86; P.Clark, 1977, pp.189-91, 199, 214-16, 220. Strangely, two men given a licence in Witham in 1628 were taken to court 18 months later for teaching without one, on the grounds that curate Thomas Young had 'licence only to teach himself' (L.M.A. DL/C/322, p.81; Guildhall MS 9537/13/19v, 9539A/1/7v, 12v).

52 *Villages:* Terling and Kelvedon in 1587, Fairstead and Rivenhall in 1592, Faulkbourne in 1599, Great Braxted in 1601 (L.M.A. DL/C/334, ff.141, 143, DL/C/335, f.92, DL/C/337, f.19v, DL/C/338, f.35). *Witham:* L.M.A. DL/C/340, f.63, DL/C/334, ff.141, 143, DL/C/341, f.141; Guildhall 9539A/1/12v. *Stopgap for clergy:* Collinson, 1982, p.98. Witham's Christopher Webb, 1628 (Guildhall MS 9539A/1/7v; *Alumni Oxoniensis*), and George Eatney, 1637 (Guildhall MS 9539A/1/77v, 114v; L.M.A. DL/C/344, f.79).

53 E.R.O. D/ACW 5/231 (will by Richard Redman); E.R.O. D/ACA 18, f.232v et al.

54 Guildhall MS 9539B/14, 9537/24/140v, 9583/2, part 3, f.125v; *O.E.D.* In c.1760, boys' and girls' boarding schools began to advertise in Witham. Church schooling began here in 1787, with new Sunday and Day Schools (*Ipswich Journal*, 20 Oct.1759, 10 Jan.1761; E.R.O. D/P 30/1/2A).

55 P.R.O. SP 16/252/67i-ii; Ford, 'Literacy', pp.22-37; Thomas, 1986, pp.99-104 (argues that many more could read type than has sometimes been thought); Barry, 1995, pp.69-94 (summarises the literature about the history of literacy).

56 Cressy, 1980, pp.47-48. *Clergymen etc.:* E.R.O. D/ACW 13/320 (Cyprian Nicholls, 1642; studied at Cambridge but died before ordained - see P.R.O. PROB 11/178/155); E.R.O. D/ACW 15/85 (Edmund Halys, 1648, gentleman, son of former vicar); E.R.O. D/ACW 19/20 (Thomas Cox, 1675, vicar); E.R.O. D/ACW 19/80 (John Ponder, 1678, nephew of clergyman); P.R.O. PROB 11/363/74 (Thomas Brett, 1680, vicar); E.R.O. D/ACW 20/214 (George Lisle, 1685, nonconformist minister); E.R.O. D/ACW 22/108 (Ann Lisle, 1689, widow of the latter, 1689); E.R.O. D/ACW 22/102 (Priscilla Ponder, 1696, clergyman's widow). *Others:* E.R.O. D/ACW 12/141, 18/328; Gyford, 1996, p.129. *Haylin:* E.R.O. D/ACW 19/80; *D.N.B.*

57 H.L.R.O., Main Papers, H.L., 20 Jan.1641/2, petition box; Cressy, 1980, pp.2, 20, 65, 72-78, 89-96; Wrightson and Levine, 1979 and 1995.

58 E.R.O. Q/SR 318/49; P.R.O. PROB 10/776 (original of P.R.O. PROB 11/236/183); E.R.O. D/ABW 66/366; M.Spufford, 1974, pp.196-97; Cressy, 1980, pp.42, 53-61.

59 Before about 1580, genuinely original wills do not usually survive for

Essex. The same was true of Cambridgeshire (M.Spufford, 1974, p.323). Some pre-1580 Essex wills from the Commissary court are known as 'original', but they appear to be office copies. Wills from the Colchester archdeaconry court only survive before 1580 in the next stage of copying, in the register books (E.R.O. D/ACR 1-7, D/ABW various). Figure 10 calculated from E.R.O. D/ABW various; E.R.O. D/ACW 1-22. Wills proved at Canterbury, now in P.R.O., mostly do survive as originals (PROB 10), but are usually seen in the registered form (PROB 11), and are not included. Wrightson and Levine, 1979 and 1985, p.148.

[60] Cressy, 1980, pp.2, 128-29. The following Witham gentlewomen signed: Dame Katherine Barnardiston of Witham Place, 1633, Ann Jenour of Howbridge Hall, 1639, Joanna Garrard of Moat farm, 1670 (P.R.O. PROB 11/163/25/205; E.R.O. D/ACW 13/112, 18/181, 22/188, 22/14). George Robinson's main claim to fame today is that he left the largest hoard of trade tokens by a single issuer that has survived to this day in Britain; there are 150 of them (Gyford, 1996, pp.116-118; Thompson and Gyford, 'Witham hoard').

[61] *Names of churchwardens:* especially from: E.R.O. D/ACA 3-4, 6, 8, 13, 18, 20, 22, 30, 32, 40, 43-4, 48-51, 53-5, E.R.O. D/ACV 1-4, 6-8, 10-12, Guildhall MS 9537/1-16, E.R.O. D/P 30/14/1. *Signing:* especially from E.R.O. D/ABW various; E.R.O. D/ACW 2-22; H.L.R.O., Main Papers, H.L., 20 Jan.1641/2, petition box. *Wilshire:* E.R.O. D/P 30/18/3, 30/25/42; E.R.O. D/ACW 20/213; manor no.179.

[62] Names of officers from: Cockburn, 1978, Cockburn, 1982, E.R.O. calendar of assize records, E.R.O. Q/SR various.

[63] Gyford, 1996, p.129; Cressy, 1980, pp.132-37, 141; P.Clark, pp.213-14; Wrightson, pp.186-91. Occupations from a variety of sources, especially quarter sessions records (E.R.O. Q/SR) and wills.

[64] P.R.O. SP 16/358/97-98. For a description of Witham's Ship Money returns see Gyford, 1996, pp.10-12. A few people were opposed to the petition, but there was a also a very big changeover of population in Witham between the Ship Money assessment (1636) and the petition (1642), probably partly related to deaths from the plague outbreak (1638 to 1641) (Gyford, 1996, pp.6-8). Various sources (especially E.R.O. D/ACA 51-54) suggest that of the 100 people in the 1636 Ship Money assessment, 16 died by 1642, and 13 others are not found in Witham after 1636 so very probably died or moved away. Signers of the petition assessed at only one shilling were John Hasleby, cooper, William Norris, husbandman, Peter Clarke the elder, alehousekeeper, Francis Mitchell, tailor, and Edward Barry. Thomas Nicholls had his name written in for him on the petition and did not even make a mark, but he made a mark on other documents, e.g. E.R.O. D/ACW 12/25, 12/40, 18/1.

Chapter 3: Henry VIII

[1] *Cal.Pat.* 1494-1509; p.39.

[2] Haigh, 1993, pp.117-67, gives a full account of official policy changes. There was a specific group of people on the continent who were known as Protestants in 1530, but the words 'Protestant' and 'Protestantism' were not used in an English context during Henry's reign (Hope, 1987, p.1).

[3] Gyford, 1996, pp.67n, 241(#29).

[4] C.Davies, 1987, pp.78-81. *Bible:* Attitudes to different versions of the Bible illustrate the complexity of the Reformation. Catholics had always used the Latin Bible, but some English versions other than Tyndale were approved by Henry, and one became compulsory temporarily. However, the Latin Bible was reintroduced at the end of the reign. English returned under Edward. (Cross and Livingstone, 1974).

[5] M.Spufford, 1995, pp.47-52; Frearson, 1995, p.273-87; Haigh, 1993, p.53; Duffy, 1992, pp.479, 503; W.K.Jordan quoted in Hunt, 1983, p.87; Dickens, 1995, pp.161-64; Ward, 'Reformation', p.92.

[6] *D.N.B.*; Foxe, 1563. Later editions contained alterations and additions. For most purposes I have used the edition published in several volumes in 1838 (Foxe, 1838). Note that the word 'abjure' can be used in several different ways; people can simply 'abjure', or they can abjure something, such as a heresy, or they can be abjured, i.e. caused to reject something (*O.E.D.*). Most of the Essex cases from Foxe are summarised in Oxley, 1965.

[7] *Large groups:* 40 at unspecified dates between 1510 and 1527, 50 in 1521 (some from Essex), 40 from Steeple Bumpstead, 1532-33, 41 from Essex and Suffolk 1532-33, 28 including 9 from Colchester but others of unknown residence, 1532-33 (Foxe, 1838, iv, pp.174, 242-43; v, 341-42). *Named Essex places:* West Bergholt, Billericay, Birdbrook[?], Boxted,

[Steeple] Bumpstead, Chelmsford, Colchester, Dedham, Halstead, Rowhedge, St.Osyth and Stratford. *Sweeting, Brewster, Mann & men of Dovercourt:* Foxe, 1838, iv, pp.208-16, 706-707.

[8] E.R.O. D/ABW various; E.R.O. D/ACR 1-4; P.R.O. PROB 11 various. I looked at all the surviving wills which were proved in Essex; no wills proved at Canterbury have been included. Rather than count the individual wills, I estimated the total number (nearly 1,400) between 1537 and the end of Henry's reign by sampling pages in the index of wills proved in Essex (Emmison, 1958). Dickens, 1995, p.172; Palliser, 1987, p.98; Haigh, 1993, p.200; P.Clark, 1977, p.58, p.420 note 75; Plumb, 1995, p.122. Several writers have considered that 'non-committal' preambles suggest Protestant tendencies, omitting the customary Catholic statements, but others have suggested that they were ambiguous. My impression is that in Essex they were more common in areas which were more inclined towards Protestantism, but I have not carried out a detailed analysis.

[9] E.R.O. D/ABW 37/7; E.R.O. D/ACR 2/225.

[10] In defining a Protestant preamble I included only examples which refer specifically to Christ as the saviour, to the passion, or to God's 'elect', and excluded both the 'mixed' ones which include some Catholic sentiments, and the large number with brief and non-committal preambles, referring to God, rather than Christ, as the saviour. Those with Protestant preambles were: E.R.O. D/ABW 1/29, 1/40, 3/104, 8/53, 8/77, 12/22, 14/33, 14/35, 16/29, 28/50, 28/53, 33/108, 33/117, 37/47, 39/55; E.R.O. D/ACR 3/34, 3/43, 3/75, 3/80, 3/83, 3/88, 3/94, 3/95, 3/107 (two wills), 3/113, 3/120, 4/42, 4/139, 4/185, 4/205, 4/234, 4/241, 4/262; E.R.O. D/AER 5/9, 5/10, 5/16, 5/19, 5/35, 5/37, 5/45, 5/49, 5/62, 5/66, 5/84, 6/70, 6/152 (two wills), 6/153 (E.R.O. D/ABW 28/50 was not used in the statistics or the map because it has no location). Note that C.Litzenberger, 1997, pp.171-73, uses a more restrictive definition of Protestant preambles, whilst McIntosh, 1991, uses a wider one. *Kent:* P.Clark, 1977, p.58. I calculate comparable figures from him show 1.5 per cent altogether, with 0.8 per cent in the first period and 2.2 per cent in the second.

[11] *Martin:* E.R.O. D/AER 6/70. *Causton:* 'unto Cryst Jesu my maker and redemer in whome and by the merytes of whose blessyd passyon is all my holle trust of Clene remyssyon and forgvenes of my synes' (E.R.O. D/ABW 8/53). *Yeman:* 'calling to my remembrance the determinat end of this my transitory lif which god hathe apoynted me from my first creacyon and being also mindful to make preparacyon for the same, into the handes of god, trusting throw heise blode and passion to have remission of my synnes and salvacyon in the same' (E.R.O. D/ACR 4/42). *Coole:* E/ACR 3/75.

[12] Craig and Litzenberger, 'Wills'; Craig, 1996, pp.41-44; (many thanks to John Craig for assistance and for providing me with a copy of this article).

[13] The most accessible source for making 16th-century population estimates, the 1523 Lay Subsidy, omits some areas (E.R.O. T/A 427). I therefore estimated proportions of people in each hundred from figures for 1327 and 1662, which were surprisingly consistent (1327 calculated from Ward, 1983; rural areas in 1662 from Hull, 1950, p.554, urban areas 1662 calculated from microfiche of E.R.O. Q/RTh 1). The places mentioned in the text were where the proportion of county's Protestant wills in Henry's reign most exceeded the proportion of its population, as follows: Rochford hundred, c. 4 % of county's pop., 12 % of the Protestant wills. Colchester borough, 3 or 4 % of pop, 13% of wills. Tendring hundred, c.7 %, 13 % of wills. Saffron Walden borough, c. one % of pop., 8 % of wills. Liberty of Havering, one or two % of pop., 17 % of wills (i.e. 8 in number, all from Romford).

[14] *Colchester:* Ward, 'Reformation', p.89 (John Clere's 'Protestant' will of 1538, quoted in Ward, does not appear in my figures because it was proved at Canterbury). *Romford:* M.J.McIntosh, 1991, pp.188-90 (with a wider definition of a Protestant will than mine). D/AER 6/152 (two wills), 6/153, 5/10, 5/19, 5/35, 5/45, 5/66. McIntosh, wrongly has one of Robert Samuel's Protestant preambles as a mixed preamble (D/AER 6/152 (Outride)).

[15] *Witham half-hundred:* c.4 % of population, 4 % of wills. *Maldon:* Petchey, 1991, pp.190-91.

[16] *John Mell:* of Boxted, abjured in 1532, witnessed will of Stephen Frende in 1544. *John Turke:* abjured in 1532 or 1533 (no residence given), witnessed will in Romford in 1540, and wrote his own there in 1541; one of the witnesses was the priest, Robert Samuel (a Thomas Turke, perhaps relative of John, witnessed will in Romford in 1557 during Mary's reign). *John Cavell:* witnessed a Thorington will in 1546

and may have been the John Cavell of Essex, weaver, burnt at Smithfield in 1556 (Foxe 1838, v, 38, 42; viii, 105; E.R.O. D/ACR 3/95; E.R.O. D/AER 5/19, 6/152; E.R.O. D/ABW 1/40; 33/330; all wills mentioned have Protestant preambles). A study of executors and beneficiaries of wills might show more connections with Foxe's information. For Raven, Chapman and Hills see the next section.

[17] Foxe, 1838, iv, pp.174-76, v, pp.16-17, 42; E.R.O. D/ACR 4/185; Hope, 1987, pp.11, 23, Hudson, 1988, pp.475-87, Spufford, 1995, pp.23-24.

[18] Foxe, 1838, iv, pp.174, 176, 214-16; B.L. Harl.MS 421/11 (endorsement on Hacker's testimony); Haigh, 1993, pp.8-9; Collinson, 1982, p.94.

[19] *E.g.*: Oxley, 1965, pp.7-14; Hudson, 1988, pp.474-81 (quotation from p.476).

[20] Hudson, 1988, p.476; Hope, 1987, p.3; see also Haigh, 1993, pp.63-64.

[21] B.L. Harl. MS 421/11; *L & P. Hen. VIII*, iv (II), pp.1788-91.

[22] Foxe, 1838, v, pp.41-42.

[23] B.L. Harl. MS 421/34; Oxley, 1965, p.14, n.1 (points out that this must be Hills' confession); Foxe, 1838, v, p.41.

[24] Foxe, v, p.41; Haigh, 1993, pp.58-60, 64, 67, 125, 154; Hope, 1987, p.11; B.L. Harl. MS 421/34; *L & P. Hen. VIII*, iv (II), pp.1859-60, 1875-76; *D.N.B.*

[25] Foxe, 1838, v, pp.16-18; Hudson, 1988, p.477 (takes this to be the same as John Chapman of Witham); E.R.O. D/ABW 37/47; E.R.O. D/ABW 28/50 (probably 1550, from the regnal year given, in Edward's reign, not 1540 as was probably written in error). *Raven:* E.R.O. D/ACR 4/185.

[26] E.R.O. D/ABW 3/121, 33/108. 39/55; E.R.O. D/ACR 3/88; 3/107, 4/139, 4/241, 4/262.

[27] P.R.O. E 179/108/154; E.R.O. D/ACR 2/174, 4/185; E.R.O. D/DBw M86; manor nos.140-41; Listed Buildings, Witham, c.1970; Fowler, 1911, p.9; P.R.O. E 301/30/9-10; E.R.O. D/ABW 12/36.

[28] Foxe, 1838, v, pp.16-17; Hudson, 1988, p.477; Foxe, 1563; Foxe, 1570, p.1190.

[29] *Raven descent:* E.R.O D/ACR 4/185; D/ABW 31/190; D/ACW 4/123. Christopher in 1542 mentioned his children Edward, John, Katherine and Agnes; Joan in 1572 gave hers as John and Agnes, Agnes by then being married with children. An Edward, not mentioned in Joan's will (sometimes known as Edmund) inherited her real property, under the terms of Christopher's will. As Christopher had been old enough to be prosecuted in 1511, Joan may have been younger than he was. An Edmund Raven of Witham was grandson of Christopher and Joan and son of John, who left him part of his house in Church Street in 1599. E.R.O. D/ACA 25, ff.96v, 102, 104v, show Edmund died 1600 and his wife left the parish; the descriptions of the property are rather involved, but manorial records seem to show it belonging to his heirs up to 1629, and then probably the same place belonging to a later Edmund Raven who had died by 1680 and left it to his son John (E.R.O. D/DBw M26 (18 April 1601), P.R.O. LR 2/215 (also photocopy in E.R.O. D/DRa Z14), E.R.O. D/DBw M48, M28 (30 Oct.1680), manor no.141). E.R.O. D/ACR 9/269, E.R.O. D/ABR 16/88, P.R.O. RG 6/1335 show that Edmund (of Cressing) who died c.1678 and his son John were Quakers. *Gravener:* Mary Raven (daughter of John and granddaughter of Christopher and Joan) married John Gravener(2), and one of their sons was John Gravener(3) (Gyford, 1996, pp.200-202).

[30] E.R.O. D/ACR 4/262; *O.E.D.*; Hope, 1987, p.11; Bossy, 1984, p.200; Gyford, 1996, pp.71, 71n, 72.

[31] E.R.O. D/ACR 2/161, 4/185; E.R.O. D/ABW 12/86, 37/7; E.R.O. D/AER 8/146; *O.E.D.* Knight became the vicar in 1526 but only survived for about eighteen months before he died (Guildhall MS 9531/10, ff.16, 26); E.R.O. D/P 30/25/4-5; P.R.O. C 1/1004/7, 1/1023/48; Fowler, 1911, pp.8-9, 14.

[32] P.R.O. C 1/1184/5; *Visitations, Essex*, pp.236, 598; Morant, *Essex*, 1763-68, ii, p.494; E.R.O. D/DAv 26. No full returns survive for the Tendring hundred, in which Ramsey lies, in the Lay Subsidy of 1523 (P.R.O. E 179/108/153 only has the names of the collectors). The only Christopher Royden/Reydon found in the E.R.O. index was in Stanway parish, west of Colchester, assessed at 40 shillings; it possible that this was one of the 'servaunts' of Thomas Bonham esquire (E.R.O. T/A 427/1/7).

[33] P.R.O. C 142/71/152; E.R.O. D/ACR 4/262; E.R.O. D/P 30/28/14, 27 Dec.1531, 29 Oct.1536; E.R.O. D/DWe T45; manor nos.22, 132.

[34] Manor no.132; E.R.O. D/ACR 4/262; P.R.O. C 142/71/152; P.R.O. C 1/1184/5, 1/1266/6; *Visitations, Essex*, p.236; Morant, *Essex*, 1763-68, ii, pp.492-94; Morant, *Colchester*, 1768, p.124; P.R.O. PROB 11/31/29; *Feet of Fines*, vi, p.39 (John and Mary Lucas in transaction with Jerome Garrard(1) in 1586 re. Witham property); P.R.O. LR 2/215 (also photocopy in E.R.O. D/DRa Z14) (shows Jerome Garrard(1) probably owned Lucas tenement thereafter).

[35] *R.C.H.M.*, iii, p.193 & plate opposite p.176; Listed Buildings, Tendring, 1987, pp.30-31; *Visitations, Essex*, p.236; Morant, *Colchester*, 1768, pp.124-25.

[36] Hope, 1987, pp.4-10.

[37] Craig and Litzenberger, 'Wills', p.424; E.R.O. D/ACR 4/262; E.R.O. D/ABW 31/190.

[38] *Richard Knight:* 1526-29 (previously curate). Was first Witham vicar regularly witnessing wills. Oxford graduate, and a Dominican (noted preachers) (Guildhall MS 9531/10, ff.16, 26; E.R.O. D/ACR 2/155, 2/161, 2/179, 2/202, 2/274). *John Newman:* Next. Cambridge graduate, little recorded in Witham. *William Love:* 1536-60. See chapter 4 for details. *Others:* some references to 'parish priest' but probably either curates or chantry chaplains in fact (e.g. William Haven in 1530 in the will of Thomas Tilling, who left Haven a yard of a costly eastern fabric called chamlet) (E.R.O. D/ABW 37/7). *Hospitallers:* had chapel on manorial demesne on the old fortified site near Chipping Hill, but manors leased out to laymen from at least 1515 onwards (Gyford, 1996, p.66-67, 69). An interesting reference to 'vacant cells' in 1529 at 'Witham' probably means Witham in Lincolnshire (*L & P. Hen.VIII*, iv (III), p.2282).

[39] *Pannatt:* witness 1540-59 of the following (usually as curate though once as parish priest): E.R.O. D/ABW 4/97, 21/66, 33/236, 33/301, 39/134, D/ACR 3/76, 4/74, 4/97, 4/107, 4/182, 4/220. Pannatt was challenged in the court of Chancery in c.1540 by the men claiming to be the rightful chantry priest and the leaseholder of the chantry (P.R.O. C 1/1004/7; P.R.O. C 1/1023/48). It was said in 1548 that Witham had no curate, only chantry priests (Fowler, 1911, p.8). Perhaps Pannatt was still claiming to be one of the latter.

[40] St.John's (north chapel) founded 1397 (owned Ishams farm, itself called 'the chantry' in 1526); St.Mary's (south chapel), founded 1444. Some of the funds of both were used to help the poor; St.John's charitable role was allowed to continue after the dissolution: this was not a very common occurrence, however (Fowler, 1911, pp.6-10; E.R.O. D/P 30/28/14 (court for 1526); Gyford, 1996, pp.83-84, 87, 220). *General:* Haigh, 1993, pp.38-39; Duffy, 1992, pp.139-40. *Wotton:* E.R.O. D/ACR 1/34, 1/41.

[41] E.R.O. D/ABW 33/40; E.R.O. D/ACR 3/87, 4/262; Fowler, 1911, p.8; E.R.O. D/P 30/25/4-5; E.R.O. D/ACA 2, f.31v. Estimates of chantry priests who taught include one twelfth in England, and one quarter in Essex (Haigh, 1993, p.171, quoting Kreider; Oxley, 1965, p.65).

[42] E.R.O. D/ACR 1/34, 2/225.

[43] Round, 'Witham Church', p.349; E.R.O. D/ABW 33/40; E.R.O. D/ACR 2/161, 2/198; Higgs, 'Wills', p.93; Duffy, 1992, pp.393, 407; Hutton, 1987, pp.116-17; Bettey, 'Reformation', p.12.

[44] E.R.O. D/ACR 2/179, 2/225, 2/161, 1/216.

[45] Haigh, 1993, p.37 (quoting Scarisbrick, 1984, p.5); Duffy, p.393; E.R.O. D/ACR 2/202, 4/107, 6/23; Palliser, 1987, p.95; Gyford, 1996, p.50n.

[46] P.R.O. PROB 11/14/11, 11/31/29; E.R.O. D/ABW 12/36, 18/200. Joan Pye lived in a house called 'Russells' on the site now occupied by no.30 Bridge Street (comparison of will with E.R.O. D/DU 967/1-45, E.R.O. D/CT 405-405A).

[47] Warner, 1926, pp.21, 212-13, 222 (thanks to Tony Raftery for lending me this book and for advice about 'St.Paul's Walk'); E.R.O. D/ACR 1/34, 2/210, 4/185; E.R.O. D/DHt T1/24; Gyford, 1996, p.261(#163).

[48] Plumb, 1995, pp.108-14, 130-31; Marsh, 1996, pp.73-96; Hope, 1987, pp.4-5, 12; Haigh, 1993, pp.195-96; Craig, 1996, pp.32-35; P.Clark, 1977, pp.31, 42 (re.Kent, not sure about social integration, and also suggested that early Lollards were less prosperous than their successors of the 1530s and 1540s).

[49] Ward, 'Reformation', pp.84-95; Higgs, 'Wills' pp.87-100.

[50] Todd, 1995 (includes essays and commentaries relating to various points of view); Dickens, 1959; Palliser, 1971; M.Spufford, 1974; Haigh, 1987; Duffy, 1992; Haigh, 1993; M.Spufford 1995; Dickens, 1995.

[51] MacCulloch, 1986, pp.154-55; Collinson, 1991, p.11; Haigh, 1993, p.70; Duffy, 1992, p.381.

Chapter 4: Edward VI and Mary I

[1] Haigh, 1993, pp.166, 168-69, 179, 181; Oxley, 1965, pp.151-52; Hutton, 1987, pp.120-22; Morrill, lecture, 1994.

[2] P.R.O. E 315/30/44; Fowler, 1911, p.8; Oxley, 1965, p.155; Gyford, 1996, p.230; Henderson, 1986, pp.13-14; L.M.A. DL/C/319, p.86; thanks to Amanda Flather for advice on seating etc.

[3] Dickin, 'Church Goods', p.170; *Cal.S.P.Dom.* 1547-80, p.12; Oxley, 1965, p.167; *O.E.D.*; H.King, 'Inventories, iv, p.197; Duffy, 1992, pp.477, 484.

[4] C.Davies, 1987, p.94; Oxley, 1965, pp.164-67; *Acts of P.C.* 1542-47, p.407; P.R.O. PC 2/3/113.

[5] Estimate re. types of preamble in Essex during Edward's reign from E.R.O. D/ABW 1, 3-4, 8 only (i.e. surnames beginning with A, B and C), compared to total in Emmison 1958; E.R.O. D/ABW 28/131, 4/32; E.R.O. D/ACW 2/313. *Kent:* P.Clark, 1977, p.76. In diocese of Canterbury, Clark found an even greater proportion of noncommittal wills than I found in Essex. He felt that they usually had Protestant associations. There, positively Protestant and Catholic preambles in Edward's reign comprised only three and six per cent of the total respectively.

[6] E.R.O. D/ABW 25/96, 39/134; Gyford, 1996, p.77.

[7] Petchey, 1991, pp.190-91.

[8] Hutton, 1987, pp.127-33; Pogson, 1987, pp.139-56; Shakespeare, 1987, p.103; *L.&P. Hen.VIII*, xvi, p.501; *Cal.Pat.* 1557-58, pp.313-21; J.Gyford, 1996, p.67.

[9] Haigh, 1993, p.228-30; Oxley, 1965, pp.178-237, summarises most of the Essex events; Foxe, 1838, vi, pp.722, 729, 739, vii, pp.69, 86, 97-98, 118, 139, 208, 335, 342, 371, 605, 718, 748, viii, 105-107, 138-45, 151-54, 302-311, 380-97, 405-407, 420, 467, 525; Foxe, 1563, p.1104.

[10] Foxe, 1838, viii, pp.307-10, 381-93.

[11] Oxley gives Eagles as being executed in Colchester, whilst Foxe and Hilda Grieve has it as happening in Chelmsford (Oxley, pp.206-208; Foxe, 1838, pp.394-97; Grieve, 1988, pp.106-107); Foxe, 1838, viii, pp.105-107, 118-23, 208-210, 335-38.

[12] Gyford, 1985, pp.144-45; Foxe, 1838, iv, p.707, viii, pp.68-76, 97-118, 139-42.

[13] Foxe, 1838, viii, pp.151-54; E.R.O. D/ACR 6/396; E.R.O. D/ACW 5/127; Gyford, 1996, pp.186-89; Jerome was a popular Christian name amongst Puritans, possibly because they felt some affinity with the prophet Jeremiah (Hanks and Hodges, 1990, pp.175-76). In due course Jerome Garrard(1) also conferred it on his eldest son, Jerome(2) of Witham.

[14] E.R.O. D/ABW 4/22, 4/28, 4/39, 4/42, 4/48, 4/50, 4/85, 4/89, 4/92, 4/112, 4/144, 8/186, 8/188, 8/199, 8/229, 8/264, 8/272, 8/284, 12/77, 14/74, 14/106, 16/124, 18/150, 18/157, 18/219, 18/221, 21/62, 22/61, 22/62, 22/65, 23/84, 23/87, 23/98, 25/113, 25/123, 25/129, 25/158, 25/180, 27/55, 28/149, 28/164, 28/165, 28/189, 31/93, 31/96, 31/97, 31/111, 33/258, 33/319, 33/330 (same as D/AER 8/28), 33/343, 37/104, 39/144, 39/146, 39/187, 39/191, 42/4; E.R.O. D/AER 5/182 (two wills, one being Graygoose), 5/194, 5/200, 5/212, 5/216 (two wills), 5/217, 5/218, 8/1, 8/4, 8/14, 8/28 (same as D/ABW 33/330).

[15] *Kelvedon:* Miles Warner, 1557 (D/ABW 39/191). *Cressing:* John Betts, 1555, witnessed by the curate, John King (E.R.O. D/ABW 4/50). *Faulkbourne:* Richard Mabbe, 1555, witnessed by Geoffrey Jones, vicar of neighbouring White Notley, discussed later in connection with 'mixed' preambles (E.R.O. D/ABW 25/123).

[16] E.R.O. D/ABW 23/98, 31/93, 33/330; E.R.O. D/ACR 3/80, 3/107; E.R.O. D/AER 5/212, 8/1; Ward, 'Reformation', p.87. *General:* seventeen per cent of Essex parishes are represented on the map under Mary compared to only nine per cent on the similar map for the end of Henry's reign. *Colchester area:* over 40 % of the parishes in the Tendring and Winstree hundreds, and 37% of those in Lexden, occur on both maps compared to only 24% of Essex parishes as a whole. *Kent:* P.Clark, 1977, p.101.

[17] Duffy, 1992, pp.508-509; Haigh, 1993, p.201; Litzenberger, 1997, p.172; M.Spufford, 1974, p.337; Dickens, 1959, pp.220-21. In defining mixed preambles for the county survey, I omitted two 'modified' types, i.e. those mentioning the holy company of heaven but not the virgin, and those which mentioned the death and passion of 'god' but not of Christ (including the latter would not have changed the result much).

The wills included were: *Witham:* E.R.O. D/ABW 4/97, 8/91, 18/61, 18/83, 18/200, 33/236, 33/301; E.R.O. D/ACR 3/87, 3/92 (E.R.O. D/ABW 8/143, 8/195, 31/95 omitted as being of the 'modified' type). *White Notley:* E.R.O. D/ABW 1/132, 8/277, 8/281, 8/296, 18/235, 39/56. *Gosfield:* E.R.O. D/ABW 12/60, 18/134. *Pentlow:* E.R.O. D/ABW 16/111, 8/242. *Other places:* E.R.O. D/ABW 1/42, 8/274, 14/24, 14/83, 16/128, 18/91, 18/203, 22/47, 23/132, 25/81, 28/230, 33/378, 39/162, E.R.O. D/AER 8/94 (same as BW 28/230 so not counted separately).

[18] *Witham:* Calculated from E.R.O. D/ABW 4/32, 4/97, 8/91, 8/143, 8/195, 12/36, 18/36, 18/61, 18/83, 18/200, 25/96, 28/131, 31/95, 33/236, 33/301, 38/178, 39/134; E.R.O. D/ACR 3/76, 3/87, 3/92. *Other places:* E.R.O. D/ABW 14/83 and 39/162 (Blackmore and Dunmow), and E.R.O. D/ABW 12/60 and 18/91 (Gosfield and Sible Hedingham). John Dowdale, willmaker of Gosfield, witnessed a Sible Hedingham will, and Giles Gray both a Sible Hedingham will and a Gosfield one.

[19] *Jones: Alumni Cantabrigiensis;* O'Boy, 1995, pp.36-38, 50. Reverend David Nash has suggested that the (unknown) dedication of White Notley church may have been abandoned because of Catholic associations (letter from Reverend Nash, 5 February 1997). E.R.O. D/ABW 1/132, 3/184, 8/277, 8/281, 8/296, 13/28, 13/36, 18/235, 25/123, 31/106, 31/135, 39/56, 39/62, 39/214. *Jolly:* E.R.O. D/AMR 2/64 (twice; preambles probably curtailed in the register); E.R.O. D/ABW 3/60, 8/242, 16/111. There may be others in other parishes; I just checked Jolly and Jones' own parishes, my own surveys, and various printed indexes. *Popley:* E.R.O. D/ABW 28/230.

[20] E.R.O. D/ABW 4/97, 8/91, 8/143, 18/61, 18/83, 18/136, 21/66, 33/236, 33/301, 39/134; *O.E.D.*; *L.& P. Hen.VIII*, xx, p.427; *Cal.Pat.* 1550-53, p.332.

[21] Guildhall MS 9531/11, f.32v (gives Love appointed in 1536; Wiles, 1911, p.31 erroneously has him arriving in 1538); Anglin, 1965, p.224; Oxley, 'Benefice Farming', p.8; Guildhall MS 9531/12 I/221; Guildhall MS 12737. Information about Rivenhall from Reverend Nash (letter of 5 February 1997). Clergy who married under Edward were disqualified under Mary, which may have affected about 15 per cent of English clergy. Hilda Grieve showed that under Mary's reign nearly a third of the Essex vacancies arose from removal, most of them because they had married (Haigh, 1993, p.228; Grieve, 'Clergy', pp.141, 148).

[22] P.R.O. C 1/1353/7, 1320/30, 1168/89-90; P.R.O. REQ 2/94/31. For Witham Place see Gyford, 1996, pp.84-87. A lease of the rectory in 1564 refers to 'Thomas Smithe or Jaram Songer' as previous holders (Guildhall MS 9531/13, f.48v).

[23] E.R.O. D/ACR 3/54, 5/20; E.R.O. D/ABW 18/136, 18/200, 25/96.

[24] Grieve, 'Clergy', pp.141-69; O'Boy, 1995, pp.205-209; E.R.O. D/AER 8/146; E.R.O. D/ACR 6/23. The E.R.O. Personal Names Index does not include anyone called William Love at the right time to be 'young William Love', though there is an Oliver Love of Moulsham, Chelmsford, who could possibly be the one in the vicar's will; he was accused with others of reaping and taking away the oats and rye of a Chelmsford man (E.R.O. Calendar of Queen's Bench Indictments, p.32).

[25] E.R.O. D/AER 8/146.

[26] *Armond:* Gyford, 1996, pp.144, 193-95; E.R.O. D/ACR 6/23 (thanks to Margaret Spufford for comment on this will, letter of 16 October, 1992). For this period we only have registered copies of the wills proved in the Colchester archdeaconry, and their preambles all appear to have been abbreviated. *Harte:* E.R.O. D/ABW 18/35, 18/200, 25/29, 28/131, 33/40; D/ACR 2/179, 2/210, 3/68, 3/76, 4/11, 4/74, 4/97, 4/107, 4/197, 4/220, 4/244, 5/20, 6/23; E.R.O. D/AER 8/146.

[27] E.g. Haigh, 1993, pp.166, 204-205, 235; Palliser, 1987, pp.99-101; Duffy, 1992, pp.503, 523; M.Spufford, 1974, p.248. For a summary of others' views see Haigh, 1987.

[28] Byford, 1988, p.100; Duffy, p.479; Haigh, 1993, pp.228-34; Alexander, 1987, p.167.

[29] Byford, 1988, pp.13-15, 81-83; O'Boy, 1995, pp.207-208.

Chapter 5: Elizabeth I (part 1 - 1558-c.1583)

[1] Duffy, 1992, pp.567-68, 588; Haigh, 1993, p.280, see also pp.238-42, 252, 279-80.

[2] There are a large number of publications discussing 'Puritanism' and/or 'Protestantism', especially by Professor Patrick Collinson and

Peter Lake. Some authors have refined their own views over the years. For a summary see Haigh, 1984, pp.18-25. See also for instance: Collinson, 1982; Collinson, *Puritanism*, 1983; Collinson, 1984; Lake, 1982; Lake, 1995; Tyacke, 1995.

[3] Byford, 1988, p.149; Petchey, 1991, pp.196-245; Wrightson and Levine, 1985, pp.197-220.

[4] Wrightson, 1996, pp.26-27.

[5] Gleason, 1969, pp.9-10, gives an extract from the diary of a Kent magistrate in the 1580s, illustrating the range of duties and how they were carried out. P.Clark, 1977, pp.114-18 summarises these also.

[6] *Magistrate and judge, 1564-82:* P.R.O. ASSI 35/6/5 to 35/24/2, passim. *Magistrate only, 1583-84:* ASSI 35/25/1, 35/26/2.

[7] Morant, 1763-68, ii, pp.114, 117. *Fortescue:* P.R.O. ASSI 35/1/3 to 35/18/8, passim, and E.R.O. Q/SR 31/37, 39/9-10, 41/22, 54/10-11, 56/40. Faulkbourne Hall also provided a 20th-century chairman of the Witham bench, who retired only recently. *Harvey:* P.R.O. ASSI 35/12/6 to 35/43/2, passim, and E.R.O. Q/SR 41/22, 54/6-8, 54/10-11, 56/40, 66/49-64, 78/26, 79/61-62, 84/70, 84/82, 84/85-92, 117/31, 144/101, 148/161, 152/28, 152/46, 152/139.

[8] Webb, *Parish and County*, 1924, pp.289, 456-60, 483; P.R.O. ASSI 35/1/3 to 35/16/4, passim, 35/18/8 to 35/23/2, passim; E.R.O. Q/SR 8/26 to 58/59, passim, and 59/1 to 78/8; Wrightson, 1980, pp.26-29

[9] Webb, *Parish and County*, pp.291-92, 463, Walter, lectures, 1994; Allen, 1974, pp.xiii-xiv.

[10] Webb, *Parish and County*, pp.489-90. *Choppin:* E.R.O. Q/SR 3/88, 11/17, 16/38, 17/48. *Garrard:* E.R.O. Q/SR 39/9-10, 41/22; Gyford, 1996, pp.186-92; Hanks and Hodges, 1990.

[11] Harrison, 1877, p.103; e.g. E.R.O. Q/SR 17/48, 41/22, 56/37; P.Clark, 1977, pp.115-16, 145; Webb, *Parish and County*, 1924, p.493.

[12] Gyford, 1996, pp.2, 34-35; Wrightson, 1980, pp.26-27; E.R.O. D/P 30/28/14; E.R.O. D/DDc T82.

[13] E.R.O. D/AER 8/146; Guildhall MS 9531/13, ff.117v, 237; E.R.O. D/ACA 16, f.24v; ACA 20, f.2 et al; E.R.O. D/DBw M28, 13 Oct.1684; E.R.O. D/ACW 15/85; Copy of will of Deborah Eatney (in custody of Chelmsford Friends' Meeting).

[14] Haigh, 1993, p.249; E.R.O. D/ACA 4, f.50v; E.R.O. D/ABW 29/26; E.R.O. D/ACR 6/45, 6/79, 6/99, 6/116, 6/355, 7/143, 7/220; E.R.O. D/ACW 2/28, 2/232, 2/333, 3/336, 3/373; *Feet of Fines*, vi, pp.13, 33; E.R.O. Q/SR 33/25, 34/34; Guildhall MS 9531/13, f.102. See chapter 7 for Halys's son Edmund.

[15] Peel, ii, pp.158, 161 (Davids, 1863, p.94 has the same list but omits some of the details about Halys). The vicarage had been valued at £22 per year in 1535, and a previous lease, in 1548, was also made for this amount (*Valor Eccl.*, i, p. 445; Guildhall MS 9531/12, f..221); Collinson, 1984, pp.184-86; Pressey, 'Records', pp.5-6; Haigh, 1993, pp.268-69.

[16] E.R.O. D/ACR 7/143 (others similar except two later ones also mentioned the forgiveness of sins (E.R.O. D/ACW 2/28, 2/333).

[17] E.R.O. D/ABW 31/219; E.R.O. D/ACR 7/57, 7/157; E.R.O. D/ACW 2/313.

[18] Guildhall MS 9537/3/86, 9537/5/93v; E.R.O. D/ABW 4/365, 12/171, 16/246, 23/309, 29/31, 34/259; E.R.O. D/ACR 6/99, 6/116; Davids, 1863, p.95.

[19] L.M.A. DL/C/333, f.89v; E.R.O. D/Y 2/4, p.207; Grieve, 1994, pp.10-11; E.R.O. D/ACW 4/31; Gyford, 1996, pp.194, 197-98.

[20] Collinson, 1984, pp.178-89.

[21] E.R.O. D/ACR 5/66, 5/86, 5/119, 6/23, 6/45, 6/51, 6/79, 6/99.

[22] Wrightson and Levine, 1979 and 1995, p.155.

[23] E.R.O. D/ABW 31/190; Foxe, 1838, v, p.42; manor no 141. Joan's identity as Christopher's widow is amplified in the notes to chapter 3. E.R.O. D/DBw M26, 17 April 1591; B.L. Add.Ch.41526; Morant, *Essex*, 1763-68, ii, p.144; Gyford, 1996, pp.67-68; Ryan, 1993.

[24] P.R.O. PROB 11/67/14 (summarised, without the preamble, in E.R.O. T/G 6/5); E.R.O. D/P 30/28/14, 25 July 1569, 29 Oct.1570; *Feet of Fines*, vi, pp.32, 115; E.R.O. D/ACA 3, f.129v; E.R.O. D/ACR 6/116; E.R.O. D/ACW 4/123.

[25] E.R.O. D/ABW 9/230, 31/219, 32/1; E.R.O. D/ACR 7/57, 7/240; E.R.O. D/ACW 2/313; Foxe, 1563, pp.510-11; Foxe, 1570, p.1186; Pressey, 'Records', pp.7-8; Craig and Litzenberger, 'Wills', Craig, 1996. Happily I recognised the words of the Witham preambles in the talk by John Craig on which the latter article is based (they also appear in Dickens, 1959, pp.216-17). Many thanks to John Craig for his assistance in this and many other matters.

[26] E.R.O. D/ACR 7/240; E.R.O. D/ACW 3/321 (these two wills of

Rochester and Shaa are quoted in Wrightson and Levine, 1979 and 1995, p.153, though the relationship of the two men and the use of Tracy's words are not mentioned there); Cross and Livingstone, 1974.

[27] Gyford, 1996, pp.74, 77; D/ACR 6/396, 7/205; E.R.O. D/ABW 9/230; E.R.O. D/DWe T45. The name John Glascock was a common one and its holders are hard to disentangle. Another one, from Roxwell, was clerk of assize to Judge John Southcott of Witham (P.R.O. PROB 11/69/24; Cockburn, 1985, pp.5, 9).

[28] Cliftlands, 1987, p.246; Gyford, 1996, pp.76-77, 144; P.R.O. REQ 2/107/47; E.R.O. D/ABW 31/219; manor no.202; E.R.O. D/DBw M26, 21 April, 1593; E.R.O. D/ACA 20, ff.143, 202 et al.; E.R.O. Q/SR 128/22, 128/23; Jameson, 'Monument', pp.39-43. Robert Richholde's mansion house has not been identified; his tenement backed onto his croft, which was Batford Croft, probably the area now occupied by Lawn Chase.

[29] E.R.O. D/ACW 2/313; E.R.O. D/ABW 28/131, 4/32; E.R.O. D/P 30/25/64; E.R.O. Q/SR 58/6; P.R.O. ASSI 35/24/1.

[30] E.R.O. D/ACR 7/57; E.R.O. D/ACA 2, f.49, ACA 18, f.132v; E.R.O. D/P 30/28/14, 29 Oct.1570.

[31] Morant, *Essex*, 1763-68, ii, p.131; Peel, 1915, i, pp.28-35.

[32] Samaha, 1974, pp.18-22; P.R.O. ASSI 35/2/5, 35/9/2, 35/11/4, 35/12/4, 35/15/3, 35/15/7; J.A.Sharpe, 1987, p.309.

[33] E.R.O. Q/SR 7/10, 19/5, 32/2, 41/10, 44/33, 56/37, 64/24, 73/60; *O.E.D.*

[34] E.R.O. D/ACA 3, f.45, ACA 4, f.137v, ACA 5, f.57, ACA 6, ff.9 et al., 68, ACA 7, ff.95v, 96v, 97, 133v, 145, ACA 8, ff.100, 283, ACA 9, ff.17, 25v, 182v, ACA 12, f.26v et al.; Collinson, 1982, pp.207-12; see also Carlson, 1995, pp.171-74.

[35] Byford, 1988, p.118; see also Petchey, 1991.

[36] Byford, 1988, pp.407-16, 433; Hunt, 1983, p.219; McIntosh, 1991, p.193.

Chapter 6: Elizabeth I (part 2 - c.1583-1603)

[1] J.A.Sharpe, 1987, p.13; Samaha, 1974, pp.36, 112, 168; Wrightson, 1988, pp.142-45; Samaha, 1974, pp.18-22; P.Clark, 1977, pp.221-68 (discusses the comparable crisis in Kent); E.R.O. D/ACA 22, f.207v; E.R.O. D/ABW 35/159; manor nos.160-61, 202, 205; E.R.O. Q/SR 183/82.

[2] 35 Elizabeth, c.1 & 2; 27 Elizabeth, c.2; Petchey, 1991, pp.196-223; Byford, 1988, pp.55-75, 192-274.

[3] Wrightson and Levine, 1979 and 1995, p.113; Cockburn, 1978; P.Clark, 1977, pp.116-19, 144-46; Wrightson, 1988, pp.151-55; Williams, 1984, pp.136-38.

[4] Gyford, 1996, pp.91, 173-80; E.R.O. Q/SR 84/70, 84/82, 84/85, 84/92, 114/43. 115/100, 117/31, 118/63, 119/54-56, 122/32, 122/42, 124/63, 126/39, 141/36, 142/40, 144/68, 144/101, 144/103, 148/161, 150/8, 152/28, 152/46, 152/113-15, 152/139, 156/58. *Residences:* from Morant, *Essex*, 1763-8, ii, pp.138, 146, 173 (Ayloffe, Wiseman, Huddleston), E.R.O. Q/SR 117/72, 137/1, 143/57 (Chiborne, Sams, Tuke). *Wiseman:* P.R.O. ASSI 35/42/1.

[5] E.R.O. Q/SR 141/34, 144/91, 144/101, 144/103, 144/111, 145/43-45, 146/22, 149/33-35, 149/37-38, 150/24, 152/51, 152/82, 152/118, 152/144, 153/55, 156/58, 163/11, 163/42-43, 165/42-48, 165/50, 173/51, 173/67, 174/32-34, 174/89-90, 175/93, 176/27-28, 177/26, 178/39-41, 178/104, 180/73, 181/36. *Bishops of London as magistrates:* P.R.O. ASSI 35/5/3, 35/13/5, 35/21/7, 35/37/2, 35/39/2 et al. Gleason, 1969, pp.15-16, 23, 49, 51, 53-55.

[6] P.R.O. ASSI 35/11/4, 35/24/1 to 35/40/1 passim; E.R.O. Q/SR 111/96; E.R.O. D/ACW 5/231; Round, 'Aylett', pp.26-34.

[7] E.R.O. D/DBw M26; P.R.O. LR 2/215 (also photocopy in E.R.O. D/DRa Z14); E.R.O. D/ACW various; E.R.O. D/ABW various; E.R.O. D/ACA various (for signatures and marks, churchwardens, and some dates of death).

[8] Guildhall MS 9531/13, f.237, 9531/14, f.101v; E.R.O. D/ACA 16, ff.46v, 80, 85; L.M.A. DL/C/334, f.258v; *Alumni Cantabrigiensis*; Harrison, 1877, pp.111-12; Collinson, 1982, pp.94, 124-25 (quoting Hertfordshire R.O. ASA 5/5/95, ASA 7/11/110); Haigh, 1993, p.271; E.R.O. T/A 547; Fowler, 1911, p.31; Cross and Livingstone, 1974, pp.342-43; *O.E.D.*

[9] L.P.L. MS 2442, f.3 (Witham worth £66 13s.4d. per year, Bigrave £80); E.R.O. D/ACW 3/371, 5/43; E.R.O. D/ACA 18, ff.161, 186, 187v et al., ACA 20, ff.215, 233; E.R.O. T/A 547; Fowler, 1911, p.31; Byford,

1988, pp.104, 307-308, 339-41.
10 E.R.O. D/ACA 22, f.161.
11 E.R.O. D/ACA 16, ff.79v, 185, 205 et al., ACA 18, ff.4, 29v, 38v, 71v, 195v, 209v et al., ACA 22, f.40v; E.R.O. D/ACV 2, ff.8, 25v, 46v, 62, 84v, 113, 172, ACV 3, ff.54v, 71.
12 L.M.A. DL/C/335, f.92; E.R.O. Q/SR 124/63-63a, 124/68-71, 125/2, 126/2-2a; E.R.O. D/ACA 20, ff.282, 291, 296v, and loose sheet; E.R.O. D/ABW 40/198; manor no.136 (house of Christopher Greene).
13 L.M.A. DL/C/303, p.741; E.R.O. D/ACA 18, f.232v, ACA 20, ff.6, 25; E.R.O. D/ACW 3/156; P.Clark, 1977, p.192; Craig, 'Spitlehouse', p.54.
14 E.R.O. D/ACA 16, ff.5v, 109v et al.; ACA 18, ff.98, 175, 202v, 209v; ACA 20, ff.45v, 66v, 117 et al., ACA 25, f.185; Guildhall MS 9537/8/30v, 9537/9/117. Day wrote only one will in his second stay in Witham, for John Lowe of Howbridge Hall in 1595, with a fairly standard preamble, though it did provide 6s.8d. for 'a godly preacher to make a sermon' at the funeral (E.R.O. D/ABW 23/309).
15 E.R.O. D/ABW 40/198, D/ACW 4/31, 4/123; E.R.O. D/ACA 16, f.133v et al., ACA 25, f.149 (has Armond with goods of over £80); E.R.O. D/P 30/25/64.
16 P.R.O. ASSI 35/32/2, 35/39/1; Samaha, 1974, p.20; P.King, 1984, p.38.
17 E.R.O. Q/SR 141/34, 144/91, 144/103.
18 P.R.O. ASSI 35/29/2, 35/31/1-2, 35/35/2, KB 9/690/2; E.R.O. Q/SR 160/34; E.R.O. D/ACA 30, f.159, ACA 40, ff.101, 121v, 122v; E.R.O. D/ABW 23/309.
19 J.A.Sharpe, 1977, pp.100-101; P.King, 1984, pp.104-108; Gyford, 1982, pp.75-76; E.R.O. D/ABW 31/95; C.Johnson, lectures 1984-85; Petchey, 1991, pp.196-223.
20 P.R.O. ASSI 35/25/1, 35/26/2; Slack, 1972, p.169; E.R.O. Q/SR 112/70.
21 E.R.O. D/Y 2/9, p.381.
22 E.R.O. D/P 30/28/14, 21 April 1572, 7 Oct.1585; E.R.O. D/DBw M26, 6 April 1583, 17 April 1585, 22 April 1587, 13 April 1588.
23 E.R.O. D/ACA 20, ff.67v, 132, 142 et al.; C.Johnson, lectures, 1984-85.
24 E.R.O. Q/SR 111/96. *Mary Martin:* E.R.O. D/ABW 31/190; E.R.O. D/ACA 22, ff.187, 230 et al. *William Freeborne:* Gyford, 1996, p.218. *Henry Brooke:* E.R.O. D/ACA 20, f.175 et al. *Miles Dawson:* E.R.O. Q/SR 152/114-15, 235/49. *Simon Greene:* E.R.O. D/ACA 16, f.86v, ACA 20, f.319v. *Joan Lockier:* E.R.O. D/ACA 20, f.110 et al.
25 E.R.O. D/ACA various; E.R.O. D/ACV 1-2; Guildhall MS 9537/5-9; L.M.A. DL/C/336, f.62v; Guildhall MS 9537/7/63; E.R.O. D/ABW 40/198; E.R.O. D/ACW 4/123 (thanks to Margaret Spufford for comments on these wills).
26 E.R.O. D/ACA 12, f.96v, ACA 13, f.117v, ACA 16, f.135, ACA 18, f.8, ACA 20, ff.115, 233, 318, ACA 22, ff.130v, 208v, 259, 282, 330v-31, ACA 25, f.110v, ACA 27, f.44. Wardens role from E.R.O. D/ACA various.
27 Collinson, 1984, pp.169-70; E.R.O. D/ACA 13, ff.94v, 118v, 136v, 162v et al., ACA 22, ff.207v et al., 253v, ACA 25, f.205v, ACA 27, ff.3v, 17v et al.; E.R.O. D/ACV 2, f.172. Thanks to John Craig for the point about language.
28 Fowler, 1911, p.13; E.R.O. D/ACA 25, ff.177, 192, 194, 197; L.M.A. DL/C/303, p.743; Deedes and Walters, 1909, pp.86-99, 452-53; E.R.O. D/ACR 2/160, 2/179; P.R.O. PROB 11/18/12.
29 Calculated from E.R.O. D/ACA 3-27, disregarding figures for 1570, 1581-82, 1584, 1586-87, 1593, where over one third of the year is missing, except that 1587 is included in the figures for the whole archdeaconry; Byford, 1988, p.381.
30 Wrightson and Levine, 1979 and 1985, p.127; Ingram, 1984, pp.185-86.
31 Underdown, 1985, pp.53, 60; E.R.O. D/ACA 16, ff.22v, 86v, 104v, 109, 232, ACA 18, ff.148, 205 et al., ACA 20, ff.5v, 319v et al., ACA 22, f.207v, ACA 27, f.7; P.R.O. PROB 11/107/35.
32 E.R.O. D/ACA 13, f.58v, ACA 16, ff.138, 146 et al., ACA 22, f.324v; *O.E.D.*; E.R.O. D/DBw M26, 13 April 1588, 17 April 1591, 17 April 1596, 14 April 1599; E.R.O. D/ACW 3/184; manor no.25.
33 E.R.O. D/ACA 16, ff.86v et al., 111 et al., ACA 18, ff.39, 46v, 53v et al., 61 et al., 180v et al., 234 et al, ACA 20, ff.143 et al. 175 et al., 202 et al., 319v et al.; ACA 25, f.110 et al., 115, 117, 133, 138 et al., ACA 49, f.15.
34 E.R.O. D/ACA 16, ff.9v et al., 22v et al., ACA 20, ff.121v et al., 132 et al., 143 et al., 152 et al.; E.R.O. Q/SR 144/111.

35 E.R.O. D/ACA 16, ff.7, 22v, 43, 111, 138, 185, 204v, ACA 18, f.4 et al., ACA 20, f.203v, ACA 25, ff.56, 194 et al.; E.R.O. D/ACW 7/116.
36 E.R.O. D/ACA 22, ff.275v, 290 et al., ACA 25, ff.56v, 141, ACA 27, ff.45, 53v et al.; E.R.O. D/DBw M83, p.280.
37 E.R.O. D/ACA 20, f.67v et al., ACA 40, f.34.
38 O'Boy, 1995, pp.15-16, 26, 103-104, 112, 119-20, 134-37, 172-73.
39 E.R.O. D/Y 2/4, p.207; E.R.O. Q/SR 172/56; Grieve, 1994, pp.10-11; E.R.O. D/ACW 4/31, 11/248; P.Ryan, 'Returns', pp.48-51; Gyford, 1996, pp.193-200; Haigh, 1984, pp.202-203; O'Boy, pp.34-35; 27 Elizabeth, c.2; 35 Elizabeth, c.1 & 2; Haigh, 1993, pp.252-63; Anglin, 1965, p.101; Collinson, *Puritanism*, 1983, p.22; Collinson, lecture, 1990.
40 Gyford, 1996, pp.237-38(#70). On Friday 5 July Armond was said to have been working on 'Sunday was fortnight'. This could be either 14 or 23 June, just before or just after the Armada sighting on Wednesday 19th (E.R.O. D/ACA 16, f.111).
41 *D.N.B.*; Gyford, 1996, p.174; Morris, 1872, p.384; P.R.O. PROB 11/69/6/24 (thanks to Margaret Spufford for commenting that the preamble of this will is 'thoroughly Protestant', letter of 16 October 1993). Knell, 'Southcott', p.2, suggests that an undated list of names of recusants which includes 'Southcott of Merstham ... gent.', relates to the judge, but it seems more likely to me to relate to his son John.
42 O'Boy, 1995, pp.36-37, 42-48, 158-59, 172, 251, 259; Edwards, 1975, pp.9-10, 29-30; *D.N.B.*; Knell, 'Southcott', pp.2-9; Morris 1872, pp.385-86.
43 Morris 1872, pp.383-84; P.R.O. PROB 11/69/6/24; Gyford, 1996, p.178.
44 Gyford, 1996, p.178; E.R.O. Q/SR 107/51, 110/62, 111/66; P.R.O. PROB 11/69/6/24; E.R.O. D/ACA 16, ff.7v et al., 111, 118, 129, 135-35v, 144v, 153, ACA 22, ff.189v et al., 347 (presentment of Mrs.Southwell of Little Totham, which could not be dealt with as 'she is in Witham').
45 E.R.O. Q/SR 144/27, 147/13, 158/20; E.R.O. D/ACA 22, ff.266, 269v, 280, 285, 291, 331 et al., ACA 25, ff.110, 115, 138, 148 et al.; L.M.A. DL/C/618, p.304. The word 'recusant' was used twice in connection with presentments of Thomas Bayles himself, but these seemed actually to refer back to earlier occasions when he had only been presented in connection with not having his wife and servants at church (E.R.O. D/ACA 25, ff.138, 158). In 1604 he appeared with a list of people some of whom were said to refuse communion, but it is not clear whether that was his offence too (E.R.O. D/ACA 27, f.123v). He was said to have been 'now of Ulting' in 1600 but this seems to have been temporary (E.R.O. D/ACA 25, f.148).
46 E.R.O. D/ACA 27, ff.196, 196v; Q/SR 163/31, 163/102, 171/61d; E.R.O. D/ACA 27, ff.7v, 115v, 121-21v; L.M.A. DL/C/618, pp.300-302; Anglin, 1965, pp.102-103.
47 E.R.O. Q/SR 163/31, 163/102, 165/42, 165/47, 171/61d, 173/71, 176/4, 176/17, 177/91, 177/98, 179/61, 180/52, 182/46; E.R.O. D/ACA 30, ff.124, 178, 234v, 241; L.M.A. DL/C/305, f.151v, DL/C/307, p.267.
48 O'Boy, 1995, p.104. First noted in Witham: *Thomas Campion, 1585:* E.R.O. D/ACA 22, f.187. *William Campion, 1592:* E.R.O. Q/SR 122/44, 123/2-3. *Nicholas Ridgley, 1586:* P.R.O. PROB 11/69/6/24. *Mr.and Mrs.Bayles, 1597:* E.R.O. D/ACA 22, f.266.
49 Manor no.41, E.R.O. D/ACA 27, ff.7v, 115v et al., 196v, ACA 30, f.14v et al.; L.M.A. DL/C/618, pp.301-302, 565, DL/C/617, p.893.
50 E.R.O. D/ACA 22, ff.187 et al., 207v, 224v, 230, 275v, 330v; ACA 25, f.56v; E.R.O. Q/SR 156/58; *D.N.B.*
51 E.R.O. D/ACA 5, ff.57, 76v et al.; ACA 7, ff.97, 125v et al.; ACA 13, ff.93, 102v et al., E.R.O. ACA 16, ff.2, 2v; ACA 18, ff.39, 45v, 46v, 69, 77 et al., ACA 22, ff.110v, 111v, 193; E.R.O. 27/7v.
52 P.R.O. P.R.O. ASSI 35/2/5; J.A.Sharpe, 1987, pp.309-315; Macfarlane, *Witchcraft*, 1970, pp.200-206; Wrightson, 1988, p.202-203.
53 E.R.O. D/ACD 1, ff.36v-37v et al.; E.R.O. D/ACW 2/28; E.R.O. D/ACA 16, ff.111, 123 et al., 149, 205 et al., ACA 18, f.45, ACA 20, f.78 et al.; P.R.O. ASSI 35/30/1.
54 E.R.O. D/ACA 16, f.184v; P.R.O. ASSI 35/34/1.
55 O'Boy, 1995, pp.1-32, 138-41, 173-74, 237-40.
56 Ingram, 1996, pp.47-88, esp.pp.77-78; Wrightson and Levine, 1979 and 1995, pp.155-57, 176-77, 180-81, 186-220.

Chapter 7: James I

1 Wrightson and Levine, 1979 and 995, pp.113-14, 116; Davids, 1863,

pp.127-33; *D.N.B.* (Richard Bancroft); Cross and Livingstone, 1974, pp.125, 617; Sharpe, 1987, pp.12-15; Hunt, 1983, pp.108-109, 112, 161-66; P.Clark, 1977, pp.304-307.

2 Gyford, 1996, pp. 145-47, 155-57, 221; E.R.O. Q/SR 183/65, 184/81; E.R.O. D/ACA 30, f.241.

3 Elizabeth was widow of John Archer, recently deceased Witham gentleman. Their house, location of the 'riot', was where the Avenue now joins Newland Street (the Avenue itself had not yet been laid out). Total value of Archer's Essex property was said to be about £160 per year. Elizabeth and her prospective son-in-law Richard Gwynne, of Norfolk, were threatened through their locked doors by the 'well horsed and armed' visitors, who mentioned Elizabeth's wealth, possibly the issue at stake. A crowd gathered, and the visitors went off to an inn with the parish constable, haberdasher Robert Allen. Gwynne took Allen to court for neglect of duty (P.R.O. STAC 8/152/4; P.R.O. PROB 11/119/9; manor no.46)

4 Suffolk R.O. EXY 4/V.4; Almack, 'Kedington', pp.137-38; Gyford, 1996, p.181; E.R.O. D/ACA 27, f.29; P.R.O. PROB 11/116/104; Bodleian library, Rawlinson MS Essex 6, ff.125 et al. Judge Southcott left lease of rectory to son John esquire (1595); another granted by the bishop in 1604 to Thomas Barnardiston for the life of Katherine (P.R.O. PROB 11/69/6/24; Guildhall MS 12737). Judge Southcott's London home was in Carter Lane in St.Gregory's parish, whose church abutted old St.Paul's and stood only a few yards from St.Michael le Querne, church of Dame Katherine and her father Thomas Banks (who died 1598) (P.R.O. PROB 11/69/24; 11/91/48/372; 11/163/25/205). John Southcott esquire lived in Bulmer, on the county boundary like the Barnardiston estates etc., though further east.

5 E.g. Collinson, *Godly People*, 1983, pp.273-87, describing the life of Ann Lock, during the later 16th century (some of it in the Cheapside area where Katherine's family, the Banks, lived) (thanks to Amanda Flather for this reference).

6 Mostly new research since Gyford, 1996, pp.181-84. Main sources are: P.R.O. PROB 11/87/6/46, 11/91/48/372, 11/108/80/229, 11/133/1/1, 11/133/12/96, 11/135/1/1, 11/158/84/156, 11/163/25/205, 11/182/14/101; E.R.O. D/ACW 14/159; E.R.O. T/P 252/4 (this misses out a whole generation including Sir Thomas Barnardiston); Norfolk R.O., N.C.C. will, 200 (Ponder, Thomas Some, 1569); Suffolk .R.O. FL 535/4/1; Guildhall MS, Noble Collection C78; Almack, 'Kedington'; Beaven, 1913; *D.N.B.*; *East Anglian Notes and Queries*, N.S., iii; *Visitations, London*; Bodleian MS Rawlinson Essex 6, f.125; Bodleian MS Rawlinson Essex 22, f.155; Pearl, 1961; R.R.Sharpe, 1894; Shipps, 1971, pp.80, 234-35. Thanks to Dr.Vanessa Harding and Dr.Jeremy Boulton for information about publications on London.

7 Huelin, 1996, pp.ix, 20; Guildhall MS 5265; P.R.O. PROB 11/163/25/205, 11/168/82/298; Dobson and Walker, pp.102, 131; D/P 11/1/1; P.R.O. ASSI 35/5/8/3, 35/50/T/43, 35/73/H/S; Beaven, 1913; Guildhall MS, Noble Collection C78; E.R.O. Q/SR 148/4, 186/121, 191/104, 268/42. The Barbers' Company no longer has the cup and it may have been pawned with other items in 1711. I have not managed to trace the relationship of Katherine's family with the Catholic Banks of Hadstock, though Katherine Banks, daughter of George, her cousin, was said to be of Hadstock when she died unmarried in 1636. Richard later challenged wills of John Banks and Dame Katherine; names of other relatives also included with him included that of Katherine against John. The case was not pursued and few details survive (P.R.O. PROB 11/164/98/323, 11/159/65/509; P.R.O. 11/171/87; P.R.O. PROB 29/29, f.339 et al., 29/30, f.31, 29/31, f.240).

8 P.R.O. PROB 11/91/48/372, 11/158/84/156. John Banks left his daughter Ann £8,000 if she survived; she did, marrying Edmund Waller at St.Margaret's, Westminster, in 1631. For the Mercers, and for Banks' other silverware, see: Collinson, *Godly People*, 1983, p.278; Pearl, p.242; Huelin, *Mercers*, frontispiece and pp.6, 13-14; Doolittle, 1994, p.48-51; Lane, 1985, pp.24-25, 38-39, 46-47; Imray, 1991, p.339, 379-85; Carlyle, 1993; Carlyle, 1994; Mercers' Company, 1880, pp.16-17. Further information kindly provided by Ursula S.Carlyle, Curator and Deputy Archivist, Mercers' Hall.

9 P.R.O. PROB 11/91/48/372, 11/135/1/1, 11/158/84/156; 11/87/6/46; 11/163/25/205; Guildhall MS 2895/1; Beaven, 1913; *East Anglian Notes and Queries*, N.S., iii.

10 P.R.O. PROB 11/116/104, 11/163/25/205, Almack, 'Kedington', pp.134-42; L.M.A. DL/C/323, p.79. Nathaniel, Sir Thomas's second son, was born 1588 (*D.N.B.*). Arthur was the third son. Almack, and

T.Webster, 1994, p.2, refer to the Geneva upbringing of Sir Thomas's father, Sir Thomas the elder (who died 1619). Webster stresses the 'puritan haven' which the latter provided at Clare in Suffolk, whilst Almack (p.134) suggests that his Puritanism waned towards the end of his life. Sir Thomas Barnardiston's and Sir William Ayloffe's fathers were cousins; the Ayloffes of Great Braxted, adjoining Witham, were anti-Puritan (see later in this chapter).

11 B.L. Harl. MSS. 386, f.24 (transcribed in E.R.O. T/A 481) gives Towse living at Witham and is dateable as 1614 by the details (no year given but gives February 23 as a Wednesday, which puts it in 1614). P.R.O. ASSI 35/57/2, 35/62/2, give Towse's house in Witham in 1615 and 1620. Katherine's date of birth is unknown, but she was old enough to marry Bartholomew Soame before he died in 1595; Bartholomew was still under 21 when his father died in 1569 (P.R.O. PROB 11/87/6/46; Norfolk R.O., N.C.C. will, 200 (Ponder, Thomas Some, 1569)).

12 Thomas Soame died at Beetley in 1569 (Norfolk R.O., N.C.C. will, 200 (Ponder, Thomas Some, 1569)); Towse was 'of Hingham' in 1571; for more about him see Sorlien, 1976, pp.9-10, 55, 75, 76, 78, 114, 319, and Underwick 1896-98, i, pp.281-449 passim, ii, pp.xv, lxiii, 5-109, 338-342 passim; neither work mentions his marriage to Dame Katherine Barnardiston.

13 P.R.O. PROB 11/163/25/205; Underwick, 1896-98, ii, note on p.xv; card index in Colchester branch of E.R.O.; E.R.O. Q/SR 242/105; *O.E.D.*; Benton, Galpin and Pressey, 1926, pp.291-92, and plate xxi opposite p.198; Hunt, 1983, p.124.

14 P.Clark, 1983, p.172; Gleason, 1969, pp.72-74.

15 *Sterne*: E.R.O. Q/SR 163/11, 163/42-43, 165/42-48, 165/50, 173/51, 173/67, 174/32-34, 174/89-90, 175/93, 176/27-28, 177/126, 178/39-41, 178/104, 180/73, 181/36. *Towse*: P.R.O. ASSI 35/35/2, 35/58/2 (magistrate by 1593); E.R.O. Q/SR 221/88, 240/93-94, 241/66, in 1618 and 1623 (only Witham recognisances signed in James' reign); E.R.O. Q/SR 228/10, 230/18, 246/136 (other involvement in Witham cases); E.R.O. Q/SR 209/68, 209/108, 210/111, 213/42, 213/92, 219/12-13, 222/78, 233/71, 230/102, 234/143, 238/1, 240/92, 240/94, 242/105, 243/47 (cases from other places 1615 to 1625); E.R.O. Q/SR 152/17, 198/122 (complaints about roads in Great Waltham and Takeley areas, 1601 and 1612).

16 E.R.O. Q/SR 241/66; *Visitations, Essex*, p.705; Petchey, 1991, pp.239-40 (Allen and his wife as friends and relatives of Puritan John Shipton of Maldon); E.R.O. D/ACW 10/6; *Exact and True Diurnal*, 1642, p.8 (Brooke). The Brookes were successive bailiffs of the half-hundred.

17 *Allen*: Morant, *Essex*, 1763-68, ii, p.131; Peel, 1915, i, pp.28-35; E.R.O. Q/SR 233/110, 235/99, 235/113, 235/147, 236/89, 239/81. *Wiseman*: P.R.O. ASSI 35/51/2; E.R.O. Q/SR 191/68, 203/92, 204/59, 205/98, 207/79, 210/83, 210/97, 212/82, 214/68, 215/105, 220/44, 227/71, 229/16, 234/154, 235/63, 242/78, 243/62, 244/31, 244/63, 247/83, 318/62 (last Witham recognisance of his, in 1642); Quintrell, 'Gentry', x, p.123; Morant, *Essex*, 1763-68, ii, pp.146-47; E.R.O. D/P 107/1/1 (burial, 12 March 1654). *Nevills*: P.M.Ryan, 1993, pp.13, 16.

18 Cockburn, 1978; Cockburn, 1982; E.R.O. D/ACW 3/184; P.R.O. PROB 11/107/35; D/ACA 27, f.7v et al., 188 et al.; L.M.A. DL/C/618, p.301; D/ACA 30, f.245v, ACA 32, f.3v et al.; P.R.O. ASSI 35/50/2 to 35/64/1, passim.

19 P.R.O. STAC 8/152/4.

20 E.R.O. T/A 547; Fowler, 1911, p.31; L.M.A. DL/C/618, pp.219-304 (the marginal notes are not signed, but appear in the same hand at courts held under various other surrogates, so they were not written by those surrogates. They are not in the same hand as the main court record). L.M.A. DL/C/305, f.150v; *Alumni Cantabrigiensis*.

21 Guildhall MS 9531/14, f.101v; E.R.O. T/A 547; *Alumni Oxoniensis*; Oxley, 'Benefice Farming', pp.7, 10; L.M.A. DL/C/619, p.279, DL/C/323, pp.79-82, DL/C/310, p.398; P.R.O. PROB 11/129/7; Fowler, 1911, p.25. Tinley's tomb was said to be of grey marble, on the floor of the chancel 'just before the Communion table' (early 18th cent.). Still present in 1937, but probably hidden now (E.R.O. T/P 195/10, 38). *Kelly*, 1937; *D.N.B.*; E.R.O. D/DU 65/89; Underdown, 1985, pp.47, 71, 94; P.R.O. PROB 11/163/25/205.

22 P.R.O. P.R.O. PROB 11/163/25/205, 11/144/78; Hill, 1970, p.42; correspondence with county Record Offices of Bedfordshire and Northamptonshire, September 1987; Guildhall MS 9531/14, ff.208, 218v; E.R.O. T/A 547; *Alumni Oxoniensis*; E.R.O. D/ACA 40, f.101v.

23 Anglin, 1965, pp.207-209; E.R.O. D/ACV 3, ff.54v, 71, D/ACV 4, f.27v, 46v, 69, 133v et al.; E.R.O. D/ACA 30, f.169v.

24 *Alumni Cantabrigiensis*; P.R.O. PROB 11/163/25/205, 11/157/31; E.R.O. D/ACW 5/231; B.L. Harl. MSS. 386, f.24 (transcribed in E.R.O. T/A 481) (no year given but has Feb.23 as Wednesday, making it 1614); Shipps, 1971, pp.84-87, & Appendix IV; Almack, 'Kedington', p.136.

25 E.R.O. D/ACV 4, f.174; Guildhall MS 9537/11; E.R.O. D/DA T550; P.R.O. PROB 11/163/25/205, 11/144/78; Shipps, 1971, pp.9-10, 105-106, 125; E.R.O. D/ACW 10/151, 9/187; E.R.O. D/ACA 33, ff.19v, 130; L.M.A. DL/C/319, p.36.

26 E.R.O. D/DBw M26, 22 April 1587 (gives Edmund Halys as Edward's son); E.R.O. D/ABD 3/17, and E.R.O. D/ACD 7, f.59 (give Edmund born in Witham, aged 58 in 1622 and 71 in 1635); E.R.O. D/ACW 15/85 (gives him 'almost' 84 in 1648); Webb, *Manor and Borough*, 1924, pp.318, 324; Martin, 1959, pp.36-37, 74-75; Byford, 1988, pp.279, 304. A series of lucky chances led to the tracing of Halys to London and Colchester in the following: Guildhall MS 15857/1/87v, 15857/1/122; E.R.O. D/DRe Z9; E.R.O. D/B 5 Cr 142 (Harrod, 1865, part 2, p.3, gives Earnesbie erroneously as Carnesbie); E.R.O. D/Y 2/7/295; P.R.O. PROB 11/73/16; E.R.O. D/P 138/1/6; E.R.O. D/B 5 Cb 2/3, Cr 150.

27 E.R.O. D/ACA 16, f.46v, ACA 20, f.2 et al.; E.R.O. D/ACD 7, f.59; E.R.O. D/ABW 40/198; E.R.O. D/DU 967/1-2 (witnessing a Witham document as early as 1590, but may have been only as an owner).

28 *Witham wills*: E.R.O. D/ACW 4/123, 4/177, 4/207, 4/226, 4/279, 5/195, 6/12, 6/126, 7/152, 7/232, 8/29, 8/84, 8/252, 8/279, 9/107, 9/128, 10/6, 10/72, 10/192, 11/8, 11/9, 11/238, 11/248, 11/264, 12/25, 12/39, 12/98, 12/144, 12/169, 12/214, 12/245, 13/112, 14/127, 14/194. *Other documents*: E.R.O. D/DU 967/2, 967/4; E.R.O. D/DC 41/482-83; E.R.O. D/DB 89; E.R.O. D/DA T550; E.R.O. D/DHt T302/5; E.R.O. D/DU 308/1; E.R.O. D/DRa T107. *E.g.s in Faulkbourne and Rivenhall*: E.R.O. D/ACW 11/80; E.R.O. D/ABW 56/283. *Own will*: E.R.O. D/ACW 15/85.

29 *Feet of Fines for Essex*, vi, p.98; E.R.O. D/DBw M26, 1587-1603 various; manor nos.12, 13; Gyford, 1996, pp.11-12; E.R.O. D/ACW 18/45; E.R.O. D/P 30/25/65; Guildhall MS 9537/13/19v, 9539A/1/7v; L.M.A. DL/C/322, pp.81-82, 89, 96.

30 E.R.O. D/ABW 40/198; E.R.O. D/ACW 4/123, 15/85; P.R.O. PROB 11/73/16.

31 P.R.O. STAC 8/152/4; E.R.O. D/ACW 15/85; E.R.O. D/ACA 43, f.174; E.R.O. Acc. A9368; H.L.R.O., Main Papers, H.L., 20 Jan.1641/2, petition box.

32 E.R.O. D/ACW 15/85; manor nos.12, 13, 90; E.R.O. D/P 30/1/1 (gives Paul Gattaway as a Quaker at his death in 1692); E.R.O. D/DBw M28, 13 Oct.1684; P.R.O. RG 6/1335 (gives Quaker marriage of Deborah Davies, 1679); extract from Deborah Eatney's will (in custody of Chelmsford Friends' Meeting).

33 L.M.A. DL/C/340, f.63, DL/C/341, ff.20, 141; Guildhall 9537/11/20; E.R.O. D/ACW 5/231; *Alumni Cantabrigiensis*; D.N.B. Redman may have come to Witham after posts in Hertfordshire and London, and possibly subsequently returned to his native Lancashire, where he benefited from some affinity with the Parliamentarians.

34 E.R.O. D/ACA 27, ff.76 et al., 80v, 114v, ACA 30, f.159, ACA 34, f.31 et al., ACA 37, f.97, ACA 40, f.101 et al., ACA 43, f.57 et al., ACA 54, f.35v; manor no.56; E.R.O. Q/SR 141/36, 141/126, 160/34; E.R.O. D/ABW 23/309; L.M.A. DL/C/319, p.85.

35 E.R.O. D/ACW 7/232.

36 E.R.O. D/ACA 43, f.94, ACA 45, ff.109v, 113v, 120. But there were a few long preambles for people who were less prosperous, such as brazier John Hatch, who lived in Maldon Lane, and bailiff Alexander Brooke of the White Hart (E.R.O. D/ACW 12/144, 10/6). Hatch's cottage in Maldon Lane is where roundabout is now, William Wood's was on the site now no.39 Chipping Hill (manor nos.40, 135).

37 E.R.O. D/ACA 27, ff.114v-115v et al.; L.M.A. DL/C/618, pp.299-304, 565; Wrightson and Levine, 1979 and 1995, pp.113-14, 116.

38 E.R.O. D/ACA 27, ff.114v, 118v; L.M.A. DL/C/618, p.299, DL/C/305, f.151. *Other references re.church rates (1602-1605)*: E.R.O. D/ACA 25, f.192, ACA 27, ff.7, 20v, 23, 29; L.M.A. DL/C/618, pp.303-304. *Other references re.church fabric (1602-1605)*: E.R.O. D/ACA 25, ff.194, 205v, ACA 27, ff.3v, 17v, 39v, 47v, 128, 136, 144, ACA 30, ff.2, 7v, 12v.

39 Wrightson and Levine, 1979 and 1995, p.106; E.R.O. D/ACV 2, ff.106, 113, 172, D/ACV 3, ff.12v, 36, 54v, 71, D/ACV 4, ff.27v, 46v; E.R.O. D/ACA 25, f.46v, ACA 27, ff.3v, 29, 31, 81v, 102, 108, 110v, 156; E.R.O. Q/SR 171/61d. E.R.O. D/ACW 4/226 (will of Gravener(1), has space for a mark, but no mark; it is probably a copy,

but it implies he was not expected to be able to sign); E.R.O. D/ABW 27/146 (with signature of John Savill); E.R.O. D/ACV 1, f.63; Webb, *Parish and County*, p.22.

40 E.R.O. D/ACA 30, ff.123v et al., 229v, ACA 32, ff.65v, 258v; E.R.O. D/ACW 4/226; E.R.O. D/ACV 4, ff.133v, 155; L.M.A. DL/C/339, f.182; Cliftlands, 1987, pp.200-202; Gyford, 1996, pp.200-201 (here I naively thought that 'caveat' written in the Act book against the death of John Gravener(2), meant 'beware'; in fact it means that the matter was referred to another court; see Anglin, 1965, pp.185-86, and Chapman, 1992, p.49, for more about the caveat).

41 E.R.O. D/ACA 30, ff.152v, 160v et al., 258, ACA 32, ff.17, 31v, 52, 127, 169; L.M.A. DL/C/619, pp.294, 378, 479.

42 E.R.O. D/ACA 32, ff.243v-44, 253v, ACA 34, ff.31-31v; Guildhall MS 9537/12; L.M.A. DL/C 323, pp.74-82, DL/C/621, pp.147, 154-56.

43 E.R.O. D/ACA 34, ff.136, 176v, ACA 40, ff.10, 83v, 215, ACA 44, f.131; L.M.A. D/C/323, p.79, DL/C/621, pp.288, 292, 308, 335, 392, 401; E.R.O. D/ACW 7/152; E.R.O. D/DBw M26, 18 April 1601; E.R.O. D/P 30/25/10; Wrightson, 1980, pp.41-44.

44 Figures in figure 18 calculated from E.R.O. D/ACA various. Cases re. sexual relations were: *1569-1609*: E.R.O. D/ACA 3, f.45, ACA 13, f.31v, ACA 16, f.16v, 103v, ACA 20, ff.153, 204, ACA 25, f.102, ACA 30, f.116. *1611-19*: E.R.O. D/ACA 32, f.132, ACA 34, ff.63v, 249, ACA 37, ff.39v, 97, ACA 40, ff.11v, 112, 126 (2 cases), 147. *Terling*: Wrightson and Levine, 1979 and 1995, pp.126-27.

45 People said to be cohabiting: *William Appleford*: weaver (E.R.O. Q/SR 234/154). *Thomas and Elizabeth Complin*: theft (E.R.O. Q/SR 330/64). *Nathaniel Garrard*: tailor, constable, surveyor, parish officer, Ship Money (E.R.O. Q/SR 317/52, 278/22, 341/8; 315/76; P.R.O. SP 16/358/97-98). *Robert and Helen Gravener*: base child, drunk, not rec. commun. (E.R.O. D/ACA 37, f.179, ACA 43, f.57v, ACA 45, f.304). *Richard and Amy Lock*: webster (weaver), assault (P.R.O. ASS 35/51/2). *Edward Spradborough*: comber, absent from church, drunk (E.R.O., Q/SR 242/78; E.R.O. D/ACA 40, f.216, ACA 43, f.57v).

46 P.Clark, 1983, pp.172-74; P.R.O. ASSI 35/62/2; E.R.O. Q/SR 213/41; Wrightson, 1988, pp.167-69; Cliftlands, 1987, p.377 (quoting communication from Keith Wrightson).

47 *Licences*: E.R.O. Q/SR 166/163; see also Q/SR 171/81; 175/94. *Disorderly alehouses*: E.R.O. Q/SR 167/15, 170/69, 185/56, 187/65, 213/41, 214/51, 222/11, 223/50, 226/10, 229/52, 230/25, 232/16, 236/31, 239/27, 240/93, 243/28, 243/62, 245/31, 246/50, 247/50; P.R.O. ASSI 35/62/1, 35/62/2, 35/63/1.

48 P.Clark, 1983, pp.154-55; E.R.O. D/ACA 16, ff.22v, 138, ACA 37, ff.144, 152, 185v, 189v (3 cases), ACA 40, ff.84, 159v, 212, 215, ACA 43, ff.57, 57v, 163, ACA 44, f.34; L.M.A. DL/C/323, pp.79-80, DL/C/621, pp.154-55.

49 P.Clark, 1983, p.145; E.R.O. D/Y 2/4, p.107-110; *Acts of P.C.* 1621-23, 337, 387.

50 *Fair*: P.R.O. C 66/2063, no.3. *Sunday drinking*: E.R.O. D/ACA 16, ff.22v, 138, ACA 37, ff.144, 152, 185v, 189v (3 cases), ACA 40, ff.84, 159v, 212, 215, ACA 43, ff.57, 163, ACA 44, f.34. Note in a few of these cases, it is not actually stated that the day concerned was Sunday, but this has been checked in Cheney, 1948.

51 E.R.O. D/ACA 40, f.159, ACA 43, ff.57, 163.

52 E.R.O. Q/SR 240/93, 245/31. *William Purcas*: E.R.O. Q/SR 236/31, 245/31, 271/10; E.R.O. D/ACA 40, f.112v, ACA 43, f.103, ACA 44, f.92, ACA 45, f.37v, ACA 54/21v. *Francis Ellis*: E.R.O. Q/SR 228/10, 236/16, 239/27, 243/28, 243/62, 245/31, 247/50; P.R.O. ASSI 35/51/1, 35/56/5, 35/62/1-2, 35/63/1; P.R.O. ASSI 35/69/1/93, 35/71/2/8, 35/71/3/12, 35/72/1/66, 35/72/1/87; E.R.O. D/ACA 30, f.97.

53 E.R.O. Q/SR 245/31. Characteristics of the 17 men were: *Ship Money assessment, 1636*: (median for town = 3s.): 8 probably still alive and in Witham then, of whom William Brooke, 4s., 5 men between 1 and 2s. and 2 not included (P.R.O. SP 16/358/97-98). *Value of goods at death*: (median for town 1587-1640 = £23): known for 7, of whom median value £23 (Gyford, 1996, pp.17-18). John Markes, maltster had £252. *Property*: at least 11 owned some, usually just one tenement. *Literacy*: signing ability known for 13, of whom 7 could sign (high - similar to rate for churchwardens) (sources various).

Individual information is : *Rooke Allen*: E.R.O. D/ACW 16/239; E.R.O. Q/SBa 6/8; E.R.O. Q/SR 210/83, 228/10, 239/27, 243/28, 328/44; E.R.O. D/ACAc 1, f.3; 1642 petition; still in Witham 1636 but not in Ship Money. *Richard Barry*: E.R.O. Q/SR 122/43-45; manor no.63; last known in 1632 (E.R.O. D/ACA 48, ff.164v, 194). *Josias*

Beecham: only known in this case, 1624. *John Brewer and John Brewer senior:* E.R.O. Q/SR 205/98, 222/11, 223/50, 233/125, 251/23, 255/28, 256/30, 263/83; one in Ship Money (2s.); both still alive 1624 (E.R.O. D/ACA 44, f.147). *Alexander Brooke:* E.R.O. D/ACW 4/207, 10/6; E.R.O. Q/SR 166/163, 171/81, 175/93,177/26, 236/89, 241/66; E.R.O. D/ACA 45, f.105v; E.R.O. D/DBw M27, 17 April 1626; died 1625. *William Brooke:* E.R.O. D/ACW 14/275; E.R.O. Q/SR 246/50-51, 318/62; E.R.O. D/DU 967/4; in Ship Money (4s.) *Peter Clarke:* E.R.O. Q/SBa 1/42; E.R.O. Q/SR 228/10, 239/27; E.R.O. D/DBw M27, 2 April 1627; 1642 petition; in Ship Money (1s.). *Jeffrey Cottis:* E.R.O. D/ACW 11/20, 11/264; E.R.O. Q/SR 295/61, 310/33; manor no.27; E.R.O. D/DHt T302/5; still in Witham 1636 but not in Ship Money. *Francis Ellis:* E.R.O. Q/SR 243/62; P.R.O. ASSI 35/51/1, 35/56/5, 35/62/1; P.R.O. ASSI 35/69/1, 35/71/2-3, 35/72/1; E.R.O. D/DBw M27, 17 Oct.1625; 1642 petition; in Ship Money (1s.6d.). *Richard Freeborne:* E.R.O. D/ACW 4/227, 228/10; E.R.O. D/ACA 45, f.120; died 1625. *John Kemett:* E.R.O. Q/SR 255/28; P.R.O. ASSI 35/71/2-3, 35/72/1; E.R.O. D/DBw M27, 17 Oct.1625, 17 April 1626, 2 April 1627; last known 1630. *Robert King:* E.R.O. D/ACW 5/236, 7/164, 10/82; E.R.O. Q/SR 228/10; E.R.O. D/ACA 40, f.84, ACA 45, f.71v; died 1625. *John Markes:* E.R.O. D/ACW 7/249, 8/252, 12/25; E.R.O. D/ACA 49, f.167v; P.R.O. ASSI 35/71/3; died 1633. *John Peachie:* E.R.O. D/ACW 12/245; E.R.O. Q/SR 170/69, 175/94, 177/126, 178/104, 228/10, 259/9, 275/33; P.R.O. ASSI 35/71/2-3; E.R.O. D/ACA 52, f.34v; E.R.O. D/DBw M27, 17 Oct.1625, 2 April 1627; in Ship Money (1s.8d.). *William Purcas:* E.R.O. D/ACW 15/309; E.R.O. Q/SR 236/31, 271/10; E.R.O. D/ACA 43, f.57, ACA 44, f.92; E.R.O. D/ALV 1, f.26; in Ship Money (1s.). *William Salter:* E.R.O. D/ACW 5/195, 11/20; E.R.O. Q/SR 177/42-43, 177/126, 183/83, 228/10, 244/9, 261/27; E.R.O. D/ACA 49, f.15; E.R.O. D/DBw M26, 20 May 1592; died 1633.

54 Re. 15 individual drinkers: only William Purcas appeared twice 1615-25; he also ran an alehouse. Only one known property owner, 2 known able to sign, 4 with known occupations (carpenter, sawyer, comber, husbandman). One (Edward Gould) was unauthorised teacher. 6 absentees from church, 2 cohabitees before marriage. Only 3 known in town 1636, of whom none in Ship Money (P.R.O. SP 16/358/97-98).
    Individual information is: *Nicholas Burgess:* carpenter (Q/SR 236/72). *Thomas Cofield:* not at church (D/ACA 46, f.22v). *William Freeborne:* sawyer; not rec. communion (E.R.O. Q/SR 235/63; E.R.O. D/ACA 45, f.304). *Edward Gould:* teacher (D/ACA 27, f.76). *Robert Gravener:* base child, incont. bef marr, not rec commun. (E.R.O. D/ACA 37, f.179, ACA 40, f.126, ACA 45, f.304). *Thomas Saffold:* to Terling church (E.R.O. D/ACA 45, f.180v). *Robert Saunders:* husbandman; signed, absent from church (2) (E.R.O. Q/SR 232/20; E.R.O. D/ACW 7/152; E.R.O. D/ACA 45, f.181). *Edward Spradborough:* comber, incont bef marr, absent from church (E.R.O., Q/SR 242/78; E.R.O. D/ACA 34, f.249, ACA 40, f.216). *Matthew Spradborough:* left tenement by father; signed (E.R.O. D/ACW 5/195; E.R.O. D/ACA 44 (loose sheet)).

55 E.R.O. D/ACA 16, f.138.

56 E.R.O. Q/SR 222/11, 223/50, 230/25; *Cal.S.P.Dom.* 1633/4, 328; P.R.O. SP 16/252/67, 67i; manor no.7.

57 E.R.O. D/ACA 32 (unnumbered page at end), ACA 34, ff.10, 91, ACA 37, ff.102v, 144, 152, ACA 40, ff.83-84, 126, 215-16, ACA 43, ff.57, 163, ACA 45, ff.91v, 93v; Cheney, 1948; L.M.A. DL/C/323, pp.79-80; Guildhall MS 9537/12/18-18v; E.R.O. D/ALV 1, f.18.

58 E.R.O. D/ACW 11/248; manor no.50; E.R.O. D/ACA 40, ff.83, 83v, 126-27, 215-16, ACA 43, f.163, ACA 45, ff.93v, 109v et al.; E.R.O. D/DBw M27, 17 Oct.1625; L.M.A. DL/C/323, p.79.

59 L.M.A. DL/C/621, pp.154-56. Of the 13, 2 were women, 5 were men of unknown occupation, and the others were an alehousekeeper, a tanner, a carpenter, a yeoman, a weaver, and a comber.

60 E.R.O. T/P 196/4. Thanks to Amanda Flather for advice on pews and seating. Patrick Collinson has written that 'disputes over seating were endemic in parish life and they normally reflected contests for social precedence' (Collinson, 1982, pp.141, 188). For Essex examples see Pressey, 'Seating', E.R.O. D/ACA 43, ff.174, 182v, ACA 44, ff.5v, 12v; E.R.O. T/P 196/4.

Chapter 8: Forced Loan, and St.Patrick's Day 1628

1 *Main original sources:* P.R.O. SP 16/96/39, 39i, depositions taken locally

and forwarded to the Privy Council (f.94 is mis-filed and concerns some other unidentified place); P.R.O. PC 2 various, records of the Privy Council; E.R.O. T/A 278 (microfilm of Bodleian Library MS. Firth C4), Lieutenancy Book, 1608-1639, mainly a letter book, with copies of inward and outward letters to and from the Essex Deputy Lieutenants, and some memoranda; Bodleian Library MS. Top.Essex e.10/2, notes on the latter, made by C.H.Firth and copied by Revd.Andrew Clark in 1909, referred to by some authors but I have not used them. *Printed sources:* Acts of P.C. 1627-28, Cal.S.P.Dom. 1627-28, 1628-29. *Research publications:* Ashton, 'St.Patrick', discusses the Catholic perspective; Aylmer, 'Communication', refutes suggestion that over 30 people were killed; A.Clark, 'Lieutenancy', summary of E.R.O. T/A 278; Hunt, pp.212-13, part of discussion of political developments in Essex; Quintrell, 'Gentry', relates Witham events to Essex gentry; Quintrell, 1993 (an edition of E.R.O. T/A 278). *My main additions:* a review of the dating of some documents before St.Patrick's day, and of motives including the influence of the Forced Loan; use of petitions from Leicestershire R.O. (for which thanks to Pat Ryan); further use of letter from Sir Thomas Wiseman (B.L. Add.MS. 34679, f.61); use of more detail from depositions and Witham background; continuation of the story later into 1628.

2 Sharpe, 1987, p.15; Cust, 1987, pp.198-201; Hunt, 1983, pp.178-90.

3 Cust, 1987, pp.13-18; Hunt, 1983, pp.202-206; P.Clark, 1977, pp.329-30.

4 *Figure 19:* calculated from P.R.O. E 401/2322-24, P.R.O. SP 16/76/13, 13i-iii, P.R.O. SP 16/54/47, 47i. *William Sams: Exact and True Diurnal,* 1642, pp.6, 8; *True and perfect Diurnall,* 1642, no.11, p.6. *Jeremy Armond and William Warren esquire:* defaulters from Witham parish February 1627, but not in list August 1627. Armond said elsewhere to have left Witham by December 1626. Warren not known in Witham, and possibly some confusion with Walton (which happened sometimes), where one of this name later bailiff (E.R.O. D/ACA 45, ff.235, 248v, 260). *William Ward:* goods worth a substantial £156 at death later in 1628 (would have included his brewing equipment). Court appearances 1617 and 1628 re. church rate, unlicensed alehouse, and working at Easter and Whitsun (E.R.O. D/ACA 40, f.70, ACA 45, ff.304, 312v, ACA 46, f.135v; E.R.O. Q/SR 243/28; E.R.O. D/ALV 1, f.26; E.R.O. D/ACW 11/20).

5 Cust, 1987, pp.260-306 (pp.263-65 for Witham half-hundred, 272-73 for the cloth industry).

6 Gyford, 1996, p.202; Almack, 'Kedington', pp.139-40; *D.N.B.* Sir Nathaniel Barnardiston was born in 1588, and John Gravener(3) some time after 1590 (E.R.O. D/ACW 5/234).

7 E.R.O. D/Y 2/3, p.55; E.R.O. T/A 278/428-43; Quintrell, 1993, pp.lvii-lx. At the end of 1627 the active Deputies appeared to be: Sir William Maynard (since 1613, resigned later in 1628); Sir Thomas Fanshaw (since 1625); William Smith/Nevill of Cressing Temple (since 1625, resigned c.February 1628); Sir Henry Mildmay of Moulsham (since 1626); Sir Gamaliel Capel (since 1626); Sir Thomas Edmondes (since 1626). Note also that Sir John Deane had died in 1626 (E.R.O. D/DAc 163).

8 P.R.O. SP 16/91/86; Leicestershire R.O. DE 220/208, 220/207, 220/209; E.R.O. T/A 278/428; P.Clark, 1977, pp.329-30 (describes tension in Kent between residents and billetted Irish soldiers); E.R.O. T/A 278/434.

9 E.R.O. T/A 278/429, 432, 434-35, 442-43, 445-46, 448-49; E.R.O. D/Y 2/8, pp.259, 263, 265, 269, 277; E.R.O. D/Y 2/9, pp.127, 143, 151, 155, 163, 167, 171, 175, 179; E.R.O. D/Y 2/5, pp.87-89; P.M.Ryan, 1993, pp.13-16. In February the King asked Essex magistrates to raise £6,057 more for the war in Ship Money, but then rescinded this and recalled Parliament instead (E.R.O. T/A 278/451-54).

10 E.R.O. T/A 278/429, 431-33, 436-37, 441-43, 449, 451; *Acts of P.C. 1627-28,* pp.237-28, 253.

11 E.R.O. T/A 278/427-29, 437, 441-42.

12 E.R.O. T/A 278/448; *Cal.S.P.Dom.* 1627-82, p.536; P.R.O. SP 16/91/86, 86A (petition from Witham to the Privy Council); Leicestershire R.O. DE 220/207 (same but looks like a draft). Editors of the former and a later user of the latter have appended the date 31 January; this disputed by Aylmer who says it must have followed the Privy Council's proposal of 3 February (Aylmer, 'Communication', p.141, note 18). But seems possible Witham heard of proposal earlier and prepared their petition accordingly. This idea supported by this petition not naming the other places proposed by the P.C., as later ones do. Petition claimed one of the Deputies lived near Witham;

presumably William Smith/Nevill (who had actually resigned) or one of the Sir Henry Mildmays, of Little Baddow, six miles away.

[13] E.R.O. T/A 278/444; *Acts of P.C.* 1627-28, p.264; P.R.O. SP 16/92/86; *Cal.S.P.Dom.* 1627-28, p.555. Exact response of the other places to the Forced Loan not calculable, but Braintree and Chelmsford both had a number of resisters; in Chelmsford area seven of them were threatened in March 1627 with being impressed as soldiers and sent off from Harwich to serve the King of Denmark (Cust, 1987, pp.260, 270-74; Grieve, 1994, pp.33-35; P.R.O. SP 16/76/22i-ii; P.R.O. SP 16/57/1).

[14] Hunt, 1983, p.202 (and note 82); *Acts of P.C.* 1627-28, p.282; E.R.O. T/A 278/454-55. The letter appears later in the letter book, but as the latter was compiled in 1639 from several sources, its arrangement is difficult to interpret (Quintrell, 1993, pp.xlv-xlix).

[15] P.R.O. SP 16/92/85, 85i-iv; *Cal.S.P.Dom.* 1627-28, p.554. Editor of calendar suggests 10 February for this Maldon petition; Aylmer says it would have preceded the Privy Council's letter of 3 February (Aylmer, 'Communication', p.141, note 13). But actually one of the accompanying complaints relates to an event on 8 February, so the 10th is more probable. The Witham jurors had convicted Brownesword of forestalling (E.R.O. D/B 3/3/208/25).

[16] *Acts of P.C.* 1627-28, p.335; E.R.O. T/A 278/449-50, 455-56; P.R.O. SP 16/96/39; *Cal.S.P.Dom.* 1628-29, p.24. As Aylmer, says, the calendar wrongly gives 18 March, which was after St.Patrick's day, as the reported date of the move (Aylmer, 'Communication', p.144, note 25); Quintrell, 1993, p.lx. At the end of February five companies had been transferred from north-east Essex to Norfolk, naturally causing little concern in Essex (E.R.O. T/A 278/445-46). Sir Henry Mildmay of Moulsham was an earlier appointment as Deputy Lieutenant; the new ones were of Graces in Little Baddow, and of Wanstead.

[17] P.R.O. SP 16/92/59; *Cal.S.P.Dom.* 1627-28, p.549. Refers to the petitioner as 'I'. The calendar prints the letter as from the Deputy Lieutenants, but it is not in their letter book. The dating is difficult; it seems to be urging Buckingham not to relieve Maldon, suggesting it preceded the move, but it says the Privy Council had already 'removed [the soldiers] to Witham'. Elsewhere it says Witham was the place where 'they are comanded', so perhaps it was written between the command and the move, i.e. between 6 and 8 March. However, the calendar editor and Aylmer suggest 7 February, taking the 'command' to be the earlier letter of 3 February (Aylmer, 'Communication', p.142).

[18] Petchey, 1991, pp.13-21; B.L. Add.MS. 34679, f.61 (Ongar, Epping and Hatfield Broadoak were the places said to be defective in their payments).

[19] Leicestershire R.O. DE 220/209 (the towns 'most fitt' were [Saffron] Walden, Brentwood, Harlow, Wethersfield, Hedingham; the ones which were 'the fittest' were Maldon, Halstead, Epping); Gyford, pp.11, 190-91, 202.

[20] P.R.O. SP 16/96/39, 39i. This includes three depositions wrongly filed, about an argument involving soldiers on the same day but not about Witham; they mention a mayor and a city (f.94). E.R.O. T/A 278/455-56 has another copy of the statement from the two Mildmays. The following times are mentioned in the various depositions: *8 or 9 a.m.,* soldier spoke to Hussey about ribbons. *9 or 10 a.m.,* Wisemans arrived. *10 or 11 a.m.,* Zebland saw Creswell go into house with musket. *About 1 p.m.,* Haven came home. *About 4 p.m.,* soldiers and Carew at Hopkinson's door.

[21] Manor no.31; E.R.O. Q/SR 245/32, 255/28; E.R.O. D/ACA 20, ff.175, 319v, ACA 37, f.144, ACA 43, f.67v et al.; P.R.O. ASSI 35/71/2-3, 35/72/1; E.R.O. D/ACW 11/86.

[22] E.R.O. Q/SR 251/23. For other disputes of Hussey's see: E.R.O. Q/SR 167/9, 167/26-27; E.R.O. D/ACA 40, ff.83v, 126 et al., ACA 51, f.103v, ACA 52, f.84, ACA 53, ff.74v, 99 et al., E.R.O. Q/SBa 2/41 (another extortion accusation; in recruiting and collecting for 'pressed' soldiers in 1640, Hussey asked money from labourer Thomas Slater twice over; he pleaded that he forgot to record the first sum because of 'the multitude of his busness').

[23] *Acts of P.C.* 1627-28, pp.350, 352, 354; B.L. Add.MS. 34679, f.61; P.R.O. PC 2/38/31, 35, 38; Birch, 1848, p.332. Hunt 1983, p.212, refers to Sir Thomas as Sir William in error, he refers to Birch but not *Acts of P.C.*; he also quotes an apparently unrelated document (P.R.O. SP 16/94/35).

[24] Manor no.7; L.M.A. DL/C/342, f.205v (gives Sir Thomas 1624 as a recusant promising to reform).

[25] Gyford, 1996, p.139.

[26] This evidence (of yeoman Gregory Shetlewood and husbandman Edmund Biggs) referred to 'Haswiefe Hopkins a sadler'; we know from other evidence that John Hopkins, otherwise known as Hopkinson, was a saddler.

[27] P.R.O. SP 16/96/39, 39i; E.R.O. calendar of assize records (names magistrates); Morant, 1763-68, ii, p.156; Round, 'Aylett', pp.26-27; L.M.A. D/CL/624, p.418; E.R.O. T/A 278/455-57; *Acts of P.C.* 1627-28, p.355. George Creswell was robbed in 1634 of items including a gold ring, two silver rings, two silver spoons, and a silver bracelet (P.R.O. ASSI 35/76/3).

[28] Birch, p.331; Aylmer, 'Communication' pp.139-48; *L.J.* iii, p.700; *Acts of P.C.* 1627-28, pp.361-62 (those summoned were William Wiseman, Captain Carew, a soldier called 'Buller' (probably 'Butler' whom William Haven claimed to have attacked him), William Haven (constable), Alexander King (blacksmith with the musket), John Hussey (owner of the dog), and William Johnson (tied the crosses onto it); *Acts of P.C.* 1627-28, p.389.

[29] E.R.O. T/A 278/458; *Acts of P.C.* 1627-28, pp.370-71, 373. Aylmer implies that mid April was the end of the financial negotiations, but as seen, they continued (Aylmer, 'Communication' p.146).

[30] E.R.O. T/A 278/465. The Deputies also wrote to the Lord Treasurer, reminding him of the 'many promises' received from the Privy Council on the matter (E.R.O. T/A 278/466).

[31] E.R.O. T/A 278/468; *Acts of P.C.* 1628-29, pp.102-103.

[32] E.R.O. T/A 278/471-73; *Acts of P.C.* 1628-29, p.249; Quintrell, 'Gentry, p.125; P.R.O. SP 16/358/97-98 (has a heading 'out-dwellers' between the surnames beginning with 'B' and those beginning with 'C' in its alphabetical list, but not only is it unlikely that all those with names C to Z were outdwellers, but many of them are known Witham residents).

[33] Hunt, 1983, p.202 (and note 82), p.204 (table 14, puts one part of Witham's payment figures into Winstree), p.208 (and note 108). The sources quoted by Hunt do not support his claim that Witham resisted the Loan, i.e. P.R.O. SP 16/91/86, SP 16/92/86, SP 16/76/13, 13i-ii, 16/76/22iii, SP 16/57/1 (latter refers to Chelmsford, not Witham).

[34] Quintrell, 'Gentry' pp.124-25.

[35] On 5 March 1628 Garrard(2) and his wife were before the Bishop's Consistory for, inter alia, being 'often absent' from Witham church (E.R.O. D/ALV 1, f.25v). On 12 March Sir Thomas Wiseman wrote about Garrard being asked by the Deputies to prepare a petition (B.L. Add.MS. 34679, f.61).

Chapter 9: Charles I (part - 1625-1640)

[1] Gyford, 1996, pp.147-48; Walter, 1980, pp.48-49; E.R.O. T/A 278/501-504 (501 refers to '2 or 300 people of Bocking Braintree and Witham', and 503 to 'the people from Witham, Braintree, Bocking &c.); E.R.O. D/B 3/3/308 (refers to 'Divers women to the number of above a hundred, of Maldon, Heibridge and Witham').

[2] E.R.O. T/A 278/525-28, 278/530-31; E.R.O. D/ACA 49, f.14v, ACA 51, f.103v; Gyford, 1996, pp.6-8; E.R.O. Q/SR 249-318; P.R.O. ASSI 35/68-83; J.A.Sharpe, 1983, pp.214-15; Wrightson, 1988, pp.142, 146-48. Pasfield was also in trouble for ill-treating his apprentice etc. (Gyford, 1996, p.227).

[3] J.A.Sharpe, 1987, pp.12-17, 238; Barker, 1976, pp.7-9; Walter, lecture, 1994 (this pointed out that there is some discussion amongst historians about the significance of Arminianism in this context).

[4] Hunt, 1983, pp.196-97, 256-57; H.Smith, *History,* pp.30-35; Shipps, 1971, pp.17-18, 34-35, 60-62, 105-106, 115-18; Walter, lecture, 1994.

[5] E.R.O. D/ACA 39, f.140, ACA 40, f.62, E.R.O. D/ABA 1, f.60. Also subsequent court records. Before taking up his official positions, Robert Aylett sometimes presided as a temporary substitute, and also whilst the archdeacon's post was vacant (e.g. E.R.O. D/ACA 39, ff.121, 130v, 133v, ACA 40, f.54; E.R.O. D/ABA 1, ff.1, 39). Chapman, 1992, p.31; Round, 'Aylett', pp.26-34 (does not mention Aylett as archdeacon's official, and nor do other commentators). For Henry King see *Alumni Oxoniensis; D.N.B.* It was not unknown for archdeacon's officials to be the bishop's commissary also (e.g. see Anglin, 1965, pp.36-37 re. William Bingham during the 1570s), but Aylett was in post for an unusually long time.

[6] E.R.O. D/ACA 47, f.148; E.R.O. Acc.A9368. In 1626, Aylett attended 63 sittings of the Archdeacon's and the Bishop's Commissary court, over half the total. Another lawyer, Christopher Wivell, took charge at

about one sixth (all N.W.Essex), the rest were shared by clergymen (most one or two each, except William Pease, vicar of Great Burstead, who took nearly all Commissary courts in Billericay (E.R.O. D/ACA 45; E.R.O. D/ABA 3).

[7] E.R.O. D/ACW 5/231 (comparison with chart opposite p.26 in Round, 'Aylett', though Round gives Leonard as of Rivenhall, because his father William was there); *Visitations, Essex*, pp.526-27; D/P 133/1/1.

[8] Round, 'Aylett', pp.27-30; P.R.O. SP 16/350/54, 16/351/100 (the archbishop's Vicar General was Sir Nathaniel Brent, as distinct from Arthur Duck who was Laud's Vicar General when he was bishop of London); P.R.O. SP 16/96/39i; Round, 'Aylett', pp.33-34; P.R.O. SP 16/350/54; House of Lords Record Office, Main Papers, H.L., 20 Jan.1641/2 (petition box); Round, 'Aylett', p.34; P.R.O. ASSI 35/84/2/41, 35/85/5/58, 35/92/2/21, 35/93/2/21, 35/94/1/38, et al.; *Acts & Ords. of Interr.*, i., pp.85-91, 106-110, 168-70, 223-29, 291-92. Information about Aylett's memorial kindly provided by Reverend David Nash.

[9] *Towse:* E.R.O. Q/SR 252/69, 255/55, 255/104, 255/109, 256/78, 256/101, 258/43, 263/83, 264/77, 266/49-50, 266/102 (note that no recognisances appear to survive 1630-35); P.R.O. ASSI 35/76/2/108; Sorlien, p.319. *Nevill, Wiseman, Ayloffe:* E.R.O. Q/SR 293/54, 293/57, 295/52, 295/61-62, 296/56, 297/92, 300/59, 305/64, 307/94, 308/82, 310/30-31, 310/33, 311/64, 312/87, 312/89, 312/98, 312/118, 315/68, 315/76, 316/66, 317/59-60, 317/62, 317/68, 318/62; Quintrell, 'Gentry', p.121; J.Walter, lectures, 1994 (gave Nevill married into a Catholic family in Leicestershire and with a Jesuit priest at his home in that county); P.M.Ryan, 1993, pp.13, 16, 21; P.R.O. SP 16/350/54; Morant, 1763-68, p.107; further information from Pat Ryan and Leicestershire Record Office. Sir Thomas Wiseman was overseer of Catholic John Southcott's will in 1637 (E.R.O. D/DP F244).

[10] P.R.O. ASSI 35/71/2 in E.R.O. calendar of assize records (the latter also gives officers' names); E.R.O. Q/SBa 2/53; *Exact and True Diurnal*, pp.6, 8; *True and perfect Diurnall*, p.6.

[11] E.R.O. D/ACW 11/248; E.R.O. D/ACR 6/23; E.R.O. D/ACW 4/31; Grieve, 1994, pp.10-11 (gives Richard Brodway, George Armond(2)'s brother-in-law, as a suspected papist).

[12] As seen in chapter 2, in 1604 clergymen were given powers to intervene if they and the parishioners did not agree, and in 1636 it was said rather ambiguously of Witham's Thomas Freshwater that he had been 'lawfully elected and chosen by the minister'. He refused to take office (E.R.O. D/ACA 51, f.249, ACA 52, f.3 et al.).

[13] H.L.R.O., Main Papers, H.L., 20 Jan.1641/2, petition box, and: *William Skinner:* E.R.O. D/ACW 9/128. *Philomen Wistocke:* E.R.O. D/ACW 9/187. *Arthur Barker:* E.R.O. D/ACW 10/72. *Richard Barnard:* E.R.O. D/ACW 13/218. *Jerome Skingley:* E.R.O. D/ACA 53, f.19.

[14] P.R.O. SP 16/358/97-98; Carlson, p.175.

[15] P.R.O. PROB 11/163/25/205.

[16] Her will included bequests to her cousins and their children of surname Banks, Biggs, and Pettitt, her sisters and/or their husbands of surname Deane, Titchborne and Draper, and her nieces and their husbands and families, of surname Mildmay, Goodwin, Rolfe, Mountjoy and Foge (P.R.O. PROB 11/163/25/205; further information about relationships from P.R.O. PROB 11/158/84/156). The minister at St.Mary Colchurch 1593 to 1638 was Richard Cowdall, nearly 80 years old in 1629, when he and others defended his curate for not baptising in the form required by Laud (*Alumni Cantabrigiensis*; *Cal.S.P.Dom.* 1629-31, pp.25, 142).

[17] P.R.O. PROB 11/158/84/156; Huelin, 1996, pp.ix, 20. Sir Richard Deane, her late sister's husband, owed her £300 'on bond'. He, her brother John, and her brother-in-law Robert Titchborne, were trustees re. her marriage agreement with William Towse. Her niece's husband Robert Mildmay was trustee of her purchase of manor and tithes of Cretingham in Suffolk in 1627. Godchildren mentioned in her will probably from the Banks side were Thomas Deane and Mary Scott. Katherine Banks of Hadstock, who she was to bring up, was daughter of George, her cousin, son of her uncle William. Her cousins Christopher Banks, gentleman, and Ann Biggs, together with Ann's husband John, were her 'servants' and received considerable bequests. Another servant, Elias Pettitt, may have been the son of her cousin Thomas Pettitt (P.R.O. PROB 11/163/25/205, 11/158/84/156; Suffolk R.O. E1/49).

[18] P.R.O. PROB 10/513 (original will); P.R.O. PROB 11/163/25/205 (register copy).

[19] P.R.O. SP 16/351/100; Webster, 1994, pp.1-2, 10, 14-15; Cross and Livingstone, 1974; Shipps, 1971, p.92.

[20] P.R.O. SP 16/351/100; J.R.Smith, 1992, p.12; H.Smith, 'Sequence', p.70; H.Smith, *History*, pp.42-43, 114, 129, 147-48, 170, 346; *Alumni Cantabrigiensis*. Note that Hunt, 1983, p.285 and index, confused Nehemiah with Nathaniel Rogers, Puritan curate of Bocking and an early emigrant to America.

[21] *Alumni Cantabrigiensis; D.N.B.*; Shipps, 1971, pp.37-58. Preston claimed to be curate September 1628, had no licence, and was given one. By 1630 Thomas Young was curate (Guildhall MS 9537/13/19v; Guildhall MS 9539A 1/10v; L.M.A. DL/C/343, ff.44, 87).

[22] Shipps, 1971, pp.150-52; E.R.O. D/ACW 11/288; Guildhall MS 9537/15, 9539A 1/88v.

[23] *Arthur Barker:* see later in this chapter. *Elizabeth Armond:* see George(2) earlier in this book, and Gyford, 1996, pp.194, 197. *Joan Nicholls:* E.R.O. D/ACW 8/252, 12/40; E.R.O. D/ACA 49, ff.183, 229.

[24] Shipps, 1971, pp.127-30; Gyford, 1996, pp.223-24, 265(#314). The money was to come from the income from the rent of what is now Barnardiston House (no.35 Chipping Hill). The terms are confused but seem to imply it was conditional on the inhabitants themselves providing for Sunday afternoon preaching.

[25] Conversations with Bill Cliftlands, c.1982-92 in 'Vic's nook' in one of the earlier manifestations of Essex Record Office; Cliftlands, 1987.

[26] Venn was uncertain about the Witham Wright's origins (*Alumni Cantabrigiensis*). His suggestion for him is too old (matric. 1585, M.A. 1592; the Witham Wright lived till 1668). Instead I decided his Francis Wright of Yorkshire, Queen's College (Cambridge) and Finchley, must have come to Witham after Finchley.

My explanations: (a) only one ordination of a Francis Wright in the diocese's Ordination Register 1601-28, i.e. November 1621, aged 25, born Ripon in Yorkshire, graduate of Queen's College (Guildhall MSS 9535A, 9535/2, f.225). (b) Francis Wright, M.A., appointed to Finchley in 1622. His signature in Finchley parish register is the same as the Witham Wright's signature of 1637 and 1642 (Guildhall MS 9628/4; P.R.O. SP 16/540(2)/237). (c) Finchley register has no entries in 1625, after which it recommences in a new format (now in Latin) (L.M.A. DRO 32/A1/1). Francis Wright, M.A., appointed to Witham 11 November 1625, and a new rector to Finchley a month later (P.R.O. E 331/12, m.14). Bishop was patron of both parishes (note the Bishop's Certificates (P.R.O. E 331), supplement gap (1621-25) in Bishop's Register (Guildhall 9531/14)). (d) Francis Wright, M.A., of Witham, was also rector of Wennington in 1626, proving the Witham man did have a degree, cementing link with earlier references (Rymer, 1726, p.670). May only have held Wennington briefly (E.R.O. T/A 547/1 is unclear).

Yorkshire: information kindly provided by John Hebden of Ripon Historical Society, and Bill Petchey, about nature of Ripon area; the former also gave baptism at Newby of Francis Wright son of Francis, Feb.4 1594 (Old Style).

[27] Collinson, 1982, pp.69, 94-95; Twigg, 1987, pp.42-43, 92-93 (there survive some lists of pupils of Queens' from these years, but they are incomplete and do not include Wright (information kindly provided by Dr.M.Milgate, archivist of Queens' College).

[28] L.M.A. DL/C/345, f.91; 'Liber Scholae Colcestriensis', p.257; Guildhall 9583/2, part 3, f.124v, 9628/4 (not quite clear whether Wright had rebuilt the whole house by 1637 or just the stable, but house seemed larger in 1637 (e.g. ten upper rooms), than in 1610 (probably 4 upper rooms)).

[29] P.R.O. C 93/16/2, 93/17/8, 93/45/38; E.R.O. D/P 30/25/3; E.R.O. D/ACW 11/264, 12/39.

[30] Cressy, 1980, p.171; Guildhall MS 9537/13/19v; Guildhall MS 9539A 1/7v, 1/12v; E.R.O. D/ACA 30, f.50 (gives John Totteridge, son of Thomas, in 1605). *Webb:* E.R.O. T/A 547; *Alumni Oxoniensis*; Shaw, ii, p.310; *C.J.* iii, p.32. Had left Braxted for Hertfordshire by 1642, but returned to visit in that year and was said to have spoken 'dangerous words against the Parliament', lavishly praising the bishops and urging their return (*True and perfect Diurnall*, p.8). He died 1669 leaving his rectory house in ruins and his wife impoverished, with 'noe visible estate' (B.L. Add. MSS. 1569-70; L.M.A. DL/C/345, ff.64, 90). *Halys and Totteridge:* E.R.O. D/ACA 30, f.50; L.M.A. DL/C/322, pp.81-82, 89, 96, DL/C/343, f.87. *Eatney:* E.R.O. D/ACA 48, ff.109v-110, ACA 49, f.14, ACA 52, f.34v; Guildhall MS 9539A 1/77v. Curate of Tollesbury 1640, nominated to Greenstead 1648 (*Alumni Cantabrigiensis*; Guildhall MS 9539A 1/114v). *Prost:* as curate (with Francis Wright), signed survey of vicarage property February 1638 (Guildhall MS 9628/4). No more

found about him in Witham. His father's will of 1637 mentions him (E.R.O. D/ACW 13/81).

[31] P.R.O. E 133/12, m.13 (appointment 13 November 1624). Entries in a new hand in the Terling parish register, which may or may not have been Weld's, begin 13 February 1625; registers were not always written by the incumbent (E.R.O. D/P 299/1/3). Several people have written about specific aspects of Weld's life in Essex, notably: Davids, 1863, pp.574-75; Davids, 'Weld', pp.405-407; Howell, 'Weld', pp.303-306; Wrightson and Levine, 1979 and 1995, esp. pp.137-39, 160-61, 179-80 (esp. role in Terling); Webster, 1997, esp. pp.188-90 (esp. re. suspension etc., on which subject we seem to have followed each other through the diocesan records). I have gratefully consulted these works but have also looked at the original sources throughout where possible and added more, so I have quoted from these sources where appropriate.

[32] *Alumni Cantabrigiensis*; Almack, 'Kedington', p.138; Collinson, 1982, pp.164, 184; Shipps, pp.72-104 (in 1629 Fairclough took the rectory of Kedington on the death of Abraham Gibson, former Witham curate); E.R.O. T/A 547; P.R.O. PROB 11/158/84/156, 11/168/82/298 (Joan Mildmay's parents were Sir Richard Deane, and Mary, nee Banks (deceased, Dame Katherine's sister)). E.R.O. D/P 299/1/3 (baptism of John Weld, 6 June 1625); P.R.O. PROB 11/163/25/205.

[33] Young, 1846, pp.511-14.

[34] Gyford, 1996, p.183 (re. coach); E.R.O. D/ACA 45, ff.179v-181. At other times Lea was said to be absent from church, frequenting other churches, not paying church rates, and again refusing to kneel at communion (E.R.O. D/ACA 46, ff.3v, 84v et al.)

[35] E.R.O. D/ACA 48, f.42, ACA 45, ff.179v-181, 194v-195, 201v.

[36] Out of the 18 men, no occupation was known for 12, indicating lack of status. The others were a butcher, a joiner, a husbandmen, two weavers, and a clothier. There were also 6 women. Of those with known ability, nearly three-quarters could sign names (H.L.R.O., Main Papers, H.L., 20 Jan.1641/2, petition box; E.R.O. D/ACW 7/152, 7/249, 9/128, 9/187, 22/159). *Pledger:* only suspect in Ship Money 1636 (P.R.O. SP 16/358/97-98); E.R.O. D/ALV 1, f.26, D/ALV 2, f.133v; L.M.A. DL/C/319, p.88; see chapter 11 for George Pledger. *Skinner:* E.R.O. D/DBw M27, 2 April 1627; E.R.O. D/ACA 46, f.84v, ACA 49, f.46v.

[37] E.R.O. D/ACW 5/127; R.Allen, 1606.

[38] E.R.O. D/ALV 1, ff.25v, 44v; E.R.O. D/ACA 45, ff.235, 248v, 303v, 320, 329; Cliftlands, 1987, p.157.

[39] E.R.O. D/ALV 1, ff.25v-26v, 44v.

[40] L.M.A. DL/C/338, ff.183v, 219 (conditions on such dispensations ensured sufficient attendance at the home parish church to incur obligation to pay tithes and rates, and to take parish office if asked); Collinson, 1982, pp.212-13, 249-50.

[41] E.R.O. D/ALV 1, ff.5v-26v.

[42] E.R.O. Q/SR 261/21; E.R.O. calendar of assize records.

[43] Q/SR 257/76-77 (discussed by Wrightson and Levine, 1979 and 1995, pp.137-39).

[44] Guildhall MS 9537/13, f.19; L.M.A. DL/C/624, p.415 (Webster, 1997, pp.188-89, does not mention the hearing of December 1628, and says that the Archdeacon's court hearing of June 1629 about Peters was the origin of Laud's knowledge of Weld, though the September 1628 reference is mentioned in a footnote); Young, p.513; Johnson, 1989-90, pp.293-95; E.R.O. D/ACW 9/179 (will of Thomas Bridges, Coggeshall clothier, father of Priscilla Gravener, John(3)'s wife).

[45] E.R.O. D/ACA 46, f.180, ACA 47, f.5; separate sheet with D/ACA 47 (dated last of June 1629); Guildhall MS 9531/15, f.21v; *D.N.B.*; P.R.O. SP 16/151/45; J.R.Smith, 1992, pp.28-30; Gyford, 1996, p.6.

[46] Massachusetts Historical Society, ii, 1931, pp.227, 336; E.R.O. D/ACA 47, ff.11v, 19, 92v, 94v, 105, 106v, ACA 48/29v; *Cal.S.P.Dom.* 1629-31, p.391; Guildhall MS 9531/15, f.23 (other such investigations in the diocese on ff.21-26, 38-41 passim); Young, 1846, pp.518-20; L.M.A. DL/C/322, pp.105, 113. Robert Mildmay's cousin Thomas Mildmay of Barnes in Springfield, married Alice or Agnes Winthrop, John Winthrop's aunt. The Barnardistons were also very distantly related to the Winthrops through the Cloptons of Suffolk, in that Dame Katherine's husband Sir Thomas was a half-cousin of Ann Clopton, wife of Sir William Clopton of Kentwell Hall, Long Melford (see appendix 2, pages 163-66). John Winthrop's short-lived second wife was the sister of another William Clopton, of Groton. The Melford and Groton Cloptons shared an early 16th-century ancestor, Sir William Clopton of Kentwell (died 1530). (*Visitations, Essex; D.N.B.;* Muskett, 1900).

[47] L.M.A. DL/C/319, pp.84-85, 89; Guildhall MS 9531/15, ff.23v-24v; E.R.O. D/ACA 48, ff.52, 61; D/P 299/1/3; Massachusetts Historical Society, ii, 1931, pp.58-60; Young, 1846, pp.521-22.

[48] Guildhall MS 9531/15, f.24v; E.R.O. D/ACA 48, ff.13v, 90 et al., 147v, 166-66v; L.M.A. DL/C/319, p.81. A Nathaniel Bosse was admitted again as curate of Terling in 1680; I do not know the relationship (Guildhall MS 9537/22, f.17v).

[49] L.M.A. DL/C/319, pp.81, 89; B.L. Harleian MS 4130, ff.81v, 88, 89 (pencilled numbers) (also quoted in Gardiner, 1886, pp.260, 264); B.L. Sloane MS 922, ff.90-93; Massachusetts Historical Society, iii, 1943, pp.93, 115, 128, 129, 245; Howell, 'Weld', p.306; Banks, 1930, p.96; N.E.H.G.S., *Register,* ii, p.53. Weld's son Edmund was baptised in Terling July 1631 (D/P 299/1/3). T.W.Davids suggested Weld was in Terling till end of March 1632, when Stalham arrived, because a change of handwriting in the parish register then (Davids 'Weld', p.405). Actually the writing had already changed in May 1630, though the new clerk had a rather similar hand to the former one (which had begun February 1625) and continued to write Thomas Weld's name on each page but in a different form. In any case various sources suggest non-clergy often wrote registers (e.g. Guildhall MS 9583/2, part 3, f.124).

[50] L.M.A. DL/C 319, p.81 (the name of the other neighbour is either illegible or not given. Webster, 1997, p.189, erroneously puts the 'neighbours' suggestion at the end of 1630 instead of December 1631, and has it coming from Weld himself as a defence; in fact the record does not indicate that Weld was present, and he had probably left the country by this time. It must in reality have been an attempt by the court to round up his associates for interrogation, probably unsuccessfully); B.L. Harleian MS 4130, f.90 (pencilled numbers) (also quoted in Gardiner, 1886, p.264).

[51] We know of Robert Gamlin elder and younger and their families in Roxbury, Massachusetts, from New England information. The elder had a daughter Mary with him, and the younger a wife Elizabeth and stepson, John 'Mayo' (Elizabeth's son) (N.E.H.G.S., *Register,* ii, p.53, iii, pp.92-93, iv, p.272, v, p.334, vi, p.183, xii, pp.274-75, 343, xxxv, pp.22, 241-42; Farmer, 1829, p.116). However, their British origins and emigration have been subject to writers quoting inaccurately from each other, causing two suspect traditions, i.e. (a) the two Robert Gamlins lived at East Malling in Kent at the time of their emigration, and (b) both sailed on the *William and Francis* with Thomas Weld in 1632. In fact note the following.

Re. Kent: contemporary notebook in 1640, published 1885, quotes 'John Mayo' formerly of 'Marroling in Kent', father of Thomas, and grandfather of John the emigrant (Lechford, 1885, pp.295-96). It does not give Thomas or John the emigrant themselves as being of Kent, but Pope in 1900 used it to say Thomas was of 'Marroling', and Banks in 1937 used Lechford and Pope to say Robert Gamlin and John Mayo the emigrant were of East Malling (Pope, 1900, p.180; Banks, 1937, p.81).

Re. the William and Francis: Winthrop's journal, put into print in 1908, gives arrival of ship in New England June 5 1632, having left London March 9, with about 60 passengers; he names only Messrs.Weld, Batchelor and Winslow (Hosmer, 1908, i, pp.80-81). A quite separate manuscript list in England, giving passengers awaiting departure from an unspecified place on an unspecified ship on March 7 1632, has been published several times (probably first by Drake in 1860 (Drake, 1860, p.11, also Hotten, 1874, p.149, Tepper, 1980, p.13). It includes an Edward Winslow and a Robert Gamlin (though not Weld or Batchelor). Because of Winslow, it has come to be assumed that this list names passengers on the *William and Francis,* e.g. Savage said Gamlin the younger was on it and possibly the elder, and Banks said both were there (Savage, ii, 1860, p.244; Banks, 1930, p.96).

I found (a) Robert Gamlin the younger and his stepson John Mayo lived in Coggeshall, Essex at the time of their emigration, and Robert the elder very probably in Terling, Essex (b) the elder Robert Gamlin could possibly have sailed with Weld on the *William and Francis,* the younger Robert and his wife and John Mayo went separately later. Explanation as follows.

Re. Essex: Robert Gamlin the younger and household: contemporary New England sources say John Mayo was aged eleven in 1640 and his father had been Thomas (N.E.H.G.S., *Register,* xxxv, pp.241-42, Lechford, 1885, pp.295-96). In Coggeshall, England, Thomas Mayhew married Elizabeth (23 September 1628); they had a son John (12 June 1629), then Thomas died (24 October 1629). Elizabeth married Robert Gamlin 31 January 1633 (E.R.O. D/P 36/1/1). *Robert Gamlin the elder:* the link with Essex is more tenuous. His only family emigrating was his daughter Mary (a 'gracious maiden' who died of smallpox 1633) (N.E.H.G.S., *Register*, xxxv, p.241). So he could be Robert Gamlin whose wife and daughter were buried Terling 22 March 1627 (wife of Goodman Gamblin) and 13 June 1628. There was a Thomas Gamlin in Terling also, but his wife was still alive after 1627 (E.R.O. D/P 299/1/3). *Both Roberts:* neither Robert Gamlin appears to be in the Ship Money returns in England dated 1636 (P.R.O. SP 16/358/97-98), which may help to support idea that they emigrated from Essex, though the returns only include the middling and upper ranks.

Re.emigration date: the manuscript list that may or may not relate to the *William and Francis* in 1632 only has one Robert Gamlin. Robert the younger married in Coggeshall several months after the *William and Francis* arrived in New England. A New England source describes the arrivals of the two Roberts differently, i.e. the elder 'in the year 1632', the younger 'the 20th of the 3d month' (no year, though a child was born to the latter 24th of 4th month 1634). Robert the elder was made freeman of Massachusetts 14 May 1634 (the same day as Thomas Hooker), and Robert the younger 3 September 1634 (N.E.H.G.S. *Register*, xxxv, pp.241-42, iii, pp.92-93).

[52] L.M.A. DL/C/319, pp.5-179, of which pp.83-90 relate to Witham; conversation with Bill Cliftlands. *Terling:* L.M.A. DL/C/319, pp.84-85 (12 people (including 5 couples) specifically, and p.89 which says 'all the aforesaid parties and their wives' were absent during some of August and September, could possibly include another 5 couples, including churchwardens William Baxter and William Haven). For Arthur Duck see *D.N.B.*

[53] *Garrard:* manor no.128; P.R.O. PROB 11/163/25/205. *Haven:* Besse, 1753, p.199 (gives William Havens and John Havens at a meeting broken up at Colchester in 1663); Fitch, *Quakers*, pp.55, 151 (other people called William Haven); in correlating these, note there were an elder and younger in Witham in 1640s (H.L.R.O., Main Papers, H.L., 20 Jan.1641/2, petition box, E.R.O. Q/SR 322/54). *Baxter:* nanor no.44 (part); P.R.O. PROB 11/163/25/205; E.R.O. D/ACD 7, f.101.

[54] E.R.O. D/ACA 48, ff.42, 83v, et al. Wright never went to court and the case was left to stand in November.

[55] Garrard relatives were Jerome (2) and his wife, Robert(2) (Jerome's son) and his wife, John(2) (Jerome's brother), Jeremiah Bromley (Jerome's brother-in-law), Thomas Bromley (Jerome's nephew) and his wife, (Gyford, 1996, p.187). Of the twelve men, there were two gentlemen/yeomen, four clothiers, one joiner, one cordwainer, one tallowchandler, and one alehousekeeper/teacher.

[56] L.M.A. DL/C/319, pp.251-53, 312-14, 339-41.

[57] E.R.O. D/ACA 48, ff.109v-110, ACA 49, f.14.

[58] E.R.O. D/ACA 48, ff.168, 195, and loose sheet in E.R.O. D/ACA 48.

[59] E.R.O. Acc.A9368; E.R.O. D/ACA 49, ff.190v, 206v, 225.

[60] E.R.O. Acc.A9368 (covering dates and courts have been written on the sheets since, but these are unreliable, as one, relating to the Archdeaconry, conflicts with the original heading, which gives Aylett as commissary). The 'mystery' list includes Mrs.Mayhew, widow, of Terling ('Mrs.' indicating some status), probably the Elizabeth whose husband Mr.Francis 'Maiow' was buried at Terling 7 May 1630. She remarried 3 October 1633 Mr.John Smith. Hence my suggested dating for the list as between 1630 and 1633 (E.R.O. D/P 299/1/3; E.R.O. D/ACA 49, ff.120, 133v, 151). No connection discovered with Coggeshall Mayhews discussed earlier re.Gamlins and Thomas Weld. *'Servants':* Christopher Banks (her cousin), John Biggs (her executor and husband of her cousin Ann), William Matthew (her 'ancientest servant') (P.R.O. PROB 11/158/84/156; 11/163/25/205). *Witham residents:* of those in 1636 Ship Money, all except three were above the median of 3s.(P.R.O. SP 16/358/97-98). Some craftsmen including three blacksmiths. Garrard family were Jerome(2), Robert(2) and Thomas Bromley. Four later signers of the Royalist petition (H.L.R.O., Main Papers, H.L., 4 Jan.1642/3).

[61] E.R.O. Acc.A9368 (contemporary heading gives Aylett as bishop's commissary). Not clear whether Aylett was levying the fines, or censuring non-payment of earlier fines. The twelve married couples all fined 4s. per couple, the three individuals 2s., and the rest 4s. About half had not paid, and half only paid part; no-one had paid in full. Of the 18 on the 1636 Ship Money, all except 3 were above the median of 3s. (those not on the assessment were probably absent, or had died, rather than being poor) (P.R.O. SP 16/358/97-98). Royalist petition included John Greene, John Markes, Jeffrey Whale (H.L.R.O., Main Papers, H.L., 4 Jan.1642/3). In addition Mrs.Ann Jenour earlier had the

Catholic Lord Petre of West Horndon as trustee of her marriage settlement (E.R.O. D/DP T177).

[62] E.R.O. D/ALV 2, f.133v; E.R.O. D/ACW 14/165. *Turner:* 4s. in 1636 Ship Money Witham (median 3s.) (P.R.O. SP 16/358/97-98); over £12 in specific bequests in his will, 1646 (E.R.O. D/ACW 14/165). *Allen and Skingley:* in Presbyterian 'classis', of 1647 (*Division*, 1648).

[63] E.R.O. D/ACA 50, ff.40, 138, ACA 51, f.6; E.R.O. D/ALV 2, f.25v; E.R.O. D/P 30/25/65; manor no.3.

[64] Wrightson and Levine, 1979 and 1995, pp.159-64; Smith, *History*, pp.37, 41, 43-46; *Summe of a Conference*, 1644; P.R.O. PROB 11/163/25/205; E.R.O. D/ACA 50, ff.137v, 138, 146v, 147 et al., 165v et al., ACA 51, ff.103v, 104; manor no.28.

[65] E.g.: E.R.O. Q/SR 177/97-98, 182/46, P.R.O. ASSI 35/50/2, 35/60/1, 35/67/4/11. Also note death and will of John Southcott, gentleman, of Little Totham, 1627 (E.R.O. D/ACA 45, f.109v and P.R.O. PROB 11/152/74).

[66] Knell, 'Southcott', p.9; E.R.O. D/ACA 49, f.158, ACA 50, f.137v, ACA 51, ff.6, 104, 248v et al.; E.R.O. Q/SR 284/10, 286/20, 293/37, 294/24, 294/28; Walter, 1996, pp.127-32.

[67] E.R.O. D/DU 465/1; E.R.O. D/ACA 52, ff.2, 84, ACA 54, ff.15v, 154v et al.; E.R.O. Q/SR 295/9, 305/25, 305/26, 307/38, 311/12, 313/38, 316/28; P.R.O. ASSI 35/80/3, 35/81/1, 35/81H, 35/83/3, 35/83/9, 35/84/2.

[68] *Cal.S.P.Dom.* 1633-34, p.328; P.R.O. SP 16/252/67, 67i, 67ii. Barrett's working history was as follows: an ordinary mariner for 19 years (of which 5 in Maldon and one in Wivenhoe) pressed into naval service for three years; about two years in the East Indies with the East India Company; two months in Suffolk; a summer living in Dover and working on a ship plying between there and Newcastle; then in Blackwall yard in London, for the East India Company again; lastly, about a week on some coal ships near Blackwall.

[69] E.R.O. Q/SR 222/11, 223/50, 233/125, 245/32, 255/28, 256/30, 256/78, 256/101.

[70] P.R.O. SP 16/261/10, 18v, 34, 39, 40v, 48v, 51v, 64v, 67v, 77v, 86v, 99, 128v, 192, 194v, 201v, 209v, 218v, 228, 231v, 236v, 277, 278v; P.R.O. SP 16/324/14, 16/324/20; *Cal.S.P.Dom.* 1634-35, pp.49, 114, 121, 126; *Cal.S.P.Dom.* 1635, pp.206, 214, 217; *Cal.S.P.Dom.* 1635-36, p.98; L.M.A. DL/C/319, pp.85, 87; E.R.O. D/ACA 50, f.146v et al., ACA 51, f.104 et al.; P.R.O. SP 16/251/40v.

[71] Bodleian MS Rawlinson A.128, ff.30, 34v-35 (also quoted in Gardiner, 1886, pp.280, 296); *D.N.B.*

[72] Bodleian MS Rawlinson A.128, f.38 (also quoted in Gardiner, 1886, pp.304); P.R.O. SP 16/261/18v, 39, 51v, 231v. *Alexander:* H.L.R.O., Main Papers, H.L., 20 Jan.1641/2 (petition box), and Jan.1642/3; unsuccessfully presented for absence from church 1639, no obvious ideological motive (E.R.O. D/ACA 53, f.217). *Parker:* E.R.O. Q/SR 286/36; father in bastardy case 1624 (E.R.O. D/ACA 44, f.120v; E.R.O. Q/SR 246/136); Ship Money 1636 at 4s. (Witham median 3s.); only known office, manorial aletaster 1625 (P.R.O. SP 16/358/97-98; E.R.O. D/DBw M27, 17 Oct.1625). *Greene:* P.R.O. PROB 11/144/78; Ship Money at £1, sixth highest in Witham (P.R.O. SP 16/358/97-98); E.R.O. Q/SR 265/64; H.L.R.O., Main Papers, H.L., 4 Jan.1642/3; *L.J.* vi, p.24. *Thursby:* gentleman in Witham 1633 (E.R.O. Q/SBa 2/17); 'late of Bocking now of Witham' 1634 (E.R.O. T/A 408 (transcript of B.L. Harl.MS.2240)); Ship Money 1636 at 8s. (P.R.O. SP 16/358/97-98); died in 1637 (L.M.A. DL/C/344, f.13v); Christopher's mortgage (E.R.O. D/DB T192); a Mrs.Thursby in Witham 1640s (E.R.O. Q/SR 318/49, 322/54). *Mootham:* In Ship Money in Witham in 1636, but no earlier references; died 1637 when father from Great Tey (P.R.O. SP 16/358/97-98; E.R.O. D/ACA 52, f.59v).

[73] E.R.O. T/A 547; Davids, 1863, pp.363, 521; B.L. Add.5829/38, quoted in Cliftlands, 1987, p.212.

[74] *Later sequestered:* Robert Senior of Feering, Thomas Stevens of South Hanningfield, John Woolhouse of West Mersea, Joseph Bird of Belchamp Otten. *Other compurgators:* Thomas Haggar of Tilbury by Clare (died before the sequestrations), Israel Edwards of East Mersea (kept his living until 1650) (*Alumni Cantabrigiensis;* Smith, *History*, pp.58, 111-12, 115, 118, 125-27, 153-55, 302, 313, 386-87, 408; Smith, 'Sequence', pp.37, 51, 85, 97-98; Davids, 1863, pp.301, 348-51, 391); P.R.O. SP 16/261/228, 231v, 277.

[75] P.R.O. SP 16/351/100; Guildhall MS 9537/15, f.15, 9628/4. *Skingley and Bunting:* 16s. and 18s. respectively in 1636 Ship Money (P.R.O. SP 16/358/97-98); Gyford, 1996, p. 74; E.R.O. D/ACA 48, f.127 et al. *Skingley:* evidence to Parliament against Royalist clergyman Edward

Strutt of Faulkbourne, 1644, witnessed will of 'schismatic' Solomon Turner, one of the Presbyterian 'classis' 1647 (E.R.O. D/ACW 14/165; *Division*, 1648). *Prost:* Guildhall MS 9628/4; Webster, 1994, p.2; E.R.O. T/R 91, p.89; *L.J.* vi, p.24. *Plague:* Gyford, 1996, pp.6-8.

[76] E.R.O. D/ACA 45, ff.180v (John Hasleby, cooper), ACA 51, f.174 (Francis Mitchell, tailor); ACA 52, f.255v (Henry Wood, clothier). Even these individual drunkards included three men in 1636 Ship Money (Hasleby and Mitchell, 1s., and Wood 4s; Wood was an enemy of Jerome Garrard(2), so it was possibly a personally inspired accusation) (P.R.O. SP 16/358/97-98).

[77] E.R.O. D/ABA 9, f.4v.

[78] Manor no.137; E.R.O. D/ACA 52, f.255v, ACA 53, ff.3, 74v, 119-119v, ACA 54, f.73; Wrightson, 1996, p.29.

[79] E.R.O. D/ACA 40, ff.84 et al., 216 et al, ACA 43, ff.57, 61, ACA 44, f.92 et al., ACA 45, f.37v et al., f.93v et al., ACA 54, ff.21-21v, 34-34v, 65; E.R.O. Q/SR 236/31, 245/32, 271/10; E.R.O. D/ALV 1, f.26 et al. Other suspects were Thomas Peachie, probably a weaver (E.R.O. D/ACW 12/245), John White, Robert White, who sold cherries on Sunday 1635 (E.R.O. D/ACA 50, f.211), Lewis Williams, a tailor.

[80] Manor nos.140, 134; E.R.O. D/ACA 54, ff.21v-22. At this time there were two Jerome Greenes, probably both husbandmen, one said to live 'at the pond' and the other 'on the hill' (the latter probably the site now no.39 Chipping Hill). Another Jerome Greene of Witham died in 1626, referring to four other men of the same name in his will, but with no information on relationships between them (E.R.O. Q/SR 318/49; manor nos.133, 135 (135 had probably been sold to the Barnardiston charity by this time); E.R.O. D/ACW 10/216; Guildhall MS 9628/4).

[81] P.R.O. SP 16/327/101; E.R.O. D/ACA 53, ff.217v-218, 233.

[82] E.R.O. Q/SR 311/46-51; Cliftlands, 1987, pp.149-51; Walter, lectures, 1994; Walter, lecture, 1995; L.M.A. DL/C/319 p.85; E.R.O. Q/SR 326/10; E.R.O. Q/SBa 2/41; P.R.O. PC 2/52/699-700.

[83] Underdown, 1993, especially pp.24-26, 40, 43, 58-59, 103, 130, 138, 147-55, 173-55, 186-87; Wrightson, 1980, pp.39-46.

[84] Manning, 1991, pp.7-47; E.R.O. T/A 547; information on Lucas kindly supplied by Pat Lewis; Grace, 1996, pp.97-119; Shipps, 1971, pp.142-43, 216-42, 258-66, 288-99, 319-23, 333; Wrightson and Levine, 1979 and 1995, pp.160, 175-78, 180-82, 186-220 (the latter a discussion of more recent writing, in the 1995 edition only); Underdown, 1993, especially pp.24-26, 40, 43, 58-59, 103, 130, 138, 147-55, 173-75, 186-87; *Cal.S.P.Dom.* 1635, p.100, quoted in Shipps, 1971, pp.92, 201; J.A.Sharpe, 1977, p.108; Johnson, 1989-90, pp.309-10; Ingram, 1984, pp.1-9; Petchey, 1991, pp.231-35; Shipps, 1971, p.319.

[85] In the 1636 Ship Money assessment as a whole, most of the Witham people even with lower assessments displayed one or more signs of respectability or a settled life. Others, perhaps the same number again, were not listed at all, as being too poor (though criteria are not known). *Re. the 45 people at the lowest end of the assessment (1s.to 2s.):* For none of them is there a surviving reference as a pauper. Over a quarter are known to have been able to sign their name. A half held property by leasehold or freehold (usually the latter). 80 per cent had one or more of the following attributes:- property; parish office; their own business; ownership of goods worth over £20 in total, or a horse, or a gold ring. With the addition of two more criteria, i.e. liability to pay rates or to provide labourers for parish road repairs, the proportion reaches over 90 per cent. People assessed at 1s. did not differ much from those at 2s. in these respects. All the figures for these matters would be higher in reality, i.e. if there were more surviving records, and/or if the people had lived longer; nearly a sixth of them died during the four years after the 1636. (P.R.O. SP 16/358/97-98; other information from various sources).

[86] Names from P.R.O. SP 16/358/97-98; for occupations see Gyford, 1996, p.11. *Office holders, i.e. names in capitals:* at one time magistrates, half-hundred officials, churchwardens, parish officers acting against Jane Earle for not going to church in 1641, sequestrators (1643), signatories to alehouse return (1644), and/or in classis (1647). *Qualifications for Royalist column:* suspected of supporting or associating with vicar Francis Wright, collecting arms for Henry Nevill in 1642, being a royalist, or being a Catholic; having name on 'royalist' petition of 1643. *Qualifications for appearing in the 'Parliamentarian' column:* churchwarden acting against authorities; parish officer acting against Jane Earle 1641; signatory to alehouse return 1644; witness to will of Solomon Turner, 'schismatic', 1646; in classis 1647; associate of Dame Katherine Barnardiston; accused of gadding to Terling church, wearing hat in church, not kneeling or standing at right part of church service, or sleeping in

church; witness against vicar Francis Wright in court; signer or maker of own mark on Parliamentarian petition of 1642 (names which were entered in by someone else, i.e 'forged' have been ignored).

[87] Collinson, 1982, pp.104, 185; Cliftlands, 1987; J.A.Sharpe, 1986, pp.253-73.

[88] Richard Deane and Sir Robert Titchborne (*D.N.B.*; Guildhall Noble Collection C78). See appendix 2 (pages 163-66) for their relationship to Dame Katherine Barnardiston, and for information about the role of her other relatives.

Chapter 10: the Long Parliament and the Civil War

[1] I am most grateful to David Appleby for many helpful comments on this chapter, and also for past assistance. The literature on the history of the Civil War period is vast. For the background to this chapter, I have particularly used: Cliftlands, 1987; Holmes, 1974; Manning, 1991; Morrill, 1980; Morrill ,1991, especially chapters by J.Morrill and J.Walter; Reay, 1985, pp.81-100; J.A.Sharpe, 1986; J.A.Sharpe, 1987, (quotation from p.17); Wrightson, 1988.

[2] *L.J.* v, pp.506-507; Holmes, pp.224-25; B.L. Thomasin Tract E88(15); Morrill, pp.57, 73, 85-87.

[3] Clarke, *Siege*, pp.5-6; Penn, 1888; *L.J.* x, pp.373-74; *Cal.S.P.Dom.* 1648-49, p.121. Declarations from Essex about the army include: *New Found Stratagem*, 1647; *Declaration of the Army*, 1647; *Letters from Saffron Walden*, 1647; *To the Right Honorable ... Sir Thomas Fairfax*, 1647. A contemporary Royalist account of the Second Civil War is Carter, 1650 (also 2nd edition, 1789).

[4] *D.N.B.*; Guildhall Noble Collection C78. Deane died in a naval battle against Dutch, 1653. Sir Robert Titchborne sentenced to death in 1660 after the Restoration, but with others reprieved and imprisoned. See appendix 2 (pages 163-66) for relationship to Dame Katherine. I have avoided using the technical terms for the various periods which I understand are as follows: *Interregnum:* 1649-60, between the reigns of the two Charles's; *Commonwealth:* sometimes used for Interregnum but was technically only 1649-53, between execution of King and the Protectorate; *Protectorate:* 1653-59 when the Cromwells were Protectors.

[5] *C.J.* ii, pp.21, 54; Shaw, 1900, ii, pp.175-79, 184-204; Morrill, 1991, p.56.

[6] Davids, 1863, pp.214-16; *Division*, 1648.

[7] Holmes, 1974, pp.22-23, 26; H.L.R.O., Main Papers, H.L., 20 Jan.1641/2, petition box; *L.J.* iv, p.523; *Declaration ... illegall Writt*, 1642. Hull, 1950, p.554, gives c.19,000 households in 'rural' Essex in 1662 Hearth Tax, and I have estimated about 1,950 in the towns that he didn't count as rural (Colchester, Harwich and Dovercourt, Maldon, Saffron Walden, Thaxted and Brightlingsea. Resulting total c.21,000 households in 1662, so c.20,000 in the 1640s, and so perhaps c.100,000 people. Note that Great Bentley is not included in the 1662 return at all (E.R.O. Q/RTh 1).

[8] P.R.O. SP 16/491/77; B.L.Egerton MS. 2651, ff.118-19.

[9] Morrill, 1980, pp.34-35; Walter, 1991, pp.109-110, 121; Walter, 1996, pp.132-38; Morant, *Colchester*, 1768, p.54; Ryves, 1971, pp.124-29, 133-154, 226-28; *L.J.* v, pp.318, 331, 365, 388, vi, p.19; Walter, lectures, 1994; *Declaration ... appeasing*, 1642; E.R.O. Q/SBa 2/47. John Walter's study of these attacks and their background is hopefully to be published soon (*Colchester Plunderers*, C.U.P.).

[10] *Attack: Cal.S.P.Dom.* 1671-72, p.58; P.R.O. SP 29/295/100 (or 112) (in this, over 20 years afterwards, Bayles puts the date as St.Bartholomew's day and the day after the Lucas attack, but St.Bartholomew's is 24 August, 2 days after the date given by Morant for the Lucas affair); *C.J.* ii, p. 881; personal communications from John Walter. Note that Hunt mistakenly gives Bayles as minister of Witham and the date as December (Hunt, 1983, p.306). *Bayles' past:* made magistrate by the King c.1641, removed by Parliament 1642 (P.R.O. ASSI 35/83/9/83, 35/83/3/65, 35/84/2/41, 35/85/5; E.R.O. Q/SR 144/27, 147/13, 158/20, 314/139, 318/161, 319/118). Name on 'Royalist' petition of 1643, not on pro-Parliament one of 1642 (B.L.Egerton MS. 2651, ff.118-19; H.L.R.O., Main Papers, H.L., 20 Jan.1641/2, petition box; and 4 Jan.1642/3). *Southcott connections:* Bayles represented Witham's vicar and churchwardens at Chancery hearing re.a charity, c.1639, and some of the documents were said to have been discovered amongst Southcott family papers (E.R.O. D/P 30/25/3; P.R.O. C 93/16/2, 93/17/8). He was one of valuers for probate re.John Southcott 1637; the other three were prominent Witham Puritans

(E.R.O. D/DU 465/1). In 1650, seems to have been both agent of Southcotts and lessee of their estates in Surrey, after sequestration by Parliament (*Cal.Cttee.for Compounding*, iii., pp.1935-37). *After 1660: Cal.S.P.Dom.* 1671-72, p.58; P.R.O. SP 29/295/100 (or 112). *Earlier Bayles c.1600:* E.R.O. Q/SR 144/27, 147/13, 158/20; E.R.O. D/ACA 22, ff.266, 269v, 280, 285, 291, 331 et al, ACA 25, ff.110, 115, 138, 148 et al., 158; L.M.A. DL/C/618, p.304. See chapter 6. The earlier Thomas Bayles was called a 'recusant' but possibly only his wife and servants were. Was said to be 'now of Ulting' in 1600 but this was temporary.

[11] *Cal.S.P.Dom.* 1641-43, p.377; P.R.O. SP 16/491/128. The magistrates were Thomas Bendish and George Gent.

[12] Morrill, 1980, pp.55-56, 68; Quintrell, 1962; *Acts & Ords. of Interr.,* i., pp.85-91, 106-110, 168-70, 223-29, 291-92; B.L.Thomasin Tract E65(9); *L.J.* v, p.632-33; *Visitations, Essex,* p.339; Howard, 1888, p.339; Walter, 1991, pp.112-13; Wrightson, 1988, pp.154-55; Morrill, 1980, pp.118-19, 121. Information about Jeremy Aylett's residence kindly provided by Reverend David Nash. After Aylett's release from prison, there was a further property dispute, about which he complained of being 'many times drawn up to London from the public service, to his no small trouble, vexation and charge'. He found this even more troublesome when he became a member of the Essex County Committee (*L.J.* vi, pp.173, 193, 204, 223, 374, 548, 609; *C.J.* iii, p.231; Hist.MSS.Com. 4, *5th Rep. House of Lords,* p.104; Hist.MSS.Com. 5, *6th Rep. House of Lords,* p.16).

[13] P.R.O. ASSI 35/83/3/65, 35/84/2/41, 35/85/5, 35/88/4/15, 35/91/8/49, 35/98/2/26, 35/99/1/32; D.H.Allen, 1974, p.xxvii; E.R.O. Q/SR 330/45-46, 330/64, 332/34, 332/68, 335/34, 337/41, 345/79, 346/54, 350/45, 352/94, 354/48, 355/50, 356/48, 356/92, 360/42, 360/74, 361/58, 363/21-23, 366/78, 367/55, 369/74, 370/50, 371/37, 376/51, 376/54-55, 377/47; D/P 107/1/1. Information about Aylett's memorial kindly provided by Reverend David Nash.

[14] P.R.O. ASSI 35/85/5/58 et al.; P.R.O. PROB 11/163/25, 11/246/163; Bodleian MS Rawlinson Essex 6, f.125; Bodleian MS Rawlinson Essex 22, f.155; E.R.O. Q/SBa 2/65, 2/67 (show Arthur Barnardiston collecting depositions from Upper Yeldham and from Bocking); E.R.O. Q/SR 323/83, 327/60, 331/49, 338/30, 338/31, 344/52, 350/113, 358/72 (recognisances signed by him for people from Gosfield, Castle Hedingham, Bocking, Lamarsh, Toppesfield, Finchingfield, Stisted, Gestingthorpe, Little Maplestead and Halstead, in 1644-51 and 1653); E.R.O. Q/SR 351/90, 351/62-63, 356/44, 357/46, 357/47 (recognisances signed by him for people from Terling, Boreham, Hatfield Peverel and Witham in 1653); E.R.O. D/Y 2/7, pp.35, 39, 189; *D.N.B.*; Almack, 'Kedington', p.138; Shipps, 1971, p.94; Underwick, ii, p.365.

[15] E.R.O. calendar of assize records; E.R.O. Q/SBa 2/53.

[16] *Brooke:* E.R.O. calendar of assize records; *Exact and True Diurnal,* 1642, pp.6, 8; *True and perfect Diurnall,* 1642, p.6; E.R.O. D/ACW 14/275; B.L. Egerton MS. 2651, ff.138-39; E.R.O. D/ACW 15/203; E.R.O. D/DBw M85; E.R.O. D/DBw M28 (25 April 1656). *Starke:* Robinson appeared on the 1643 'peace' petition. See chapter 11 for Richard Swinborne. *Bunny:* H.L.R.O., Main Papers, H.L., 4 Jan.1642/3; some family connection between William and Robert Bunny but details unclear (E.R.O. D/ACW 12/39). *Mootham:* P.R.O. SP 16/261/18v; E.R.O. D/ACW 11/238; E.R.O. D/ACA 52, f.59v; E.R.O. D/DBw M28 (29 April 1656, 13 Dec.1659).

[17] Roberts, 1989, pp.12-13 (thanks to David Appleby for this reference); H.L.R.O., Main Papers, H.L., 8 June 1642; *L.J.* v, pp.143, 445; B.L.Egerton MS. 2651, f.123; Grieve, 1994, pp.55-60; *Instructions agreed,* 1642; *Declaration.... his Maiesties Proclamation,* 1642; Holmes, p.94; P.R.O. SP 28/129, pt.4; E.R.O. Q/SR 326/10 (reference from Bill Cliftlands).

[18] E.R.O. Q/SBa 2/78; P.R.O. PROB 11/248/317; E.R.O. Q/SO 1, f.13v; E.R.O. D/ACW 18/226, 19/219; E.R.O. D/ACAc 2, ff.21, 75v; E.R.O. D/P 30/1/1. Another more prosperous Thomas White was in Witham, but unlikely he would have been a foot soldier; he was a ratepayer, sometimes called yeoman, could sign, was son-in-law of blacksmith John Adcock, from whom White's children inherited the forge and other property. One Thomas had a two-hearth house 1662-73 (probably this one), the other died 1672 (probably the soldier) (E.R.O. Q/SR 318/49, 366/78; E.R.O. D/ACW 16/71; P.R.O. PROB 11/236/166; E.R.O. D/DBw M28, 17 Sept.1669; E.R.O. Q/RTh 1/29, 5/18, 8/9, 9/7).

[19] E.R.O. Q/SR 322/74, 322/115-16, 323/80. *Coe:* also in trouble later 1638 for not receiving the Communion at Easter; this dismissed as he had been in Suffolk with his father (E.R.O. D/ACA 53, ff.119, 133,

217). His cottage in Mill Lane was north of 'Holleways' (Gyford, 1996, p.164). *Goulston:* B.L. Egerton MS. 2651, ff.138-39. Not found in Witham before 1643. May have lived in Blunts Hall area; owned land in that manor and in Hatfield Peverel. One report has him leasing Witham tithes, but others say this was John Goulston (E.R.O. D/P 30/28/14, 12 April 1669, 8 Jan.1691; manor no.19; Fowler, 1911, p.5; Guildhall MS 12737; L.P.L. MS COMM XII a/8, a/12). 7 hearths in 1662, 5 in 1670 and 1673. Lent £60 to Thomas Nethercoate, Witham clothier, some time before 1651. Trustee of Newland Street almshouses and Barnardiston charity. Later witnessed wills of Quaker John Freeborne (1674), and vicar Thomas Cox (1675) (E.R.O. Q/RTh 1/29, 5/18, 8/9, 9/7; P.R.O. PROB 11/218/193; E.R.O. D/P 30/25/67-68, 30/25/42; E.R.O. D/ACW 18/328, 19/20).

[20] *L.J.* v, p.529; H.L.R.O., Main Papers, H.L., 4 Jan.1642/3; *Humble Petition,* 1642/3. Many thanks to John Walter for pointing this petition out.

[21] B.L.Egerton MS. 2651, ff.138-39. Thanks to David Appleby for discussing this episode and explaining that it was not unknown for prosperous Royalists and Catholics to pull strings in this way.

[22] *Cal.Cttee.for Money,* ii, p.622.

[23] P.R.O. SP 16/350/54, 16/76/13i-ii; SP 16/54/47; Gyford, 1996, p.68; P.M.Ryan, 1993, pp.14-17; *Exact and True Diurnal,* 1642, pp.6, 8; *True and perfect Diurnall,* 1642, pp.6, 8 (refers to message from 'Waltham' in Essex, September 1642, but said to be 3 miles from Cressing Temple, so must mean Witham); P.R.O. E 401/2322; Guildhall MS 9537/13/19v, 9539A 1/7v; H.L.R.O., Main Papers, H.L., 20 Jan.1641/2, petition box; and 4 Jan.1642/3; *Cal.Cttee.for Compounding,* ii, p. 863; *C.J.* ii, pp.814, 953; Holmes, 1974, pp.38, 247. *William Brooke:* E.R.O. D/ACW 14/275; E.R.O. calendar of assize records, 1626-47. *Hinde Goodale:* E.R.O. D/DBw M27, 17 Oct.1625, 17 April 1626, 12 April 1627; E.R.O. Q/SR 318/49.

[24] E.R.O. D/DDc T81; E.R.O. D/DBw M85. Alleged that missing rolls caused next steward to treat Chipping and Newland as one manor in error, because of absence of previous examples. Distinction important to entry fines (Gyford, 1996, p.66). John Walter suggests allegations about confiscation of manorial records may arise from propaganda, and possibly instead there had been no courts whilst the lord was absent (Walter, 1991, p.112). Most of the Witham rolls back to 1604 were already missing by 1656 (E.R.O. D/DBw M26-28, M86).

[25] Morris, 1872, pp.388-96. The Earl of Essex had died in 1646 and had for several years been separated from his second wife Elizabeth (*D.N.B.*).

[26] Morris, 1872, pp.398-99; *Cal.Cttee.for Compounding,* iii, pp.1935-37 (Bill Cliftlands kindly pointed out the reason for the Southcotts' smaller sequestration figure); P.R.O. E 112/178/96; E.R.O. Q/RRp 1, m.3.

[27] E.R.O. Q/SR 316/66, 317/68, 318/62, Easter, Midsummer and Michaelmas 1642 (last Witham recognisances signed by Sir Benjamin Ayloffe, Henry Nevill and Sir Thomas Wiseman respectively); *C.J.* ii, pp.941-42; *Aylett letters,* 1908, introduction and letters i, iv.

[28] *Cal.Cttee.for Compounding,* ii, pp.848-49; *Aylett letters,* 1908, letters i, iii.

[29] Cliftlands, 1987, pp.195-97, 377-80; Walter, 1991, p.113; *C.J.* ii, p.54; Shaw, 1900, ii, pp.177-78; Notestein, 1923, p.261.

[30] E.R.O. Q/SBa 2/45; E.R.O. Q/SR 315/76. See Gyford, 1996, p.56 for Jane Earle, and pp.155-56 for John Freeborne. Posts of the men are unspecified; Robert Garrard(2) and Philip Pledger named first so perhaps churchwardens. *Cage:* 19th-century site corner of Mill Lane; whether here also in 17th century unkown (E.R.O. T/P 116/83; Chelmsford Library ZP 025.175).

[31] E.R.O. D/ACA 54, ff.21, 44 et al. *John Freeborne:* Penney, 1907, p.97. *William Freeborne:* Gyford, 1996, pp.6, 234(#21-22); Hotten, 1874, pp.279, 281; N.E.H.G.S. *Register,* iii., p.93, Stratton, 1951, pp.190-91.

[32] H.L.R.O., Main Papers, H.L., 20 Jan.1641/2, petition box (the parishes not named, so only identifiable from the people's names); Holmes, 1974, p.26; P.R.O. PC 2/43/442, 456.

[33] E.R.O. Q/RTh 9/7; P.R.O. SP 16/358/97-98, 16/261/18v; Carlson, 1995, p.172. Petitioners seem to have been householders; for instance widows and single women included but not married women. Order of names does not indicate a walk down the street. Alexander signed whilst Parker's name was written in.

[34] The proportions of petitioners who appeared the Ship Money returns of 1636 were as follows (overall median assessment for the Ship Money was 3 shillings): 44 % of those who signed (median 4 shillings), 15 % of those making marks (median 2 shillings), 15 % of those whose names were written in (median 2 shillings); (all the figures appear rather low;

there were an above-average number of deaths between 1636 and 1641, probably due to plague (P.R.O. SP 16/358/97-98); Gyford, 1996, pp.6-7, 12). Of the names written in, 12 (12 %) are known to have been paupers and/or were later exempted from paying the 1673 Hearth Tax (E.R.O. Q/RTh 9/7).

35 H.L.R.O., Main Papers, H.L., 4 Jan.1642/3; Davids, 1863, pp.51, 252, 262, 449-50, 522. Fewer than half of the petitioners were in 1636 Ship Money. For these, median assessment was 3s.6d./4s.(parish median was 3s.) (P.R.O. SP 16/358/97-98). *Paupers:* E.R.O. Q/SR 322/54 (William Allen, butcher); E.R.O. D/ACA 50, f.190v (Nicholas Greene); E.R.O. D/ACA 54, f.65 (Thomas Peachie).

36 *On both petitions and better off:* included Thomas Parker (yeoman, 11s. in Ship Money); grocer William Robinson (will-writer, 5 hearths 1662; for some reason not in Ship Money) (P.R.O. SP 16/358/97-98; P.R.O. PROB 11/248/317; E.R.O. D/ACW 9/128-18/36 passim). *On both petitions and poor (all marks on earlier petition):* William Allen (butcher) (E.R.O. Q/SR 322/54); Thomas Peachie (weaver) (E.R.O. D/ACA 54, f.65); Henry Pickett the younger (weaver) (E.R.O. Q/RTh 5/18). *On both petitions, otherwise known for drink and disorder, marks or written in on earlier petition:* Rooke Allen (husbandman/victualler) (E.R.O. Q/SR 210/83, 245/31, 376/54; E.R.O. D/ACA 37, f.102v); William Purcas (bricklayer) (E.R.O. Q/SR 236/31, 245/31, 271/10; E.R.O. D/ACA 43/57, ACA 45/37v; E.R.O. D/ALV 1, f.26); William Revell (tailor/victualler) (P.R.O. ASSI 35/62/1-2, 35/63/1, in Cockburn, 1982; E.R.O. D/ACA 40, f.215v, ACA 46, f.22v). *John and Nicholas Greene:* E.R.O. Q/SR 313/33, 359/26; E.R.O. D/ACA 50, ff.176v, 190v; Gyford, 1996, p.159.

37 E.R.O. Q/SR 315/68; Davids, 1863, p.218; H.L.R.O., Main Papers, H.L., 1 May 1643, Sequestration Order, 6 April 1643 (says Wright 'not preached in [Witham] church for the space of twelve Monthes last past'); White, 1643, p.26; Smith, *History*, p.129. *John Heron:* ordained 1635, then curate in Suffolk. By August 1640 curate of Moze, north-east Essex, son baptised there October 1641. Vicar of Kirby le Soken nearby 1645, stayed after Restoration, died there 1679. Also known as Hearne. Only Witham connection found was 1643 petition (*Alumni Cantabrigiensis*; E.R.O. T/A 547; Davids, 1863, p.299; E.R.O. D/P 285/1/1). *Carter Lane:* P.R.O. SP 16/540(2)/237; P.R.O. PROB 11/69/6/24. Much recommended City of London Youth Hostel now in same street (good-value restaurant open to non-members).

38 B.L.Egerton MS. 2651, ff.138-39; H.L.R.O., Main Papers, H.L., 23 June 1660, Petition of Francis Wright; H.L.R.O., Main Papers, H.L., 1 May 1643, Sequestration Order, 6 April 1643; *C.J.* iii, p.32; White, 1643, p.26.

39 H.L.R.O., Main Papers, H.L., 29 April & 1 May 1643; *L.J.* vi, pp.15, 21, 24; Cliftlands, 1987, pp.251, 360; P.R.O. PROB 11/163/25; P.R.O. SP 16/261/57, 16/261/231v; H.L.R.O., Main Papers, H.L., 4 Jan.1642/3; B.L. Egerton MS. 2651, ff.138-39; Guildhall MS 9628/4; E.R.O. D/ACW 13/81; T.Webster, 1994, p.2; E.R.O. D/ACA 47, ff.119, 129v, 140v; Davids, 1863, p.521.

40 H.L.R.O., Main Papers, H.L., 1 May 1643, Sequestration Order, 6 April 1643; Smith, *History*, pp.44-49, 53; P.R.O. SP 16/351/100; L.P.L. MS COMM vol. XII a/8; Smith, 'Sequence', pp.71-72; *Alumni Oxoniensis*; Smith, *History*, pp.303, 383; Davids, 1863, p.519. *Rowles:* formerly Jesus College, Oxford, rectory of Wavendon, Buckinghamshire. *Ludgater:* probably from Wales; rector of Great Birch 1643.

41 *Brewer:* E.R.O. Q/SBa 6/8; E.R.O. D/ACW 16/20. *Halys:* E.R.O. D/ACW 15/85; *Rowles:* P.R.O. PROB 11/225/27. *Ludgater:* P.R.O. PROB 11/263/147; E.R.O. D/ACW 16/111, 16/114.

42 H.L.R.O., Main Papers, H.L., 1 May 1643, Sequestration Order, 6 April 1643; Walter, 1991, p.113; P.R.O. SP 16/358/97-98. *William Allen:* two Witham men of this name, the other, a butcher, being 'poor' 1644, so not the sequestrator (E.R.O. Q/SR 318/49, 322/54).

43 Cliftlands, 1987, p.251; H.L.R.O., Main Papers, H.L., 4 Jan.1642/3; D.H.Allen, 1974, p.181; E.R.O. Q/SBa 2/81.

44 H.L.R.O., Main Papers, H.L., 20 Jan.1641/2, petition box; H.L.R.O., Main Papers, H.L., 4 Jan.1642/3. *Parker:* three times in Archdeacon's court 1636-40, not receiving Communion, letting servants plough in service time, and not paying rates (dismissed each time) (E.R.O. D/ACA 51, f.104, ACA 53, f.102v, ACA 54, f.143). *Burchard:* E.R.O. D/ACW 11/80, 11/264, 14/194; Gyford, 1996, pp.254-55(#89). *Skingley:* E.R.O. D/ACA 48, f.127 et al. Gave evidence to Parliament against Royalist clergyman Edward Strutt of Faulkbourne 1644, witnessed will of 'schismatic' Solomon Turner 1646, in Presbyterian

'classis' 1648 (E.R.O. D/ACW 14/165; *Division*, 1648). Re.Fordham see P.R.O. PROB 11/218/193, 11/290/208. *Allen:* E.R.O. D/ACW 14/165; E.R.O. calendar of assize records; E.R.O. D/P 107/1/1. *John Freeborne:* E.R.O. Q/SR 317/68; Gyford, 1996, pp.254-55(#89).

45 Guildhall MS 9583/2, part 3, f.124 (in 1664 previous font had been 'spoyled', no reason given); *Cal.S.P.Dom.* 1648-49, p.121; Grieve, 1994, pp.61-67, 72-80; Storey, 1994; Ralph, 1947; Macfarlane, 1976, pp.282, 422, 428, 433-34, 447, 452. *Johnson:* 'Goodman Johnson' accommodated meetings in Earls Colne March 1647, September 1648, about to leave the parish 1648 so possibly to Witham (Macfarlane, 1976, pp.89, 138). 'Cousin Johnson' visited Josselin September 1651 ('cosin' not necessarily a cousin in modern sense) (p.256). Witham's Edward Johnson first mentioned in the town 1662 (E.R.O. Q/RTh 1/29). Had grandchildren when died 1669. Josselin not mentioned in his will (E.R.O. D/P 30/1/1; E.R.O. D/ACW 18/26; note that the registered version of latter, D/ACR 8/140, only contains half the will). Some references to people called Edward Johnson in Earls Colne 1630s, 1651, and 1680s (T/P 271).

46 E.R.O. Q/SBa 6/8/11 (John Gravener(3) did not sign); Davids, 1863, pp.214-16; *Division*, 1648 (Witham half-hundred part of the 'Fourteenth Classis' of Essex which also included Thurstable and Winstree hundreds, and borough of Colchester borough); Shaw, 1900, ii, pp.429-30. *Risbridge classis and Dame Katherine Barnardiston:* Sir Nathaniel and Sir Thomas Barnardiston (her stepson and stepgrandson), Sir William and John Soame of Little Thurlow and Little Bradley respectively (her nephew and great nephew); ministers included Richard Blackerby of Great Thurlow, and Samuel Fairclough of Barnardiston and Kedington.

47 E.R.O. Q/SBa 6/8/11, Q/SBa 2/58; Wrightson and Levine, 1979 and 1985, p.116; E.R.O. D/ACA 54, ff.21v-22; E.R.O. Q/SR 328/44, 329/62, 360/42, 360/74, 363/9, 363/16, 363/23, 365/50; P.R.O. ASSI 35/87/2, 35/88/9, 35/92/2, 35/94/1, 35/94/T, 35/95/2. Richard Earmesby's will of 1662 shows that he still had the Blue Anchor in Heybridge then (E.R.O. D/ACW 16/182). *Fairs:* P.R.O. C 66/2063, no.3. In August 1669 the lord of the manor wanted to revive the fairs and wrote that 'they have beene discontinued about 30 yeares yett some Inhabitants doe remember what dayes they were kept the one being on Holyrood day', i.e. 14 September (E.R.O. D/DBw M85, 14 Aug.1669).

48 E.R.O. Q/SR 318/49, 322/54, 349/26. *Surveyors:* all signed the Royalist 'peace' petition of 1643 (H.L.R.O., Main Papers, H.L., 4 Jan.1642/3).

49 E.R.O. D/P 30/25/67. *Surveyors:* still about 1652, prosperous enough to be eligible. Whale died c.1654 (P.R.O. PROB 11/236/183). Robinson continued in various roles. As seen, Alexander Freeborne became master of the Chelmsford House of Correction 1660. *Graveners:* Gyford, 1996, pp.201-202. *Skingley:* see earlier. *Petition:* H.L.R.O., Main Papers, H.L., 20 Jan.1641/2, petition box; brewer Thomas Barker signed, fathers of George Pledger and Robert Burchard(4) made a mark and signed respectively (i.e Philip and Robert(3) respectively). *Goulston:* E.R.O. Q/SR 322/74.

50 *Abraham Lake (with son Robert):* yeoman, Benton Hall, first known in Witham 1651, dissent 1663 & 1664 (P.R.O. ASS 35/92/1; E.R.O. Q/SR 399/98; E.R.O. D/ACA 55, pp.16, 148 et al.). *Thomas Goodman (with son Thomas):* yeoman, first known 1644; dissent 1661, i.e. Robert Billio, nonconformist minister, witnessed his will (E.R.O. Q/SR 322/54; D/ACW 17/8). *Robert Edwards:* first known appearance 1652, i.e. this one (E.R.O. D/P 30/25/67). *Thomas Chipperfield:* yeoman, first known appearance 1652, i.e. this one and another; dissent 1664 (E.R.O. D/P 30/25/67; E.R.O. Q/SR 352/30, 399/26, 32).

51 E.R.O. D/ACW 11/248. Robert Jackson(1)'s grandfather Thomas Brodway probably in London at time of the petitions (1642 and 1643) and his father Adam had died. His mother Abigail did not participate (H.L.R.O., Main Papers, H.L., 20 Jan.1641/2, petition box; H.L.R.O., Main Papers, H.L., 4 Jan.1642/3).

52 E.R.O. Q/SBa 2/83/11; E.R.O. Q/SO 1. *First appearance in 1653:* Edward Acton, Robert Barwell(1), Jonas Gray, John Harris, Henry Lees, John True (probable husband of Elizabeth, for whom see chapter 11), Richard True.

53 See Gyford, pp.254(#76), 205 (re.Coggeshall origins); Wrightson and Levine, 1979 and 1995, p.163; Grieve, 1994, pp.60-62, 74-75. *Turner:* E.R.O. D/ALV 2, f.133v; E.R.O. D/ACW 14/165. *Quaker wills:* e.g. E.R.O. D/ACW 18/328, 19/1. *Nonconformist wills:* E.R.O. D/ACW 19/46, 20/214, 21/152. *Preamble missing or noncommittal, 1650s:* PROB 11/225/27, 11/261/18; 11/283/577, 11/263/147, 11/281/513; E.R.O.

D/ACW 16/20, 16/62. *Longer peambles, 1650s:* E.R.O. D/ACW 15/309; P.R.O. PROB 11/218/193, 11/236/166, 11/248/317 (Robinson); P.R.O. PROB 11/236/183 (Whale). Robinson and Whale on 'peace' petition, 1643 (H.L.R.O., Main Papers, H.L., 4 Jan.1642/3). *General:* see figure 4, chapter 2. Probably fewer wills in 1650s than before, probate being more costly in the absence of local courts.

[54] Peters, 1996, pp.141-65; T.A.Davies, 1986, p.79, quoting Penney, 1907, pp.92, 96-97; Reay, 1985, pp.7-10; Besse, 1753, pp.190-91; Penney, 1924, pp.89, 110; D.H.Allen, 1974, p.88.

[55] P.R.O. RG 6/1335. *Howlett:* first child born London 1647, second Witham 1649. In 1651 John Howlett one of 16 men promising to finish work on roads. Produced own tokens 1667, died in 1669. Widow Elizabeth one-hearth house 1670, 1673, exempt from Hearth Tax. Subsequent life unknown. No known prosecution as Quakers, although John and another man guaranteed Elizabeth's appearance at quarter sessions 1654 (reason unknown) (E.R.O. Q/SR 349/26; Lucas, 'Witham', p.112; E.R.O. Q/RTh 1/29, 5/18, 8/9, 9/7; E.R.O. Q/SR 361/58). *Pledger:* E.R.O. D/ACW 18/328 gives Jane Pledger, wife of George, as daughter of John Freeborne. *Winkfield:* Elizabeth, daughter of John Harding of Witham (little known); her grandfather (d.1656) and great grandfather (d.1624) were both Witham maltsters called John Hull; the former put his name to the royalist 'peace' petition in 1643 (P.R.O. PROB 11/256/218; D/ACW 9/128; E.R.O. Accession A9012 (D/NF 1 addl.); H.L.R.O., Main Papers, H.L., 4 Jan.1642/3). Nicholas's father Peter(2), was also a gardener, grandfather Peter(1) probably a weaver and gardener. Latter alleged absent from church 1628 (also his brother Richard 1611); reasons unknown but others at the time well-known as Puritans (E.R.O. D/ACW 16/18; E.R.O. Q/SBa 2/17; E.R.O. D/ACW 12/169; E.R.O. D/ALV 1, f.25v, E.R.O. D/ACA 34, f.31). Nicholas one hearth 1662, 1670, 1673 (probably on site now George public house, no.36 Newland Street. Also occupied c.20 acres land in 4 pieces near town centre, and 30 acres in Faulkbourne (E.R.O. Q/RTh 1/29, 5/18, 8/9, 9/7; manor nos.1, 43, 84, 195, 200, 201; E.R.O. Accession A9012 (D/NF 1 addl.), deeds of cottage in Witham from 1682; E.R.O. D/P 30/1/1).

[56] Besse, 1753, pp.192-83; Penney, 1924, p.177.

[57] E.g. the introduction to Manning, 1991, pp.7-47; Walter, lectures, 1994; T.Webster, 1994, pp.7-9; Cust and Hughes, 1994.

[58] Grieve, 1994, pp.60-62, 74-75.

Chapter 11: Charles II, James II, William and Mary

[1] *Aylett letters,* 1908, letter ii; *D.N.B.* Sir Robert Titchborne was sentenced to death 1660 but with some of his other colleagues reprieved. Spent the rest of his life in prison, died in the Tower in 1682.

[2] Newly restored Royalist clergymen who supervised the courts as surrogates included John Michaelson of Chelmsford, and Christopher Webb of Gilston in Hertfordshire (teacher in Witham over thirty years previously) (E.R.O. D/ABA 10 (e.g. ff.17v, 20)).

[3] 13 & 14 Charles II, c.1; 16 Charles II, c.4; 35 Elizabeth, c.1; Wrightson, 1988, pp.219-20; Phillipson, lxxvi; Sharpe, 1987, pp.333-34; O'Leary, 'Election', pp.9-16; Caunt, 'Parliament', pp.187-90; E.R.O. D/DKw O4. Successful candidates were Colonel Henry Mildmay of Graces, Little Baddow, and John Lamotte Honywood of Marks Hall.

[4] 1 William and Mary, c.18. Summary from various sources, especially: Sharpe, 1987, pp.331-40; Taylor, 1962, pp.4-13; E.R.O. Q/SO 2/240; *Victoria History,* ii, 1907, pp.71-73; *D.N.B.*

[5] Allen, 1974, pp.xxxiii-xli; E.R.O. calendar of assize records; E.R.O. D/P 30/14/1. Morant, *Essex,* ii, 1763-68, pp.114, 126, 139, 147, 152. *John Godbold (till late 1660s):* E.R.O. Q/SR 376/51, 376/54-55, 377/47, 390/61, 391/29, 411/79, 414/67. *Sir William Ayloffe (till 1675):* E.R.O. Q/SR 398/53. *Henry Ayloffe (after 1684):* E.R.O. Q/SR 446/157-59, 448/268-72, 449/129-30A, 449/138-39, 454/85, 455/30, 470/41, 474/25, 474/27, 500/14, 500/16, 505/12, 508/15, 512/7, 513/2, 514/19, 526/24, 526/26, 533/2, 533/12-13. *Sir William Wiseman:* E.R.O. Q/SR 399/98-99 (prosecution of George Lisle, nonconformist minister). Thanks to the Reverend David Nash for information about the Wisemans. *Sir Thomas Adby (till 1675):* Q/SR 387/56, 399/98-99, 401/109, 423/83, 430/80. *Thomas Roberts (till 1681):* E.R.O. Q/SR 416/85, 417/48-49, 430/98. *Sir Thomas Darcy (after c.1685):* E.R.O. Q/SR 448/334-35, 453/61, 458/31, 468/8.

[6] Morris, 1872, pp.399-400, 410; P.R.O. ASSI 35/128/2/14, 35/131/1/34; E.R.O. Q/SR 457/27, 458/4, 458/39; E.R.O. D/P

30/14/1 (5 Dec.1687, indenture of Mary Bilboe). I have never managed to find any reference to a Foster as a sheep stealer at this time, so perhaps the prosecution did not proceed.

[7] Calculated from E.R.O. calendar of assize records. E.R.O. Q/SR 541/24, 544/36, 544/40, 552/37, 557/37 et al. For Newman Barwell see Gyford, 1996, pp.207-208.

[8] E.R.O. calendar of assize records. Until around 1680 the changeover was arranged so that the two men did not both leave office at the same time, whilst after about 1680 they were both replaced together. For some of the constables I know definite residences in other parishes, whilst for others I only know that they do not appear in Witham records There were Burchards in other parishes, particularly Terling, so it is possible that even constable Robert Burchard did not come from Witham. *Abraham Lake:* E.R.O. Q/SR 399/98; E.R.O. D/ACA 55, pp.16, 148 et al. *Dalton Clarke:* Gyford, 1996, p.60.

[9] E.g. see Craig, 'Co-operation'. *Status of known Witham office-holders 1666 to 1680:* median number of hearths in 1673 Hearth Tax were: aletasters 2; parish constables 2; overseers of the poor 4-5, churchwardens 4 (Q/RTh 9/7). Those unable to sign out of the total of known writing ability were: churchwardens (3 out of 25, i.e. Richard Swinborne, innkeeper and Robert Wilshire, glover (twice)); overseers (2 out of 13, i.e. John Moore, miller and James Chaplin). Limited evidence about signing ability of constables and alehousekeepers shows more known to be able to sign than not to be so able. *Shakerley:* E.R.O. D/P 30/14/1; E.R.O. D/ACV 9A, ACV 9B, f.92, ACV 11; E.R.O. D/ACW 22/38; Gyford, 1996, p.137. *Parish constables:* E.R.O. D/DBw M28-29. These manor court rolls name 8 different pairs 1662 and 1687. At some courts, no election was recorded, so possibly previous holders continued, but there were other people said to be parish constables but not appearing in the rolls (ASS 35/109/3/106, 35/112/9/26 give John Morin and John Norton in 1670). In some places by this time, magistrates were choosing parish constables as the manorial system declined (Webb, *Parish and County,* 1924, pp.27-28). *Wall:* Q/SR 399/122; E.R.O. D/ACA 55, p.347. *Richmond:* E.R.O. Q/SR 402/26; E.R.O. D/ACW 20/244; E.R.O. D/P 30/1/2; Gyford, p.121. Another Thomas Richmond, a grocer, probably the tanner's son, also a Quaker, died 1698 (P.R.O. PROB 11/446/174).

[10] Webb, *Parish and County,* 1924, pp.30-32, 111-12. Main source of information for identity of Witham overseers is E.R.O. D/P 30/14/1, with some from other parish records etc. *Possible nonconformist overseers:* Jerome Garrard(3) (1664) (E.R.O. D/ACA 55, p.62); Edward Johnson (1664) (E.R.O. D/ACA 55, pp.16, 62). *Quaker overseers:* John Hull (c.1664 and 1680), Robert Barwell(1) (1671 and 1677), George Pledger (1673), John Moore (1676), John Baker (1699) (information about Quakerism from various sources). *Priscilla Chipperfield:* E.R.O. D/P 30/14/1 (this also shows widow Mary Porter as overseer in 1733); Gyford, 1996, pp.74-75; Webb, *Parish and County,* 1924, pp.15-17.

[11] Gyford, 1996, pp.90-91, 146-49. Identity of churchwardens mostly from E.R.O. D/P 30/14/1, E.R.O. D/ACV 6-12. The practice whereby some of the wardens reappeared in the post after a few years was also noted at this time in Cambridgeshire by Eric Carlson. He felt the fewer people thereby becoming wardens to have a higher relative status in the community than before 1640 (Carlson, 1995, pp.176-78, 187-88, 195-99). In Witham there had already been wardens of fairly high status before 1640 also; those of high status 1660 onwards therefore were nothing radically new, though they also probably reflected the polarisation in the parish's social structure as a whole.

[12] *Articles of Enquiry,* 1664; Guildhall MS 9583/2, part 3, ff.124-25v. The church had already been reported as out of repair by the previous churchwardens during 1663 (E.R.O. D/ACA 55, p.13).

[13] E.R.O. D/ACA 48, f.42; E.R.O. D/ACW 11/300, 17/201; E.R.O. D/P 30/25/67; E.R.O. Q/SBa 2/83/11; E.R.O. D/P 30/1/1; Guildhall MS 9583/5.

[14] Hist. MSS.Com. 6, *7th Report,* p.1086; Smith and Hope, 'Clergy'; Guildhall MS 9537/16; H.L.R.O., Main Papers, H.L., 23 June 1660, Petition of Francis Wright; letter from Assistant Clerk of the Records, House of Lords Record Office, 4 June 1986.

[15] L.M.A. DL/C/319, pp.84-85, 87-90.

[16] Guildhall MS 9567/7 (sundry diocesan papers, which include the stray document about Wright which is in the form of abstracts of various depositions; shows it is always worth looking at collections marked 'sundry' or 'miscellaneous'!). In addition Wright's son, 'Francis Wright junior, gentleman', now in his twenties, was asked to appear at quarter sessions to 'answer the inhabitants of Witham' in 1661 (reason

and outcome unknown) (E.R.O. Q/SR 390/61; 'Liber Scholae Colcestriensis' (gives Francis and Thomas Wright, sons of Francis, aged 12 and 9 respectively in 1641).

[17] E.R.O. D/ACA 55, pp.13, 111, 149, 182, 210, 347; Guildhall MS 9537/16, 9537/17, 9583 I, 9583/2, part 3, ff.124-25v. *Parish register:* The churchwardens claimed there was a register for baptisms and burials and 'to our knowledge those concerned in keeping of them have done their duty' (Guildhall MS 9583/2, part 3, f.124). It must have either been lost or abandoned soon afterwards; the register which survives today begins continuous entries in January 1665 (E.R.O. D/P 30/1/1). It also includes some baptisms by Wright's successors of 'such as were unbaptised for some yeares before Mr.Harper came to be Minister'; seeming to confirm the wardens' allegations. There are also some mixed entries of baptisms that seem to have taken place at various earlier dates, perhaps in other churches. The whole register is very confused. However, there appear to be two full years' entries during Wright's incumbency, 1666 and 1667, in which 15 and 20 baptisms respectively took place. Full year's entries under John Harper were 1671 and 1672, during which 41 and 47 baptisms took place.

[18] P.R.O. E 112/398/238, 112/398/263 (includes a list of what was alleged to be owed, expressed in money, and evidence of ten of the accused in 1668), 112/402/642 (includes the evidence of five of the accused in 1664). Out of the twenty different people accused, there were two Quakers (Nicholas Winkfield and John Freeborne), and up to six nonconformists (Abraham and John Lake, Thomas and Richard Chipperfield, Thomas Goodman, and Henry Burche (who possibly married Elizabeth Read)).

[19] Guildhall MS 11,185. There are some Act books of the Consistory court surviving for this period but they deal almost entirely with London, and the few Essex entries do not relate to Witham (L.M.A. DL/C/328-29, 625-26). The relevant Bishop's Register does not mention anything about Wright's removal (Guildhall MS 9531/16).

[20] E.R.O. D/P 30/1/1; L.M.A. DL/C/345, f.91; Guildhall MS 9531/16, f.133; Tatham, 1911, pp.177, 228; J.Walker, 1714, p.397.

[21] *Alumni Cantabrigiensis;* Guildhall MSS 9531/16, ff.133v, 149, 9531/17, f.44, 9537/18, f.30, 9539A/3, f.28v.; E.R.O. D/P 30/1/1.

[22] L.M.A. DL/C/345, f.91 (this copy of the agreement of 1672 has no precise date or signature, so it is not known whether it was formally completed); Guildhall MS 9539A/3, f.37; E.R.O. Q/RTh 1/29, 5/18, Q/RTh 8/9 (the latter is dated 1673; the other return which is also nominally dated 1673, E.R.O. Q/RTh 9/7, still gives four hearths, but it still has the vicar as Harper, so probably in fact dates from before 1673); E.R.O. D/DBw M101 (earliest surviving court records of Vicarage manor, beginning in 1672); E.R.O. D/ACW 18/282, 19/20. By this time clergymen were beginning to be replaced as writers of wills by lawyers, but Cox probably wrote the will of Daniel Spradborough of the Spread Eagle (E.R.O. D/ACW 18/278), and Brett wrote two wills (E.R.O. D/ACW 19/81, 19/132). Some references call Cox John Cox, but to judge from this will and local records, his name was Thomas (*Alumni Cantabrigiensis;* E.R.O. T/A 547).

[23] *Brett:* was only ordained in 1666 and his will mentioned no wife or children; Guildhall MSS 9537/21, f.35, 9540/2, f.3; P.R.O. PROB 11/363/74; L.M.A. DL/C/345, f.21; Venn, *Alumni Cantabrigiensis.* *Nussey:* may have been son of a former rector of Beaumont in north-east Essex (E.R.O. D/P 285/1/1 - Benjamin Nussey baptised 25 July 1626). *Countess Lavall:* Gyford, 1996, pp.175-77; E.R.O. D/DP T215; Q/SPb 1/20v.

[24] E.R.O. T/A 547; Guildhall MSS 9531/17, f.62v, 9537/23; L.M.A. DL/C/345, f.204; E.R.O. T/P 195/10, pp.48-49; Fowler, 1911, pp.28, 32. P.R.O. PROB 11/586/167; Compton's coat of arms remained in the church until the mid-nineteenth century; it was then moved to the vestry, and subsequently lost.

[25] E.U.L. EQ 22, p.20; L.M.A. DL/C/345, f.134v; E.R.O. D/ACV 9B (showing that in 1685 it was reported that 'the Church and Steeple are now repairing', though 'one Butteress on the North side of the Church being down, and the other Decaying they must be repaired'); E.R.O. D/P 30/6/1; E.R.O. T/P 195/10, p.37. The largest donations in 1704 (over £20 each) were given by John Bennett, lord of the manors of Chipping and Newland, and William East of the Middle Temple, owner of the rectorial tithes. There were also members of the Barnardiston and Nevill families, influential in Witham's past.

[26] Fowler, 1911, p.15; E.R.O. D/P 30/25/12-18; P.R.O. C 93/17/8, 93/45/38; L.P.L., F.P.Compton 1, f.52; Morant, *Essex,* ii, 1763-8, p.111; L.M.A. DL/C/345, f.91; P.R.O. PROB 11/417/191; P.R.O. C

11/1459/32; 11/1510/47; P.R.O. C 33/374/354, 33/374/356, 33/374/376, 33/374/467; E.R.O. D/DBw M68, p.6; E.R.O. D/DBw M71, p.2. John Bennett the elder bought the manors 1668 and his son John inherited 1670. In 1669 John the elder tried to extract a 'deodand' from a Cambridgeshire waggoner and from Robert Barwell(1), on the grounds that a man had died in the manor of Newland, from injuries received when he was run over by a waggon drawn by four horses and carrying some of Barwell's oil. His son probably introduced new 'customs' about payments from entrants into property (P.R.O. E 112/397/184; Gyford, 1996, p.68).

[27] P.R.O. PROB 11/586/167 (at first Warley left his 'Library of Printed Books unless Duplicates' to the master and fellows of Clare Hall in Cambridge, but this was amended by a codicil so that instead they were to have £50 when they began to build a new chapel and another £50 towards the building of a 'New Theater'); Elham [Kent] Parish Magazine, December 1984 (Anne Brambleby kindly pointed this out); E.R.O. D/ACW 28 (Deborah Warley); manor no.156; *Charity Commissioners Report,* p.914; Fowler, 1911, p.22; E.R.O. D/P 30/25/92. Lilly Butler, vicar 1762-82, who took the school money, became chaplain to the Duke of Buckingham in Ireland, and Dean of Ardagh; he died in Boulogne in 1792 (*Alumni Cantabrigiensis,*).

[28] *Alumni Cantabrigiensis;* E.R.O. D/P 30/25/90, 91; E.R.O. D/DA T549; E.R.O. D/P 30/1/1; Gyford, 1996, pp.187, 191-92; Guildhall MSS 9539B, f.14, 9537/16, ff.17, 18v, 9537/18, f.27v; 9537/19, f.23, 9583/2, part 3, f.125v. Thomas Ponder was probably ordained in 1637. In 1654 he and his wife had lived at Stoke by Nayland in Suffolk. Venn gives him as curate of Witham as well as of Cressing in 1664, but this probably arises from a misinterpretation of the entry as schoolmaster at Witham in the same year. The churchwardens' presentment of that year says that there was no curate in Witham. In 1669 Ponder may have been about to leave Cressing, as the vicar was ordered to get a new curate (Guildhall MS 9537/16, f.18v, 9583/2, part 3, ff 124-25v). *Wills witnessed by Ponder:* E.R.O. D/ACW 18/112, 18/140, 18/226, 18/318, 18/357, 19/18, 19/80, 19/112. He also witnessed other documents such as apprenticeship indentures (E.R.O. D/P 30/14/1; E.R.O. D/P 30/18/3). *House, poverty, bequests etc.:* E.R.O. Q/RTh 1/29, 5/18, 8/9, 9/7; Guildhall MS 9538B, f.14; E.R.O. D/ACAc 2, f.74; E.R.O. D/P 30/1/1; E.R.O. D/ACW 19/46, 19/80, 22/102; *D.N.B;* manor no.102 (see also 170, 173); E.R.O. D/P 30/1/2. The two books were 'Geography' by Peter Haylin, and a set of sermons by Lancelot Andrewes.

[29] *Howe: Alumni Cantabrigiensis;* E.R.O. D/ACW 19/18. *Burchard:* Guildhall MS 9537/24, f.140v; E.R.O. D/ACW 14/194, 20/100 (probably wills of Robert Burchard(5)'s grandfather and father respectively); manor no.1; P.R.O. PROB 11/586/167; E.R.O. D/P 30/25/93; E.R.O. D/P 30/1/2 (11 June 1738, burial of 'Mr.Robert Burchard, formerly schoolmaster', aged 88); E.R.O. T/A 778/2 (microfilm of Guildhall MS 25750/1). In 1722 it was said that the children were 'only taught to read and write' at Burchard's school, but it was 'duly manag'd and attended'.

[30] *Trustees:* E.R.O. D/P 30/25/43. Nonconformists were Robert Garrard(2), Jerome Garrard(3); Quakers were Robert Barwell(1) and John Freeborne. *Figure 24:* calculated from E.R.O. Q/RTh 9/7. The householders liable to pay were about 40 per cent of the total of the total number in the town, the other 60 per cent being exempt.

[31] Guildhall MS 10,925B; E.R.O. T/A 420; *Victoria History,* ii, pp.70-71, iv, p.311; the 'census' related to the Province of Canterbury.

[32] *Travellers:* Besse, 1753, pp.194-7; *C.J.* viii. 39; Barclay, 1839 (Caton's visit to Witham is the first by a traveller of which there is a surviving record. He had been to the Colchester area several times from 1659 onwards, often during journeys to and from Holland). *Essex:* Cliftlands, 1987, p.165. Hull found Quakers in c.15 per cent of Essex parishes from Archdeaconry records alone 1662 to c.1690 (Hull, 'Early Friends', and 'More Friends'). *Witham registers etc.:* P.R.O. RG 6/1335; note that though Chelmsford was ultimately part of Witham Monthly Meeting, the registers do not show Quaker activity there in 1660s. In particular there is no evidence that Alexander Freeborne, John's nephew, gaoler at Chelmsford House of Correction, was a Quaker, and it seems unlikely as he was appointed by the new Royalist magistrates as gaoler after they had removed his predecessor; Hilda Grieve's suggestion that he was a Quaker was probably based on his relationship to John (his uncle, not his father as she suggests; John's father was a different Alexander) (Grieve, 1994, pp.85-86; Gyford, 1996, p.155).

[33] Guildhall MS 9583/2, part 3, ff.124v-125; 13 & 14 Charles II, c.1,

[34] section iv (gives power to individual justices to imprison Quakers offending under the Act); E.R.O. Q/SR 402/25-26 (these reports of the convictions were filed with the main quarter sessions records, but it is probable that this did not always happen). The fact that the men who came from Witham men were Quakers is revealed by various other records.

[34] Women did take part in early Quaker worship; one had been preaching at a meeting visited by William Caton in 1663 just before he came to Witham (Barclay, 1839, p.119). Later evidence suggests that in due course they more frequently held separate meetings; e.g. in 1698 the Witham grocer Thomas Richmond referred in his will to the Men's and Women's Meetings in London in 1698 (P.R.O. PROB 11/446/174).

[35] *Men at the meeting:* for more information see Gyford, 1996, pp.121 (Richmond), 124 (Pledger), 155-56 (Freeborne and Gardner), 205-206 (Barwell). Quotation about Freeborne from Friends House Library, Portfolio 17, item 3. Since I wrote the 1996 book I have found a reference to Barwell possibly being the owner of some 'trayne oil', i.e. oil extruded from wool, in a dispute about deodand in the manor of Newland in 1669 (P.R.O. E 112/398/238). This suggests he was still working as a clothier. *Rates:* E.R.O. Q/SR 402/26; E.R.O. D/ACA 55, p.348 (some of the presentations from other parishes in this volume were said to have been made by the churchwardens, but not the ones from Witham).

[36] *Elizabeth True:* probably lived in the house now nos.53/55 Chipping Hill. Father was Robert Clarke (died 1640 and left her £10), her husband John True (died 1657 and left her £150), her brother Peregrine Clarke of Kersey in Suffolk (died 1679 and left her two tenements in Chipping Hill, in return for loaning him some money). Her daughter Elizabeth had a Quaker wedding, she made a bequest to the Quaker poor in her will of 1705 and was recorded as a Quaker in the burial register of St.Nicholas church (manor no.136; E.R.O. D/ACW 13/258; P.R.O. PROB 11/263/147, 11/362/56; E.R.O. Accession A9012 (D/NF 1 addl.); P.R.O. RG 6/1335; E.R.O. D/ACW 23/147; E.R.O. D/P 30/1/2). Her properties were: manor nos.131, 134-36, 182; Vicarage manor, nos.4, 16, 17, 18 (E.R.O. D/DBw M101).

[37] E.U.L. EQ 22, pp.10, 24, 66. For the 17th-century relationships etc. see P.R.O. RG 6/1335, E.R.O. D/ACW 19/290, 21/24, 27/35. The probable connection between the 16th and 17th-century Ravens through the descent of property is explained in the notes of chapter 3.

[38] P.R.O. RG 6/1335; E.R.O. D/NF 1/1/1; E.R.O. Accession A9012 (D/NF 1 addl.); E.R.O. D/ACW 18/328); E.R.O. D/AEA 44, f.113v; Friends House Library, Portfolio 17, item 3 (refers to John Freeborne as having been 'nere 80 years' at his death in 1675); Penney, 1924, p.249.

[39] *Gattaway:* E.R.O. D/ALV 7. The accusation did not call him a Quaker, but he was distrained in 1683 for being at a meeting (E.U.L. EQ 22, p.20) (also summarised in Besse, 1753, pp.205-207), received part of bequest for Quaker poor 1688 (E.R.O. D/NF 1/1/1), and was called a Quaker in parish burial register, 1692 (E.R.O. D/P 30/1/2). In some other parishes, there were unauthorised teachers actually referred to as Quakers (Hull, 'Early Friends', p.69). *Meeting house:* E.R.O. Accession A9012 (D/NF 1 addl.) (in about 1690 it was said that there was 'resting and remaining in the hands of John Baker 39 shillings which was left of the money which he received for the bilding of the house'); manor no.59; P.R.O. RG 6/1335; information kindly provided by Friends' House in 1983. *Richmond:* P.R.O. PROB 11/446/174.

[40] *England:* 30-40,000 members, c.5 million population. *Essex:* 1,283 members 1655-64, with 600 more 1665-74, out of population c.126,000 (T.A.Davies, 1986, pp.32-33; Burley, 1957, p.399; Scott, 1991, p.3.). *Witham:* figures as shown in figure 25 calculated from E.R.O. Q/RTh 9/7 and miscellaneous information about identity of Quakers (including P.R.O. RG 6/1335, E.R.O. D/P 30/1/1, E.R.O. Accession A9012 (D/NF 1 addl.)); Gyford, 1996, pp.146, 148-49. Amongst payers of the tax, Quakers figured equally well in the 1662 returns, but these do not give information about people who were exempt from paying (E.R.O. Q/RTh 1/29).

[41] *Trustees and overseers:* E.R.O. D/P 30/25/43; E.R.O. D/P 30/15; E.R.O. D/P 30/14/1; E.R.O. D/P 30/18/1; E.R.O. D/DBw M28, 1 May 1671. *Oaths:* P.R.O. E 112/397/184, 112/398/263, 112/402/642 (Barwell and Winkfield); P.R.O. PROB 6/73, f.179, 6/79, f.167 (Barwell). *Moore:* E.R.O. D/ACW 22/168; E.R.O. D/DDc T81; E.R.O. D/P 30/18/3; E.R.O. Q/SR 462/30.

[42] *Freeborne and Gardner etc.:* E.R.O. D/ACW 18/328, 19/1; P.R.O. RG 6/1335; E.R.O. D/NF 1/1/1. Pledger was Freeborne's executor and

still had the £30 when Elizabeth died. She left it to Todd, her own executor, to bring up her two younger children, and to put John out as apprentice to a 'copper [cooper?] or shoemaker'. The meeting recorded that Todd 'did condescend to leave the difference between George Pledger and him concerning Elizabeth Gardner to the consideration of Friends'.

[43] *Quarterly Meeting:* E.R.O. T/A 423/7; E.R.O. D/NF 1/1/1 (it was probably for the purpose of collecting for the poor that the names of 18 men were noted as collectors in 1696). *Thomas Richmond:* E.R.O. D/ACW 20/244; E.R.O. D/NF 1/1/1; E.R.O. D/P 30/1/2. Philip, also a Quaker, probably lived in Writtle. Recipients were widow [Margaret] Cockerill (died 1691), Paul Gatward [Gattaway] (died 1692), George Cottis, Alex.[?] Francis (died 1690), John Burton (E.R.O. D/P 30/1/2, P.R.O. RG 6/1335). Cockerill, Cottis and Francis lived in Barwell properties (manor nos.180, 56, 29). *Jane Woodcock:* E.R.O. D/ACW 20/271.

[44] Copy of will of Deborah Eatney (in custody of Chelmsford Friends' Meeting); E.R.O. D/DBw M28, 13 Oct.1684; E.R.O. D/ACW 15/85; P.R.O. RG 6/1335; E.R.O. D/NF 1/1/1; E.R.O. D/ACW 21/55; Edward Halys's son was Edmund, who died in 1648 (discussed in chapter 7). Edmund's daughter Margaret married Samuel Davies, son of Dorothy Davies (whose second husband was yeoman William Nicholls). Samuel's daughter was Deborah, who married Edward Eatney in 1679; he was from Mundon, After Deborah's death Edward went to Fuller Street in Fairstead.

[45] E.R.O. D/ACW 23/147; P.R.O. PROB 11/446/174, 11/477/159. The memorial in St.Nicholas church to Robert Barwell(2) in 1697 says that both his parents, Robert(1) and Martha(1), were then over 80.

[46] P.R.O. E 112/398/238, 112/398/263, 112/398/315, 112/402/642 (same case as 112/398/238;has Winkfield's evidence). For nonpayment of tithes by Essex Quakers see T.A.Davies, 1986, pp.83-89, 115-118.

[47] E.U.L. EQ 22, p.20 (also summarised in Besse, 1753, pp.205-207). In the previous year William Shepard of Wickham Bishops, son-in-law of Robert Barwell(1), had kitchen equipment and furniture taken for non-payment of tithes (p.18). Many other similar reports made a point of recording how much more had been taken in distraint than was actually owed in fines.

[48] Gyford, 1996, pp.146, 149, 199-200.

[49] *Freeborne:* E.R.O. D/ACW 18/328, 19/1. *Pledger:* E.R.O. D/ACW 21/8; E.R.O. D/NF 1/1/1; P.R.O. RG 6/1335; E.R.O. D/P 30/1/1. The relevant part of St.Nicholas church burial register is missing at time of George's death. Jane's burial is recorded there; she was not described a Quaker but this was just before such descriptions started being added. *Nicholls:* Manor no.97; E.R.O. Q/SR 402/26; E.R.O. Accession A9012 (D/NF 1 addl.); P.R.O. RG 6/1335; E.R.O. D/ACW 19/20, 21/24, 21/35, 22/272; E.R.O. D/P 30/1/1; E.R.O. D/ACV 12; E.R.O. D/P 42/1/1. *Gattaway:* A Paul Gattaway had a child baptised Witham 1677; must have been Paul junior as Paul senior the Quaker was already adult 1648 when he witnessed Edmund Halys' will (E.R.O. D/P 30/1/1; E.R.O. D/ACW 15/85).

[50] P.R.O. PROB 6/73, f.179, 6/79, f.167; E.R.O. D/P 30/1/2; P.R.O. RG 6/1335; E.R.O. D/P 30/14/1; Guildhall MS.9532/1/95; Fowler, 1911, pp.19-20; E.R.O. T/P 195/10 (gives Newman Barwell with 'his owne seat' in the church in 1706); E.U.L. EQ 22, pp.111, 125, 131. The John Raven in question was son of John the elder (who d.1709); Edmund Raven, probably John the younger's cousin, was also distrained by Newman Barwell (p.100, 109).

[51] P.R.O. PROB 11/477/159; E.R.O. D/ACW 23/147; P.R.O. RG 6/1335; E.R.O. D/P 30/1/2; P.R.O. RG 6/1335; E.R.O. D/P 30/1/2. *Witham burials:* The relationship between St.Nicholas church parish burial register and that of the Quakers is not clear. The church probably tried to record all burials, wherever they took place. From about 1680 onwards the parish register has 'quaker' against some of its entries. In less than half of these cases there is a parallel entry in the Quaker burial register suggesting a burial in the Quaker ground. In a few other cases people mentioned in the Quaker register also appear in the St.Nicholas register but are not given there as Quakers. *Feering:* John Raven's will, written 1708, left 'the piece of ground on Feering Hill now used as a burying place for people called Quakers' to two Kelvedon men in trust as a Quaker burying place 'for ever'. He owned property in several other parishes (E.R.O. D/ABR 16/88). When the surviving Feering parish register recommences in 1707 after a gap, it includes several burials said to have taken place 'in the Quakers burying place in Feering'. They include John Raven himself in 1709 (whose executor paid a fine for not

producing an affidavit that he had been buried in wool), and another was Margaret Raven in 1707, probably a relative from Maldon. In the Quaker registers of Coggeshall Monthly meeting in which Feering lay, references to burials at the Feering ground only survive from 1732 onwards (P.R.O. RG 6/1189).

[52] E.U.L. EQ 22, p.46. Other places in the Monthly meeting had six couples giving birth in the 1660s, but over twenty between 1700 and 1710, particularly Maldon and Chelmsford. A meeting was established in Moulsham in Chelmsford in 1670, with a meeting house built there in 1701, Billericay built a new meeting house in 1697 (P.R.O. RG 6/1335, 6/1292, 6/659, 6/54; E.R.O. D/NF 1/1/1, 1/3/1; Grieve, 1994, pp.86-87); E.R.O. D/P 30/14/1. *Election:* Poll book for 1693/4 (typescript in E.R.O.); Caunt, 'Parliament', pp.187-90. Sir Charles Barrington of Hatfield Broadoak was the victorious Tory. Altogether 28 Witham men supported him and 20 opposed him. Ex-Quakers amongst the supporters were George Pledger (younger), Matthew Nicholls and Richard Cooper; although Cooper lived in Hatfield Peverel, his entitlement to vote came from his ownership of some property in Witham.

[53] In particular see: Phillipson, lxxvi and lxxvii (the latter, pp.2-4, 9, shows in Cambridge a process of ageing and decline, but more noticeably in the early 18th century); Reay, 1985; Scott, 1991 (pp.3, 9, shows in York a pattern of first generation Quakers not being replaced, though only amongst gentry members; pp.14, 16, emphasises parallels between Quakerism and Puritanism); Stevenson, 1995; T.A.Davies, 1986, pp.301-308 (a new book from Adrian Davies is to be published during 1998 showing the development of his findings and his thoughts since he wrote this thesis); Wrightson and Levine, 1979 and 1995, pp.164-68.

[54] In the volume E.R.O. D/ACA 55, some of the presentations from other parishes are said to have been made by the churchwardens, but not those from Witham. Davids, 1863, pp.512-15; Matthews, *Calamy*, 1934, p.55; E.R.O. D/ACW 17/8; E.R.O. D/ACA 55, p.16; Earnshaw, 1988, pp.3-5; Beale 1989.

[55] E.R.O. D/ACA 55, pp.16, 62; Davids, 1863, pp.479-84, 552.

[56] Matthews, *Calamy*, 1934, p.325; H.Smith, *Ecclesiastical history*, p.382; Davids, 1863, pp.449-50; Turner, 1911, ii, p.934; E.R.O. D/ACW 22/188. Information about Rivenhall kindly provided by the Reverend David Nash. E.R.O. D/ACA 55, pp.15-16 (p.15 refers to a William Lake but this probably an error; there was no William Lake amongst the main inhabitants at this time, and the fuller entry on p.16 gives Abraham). E.R.O. Q/SR 399/26-27, 399/32, 399/98-99, 122. Q/SR 399/26 and 399/27, indictments for the two meetings, are endorsed 'to be removed by certiorari', whilst 399/32, another indictment for the barn, is endorsed 'to be quashed', perhaps because it duplicated the other one. Q/SR 399/26 and 399/32 give the barn as 'of Thomas Chipperfield, yeoman', 399/98 gives it as 'belonging to a house called the Place', and 399/99 as 'at Witham Place'. The barn which is now part of the Community Centre appears from its structure to have been built as a house in the grounds of Witham Place in the 16th century; it is not clear when it stopped being used as a house and became a barn (E.R.O. D/CT 405, 405A, plot no.630A; E.R.O. D/DP T215; thanks to Pat Ryan for advice about the building).

[57] E.R.O. Q/SR 399/98-99; P.R.O. KB 9/896/489; P.R.O. KB 29/314, ff.85, cxv; P.R.O. ASSI 35/104/5/42, 35/105/1/16; E.R.O. D/ACA 55, pp. 213, 346-47 et al. Wall's grocery business mainly dealt in fabrics; there survives an inventory of his goods (P.R.O. PROB 4/408; Gyford, 1996, pp.15-16, 134).

[58] Taylor 1962, p.11; Matthews, *Calamy*, p.325; Turner, 1911, ii, p.934; *Cal.S.P.Dom.* 1672, 99, 101, 199-200; P.R.O. SP 29/321/289, 319; P.R.O. SP 44/38A/142, 44/38A/155; manor no.136 (Elizabeth True). I decided not to use the term Presbyterian to describe the nonconformists during this period in general as it seemed to imply too precise an organisation. E.R.O. D/P 30/1/2; E.R.O. D/ACW 20/214, 22/188; the tablet commemorating the Lisles was originally on the north wall of the chancel and so has been moved at some time (Fowler, 1911, p.21).

[59] *Cal.S.P.Dom.* 1672, 99, 101; P.R.O. SP 29/321/289; P.R.O. SP 44/38A/142; E.R.O. D/DBw M63 (no.119, later manor no.131); E.R.O. D/ACW 18/26, 21/152; Smith, *Ecclesiastical history*, p.406; Matthews, *Calamy*, p.477; E.R.O. Q/SO 2, f.240; manor no.131; PROB 11/362/56.

[60] Matthews, *Calamy*, 1934, p.477; E.R.O. D/ACW 18/13, 20/214, 21/152. Witnesses of Taylor's will were Ann Lisle, George's widow,

Frances Hemming, the Lisles' daughter (E.R.O. D/DBw M29), and Aaron Cracknell, husband of their granddaughter (E.R.O. D/DBw M68, p.10). Taylor's first house was occupied by John Baker, a Quaker grocer, by 1686 (E.R.O. D/DBw M66, manor no.131). The location of his second house is unknown.

[61] E.R.O. D/ACW 19/46, 18/13 (in the latter, Ann Sharpe's daughter is given as Ann, wife of Edmund Taylor, and her 'sister' as Rose Garrard - this could have meant sister-in-law); Gyford, 1996, pp.191-92; E.R.O. D/P 30/25/43.

[62] E.R.O. Q/RTh 1/29, 5/18, 8/9, 9/7; manor nos.46-47; E.R.O. D/DHh P1; E.R.O. D/DKw O4; Caunt, 'Parliament', pp.187-90; E.R.O. D/ACW 20/172; E.R.O. D/ACAc 1/140; E.R.O. T/M 35; E.R.O. D/P 30/15; E.R.O. D/ACW 18/26 (has the whole of Edward Johnson's will whereas the registered version, D/ACR 8/140, only has half); Macfarlane, 1976, pp.549, 614, see also pp.491, 580; Macfarlane, 1970, pp.27-30; Wrightson and Levine, 1979 and 1995, p.168. Nearly twenty of Witham's freeholders made the journey to Chelmsford to vote in the election, but for most we do not know their religious affiliation.

[63] Wrightson and Levine, 1979 and 1995, pp.168-69; E.R.O. D/ACAc 2, f.77v; Gyford, 1996, p.19; E.R.O. D/P 30/1/1; E.R.O. Q/SR 399/26, 32, 99. The Toleration Act of 1689 allowed that if the parish chose a dissenter as churchwarden, the elected person could choose a deputy if they wished (1 William and Mary, c.18). Thomas and Priscilla Chipperfield had three children baptised as soon as Wright's successor, John Harper, arrived in 1670, one born in 1657 (perhaps a time of confusion?), and the others in Wright's time, 1660 and 1667 (E.R.O. D/P 30/1/1). Jonas Warley was appointed in August 1680, two months before Thomas Chipperfield died but may not have arrived straight away (E.R.O. D/P 30/1/1). One of the rooms in Chipperfield's farmhouse at Powershall was called a chapel but it did not include any special furniture and may have been a relic of an earlier occupant (P.R.O. E 112/649/358).

[64] *Articles of Enquiry,* 1664; Guildhall MS 9583/2, part 3, ff.124-25v.

[65] I.e. Thomas Johnson, son of Edward, John Goodman, son of Thomas, and John Lake, son of Abraham (warden 1684, just before his father's death in 1686) (D/ACV 7, ACV 8, ff.10v, 11v, 47, 59, 88v, 271; E.R.O. D/P 30/14/1; E.R.O. D/ACW 17/8, 23/138, 24/17; E.R.O. D/P 30/1/1; Gyford, 1996, pp.78-79). Also gentleman Aaron Cracknell, husband of George Lisle's granddaughter Ann, was a warden 1695. He had been witness to the will of vicar Thomas Brett during Lisle's life-time, in 1680 (P.R.O. PROB 11/363/74; E.R.O. D/DBw M68, p.10, gives Ann Cracknell as George Lisle's granddaughter). The Cracknells eventually took over the Lisle's house after the death of Ann Lisle (manor no.132).

[66] E.R.O. D/NC 3/30; E.R.O. D/P 30/25/22; E.R.O. D/ACV 8. The Collins Lane meeting house was a 'large room formerly six chambers', probably on the upper floor as there were several rooms under it (E.R.O. D/DU 191 addl.; manor no.104; E.R.O. D/ACW 30 (Jacob Pattisson)). Identities of the people who were connected with the Collins Lane building, such as Edmund Collins, one-time owner, suggest that it was a nonconformist rather than a Quaker meeting house (E.R.O. D/NC 3/9, 3/30 show that Edmund Collins built the new building in 1715).

[67] E.R.O. T/A 420; E.R.O. Q/SR 414/31; E.R.O. D/P 30/25/43; Morris, 1872, p.405. Sir John may have been absent from the town for a while during the early 1660s (E.R.O. Q/RTh 1/29, 5/18, 8/9, 9/7; the latter three dated 1670 and 1673 show the Southcotts in an 11-hearth house; there are no Southcotts in the first one, in 1662, when the only 11-hearth house was occupied by '--- Nurse', probably Benjamin Nussey).

[68] Q/SPb 1/20v; Gyford, 1996, pp.175-77, 180; Hist.MSS.Com.6, *7th Rep. Appendix*, p.505; P.R.O. ASSI 35/131/1; E.R.O. Q/SR 467/94; E.R.O. D/P F339; P.R.O. C 93/45/38; E.R.O. D/P 30/25/22, 30/25/45; Rowe, 1996, p.188; Henderson, 1988.

[69] Guildhall MS 9583/2, part 3, ff.124-25; E.R.O. D/ACA 55, pp.110-11, 346-48; E.R.O. D/P 30/1/1; Gyford, 1996, pp.203, 262(#196); Guildhall MS 9583/5.

Chapter 12: Post script

[1] E.g. see Haigh, 1984, pp.1-25.

[2] P.Collinson, 'Critical conclusion', 1995, p.391.

SOURCES

BIBLIOGRAPHY
of books, articles, theses, talks, etc. referred to in the above notes

This list includes everything other than original documents (for which see the separate list on page). It serves as a
    key to the abbreviated versions of these items in the notes.

Most items are referred to in the notes by the name of the author and the date, and listed below under the name of
    the author.

Articles in journals, and books with no date of publication, are referred to in the notes by the name of the author
    and an abbreviated title, and listed below under the name of the author.

Calendars of public records etc., standard works of reference, and works whose author is unknown, are referred to
    in the notes by an abbreviated title, and listed below under that abbreviated title, with fuller details in square
    brackets afterwards.

Lower case Roman numerals relate to volume numbers.

Acts & Ords. of Interr. [C.H.Firth and R.H.Rait, *Acts and Ordnances of the Interregnum, 1642-60*].

[Acts of Parliament are shown in the form 16 Charles II, c.4, the first number indicating the regnal year and the second the chapter]

Acts of P.C. [Various editors, *Acts of the Privy Council of England*, H.M.S.O.; volumes described by years covered].

G.Alexander, 'Bonner and the Marian Persecutions', in C.Haigh (ed.), *The English Reformation Revised*, C.U.P., 1987.

D.H.Allen, *Essex Quarter Sessions Order Book, 1652-61*, Essex Record Office, 1974.

R.Allen, *The doctrine of the Gospel by a plaine and familiar interpretation of the particular points or articles thereof*, 1606.

R.Almack, 'Kedington alias Ketton and the Barnardiston family', *Suffolk Archaeology*, iv.

Alumni Cantabrigiensis [J.and J.A.Venn, *Alumni Cantabrigiensis*, i, C.U.P., 1927].

Alumni Oxoniensis [J.Foster, *Alumni Oxoniensis, 1500-1714*, Parker, 1891].

J.P.Anglin, 'The court of the archdeacon of Essex, 1571-1609: an institutional and social study', University of California, Los Angeles, Ph.D. thesis, 1965.

Articles of Enquiry concerning matters ecclesiastical within the diocese of London, in the primary Episcopal Visitation of the Right Reverend Father in God Humfry Lord Bishop of London, 1664.

R.Ashton, 'St.Patrick's Day at Witham 1628', *Essex Recusant*, xxiii.

The Aylett letters, being four letters written in the 17th Century to the Cavalier Captain John Aylett of Virginia ..., privately published by Francis T.A.Junkin, Chicago, 1908 (photocopy in Essex Record Office library).

G.E.Aylmer, 'Communication - St.Patrick's Day 1628 in Witham, Essex', *Past and Present*, no.61.

C.E.Banks, *The Planters of the Commonwealth*, 1930.

C.E.Banks, *Topographical Dictionary of 2885 English Emigrants to New England, 1620-50*, 1937.

J.Barclay (ed.), *A Select series, topographical, narrative, epistolary and miscellaneous, chiefly the productions of early members of the Society of Friends ...*, vi, *Journal of the Lives and Gospel Labours of William Caton and John Burnyeat...*, Harvey and Dalton, 1839.

W.A.Barker, *Religion and Politics, 1559-1642*, Historical Association, 1976.

J.Barry, 'Literacy and Literature in Popular Culture: Reading and Writing in Historical Perspective', in T.Harris (ed.), *Popular Culture in England, c.1500-1850*, Macmillan, 1995.

P.Beale (ed.), *A concise dictionary of slang and unconventional English*, Routledge, 1989.

A.B.Beaven, *The Aldermen of the City of London*, ii, Corporation of the City of London, 1913.

G.M.Benton, F.W.Galpin and W.J.Pressey, *The Church Plate of the County of Essex*, Benham, 1926.

J.Besse, *A Collection of the Sufferings of the People called Quakers*, 1753.

J.Bettey, 'The Reformation and the Parish Church: Local Responses to National Directives', *The Historian*, no.46.

T.Birch, *The Court and Times of Charles the First*, 1848.

J.Bossy, 'Godparenthood: the Fortunes of a Social Institution in Early Modern Christianity', in K.von Greyerz, *Religion and Society in Early Modern Europe 1500-1800*, Allen and Unwin, 1984.

Revd.J.Bramston, *Witham in Olden Time: Two lectures delivered at the Witham Literary Institution*, Meggy and Chalk, 1855.

E.R.Brinkworth (ed.), *The Archdeacon's Court*, i, Oxfordshire Record Series 23, 1942.

K.H.Burley, 'The Economic Development of Essex in the later Seventeenth and early Eighteenth centuries', London University Ph.D. thesis, 1957.

M.Byford, 'The Price of Protestantism: Assessing the Impact of Religious Change on Elizabethan Essex: the Cases of Heydon and Colchester, 1558-1594', Oxford University Ph.D. thesis, 1988.

C.J. [*Journal of the House of Commons*].

Cal.Cttee.for Compounding [Everett Green (ed.), *Calendar of State Papers, Domestic: Committee for Compounding with*

Delinquents, etc., H.M.S.O.]

Cal.Cttee.for Money [Everett Green (ed.), *Calendar of State Papers, Domestic: Committee for the Advance of Money*].

Cal.Pat. [Various editors, *Calendar of Patent Rolls*, H.M.S.O.; volumes described by years covered].

Cal.S.P.Dom. [Various editors, *Calendars of State Papers, Domestic*, H.M.S.O.; volumes described by years covered].

A.J.Camp, *Wills and Their Whereabouts*, priv.pub., 1974.

E.Carlson, 'The origins, functions and status of the office of churchwarden, with particular reference to the diocese of Ely', in M.Spufford, (ed.), *The world of rural dissenters, 1520-1725*, C.U.P., 1995.

U.S.Carlyle, *The Company Plate*, Mercers' Company, 1993.

U.S.Carlyle, *The Mercers' Company*, Mercers' Company, 1994.

M.C[arter], *A True and Exact Relation of that as Honourable as Unfortunate Expedition of Kent, Essex and Colchester, 1648*, 1650.

G.Caunt, 'Essex in Parliament no.7: Whigs and Tories', *Essex Journal*, ii.

C.R.Chapman, *Ecclesiastical Courts, Their Officials and Their Records*, Lochin, 1992.

Charity Commissioners' Report [*The Reports of the Commissioners Appointed in pursuance of Various Acts of Parliament to enquire concerning Charities in England and Wales relating to the County of Essex 1819-37*, Henry Gray, n.d.]

G.Chaucer, *The Canterbury Tales*, Penguin.

C.R.Cheney, *Handbook of Dates for Students of English History*, Royal Historical Society, 1948.

Revd.A.Clark, 'A Lieutenancy Book for Essex: 1608-1631 and 1637- 1639', *Essex Review*, xvii.

P.Clark, *English Provincial Society from the Reformation to the Revolution: Religion, Society and Politics in Kent, 1500-1640*, Harvester, 1977.

P.Clark, *The English Alehouse: a Social History 1200-1830*, Longman, 1983.

D.T-D.Clarke, *The Siege of Colchester, 1648*, Colchester Borough Council, n.d.

W.Cliftlands, 'The "Well-Affected" and the "Country": Politics and Religion in English Provincial Society, c.1640-c.1654', Essex University Ph.D. thesis, 1987 (microfilm copy in Essex Record Office, ref. T/Z 413).

J.S.Cockburn (ed.), *Calendar of Assize Records, Essex Indictments, Elizabeth I*, H.M.S.O., 1978.

J.S.Cockburn (ed.), *Calendar of Assize Records, Essex Indictments, James I*, H.M.S.O., 1982.

P.Collinson, *The Religion of Protestants: the Church in English Society 1559-1625*, Clarendon, 1982.

P.Collinson, *English Puritanism*, Historical Association, 1983.

P.Collinson, *Godly People*, Hambledon, 1983.

P.Collinson, 'The Elizabethan Church and the new religion', in C.Haigh (ed.), *The reign of Elizabeth I*, Macmillan, 1984.

P.Collinson, 'Godly Preachers and Zealous Magistrates in Elizabethan East Anglia: the Roots of Dissent', in E.S.Leedham- Green (ed.), *Religious Dissent in East Anglia [I]*, Cambridge Antiquarian Society, 1991.

P.Collinson, 'Critical conclusion', in M.Spufford (ed.), *The world of rural dissenters, 1520-1725*, C.U.P., 1995.

P.Collinson, lecture on 'Roots of Nonconformity in Essex and East Anglia 1570-1640', at Essex University (Annual Local History Lecture), 9 May 1990.

J.Craig, 'The Christian Brethren in Suffolk', in D.Chadd, *Religious Dissent in East Anglia III*, Centre of East Anglian Studies, 1996.

J.Craig, 'Margaret Spitlehouse, female scrivener', *Local Population Studies*, xlvi.

J.Craig, 'Co-operation and initiatives: Elizabethan churchwardens and the parish accounts of Mildenhall', *Social History*, xviii.

J.Craig and C.Litzenberger, 'Wills as Religious Propaganda: the Testament of William Tracy', *Journal of Ecclesiastical History*, xliv, no.3.

D.Cressy, *Literacy and the Social Order: Reading and Writing in Tudor and Stuart England*, C.U.P., 1980.

F.L.Cross and E.A.Livingstone (eds.), *The Oxford Dictionary of the Christian Church*, O.U.P., 1974.

R.Cust, *The Forced Loan and English Politics 1626-1628*, O.U.P., 1987.

R.Cust and A.Hughes (eds.), *Conflict in Early Stuart England*, Longman, 2nd impression, 1994.

D.N.B. [L.Stephen and S.Lee (eds.), *Dictionary of National Biography*, 1908 1909].

T.W.Davids, *Annals of Evangelical Nonconformity in the County of Essex*, Jackson, Walford and Hodder, 1863.

T.W.Davids, 'The Rev.Thomas Weld', *New England Historical and Genealogical Register*, October 1882.

C.Davies, '"Poor persecuted little flock" or "Commonwealth of Christians"; Edwardian Protestant concepts of the Church', in P.Lake and M.Dowling (eds.), *Protestantism and the National Church in Sixteenth Century England*, Croom Helm, 1987.

T.A.Davies, 'The Quakers in Essex 1655-1725', Oxford University D.Phil. thesis, 1986.

A Declaration of the Army under his Excellency Sir Thomas Fairfax as it was lately presented at Saffron Walden in Essex ..., 1647.

A Declaration of the Lords and Commons in Parliament concerning his Maiesties Proclamation, and the Declaration of the County of Essex to the Earl of Warwick ..., 1642.

A Declaration of the Lords and Commons in Parliament concerning an illegall Writt sent to the High Sheriff of Essex ..., 1642.

A Declaration of the Lords and Commons assembled in Parliament for the appeasing and quietting of all unlawfull Tumults and Insurrections in the severall Counties of England, and Dominion of Wales, 1642.

C.Deedes and H.B.Walters, *The Church Bells of Essex: their founders, inscriptions, traditions and uses*, 1909.

A.G.Dickens, *Lollards and Protestants in the Diocese of York, 1509- 1558*, O.U.P., 1959.

A.G.Dickens, 'The early expansion of Protestantism in England 1520-1558', in Todd, M. (ed.), *Reformation to revolution: politics and religion in early modern England*, Routledge, 1995.

E.P.Dickin, 'Embezzled Church Goods of Essex', *Transactions of the Essex Archaeological Society*, N.S., xiii;

The Division of the County of Essex into severall Classes, together with the names of the Ministers and others fit to be of each Classis ..., 1648.

J.Dobson and R.Milnes Walker, *Barbers and Barber-Surgeons: a history of the Barbers and Barber-Surgeons' Companies*, Blackwell.

I.Doolittle, *The Mercers' Company 1579-1959*, Mercers' Company, 1994.

S.G.Drake, *Result of some researches among the British Archives ... Founders of New England*, 1860.

E.Duffy, *The Stripping of the Altars: Traditional Religion in England c.1400-c.1580*, Yale University Press, 1992.

M.G.L.Earnshaw, *The Church on Market Hill*, Essex

Electronic Interface, 1988.

East Anglian Notes and Queries.

A.C.Edwards, *John Petre*, Regency Press, 1975.

F.G.Emmison (ed.), *Wills at Chelmsford*, British Record Society, i-ii, 1958-61.

F.G.Emmison, *Elizabethan Life*, ii, *Morals and the Church Courts*, Essex Record Office, 1973.

F.G.Emmison, *Elizabethan Life*, v, *Wills of Essex gentry and Yeomen*, Essex Record Office, 1980.

N.Evans, 'The descent of Dissenters in the Chiltern Hundreds', and 'The impossibility of tracing dissent through time in thirty-six parishes in the Essex, Cambridgeshire, and Suffolk borders', in M.Spufford (ed.), *The world of rural dissenters, 1520-1725*, C.U.P., 1995.

An exact and True Diurnal of the Proceedings in Parliament, from the 29 of August, to the 5 of Septemb., 1642, 1642.

Feet of Fines [Various editors, *Feet of Fines for Essex*; i-iv pub. by Essex Archaeological Society; v-vi pub. by Leopard's Head Press].

J.Farmer, *A Genealogical Register of the First Settlers of New England*, 1829.

S.H.G.Fitch, *Colchester Quakers*, Stanley G.Johnson, n.d.

W.Ford, 'The Problem of Literacy in Early Modern England', *History*, lxx.

R.C.Fowler, *The Church of St.Nicholas, Witham*, Wiles, 1911.

J.Foxe, *Actes and Monuments of these latter and perillous dayes ...*, first edition, 1563.

J.Foxe, *The second volume of the Ecclesiastical history, conteyning the Actes and Monumentes of thynges passed ... Inlarged by the author*, 1570.

J.Foxe (S.R.Cattley (ed.)), *The Acts and Monuments of John Foxe*, Seeley and Burnside, 1838.

M.Frearson, 'Communications and the continuity of dissent in the Chiltern Hundreds during the sixteenth and seventeenth centuries', in M.Spufford (ed.), *The world of rural dissenters, 1520-1725*, C.U.P., 1995.

S.R.Gardiner, *Reports of Cases in the Courts of Star Chamber and High Commission*, Camden Society, 1886.

J.H.Gleason, *The Justices of the Peace in England 1558-1640; a later Eirenarcha*, O.U.P., 1969.

Richard Gough, *History of Myddle*, Penguin, 1981.

F.Grace, '"Schismaticall and Factious Humours": Opposition in Ipswich to Laudian Church Government in the 1630s', in D.Chadd, *Religious Dissent in East Anglia III*, Centre of East Anglian Studies, 1996.

H.E.P.Grieve, *The Sleepers and the Shadows: Chelmsford, a Town, a People and its Past*, i, Essex Record Office, 1988.

H.E.P.Grieve, *The Sleepers and the Shadows: Chelmsford, a Town, a People and its Past*, ii. Essex Record Office, 1994.

H.E.P.Grieve, 'The Deprived Married Clergy in Essex, 1553-1561', *Transactions of the Royal Historical Society*, xxii.

J.Gyford, 'Men of Bad Character: Property Crime in Essex in the 1820s', Essex University M.A. thesis, 1982.

J.Gyford, *Domesday Witham*, Janet Gyford, 1985 (also on www.gyford.com/domesday).

J.Gyford, *Witham 1500-1700: making a living*, Janet Gyford, 1996.

C.Haigh (ed.), *The reign of Elizabeth I*, Macmillan, 1984.

C.Haigh (ed.), *The English Reformation Revised*, C.U.P., 1987.

C.Haigh, *English Reformations: Religion, Politics and Society under the Tudors*, O.U.P., 1993.

P.Hanks and F.Hodges, *A Dictionary of First Names*, O.U.P., 1990

Harrison, W. [F.J.Furnivall, ed.], *Harrison's Description of England in Shakspere's Youth; being the second and third books of his Description of Britaine and England; edited from the first two editions of Holinshed's Chronicle, A.D. 1577, 1587: part i, the second book*, N.Trübner & Co. for the New Shakspere Society, 1877.

H.Harrod, *Report of the Records of the Borough of Colchester*, 1865.

T.A.Henderson, *The Parish Church of Saint Nicolas, Witham, Essex*, Witham P.C.C., 1986.

T.[A.]H[enderson], 'The Early Days of the Church of the Holy Family in Witham', *Parish Magazine, Saint Nicolas, Witham*, December 1988.

L.Higgs, 'Wills and religious mentality in Tudor Colchester', *Essex Archaeology and History*, xxii.

C.Hill, *God's Englishman: Oliver Cromwell and the English Revolution*, History Book Club, 1970.

Hist.MSS.Com. [Royal Commission on Historical Manuscripts, *Reports*].

C.Holmes, *The Eastern Association in the English Civil War*. C.U.P., 1974.

A.Hope, 'Lollardy, the stone the builders rejected ?', in P.Lake and M.Dowling (eds.), *Protestantism and the National Church in Sixteenth Century England*, Croom Helm, 1987.

J.K.Hosmer (ed.)), *Winthrop's Journal "History of New England" 1630-1649*, i, Scribner, 1908.

J.C.Hotten (ed.), *Original lists of Persons of Quality ... who went from Great Britain to the American Plantations, 1600-1700*, Chatto and Windus, 1874.

J.J.Howard (ed.), *A Visitation of the County of Essex ... by Sir Edward Bysshe*, Mitchell and Hughes, 1888.

R.Howell, 'Thomas Weld of Gateshead: the return of a New England Puritan', *Archeologia Aeliana*, 4th series, xlviii, p.303-32.

A.Hudson, *The Premature Reformation: Wycliffite Texts and Lollard History*, Clarendon, 1988.

G.Huelin, *Vanished Churches of the City of London*, Corporation of London, 1996.

G.Huelin, *Think and Thank God: the Mercers' Company and its Contribution to the Church and Religious Life since the Reformation*, Mercers' Company, n.d.

F.Hull, 'Agriculture and Rural Society in Essex, 1560-1640', Ph.D. thesis, 1950.

F.Hull, 'Early Friends in Central and Northern Essex', *Essex Review*, lvi.

F.Hull, 'More Essex Friends of the Restoration period', *Essex Review*, lvii.

The Humble Petition of the Inhabitants of the County of Essex to His Majesty, with His Majesties Gratious Answer thereunto. Also the Petition Presented by the Inhabitants of the aforesaid County to both Houses of Parliament, 1642/3.

C.R.Humphery-Smith (ed.), *The Phillimore Atlas and Index of Parish Registers*, Phillimore, 1995.

W.Hunt, *The Puritan Moment: the Coming of Revolution in an English County*, Harvard University Press, 1983.

R.Hutton, 'The Local Impact of the Tudor Reformations', in C.Haigh (ed.), *The English Reformation Revised*, C.U.P., 1987.

J.Imray, *The Mercers' Hall*, Mercers' Company, 1991.

M.Ingram, 'Religion, Communities and Moral Discipline in Late Sixteenth- and Early Seventeenth-Century England: Case Studies', in K.von Greyerz, *Religion and Society in Early Modern Europe 1500- 1800*, Allen and Unwin, 1984.

M.Ingram, 'From Reformation to Toleration; Popular

Religious Cultures in England, 1540-1690', in T.Harris (ed.), *Popular Culture in England, c.1500-1850*, Macmillan, 1995.

M.Ingram, 'Reformation of manners in early modern England', in P.Griffiths, A.Fox, and S.Hindle (eds.), *The experience of authority in early modern England*, Macmillan, 1996.

Instructions agreed upon by the Lords and Commons assembled in Parliament For ... Members of the House of Commons, and Deputie-Lieutenants for the County of Essex ..., 1642.

C.Jameson, 'Never a dull moment!: some stories behind a monument in a small Essex church', *Essex Family Historian*, no.86.

C.Johnson, 'A Proto-Industrial Community Study: Coggeshall in Essex, c.1500-c.1750', Essex University Ph.D. thesis, 1989-90.

C.Johnson, lectures on 'A Social History of the Woollen Industry', at W.E.A., Colchester Branch, 1984-85.

Kelly's directory, Essex (1937).

H.W.King, 'Inventories of Church Goods, 6th Edw.VI', *Transactions of the Essex Archaeological Society*, O.S., iv, p.197.

P.J.R.King, 'Crime, Law and Society in Essex 1740-1820', Cambridge University Ph.D. thesis, 1984.

L.& P. Hen.VIII, [Various editors, *Letters and Papers, Foreign and Domestic, Henry VIII*, H.M.S.O.].

P.R.P.Knell, 'The Southcott family in Essex, 1572-1642', *Essex Recusant*, xiv.

L.J. [*Journal of the House of Lords*].

P.Lake, *Moderate puritans and the Elizabethan church*, C.U.P., 1982.

P.Lake, 'Calvinism and the English Church 1570-1635', in Todd, M. (ed.), *Reformation to revolution: politics and religion in early modern England*, Routledge, 1995.

R.Lane, *The Mercers' Company Plate*, Mercers' Company, 1985.

J.Lawson and H.Silver, *A Social History of Education in England*, Methuen, 1973.

T.Lechford, *Notebook kept by Thomas Lechford, esquire, lawyer, in Boston Massachusetts Bay from June 27 1633 to July 29, 1641*, C.U.P., 1885.

Letters from Saffron Walden to the Generalls Head Quarters by way of Apologie and Vindication of the Army, 1647.

'Liber Scholae Colcestriensis', *Transactions of the Essex Archaeological Society*, NS, ii.

Listed Buildings, Tendring, 1987 [Department of the Environment, 'List of Buildings of Special Architectural and Historic Interest: District of Tendring, Essex: Parishes of Beaumont ...', unpublished report, 1987].

Listed Buildings, Witham, c.1970 [Ministry of Housing and Local Government, 'Historic Buildings, Survey Report, Witham', unpublished report, c.1970].

C.Litzenberger, *The English Reformation and the Laity: Gloucestershire 1540-1580*, C.U.P., 1997.

W.J.Lucas, 'Witham, Essex', *Transactions of the Essex Archaeological Society*, N.S., iv.

MacCulloch, D., *Suffolk and the Tudors: Politics and Religion in an English County 1500-1600*, Clarendon, 1986.

A.Macfarlane, *Witchcraft in Tudor and Stuart England: A Regional and Comparative Study*, Routledge and Kegan Paul, 1970.

A.Macfarlane, *The Family Life of Ralph Josselin, a seventeenth-century clergyman: an essay in historical anthropology*. C.U.P., 1970.

A.Macfarlane (ed.), *The Diary of Ralph Josselin 1616-1683*, O.U.P., 1976.

M.J.McIntosh, 'Social Change and Tudor Manorial Leets', in J.A.Guy and H.G.Beale (eds.), *Law and Social Change in British History*, Royal Historical Society, 1984.

M.J.McIntosh, *A community transformed: the manor and Liberty of Havering, 1500-1620*, C.U.P., 1991.

B.Manning, *The English People and the English Revolution*, second edition, Bookmarks, 1991.

C.Marsh, 'In the Name of God ? Will-making and Faith in Early Modern England', in G.H.Martin and P.Spufford (eds.), *The Records of the Nation*, Boydell and B.R.S., 1990.

C.Marsh, 'Nonconformists and their Neighbours in Early-Modern England: s Tale of Two Thomases', in D.Chadd, *Religious Dissent in East Anglia III*, Centre of East Anglian Studies, 1996.

Massachusetts Historical Society, *Collections*, Third series, xxi, ii and iii, 1931, 1943.

Mercers' Company, *Return to the Royal Commission on Livery Companies*, 1880.

G.Martin, *The Story of Colchester from Roman Times to the Present Day*, Benham, 1959.

A.G.Matthews, *Calamy Revised*, Clarendon, 1934.

A.G.Matthews, *Walker Revised*, Clarendon, 1948.

P.Morant, *The History and Antiquities of the County of Essex*, 1763-68.

P.Morant, *The History and Antiquities of the most ancient Town and Borough of Colchester*, 2nd edn., 1768.

J.Morrill, *The Revolt of the Provinces: Conservatives and Radicals in the English Civil War, 1630-1650*, Longman, 1980.

J.Morrill (ed.), *The Impact of the English Civil War*, Collins and Brown, 1991.

J.Morrill, lecture on 'William Dowsing and Civil War Iconoclasm in East Anglia', at the Third Symposium on the History of Religious Dissent in East Anglia', 10 April 1994.

J.Morris (ed.), *The Troubles of Our Catholic Forefathers Related by Themselves*, Burns and Oates, 1872.

N.E.H.G.S., *Register* [New England Historic Genealogical Society, *The New England Historical and Genealogical Register*, 1842-]

R.Newcourt, *Repertorium or an Ecclesiastical Parochial History of the Diocese of London*, 1708-10.

A New Found Stratagem framed in the Old Forge of Machivilisme, and put upon the Inhabitants of the County of Essex, 1647.

W.Notestein (ed.), *The Journal of Sir Simonds D'Ewes: from the beginning of the Long Parliament to the opening of the trial of the Earl of Strafford*, Yale University Press and O.U.P., 1923.

O.E.D. [*Oxford English Dictionary*, Clarendon, 1933].

M.W.O'Boy, 'The Origins of Essex Recusancy', Cambridge University Ph.D. thesis, 1995.

J.G.O'Leary, 'The Election of Two Knights of the Shire in 1679', *Essex Review*, lxv.

J.E.Oxley, *The Reformation in Essex*, Manchester University Press, 1965.

J.E.Oxley, 'Benefice Farming in Tudor Essex', *Essex Journal*, xxvi.

D.M.Palliser, *The Reformation in York, 1534-1553*, Borthwick Papers no.40, University of York, 1971.

D.M.Palliser, 'Popular Reactions to the Reformation during the years of Uncertainty 1530-70', in C.Haigh (ed.), *The English Reformation Revised*, C.U.P., 1987.

'Parish Magazine', Saint Nicolas, Witham, August 1944.

V.Pearl, *London and the Outbreak of the Puritan Revolution: City*

Government and National Politics, 1625-43, O.U.P., 1961.

A.Peel (ed.), The Seconde Parte of a Register, being a Calendar of Manuscripts under that title intended for publication by the Puritans about 1593, and now in Dr.Williams's Library, London, C.U.P., 1915.

A.Penn, The Story of the Siege of Colchester, Wiles, 1888.

N.Penney (ed.), First Publishers of Truth, 1907.

N.Penney (ed.), Journal of George Fox, J.M.Dent, 1924.

W.J.Petchey, A Prospect of Maldon, 1500-1689, Essex Record Office, 1991.

K.Peters, 'Quaker Pamphleteering and the Origins of the Quaker Movement in East Anglia, 1652-1656', in D.Chadd, Religious Dissent in East Anglia III, Centre of East Anglian Studies, 1996.

L.Phillipson, 'Quakerism in Cambridge before the Act of Toleration (1653-1689)', Proceedings of the Cambridge Antiquarian Society, lxxvi.

L.Phillipson, 'Quakerism in Cambridge from the Act of Toleration to the end of the Nineteenth Century' (1689-1900)', Proceedings of the Cambridge Antiquarian Society, lxxvii.

D.Plumb, 'The social and economic status of the later Lollards', and 'A gathered church ? Lollards and their society', in M.Spufford (ed.), The world of rural dissenters, 1520-1725, C.U.P., 1995.

R.H.Pogson, 'Revival and Reform in Mary Tudor's Church: a Question of Money', in C.Haigh (ed.), The English Reformation Revised, C.U.P., 1987.

C.H.Pope, The Pioneers of Massachusetts, 1900.

W.J.Pressey, 'The Apparitor in Essex', Essex Review, xlvi.

W.J.Pressey, 'Essex Affairs Matrimonial', Essex Review, xlix.

W.J.Pressey 'Colchester Archdeaconry Visitations- 1588', Essex Review, xxxii.

W.J.Pressey, 'The Essex Churchwarden', Essex Review, li.

W.J.Pressey, 'The Records of the Archdeaconries of Essex and Colchester', Transactions of the Essex Archaeological Society, N.S., xix.

W.J.Pressey, 'Some seating experiences in Essex Churches', Essex Review, xxxv.

W.J.Pressey, 'The Surplice in Essex', Essex Review, xlv.

D.W.Pryke, 'A New Seventeenth Century Trade Token in Lead', Numismatic Circular, no.105(8), p.283.

J.S.Purvis, An Introduction to Ecclesiastical Records, St.Anthony's Press, 1953.

B.W.Quintrell, 'The Divisional Committee for Southern Essex during the Civil Wars and its part in local administration', Manchester University M.A. thesis, 1962.

B.W.Quintrell (ed.), The Maynard Lieutenancy Book, 1608-1639, Essex Record Office, 1993.

B.W.Quintrell, 'Gentry Factions and the Witham Affray', Essex Archaeology and History, 3rd series, x.

R.C.H.M., [Royal Commission on Historical Monuments (England): An Inventory of the Historical Monuments in Essex, H.M.S.O., 1916-23].

P.L.Ralph, Sir Humphrey Mildmay: Royalist Gentleman, Rutgers U.P., 1947.

B.Reay, The Quakers and the English Revolution, Temple Smith, 1985.

To the Right Honorable, Excellent, Worthy and Pious Sir Thomas Fairfax ... the Petition of the well-affected in the County of Essex, 1647.

K.Roberts, Soldiers of the English Civil War (1): Infantry, Osprey, 1989.

J.H.Round, 'Dr.Robert Aylett', Transactions of the Essex Archaeological Society, N.S., x.

J.H.R[ound], 'Witham Church', Transactions of Essex Archaeological Society, N.S., x.

J.Rowe, 'The 1767 Census of Papists in the Diocese of Norwich: The Social Composition of the Roman Catholic Community', in D.Chadd, Religious Dissent in East Anglia III, Centre of East Anglian Studies, 1996.

P.Ryan, 'Diocesan Returns of Recusants for England and Wales, 1577', Catholic Record Society, xxii.

P.M.Ryan, 'Cressing Temple: Its History from Documentary Sources', D.D.Andrews (ed.), Cressing Temple: a Templar and Hospitaller manor in Essex, Essex County Council, 1993.

T.Rymer, Foedera, xiii, second edition, 1726.

[B.Ryves (ed.)], Mercurius Rusticus, reproduced in R.Jeffs (ed.), The English Revolution III: Newsbooks 1, Oxford Royalist Volume 4, Cornmarket, 1971.

J.Samaha, Law and Order in Historical Perspective: the Case of Elizabethan Essex, Academic Press, 1974.

J.Savage, A Genealogical Dictionary of the First Settlers in New England, Little, Brown and Co., 1860-62.

J.J.Scarisbrick, The Reformation and the English People, O.U.P., 1984.

D.Scott, Quakerism in York, 1650-1720, Borthwick Papers no.80, University of York, 1991.

J.Shakespeare, 'Plague and Punishment', P.Lake and M.Dowling (eds.), Protestantism and the National Church in Sixteenth Century England, Croom Helm, 1987.

J.A.Sharpe, 'Crime and Delinquency in an Essex Parish 1600-1640', in J.S.Cockburn (ed.), Crime in England 1500-1800, Methuen, 1977.

J.A.Sharpe, Crime in seventeenth-century England, a County Study, C.U.P., 1983.

J.A.Sharpe, 'Scandalous and Malignant Priests in Essex: the Impact of Grassroots Puritanism', in C.Jones, M.Newitt and S.Roberts (eds.), Politics and People in Revolutionary England, Blackwell, 1986.

J.A.Sharpe, Early Modern England: A Social History 1550-1760, Edward Arnold, 1987.

R.R.Sharpe, London and the Kingdom, Longman, 1894.

W.A.Shaw, A History of the Church during the Civil Wars and under the Commonwealth, 1640-60, 1900.

K.W.Shipps, 'Lay Patronage of East Anglian Puritan Clerics in Pre-Revolutionary England', Yale University Ph.D. thesis, 1971.

P.Slack, 'Poverty and Politics in Salisbury 1597-1666', in P.Clark and P.Slack (eds.), Crisis and Order in English Towns 1500-1700, Routledge and Kegan Paul, 1972.

H.Smith, The ecclesiastical history of Essex under the Long Parliament and Commonwealth, Benham, n.d.

H.Smith, 'The Sequence of the Parochial Clergy in the County of Essex 1640-44', typescript in Essex Archaeological Society Library (copy in Essex Record Office), n.d.

H.Smith and T.M.Hope, 'Essex Clergy in 1661', Bramston MSS, n.d., (xerox in Colchester Library).

J.R.Smith, Pilgrims and Adventurers: Essex (England) and the Making of the United States of America, Essex Record Office, 1992.

R.P.Sorlien (ed.), The Diary of John Manningham of the Middle Temple 1602-1603, University of Rhode Island, 1976.

M.Spufford, Contrasting Communities: English Villagers in the Sixteenth and Seventeenth Centuries, C.U.P., 1974.

M.Spufford, (ed.), The world of rural dissenters, 1520-1725, C.U.P., 1995.

P.Spufford, 'The comparative mobility and immobility of Lollard descendants in early modern England', in M.Spufford (ed.), *The world of rural dissenters, 1520-1725*, C.U.P., 1995.

B.Stevenson, 'The social and economic status of post-Restoration dissenters, 1660-1725', and 'The social integration of post-Restoration dissenters, 1660-1725', in M.Spufford (ed.), *The world of rural dissenters, 1520-1725*, C.U.P., 1995.

L.Stone, 'The educational revolution in England', *Past and Present*, xxiv.

M.Storey (ed.), *Two East Anglian Diaries 1641-1729: Isaac Archer and William Coe*, Boydell, 1994.

B.L.Stratton, *Sherman and Allied Families*, privately published, 1951.

A summe of a Conference at Terling in Essex, January 11, 1643, 1644.

M.Takahashi, 'The Number of Wills proved in the Sixteenth and Seventeenth Centuries', in G.H.Martin and P.Spufford (eds.), *The Records of the Nation*, Boydell and B.R.S., 1990.

A.Tarver, *Church Court Records: an introduction for family and local historians*, Phillimore, 1995.

G.B.Tatham, *Dr.John Walker and the Sufferings of the Clergy*, C.U.P., 1911.

J.H.Taylor (ed.), *1662 and its Issues*, Congregational Historical Society, 1962.

R.Taylor, *Collecteanea II*, (Record Society xxiii), Somerset Record Society, 1928.

M.Tepper, *Passengers to America*, Genealogical Publishing, 1980.

K.Thomas, *Religion and the Decline of Magic*, Weidenfeld and Nicholson, 1971.

K.Thomas, 'The Meaning of Literacy in Early Modern England', in G.Baumann (ed.), *The Written Word: Literacy in Transition*, Clarendon, 1986.

R.H.Thompson and J.Gyford, 'The Witham hoard of 17th-century tokens and George Robinson the issuer', *Essex Archaeology and History*, xx.

M.Todd, (ed.), *Reformation to revolution: politics and religion in early modern England*, Routledge, 1995.

A True and perfect Diurnall of the passages in Parliament, from Nottingham, Ashby and Leicester, and other parts, 1642, no.11.

G.L.Turner, *Original Documents of Early Non-conformity under Persecution and Indulgence*, 1911.

J.Twigg, *A history of Queens' College, Cambrige, 1448-1986*, Boydell, 1987.

N.Tyacke, 'Puritanism, Arminianism and counter-revolution', in Todd, M. (ed.), *Reformation to revolution: politics and religion in early modern England*, Routledge, 1995.

D.Underdown, *Revel, Riot and Rebellion: Popular Politics and Culture in England, 1603-1660*, O.U.P., 1985.

D.Underdown, *Fire from Heaven: Life in an English Town in the Seventeenth Century*, Fontana, 1993.

F.A.Underwick (ed.), *A Calendar of the Inner Temple Records*, Masters of the Bench, 1896-98.

Valor Eccl. [J.Caley and Rev.J.Hunter (eds.), *Valor Ecclesiasticus. temp. Henrici VIII, auctoriatate regia institutus*, Record Commissioners, 1810-34].

The Victoria History of the County of Essex, ii, Archibald Constable and Co., 1907.

The Victoria History of the Counties of England; a History of the County of Essex, (ed. W.R.Powell), iv, University of London, Institute of Historical Research, 1956.

Visitations, Essex [W.C.Metcalfe (ed.), *Visitations of Essex*, Harleian Society, 1878].

Visitations, London [J.J.Howard, *The Visitation of London, 1633, 1634 and 1635*, Harleian Society, 1883].

G.Walker, 'Heretical Sects in Pre-Reformation England', *History Today*, xliii.

J.Walker, *An Attempt towards recovering an account of the numbers and sufferings of the clergy of the Church of England, Heads of Colleges, Fellows, Scholars etc., who were Sequester'd, Harras'd, &c. in the late Times of the Grand Rebellion*, 1714.

J.Walter, 'Grain riots and popular attitudes to the law: Maldon and the crisis of 1629', in J.Brewer and J.Styles, *An Ungovernable people: the English and their law in the 17th and 18th centuries*, Hutchinson, 1980.

J.Walter, 'The Impact on Society, a World Turned Upside Down ?', in J.Morrill (ed.), *The Impact of the English Civil War*, Collins and Brown, 1991.

J.Walter, 'Anti-Popery and the Stour Valley Riots of 1642', in D.Chadd, *Religious Dissent in East Anglia III*, Centre of East Anglian Studies, 1996.

J.Walter, lectures on 'The Civil War in Essex and Suffolk', at W.E.A. Essex Federation's day-school, 23 April 1994.

J.Walter, lecture on 'Superstition and sedition: riot and religion in Civil War Essex' (Kenneth Newton Memorial Lecture), 9 November 1995.

J.C.Ward (ed.), *The Medieval Essex Community: Lay Subsidy of 1327*, Essex Record Office, 1983.

J.C.Ward, 'The Reformation in Colchester, 1528-1558', *Essex Archaeology and History*, xv, pp.84-95.

S.A.Warner, *St.Paul's Cathedral*, S.P.C.K., 1926.

S.and B.Webb, *English Local Government from the Revolution to the Municipal Corporations Act: the Parish and the County*, Longmans Green, 1924.

S.and B.Webb, *English Local Government from the Revolution to the Municipal Corporations Act: the Manor and the Borough*, Longmans Green, 1924.

T.Webster, *Godly clergy in early Stuart England: the Caroline Puritan Movement c.1620-1643*, Cambridge University Press, 1997.

T.Webster, *Stephen Marshall and Finchingfield*, Essex Record Office, 1994.

J.White, *The First Century of Scandalous, Malignant Priests ...*, 1643.

P.Williams, 'The Crown and the counties', in C.Haigh (ed.), *The reign of Elizabeth I*, Macmillan, 1984.

K.Wrightson, 'Two concepts of order; justices, constables and jurymen in seventeenth-century England', in J.Brewer and J.Styles (eds.), *An Ungovernable People: the English and their law in the seventeenth and eighteenth centuries*, Hutchinson, 1980.

K.Wrightson, *English Society 1580-1680*, Hutchinson, 1988.

K.Wrightson, 'The politics of the parish in early modern England', in P.Griffiths, A.Fox, and S.Hindle (eds.), *The experience of authority in early modern England*, Macmillan, 1996.

K.Wrightson and D.Levine, *Poverty and Piety in an English Village: Terling 1525-1700*, first edition, Academic Press, 1979, second edition with addition of 'Postscript: Terling Revisited', O.U.P., 1995.

A.Young (ed.), *Chronicles of the First Planters of the Colony of Massachusetts Bay, 1623-1636*, 1846.

ORIGINAL DOCUMENTS USED: select list

Most of the reference numbers given here are general prefixes only; individual documents usually require additional identifying numbers.

BODLEIAN LIBRARY, MANUSCRIPTS
Firth C4   Lieutenancy Book
(microfilm in E.R.O., T/A 278)

BRITISH LIBRARY, DEPARTMENT OF MANUSCRIPTS (formerly British Museum)
Individual documents as quoted in the notes.

ESSEX UNIVERSITY LIBRARY
Friends' collection
EQ 22   Sufferings in Essex.
Other items on microfilm in E.R.O. T/A 423.

ESSEX RECORD OFFICE
Ecclesiastical records:
Several jurisdictions
A9368   Assorted papers
Consistory of Bishop of London
D/ALV   Act Books
Commissary of Bishop of London
D/ABA   Act books
D/ABD   Depositions
D/ABR 4   Will register/Act book
D/ABV   Visitations
D/ABW   Wills
Archdeaconry of Colchester
D/ACA   Act books
D/ACAc   Probate and administration acts
D/ACD   Depositions
D/ACR   Will registers
D/ACV   Visitations
D/ACW   Wills
Archdeaconry of Essex
D/AER   Will registers
D/AEV   Visitations
Archdeaconry of Middlesex
D/AMR   Will registers
D/AMV   Visitations
Diocesan records
D/CT 405   Tithe award and map, Witham, 1839
Estate and Family Archives
D/DBw M   Manorial records, Witham
Nonconformist records
D/NC 3   Witham Congregational Church
D/NF 1 and Accession A9012
     Witham Monthly Meeting of Society of Friends (Quakers)
Parish records
Terling
D/P 299/1   Parish registers
Witham
D/P 30/1   Parish registers
D/P 30/14/1   Apprenticeship indentures
D/P 30/18   Overseers, miscellaneous papers
D/P 30/25   Records of charities
D/P 30/28/14   Blunts Hall manor
Essex historians' manuscripts
D/Y 2   Morant manuscripts
Quarter Sessions
Q/RTh   Hearth tax returns
Q/Sba   Sessions bundles
Q/SO   Order books
Q/SPb   Process books of indictments
Q/SR   Sessions Rolls. References to these in the notes generally relate to the typescript calendar, also in E.R.O., though on a few occasions I have also consulted the original rolls
Transcripts etc.
T/A 42, 42A   Ship Money returns, 1636 (and index)
T/A 278   Lieutenancy Book
T/A 420   Bishop Compton's census, 1676
T/A 423   Quarterly meeting records, Society of Friends (Quakers)
T/A 427   Lay Subsidy returns, 1520s (inaccurate)
T/A 547   Newcourt's Repertorium updated
T/B 71   Witham manorial records
T/P 195   Holman's history of Essex
T/P 196   H.W.King's collection
Calendar of Assize rolls 1625-1714
Calendar of Quarter Sessions rolls 1556-1714

GUILDHALL LIBRARY, MANUSCRIPTS
Ecclesiastical records, diocese of London
9531   Bishops' registers
9532   Vicar General's books
9535   Ordinations
9537   Visitations
9539-40   Subscription books
9583   Churchwardens' presentments
9628   Parish terriers
9657   Sundry papers
11,185   Sequestration bonds
12,737   Deeds of rectory
Noble Coll.   Biographies

HOUSE OF LORDS RECORD OFFICE
Main papers, H.L.
Petitions
20 Jan.1641/2 (petition box)
8 June 1642
4 Jan.1642/3
Items re.Francis Wright
6 April 1643, bond
23 June 1660, petition

LAMBETH PALACE LIBRARY
Individual documents as quoted in the notes

LEICESTERSHIRE RECORD OFFICE
DE 220/208, 220/207, 220/209
     Draft petitions

LONDON METROPOLITAN ARCHIVES (formerly Greater London Record Office)
Ecclesiastical records, diocese of London
DL/C 300-27, 614-24   Consistory Court Act Books
DL/C 331-345   Vicar General's books

PUBLIC RECORD OFFICE
Assizes, Home circuit
ASSI 35   Assize rolls. References to these in the notes from 1558-1625 usually refer to the printed calendars in Cockburn, 1978 and 1982 (for which see the bibliography), whilst from 1625-1714 they refer to the typescript calendar in E.R.O.
Chancery
C 1   Early Chancery proceedings
Exchequer
E 101   Accounts, various
E 112   Bills, answers etc.
E 179/108/154   Lay Subsidy, 1520s, for which also see E.R.O. T/A 427
E 301   Chantry certificates
E 331   Bishops' certificates
E 401   Receipt books
Privy Council
PC 2   Privy Council Registers
Prerogative Court of Canterbury
PROB 6   Administration books
PROB 10   Wills
PROB 11   Will registers
PROB 29   Act books
Court of Requests
REQ 2   Proceedings
General Register Office
RG 6   Registers of Society of Friends (Quakers)
State Paper Office
SP 16   State Papers Domestic, Charles I, including SP 16/358/97-98, Essex Ship Money returns (also see E.R.O. T/A 42, 42A).

INDEX

The alphabetical order of entries is in the 'letter-by-letter' style, e.g. Virginia comes before Virgin Mary.

I have tried to break up the entries in various ways, e.g. by subheadings, but some of them were hard to divide, and are longer than is really advisable.

In the subheadings, subject references come first, followed by proper names (i.e. of people and places).

Page numbers with asterisks (*) show entries which relate to drawings or figures, or their captions.

Proper names are given in the form which was most frequently used. Common variants are put in brackets afterwards. Some cross-referencing is given if the variants appear some distance away from each other in the index.

If anyone else has experienced trauma as a result of indexing using *Word*, I'd be most interested to know !

Place names:

Parishes are in Essex unless otherwise indicated.

Buildings, fields etc. are in Witham unless otherwise indicated. Modern street numbers are given in the order in which they appear on the ground, usually odds first, then evens. Places which only have names and not numbers follow them.

Counties are 'old' pre-1974 counties.

Maps are only indexed for their subject matter, not for the individual places shown on them.

Personal names:

Names of contemporary historians are only indexed if some of their work is described. Those to whom I have mentioned gratitude for other reasons are not indexed, but nevertheless appreciated !

People named are from Witham unless otherwise indicated. Those not from Witham usually have another place of residence given. If their residence is not known or not relevant, they instead have an office or occupation which hopefully makes it reasonably clear that they are not from Witham (such as 'archdeacon' or 'historian').

Sometimes distinctions such as 'the elder' (eldr.) are given to help distinguish people of the same name, even if this term was not used by the person's contemporaries.

Most of the Witham people referred to in this book also appear in *Witham 1500-1700: Making a Living*. The index to that book gives dates and occupations for them.

End notes:

The end notes are only indexed if they include material which would not be obvious from the main text. The number of the note appears in the form (#44) after the page number.

Abbreviations:

Abm.	Abraham	Dor.	Dorothy	Jas.	James	Prisc.	Priscilla
Alex.	Alexander	Edm.	Edmund	Jeff.	Jeffrey	Rich.	Richard
Andr.	Andrew	Edw.	Edward	Jer.	Jerome	Robt.	Robert
Anth.	Anthony	eldr.	elder	Jn.	John	Saml.	Samuel
Arth.	Arthur	eldst.	eldest	Jos.	Joseph	Steph.	Stephen
Barb.	Barbara	Eliz.	Elizabeth	Kath.	Katherine	Sus.	Susan,
Barth.	Bartholomew	Franc.	Francis	Laur.	Laurence		Susannah
Ben.	Benjamin	Geoff.	Geoffrey	Marg.	Margaret	Thos.	Thomas
Chris.	Christopher	Gilb.	Gilbert	Mat.	Matthew	w.	wife
Clem.	Clement	Geo.	George	Nath.	Nathaniel	Wm.	William
Cuth.	Cuthbert	Hen.	Henry	Nich.	Nicholas	ygr.	younger
Danl.	Daniel	Humph.	Humphrey	Phil.	Philip	ygst.	youngest